978-3-8382-0806-0

AF085638

JOURNAL

OF

SOVIET AND POST-SOVIET

POLITICS AND SOCIETY

Vol. 1, No. 2 (2015)

Double Special Issue

Back from Afghanistan:

The Experiences of Soviet Afghan War Veterans

Martyrdom and Memory in Eastern Europe

JSPPS 1:2 (2015)

GENERAL EDITOR AND ISSUE EDITOR-IN-CHIEF:

Julie Fedor, University of Melbourne

CONSULTING EDITOR:

Andreas Umland, Institute for Euro-Atlantic Cooperation, Kyiv

GUEST EDITORS:

Felix Ackermann, European Humanities University, Vilnius

Uilleam Blacker, University College London

Michael Galbas, University of Konstanz

Bibliographic information published by the Deutsche Nationalbibliothek
The Deutsche Nationalbibliothek lists this publication in the Deutsche Nationalbibliografie; detailed bibliographic data are available on the Internet at http://dnb.dnb.de.

Bibliografische Information der Deutschen Nationalbibliothek
Die Deutsche Nationalbibliothek verzeichnet diese Publikation in der Deutschen Nationalbibliografie; detaillierte bibliografische Daten sind im Internet über http://dnb.d-nb.de abrufbar.

Cover picture: © Anna Reich. Jonas Vaitkūnas in his bedroom. Vilnius, Lithuania.

Journal of Soviet and Post-Soviet Politics and Society Vol. 1, No. 2 (2015)

Stuttgart: *ibidem*-Verlag / *ibidem* Press

Erscheinungsweise: halbjährlich / Frequency: biannual

ISSN 2364-5334

Ordering Information:
Subscription (two copies per year): € 58.00 / year (+ S&H: € 4.00 / year within Germany, € 7.00 /
year international). The subscription can be canceled at any time.

Single copy or back issue: € 34.00 / copy (+ S&H: € 2.00 within Germany, € 3.50 international).

© *ibidem*-Verlag / *ibidem* Press
Stuttgart, Germany 2015

Printed in the EU

CONTENTS

Back from Afghanistan:

The Experiences of Soviet Afghan War Veterans

GUEST EDITED BY

FELIX ACKERMANN AND MICHAEL GALBAS

Back from Afghanistan: Experiences of Soviet Afghan War Veterans in Transnational Perspective

Felix Ackermann and Michael Galbas

This special issue is aimed at discussing how states and societies have addressed the consequences of the Soviet–Afghan War (1979–89), not only during the Soviet period but also in the aftermath of 1991.[1] The primary intention is to analyze the different strategies used for (re)integrating veterans of an asymmetric war into society in a radically changing international context, which covers a period beginning with the break-up of the USSR and ending with current developments in the successor states, including the ongoing war in

---

[1]   For these topics and the Soviet–Afghan War in general see also: Paul Robinson and Jay Dixon, *Aiding Afghanistan: A History of Soviet Assistance to a Developing Country* (London: Hurst & Co, 2013); Rodric Braithwaite, *Afgantsy: The Russians in Afghanistan 1979–98* (Oxford: Oxford University Press, 2011); Artemy Kalinovsky, *A Long Goodbye: The Politics and Diplomacy of the Soviet Withdrawal from Afghanistan, 1980–1992* (Cambridge, MA: Harvard University Press, 2011); Homayun Sidky, "War, Changing Patterns of Warfare, State Collapse, and Transnational Violence in Afghanistan: 1978–2001", *Modern Asian Studies* 41, no. 4 (2007): 849–88; Gregory Feifer, *The Great Gamble: The Soviet War in Afghanistan* (New York: HarperCollins Publishers, 2009); Lester W. Grau and Michael A. Gress (eds), *The Soviet-Afghan War: How a Superpower Fought and Lost* (Lawrence, KS: University Press of Kansas, 2002); Antonio Giustozzi, *War, Politics and Society in Afghanistan, 1978–1992* (Washington, DC: Georgetown University Press, 2000); Douglas A. Borer, *Superpowers Defeated: Vietnam and Afghanistan Compared* (London: Cass, 1999); Mark Galeotti, *Afghanistan: The Soviet Union's Last War* (London: Frank Cass, 1995); Aleksandr A. Liakhovskii, *Tragediia i doblest' Afgana* (Moskva: GPI, 1995); Manfred Sapper, *Die Auswirkungen des Afghanistan-Krieges auf die Sowjetgesellschaft: Eine Studie zum Legitimitätsverlust des Militärischen in der Perestrojka* (Münster, Hamburg: Lit., 1994); Henry S. Bradsher, *Afghanistan and the Soviet Union* (Durham, NC: Duke University Press, 1983); and the forthcoming volume: Tanja Penter and Esther Meier (eds), *Sovietnam: Die UdSSR in Afghanistan 1979-1989* (Paderborn: Ferdinand Schöningh Verlag, in press).

Eastern Ukraine.[2] Beyond a normative concept of successful (re)integration, contributors address the many contradictions between the soldiers' self-perceptions, their post-war experiences, and the changes faced by the veterans in the new post-war and post-Soviet social settings.[3] Certain specific features of the Soviet–Afghan conflict, such as its asymmetric nature, and the unwillingness of Soviet officials to address the violent character of the Soviet invasion, have had a long-term impact on the veterans of the war. Furthermore, this impact has later resurfaced in different ways in the newly emerging post-Soviet societies.[4] By bringing together new original

[2]   For reintegration strategies of Soviet Afghan veterans into Soviet society see also Karen Petrone, "Coming Home Soviet Style: The Reintegration of Afghan Veterans into Soviet Everyday Life", in *Everyday Life in Russia Past and Present*, eds. Choi Chatterjee, David L. Ransel, Mary Cavender, and Karen Petrone (Bloomington: Indiana University Press, 2015), 350–67; J. Riordan, "Disabled Afgantsy: Fighters for a Better Deal", in *Social Change and Social Issues in the Former USSR*, ed. Walter Joyce (Basingstoke: Macmillan, 1992), 136–57. In this context, it would also be worth analyzing the handling of the war experiences by the Afghan people—an undertaking that is however outside the field of expertise of the contributors to this issue.

[3]   For this field of research in other contexts, see also Beatrice De Graaf and George Dimitriu and Jens Ringsmose (eds), *Strategic Narratives, Public Opinion and War: Winning Domestic Support for the Afghan War* (London: Routledge, 2015); Benjamin Ziemann, *Contested Commemorations: Republican War Veterans and Weimar Political Culture* (Cambridge: Cambridge University Press, 2013); Anne Demers, "When Veterans Return: The Role of Community in Reintegration", *Journal of Loss and Trauma: International Perspectives on Stress & Coping* 16, no. 2 (2011): 160–79; Karen J. Burnell, Peter G. Coleman, and Nigel Hunt, "Coping with Traumatic Memories: Second World War Veterans' Experiences of Social Support in Relation to the Narrative Coherence of War Memories", *Ageing and Society* 30, no. 1 (2010): 57–78; Neil Jeffrey Diamant, *Embattled Glory: Veterans, Military Families, and the Politics of Patriotism in China, 1949–2007* (Lanham, MD: Rowman & Littlefield Publishers, 2009); David A. Gerber, "Disabled Veterans, the State, and the Experience of Disability in Western Societies, 1914–1950", *Journal of Social History* 26, no. 4 (2003): 899–916.

[4]   We are grateful to the participants of the "Back from Afghanistan" workshop held at European Humanities University in Vilnius on 12–13 February 2015 with the support of the German Academic Exchange Service DAAD. A short report can be found here: M. Mirschel, "Tagungsbericht: Back from Afghanistan. Workshop on the experiences of veterans from the war in Afghanistan in Tajikistan, Ukraine, Belarus, Russia, Lithuania and Germany, 12.02.2015 – 13.02.2015 Vilnius", *H-Soz-Kult*, 5 September 2015, http://hsozkult.geschichte.hu-berlin.de/index.asp?id=6144&view=pdf&pn=tagungsberichte&type=tagungsberichte. We particularly wish to thank Tomas Balkelis, Aliaksej Bratochkin, Fabio

research on Ukrainian, Russian, and Tajik veterans we set out here to examine and compare the impact of the Soviet–Afghan War from a transnational perspective, across different post-Soviet contexts.

From the perspective of conscripts from the European parts of the Soviet Union, this was a war that took place in a remote country; yet the war had a substantial impact on the different home societies, both before and after the soldiers returned from Afghanistan.[5] This special issue analyzes this impact with an emphasis on the ways in which the veterans dealt with the violent experience of the Soviet–Afghan War and its consequences in different Soviet and post-Soviet societies. The different contributions take into consideration the social, legal and media strategies applied with a view to (re)integrating the (often traumatized) veterans in radically changed political contexts after the dissolution of the USSR.[6] In this introduction we give a brief overview of the research on the war itself; we draw some parallels with the war in Afghanistan in the early 21st century; and finally, we formulate some relevant questions for the future study of the impact of war in a transcultural perspective.[7]

Balfetti, and Jan C. Behrends for providing feedback on the presented texts. All websites cited in this article were accessible on 21 July 2015.

[5]   German veterans of the Second World War became active in shaping the imagination of the war in the earlier years of the Federal Republic of Germany; see: B. Schwelling, „Krieger in Nachkriegszeiten – Veteranenverbände als geschichtspolitische Akteure der frühen Bundesrepublik", in *Geschichtspolitik: Wer sind ihre Akteure, wer ihre Rezipienten?*, eds. Claudia Fröhlich and Horst-Alfred Heinrich (Stuttgart: Franz Steiner Verlag, 2004), 69–80.

[6]   A first version of this introduction was presented as part of the panel "Learning from the Soviet Union? Strategies of Social Inclusion of Afghan War Veterans", organized by the authors during the 50th Convention of German historians in Göttingen on 25 September 2014. A short report can be found here: „HT 2014: Von der Sowjetunion lernen? Der gesellschaftliche Umgang mit Veteranen des Sowjetisch-Afghanischen Krieges", 23–26 September 2014, Göttingen, *H-Soz-Kult*, 10 October 2014, http://hsozkult.geschichte.hu-berlin.de/tagungsberich te/id=5619.

[7]   For an analysis of the impact of wars in a transcultural perspective, see also Julia Eichenberg and John Paul Newman (eds), *The Great War and Veterans' Internationalism* (London: Palgrave Macmillan, 2013).

The Soviet–Afghan War and its Consequences

When Soviet troops entered Afghanistan on 25 December 1979, the last large-scale battle of the Cold War started. The declared official goal of the invasion was to uphold Soviet influence and the establishment of public order in a neighboring country troubled by a civil war that had been dragging on for years.[8] The Soviet troops were issued no direct order to fight in Afghanistan. Rather, they were supposed to be overseeing central infrastructure construction projects, training the Afghan army, and providing logistical support for its fight against the Mujahidin. Within a single decade, the Soviet Union sent in total over 600,000 military and civil personnel to Afghanistan. Almost immediately after the invasion, it became clear that the Soviet military presence had only provoked a further deepening of the civil war: instead of bringing peace to Afghanistan, the Soviet Union had become a party to the Afghan conflict in its own right. This had further military consequences.[9] The Mujahidin commanders focused on the deployment of guerrilla tactics, which resulted in about 15,000 Soviet casualties across the course of the war.[10] Eventually, having failed to achieve any of its strategic goals, the Soviet leadership finally decided to withdraw its troops and ended the intervention officially on 15 February 1989.

In addition to the human losses caused by the war, the Soviet decision to violate the Afghan border had a negative impact on the reputation of the Soviet state and its institutions, both within and outside the Soviet Union. Formally the intervention was presented as an act of internationalist brotherly help for a friendly society and

---

[8]   Robert Johnson, *The Afghan Way of War: Culture and Pragmatism: A Critical History* (London: Hurst & Co, 2011), 208; Artemy Kalinovsky, "Decision-Making and the Soviet War in Afghanistan. From Intervention to Withdrawal", *Journal of Cold War Studies* 11, no. 4, (2009): 46–73; David N. Gibbs, "Reassessing Soviet Motives for Invading Afghanistan: A Declassified History", *Critical Asian Studies* 38, no. 2 (2006): 239–63; Aleksandr A. Lyakhovskiy, "Inside the Soviet Invasion of Afghanistan, and the Seizure of Kabul, December 1979", *CWIHP Working Paper* 51 (January 2007).

[9]   See Gregory Barnes, *The Soviet–Afghan War 1979–89* (Oxford: Osprey Publishing, 2012).

[10] Grigorii Krivosheev, *Rossiia i SSSR v voinakh XX veka: Poteri vooruzhennykh sil. Istorio-statisticheskoe issledovanie* (Podol'sk: GUP MO, 2005), 611–19.

an act of self-defense according to the UN Charter.[11] Domestically, the obvious contradiction between the war's official image and its reality served to multiply the doubts of ordinary Soviet citizens regarding the legitimacy not only of Soviet intentions in Afghanistan but also of Soviet institutions per se.[12] In 1980 the United Nations General Assembly condemned the Soviet intervention and "appeal[ed] to all States to respect the sovereignty, territorial integrity (...) of Afghanistan."[13] Therefore, even while limited to the territory of Afghanistan, this war had global consequences since it put an end to attempts to contain the Cold War. The United States declared the Soviet intervention an expansionist move.[14] Even if the US were formally not directly involved in the conflict, they did provide financial support and weapons to the Mujahidin. Both superpowers reinforced their parallel nuclear programs during the conflict. In addition, many (Western) countries protested against the war and consequently boycotted the 1980 Moscow Olympic games. Moreover, from a midterm perspective, it is clear that the economic impact of the Soviet–Afghan War was one of the factors that weakened the Soviet Union in general, by worsening the situation in the course of the 1980s. Thus, we view this war as an accelerating factor, but not as the cause of the dissolution of the Soviet Empire.[15]

---

[11]   Pierre Allan and Dieter Kläy have edited a collection of documents concerning the Soviet–Afghan War: Pierre Allan and Dieter, *Zwischen Bürokratie und Ideologie: Entscheidungsprozesse in Moskaus Afghanistankonflikt* (Bern, Stuttgart, Wien: Paul Haupt Verlag, 1999); see also Grau and Gress (eds), *Soviet–Afghan War*.

[12]   Braithwaite, *Afgantsy*, 330.

[13]   "The Situation in Afghanistan and its Implications for International Peace and Security", *6th Emergency Special Session* (convened by the UN Security Council), 10–14 January 1980, http://www.un.org/ga/sessions/emergency.shtml.

[14]   The US President Jimmy Carter asserted that: "This invasion is an extremely serious threat to peace because of the threat of further Soviet expansion into neighboring countries in Southwest Asia and also because such an aggressive military policy is unsettling to other peoples throughout the world"; "Address to the Nation on the Soviet Invasion of Afghanistan," 4 January 1980, *The American Presidency Project*, http://www.presidency.ucsb.edu/ws/?pid=32911.

[15]   An analysis of the political, social and economic consequences and related debates can be found here: William Maley, *The Afghanistan Wars* (New York: Palgrave Macmillan, 2009); Rafael Reuveny and Aseem Prakash, "The Afghanistan

The Soviet intervention and the subsequent withdrawal had various effects on Afghanistan itself and on neighboring societies.[16] After 1989 the Taliban gained more influence in Afghanistan. It was their support for Al Qaeda before the terrorist acts of September 11 that gave the formal occasion for an intervention of several NATO member states in Afghanistan. In October 2001 the US jointly with Great Britain launched "Operation Enduring Freedom", which was profiled as a war against terror. Afterwards, the "International Security Assistance Force" (ISAF) was launched in December 2001 and formally organized as a stabilizing and training mission for the Afghan army and security forces.[17]

The Soviet and the more recent war in Afghanistan share certain features.[18] Generally, the Soviet leadership had decided, much as ISAF would later do, to uphold only a minimum level of security and public order in Afghanistan. Securing strategically important locations and training the Afghan army were among the top priorities

---

War and the Breakdown of the Soviet Union", *Review of International Studies* 25 (1999): 693–708.

[16]   See Larry P. Goodson, *Afghanistan's Endless War: State Failure, Regional Politics, and the Rise of the Taliban* (Seattle, WA: University of Washington Press, 2001).

[17]   The mission was officially completed at the end of 2014. Among the armies engaged in this ISAF were the German army, and armies from all around the world—from Canada, France, Italy, and Poland, and from Jordan, South Korea, and Australia. The coalition's military fatalities across both operations in Afghanistan numbered 3,487. For the Bundeswehr the ISAF brought the largest number of casualties in its history to date; „Todesfälle im Auslandseinsatz", *Bundeswehr* official website, July 2014, http://www.bundeswehr.de/portal/a/bwde/!ut/p/c4/04_SB8K8xLLM9MSSzPy8xBz9CP3I5EyrpHK9pPKUVL301JTU-vOzUPL2S_JTU4rTE1Jyc1PjM3PjUzLzixJIq_YJsRoUAEK3m7A!!/#par4.

[18]   For comparative overviews of the two interventions, strategies, and efforts see: Peter Tomsen, *The Wars of Afghanistan: Messianic Terrorism, Tribal Conflicts, and the Failures of Great Powers* (New York: Public Affairs, 2011); Martin Kipping, *State-Building: Erfolg und Scheitern in Afghanistan* (Baden Baden: Nomos Verlagsgesellschaft, 2011); Peter Marsden, *Afghanistan: Aid, Armies and Empires* (London: I. B. Tauris, 2009); Abdulkader H. Sinno, *Organizations at War in Afghanistan and Beyond* (Ithaca, NY: Cornell University Press, 2008). An analysis of arguments used by Soviet and NATO officials during their interventions in Afghanistan can be found here: Katja Mielke and Conrad Schetter, „Wiederholt sich Geschichte? Die legitimatorischen Deutungsmuster der Intervention in Afghanistan 1979 und 2001", *Peripherie. Zeitschrift für Politik und Ökonomie in der Dritten Welt* 29, no. 116 (2009): 448–68.

shared by the leaders of both interventions. The number of soldiers present in the Hindu Kush across the two interventions was also comparable.[19] A further structural similarity might be found in the euphemistic treatment of the war that characterized early public representations of both interventions. The evasive rhetoric used in reporting the more recent war was in some ways reminiscent of the 1980s Soviet discourse on "fraternal aid". Thus, for example, in the early 21st century the employment of Bundeswehr soldiers in Afghanistan was initially presented in the German public sphere as a kind of militarily secured form of developmental aid.[20] A debate over whether this was a full-fledged war was initiated only after the first troops returned and the first soldier was killed.[21] Subsequently the German federal government changed tack and now for the first time described the war as "armed conflict in the sense of humanitarian international law", but not as "war".[22] In such attempts to camou-

---

[19]   The Soviet contingent had varied between 80,000 and 100,000 soldiers per year. In 2010 ISAF enlarged its contingent from 70,000 to 130,000; Viktor Rudenko (ed.), *Ty v pamiati i serdtse moem, Afganistan: Materialy voenno-prakticheskoi konferentsii, posviashchennoi 15-i godovshchine vyvoda Ogranichennogo kontingenta sovetskikh voisk iz Afganistana* (Voronezh: Kalita-R, 2004), 60; "Facts and Figures", *ISAF* official website, October 2009, http://www.nato.int/isaf/docu/e pub/pdf/placemat_archive/isaf_placemat_091001.pdf; "Facts and Figures", *ISAF* official website, November 2010, http://www.isaf.nato.int/images/stories/File/ Placemats/15%20NOV.Placemat%20page1-3.pdf.

[20]   For example, particular stress was placed in official sources on the building of girls' schools and fountains in an attempt to detach the violent character of the ongoing war from the image of the intervention in Afghanistan.

[21]   It was only the ensuing debate that changed the public perception of the intervention in Germany. See Kaare Dahl Martinsen, „Totgeschwiegen? Deutschland und die Gefallenen des Afghanistan-Einsatzes", *APuZ* 44 (2013), http://www.bp b.de/apuz/170806/deutschland-und-die-gefallenen-des-afghanistan-einsatzes? p=all.

[22]   See „Regierungserklärung des Außenministers zum Bundeswehr-Einsatzes in Afghanistan", *Die Bundesregierung*, 10 February 2010, http://www.bundesregie- rung.de/ContentArchiv/DE/Archiv17/Regierungserklaerung/2010/2010-02-10- westerwelle-regierungserklaerung-afghanistan.html. In April 2010 the German Minister of Defense, Karl-Theodor zu Guttenberg, first mentioned the term "war", but in a non-legal sense: "Even if not everybody will like it. Facing the ongoing fights in parts of Afghanistan, one can colloquially—and colloquially only—speak of a war"; „Guttenberg spricht von Krieg", *Deutsche Welle*, 4 April 2010, http://www.dw.de/guttenberg-spricht-von-krieg/a-5432108.

flage the real nature of the war we see a parallel to the Soviet representation of the intervention in Afghanistan back in the 1980s. In
the Soviet case there was an internal official order on precisely how
to label the "brotherhood" and "solidarity" of the Soviet and Afghan
peoples, in order to hide the violent nature of the intervention and
to avoid its being perceived by the Soviet society and the international community as an expansionist move.[23]

An important difference between the two cases arises out of
the Soviet attempt, throughout the greater part of the war, to avoid
reporting any casualties whatsoever. Throughout the 1980s, coffins
bearing the mortal remains of soldiers fallen in combat were returning to all the Soviet republics. Instead of addressing the resulting
family sorrow and loss as an effect of the war, the Soviet media coverage stressed the civil achievements as an effect of internationalist
solidarity. It was only towards the end of the war that texts condemning the violence and its consequences were published in the
Soviet press. The title of Svetlana Aleksievich's documentary novel
Zinky Boys,[24] for example, became a metaphorical phrase for the violence in Afghanistan recognized all over the Soviet Union. The official Soviet press coverage of the war also changed over time. Because of perestroika and glasnost a critical social debate about the
war and the trauma experienced by the Soviet soldiers gained mo-
mentum.[25] The Committees of Soldiers' Mothers made the deaths of
their sons a public issue for the first time. Popular accounts such as

---

[23] Martha Vogel, *Roter Teufel - mächtiger mugahid. Widerstandsbilder im sowjetisch-afghanischen Krieg 1979–1989* (Wien: Böhlau, 2008), 26; Esther Meier, *Eine
Theorie für „Entwicklungsländer": Sowjetische Agitation und Afghanistan 1978–
1982* (Berlin: LIT, 2001), 85–88. We thank Markus Mirschel for this suggestion.
[24] Previews of the book were published first in Russian in the Soviet Union after
the war in different newspapers such as *Druzhba narodov* and *Komsomol'skaia
pravda*. After publication, the book generated worldwide interest and was translated into many other languages; Svetlana Aleksievich, *Tsinkovye mal'chiki*
(Moskva: Golosa utopii, 1990); in English: *Zinky Boys: Soviet Voices from the
Afghanistan War* (New York: W. W. Norton & Company, 1992), in German:
Zinkjungen. Afghanistan und die Folgen (Frankfurt am Main: Fischer, 1992).
[25] See Julie Elkner, "Dedovshchina and the Committee of Soldiers' Mothers under
Gorbachev", *The Journal of Power Institutions in Post-Soviet Societies* 1 (2004),
http://pipss.revues.org/243.

Aleksievich's documentary writings established a highly critical perspective on the individual price paid by the many conscripts sent to Afghanistan: the long-term presence of violence in the everyday life of the returnees, and its impact, on a small scale, on individual families, and on a large scale, on Soviet society as a whole.

We see a further parallel in the political decisions that were made to withdraw troops in the late 1980s and in the early 21st century even though or rather precisely because no military victory was in sight. Both sets of troop withdrawals were based on a certain degree of acceptance of the following issues: 1) the intervention had been based on false assumptions about the military, political, and social situation in Afghanistan; 2) even a large military presence would not be able to guarantee a lasting stability; and 3) the intervention lacked legitimacy in the eyes of a considerable share of inhabitants of Afghanistan themselves. As early as in the mid-1980s, the Soviet leaders recognized that Soviet troops would not be able to establish a Soviet type of socialism in Afghanistan, even in the long run.[26] With their support of Mohammad Najibullah in 1986 they opted instead for a president who would try to consolidate society around his version of "pragmatic nationalism".[27] A similar change in operational strategies can also be observed in the history of ISAF. From 2010 ISAF made a stronger push for political reconciliation between rival groups instead of concentrating on fighting against the Taliban with military force.[28] Finally, both in 1989 and

---

[26] See Sapper, *Die Auswirkungen auf den Afghanistankrieg*, 260–88.

[27] Kalinovsky, *Long Goodbye*, 93–121.

[28] Therefore, the responsibility for security passed into Afghan hands and ISAF contingents were diminished. Cf. "Security Council Extends International Security Assistance Force in Afghanistan for One Year to Help Build Afghan Security Sector", *UN Security Council*, 13 October 2010, http://www.un.org/press/en/2010/sc10049.doc.htm. Furthermore, the German Federal Minister of Foreign Affairs, Guido Westerwelle, said during a speech to the Bundestag in 2012 that: "Reconciliation and mutual understanding among the Afghan people themselves are the core options for securing a long term peace in Afghanistan. (...). Our strategy (...) is based on the insight that there will be no military solution, but only a political solution to the conflict. (...). It is fully clear, this intervention, which started 11 years ago, shall not last another ten or twenty years. This is common sense"; „214. Sitzung des Deutschen Bundestags", *Plenarprotokoll* 17/214, 13 December 2012, 26331, http://dipbt.bundestag.de/dip21/btp/17/17214.pdf.

2014 the troop withdrawals were carried out based on political decisions taken because the outside societies involved in Afghanistan
were no longer willing to pay the high price of human loss and the
huge material costs of the interventions.

Even given all the parallels above, there are obvious differences when it comes to the soldiers who fought the two wars. The
most striking difference is between the large-scale conscription
army deployed in the Soviet case and the compact professional military contingents that participated on behalf of several states in "Operation Enduring Freedom" and ISAF. Together with technological
changes this resulted not only in a remarkable difference in terms of
the soldiers' equipment. Thus, the Soviet system of conscription
brought thousands of barely prepared soldiers to Afghanistan. Many
of them did not know in advance that they were about to operate in
a full-fledged war and were not familiar with the regional specifics.
In addition, most of them would not, if given the choice, have opted
for risking their lives for the sake of "international solidarity". In
many cases conscripts experienced service in the Soviet army and in
the Soviet–Afghan War in particular as a kind of forced migration
and slave labor. This is obviously very different from the case of the
early 21st century professional armies, whose soldiers are by definition volunteers who decide to join the armed forces knowing that
they will likely be exposed to violence in one of the global conflict
"hot spots". The public discourses in the US and Western Europe on
psychological consequences such as post-traumatic stress disorder
(PTSD) and new programs of social care for veterans also reflect a
considerably higher social awareness of the risks that the soldiers
shoulder when returning from wars to their families.

The Return of Soviet Soldiers to New Post-Soviet Republics

The return of the last veterans from Afghanistan in 1989 was an important part of the political upheaval that helped to bring about the
dissolution of the Soviet Union.[29] In a first phase after the break-up
of the Union in 1991, the Afghanistan veterans were mostly left to

---

[29]   See Reuveny and Prakash, "Afghanistan War", 700–4.

deal with the new circumstances on their own. Next, newly emerging veterans' organizations started to fight over resources, particularly in Russia, in an attempt to gain political influence, recognition, and social rights.[30] Due to a lack of state support, some veterans used their Afghanistan networks in order to establish new criminal structures.[31]

After the collapse of the Soviet Union, the formal legal recognition of the returning soldiers' rights as "veterans" was established to various degrees in the newly independent states in the mid-1990s. It was only then, when the process of recognition in new nationally defined contexts started, that the *afgantsy*, as the Soviet veterans of the Soviet–Afghan War were unofficially called, gained legal and social rights. In the Russian Federation former combatants were granted a new legal status by law in 1995. Thus, the veterans gained pensions in the event of long-term injuries, and a certain minimum level of public medical care.[32] However, to this day the *afgantsy* do not enjoy legal equality with the veterans of the Great Patriotic War, and have access to a lower level of social benefits.

A rising level of cooperation with state institutions on the part of veterans' organizations in Russia, aimed at gaining more recognition from the state, can be observed from the 2000s onwards. In the frame of the resulting new public-private partnership between the state and veterans' organizations a joint vision of the history of the Soviet–Afghan War has likewise emerged. As part of this vision, representatives of both the state and the major veterans' organizations have joined forces to draw a heroic picture of the Soviet intervention. Critical aspects such as the physical and psychological consequences for the soldiers as well as strategic and tactical mistakes made by both political and military leaders have been excluded from this heroic image. In Putin's Russia state actors have deployed this picture of the war especially to support a new national patriotic identification with the state. At the same time representatives of the

---

[30]   See Michael Galbas' paper in this issue.

[31]   See Serguei Alex. Oushakine, *The Patriotism of Despair: Nation, War, and Loss in Russia* (Ithaca, NY: Cornell University Press, 2009).

[32]   "Federal'nyi zakon N 5-f3 'O veteranach' ot 12 yanvaria 1995", *Rossiiskaia gazeta*, 15 January 1995, http://www.rg.ru/1995/01/25/zakon-dok.html.

state offered the veterans a changed function in the public dis-course—something we would describe as a kind of official co-opta-tion of the veterans, who were promised greater recognition and so-cial re-integration in exchange for their loyalty. For those veterans who were members of organized veterans' groups, the cooperation with the state offered the prospect of a higher level of retrospective social approval for the Soviet intervention in Afghanistan and con-stantly a higher level of social acceptance and a higher social status for the war's veterans.

In other post-Soviet republics the picture is quite different. In Ukraine the *afgantsy* were also dissatisfied with the welfare and de-manded political and social support from the state throughout the 1990s. But in contrast to the Russian case, in Ukraine this initially did not lead to tighter cooperation with state agencies. On the con-trary, we saw *afgantsy* becoming highly active during the Maidan protests, where they supported first the protesting students and later the popular demand for Yanukovych's dismissal.[33]

In the Baltic states *afgantsy* are organized and active, but they do not make their claims for social rights public. In these societies the deployment of Lithuanian, Latvian, and Estonian conscripts in the Soviet–Afghan War is not easily combined with the dominant narratives of national pride. Nevertheless the veterans from Lithua-nia, for example, were able to gain some legal recognition as victims of totalitarian rule. Some insights into the conditions of their lives today are given by the visual anthropologist Anna Reich in her photo essay about Lithuanian veterans from the Soviet–Afghan War at the end of this issue.

In the nearby Republic of Belarus the newly arisen veterans' organizations developed different strategies and approaches to deal with state structures in order to gain social benefits from the 1990s onwards. On the one hand, several of the organizations have openly criticized the social policies of the Lukashenka administration. This became particularly challenging in 2007 after a new law was issued

---

33   Yu. Butusov, "Afhantsi Maidanu: Vymoha odna—povnoe perezavantazhennia vlady," *Dzerkalo Tyzhnia* (Ukraine), 7 February 2014, http://gazeta.dt.ua/inter-nal/afganci-maydanu-vimoga-odna-povne-perezavantazhennya-vladi-_.html. See also Iryna Sklokina's paper on the *afgantsy* in Ukraine in this issue.

canceling all forms of special social welfare measures for Afghan veterans.[34] Due to the oppositional spirit of these associations their access to financial resources and to a broader public sphere beyond the Internet has been denied by the Lukashenka regime.[35] Therefore, apart from oppositional media channels such as internet portals, these organizations have almost no resources for organizing public activities beyond the ultra-local level or for providing material support for their members. On the other hand, those organizations which cooperated with the regime from the very beginning have succeeded in gathering enough resources not only to support their members but also to bring their memories and experiences into public space. The most prominent example of this is the foundation "Afghan Memory" (*Pamiat' Afgana*), which runs a military recreation park near Minsk called "The Stalin Line" (*Liniia Stalina*). This park not only glorifies the defense of Minsk in 1941, but also uses military equipment dating to the Soviet–Afghan War for the purposes of "patriotic education of the youth".[36]

These examples illustrate how much variation there has been in dealing with the Soviet–Afghan war experience across the newly independent states after the collapse of the Soviet Union. In order to gain insights into the handling of the Soviet–Afghan war experiences by the veterans within the Soviet Union, we open this special issue with Yaacov Ro'i's article "The Varied Reintegration of the Afghan War Veterans in their Home Society". Ro'i shows the very different paths of *afgantsy* returning from war in Afghanistan into the Soviet society. In this context he analyzes the factors that affected the re-acclimatization of the *afgantsy* into civilian life. Based on this, Ro'i highlights the fact that the strategies used in the reintegration of the veterans were not only the result of conscious choice but depended to a large degree on objective conditions such as the timing

---

[34]   Ye. Smirnov, "Konstitutsionnyi sud abiazan vosstanovit'nai prava", *Afganiets, Spetsial'nyi vypusk*, nos 3–4 (2008).

[35]   "Afgantsy trebuiut ot Miasnikovicha vernut' l'goty", *Belorusskii partizan*, 9 September 2013, http://www.belaruspartisan.org/politic/241603/.

[36]   See also Felix Ackermann, „Wem gehört der Große Sieg? Die öffentliche Aushandlung der Erinnerung an den Zweiten Weltkrieg in Belarus", *Zeitgeschichte-online*, July 2014, http://www.zeitgeschichte-online.de/geschichtskultur/wem-gehoert-der-grosse-sieg.

of their return home, for example, before or after the emergence of glasnost and perestroika.

In our understanding, the specifics of the returning veterans' different responses and experiences are shaped by the asymmetry of the war in combination with the Soviet denial and refusal to recognize its character as a full-fledged war. It was this denial in particular which made it hard for political and social actors to make sense of the Soviet–Afghan War and even more of its casualties. Did the veterans actually support the development aid that they were providing by force of arms? Or could they even be seen as heroes, whose actions in Afghanistan might be viewed as a defense of the fatherland comparable to the feat of the veterans of the Great Patriotic War? To this day, the last Soviet war remains in the shadow of the Great Patriotic War—in particular because, first, the Soviet–Afghan War directly affected only a part of the Soviet society and, second, this was not a war that could be classed as a military success. The Soviet victory in the Great Patriotic War thus constitutes a much more valuable political asset, and hence its ongoing use in societies such as Russia and Belarus today as a central point of reference for further political engineering of post-Soviet national identities.[37]

Four Dimensions of the Collective *Afgantsy* Experience

The contributors to this special issue focus on the question of how the collective experiences of the *afgantsy* influenced them in navigating the radically changing social and political context in the late 1980s and beyond. We regard the veterans as a social group, spread across all of the former Soviet republics and united by a shared set of experiences, which makes them one of the last Soviet generations

---

[37]   See Lev Gudkov, "The Fetters of Victory: How the War Provides Russia with its Identity", *Eurozine* (2005), http://www.eurozine.com/articles/2005-05-03-gudkov-en.html?filename=article/2005-05-03-gudkov-en, first published in *Neprikosnovennyi zapas* 40, nos 2–3 (2005); Thomas Sherlock, *Historical Narratives in the Soviet Union and Post-Soviet Russia: Destroying the Settled Past, Creating an Uncertain Future* (New York: Palgrave Macmillan, 2007).

shaped by a particular historical moment.[38] These shared experiences include their service in the Soviet army, their (mostly forced) deployment in Afghanistan, and their return to their homes in the 1980s, at a time when glasnost, perestroika, and the decision to withdraw were either about to be launched or had already changed the configuration in which the Soviet–Afghan War was discussed in public. Thus, the *afgantsy* were caught between sharply contrasting attitudes towards and policies on the war. Furthermore, with the dissolution of the Soviet Union the *afgantsy* now had to find their place in the societies of the newly independent states.

In order to consider how the veterans dealt with these experiences within different political and social settings, the contributors to this issue analyze four key dimensions of this issue. First, they examine how the veterans organized in network structures, which helped to preserve their experiences from the war and then transmit them into post-Soviet contexts. Our authors address how both the specific set of veterans' experiences and their networks have been used as social capital with a view to gaining recognition in the newly emerging states. Second, the contributors look at the ways in which veterans' groups have competed with each other for state support and recognition, and the role that *afgantsy* have occasionally played in giving support and legitimacy to state structures. The latter point is especially relevant to contexts where state structures have suffered from a lack of legitimacy, including in Tajikistan in the early 1990s and during the Euromaidan protests in Ukraine in 2013/14. Third, the articles focus on how narratives about the Soviet–Afghan War have changed in these different settings, and on the specific forms acquired by the general frame for remembering the Soviet–Afghan War in particular given societies. Finally, the authors explore the transnational dimensions of these developments. Without physically changing location, the *afgantsy* were transferred in 1991 into separate and in many ways new and different contexts, which were now formally organized as nation states. However, at the same time, transnational links among the veterans also remained in place.

---

[38]   See Sapper, *Die Auswirkungen des Afghanistan-Krieges auf die Sowjetgesellschaft*, 148–50.

How did this post-imperial setting influence the veterans' networks? To what extent did pre-1991 links remain important? And perhaps even more importantly, how does the imperial frame of the war experience still structure the relationship between the *afgantsy* in different settings?

The present issue addresses these questions by dealing with three different cases, examining the situation of Afghan veterans in Russia, Ukraine, and Tajikistan. First, Markus Göransson's paper on the Tajik case focuses on the impact of state dissolution in the early 1990s, which meant that the *afgantsy* had to choose which side to support in an emerging civil war. Göransson depicts how, during the 1980s, the common experience in the war in neighboring Afghanistan created a horizontal community of veterans that cut across regional, religious, and national identities. For the most part these horizontal links did not last. During the state crisis of the 1990s and beyond, the regional identities of the *afgantsy* were strengthened in particular as the mobilization of veterans' networks in the conflict took place mainly in local settings.

Next, Michael Galbas in his paper "'Our Pain and Our Glory': Social Strategies of Legitimization and Functionalization of the Soviet–Afghan War in the Russian Federation" examines the development of the relationship between state institutions and the veterans in Russia. He traces the transition of Russian *afgantsy* organizations from their beginnings as potentially oppositional structures to a situation in which they increasingly became part of the state apparatus transmitting social welfare. He argues that in exchange for this exclusive position vis-à-vis the state apparatus, Afghan veterans' organizations became a loyal pillar supporting the government's attempts to reshape the historical imagination of Russia as a glorious historical entity.

An example of the ways in which the relationship between state and veterans differs in the respective successor states of the Soviet Union is provided by Iryna Sklokina's article "Veterans of the Soviet–Afghan War and the Ukrainian Nation-building Project: from Perestroika to the Maidan and the War in Donbas". In her analysis, Sklokina is interested in particular in the behavior of the Ukrainian *afgantsy* during state crises such as the events following the Euromaidan in 2013/14. In this context, she uncovers a certain breakdown in the emotional bonds that had previously linked the *afgantsy* in Ukraine as "former Soviet veterans of the war in Afghanistan". Whereas some veterans supported the process of nation-building and the change of the political sphere in Ukraine, in contrast, others understand their personal Afghanistan experience as a part of the greatness of Russia and lean more towards the Russian imperial project.

All of the papers presented here describe various strategies employed by the *afgantsy* in different environments in order to navigate the changing social and political contexts in the late 1980s and beyond. In a final comment Jan C. Behrends points out that the Afghanistan veterans had in common a fight for public recognition and social entitlements as well as being bonded by the experience of violence and their willingness to use it to achieve their goals. Therefore, Behrends considers the Soviet–Afghan War as the starting point for a history of violent entanglement that shaped the (post-) Soviet experience and has become particularly visible in the ongoing war in Eastern Ukraine. We see the Tajik, Russian, and Ukrainian cases covered in this special issue as just the beginning of a larger transcultural comparison incorporating additional perspectives and, in particular, covering the Afghan side of the war. Already at this stage it has been shown, that the long-term impact of the Soviet–Afghan War on post-Soviet societies and politics is not to be underestimated. The strategies of civil integration adopted by many veterans and the further employment of the military experience in post-Soviet conflict by other *afgantsy* are two sides of the same coin.

The Varied Reintegration of the Afghan War Veterans in Their Home Society

Yaacov Ro'i

Abstract: This article looks at the adaptation of the Soviet Afghan war veterans to Soviet civilian life in the unsettled 1980s. It discusses their problems as they sought to make the transformation from the war to a "normal" existence as regular Soviet citizens at a time of instability and economic and political crisis. In doing so, it explains how and why they opted for, or were channeled into, different directions, and suggests that it many cases it was not their own individual inclination or choice, but rather a wide gamut of constraints and external forces that propelled them into a given trajectory.

"We came home anticipating a celebration," veteran of the Soviet–Afghan War Ruslan Umiev said two years after coming back from Afghanistan. "But," he went on,

> we landed in yet another war—a moral one. It's not a question of material well-being, although none of us got rich in this war. Nor has anyone told us what it was all about—an aid mission or a miscalculation? We have difficulty finding friends, we have difficulty being understood. ... Who are we—Afgantsy-soldiers, internationalists, or some guys who messed up the fate of other people as well as their own? We are constantly asked these questions—at work, on the street, at home. We ask ourselves these same questions.[1]

This article sets out to look at the different paths taken by the Afghan war veterans as they sought to resolve these issues and reintegrate into their home societies. It will try to explain why their reintegration was as varied as it in fact was, since at first glance, the great

---

[1]   Gennadii Zhavoronkov, "Afganistan: vzgliad iz 1980-go goda," *Moskovskie novosti*, 23 July 1989, 9.

majority of them had much in common, having undergone an identical formative experience. They had been sent to Afghanistan just a year or so after finishing school in a very stereotyped and rigid education system, without for the most part having had time to study or take up a profession, let alone to shape their personality or individuality. They returned to their Soviet homeland as young men in their early twenties after undergoing one and a half to two years in a particularly brutal and cruel war in a foreign and very different country; indeed, almost all of them had friends or at least knew people who had been killed, often in front of their very eyes, a large number of them over ten such people.[2] Their successful adaptation to civilian life was therefore not a foregone conclusion and their endeavor to do so and the different paths they chose or that came their way to attain that end are the topic of our present discussion.

Indeed, I argue that in many instances the variety was not the result of any conscious choice on the part of the *afgantsy*. Often it emanated from options thrown their way by such objective contingencies as the timing of their return home, with those returning under glasnost and perestroika encountering conditions very different from those who came back earlier. Frequently, too, it was the outcome of a lack of options given the circumstances of the society to which they came back, for example in the case of those who returned to the countryside, especially in the periphery. In many cases, the veterans' own psychological condition also precluded any free choice.

Intending in the early 1990s to research the Soviet domestic implications of the Soviet–Afghan War, I needed to understand who exactly the *afgantsy* were, how they perceived their experience in Afghanistan, the way it influenced them as private individuals and as Soviet citizens, and how they re-acclimatized to civilian life in the Soviet Union. With this end, I conducted a survey of over 220 veterans in the first half of the 1990s in eleven of the Soviet Union's fifteen successor states (all indeed except Georgia and the three Baltic

---

[2]   Of my interviewees, 95 percent knew people who had been killed; 39 percent more than ten such cases. In addition to the grief that this often entailed, especially when those killed were close friends, these experiences entailed an enhanced sense of one's own insecurity and vulnerability.

states from which less than five percent of those who fought in Afghanistan actually came).[3] The survey was based on snowball sampling methods, starting with *afgantsy* clubs around the former Soviet Union. The interviews were grounded in a set questionnaire. Since the focus of these interviews was far broader than that of the present article and since a great deal has been written about the *afgantsy* both in the former Soviet Union or its successor states and in the West, I have necessarily had resort to many of these sources to supplement my own findings.[4]

The aim of this article is to draw a more nuanced picture of the Soviet Afghan war veterans, who were frequently perceived by Soviet society as bing a homogeneous group, distinct from regular citizens,[5] and were duly dubbed by various epithets: drug addicts, criminals, heroes—to name just the most popular. My research, however, indicates that most of the veterans refute the idea that there was any typical *afganets* or characteristic *afganets* mentality despite their common background. My interviewees tended, however, to agree that the veterans could be classified in several groupings specified in my questionnaire. A total of 18.4 percent accepted their classification in two sub-groups—the so-called "lost generation" who resorted to drugs, crime, and violence, and those determined to help transform society; while 54.8 percent said they could be divided into three categories: those who returned with an active civic position; the so-called "lost generation"; and those indistinguishable from the population at large. Even among the 26.9 percent who denied altogether that there was a typical *afganets*, up to 35

---

3   I would like to express my gratitude to Roman Zolotaretskii, my then research assistant, who conducted the bulk of the fieldwork.

4   The most important of these works were probably: Svetlana Alexievich, *Zinky Boys: Soviet Voices from the Afghanistan War* (London and New York: W. W. Norton, 1992), which, although reflecting the mood in a certain sector of Soviet society in the period immediately following the war's end—it was originally published in Russian in 1990—is an authentic collection of the voices of veterans and their families; and Mark Galeotti, *Afghanistan: The Soviet Union's Last War* (London: Frank Cass, 1996), widely acknowledged as a leading study on the Soviet-Afghan War.

5   See, for example, V. Znakov, "Psikhologicheskie issledovaniia stereotipov ponimaniia lichnosti uchastnikov voiny v Afganistane," *Voprosy psikhologii*, no. 4 (1990): 108–16.

percent attributed to members of their group certain features or inclinations listed explicitly in the questionnaire. These sub-divisions
were designed to throw light on the ways and the extent to which
the *afgantsy* adapted to civilian life or were accepted into their home
surroundings.

The majority, in fact, ultimately found their niche in civvy
street even if they did not fulfill the Komsomol daily organ's ambitious definition of the "found generation" as those who re-integrated
into civilian life, took up key positions in Komsomol committees,
helped restructure the education of the young, created clubs for reservists, entered higher education, and played an active part in perestroika.[6]

The *afgantsy* belonged to different nationalities; came from a
wide variety of surroundings, although most came from villages, *kolkhozy*, and small towns, and were sons of blue-collar workers, farmers, and junior white-collar employees;[7] had had a variety of experiences in Afghanistan, the main divide being between those who had
participated directly in fighting and those who had not; and returned at different times, those coming back before glasnost and
those coming back under glasnost arriving in rather dissimilar societies. Naturally, too, comprising a relatively large group of people—
estimated at anywhere between 620,000 and approximately one million[8]—they could hardly be expected to reintegrate in their home
society in the same way.

---

[6]   *Komsomol'skaia pravda*, 27 June 1986 and 14 May 1988.
[7]   Mikhail Reshetnikov, Rector of the East European Institute for Psychoanalysis
in St. Petersburg, cited in "'Afganskii sindrom'—eto navsegda", *Rosbalt*, 14 February 2009, http://www.rosbalt.ru/piter/2009/02/14/618431.html (accessed 12
April 2015).
[8]   The number of Soviet military personnel who served in Afghanistan has not
been convincingly or ultimately ascertained, estimates ranging from 525,000 to
one million. In 1991 MPA (Main Political Administration) Chief Colonel-General
Nikolai Shliaga said there were 540,000 *afgantsy* in the Soviet Union; "Skol'ko
nas?", *Pobratim*, no. 11 (1991)—obviously this did not include the 15,000 or so
who had been killed. The official figures published by the Russian Federation
Ministry of Defense speak of a total of 620,000 Soviet servicemen in Afghanistan
from December 1979 through February 1989, of whom 525,000 soldiers had
served in the 40th Army, 90,000 were border troops and members of other KGB
units, and 5,000 Interior Ministry troops; *Rossiia i SSSR v voinakh XX veka: Poteri vooruzhennykh sil. Statisticheskoe issledovanie pod obshchei redaktsiei G.*

A paper prepared for the Supreme Soviet Committee for the Affairs of Internationalist Soldiers in 1991 discussed the veterans' heterogeneity—in their acknowledgement of the war, their value orientation, and their conduct in Afghanistan and back home. Their views of the war diverged, some recognizing its tragic nature, others perceiving it as a heroic epic; while some sought to preserve their sense of self-worth, others contented themselves with the status of legionnaire; some actually carried over their animosity toward the "adversary" in Afghanistan, found his equivalent at home (usually a local official) and were ready to destroy him.[9] Thirteen percent of my interviewees, responding to a multiple-choice question, visualized themselves on returning home as insufficiently appreciated heroes; 34 percent—as people to whom society owed a debt; and 53 percent—as pawns in a political game.

Having different views of themselves, of the war, and of Soviet society, the *afgantsy* embarked on various paths as they re-integrated. It took them varying periods of time to overcome the moral and psychological upheaval they had experienced. Some never did,[10] while others, especially perhaps in rural areas and in the country's southern periphery, moved ahead as if they had undergone a regular bout of army service. The difficulties the *afgantsy* encountered were more considerable than those known to troops returning from a prolonged period of war the world over, enhanced as they were by the upheavals that shook their home society in the latter half of the 1980s that entailed political uncertainty, economic crisis, and an ideological and ideational vacuum.

Krivosheeva (Moscow: Olma-press, 2001). No sources for these suspiciously round figures are given. Gorbachev, however, spoke of one million and a number of observers have agreed with this higher figure. My own estimate is around 750,000.

9   "Problemy sotsial'noi reabilitatsii uchastnikov voiny v Afganistane" [1991], n.a., 18–19. I was given this paper by Pavel Shetko who headed the commission.

10 There are no statistical data, nor even estimates, for those who remained mentally disabled and so disqualified from any genuine reintegration in society.

Welcome Home?

While in Afghanistan, most soldiers merely wanted to survive and return home. Just a few had qualms even then, and the seriously wounded were actually reluctant to go home.[11] But the *afgantsy* did not find the home they had been yearning for. "You never really return home," one of them is recorded as saying.

Those who came back early on in the war, one of my interviewees noted, were greeted as heroes.[12] But after the first years, this changed—although Soviet government policy dictated that local communities "conduct 'welcome home' ceremonies, ... largely meaningless, empty rituals," that the *afgantsy* called "the 'false face of welcome'."[13]

Over time, the overriding sentiment of the returning *afgantsy* was almost certainly anger. They were angry at the way they had been sent to, and prepared for, Afghanistan. They were angry at the way they had been lied to and at the lies that continued to be told about the war.[14] If the lurid side of the war, including the fact that Soviet planes and helicopters sometimes attacked Soviet troops, were to be pushed under the carpet, one *afganets* said in reaction to Andrei Sakharov's call for the entire truth about the war, "our children may also want, when they read about it, to take part in a war."[15]

In particular perhaps, the veterans were angry at the rapportage on the war in the Soviet press and at the treatment they received from officialdom. One soldier told journalist Artem Borovik already in Afghanistan that the Soviet papers "write such crap it

---

[11]   Alexievich, *Zinky Boys*, 38, 138, and 146. The invalids had their own special path, challenges, and struggle but for lack of space, I shall not discuss this in the present paper.

[12]   Author's interview with Ikhtior Tashpulatov, Chairman of the Afghan War Veterans' Association, Bukhara Oblast', 26 May 2014. The interviewee served in Afghanistan in 1982–83.

[13]   Larry Heinemann, Introduction, in Alexievich, *Zinky Boys*, xiii; see also Gennady Bocharov, *Russian Roulette: Afghanistan Through Russian Eyes* (New York: HarperCollins, 1990), 44–46.

[14]   "Many of my friends are dead," one former soldier tells us, "and sometimes I envy them because they'll never know they were lied to about this disgusting war—and no one can ever lie to them again"; Alexievich, *Zinky Boys*, 27–28.

[15]   *Moskovskie novosti*, no. 30, 23 July 1989, 9.

makes you sick."[16] Of my interviewees, only four percent thought the reporting of the war in real time reflected the reality.

Certainly, the attitude of the authorities toward the returning veterans as reflected both in the media and in the practical, material sphere was at best ambiguous. On the one hand, they had participated in a "hidden" war (to use the term favored by Borovik); on the other hand, as of 1983, it was formally recognized that they were owed a debt and were entitled to material benefits, *l'goty* (lit. privileges). The decree of 17 January 1983 to this effect was the first official document to recognize soldiers of the 40th Army, the "limited contingent of Soviet troops" fighting in Afghanistan, as servicemen fulfilling an assignment of the Soviet state.[17] Yet, "the decree was not published, trapped in the limbo of this undeclared war," and as a result often ignored. (In Uzbekistan, the situation seems to have been better than in the RSFSR, several *afgantsy* with whom I spoke there testifying that they actually began receiving their privileges in the mid-1980s; one *afganets* actually showed me the card entitling him to *l'goty* dated April 1984.[18]) Not until 1988 did public decrees detail the benefits and privileges due at least to the invalids, although by then, lack of funds, the general chaos of Soviet administration, and the poor state of the Soviet health system frequently precluded any adequate treatment even for them. As Galeotti has noted, the relevant authorities tended still to be totally ignorant of the legislation on veterans' rights and those that were aware of their responsibilities toward veterans, war invalids, and bereaved families "often took the official silence to be a signal of the lack of priority to

---

[16]   *Ogonek*, no. 4 (January 1988): 12.

[17]   N. Yu. Danilova, "Voennosluzhashchie, voiny-internatsionalisty, veterany: dinamika pravovogo statusa," *Sotsiologicheskie issledovaniia* no. 10 (2001): 77–85. The actual resolution—of the CPSU CC and the Council of Ministers—was entitled: "Benefits for the servicemen, workers and employees on the staff of the Limited Contingent of Soviet Troops on the territory of the Democratic Republic of Afghanistan, and their families." The decree underwent an amendment on 26 July 1984.

[18]   Author's interview with Tuimurod Akebirov, Bukhara, 26 May 2014.

be granted the issue."[19] The cavalier fashion in which officialdom related to the *afgantsy* was widely acknowledged and even given publicity in the media.[20]

Many *afgantsy* were similarly infuriated—and humiliated—by the labels attached to them (junkies, rapists) and by the accusations hurled at them by a society that toward the end of the 1980s looked upon the war as a national disgrace and blamed the soldiers who had fought it. They felt misunderstood in face of the widespread refusal to acknowledge the hardships and sacrifices to which they had been consigned in a backward and unfriendly foreign country. Young boys, one of them said, had been "taken from their homes, had a gun stuck in their hands and [been] taught to kill. They were told they were on a holy mission and that their country would remember them. Now people turn away and try to forget the war, especially those who sent us there in the first place."[21] In some places they encountered gibes, such as "Only fools go to Afghanistan," or were told they had stolen the medals they wore.[22]

A charge that was particularly stinging was that they had lost the war. "Who says we lost the war? Here's where we lost it, back home, in our own country."[23] In the words of the song "Afghan Syndrome" of the punk-rock troupe "Grazhdanskaia oborona", losing the war meant to be ashamed of one's medals, to be shunned like a thief, to live like a spring with a hand on the trigger.[24] The ultimate blow—and insult—came in December 1989 when the Congress of People's Deputies condemned the war as a political and moral mistake that ineluctably stigmatized its veterans, in the words of one *afganets*, as "the victims of a political adventure."[25]

---

[19]   Galeotti, *Afghanistan*, 74–79 and 86.

[20]   E.g., *Pravda*, 4 April and 5 August 1987.

[21]   Alexievich, *Zinky Boys*, 26. Stories abound of the hurt feelings and sense of cruel injustice the veterans felt on their return home and in the following years, for example, ibid., 69, 113, 148-50 and 160-1.

[22]   *Sotsialisticheskaia industriia*, 26 June 1988, quoted *Radio Liberty* 425/88, 19 September 1988.

[23]   Alexievich, *Zinky Boys*, 160-61.

[24]   "Afganskii sindrom", *Grazhdanskaia oborona* official website, http://www.groborona.ru/texts/1056965230.html#ixzz3XAFaDllH (accessed 12 April 2015). The song appeared in 1990.

[25]   *Dialog* (Tashkent) no. 11 (1991), 52.

While the loyalty of some *afgantsy* to the Soviet regime and mother country was unimpaired by their ordeals, others acquired new perceptions. The secretary of the Supreme Soviet committee on the veterans stressed that the *afganets* "looks at the society which sent him to his death through different eyes."[26] Many *afgantsy* could no longer stomach the falsehoods that Soviet society seemed to be based upon. The lies in the media "opened my eyes," one of them said. "Afghan cured me of the illusion that everything's OK here, and that the press and television tell the truth... I wanted to do something specific,... speak out, tell the truth, but my mother stopped me. 'We've lived like this all our lives,' she said." Or another testimony: "It was quite a shock for me, the black marketeers, the mafia and the apathy—but they won't let us get on and do something serious about it."[27]

Well before the war's end, different perspectives were manifest among the *afgantsy* regarding both the war and the regime that had consigned them to Afghanistan. In 1986, one veteran wrote to a newspaper that "not everyone believes the old cliché that an 18-year-old youngster is happy to fulfill his internationalist duty in Afghanistan."[28] His doubts evoked "a torrent of 'ferocious and virulent letters'" from fellow *afgantsy* who insisted that "internationalism is not only a political concept, but first and foremost, a moral virtue, like honesty, decency and intelligence."[29] Another, who had completed a year of higher education prior to being enlisted and returned to his studies on demobilization in 1986, decided he wanted out; after all the rottenness he had seen in Afghanistan, where officers stole "everything they could lay their hands on," he decided there was no future in the Soviet Union. Regarded as a hero at the Moscow institute where he studied, he was unable to persuade people, especially

---

[26]   *Pobratim* no. 6 (1990), 2.
[27]   Alexievich, *Zinky Boys*, 21 and 189.
[28]   *Sobesednik*, no. 50 (December 1986), 8.
[29]   *Sobesednik*, no. 23 (June 1987), 3, quoted in Jim Riordan, "'Afgantsy'—Return of the Lost Generation," unpublished paper, 5.

professors and others of the older generation, that there was noth-ing good, heroic or nice about the war.[30]

As time passed, the reality of their daily existence, on the one hand, and of the deteriorating situation around them, on the other, slapped the *afgantsy* in the face. On the personal level, they found themselves increasingly misunderstood, judged, marginalized. On the broader, public level, the lies about the war in the media opened their eyes to the falsity on which the Soviet system was based.

Acclimatization: to Swim or Flounder in the Maelstrom of Perestroika?

Settling back into civilian life entailed finding work or entering fur-ther education; acquiring accommodation; and learning to live with one's experiences and memories. Often the third goal was the hard-est to achieve.

For many *afgantsy* the war did not end with their return. Af-ghanistan stayed with them, "followed them home, plaguing them as they tried to adapt to a new life."[31] For years, they couldn't sleep, they had nightmares. Alexievich cites many such cases. In the words of a nurse, for example, "all of us who were there have a graveyard of memories." And a former private testified, "Two years after I got home I was still dreaming I was at my own funeral... or else waking up in a panic because I had no ammo to shoot myself with."[32] Many were frightened to go out of the house for months and sometimes longer. A nurse who went there in 1980 said a decade later, "don't tell me the war's over now... I'll be haunted by Afghanistan for the rest of my life. ... You try and live a normal life, the way you lived before. But you can't." The men "came home, fell in love, had kids—but none of it really helped. Afghanistan was more important than anything else." A woman who had served there as an NCO in the

---

[30]   Author's interview with Vadim Altskan, 24 June 2014. Vadim, who hailed from Khmel'nitsky in Ukraine, had been enlisted at the end of his first year at uni-versity.

[31]   Oleg Sarin and Lev Dvoretsky, *The Afghan Syndrome: The Soviet Union's Vi-etnam* (Novato, CA: Presidio, 1993), 148.

[32]   Alexievich, *Zinky Boys*, 24 and 146.

security service was even more pessimistic: "This war will never be finished—our children will go on fighting it."[33] These sentiments that are common to war veterans, particularly to those who go to war at a very young age and who spend protracted periods in constant fear of death, appeared incongruous to a society whose term of reference was the Great Patriotic War that was a very different war, fought in totally different circumstances, and in which the entire population was enlisted. Nor was the *afgantsy's* condition recognized as demanding medical or other treatment until the very end of the war.

Hundreds and perhaps thousands of soldiers who returned before the war was over reportedly "stormed" the military commissariats demanding to be sent back to the war, either because they longed for the action or the camaraderie of Afghanistan or because they felt unwanted at home.[34] Some veterans sought to find the action they needed by going to places within the Soviet Union where there were risk and perils, "craving for real life instead of mere existence."[35] They were in evidence wherever there was danger or fighting. One Ukrainian veteran volunteered to go to Chernobyl, then to the scene of the earthquake in Armenia (1989), and finally went to work at the Ministry for Emergency Situations.[36] Another, from Minsk, volunteered to go to Transdniestria when fighting broke out there (November 1990) because he wanted to go on fighting.[37]

The war had transformed the *afgantsy*, changing many of them irremediably. In the words of a psychologist who had served

---

[33]   Ibid., 26 and 149.

[34]   David Gai and Vladimir Snegirev, *Vtorzhenie: Neizvestnye stranitsy neob"iavlennoi voiny* (Moskva: IKPA, 1991), 253; *Sobesednik*, no. 3 (January 1988), 11. For one who, demobilized in 1982, succeeded in returning in 1984, see *Ogonek*, no. 4 (January 1988), 12.

[35]   Alexievich, *Zinky Boys*, 128.

[36]   Svetlana Gollands, "Afganskii nadlom: kak zhivut ukrainskie soldaty neob"iavlennoi voiny", *Argumenty i fakty* (Ukraine), 16 February 2012, www.aif.ua/society/people/963886 (accessed 1 April 2015).

[37]   "Peremolotyi Afganistanom: istoriia minchanina, kotoryi vyzhil na voine, no tak i ne privyk k miru", *Onliner* (Belarus), 11 February 2015, http://people.onliner.by/2015/02/11/afgan (accessed 1 April 2015).

in Afghanistan, coming into contact with the totally novel conditions of Afghanistan and the war had brought about a change in, indeed a break with, their previous personality and values. They had had perforce to shake off the shackles and the illusions that had surrounded them at every turn as they grew up in the Soviet Union and to fend for, and rely on, themselves. The *afgantsy* thus returned with new attributes—and illusions—and a new mental structure that nobody in the Soviet Union needed. This applied especially to those coming back at or toward the war's end, who returned to a society that welcomed the termination of this unpopular war and did not know how to handle people who took pride in having participated in it and expected some sign of gratitude for just that. The situation was made even more complicated by the fact that the veterans' new tough and uncompromising personality was more rigid than the immature one they had taken to Afghanistan and accordingly difficult to change.

The same psychologist discerns two distinct stages in the veterans' adaptation. The first was that of shock, the disappointment at encountering a totally unanticipated reality, to which different people reacted in different ways. Some resolved to fight for their rights, others to unite in order to withstand together the "strange" world into which they had fallen, a third group to withdraw to alcohol and drugs, a fourth to link up with the criminal world, and so on. While a minority entered quickly into the rut of the surrounding society, most moved on to the second stage—of enhanced alienation. They became overpowered by "negative experiences and complex emotional situations" and destructive actions took over. Their conduct became inconsistent and illogical, and they took unnecessary risks. Often this led to a profound psychological crisis, even to suicide, and the *afganets* was baffled: to what precisely should he adapt as the society around him disintegrated? Some wanted to feel needed and decided to cleanse society, but to do so by endeavoring to impose their own perceptions and by resorting to illegal methods, reverting to patterns they had known during the war.[38]

---

[38]   L. V. Ol'shanskii, "Smyslovye struktury lichnosti uchastnikov afganskoi voiny," *Psikhologicheskii zhurnal*, 12, no. 5 (1991): 121–8.

Indeed, the returning veterans felt they were not like everyone else. They were more serious, "we had killed people and our friends had been killed before our eyes."[39] They could not see in new fashions or forms of dance issues that genuinely concerned them, as they did their contemporaries.[40] Many of them could no longer intermingle with their former friends, for they had had experiences—whether in the barracks or in combat—they just couldn't discuss with anyone.[41] Made to feel like outsiders, "they were confused in trying to decide what to do in order to start a normal civilian life."[42]

The *afgantsy*, like the veterans of Vietnam, "experienced prolonged emotional problems in the years following military service—Post-Traumatic Stress Disorder" (PTSD),[43] commonly known in the Soviet Union as the "Afghan syndrome". The symptoms ascribed to PTSD are precisely those characteristic of the *afgantsy*: "flashbacks, emotional numbness, withdrawal, jumpy hyperalertness or over-compensatory extroversion."[44] The incidence of psychological damage is reportedly particularly high in wars like Afghanistan: modern counter-insurgency wars and wars where soldiers fight without faith in their cause.[45] PTSD, moreover, frequently led to physical problems and early death from a wide range of illnesses.[46] Two articles published on the web in 2006 and 2013 maintained that the intensity

---

39   Author's interview with Nugzar Kakhniauri (Tbilisi), 9 September 2014; and see Introduction to this special issue.
40   *Podvig*, 34 (1989): 10–11.
41   As one person in Tashkent, many of whose contemporaries fought in Afghanistan, including her brother-in-law, told me, they returned more serious, more daring, often irritable, and none of them discussed their experiences there; interview with Nodira Mustafaeva, 21 May 2014. See also Alexievich, *Zinky Boys*, 129.
42   Sarin and Dvoretsky, *Afghan Syndrome*, 148.
43   Larry Heinemann, Introduction in Alexievich, *Zinky Boys*, xiii.
44   Galeotti, *Afghanistan*, 69.
45   There are several studies on the incidence of PTSD among American veterans of Afghanistan and Iraq in the 2000s. For example, "Anger, Hostility, and Aggression among Iraq and Afghanistan War Veterans Reporting PTSD and Sub-threshold PTSD," *Journal of Traumatic Stress*, 20, no. 6 (December 2007): 945–54.
46   Rodric Braithwaite, *Afgantsy: The Russians in Afghanistan, 1979–1989* (London: Profile Books, 2011), 321.

of physical and psychological disorders among the *afgantsy* was actually mounting. The earlier article, published anonymously, maintained that five years after the final withdrawal, 41.5 percent of the veterans were diagnosed as suffering from heart disease, 53.7 percent from intestinal disorders, and a large (unspecified) number from various nervous ailments. A decade later, in 2005, over one thousand reportedly attempted to commit suicide and in 2006, according to a "rough estimate," 100,000 were in jail.[47]

There is no consensus as to the extent of the Afghan syndrome. According to a booklet of the Ukrainian Center for Psychotherapy and Medical Ethics and the Psychological Service of the Union of Afghan Veterans (SVA), Soviet academics considered that 80 percent of *afgantsy* suffered one form or another of post-traumatic stress. The same source described the impact of PTSD on the personality, values, and conduct of the veterans, stressing that it could be expected to worsen with the passage of time.[48]

My own interviewees tended to see the picture in a more optimistic light. Over one-third (37 percent) maintained that all their personal acquaintances adjusted quickly to civilian life; another third (35 percent) said they personally knew veterans whom it took several months to readjust; 10 percent responded that some of their acquaintances needed psychological assistance but eventually reentered society; and 18 percent said they knew cases of *afgantsy* who received psychological treatment but never made it back to normalcy.[49]

The disparity may well be due to the fact that those who reported the ubiquitous nature of psychological disorders were looking particularly at Russia, Ukraine, and Belarus. Although cases were

---

47   Vladimir Pregolin, "Sindrom voiny", *Privatelife.ru*, undated, http://www.privatelife.ru/2006/0506/n5/3.html, and Stanislav Oleinik, "Afganskii sindrom", *Art of War*, 26 September 2013, http://artofwar.ru/o/olejnik_s_a/afganskij_sindrom.shtml (both accessed 1 April 2015). The latter article was authored by the deputy commander of the KGB Spetsnaz in Kabul 1984–87.
48   *Novye aspekty psikhoterapii posttravmaticheskogo stressa: metodicheskie rekomendatsii* (Kharkov: Bazovyi sanatorii "Berezovskie mineral'nye vody", 1990). According to the chairman of the Leningrad Afghan Veterans' Association, "everyone needs psychotherapy"; quoted Galeotti, *Afghanistan*, 68.
49   My questionnaire provided these four optional answers.

recorded in Central Asia and the Caucasus as well, they seem to have been rarer[50]—and not to have been professionally treated.[51] Certainly, the psycho-social impact of the war was neither uniform in content nor strength and worked on many levels, depending on the type of unit in which the soldiers served, their experiences, characters, home and social environment, and other variables. There were those who felt strengthened by the experience; in the words of one of them, "Thanks to Afghan, I became a human being."[52] "For some, it bred zeal, a compulsive need for action and approbation. But at the other end of the scale, it produced violence, maladjustment, and suicide."[53] Some drowned their problems in drink or resorted to drugs, to which a large, if not overwhelming, number of them had had recourse in Afghanistan.[54] Many *afgantsy* retired into themselves: "This feeling that I don't want to go on living gets stronger with every passing day. I have no desire to meet anyone or see anything... The same thing's happening to all the people I've kept in touch with from my time over there."[55]

The self-hate, self-disgust, guilt feeling, and social isolation, were reflected first and foremost in difficulty in forming and maintaining intimate relationships, especially when these sentiments

---

[50]   An Uzbek *afganets* with whom I spoke in 2014 said categorically that nobody among the Uzbek veterans ever had psychological problems or treatment. Most Uzbek veterans, he said, just got on with their lives. They weren't afraid of blood; they had all seen sheep being killed when they were children; author's interview with Turdibay Shadmanov, 21 and 22 May 2014. Other interviews I conducted in Uzbekistan confirm that this was the rule. I heard a similar opinion in Tbilisi; interview with Nukri Gordeziani, 13 September 2014. However, in casual conversation in Uzbekistan I did hear of people who were never able to take up a permanent job or live a normal life, and a Georgian *afganets* told me of a friend who had similar difficulties and eventually—in 2011—committed suicide.

[51]   I was told in Tashkent in 1991, for example, that not a single psychologist in the entire city worked in the field of post-traumatic disorders; interview with three *afgantsy*, 26 June 1991.

[52]   Interview with Pavel Shetko, Minsk, 25 August 1993.

[53]   Galeotti, *Afghanistan*, 70.

[54]   See, for example, *Moscow News*, 13 December 1987, 13; *Sobesednik* no.3 (January 1988), 11. There seem to be no statistics or even well-founded estimates regarding the prevalence of drink and drugs among the veterans.

[55]   Alexievich, *Zinky Boys*, 189–90.

bred into the general hostility of society, and a high rate of suicide.[56] These very same feelings brought some veterans into the fold of the Church.[57] Metropolitan Pitirim participated in several *afgantsy* fora and demonstrated manifest interest in their lot.[58] At an exhibition of *afganets* art in Moscow in 1991, the motif of crucifixion appeared in several pictures, with an *afganets* "nailed to the cross to expiate the sins of a whole people."[59] This very etching, or one similar, appeared on the cover of the booklet of poems of paratroop officer Dmitrii Semenov, *Bol'* (Pain; Moscow, 1990), in which many of the poems were of a manifestly Christian nature. And Union of Veterans of Afghanistan (SVA) organ *Pobratim* devoted considerable space to religious motifs.

By the end of the war Soviet psychologists were studying and treating PTSD; in early 1990 Director of the SVA Psychological Service Madridin Magomed-Eminov wrote a major article on "The Syndrome of the Front-Line Soldier." His basic premise was that the soldier's return home was no less psychologically critical than his dispatch to the war and meant that on returning home he had yet another, internal war to fight.[60]

The result of the moral conflict to which the soldiers were exposed during the war was that the soldiers returned home with a sharpened sense of justice and morality that made their acclimatization difficult and alienated the authorities.[61] Their "code of values" that was "at odds with civilian ethics" meant, when combined with the license to use a gun, a "heady" power of life and death which might be conducive to compulsive violence. Indeed, studies suggested "a trend towards criminality in a significant proportion of the

---

[56]   The reasons, at least the immediate reasons, for suicide were sundry. It might be despair of getting housing—see Braithwaite, *Afgantsy*, 315–16; or simply prolonged suffering—one *afganets* committed suicide in Kutaisi (Georgia) in 2012—author's interview with Konstantin Pkhakadze, 14 September 2014. For legion instances of broken relationships, see Galeotti, *Afghanistan*, 86–87.

[57]   Some soldiers in the 40th Army had already shown religious inclinations during their time of service; see P. Tkachenko (ed.), *Dorogie moi...: Pis'ma iz Afganistana* (Moscow: Profizdat, 1991), 12 and 74.

[58]   See, for example, *Pobratim*, no. 4 (1990), 5.

[59]   Galeotti, *Afghanistan*, 72.

[60]   *Pobratim*, nos 4 and 5 (1990), 5.

[61]   Oleinik, "Afganskii sindrom".

afgantsy," although it did not necessarily find expression in practice.[62] One American political analyst, commenting on the veterans' problems, said that their difficulties in finding housing and employment led them in different directions. Some became "part of the restless youth underground of punks, heavy metalists, and other informal groups"; others became "hard-liners and set up veterans' organizations dedicated to the military-political education of the youth or to violence against what they see as decadent critics of society."[63]

The difficulties the veterans encountered in entering civilian life in the latter half of the 1980s were made all the more acute by the uncertainties and chaos induced by glasnost and the economic stringency of everyday life. For perestroika undermined the traditional checks and balances that had regulated citizens' living standards and lifestyle and provided a certain sense of security.

In early 1986, the press was bringing stories of veterans deciding to take the law into their own hands to mete out justice to "money-grubbers" who evaded the courts and other anti-social elements.[64] Venting their anger, they ended up on the defendant's bench for carrying out lynch laws against people whom they felt the authorities did not punish sufficiently for their deeds. Or they might attack and even murder members of a variety of subcultures—punks, rockers, heavy-metal fans,[65] particularly semi-Westernized youth cultures, the very same fraternities with which their fellow veterans had teamed up.

My own interviews show that a rather high percentage of veterans approved resorting to force to change a situation or achieve one's ends. Indeed, the veterans tended to see their mission or role in society as that of vigilantes who aspired to rectify the wrongs they saw around them by taking the law into their own hands. Some in

---

[62]   Galeotti, *Afghanistan*, 71. Galeotti points out that the 3,000 veterans in prison in late 1989 for criminal offences—2,540 for crimes committed while in Afghanistan—did not reflect "any mass criminality."

[63]   Daria Fane, "After Afghanistan: The Decline of Soviet Military Prestige," *Washington Quarterly* (Spring 1990), 6.

[64]   E.g., *Komsomol'skaia pravda*, 8 January 1986, and *Sobesednik*, 12 March 1986.

[65]   Valerii Konovalov, "Reintegrating Afghan Veterans into Civilian Life," *Radio Liberty* 425/88, 19 September 1988.

fact became vigilantes by virtue of their employment in security organs and various organizations that wanted bodyguards or through their association with gangs (such as the Liubertsy or Kaskad) that sought to mend society by military discipline and paramilitary arts.[66]

Some veterans felt it necessary to leave their native towns and villages. Unable to reintegrate into their home surroundings, they moved elsewhere to start a new life. One soldier who returned in 1985 wrote to an army newspaper: "I did not know what to do or where to go. I did not find understanding among my friends and all my family." (His mother had died while he was in Afghanistan, one of a long list of parents who fell seriously ill or died from worry.) "My nerves started to fail. I decided to leave my native village for some place as far away as possible." Eventually, he found work in a cotton-spinning factory, where there were other *afgantsy* among whom he could find understanding.[67] The need or, at least, aspiration to be among their own led them when the opportunity arose to build—and inhabit—their own housing communes.[68]

On the surface, the *afgantsy* made different choices. Some opted for a quiet life. Others preferred to engage in public activity. Here too there were various options. Some resolved to focus on the fight for the rights they believed were their due from a state and society on behalf of which they had endured a hard war that had taken the lives of many of their comrades and crippled many more. Others were determined to assist in mending the wrongs and misdoings they saw all around them that glasnost was highlighting.

The different paths the veterans followed, then, were frequently the outcome of objective circumstances, such as the clash between the political, moral, and psychological function of the way the Soviet Union surrounded its military past with an aura of heroic myth,[69] and the mood in society in the mid- and late 1980s. But

---

[66]   Riordan, "'Afgantsy'", 24.
[67]   Sarin and Dvoretsky, *Afghan Syndrome*, 170.
[68]   For example, in Kaluga; *Sobesednik* no. 3 (January 1988): 11.
[69]   To use the summation of Mikhail Reshetnikov in a 2002 website article referred to in Braithwaite, *Afgantsy*, 323.

probably no less often they emanated from their own personal situation and context.

Career Patterns

Employers frequently hesitated to hire Afghan war veterans because
they were regarded as "difficult".[70] Eventually, however, most seem
to have found employment, apparently—judging from anecdotal evidence—in all sectors of the job market. According to Galeotti, the
job advertisements in the veterans' press (*Pobratim* 1989–91) divided
approximately into one-third for military-related work, one-third
for sales and entrepreneurial opportunities, and one-third for conventional blue-collar work.[71]

By the time the Soviet Union broke up, 70,000 veterans had
found careers in the Soviet armed forces.[72] Many, probably the great
majority, were clearly officers or NCOs who had chosen a military
career prior to serving in Afghanistan. Among others, they had the
advantage of not having to endure the psychological shock of rea-
dapting to civilian life although some had difficulty in facing the rig-
orous discipline and formalism of Soviet army life. One pilot who
returned to his native Barnaul in 1983 remained in the army for another two and one-half years, during which he constantly bickered
with his commander and his political deputy over what he considered their abuse of authority; eventually, he was discharged as unfit
for service.[73]

The higher echelons of the armed services were similarly re-
plenished with Afghan war veterans, clearly because their experience in directing combat was considered an important asset in a service that had seen relatively little fighting for well over a generation.
Several of the 40th Army's senior officers became generals, either in
the course of the war—like former helicopter regiment commander
Vitalii Pavlov and former paratroop division commander Al'bert
Sliusar'—or after it ended. Many also took up or were appointed to

---

[70]   Ibid., 319. See also "Peremolotyi Afganistanom".
[71]   Galeotti, *Afghanistan*, 57.
[72]   "Skol'ko nas?", *Pobratim*, no. 11 (1991).
[73]   Tkachenko, *Dorogie moi*, 79.

teaching positions in military academies, including Sliusar' who by 1985 headed the Riazan' Higher Paratroop Academy.[74] Others were sent to various Military Districts. Yu. Kuznetsov, a lieutenant-colonel in the paratroop forces in Afghanistan, became a Hero of the Soviet Union, a full colonel, and commander of the Central Asian Military District (MD) Panfilov Motor-Rifle Guards Division. Viktor Kot who commanded a sub-division of fighter-bombers in Afghanistan likewise returned a Hero of the Soviet Union, took over command of an air force regiment, and was shortly afterwards promoted to the rank of major-general and deputy commander of the Far Eastern MD air force.[75] Lieutenant-Colonel Ruslan Aushev became commander of a mechanized infantry division in the same MD.[76] And Boris Gromov, the last commander of the 40th Army, was appointed commander of the Kiev MD.[77]

By late 1991 too, 14,000 *afgantsy* had been recruited into the Ministry of the Interior (MVD), where, according to Gromov, by now First Deputy Minister of the Interior, they applied "professionalism acquired in Afghanistan,"[78] and another 20,000–22,000 in the emergency services, in criminal investigation units, the prosecutor's office and special squads and as security guards. They were especially strong in macho, action-centered emergency units that were "most assiduous in recruiting veterans." At first, *afgantsy* were not enlisted to the new Interior Ministry special units, the OMON, the MVD personnel department head considering their "youthful maximalism" potentially disadvantageous. Over time, however, this changed even in the center and did not apply a priori in some national republics (see below). The "alternative" law enforcement agencies where *afgantsy* served included the *druzhina*, the voluntary people's militia organized to assist the police in maintaining public order; Workers' Detachments set up to break up strikes and radical protest; and municipal militias, for instance in the Russian city of

---

74   Eight of the 21 *afgantsy* Heroes of the Soviet Union listed in the Soviet press in early 1985 were by then teaching in military academies; *Posev*, no. 4 (1985), 32.
75   *Posev* no. 2 (1986), 15.
76   *Krasnaia zvezda*, 29 June 1988.
77   Gromov, *Ogranichennyi kontingent*, 345.
78   "Skol'ko nas?"

Tol'iatti, in Dushanbe, and ultimately in Moscow. Others were drawn to the fire service and trauma para-medicine.[79] "Essentially," we are told, "national-patriotic forces want to use the 'afgantsy' as the basis of their military formations."[80]

The marked growth in the crime rate and general feeling of instability that accompanied the deterioration of the Soviet state was apparently the backdrop to the huge interest in the Soviet Union in the late 1980s in martial arts, such as unarmed combat, that became "a sure-fire money-spinner... for which the afgantsy were well prepared to cater." Against the background of the new economic freedoms, the sense of insecurity was also conducive to the mushrooming of "a private security business, providing bodyguards, private investigators, security experts and even computer data crime specialists, culminating in the founding of the Independent Society of Private Detectives in 1991" whose chair was an *afganets*. The more professional agencies refused to hire veterans, preferring people with experience in the MVD or KGB, and the *afgantsy* found their way into "the shadowy world of bodyguarding, which so often shaded directly into criminality." They in fact "acquired a reputation as bouncers and bodyguards," the Union of Veterans of Afghanistan setting up its own firm to provide security for persons and property. "Groups and individuals of every political complexion took to finding afganets minders, from the liberal Aprel' group (protected by volunteers from the Union of Democratic Afghan War Veterans) to ... Russian nationalist icon...Aleksandr Nevzorov. In the Baltic [republics], the local [Communist] Party supported the formation of the Viking cooperative, whereby local afgantsy would moonlight and protect Party buildings from nationalists at the taxpayer's expense. Afgantsy seem to have occupied a similar position within the underworld"; although none of the major criminals was an *afganets*, it "often had a respectable proportion of veteran 'soldiers'."[81] Likewise, they were easily recruited to groups like the right-wing, anti-

---

[79] Galeotti, *Afghanistan*, 59–61; Valerii Konovalov, "Reintegrating Afghan Veterans into Civilian Life," *Radio Liberty* 425/88, 19 September 1988.

[80] "Problemy sotsial'noi reabilitatsii," 11.

[81] Galeotti, *Afghanistan*, 61 and 111.

semitic Russian nationalist organization Pamiat', whose leader surrounded himself with veterans as bodyguards.[82]

Almost at the other end of the scale, rather a large number of
veterans seem to have found their way into the ranks of Komsomol-
initiated activity. In 1985, MPA head Colonel-General Aleksei Liz-
ichev cited the experience of the soldier-internationalists as a potent
weapon in the military-patriotic education (VPV) armory "to defeat
'pacifist tendencies' in Soviet youth" and the following year, the
Komsomol set up an Administration for Afghan Questions.[83] Already in the early years of the war, *afgantsy* were enlisted to speak
in schools and to discuss in the Volunteer Society for Cooperation
with the Army, Aviation, and Fleet (DOSAAF) their military service,
the lofty duty of defending the motherland, and the value of military
comradeship.[84] Now, in the latter half of the decade, this appears to
have become full-time employment. The head of an oblast' council
of veterans in Tajikistan said in 1988, "we have a particularly great
responsibility for preparing young people for military service." This
framework provided pre-conscription teen-agers "grounding" in
military arts and reservists some brush-up training, as well as instruction in useful skills—driving, electronics, first aid—and the
wider, ideological and propaganda network building and defending
the party's monopoly of authority and legitimacy. "There was money
and hence power and *blat* (influence and power[85]) in such activities,
the motors that drove any good Soviet careerist." VPV meant jobs
and "extra-curricular opportunities to collaborate with the system
which were an essential aid to lubricating the rest of one's life within
the Party-State." Not surprisingly, many delegates to the 1987 XX
All-Union Komsomol Congress had served in Afghanistan.[86]

---

82   Konovalov, "Reintegrating Afghan Veterans"; *Izvestiia*, 1 August 1987.

83   Galeotti, *Afghanistan*, 106.

84   For example, Moscow Television Service in Russian, 31 March 1984—Daily Report III, 19 April 1984, V 5–6.

85   Hedrick Smith gives a long explanation of this very crucial factor in Soviet life.
Talking of the Soviet counter-economy he writes that "*blat*—influence, connec-
tions, pulling strings" was "an essential lubricant of life"; *The Russians* (New
York: Ballantine Books, 1976), 115.

86   Galeotti, *Afghanistan*, 104–107; Andrew Ilves, "Monument to Afghanistan War
Dead Unveiled in Tajikistan," *Radio Liberty* 260/88, 24 May 1988.

Afghan veterans were given grants for professional training and retraining and admitted to university, which made entry somewhat easier for them. They received extra grants and required lower entrance marks. Those who were not Russians, however, seem not to have been enabled to continue to advanced studies in Russian universities.[87]

Alleviating the *afgantsy's* entrance into university was perceived by some veterans as designed to keep them out of trouble. One student who'd lost an arm in the war remembered how the dean "called me in to see him. 'Look,' he said, 'we gave you a place even though your grades weren't really good enough'." He was given to understand that "they were frightened of us, because they knew that if we organized we'd fight for our rights and they'd have to give us flats and so on."[88]

Many, too, went into blue-collar jobs. Those who came from *kolkhozy* and returned home may have found work in the *kolkhoz*. One veteran, who returned with one arm, had no choice other than to do menial work on his *kolkhoz* in Belarus, for pensions became increasingly unsatisfactory as the economy deteriorated and the money ran out—until he resolved to take up studies.[89]

In short, *afgantsy* entered all walks of life, with a disproportionately large number in the armed services and enforcement agencies, on the one hand, and in semi- or partially martial professions and niches, on the other hand. As they fought their way into a floundering economy, where they were seemingly disadvantaged by lost time and their singular experience, they felt an increasing need to consolidate and close ranks. In this way, they hoped to both sustain the camaraderie of Afghanistan and to create a framework for mutual assistance in an increasingly unfriendly environment.

Veteran Associations: the Salience of Collective Action

The veterans' sense of togetherness, of having a similar, even identical, fate, entailing among others a feeling of singular vulnerability,

---

[87]   Author's interview with Turdibay Shadmanov, 21 and 22 May 2014.
[88]   Alexievich, *Zinky Boys*, 56.
[89]   Interview with Pavel Shetko, 25 August 1993.

comprised the basis for the *afgantsy* clubs. These associations, however, never represented a united, coherent force. They lacked both a uniform mentality and singleness of purpose; according to Galeotti, their generally low social profile deprived them "of a single, audible voice."[90] This, although from my interviews it is apparent that the veterans believed for the most part that the *afgantsy* comprised a significant political force as the group in society that was most tightly consolidated.

At first, most *afganets* activity united veterans on a local basis and as individuals or circles of friends. The Novosibirsk *afgantsy*, for instance, set up an informal network for self-help and mutual support as early as 1983—although (more commonly) most of the early sporadic grass-root *afgantsy* clubs surfaced in 1985–86.

With the advent of state-initiated glasnost and the concomitant "enthusiasm of the Soviet people to test their new-found freedoms of speech and association, an appreciation of the unique needs of the afgantsy and of the advantages in unity began to spread." This, as Galeotti points out, was the backdrop to the "first initiatives" of the Establishment—in the form of the Komsomol—to forge and direct the 'afganets movement'," within the general trend to "replace the leash with the harness, to release society and yet channel it to economic and political reconstruction."[91]

In 1987 the draft of a new law on public organizations was prepared, and although it was not enacted, a first officially sanctioned national conference of "informal" associations (*neformaly*) took place in Moscow that same year. However, these associations only acquired full legal rights with the passing in October 1990 of the Law on Social Organizations.[92] Notwithstanding, well before the disintegration of the Soviet Union, *afgantsy* clubs surfaced at both the national and the republican, regional, and even municipal, level.

A postal survey was conducted by Galeotti in 1991–92 of nine veteran groups "ranging in size from 45 to 1,800 members, and geographically scattered from Kaliningrad to Karaganda," with over

---

90   Galeotti, *Afghanistan*, 47 and 103.
91   Ibid., 105.
92   Vera Tolz, *The USSR's Emerging Multiparty System* (New York: Praeger, 1990), 26–29.

4,400 members between them. The survey found the groups "strikingly homogeneous, combining the imperatives of self-help and military-patriotic education with a generous portion of shrewd economic and political entrepreneurship," designed to give help to the victims of the war and "other charitable causes." The central focus would invariably be "the acquisition of resources to redistribute to the needy: themselves, their friends, the parents of their fallen comrades, a characteristically Soviet mix of Robin Hood altruism and hard-hearted self-interest. As such, economics lay at the heart of the 'afganets movement'."[93]

Afgantsy working for the Perm association set up three teenager clubs for "working-class kids who would be the next generation of draftees and, had the war continued, afgantsy." Moreover, veterans liked to find "the camaraderie of the groups, the macho heroism of stories and films shown at meetings and the opportunity to test one's physical abilities."[94] In Donetsk Oblast, where the Party, Komsomol, soviet and trade union organizations enlisted veterans in political education activities and strengthening public order through Komsomol volunteer militia detachments, one in ten former internationalist soldiers was a member of a Komsomol committee or bureau in May 1987.[95] The best known club was probably "Dolg" (Duty) set up in Moscow that same year, and so called because its members had fulfilled their internationalist duty; because they felt they had a duty toward their fallen comrades, the maimed and disabled and their families; and toward the younger generation "to tell them of their duty, transmit our experience, help them prepare better for their army service and altogether to overcome life's difficulties."[96] In November 1987, a first nation-wide convention of *afgantsy*, the All-Union Gathering of Young Reservists, took place—in Ashkhabad, capital of Turkmenistan, under Komsomol auspices. It assembled some 2,000 veterans from clubs and associations throughout the country.[97]

---

93   Galeotti, *Afghanistan*, 109–10.
94   Ibid., 107.
95   *Krasnaia zvezda*, 26 May 1987.
96   *Moskvichi iz kluba "Dolg"* (Moscow: Moskovskii rabochii, 1988), 99.
97   See, for example, *Komsomolets Uzbekistana*, 30 March 1990.

For the veterans, the clubs that were at first a place where they could meet people like themselves and preserve their disparate identity in an unaccepting society, became over time primarily a framework for the fight for their rights. In the words of Hedrick Smith, the *afgantsy* associations lobbied for "proper health care, for preferred treatment as consumers, and for understanding from the home folks."[98] One invalid *afganets* insisted that the veterans "all have the same problems—lousy pensions, the difficulty of getting a flat and a bit of furniture together, no decent medicines or prostheses… If ever all that gets sorted out our veterans' clubs will fall apart. Once I get what I need, and perhaps a fridge and washing-machine and a Japanese video … that'll be it! I won't need the club any more."[99]

In parallel to developments throughout Soviet society and in the body politic, pressures began to build for the scattered community of *afgantsy* associations to unite within an umbrella formation. A consensus arose within the Afghan "movement" that it needed some "national-level body to articulate its views and… ensure that it was not overlooked at the center." This was the sense of a decision taken by the March 1990 All-Union Conference of Chairmen of Afghan Veteran Organizations.[100] However, not one, but two bodies came into being, the Union of Veterans of Afghanistan—the SVA— and the All-Union Association of Reserve Soldiers' Councils, Internationalist Soldiers and Military-Patriotic Unions.

The SVA claimed in 1991 to represent more than 300,000 *afgantsy*, to embrace over one thousand primary organizations, in every union republic except Estonia, 185 regional sections, nine republican SVAs and to have an annual budget of 7,000,000 rubles, equaling $960,000.[101] Yet, just between one-half and two-thirds were active members, the others being there simply to "ensure a place in the queue for a special flat or access to charitable food parcels with-

---

[98]   Hedrick Smith, *The New Russians* (New York: Random House, 1990), 431.
[99]   Alexievich, *Zinky Boys*, 19.
[100]   *Pobratim*, no. 4 (1990), 1. The same number of *Pobratim* published a model statute for SVA territorial branches; Ibid., 4.
[101]   "Spravka o Soiuze veteranov Afganistana," 15 June 1991.

out any real feeling of belonging to a community." Once out of uniform, many clearly preferred to perceive themselves first and foremost as "Soviets, Estonians, workers, students, Muscovites, Christians, or whatever." (Of my own interviewees, approximately one-half were members of veteran clubs.)

In the event, neither nationwide organization was capable of winning political recognition for its claims. The public mood became "increasingly angry and divided," as a result of "hunger, shortage, disillusion and an apparent policy impasse in the Kremlin." In this context, marginal groups such as the *afgantsy* received "short shrift."[102]

Afgantsy associations at the various levels continued to exist when the union republics became successor states. The founding conference of the Russian Federation SVA took place in November 1990. In 2014, the Bukhara provincial Afghan veterans' association was still continuing to convene several times a year—on February 15, the anniversary of the final withdrawal; May 9, Victory Day of the Great Patriotic War; Uzbekistan's Independence Day and "when [the] occasion arises." Its members continued to meet with *afgantsy* from different regions of Uzbekistan, from other Central Asian states, and from different Soviet successor states further away, including Russia.[103]

In March 1992 a Committee for Internationalist Soldiers Attached to the Council of the Heads of Government of the Commonwealth Member States was also established, headed by Ruslan Aushev. However, as a result of ongoing confrontation and conflicts between the successor states, coordinated activity between their respective organizations was difficult, if not impossible. For example, the United Council of the Georgian Federation of Veterans announced that the intention of the chairman of the Union of Afgantsy-Internationalists to represent Georgia in the parade planned by the Russian *Boevoe bratstvo* ("Fighting Brotherhood") for May

---

[102]   Galeotti, *Afghanistan*, 104 and 113–18.

[103]   Author's interviews with Ikhtior Tashpulatov and Tuimurod Akebirov, 26 May 2014.

2014 was no less than treason, since Abkhazia and South Ossetia were to participate as independent states.[104]

There were other reasons as well for disagreement and clashes between *afganets* organizations. One chairman of the Russian Fund for Invalids of the War in Afghanistan was killed in 1994 and two years later, a subsequent chairman met the same fate, together with 14 others, apparently in an attempt to lay hands on the spoils. A few people at the top of the Afghan veteran organizations waxed rich, only a small part of the money actually getting to the disabled ex-servicemen for whom it was intended.[105]

One summation perceived the "afganets movement" as

> taking advantage of freedoms offered by glasnost', trying to fight for some share of resources in the period of democratization, then pushed back into the ghetto in the face of hard times and disinterest on the part of society as a whole. In many ways, ... it reflected the evolution of Soviet—or at least, Russian—society, with its transition from informal groups within the existing structures to independent groupings, co-operatives and unions—a brief explosion of equal parts of idealism and pragmatism and then the slow, sullen retrenchment as times became even harder.[106]

The *Afgantsy*, Perestroika and the Break-up of the Soviet Union

There is little evidence that the majority of veterans were especially interested in politics. They were preoccupied helping one another and raising their families. According to one opinion, "Either they were so desperate to fit into mainstream society that they were too busy keeping their heads down, or they were just too tired and cynical to involve themselves in politics." The politicized *afgantsy* who stole a great deal of limelight in the postwar years were a visible minority but not insignificant minority, for "in the light of the harsh lessons learned from the experiences of war, many felt the need to

---

[104]   "Gruzinskie veterany-'afgantsy' otmezhevalis' ot marsha rossiiskogo 'Boevogo bratstva'", *Gruziia online*, 9 July 2013 (accessed 9 July 2013). The veteran organization *Boevoe bratstvo* was established by Gromov in 1997; Braithwaite, *Afgantsy*, 317.

[105]   Ibid., 317-18.

[106]   Galeotti, *Afghanistan*, 118–19.

play their role in the unfolding fate and dissolution of the Soviet Union, whether in central politics or centrifugal localism."[107]

Asked about their participation in political activity and the events or manifestations in Soviet society that led them to take part in protests, just 35 percent of my interviewees answered that they undertook political activity of any sort and over half of these were motivated by the desire to improve their own lot and that of their *afgantsy* comrades. Interestingly, 20 percent responded to the question by saying they themselves had "no problems"—ergo, no motivation for undertaking political activity.

The role of the *afgantsy* in Soviet society, however, was not determined solely by their active participation in political and social processes. According to a paper compiled in 1991, their very presence filled "a 'liberating' function... from the slumber of ignorance." They became "a catalyst of the socio-political process" occurring in the country, enabling society to realize that the national interest did not entail military expansion into a neighboring country and bringing about an enhanced "national patriotism" for the war's failure injured the national consciousness. At the same time, the *afgantsy* constituted "an obstacle to the tranquil life of a sector of the population and of many officials and a target of criticism of those inclined to see them as guilty of our social troubles."

The same paper, however, tells us that the veterans aspired "to use the various political forces to their own ends."[108] In contrast, or in parallel, another source tells us that "both the 'right' and the 'left', the new political parties and social organizations, [tried] to use the Afgantsi for their own ends, to exploit their strength, their status, and their feelings of anger and bitterness in their political games."[109] By 1990 *afgantsy* groups "campaigning for what they consider social justice" could be found maintaining "close contacts with Pamyat societies," whereas a Sakharov Union of Democratic Afghan War Veterans defended "democratic activities," including bodyguards for members of anti-Stalinist Memorial societies and other

---

[107]   Ibid., 54.
[108]   "Problemy sotsial'noi reabilitatsii", 9.
[109]   Sarin and Dvoretsky, *Afghan Syndrome*, 147 and 149.

democratic organizations that came under attack from Pamiat'.[110] Their own subculture, however, as evidenced in their songs, indicates that their sympathies were rather with the latter grouping, the songs tending to have a clearly nationalist hue—a love of Russia, romanticism, intolerance of the West and of liberal and intellectual circles at home.[111]

In the event, the Afghan veterans remained a marginal political group. The replacement of informal groups by more openly political ones in the later Gorbachev period "underpinned purely inward-looking or economic demands with a wider programme or world-view... [T]he need to pressure the State and unite to campaign for appropriate treatment of invalids fed into wider questions of political activity, of the socially just and necessary allocation of resources, and how groups could articulate their interests in wider for a."[112]

Yet, the Congress of People's Deputies of the USSR elected in spring 1989 boasted a significant contingent of *afgantsy*.[113] Some were nominated by establishment institutions, others won in straight elections, sometimes "on a clear 'afganets ticket,' stressing either military-patriotic education or abhorrence of the war." They were a veritable mix, from military candidates like Defense and State Security Committee member Colonel Valerii Ochirov to "party hack agitators" like the legless Komsomol appointee and official Serhii Chervonopys'kyi to L'viv Deputy Yurii Sorochyk and "veteran turned pacifist Vasilii Katrinich." Deputy Senior Sergeant Yurii Shatrovenko was perhaps closest to being the "'typical afganets deputy' in highlighting three areas for concern": the role of the army and its need for public support; youth affairs, "mixing authoritarian views on draft-dodging and military and civil indiscipline with an apprecia-

---

[110] Tolz, *USSR's Emerging Multiparty System*, 99, quoting *Moscow News*, no. 13 (1990).
[111] Valery Konovalov, "Pesni veteranov Afganistana," *Radio Liberty Research RS* 50/88, 6 June 1988.
[112] Galeotti, *Afghanistan*, 82–83.
[113] They accounted for 120 deputies; N. I. Pikov (ed.), *Voina v Afganistane* (Moskva: Voenizdat, 1991), 308. Galeotti gives a figure of 56, without providing a source, and is apparently mistaken.

tion of the genuine problems of finding accommodation and meaningful work." He also "appealed that the afgantsy and the country
should be told, once and for all, whose fault the war was, and see
that justice was done." This mix was typical of the platforms of *afgantsy* candidates both in the USSR and the Russian elections, incorporating "the general concerns of the time: physical conditions,
control of the organs of coercion, moral justice and the danger of
civil anarchy."[114]

Although at the outset the *afgantsy* deputies resolved to work
together, they at no stage represented a tight grouping since their
political views were often very different. However, in April 1990 the
USSR Supreme Soviet—the bicameral standing legislature elected
by the Congress of People's Deputies—set up a Committee for the
Affairs of Internationalist Soldiers headed by Pavel Shetko who had
lost an arm in the war and hurled himself into political activity. At
first, the committee was to be comprised solely of *afgantsy*, but since
they were inexperienced, it was decided to complement their number to assist in implementing its brief. Its secretary explained that
its primary assignment was to give binding statutory authority to
the various resolutions designed to assist the veterans. The committee succeeded in securing a 50 percent tax discount for *afgantsy* and
a total exemption for their organizations; it developed links with the
Ministry of Health to prepare coordinating plans for the war's invalids; began negotiations with Mossovet (the Moscow City Council)
on setting up memorials in the city. It hoped to get information on
PoWs, some of whom had already set up families of their own, so as
to inform their parents at home that they were alive, and Shetko
went to Pakistan with a delegation and brought back two prisoners.
When rioting occurred in Dushanbe in February 1990, the committee's deputy chairman went there, "knocked together *afgantsy* 'self-
defense' detachments and the situation normalized." (This, at least,
was the committee secretary's version.) Over time, there were also
working visits to the U.S. to meet Vietnam veterans and rehabilitation experts, and eventually, the Committee initiated a framework
for the care and provision of veterans. It felt that the government's

---

[114]   Galeotti, *Afghanistan*, 125–27.

draft program to help the *afgantsy* "lacked both an appropriate mechanism and an appreciation of the different needs of different veterans, as opposed to some notionally 'average' soldier-internationalist."[115]

When it came to the broader issues that were not directly related to the lot of the *afgantsy*, the veterans found themselves siding with liberals, conservatives, and radicals. Their estrangement from their peers, their contemporaries in their twenties and thirties, was accompanied by disgust at their materialism and lack of values.[116] But they were torn between the opponents of perestroika and glasnost on the grounds that Gorbachev's reforms were leading to anarchy and Western values and fashions and endeavors to put an end to the ills of Soviet society with its corruption, nepotism, and endless bureaucracy.

In parallel to strictly political activity, military or para-military activities took place in the Soviet Union's last years and *afgantsy* were visible in all or most of them. The Kyrgyzstan OMON, for example, that played a significant role in quelling the ethnic disturbances in Osh in June 1990, had *afgantsy* in its ranks from the start.[117] Soon, riot policemen became Moscow's instrument against nationalists in the local militias. This, although Gorbachev told Presidential aide Georgii Shakhnazarov in October 1990 that when "'a leader of our *afgantsy*' had told him that he must use whatever means necessary to impose order and he could then count on the army to support him," Gorbachev had replied, "'We are following another path'."[118]

In fact, the veterans showed enthusiasm defending nationalist causes in those union republics, where local politics became "tantamount to guerrilla warfare or warlordism." Nationalism was both a cause that provided ideals to which they could pledge allegiance and

---

[115]   *Pobratim* no. 6 (1990), 2; interview with Pavel Shetko, 25 August 1993; and Galeotti, *Afghanistan*, 122–24 and 127.

[116]   *Sobesednik* no. 17 (April 1987), 15; and *Avrora* no. 9 (1987), 20, quoted in Riordan, "'Afgantsy'", 22–23.

[117]   For the role and image of Afghan war veteran associations as law-enforcement agencies in Kyrgyzstan, see *Komsomolets Kirgizii*, 6 and 13 March 1991.

[118]   Archie Brown, *The Gorbachev Factor* (Oxford: Oxford University Press, 1996), 280.

offered employment "in which they could feel their experiences were an asset rather than a stigma." Some 450 veterans took part in the Tbilisi demonstration in April 1989 and *afgantsy* fought in all Georgia's wars—with Abkhazia in 1993, when they comprised a special unit and served as instructors, as other soldiers "knew nothing about fighting a war," and again in South Ossetia in 2008.[119] *Afgantsy* became heavily involved on both sides in Armenian–Azerbaijani warfare in Nagorno-Karabakh, actually leading the opposing militias. In Lithuania, veterans joined defenders of the parliament in early 1991 when Soviet troops and OMON riot police which had recruited *afgantsy* stormed key buildings in Vilnius. They trained young volunteers in urban combat skills and the Lithuanian Union of Veterans of the War in Afghanistan warned the USSR Supreme Soviet Committee for the Affairs of Internationalist Soldiers that further attacks would "meet an 'armed rebuff'." With the first moves to form a Ukrainian army, the veterans were singled out as a vital source of recruits and an active constituency of support.[120] In fall 1991 Afghan war veterans joined Adolat (Justice) Party groups that began forming in the Ferghana Valley in Uzbekistan, and were part of an informal Muslim self-government structure that helped provide material assistance to the community, introducing *zakat*, the traditional Muslim tax intended to redistribute public wealth in favor of the poor.[121]

In 1992, *afgantsy* joined the numerous military or paramilitary nationalist groupings that operated throughout the former Soviet Union (FSU)—the "Russian national legion" in South Ossetia, Chechen-Ingush insurgents, the Dniester Guard or the new Cossacks.[122] Indeed, Dzhokhar/Johar Dudayev, President of the Chechen Republic of Ichkeria, 1991–96, who had risen to the rank of major-general in the Soviet air force, participated in the war in Afghanistan, for

---

[119]   Author's interview with Nugzar Kakhniauri, 9 September 2014, and with a group of four *afgantsy* in Kutaisi, 14 September 2014.

[120]   Galeotti, *Afghanistan*, 54, 59–60 and 136–37.

[121]   See Yaacov Ro'i, "Islam in the FSU—An Inevitable Impediment to Democracy?" in Yaacov Ro'i (ed.), *Democracy and Pluralism in Muslim Eurasia* (London and New York: Frank Cass, 2004), 109.

[122]   Galeotti, *Afghanistan*, 54.

which he had been awarded the Orders of the Red Star and the Red Banner. He actually introduced and developed carpet-bombing tactics against *mujahidin* forces and participated personally in bombing their strongholds. At the same time, the Russian Interior Ministry SOBR (Special Rapid Reaction Force) in Groznyi in 1995 was composed almost entirely of Afghan veterans.[123] Chechen *afgantsy* helped their Russian counterparts locate missing Russian soldiers in the First Russo–Chechen War (1994–96) and on one occasion fraternizing between the former and a captured Russian Afghan veteran officer enabled the liberation of the officer's fifty men who had fallen into Chechen hands.[124]

The Afghan war veterans continued to play a role in the FSU's various states. In the year 2000, the anti-government Afghanistan War Veterans' Party had a separate ticket and received 8 percent of the vote in the elections to Kyrgyzstan's Legislative Assembly.[125] In Lithuania, Valdas Tutkus who had been a company commander in Afghanistan from 1983 to 1985 filled a number of senior command posts before becoming commander of the country's armed forces with the rank of Major-General from 2004 to 2009. Still in 2014, the highest-ranking officers in Uzbekistan were officers who had served in Afghanistan.[126] And in the Euromaidan protest movement in Kiev in late 2013–early 2014, the *afgantsy* were highly visible throughout the nearly four months that the demonstrations lasted.[127] Here again, Afghan veterans found themselves—as in Vilnius and Nagorno-Karabakh—fighting on both sides. (For the rationale behind the interventionism of Russian *afgantsy* in the Near Abroad, see following section.)

---

[123]   Anatol Lieven, *Chechnya: Tombstone of Russian Power* (New Haven and London: Yale University Press, 1999), 54; and "Pavel Grachev: 'Menia naznachili otvetstvennym za voinu'", *Trud*, 15 March 2001, http://www.trud.ru/article/15-03-2001/21092_pavel_grachev_menja_naznachili_otvetstvennym_za_vo.html; (accessed 17 April 2015).

[124]   Rustam Rustemark, "Chechenskie 'shurshavi' 25 let spustia", *Kavpolit*, 22 February 2014, http://kavpolit.com/articles/chechenskie_shuravi_25_let_spustja-838/ (accessed 17 April 2015).

[125]   Leonid Levitin, "Liberalization in Kyrgyzstan: 'An Island of Democracy'," in Ro'i (ed.), *Democracy and Pluralism in Muslim Eurasia*, 207.

[126]   Author's interview with Ikhtior Tashpulatov, 10 October 2014.

[127]   See Iryna Sklokina's article in this issue.

The Role of *Afgantsy* Generals in Soviet and Successor State Politics

Given the general turmoil that characterized the political arena in Gorbachev's last years and the inefficacy of sectorial, *afganets*-centered activity, the higher-placed veterans inevitably sought to participate in both all-union and national, republic-based politics. Already prior to their actual involvement some of them had begun to take sides in the mounting confrontation between those who sought to preserve the traditional Soviet body politic and the reformists led by Gorbachev's more radical advisers.

Some veteran senior officers were called upon by virtue of their military posts to deal with internal unrest. Igor' Rodionov, as commander of the Trans-Caucasus Military District, was charged with quelling the demonstration in Tbilisi in April 1989. Valentin Varennikov was sent in January 1990 to deal with the anti-Armenian pogroms in Baku, and in 1990–91, he coordinated the attempts to subdue the Baltic republics, notably in Vilnius (January 1991). The military was also becoming involved in unprecedented manner in politics. Varennikov, now Commander-in-Chief of the Ground Forces and Deputy Defense Minister, was among 53 people who called in December 1990 for a state of emergency and presidential rule in conflict zones if constitutional means proved ineffective. *Afgantsy* generals were among military leaders who accused Gorbachev of cowardice, demagogy, treachery, and responsibility for the collapse of Soviet power. This activity led ultimately to the August 1991 coup that sought to preserve the status quo without transferring new and real powers to the union republics.[128]

Gromov, who in late 1990 became First Deputy Minister of the Interior, presided over a militarization of the police forces and the expansion of the Opnaz security troops. He found himself "drifting into a hard-line camp of soldiers and bureaucrats" who, when it became clear that the CPSU was "beyond resurrection... began grafting

---

[128]   Braithwaite, *Afgantsy*, 308–11. Among others, Braithwaite quotes Valentin Varennikov, *Nepovtorimoe*, vol. 5 (Moskva: Sovetskii pisatel', 2002), 192 ff. and 230.

Bolshevik traditions [on]to a chauvinist Russian nationalism" aspiring to a Mother Russia, proud and strong, terrifying, glorious and eternal. He became involved in plans to seize power, including support for the "Word to the People," the open letter to *Sovetskaia Rossiia* that was in effect the manifesto for the 1991 August Coup. Following the Coup, he left the political arena to become deputy commander of the ground forces.[129]

Other *afgantsy* officers took the opposite side. In Galeotti's words, "Tough war hero at Boris Yeltsin's side during the August Coup, hard-talking champion of Russia's national interest, Russian Vice-President Aleksandr Rutskoi epitomizes ... the image of the afganets as political warrior prepared to surmount any obstacle, tackle any injustice." Rutskoi's "real strength... was that he made use of his Afghan pedigree," but broke away from it to "find new causes, alliances and bases of support." Rutskoi, like Gromov, rose thanks to the war, yet adopted issues far wider than purely *afganets* ones—any other option would have meant courting marginalization.[130]

A number, perhaps the majority, of senior officers who had served in Afghanistan believed that Russia had the right to protect its interests by any and every means. That meant first and foremost to intervene where necessary in defense of ethnic Russians in the other successor states. The Afghan war had taught the military how to fight "local wars"; the politicians had only to apply the strength that had been proven. Indeed, a number of young officers at lower command levels than Varennikov or Gromov, such as Lieutenant-General Pavel Grachev, who became commander of the paratroopers in late 1990 and his deputy, Major-General Aleksandr Lebed', were keen "for the Soviet army to expand the scope and role of its so-called 'projection' forces, the sort of units which ... 'can go and fight a war on someone else's territory'."[131] Interestingly, one of my

---

[129]   Galeotti, *Afghanistan*, 130–31.

[130]   Ibid., 120–21 and 138.

[131]   Ibid., 127–30 and 210. For the role of *afgantsy* generals in the Russian Federation and in Tajikistan, see the articles in this issue by Michael Galbas and Markus Göransson respectively.

Uzbek *afganets* interviewees dubbed Russian intervention in Ukraine "a new Afghan War."[132]

* * *

The paths, then, that the Afghan war veterans took on returning home and in the following years were very varied—quite apart from those who returned maimed or psychologically unable to take a "normal" route, whose future was determined by their objective condition. They were united solely in caring for fellow *afgantsy*, especially the disabled, and for families of their fallen comrades. Some did not choose the direction they took, but were guided, as it were, by external forces, such as the Komsomol, or external circumstances, particularly by failure to find accommodation and employment that suited their aspirations and qualifications, which propelled them to moving in directions they would not have otherwise chosen. For the most part, those who were able to take the decision desired above all else to find their way into the surrounding society and to shake off the stigma that that very society imposed upon them and the traumas they had endured in their military service. Over time, many, perhaps most, of them were successful in doing both, at least to a certain degree. Even those who owed their professional achievements to their Afghan experience tended to move beyond it when new and more promising opportunities arose, although those who remained in the military or security forces or surfaced in military or para-military events identified themselves and were identified by others as *afgantsy*, whatever cause they represented. As to those who took up the challenge and embarked on public activity, taking advantage of the unsettled atmosphere of the Gorbachev period and its immediate aftermath, not all agitated for change in the same direction or at the same pace or had a clear-cut agenda. While many aspired to defend the old order in whole or in part, most probably tending to be conservatives, even ultra-conservatives, and nationalists, others, like the veteran with which this

---

[132]   Author's interview with Nariman Abdullaeva, 16 May 2014.

paper opened, were convinced that "now it is necessary to defend democracy so that what happened with us will never be repeated."[133]

[133] *Moskovskie novosti*, 23 July 1989, 9.

A Fragile Movement:
Afghan War Veterans and the Soviet Collapse in Tajikistan, 1979–92

Markus Göransson[1]

Abstract: Afghan War veterans in Tajikistan showed remarkably little cohesion during the political contention that swept the republic between 1990 and 1992. Instead they fragmented along much the same political and sub-ethnic lines as the population as a whole. Successful state cooptation in earlier years had left a legacy of organizational dependence among the afgantsy, *who continued to look towards the state for organizational support and political legitimation. When state backing dried up in the early 1990s, the* afgantsy *were unable to hold ranks but were drawn into the struggles unfolding in the republic. Drawing on interviews with Afghan War veterans and other primary sources, the article traces the development of state-veteran relations in Tajikistan between 1979 and 1992 and argues that state actors were indispensable in providing organizational strength, discursive cohesion, and political legitimacy to a group shaped by socio-cultural diversity.*

"The soldier-internationalists in Tajikistan were and will always be on the side of the government and the state."[2] This was declared by Sattor Jalilov, chairman of the Dushanbe section of the Committee

---

[1]   The author is a PhD candidate at the Department of International Politics, Aberystwyth University. In 2013 and 2014, he was a Junior Research Fellow at the University of Central Asia (UCA) Dushanbe, generously assisted by Sunatullo Jonboboev, senior research fellow at the UCA, Dilovar Butabekov, head of UCA Khorugh campus, and Bohdan Krawchenko, director general of the UCA. In 2013 he was also a visiting researcher at the Academy of Sciences of the Republic of Tajikistan, where he received implausibly helpful support from Sakina Karimova. The present article is based on research undertaken for his PhD project.
[2]   Interview with Sattor Jalilov, 17 July 2013, Dushanbe.

for Soldier-Internationalist Affairs,[3] the largest association of Afghan War veterans in Tajikistan, in an interview with the author in 2013. The words reflect a discourse that is in vogue among *afgantsy* in Tajikistan today, one centered on the notion of the Afghan War veterans as defenders of the state. In public statements,[4] newspaper articles[5] and private conversation,[6] *afgantsy* representatives routinely stress the patriotism of the Tajik veterans, casting them as loyal servants of the state, ever ready to defend the "Motherland" and the legitimate political order.

The discourse is not without an important element of truth. In the recent past, Afghan War veterans have repeatedly taken action in defense of the political status quo in Tajikistan. This was so especially in the early 1990s, when the Central Asian republic was racked by severe political conflict, which eventually led to a civil war (1992–97). Responding to the turmoil, the Dushanbe *afgantsy* organization sided with the established regime. In February 1990, when violent riots swept the capital, Afghan War veterans set up security units and helped law-enforcement bodies stabilize the situation in the city. In February 1992, the leader of the Dushanbe *afgantsy*, Suhrobsho Alimov, proposed that a security agency consisting of veterans be created to carry out "law-enforcement work" on behalf of the government.[7] In April 1992, Alimov and other *afgantsy* officials offered to help the Tajik president Rahmon Nabiev to deal

---

3   Its full name in Tajik is *Kumitai kor bo jangovaroni internatsionalisti Jumhurii Tojikiston*; in Russian: *Komitet po delam voinov-internatsionalistov Respubliki Tadzhikistan*.

4   In February 2013, the Supreme Council of the Committee for Soldier-Internationalist Affairs declared in its in-house newspaper *Internatsionalist - bashardöst*: "We aim, desire and wish for the stability and prosperity of the land. As in 1992, we are soldiers, workers, and rear guards of the Constitution and are ready to support the policies of the President of the Republic of Tajikistan, the honorable Emomali Rahmon"; Shöroi olii, "Bashardöstī-vatanparastī ast", *Internatsionalist – bashardöst*, February 2013.

5   Muhiddin Rahimov, "My patrioty svoei rodiny!", *Internatsionalist – bashardöst*, February 2013.

6   The head of a local *afgantsy* organization affirmed to the author with some emotion that Afghan War veterans were ready, at a moment's notice, to take up arms "against any enemy … and to remain [fighting] until the very end"; conversation with Afghan War veteran, 2 May 2013.

7   Anon., "Vstrechi stanut traditsionnymi", *Vechernii Dushanbe*, 20 February 1992.

with mass demonstrations in the capital by placing "the necessary number of soldier-*afgantsy* at [his] disposal."[8] Time and time again during the crisis of the early 1990s, the *afgantsy* leadership volunteered to support the powers-that-be.

But if the top leadership was ready to throw in its lot with the Tajik regime, it was far less successful in mobilizing other Afghan War veterans. True, many *afgantsy* supported the government. However, many others sided with the opposition,[9] remained neutral, or fled when violence broke out.[10] Indeed, many *afgantsy* who today pride themselves on having fought for the state were, in fact,

---

8   Prezidium Soiuza Veteranov Afganskoi Voiny Respubliki Tadzhikistan, "Dumat' o sud'be naroda", *Vechernii Dushanbe*, 16 April 1992.

9   One of the most prominent is Mahmadali Hait, a former GRU operative, who was accused of espionage during the war, imprisoned, tortured, and eventually dishonorably discharged (the accusations were eventually retracted). He joined the nationalist *Rastokhez* movement in the late 1980s, where he attained the posts of general-secretary and deputy leader. After leaving *Rastokhez* in 1992, he joined the Islamic Party of Renaissance and later acted as the chief of intelligence of the opposition forces during the civil war; interview with Mahmadali Hait, 16 July 2013, Dushanbe. Other respondents, too, said they actively supported the opposition, including during the large spring 1992 demonstrations in Dushanbe. One of them said—rather implausibly—that it even seemed to him that "most of the *afgantsy* here in Dushanbe were for the opposition. Because the government was run by the Leninabad mafia. When *perestroika* started, people began to support change"; interview with Afghan War veteran, 9 May 2013, Dushanbe. Leninabad was the name of Sughd Province in the Soviet period.

10   Many *afgantsy* who hailed from the Pamir mountains in eastern Tajikistan seem to have fled Dushanbe in 1992, seeking refuge in their native region for fear of reprisals from militants. Several Pamiri respondents who worked or studied in Dushanbe left at this time. One was a former scout, who was a schoolteacher in Dushanbe when violence visited the capital, prompting him to leave for his home district of Ishkashim in the Wakhan Valley; interview, 27 August 2013, Ishkashim district. Other respondents left the country, either for Afghanistan or Russia. One *afganets*, who today runs a taxi-cum-trading business between Dushanbe and Kunduz, fled to Afghanistan at the end of 1992, having supported the opposition. He said that other *afgantsy* friends of his who had also backed the opposition likewise went to Afghanistan; interview with Afghan War veteran, 28 June 2013, Dushanbe.

members of a hodgepodge of pro-Communist militias that eventually came to be known as the Popular Front.[11] This entity declared its support for the status quo but had its own agenda and eventually succeeded in establishing itself as the new power in the country.[12]

In fact, the Afghan War veterans showed remarkably little cohesion during the political crisis. A number of veterans' associations did exist—a product of the mobilization of the *perestroika* era—but they tended to be highly localized and proved insufficient for uniting the veterans on a broader scale. The Union of Veterans of the Afghan War (SVAV), formed on 28 February 1992, claimed to represent all *afgantsy* in the country. Yet it was highly Dushanbe-centered and commanded little authority outside of the city limits. Meanwhile, many local *afgantsy* groups displayed astonishingly little organizational strength. One example is the city of Qurghonteppa, where no independent *afgantsy* organization existed until one was created under the leadership of the ex-paratrooper Bakhrom Olimov in 1993. Previously, the *afgantsy* reportedly lacked even a registry of the Afghan War veterans resident in the city.[13]

Hence, the dominant theme in the history of the Tajikistani *afgantsy* in the early 1990s was not, as Sattor Jalilov would have it, the tenacious support given by certain groups of veterans to the political status quo, but rather the disarray and decline of the *afgantsy* as a movement. This disarray and decline had many causes, including rising insecurity, the politicization of regional identities, and the

---

[11]   Jennifer Mitchell notes that "the Tajik regime did not have time to assemble a coherent armed force in the brief period between independence and open warfare, and thus the civil war featured a ragged cast of pro-regime militias, opposition guerrilla forces, foreign jihadis, Russian and Uzbek army units, Central Asian peacekeepers, and UN monitors and negotiators"; Jennifer Mitchell, *Civilian Victimisation in the Tajik Civil War: How the Popular Front Won the War and Ruined the Nation*, PhD thesis, King's College, London, 2014, 47.

[12]   Nourzhanov and Bleuer refer to the Popular Front as "anti-opposition" rather than "incumbent"; Kirill Nourzhanov and Christian Bleuer, *Tajikistan. A Political and Social History* (Canberra: Australian National University Press, 2013), 325. See also Mitchell, *Civilian Victimisation*, 76.

[13]   As was pointed out by Yokub Nazarov, acting head of the *Union of Veteran Soldier-Internationalists*, one of the two *afgantsy* organizations in Qurghonteppa: "Only through the *voenkomat* could we get in touch with each other. Only after the civil war was there an organization"; interview, 13 May 2013, Qurghonteppa.

poor communications between different parts of the republic. However, certainly the most important factor was the crumbling power of the state, which robbed the *afgantsy* of much of their organizational strength. The Soviet period brought close collaboration between Afghan War veterans and state bodies. Yet when the authority and power of those bodies declined in the early 1990s, the *afgantsy* reeled, unable to find their feet as an independent movement.

The article traces the development of state-veteran relations in Tajikistan between 1979 and 1992 and argues that *afgantsy* mobilization was fundamentally shaped by the presence or absence of effective state agency. This was true in the Soviet period, when the *afgantsy* movement took shape under the auspices of state institutions, and also in the immediate post-Soviet era, when the fracturing of state authority produced similar fragmentation among the *afgantsy*. Stressing the socio-cultural diversity of the veterans, the article highlights the indispensable role of state actors in lending discursive cohesion, organizational rigor, and political legitimacy to the collective.

In doing so, the article seeks to provide an in-depth case study of *afgantsy* mobilization in the context of the Soviet collapse. Little has been written about this topic,[14] and even less has been said about the role of veterans in the contention that pushed Tajikistan towards civil war.[15] Texts that do address these issues have tended to home

---

[14]   One exception is Mark Galeotti, who offers a broad overview of instances of *afgantsy* involvement in Soviet and post-Soviet armed violence; see Mark Galeotti, *The Impact of the Afghan War on Soviet and Russian Politics and Society, 1979-1991*, PhD thesis, London School of Economics, 1992, 79–89, 165–67.

[15]   Erica Marat mentions the *afgantsy* in the Tajik Civil War but focuses more on contemporary concerns; see Erica Marat, *The Military and the State: From Red Army to Independence* (Routledge: Abingdon, 2010). Other authors have discussed the role in the Tajik violence of the 201st Motorized Rifle Division, relocated to Tajikistan from Afghanistan, but pass over the part played by *afgantsy* who were no longer under Russian command; see Michael Orr, "The Russian Army and the War in Tajikistan", in *Tajikistan: The Trials of Independence*, eds. Mohammad-Reza Djalili, Frédéric Grare and Shirin Akiner (Abingdon and New York, NY: Routledge, 1998), 151–160; Bess A. Brown, "National Security and Military Issues in Central Asia", in *State Building and Military Power in Russia and the New States of Eurasia*, ed. Bruce Parrot (Armonk, NY: M.E. Sharpe, 1995),

in on particular instances of mobilization, eschewing the broader context and deeper history of that mobilization. This article, in contrast, tries to write the collective performances of the Tajikistani *afgantsy* in the early 1990s into the longer history of state-veteran interaction in the Tajik SSR. Certainly, the swiftness with which the veterans' movement disintegrated in 1990-92 needs to be understood against the background of state cooptation in earlier years.

The article draws on fieldwork conducted in Tajikistan in 2013 and 2014, a time when the author interviewed some eighty former participants of the Afghan War, in the cities and towns of Dushanbe, Qurghonteppa, Kulob, and Khorugh, as well as a number of smaller localities in the eastern Pamir mountains. The article also uses a large number of press reports, personal files, and official records, obtained in public archives and personal collections. Yet, the interviews are key, for no other source has been able to yield as much insight about the mobilization of the *afgantsy* in 1990–92, a topic about which sadly little written documentation exists. The interviews were conducted in a range of different settings, from the homes and workplaces of respondents to more public places, such as parks, restaurants, and teahouses, with many exchanges undertaken also on the premises of *afgantsy* organizations. The interactions varied in length, from twenty minutes to four hours, averaging around 1-1.5 hours, and covered topics including the experiences of the soldiers during the Afghan War and their trajectories between their demobilization and the turbulence of 1992. The respondents were encountered in a number of different ways: some quite unexpectedly during strolls in towns or behind the steering wheels of taxis, others through friends, academic acquaintances and—as time went on—with the help of respondents who arranged introductions to their peers.[16] The large number of interviews provided opportunities for triangulation (as did the availability of certain pertinent written sources), while repeat interviews made it possible to ask follow-up and more detailed questions in some cases.

248; Rodric Braithwaite, *Afgantsy: The Russians in Afghanistan, 1979-1989* (London: Profile Books, 2011), 305–6.

[16]   Respondents who wished to remain anonymous have been cited without their names.

The article begins with an overview of the Tajikistanis who took part in the Afghan War, stressing their diverse backgrounds and varied experiences during the war. It then moves on to the emergence of the *afgantsy* as a social group in the 1980s, much aided by the celebratory and organizational energies of the state. The final section offers a close account of three episodes of *afgantsy* mobilization in Tajikistan: in Dushanbe during the February 1990 disturbances; in Dushanbe during the protests of spring 1992; and in Qurghonteppa in the summer of 1992.

1.   The Tajik *Afgantsy*

It is not clear how many Tajikistanis took part in the Soviet–Afghan War, for neither the Soviet government nor its Russian successor has released firm figures on the republican origins of the soldiers who travelled "across the river". *Afgantsy* organizations in Tajikistan claim that 15,000 Tajikistanis participated in the war.[17] Yet, this number has not been possible to verify, nor has its ultimate source been determined. Furthermore, it is uncertain if it refers only to servicemen of the 40th Army or also to individuals who took part in the war under the banner of the KGB, the MVD, and even a number of civilian structures that dispatched personnel to Afghanistan. There are several reasons for supposing that the number is an inclusive one. One is that contemporary Tajik law counts all Tajik citizens who served or worked in Afghanistan between 1979 and 1989 as veterans.[18] Another is that the two largest Afghan War veterans associ-

---

[17]   See Lutfia Eshonkulova, "V Dushanbe pochtut pamiat' voinov-internatsionalistov", *Khovar.tj*, 14 February 2012, http://khovar.tj/rus/security/31740-v-dushanbe-pochtut-pamyat-voinov-internacionalistov.html; Marhabo Zununova, "Aktsiia pamiati pogibshikh voinov-afgantsev sostoialas' v Dushanbe", *Khovar.tj*, 27 December 2012, http://khovar.tj/rus/society/35490-akciya-pamyati-pogibshih-voinov-afgancev-sostoyalas-v-dushanbe.html. Unless otherwise stated, all websites cited here were accessible on 21 June 2015.

[18]   The formal judicial category is "Veterans of military operations on the territory of other states" (*veterany boevykh deistvii na territorii drugikh gosudarstv*), a subset of the broader category of "veterans"; *Zakon Respubliki Tadzhikistan "o veteranakh"*, 13 November 1998 (revised on 28 February 2004), paragraph 3, article 16.

ations in Tajikistan, the Committee for Soldier-Internationalist Affairs and the Union of Veteran Soldier-Internationalists, are open to any Tajik citizen who holds this status. Thirdly, the SVAV, in March 1992, just three years after the end of the war, reported only 11,000 *afgantsy* as living in Tajikistan,[19] a time when a narrower legal definition of Afghan War veteran was in force.[20] Finally, in January 1988, one year before the Soviet withdrawal, a report by the Red Crescent Society of Tajikistan stated that no more than 6,561 soldier-internationalists were registered with the *voenkomat* (military commissariat) in the republic, an astonishingly low number in view of present claims.[21] Naturally, further research needs to be done to determine the number with greater definitiveness, but it seems plausible that the number of Tajikistanis who took part in the war in a military capacity was indeed well shy of 15,000.

Those who did serve were a motley group, distinguished by military rank, military function, regional affiliation, ethnic identity, education, and social origin, to mention only a few factors. This diversity makes it difficult to speak of a typical Tajikistani *afganets*, for little united the veterans beyond the fact that they were Soviet citizens who had taken part in the Afghan War.

Importantly, the Tajikistanis were drawn from across the diverse Tajik republic. A book about veterans from Sughd Province[22] reveals that 2,862 natives of the province fulfilled their "internationalist duty" in Afghanistan.[23] This leaves many more veterans from

---

[19]   SVAV, "Obrashchenie veteranov afganskoi voiny k Prezidentu, Verkhovnomu Sovetu, pravitel'stvu i narodu Tadzhikistana", *Vechernii Dushanbe*, 16 March 1992.

[20]   See N. Yu. Danilova, "Voennosluzhashchie, voiny-internatsionalisty, veterany: dinamika pravovogo statusa," *Sotsiologicheskie issledovaniia* 10 (2001): 81.

[21]   Z. Kh. Davliatbekova, "Spravka o rabote Obshchestva Krasnogo Polumesiatsa Tadzhikskoi SSR po okazaniiu pomoshchi voinam-internatsionalistam," *Gosudarstvennii arkhiv Rossiskoi Federatsii*, 9501-16-299, 119–20. The author is grateful to Markus Mirschel for this interesting document.

[22]   Sughd Province was known as Leninabad Province during the Soviet period. For the sake of simplicity, the article will refer to places by their present names, thus Qurghonteppa not Kurgan-Tyube, Kulob not Kulyab, Hisor not Gissar, etc. The exception is the province of Qurghonteppa, which was amalgamated into the larger Khatlon province after the Soviet collapse.

[23]   Turdyboi Gafurdzhanov (ed.), *Kniga Slavy* (Chkalovsk: Vostochnyi kombinat redkikh metallov, 1999).

other parts of Tajikistan, including large groups that still reside in Dushanbe, Qurghonteppa, and the Gorno-Badakhshan Autonomous Region (GBAO), where most of the research for this investigation was undertaken.[24]

There were also important ethnic differences. Most were Tajiks, but many others were Uzbeks, Russians, Kyrgyz, or members of other minorities in the Tajik SSR. Of the 2,862 *afgantsy* in Sughd Province, as many as 865 were ethnic Uzbeks.[25] In the Kyrgyz-majority Murghob district, all but one of the 21 *afgantsy* who reside there today are ethnic Kyrgyz (the remaining one being a Pamiri Tajik).[26]

Even those who were listed as Tajik were a diverse group. A number belonged to the Pamiri minority, officially subsumed under the "Tajik" category but actually distinguished by the fact that Pamiris are generally Shia Ismaili and speak languages only distantly related to Tajik. This distinction was to become important during the early 1990s, when Pamiris joined the opposition in large numbers. Meanwhile, Tajik-speaking Sunnis were stratified by regional affiliation, a point which was also to acquire acute importance during the civil war, fought largely along regional lines.

Professional and educational distinctions set the troops apart, too. Most of the soldiers were conscripts, who, recruited at the age of 18 or 19, had only in rare cases embarked on studies of higher education. But there was also a significant number of university graduates, usually students of eastern languages (Persian and Pashto, in particular), who were deployed to Afghanistan to use their language expertise in the service of the Soviet military. These individuals were

---

[24] The deputy mayor in charge of veterans affairs in Qurghonteppa, reported 142 registered Afghan War veterans in the city (population: 75,500); interview with Soleha Kasymova, 26 April 2013, Qurghonteppa. A document obtained from the GBAO *voenkomat* in Khorugh lists 147 *afgantsy* in the province, which has 200,000 inhabitants; "Ruyikhati ishtirokchiëni internasionalisti islomii Afghoniston," Military conscription office, Khorugh, Tajikistan, undated. Sattor Jalilov claims that 1,500 *afgantsy* currently live in Dushanbe; interview, 17 July 2013, Dushanbe. The numbers are probably lower than they were before natural death, emigration, and the ravages of the civil war worked their effects.

[25] Gafurdzhanov, *Kniga Slavy*.

[26] Military conscription office, Khorugh, "Ruyikhati ishtirokchiëni internasionalisti islomii Afghoniston."

generally assigned to intelligence and interpreting functions, some-times in quite senior roles, as for instance Mahmadali Hait, who was placed in the GRU where he took part in secret negotiations with the Afghan Mujahidin leader Ahmad Shah Massoud.[27] As senior in-terpreters and intelligence officers, the graduates occupied a rather different position in the intervention than their compatriots re-cruited as conscripts.

It is indeed difficult to generalize about the roles of the Tajik-istani soldiers in the Soviet forces. Some researchers have tarred the Central Asians with the same brush, arguing that the Soviet Muslims were by and large relegated to menial functions due to concerns over their loyalty and competence.[28] Such views can be discounted. True, there were substantial numbers of Tajikistanis in less demand-ing roles, including as construction workers, caterers, and even dog trainers and warehousemen. But many others were placed in im-portant combat functions, for example as riflemen, machine-gun-ners, sappers, snipers, grenade throwers, and many more. What is most eye-catching is the wide range of roles to which Tajikistanis were assigned, both combat and non-combat ones.[29] As one ex-par-

---

[27]   Interview with Mahmadali Hait, 16 July 2013, Dushanbe.
[28]   Leo J. Daugherty III, "Ethnic Minorities in the Soviet Armed Forces—the Plight of Central Asians in a Russian-dominated Army," *The Journal of Slavic Military Studies*, 7, no. 2 (1994): 171. See also Leo J. Daugherty III, "The Bear and the Scimitar. Soviet Central Asians and the War in Afghanistan, 1979-1989," *The Journal of Slavic Military Studies* 8, no. 1 (1995): 73–96; Robert S. Mathers, "Green, Red and White. The Problems of Muslim Soldiers in Today's Russian army," *The Journal of Slavic Military Studies* 16, no. 4 (2003): 22–23.
[29]   One hundred and ninety different functions were represented among the 2,862 *afgantsy* who appear in the book from Sughd Province. They ranged from mu-sicians and woodcutters to paratroopers and intelligence-interpreters. Many were of a supportive kind. For example, 534 of the individuals in the sample served as drivers (this includes all categories of drivers: truck drivers as well as drivers of tanks, infantry fighting vehicles, APCs and others); 128 in construc-tion- or repair-related functions; and 99 as cooks or bakers. Yet many others held positions that were obviously combat-related, including as mortar-opera-tors (20), snipers (43), sappers (50), grenade throwers (73), machine-gunners (109), gun-layers (162) and riflemen (336); Gafurdzhanov, *Kniga Slavy*.

atrooper from Qurghonteppa put it, the Tajiks "served in all capacities and everywhere in Afghanistan. There was no particular position that they had, not even as interpreters."[30]

Nor is there reason to believe that Tajikistanis were necessarily at the bottom of the military pyramid in the 40th army. True, few appear to have occupied the upper echelons of the command structure (only 205, or 7.2 percent of the soldiers in the Sughdi sample held ranks of junior lieutenant or higher),[31] which may reflect the relatively low number of professional soldiers from non-Slavic backgrounds in the Soviet military at the time.[32] However, many of the rank-and-file (726, or 25.9 percent) held senior NCO ranks, from lance-corporal all the way up to sergeant major (*starshina*)—hardly a sign of an absence of trust on the part of their superiors.[33] Moreover, many of the soldiers in the Sughdi sample were given command functions, including some of the soldiers who remained privates throughout their service. Indeed, no fewer than 405 (14.3 percent) soldiers served as commanders or deputy commanders of units of varying sizes, including platoons, sections, battalions and companies. Again, this suggests that Tajikistanis were, in a significant number of cases, given leadership roles, rather than consigned to support functions in the rear.

The diversity of functions and ranks reflects the varied nature of service in Afghanistan, where the Soviet army was charged, at one and the same time, with securing supply lines, harrying Mujahidin groups, disrupting rebel communications, maintaining military bases, and carrying out other functions required to sustain the mission. In light of this, it would be imprudent to generalize about the experiences of the Central Asians who were drafted into the Soviet

---

[30]   Interview with Afghan War veteran, 2 May 2013, Qurghonteppa.
[31]   These were 2 junior lieutenants, 32 lieutenants, 83 senior lieutenants, 43 captains, 20 majors, 1 general-major, 9 lieutenant-colonels, and 6 colonels.
[32]   Ellen Jones, *Red Army and Society* (Winchester MA: Allen & Unwin, 1985), 203; Yossef Bodansky, "Muslims, High Technology, and the Soviet Military," *Cahiers du monde russe et soviétique* 25, nos 2/3 (1984): 188.
[33]   Seventy-six were demobilized as lance-corporals, 182 as junior sergeants, 361 as sergeants, 73 as senior sergeants, and 39 as sergeant majors. There were also 4 warrant officers and 1 senior warrant officer in the sample; Gafurdzhanov, *Kniga Slavy*.

intervention. As Mark Galeotti has quipped: "It makes a very real difference if you came back from a war with the Order of Lenin or an artificial leg, if your most powerful memory is of a punitive raid or guarding a medical unit dispensing supplies to villagers."[34] The "Afghan brotherhood", so celebrated by many *afgantsy* today, provides an identity and sense of camaraderie but hardly reflects the very significant distinctions that existed among the soldiers during the war.

One should not play down the fraternity that existed among many *afgantsy*, a large number of whom had endured great suffering in the Afghan deserts and mountains. Yet, as a social group, the *afgantsy* were shot through with difference. A far stronger glue than their common suffering and exploits was the recognition that the *afgantsy* later received at the hands of the state. It was state institutions, as we will see, that provided discursive and organizational cohesion to the *afgantsy* movement.

2.   The Evolution of the *Afgantsy* Movement

2.1   1979–83: The Movement Takes Shape

A large number of Tajikistanis were deployed in the early years of the war,[35] which meant that a sizable Tajik contingent was demobilized around the same time, particularly in 1983, when many soldiers reached the end of their service. One of these soldiers was Ibragim Yatimov, a former platoon commander who served in the northern Afghan provinces of Balkh and Kunduz. He recalled staying in touch with several members of his platoon after returning to the Soviet Union, where he also met other veterans who had been in Afghanistan at the same time:

> After demobilization, you know, we...we met. There were many of us. You know, for instance, in our draft there were a lot of people from Tajikistan.

---

34   Mark Galeotti, *Afghanistan—The Soviet Union's Last War* (Abingdon: Frank Cass, 1995), 46.
35   54.1 percent (1,512) of the soldiers in the Sughdi sample were called up between 1978 and 1982; Gafurdzhanov, *Kniga Slavy*.

> We met. We met often. When we came back from Afghanistan, three of us from my former unit entered university and studied together.[36]

At this time, the veterans received only limited support from state bodies. But many of them gravitated towards each other, particularly those who had served in the same units. In 1983, shortly after their demobilization, twenty-five members of Mr. Yatimov's unit gathered for a reunion in Dushanbe. Later, too, Mr. Yatimov kept in touch with some of them, and today even works with one of them in the Tajik capital. Another member of the 1981–83 cohort, a former scout from the Wakhan Valley, remained on such good terms with a number of his former comrades that he sought them out in Yekaterinburg after fleeing Tajikistan during the civil war. They helped him to find a job and he remained in Russia for a number of years, even acquiring Russian citizenship, before he eventually returned to Tajikistan.[37]

These were bonds that depended very little on official support and were sustained rather by common experience, personal acquaintance, and a sense widespread among the *afgantsy* that they stood apart from the rest of the population. Many *afgantsy* did not need official prompting to celebrate that they were veterans of the Afghan War. Yet, this identity was vested primarily in the small collectives: the former military unit, the friendship group, and the network of acquaintances forged through work and study. There existed no mechanism in pre-*perestroika* Tajikistan through which the veterans could organize themselves and articulate an Afghan War veteran identity that extended beyond the most localized level. The power to do so rested in the hands of state institutions.

2.2   1983–89: Celebration

On 17 January 1983, the Central Committee of the Communist Party of the Soviet Union and the Council of Ministers of the Soviet Union

---

[36]   Interview with Ibragim Yatimov, 21 May 2013, Dushanbe.
[37]   Interview with Afghan War veteran, 27 August 2013, Ishkashim district.

decreed that participants of the Afghan War were entitled to benefits.[38] As Nataliya Danilova has noted, this gave legal recognition to
the Afghan War veterans and brought them out of the legal and political limbo in which they had found themselves since the invasion.[39] But it also marked a turning point in official policy on the
former fighters. After the decree, the policy of silence and non-
recognition gradually gave way to a strategy of celebration.

That celebration was particularly noticeable in the press, including the youth-oriented *Komsomolets Tadzhikistana*, which began to run pieces lauding the "soldier-internationalists" in the mid-
1980s. Articles extolling the patriotic and internationalist virtues of
the young Tajikistani soldiers began to appear regularly in the newspaper at this time.[40] In sharp contrast to earlier minimalist reporting
on the war, the pages of the newspaper now filled with brief biographies of the Tajikistani soldiers, often accompanied with personal
photographs and patriotic slogans.[41]

Outside of the official press, the *afgantsy* were invited to public functions, especially on days of military importance, or were
asked to meet with teenage boys to tell them about their wartime
experiences. In 1987, the Tajik Supreme Soviet organized a "Week of
Remembrance", which was intended as an annual event for commemorating Tajikistanis who had died fighting for Soviet power at
home and abroad.[42] While the event was meant to celebrate all Tajikistanis who had died, the *afgantsy* clearly held a certain prominence as the most recent Soviet cohort who had upheld the "revolutionary, fighting traditions of the older generations."[43] As such, they

---

38   Danilova, "Voennosluzhashchie", 79.
39   Ibid.
40   See: G. Shustov, "Podvigi desantnikov", *Komsomolets Tadzhikistana*, 1 February
      1987; S. Vedeneev, "Voz'mi v primer geroia", *Komsomolets Tadzhikistana*, 23
      October 1985; E. Svidchenko, "Tverdaia postup' Nabi Akramova", *Komsomolets
      Tadzhikistana*, 9 May 1987.
41   See: K. Kholmova, "Mukhammadi Bafoev", *Komsomolets Tadzhikistana*, 31 July
      1986; I. Dudukina, "Daler Ubajdullaev", *Komsomolets Tadzhikistana*, 29 July
      1987; E. Dudukina, "Emomdzhon Rakhmonov", *Komsomolets Tadzhikistana*, 26
      July 1987.
42   Anon., "Nedelia pamiati", *Vechernii Dushanbe*, 5 May 1987.
43   M. Gulina, "My etoi pamiati verny", *Vechernii Dushanbe*, 11 May 1987.

were both invited to the main celebrations and given a commemo-rative event of their own: the Day of the Soldier-Internationalists, organized under the auspices of the Dushanbe Komsomol body.[44]

However, the public exultation was not always accompanied by hands-on support. Glaringly, many *afgantsy* did not receive their benefit cards until long after they had been granted the right to sup-port under the 1983 decree.[45] One veteran from Dangara district, for example, received his card only on 18 April 1985, almost four years after his demobilization in 1981.[46] Even some veterans who obtained the required certification struggled to secure the support to which they were entitled. A blunt article in 1986 in *Komsomolets Tadzhik-istana* dealt damning criticism of Komsomol officials in Dushanbe, who were accused of neglecting *afgantsy* and the families of dead soldiers.[47] For many Afghan War veterans, the support that was promised to them remained a pipe dream.

Nevertheless, the 1983 decree was a watershed in certain ways, for it ushered in a new pattern of interaction between the *afgantsy* and state institutions. Revealingly, the self-critical article in *Komso-molets Tadzhikistan* ended with the rhetorical question: "But what to do with those Komsomol leaders who sit with their hands in their laps waiting for instructions. Where is the initiative?"[48] The sub-text was that state bodies, especially the Komsomol, should engage closely with the *afgantsy*.

---

[44] Ibid.

[45] Galeotti, *Impact of the Afghan War*, 100; Danilova, "Voennosluzhashchie", 80.

[46] "Svidetel'stvo", Saidmurod Safaralievich Sangakov, private collection, Union of Veteran-Soldier Internationalists, Qurghonteppa, Tajikistan. There are many other examples of veterans who were granted their benefit cards with consider-able delay. One was Rakhmon Abduzhalilovich Abdurakhimov from Qurghon-teppa who received his card on 22 June 1984, more than one year after the end of his service (1981–83) and more than 18 months after the January 1983 decree. Another one was the Qurghonteppa native Azim Khamralievich Mirzaev, who was demobilized in May 1980, and received his card on 25 April 1984, i.e. almost four years after his return from Afghanistan and more than one year after the January 1983 decree; private collection, Union of Veteran Soldier-International-ists, Qurghonteppa, Tajikistan.

[47] O. Reshetnikov, "Bezrazlichie k sud'bam takikh parnei", *Komsomolets Tadzhik-istana*, 12 November 1986.

[48] Ibid.

For all their shortcomings, official bodies did become more involved in the lives of the former fighters. This was partly to administer the benefits that were guaranteed in the 1983 decree.[49] But it was also because the authorities saw in the veterans a possible asset for use in efforts of military and patriotic propaganda. Previously, World War II veterans had played the part of role models for Soviet youth. Now many of them were reaching their sixties and seventies and could no longer lay claim to the same youthful vigor. Instead, the Afghan War veterans were asked to step into their shoes, and were increasingly solicited to take part in public events,[50] meet with school pupils,[51] and help to ready teenage boys for military service,[52] much like their World War II forebears had done before. It was now the *afgantsy*'s turn to be paraded in public, idealized as model Soviet citizens, and celebrated as embodiments of socialist principles.

Conversely, some of the more ambitious *afgantsy* were quick to spot the opportunities that lay in closer collaboration with official bodies. The future SVAV chairman Suhrobsho Alimov made his name as a Komsomol leader in Dushanbe.[53] The Dushanbe *afgantsy* leader, Rizoali Odzhiev, was elected to the Congress of People's Deputies on a Komsomol ticket in 1989.[54] The deputy leader of the

---

49   Ibragim Yatimov stated in correspondence with the author that, "After the 'Resolution on benefits' in 1983, we were given certificates in 1984. Starting in 1984, it was mainly the district executive committees that took charge of the veterans. Many veterans received apartments, cars, land, bank credit, and other things... Between 1984 and 1987, the local executive bodies, Komsomol and district *voenkomaty* conducted work with the veterans of Afghanistan. The Komsomol sent the *afgantsy* to work in Tajikistan and the rest of the Union and helped them to get into institutes of higher education in colleges, technical colleges, and others"; personal correspondence with Ibragim Yatimov, 2014.

50   Svidchenko, "Tverdaia postup Nabi Akramova'"; N. Podivilova, "Vypolniaia dolg pered Otchiznoi", *Vechernii Dushanbe*, 3 April 1987; F. Guliamov, "Gotovy k sluzhbe", *Vechernii Dushanbe*, 21 April 1987.

51   Vedeneev, "Voz'mi v primer geroia".

52   Guliamov, "Gotovy k sluzhbe"; V. Podvislova, "Ikh zhizn'—podvig", *Vechernii Dushanbe*, 8 May 1987.

53   "Komitet po delam voinov-internatsionalistov", *Mezhdunarodnyi soiuz "Boevoe bratstvo"* official website, undated, http://ms-bb.ru/content/komitet-po-delam-voinov-internacionalistov-respubliki-tadzhikistan (URL currently inactive; last accessed 7 January 2015).

54   "Odzhiev Rizoali Kadamshoevich", *Poslednie deputaty poslednego Verkhovnogo Soveta SSSR po alfavitu* website, undated, http://supsov.narod.ru/HTML/D1431.HTML.

Dushanbe *afgantsy*, Shavkat Mirzoev, was a candidate member of the Communist Party in 1987, having petitioned to join it during his service in Afghanistan.[55] If the mid-1980s was a time of increased collaboration between official bodies and *afgantsy*, that collaboration went both ways.

Hence, the period between 1983 and 1989 saw the *afgantsy* emerge from medial darkness and enter the public spotlight with vigor. If the veterans had been left to find their own bearings in earlier years, they now received significant attention from Soviet officialdom. State bodies such as the *voenkomaty*, the district executive committees and the Komsomol were given augmented responsibilities for the veterans, while a public campaign got underway that celebrated the *afgantsy* as steadfast patriots and model Soviet youth. It was a time of rapprochement between the *afgantsy* and the structures of the Soviet state, both discursively, with a public *afgantsy* identity beginning to form around notions of patriotism and military honor, and organizationally, since the veterans were organized and mobilized by state bodies. On an individual level, numerous *afgantsy* attempted to use their social capital to climb the greasy poles of the Komsomol and the Communist Party, some of them doing so quite successfully. If the veterans had been fragmented and weak in earlier years, finding a sense of togetherness mainly in their small collectives, they were now cast onto the republican stage and brought into the fold of the state bureaucracy. In many ways, this was the peak of cooperation between state and *afgantsy*.

2.3   1989–90—Separation

The late 1980s saw increased activism among the *afgantsy* in the Tajik SSR. Using the new freedoms granted under *perestroika*, Afghan War veterans set up autonomous associations in parts of the republic, especially in Dushanbe and Sughd Province. As Ibragim Yatimov, a long-time *afgantsy* activist in Dushanbe, noted in correspondence with the author, "beginning in 1985–86, independent councils of Afghan war veterans were formed in many districts of

---

55   Podivilova, "Vypolniaia dolg pered Otchiznoi".

Tajikistan. For instance in 1987, in the Zheleznodorozhnii district of Dushanbe, there was such a council of veterans of Afghanistan."[56] Some of the earliest activism took place in Sughd Province. A club was formed in Khujand city in 1985, and by 1987 it had expanded into the Union of Veteran Soldier-Internationalists, which had formal ties to the provincial *voenkomat* and Komsomol.[57]

The crowning moment of the mobilization came in 1989, when the City Committee of Afghan War veterans in Dushanbe was established by a team of illustrious *afgantsy*, among them Abdukarim Afganov, Rizoali Odzhiev, Shavkat Mirzoev and Vali Saerabekov. It was set up on the basis of existing district organizations in the capital and acted as a pressure group for lobbying the city and republican authorities. Vali Saerabekov, once the secretary of the organization, explained that he and other *afgantsy* activists had decided to establish it after they realized that the rights of the veterans were not being met.[58] One of their main gripes was the shortage of housing in Dushanbe; it was felt that an independent organization would enable the *afgantsy* to defend their interests more effectively.[59]

The relaxation of press restrictions during *perestroika* also brought greater candor in the public discussions of the problems that the veterans faced. These problems included the poor provision of veteran benefits and the aloof treatment that many *afgantsy* felt that they were receiving at the hands of public officials. While some parts of the official press reported on issues of this kind,[60] arguably

---

56   Personal correspondence with Ibragim Yatimov, 2014.
57   "Istoriia obrazovaniia SVVI", *Soiuz veteranov voinov internatsionalistov Sogdiiskoi oblasti* official website, undated, http://www.internationalist.tj/index.php?option=com_content&view=article&id=75&Itemid=125&lang=ru.
58   Conversation with Vali Saerabekov, Dushanbe, 17 February 2014.
59   In an earlier interview, Saerabekov reported that the organization was successful in convincing the mayor of Dushanbe to allocate around 100 housing plots and 100 apartments in a newly-built housing complex to the veterans; interview with Vali Saerabekov, Dushanbe, 13 July 2013.
60   See: Ye. Tret'iakova, "Vchera soldat—a segodnia?", 24 February 1989; L. Ivchenko, "L'goty voinam-afgantsam", *Komsomolets Tadzhikistana*, 24 March 1989; I. Agabekov, Yu. Shitov, "My vernulis'", *Komsomolets Tadzhikistana*, 7 April 1989; M. Dzhumieva, "Kak zhivete, veterany?" *Vechernii Dushanbe*, 28 December 1989.

the most important platform for the frustrated veterans was *Paemi Dushanbe* (Voice of Dushanbe), a newspaper that was launched in January 1990 and became known for its against-the-grain editorial line. Importantly, *Paemi Dushanbe* printed articles penned by *afgantsy* themselves, which provided an immediate channel for activists such as Shavkat Mirzoev and Vali Saerabekov to express their views.[61] Gradually, the public discourse surrounding the *afgantsy* now began to change, with more and more critical views voiced publicly in the republic. The veterans were no longer the voiceless poster boys of military-patriotic propaganda; they had begun to organize and represent themselves more independently.

Yet the independence had its limits. Outside of Dushanbe, many Afghan War veterans' associations were very weak, or even non-existent. *Afgantsy* in Qurghonteppa and Khorugh reportedly lacked structures of their own and continued to rely on the organizational support of the *voenkomat*, the Komsomol, and other official bodies.[62] Even in Dushanbe, the ties between the veterans and the state remained strong. Several of the leading activists remained involved with the Communist establishment, while state institutions continued to support the *afgantsy* with facilities, organizational support, and reportedly even financing.[63] One should also not exaggerate the weight of the criticism occasionally leveled by the veterans at the state authorities. The *afgantsy* depended on having a good relationship with the institutions that oversaw and dispensed their benefits. As Saerabekov recalled, the City Committee was able to wrest housing concessions from the authorities only after its representatives met with Qahhor Mahkamov, the first secretary of the

---

[61] See: Shavkat Mirzoev and Vali Saerabek, "Az tu rozi nihon nadorem", *Paemi Dushanbe*, 2 February 1990; Vali Saerabek, "Ba jangovar khona nadodand. Charo?" *Paemi Dushanbe*, 9 May 1990.

[62] This was reported by several respondents in Qurghonteppa, including Yokub Nazarov, the acting head of the Union of Veteran Soldier-Internationalists; Bakhrom Olimov, the founder of the Qurghonteppa *afgantsy* organization; and an *afganets* who currently holds a senior position in the military conscription office of Qurghonteppa.

[63] According to Ibragim Yatimov, the Komsomol provided financial and other help to the city committee; personal correspondence with Ibragim Yatimov, 2014.

Communist Party of Tajikistan, who charged the mayor of Dushanbe with resolving the issue.[64]

So, the late 1980s saw mobilization occur at multiple speeds
among the *afgantsy*. Some localities saw the appearance of autonomous veterans associations who lobbied for the interests of their
members, while other areas witnessed little activity of this kind. Dushanbe was the center of *afgantsy* activism, equipped with a potent
city organization. But even here the veterans remained closely
linked to the state authorities, both by material need and by significant personal ties. During the turmoil that swept Tajikistan in the
early 1990s, both the uneven organization and the close state-*afgantsy* ties were to have considerable importance for the mobilization of the *afgantsy*.

3.   The Tajik Troubles, 1990–92

3.1   An Overview

The period between 1990 and 1992 was a time of growing political
contention in Tajikistan. Arguably, the first shots were fired in February 1990 when riots erupted in Dushanbe, rattling the Communist
leadership and deepening tensions in the republic. They were the
start of a long period of open contention, with pro- and anti-regime
forces increasingly locking heads. Eventually, the situation exploded
in open violence in May 1992, marking the beginning of a civil war
that was formally brought to an end only in June 1997.

Overtly, the dispute in Tajikistan pitted the Communist regime against an array of opposition groups, comprising the nationalist *Rastokhez* movement, the Democratic Party of Tajikistan, the
Islamic Revival Party, and a number of organizations with explicit
regional agendas, such as La'li Badakhshan, an advocate for increased autonomy for the Gorno-Badakhshan region in the Pamir
Mountains. Yet behind the scenes much of the initiative was held by
the leaders of patronage networks, who attempted to defend or advance their positions at a time when Soviet power was transforming,

---

[64]   Interview with Vali Saerabekov, 13 July 2013, Dushanbe.

bringing uncertainty about the future. These patronage networks were frequently regionally embedded, coinciding with the political and economic structures that had grown up in particular regions during Soviet rule.[65] As such the conflict soon acquired a regional dimension. If the Communist Party and many institutions of government were controlled by elites from Sughd Province, who also received support from actors in Kulob Province, they were increasingly challenged by groups with roots in the regions of Gharm and Badakhshan.

With little foothold in government, the opposition often resorted to street politics to give weight to its demands for political reform. In August 1991, for example, it staged a large rally in Dushanbe demanding the resignation of first party secretary Qahhor Mahkamov, who was believed to have supported the abortive putsch against Gorbachev in the same month.[66] In spring 1992, it organized new demonstrations, this time against a decision by the recently elected Communist president Rahmon Nabiev to dismiss the Pamiri interior minister Mamadayoz Navjuvonov, while it also demanded a series of political concessions, including the dismissal of the Communist-controlled Supreme Soviet.[67] The strength of the protests exposed the weakness of the government, which scrambled for means to assert its authority. Indeed, so feeble was the regime that it could not even count on the support of the interior ministry, still largely controlled by Pamiris.[68]

Violence eventually erupted in Yovon district near Dushanbe on 5 May 1992.[69] The opposition used the turmoil to move its positions forward, seizing a number of government buildings in the capital, while armed Kulobi groups in Dushanbe retreated to the south. The locus of the violence soon shifted here, particularly to the province of Qurghonteppa and the Vakhsh River Valley, where much of

---

[65]   For a discussion of the relationship between patron-client networks and regionalism see İdil Tunçer-Kılavuz, "Political and Social Networks in Tajikistan and Uzbekistan: 'Clan', Region and Beyond", *Central Asian Survey* 28, no. 4 (2009).
[66]   See Nourzhanov and Bleuer, *Tajikistan*, 229.
[67]   Ibid., 295–96.
[68]   Ibid., 307–8.
[69]   Ibid.

Tajikistan's agricultural wealth is located. This area was heavily settled by Pamiris, Gharmis, and Kulobis, many of whom had been transferred there during relocation programs in the 1930s and 1950s.[70] It soon became the site of widespread and systematic violence, as members of the different communities, often egged on by militiamen, took up arms against each other.[71] The bulk of the fighting of the war took place here during the summer and autumn of 1992, causing an unknown number of deaths and reportedly several hundreds of thousands of refugees.[72]

The *afgantsy* were drawn into the developments both in Dushanbe and Qurghonteppa, but as we will see, in very different ways. If the *afgantsy* organization in Dushanbe relied on close connections with the state executive, the veterans in Qurghonteppa established self-defense units and militia groups in the absence of formal structures of power.

3.2   The February Riots

The riots in Dushanbe in February 1990 opened a new chapter in the relations between the Dushanbe *afgantsy* organization and the state authorities. The key forces behind the riots are unknown, but it is clear that the disturbances began after anti-regime protests outside the Communist Party Central Committee headquarters in central Dushanbe descended into violence, when protesters and security forces clashed on 12 February.[73] This sparked city-wide looting and violence that persisted for several days. The authorities were paralyzed, all the more so as a group of leading politicians and members

---

70   Olivier Roy, "Is the Conflict in Tajikistan a Model for Conflicts throughout Central Asia?" in *Tajikistan: The Trials of Independence*, ed. Mohammad-Reza Djalili, Frédéric Grare and Shirin Akiner (Abingdon and New York: Routledge, 1998), 138–39.
71   For a blow-by-blow account of the violence in the south see Mitchell, *Civilian Victimisation*.
72   "Tajikistan: Tajik Refugees in Northern Afghanistan," *Human Rights Watch* official website, 1 May 1996, http://www.hrw.org/reports/1996/05/01/tajik-refugees-northern-afghanistan-obstacles-repatriation.
73   Viktor Ponomarev, "Kolokola nadezhdy", *Pravda*, 11 May 1990.

of the intelligentsia sided with the protesters, demanding the resignation of the Communist government.[74]

It was against this background that the Dushanbe *afgantsy* leader Rizoali Odzhiev appeared on republican television on 13 February and urged Afghan War veterans to gather the next day in Mironenko Park.[75] Many veterans heeded his call ("almost all" according to an article in *Pravda*[76]—"maybe five hundred" according to a veteran who took part[77]), and the meeting soon moved to the nearby Trade Union building, which houses a large conference hall. According to reports, a discussion was held here on how the *afgantsy* should respond to the disorder, followed by a vote, which was resolutely settled in favor of supporting the forces of law and order.[78]

In carrying out their pledge, the veterans drew on their military expertise. They organized themselves into small units that acted as auxiliaries to the state security bodies, patrolling the streets and guarding government and other buildings.[79] *Pravda* describes how the veterans "controlled the streets of the city day and night, mostly

---

[74]   For discussions of the February 1990 events see Aziz Niyazi, "The Year of Tumult: Tajikistan after February 1990", in *State, Religion and Society in Central Asia. A Post-Soviet Critique,* ed. Vitaly Naumkin (Reading: Ithaca Press, 1993), 262–89; Olivier Roy, *La Nouvelle Asie Centrale—ou la Fabrication des Nations* (Paris: Editions du Seuil, 1997), 212; Nourzhanov and Bleuer, *Tajikistan,* 179-91.

[75]   Vali Saerabekov credits Odzhiev with having played a key role in mobilizing the veterans; interview with Vali Saerabekov, 13 July 2013, Dushanbe. Other public appeals were also made to the *afgantsy,* including one in the mouthpiece of the Tajik Communist Party, *Kommunist Tadzhikistana,* which urged "Communists, Komsomol members, soldier-internationalists and all Dushanbe residents who hold dear the history and future of Tajikistan… to support the party and Soviet bodies, which act within the framework of the law, to deal an immediate and effective rebuff to the extremist elements"; Anon. "Sobranie aktiva," *Kommunist Tadzhikistana,* 16 February 1990.

[76]   Ponomarev, "Kolokola nadezhdy."

[77]   Interview with Ibragim Yatimov, 23 June 2013.

[78]   Ibragim Yatimov noted that "Then a decision was taken that we would support the authorities, that is, the government of Tajikistan, the CC of the Communist Party of Tajikistan, we would support them…A majority of the soldier-afgantsy, the veterans of Afghanistan, said that we should support the authorities"; interview, 23 June 2013, Dushanbe.

[79]   Ibragim Yatimov remembered: "We guarded the local government. Back then we were at the local government. We were at the railway station. They told us: 'Lads, go out, don't let these robbers attack the government agencies and institutions'"; interview with Ibragim Yatimov, 23 June 2013, Dushanbe.

with words but when necessary with their fists" and that they requisitioned radio taxis, which they used to police the city across large distances.[80] If the veterans had previously organized themselves to defend their own interests, they now took to the streets to help put an end to the violence and looting that had engulfed the capital. Indeed, the veterans acted as an additional security body, putting their military expertise and discipline at the service of the authorities.

In doing so, the *afgantsy* showed impressive organizational abilities. They set up a headquarters in the center from which they coordinated the actions of their units[81] and even took control of a bread-making factory, where veterans worked in three shifts to produce bread for the city.[82] Yet they were not alone. Throughout the crisis, they were in close contact with official bodies. According to Ibragim Yatimov, his unit met frequently with representatives of the *voenkomat* in the district where it was stationed (Zheleznodorozhnii).[83] Vali Saerabekov said that the *afgantsy* cooperated with representatives of the Communist Party in general:

> We created a headquarters then. Our headquarters worked here in the center and in all of the districts. And we were on duty at all crossings. We even dressed in special guard uniforms... But we were helped also by party bodies and people. They all immediately gathered around us. We commanded authority then. You can say that we quickly took the city under our control.[84]

This was significant, for the actions of the veterans had an obvious political dimension. The disturbances had originated in clashes between protesters and state security forces and many members of the nascent opposition believed that the protesters had been unjustly attacked. Meanwhile, some groups sought to capitalize on

---

80   Ponomarev, "Kolokola nadezhdy."
81   Interview with Vali Saerabekov, 13 July 2013, Dushanbe.
82   An untitled article in *Kommunist Tadzhikistana* reported that *afgantsy* "not only helped to protect residential buildings and order on the streets. During the most tense days in the capital, the '*afgantsy*' worked in three shifts at the bread-baking association, baking bread for the citizens of Dushanbe, then delivering it and escorting the delivery cars"; Anon., *Kommunist Tadzhikistana*, 25 February 1990.
83   Interview with Ibragim Yatimov, 21 May 2013, Dushanbe.
84   Interview with Vali Saerabekov, 13 July 2013, Dushanbe.

the riots and tried to put pressure on the government to resign. The *afgantsy* ostensibly mobilized to restore law and order but were, inadvertently or intentionally, drawn into the political fracas.

This was felt by elements within the movement itself. Not all *afgantsy* who attended the meeting in Mironenko Park approved of the decision to rally behind the government. Ibragim Yatimov was one of several who dissented:

> At the general meeting many—the majority—supported the government... I did not support it. There were also others who like me did not support it. There were maybe 500 people at the meeting and the majority supported the government... We expressed our opinion. But unfortunately we were not listened to. There were very few comrades on our side.[85]

Eventually, Ibragim joined the others and spent many days guarding the railway station and government buildings in the Zheleznodorozhnii district.[86] Yet his opposition at the February 14 meeting suggests that political divisions in the republic had begun to creep into the *afgantsy* movement, too. At a time of intense political disagreement, there were obvious political overtones to supporting the Communist Mahkamov government, even though the *afgantsy* organization claimed they were merely interested in protecting law and order regardless of who was in charge. As the conflict in Tajikistan deepened, the politicization of the *afgantsy* movement was to become ever starker.

---

[85]   Interview with Ibragim Yatimov, 23 June 2013, Dushanbe.
[86]   Interview with Ibragim Yatimov, 21 May 2013, Dushanbe.

3.3   The Meetings of Spring 1992

The collaboration between the Dushanbe *afgantsy* and the state authorities continued after the February events. In particular, the *afgantsy* leadership and the state executive developed closer working ties, especially after Qahhor Mahkamov resigned in August 1991 and another Communist official, Rahmon Nabiev, was elected president in November. Vali Saerabekov remembers Nabiev's presidency as a time when the Dushanbe *afgantsy* and the state leadership enjoyed very close relations: "Nabiev brought us very close. That is, us, the veterans of Afghanistan. He received us several times."[87] Even before Nabiev's election as president, when he was still chairman of the Supreme Soviet, he made a point of awarding top state decorations ("Orders of Glory") to Saerabekov and two other senior *afgantsy* officials for helping to halt the February 1990 riots. The fact that some two hundred other *afgantsy* who had also been promised medals for their service during the riots were overlooked may indicate where Nabiev's priorities lay.[88]

The collaboration between state and *afgantsy* acquired a more institutionalized form during this period. In February 1992, Suhrobsho Alimov, chairman of the Union of Soldier-Internationalists (SVI), met with Farukh Niiazov, chairman of the government's Defense Committee, one of the chief coercive bodies under President Nabiev's control. The two men agreed to deepen their cooperation and decided that regular meetings should be held henceforth between their organizations. Even more importantly, Nabiev announced that he was prepared to organize a "security agency" drawn from the ranks of the *afgantsy*, to be tasked with "a wide range of law-enforcement work."[89] This seemed a promise of security assistance to the fledgling government, suggesting that the *afgantsy* leadership was entering into formal relations with one of the pillars of Nabiev's power at a time when political tensions in the country were on the rise.

---

[87]   Interview with Vali Saerabekov, 13 July 2013, Dushanbe.
[88]   Ibid.
[89]   Anon., "Vstrechi stanut traditsionnymi".

The report from the meeting between Alimov and Niiazov made no mention of what the "law-enforcement work" might entail. However, this became clear two months later, when massive protests again rocked Dushanbe. Held on Shahidon Square outside the Presidential Palace, the protests were organized by opposition parties in support of a number of demands, including that the Supreme Soviet be disbanded, that multi-party elections be called, and that a new constitution be drawn-up.[90] The scale and tenacity of the meetings shook the government. As Kirill Nourzhanov and Christian Bleuer have observed, Nabiev had few coercive means at his disposal and labored under pressure from supporters not to give in to the protesters' demands.[91] The result was paralysis and tension in the capital.

In this context, the presidium of the newly-formed Union of Veterans of the Afghan War (SVAV) issued an appeal, published in *Vechernii Dushanbe* on 16 April, which called on the pro- and anti-government factions to resolve their differences peacefully. It insisted that it took no sides in the conflict—"We will not undertake to argue about who is right and who is wrong"—and urged "all political parties and movements, as well as the leadership of the state, to exercise wisdom and mutual tolerance."[92] Stressing its concern with peace and security, it made a reference to the war in Afghanistan: "We went through one war and became acquainted first-hand with all of its 'charms'. We do not want our people to experience such grief, not in return for any future reward."[93]

Yet the equanimity of the SVAV presidium had its limits. Even as it professed its neutrality, it directed most of the blame for the crisis at the opposition, which, it said, was using tactics "so extreme" that the "slightest mistake or lack of restraint by either side will lead to a tragic outcome." It, therefore, called on "all protesters...to leave the square and not be tools in the hands of politicians."[94] But it went

---

[90]   Nourzhanov and Bleuer, *Tajikistan*, 296.
[91]   Ibid, 297–98.
[92]   Prezidium Soiuza Veteranov Afganskoi Voiny Respubliki Tadzhikistan, "Dumat' o sud'be naroda".
[93]   Ibid.
[94]   Ibid.

even further. In an act of obvious political partisanship, the *afgantsy* leaders declared that they supported the efforts of President Nabiev to "stabilize" the situation in the capital. Indeed, they were even prepared to set up a contingent of Afghan War veterans under the president's control to be used towards this end. This seems to have been more than bluster. According to Vali Saerabekov and Shavkat Mirzoev, who both held senior positions in the SVAV at the time, the presidium was fully prepared to move against the protesters.[95] The two veterans say that the organization, in consultation with the government, even made preparations for such an action before Nabiev, in a last-minute change of heart, restrained them.

Of course, this needs not be read as an act of factional support for Rahmon Nabiev or the neo-Communist regime. Rather, it can be seen as an expression of fealty to the institutions of state, to which the *afgantsy* leadership retained close organizational and personal ties. On other occasions, the Afghan War veterans guarded their neutrality. During the November 1991 election, for example, they refrained from siding with either Nabiev or his main opponent Davlat Khudonazarov (in contrast to some groups of Great Patriotic War veterans who publicly endorsed Nabiev).[96] They also offered support to the government of Nabiev's successor Akbarsho Iskandarov, after Nabiev resigned in September 1992.[97] Their overt support for institutions rather than individuals was the basis for their claim that their organization "is not political, its basic goal is [to give] moral and material support to the people who went through the 'Afghan breakdown' [*afganskii izlom*]."[98]

---

[95] Interview with Vali Saerabekov, 13 July 2013, Dushanbe; telephone conversation with Shavkat Mirzoev, 21 March 2013.

[96] Dushanbe section of the Soviet Committee of War Veterans, "Obrashchenie", *Vechernii Dushanbe*, 31 October 1991.

[97] SVAV presidium, "Obrashchenie prezidiuma Soiuza veteranov afganskoi voiny Respubliki Tadzhikistan k Verkhovnomu Sovetu i pravitel'stvu respubliki, politicheskim partiiam i organizatsiiam vsemu slavnomu narodu Tadzhikistana!", *Vechernii Dushanbe*, 23 September 1992.

[98] Prezidium Soiuza Veteranov Afganskoi Voiny Respubliki Tadzhikistan, "Dumat' o sud'be naroda."

Yet in the context of the time it proved impossible to marry neutrality with support for the political status quo. For broad sections of Tajik society, the regime lacked the legitimacy that the SVAV presidium imputed to it. This applied most flagrantly to the Supreme Soviet, which had been elected during the state of emergency after the February 1990 riots and was composed almost entirely of members of the Communist Party.[99] It was no surprise that the opposition demanded its dissolution and the convening of new elections. By throwing their weight behind Nabiev, the SVAV leadership joined the fray that was engulfing the Tajik Republic.

3.4   Fragmentation

In doing so, the presidium was also at cross-purposes with sections of their own membership. The veterans were far from united behind the government. Many supported the opposition and even took part in the street protests. One of them was Ibragim Yatimov, who had spoken out against the decision to support the government during the February 1990 events. He now supported the opposition, objecting to what he saw as the "Leninabad mafia."[100] Another was Mirzo Khakimov, an Afghan War veteran and state cotton farm worker who participated in the opposition protests because, he claimed, he was being systematically cheated of the proceeds of his work by the powers-that-be.[101] Indeed, one of the leaders of the opposition was Mahmadali Hait, a former GRU operative in Afghanistan who became the intelligence chief of the United Tajik Opposition during the civil war.

But if the SVAV's authority was limited in Dushanbe, it was weakest in some of the provinces where there was little history of independent *afgantsy* organization. To all appearances, the SVAV was very Dushanbe-centered, with a leadership that comprised many of the same individuals who had led the Dushanbe committee

---

[99]   The Communist Party won 94 percent of the seats in the February 1990 elections. Nourzhanov and Bleuer, *Tajikistan*, 189.
[100]   Interview with Ibragim Yatimov, 9 May 2013.
[101]   A. Khodzhaev, "Kazhdyi sam sebe politik", *Vechernii Dushanbe*, 7 April 1992.

and with few strong links to organizations outside of the capital. Indeed, it seems to have emerged very much out of the *afgantsy* movement in Dushanbe. As Ibragim Yatimov noted: "on the basis of the district [organizations] the city [committee] was formed. And on the basis of the city [committee] the republican one was formed."[102] Eventually, the SVAV would grow into a potent structure after the civil war, but in 1992 it was still in an embryonic state. Moreover, any efforts to bring the *afgantsy* together were soon overtaken by the events of the spring and summer.

This was particularly true in some of the southern districts, where divisions along sub-ethnic and political lines tended to overwhelm any attempts at unity. A case-in-point was Qurghonteppa, the agrarian southern province, where Soviet-era population transfers had left a legacy of considerable demographic fragmentation. Here, the conflict—which exploded with vicious violence in the summer of 1992—followed largely communal lines, pitting individuals with roots in the Pamir, Gharm, and Kulob regions against each other.

The local *afgantsy*, too, appear now to have become divided along communal and kinship lines. A number of Kulobi veterans who were interviewed in the city of Qurghonteppa said they joined militia groups allied with the Kulobi-dominated Popular Front. Others who were of Gharmi or Pamiri origin reportedly fled the region or were killed. One *afganets* of mixed Kulobi-Gharmi descent fled to Afghanistan during the civil war but has since returned and is now active in the local *afgantsy* association.

Interestingly, formal veteran structures appear to have played little or no role in the mobilization of the *afgantsy* in Qurghonteppa. In its initial stages, this mobilization seems to have been a largely spontaneous affair, supported by kinship and friendship ties rather than the actions of any coordinating actor. This seems to have been true even within the main sub-ethnic communities. Several *afgantsy* of Kulobi origin denied that any attempts had been made to organize them as a group. Instead they insisted that they had established self-defense groups together with friends and relatives or had joined

---

[102]   Interview with Ibragim Yatimov, 5 August 2013, Dushanbe.

other groups after being approached by people they knew. Such was the case with one man who served as a military interpreter in Afghanistan and later worked as a policeman in Qurghonteppa. He insisted that he himself had chosen to take up arms, "to defend the state"—adding that he then approached friends, including veterans, asking them to fight.[103] His words were echoed by a former paratrooper who claimed that there was no organized attempt to recruit *afgantsy* to the Popular Front ("those who wanted to join could join")[104] while yet another veteran insisted that the militias did not deliberately recruit Afghan War veterans: "It was people themselves who organized themselves to defend their villages, their neighborhoods—and who went off [to fight]."[105]

One should be cautious about claims that the *afgantsy* picked up arms out of a wish to "defend the state", or that the militias of the Popular Front refrained from recruiting some of the most battle-trained and militarily experienced individuals around. Yet, as other research has shown,[106] the mobilization in Qurghonteppa in its initial phases did tend to be bottom-up, set in motion through local and informal structures. Certainly one reason for the grassroots mobilization of the *afgantsy* was the breakdown or absence of structures that might have provided a vehicle for organizing them. As has been noted, the respondents in Qurghonteppa claimed that there had been no autonomous *afgantsy* organization in Qurghonteppa before the civil war and that the military conscription office, the main body that had organized the *afgantsy* in Soviet times, ceased to function effectively during the violence.

So, at a time when the SVAV presidium in Dushanbe attempted to maintain unity in the ranks of the Afghan War veterans, those efforts came to naught in Qurghonteppa, where no local veterans' association existed, let alone one that answered to the republican organization—and where even the local *voenkomat* ceased to function under the pressures of the conflict. Here, the *afgantsy* fell back on other forms of relationships, mainly familial and friendship-

---

[103]   Interview with Afghan War veteran, 17 June 2013, Qurghonteppa.
[104]   Interview with Afghan War veteran, 2 May 2013, Qurghonteppa.
[105]   Interview with Afghan War veteran, 13 May 2013, Qurghonteppa.
[106]   See Mitchell, *Civilian Victimisation*, 75–76.

based, which substituted for formal channels of mobilization. There were instances where Afghan War veterans deliberately sought each other out, yet these occasions, too, seem to have depended mainly on personal connections. Indeed, the case of Qurghonteppa illustrates the frailty of the *afgantsy* movement in this early stage of the civil war. Far from mobilizing as a group, the *afgantsy* divided along the same communal lines as the rest of the population

Conclusion

The Tajikistani *afgantsy* who had fought side by side in Afghanistan did not hold ranks when political contention spread to their home republic. This was not so surprising for they had few means to reconstitute themselves as a broad-based movement when the power and authority of the state declined. Coopted by state bodies since the mid-1980s, the *afgantsy* struggled to find their feet when state power became fragmented, then declined, in the early 1990s. The decay of state power exposed the weakness of the *afgantsy* identity, as the veterans divided along much the same lines as the population as a whole. It also showed the limited mobilizing powers of the *afgantsy* movement in the absence of state agency. When the organizational support to which they had grown accustomed dried up, few other structures and organizations revealed themselves onto which they could fall back. The leadership of the Dushanbe *afgantsy* threw in its lot with the state executive, claiming—tenuously—that it formed the main locus of political legitimacy in late Soviet and post-Soviet Tajikistan. Yet many other veterans gravitated towards other sites of authority, including self-defense militias, the Popular Front, and opposition groups. Indeed, there was little prospect for the veterans to remain "on the side of the government and the state" at a time when the government and the state had ceased to be effective vehicles of power.

Much of this dynamic was peculiar to Tajikistan, where a rapid breakdown of state authority in the early 1990s followed on slow and patchy independent mobilization of the *afgantsy* in the *perestroika* period. Furthermore, regional identities, which had long been a fact of political life in Soviet Tajikistan, asserted themselves in the early 1990s with a vigor that had few parallels elsewhere in the USSR. Yet the Tajik case also points to bigger themes in the history of *afgantsy* mobilization in the (former) Soviet Union. One of these is the highly localized form that mobilization assumed in many places, with local concerns and power constellations often overwhelming aspirations towards national unity. Another is the fraught legitimacy and authority that many post-Soviet states experienced and the divisive effect that this sometimes had on *afgantsy*, whose collective identity was strongly imbued with Soviet state discourses. A third is the frequency with which *afgantsy* were drawn into political contention, with many participating in armed showdowns—including as violence specialists, as happened in Kyrgyzstan, Chechnya, and Nagorno-Karabakh. On all three counts, the Tajik case brings into relief processes that were visible also in other parts of the post-Soviet space.

"Our Pain and Our Glory": Social Strategies of Legitimization and Functionalization of the Soviet–Afghan War in the Russian Federation[*]

Michael Galbas

Abstract: *The article analyzes first, the development of the relationship between state institutions and veterans' associations from the end of the Soviet–Afghan War to the present; and second, the interactions between the veterans themselves and their organizations during this time. The paper argues that the relationship between state institutions and the organizations as well as the self-images amongst the veterans' movement have radically changed over this period. In the 1990s, the associations acted mostly in opposition to state institutions and presented themselves as victims of state abuse to remind the politicians that they had a moral responsibility for them. However, since the 2000s political actors managed to swing the veterans' organizations from political opposition over to the government camp, the two parties now share common heroic interpretations of the Soviet–Afghan War. The transformation of the veterans' self-image from victims of state abuse to heroic narratives can also be observed on the individual level of the veterans. Oral history interviews give insights into how the organizations have developed from a genuine community of entitlement into a community of values, based on militarized patterns of thought. Thus, the veterans' organizations nowadays can be seen as both a medium for and a pillar of the militaristic and patriotic political ideology and tendencies in Russia.*

On 15 January 2015, the original date set for the sentencing of the prominent anti-Putin activist Aleksei Navalny for fraud and money

---

[*] I would like to thank Hendrik Woicichowski, Florian Ernst, Nikolai Gorelov, Florian Reinhart, Niklas Ehrentreich, Julie Fedor, and two anonymous reviewers for their valuable suggestions and support.

laundering,[1] a handful of people gathered on Manezh Square in Moscow. Their intention was to show their support for the detained activist and to protest the government's actions. Yet before they could carry out their protest, they were met on the square by several thousand members of the newly formed "Anti-Maidan" movement. This was a movement established by patriotic social groups such as the "Night Wolves"[2] motorcycle club with the express aim of preventing political "riots" in Russia of the type that had taken place in Ukraine in 2014. A feature of the "Anti-Maidan" movement worth noting is the participation of two veterans' organizations from the Soviet–Afghan War: the "Russian Alliance of Veterans of Afghanistan" (RSVA)[3] and "Battle Fraternity" (*Boevoe Bratstvo*).[4] The veterans had come to support the government, just as they had done on many other occasions over the previous three decades. For example, high-ranking officers and former Afghan soldiers were involved in the resistance to the August coup of 1991.[5] However, the appearance of organizations in public is a new form of the veterans' assistance to the government.

This example of the striking visibility of organized veterans' groups in post-Soviet Russian public and political life offers a useful entry-point for exploring a range of questions about the history of relations between Afghan veterans and the state. What is the nature

---

[1]   On 29 December 2014 the judge declared that the announcement of the verdict would in fact be made on 30 December. On the verdict, see L. Smith-Spark, M. Chance and A. Eshchenko, "Kremlin Critic Alexey Navalny Arrested Hours after Sentencing", *CNN.com*, 2 January 2015, http://edition.cnn.com/2014/12/30/world/europe/russia-alexei-navalny-case/. All websites cited in this article were last accessed on 15 July 2015.

[2]   See R. Noack, "An Ultra-nationalist Russian Biker Gang is Invading Europe, and Poland isn't Happy", *Washington Post*, 25 April 2015, http://www.washingtonpost.com/blogs/worldviews/wp/2015/04/25/an-ultra-nationalist-russian-biker-gang-is-invading-europe-and-poland-isnt-happy/.

[3]   *Rossiiskii Soiuz Veteranov Afganistana.*

[4]   "Desantniki, 'afgantsy' i baikery sozdali v Rossii 'Antimaidan'", *Rossiiskii Soiuz Veteranov Afganistana* official site, 15 January 2015, http://www.rsva.ru/content/desantniki-%C2%ABafgantsy%C2%BB-i-baikery-sozdali-v-rossii-%C2%ABan timaidan%C2%BB.

[5]   Mark Galeotti, *Afghanistan: The Last Soviet Union's War* (London: Frank Cass, 1995), 182–84.

of the relationship between the state and the veterans' organizations? What aims are pursued and what positions occupied by the state institutions and the organizations within this relationship? How has this changed over the past decades, and what has driven that change? To what extent are the veterans themselves affected by the current political climate? Have the veterans been resistant to changes in the relationship between state power and their organizations?

These sets of questions are of interest in part because the political environment within which the Afghan veterans' associations operate has undergone such significant change since the associations were founded amidst the political upheaval of the Soviet Union in the mid-1980s. After the collapse of the Soviet Union, Russia underwent a dramatic transformation in political and social relations, as well as economic decline. At the end of the 1990s, economic recovery started; meanwhile, however, authoritarian tendencies became apparent in the political system, and state actors succeeded in establishing a new patriotic post-Soviet identity.[6] Based on these factors, this article aims to examine two aspects of this topic: first, the historical development of the relationship between state institutions and veterans' associations from the end of the Soviet–Afghan War to the present; and second, the interactions between the veterans themselves and their organizations during this time.

In order to examine the triangular relationship between the state, veterans' organizations, and the veterans themselves, this article analyzes the politics of history surrounding the Soviet–Afghan War in late Soviet and post-Soviet Russia, from the end of the war to the present. The historian Edgar Wolfrum defines the politics of history as "a set of public, symbolic actions based on rituals or discourses aimed at constructing an image of history and identity."[7] To develop this definition further, current research divides the politics

---

[6]   See also Stephen White, Richard Sakwa, and Henry Hale (eds), *Developments in Russian Politics 7* (Durham, NC: Duke University Press, 2010).

[7]   Edgar Wolfrum, *Geschichtspolitik in der Bundesrepublik Deutschland: Der Weg zur bundesrepublikanischen Erinnerung, 1948–1990* (Darmstadt: WBG, 1999), 32.

of history into the *material* and *instrumental levels*.[8] The material level involves the implementation of measures concerning the past of a given community. On the one hand, this includes all political action aimed at atoning for the history of predecessor regimes, such as restitution, law enforcement, and amnesty. On the other hand, the material level includes all political decisions affecting the memory of a community, such as the establishment of memorial days and ceremonies, the allocation of funds for museums and exhibition projects, or the appointing of commissions to study certain subjects. At the instrumental level, the politics of history are about the use of history in public debates for political purposes. The cultural scholar Mathias Berek has identified three such purposes commonly pursued in this context: the legitimation of institutions and of individual and collective actions; the construction of a single timeline for the members of a given group; and the mediation of identity. These three functions—legitimation, construction, and arrangement—aim to produce social coherence.[9] Using these categories, one can substantiate the extent to which an organization participates in the particulars of the politics of history and in the process, legitimizes or delegitimizes particular political aims. In this context, the politics of history can also be used for analyzing the role of the veterans' organizations in the sphere of state politics, as well as the attitudes and stances within the organizations themselves. The sociologist Birgit Schwelling points out that veterans' organizations, united by common experiences such as participation in war, transform these experiences into history and introduce them into the political process. Thereby, this process fulfills two functions: it is used externally as a tool for implementing various interests, and

---

8   Manuel Becker, *Geschichtspolitik in der „Berliner Republik": Konzeptionen und Kontroversen* (Wiesbaden: Springer, 2013), 198–200.

9   M. Berek, „Gutes oder schlechtes Erinnern? Die Notwendigkeit des Politischen in der Erinnerungskultur", in *Erinnerungskultur und Versöhnungskitsch*, eds. Hans Henning Hahn, Heidi Hein-Kircher, and Anna Kochanowska-Nieborak (Marburg: Verlag Herder Institut, 2008), 71–85. Berek uses the term „Erinnerungspolitik" instead of „Geschichtspolitik".

it is also used internally as a means of binding together the collective and for the construction and stabilization of common sentiments.[10]

By presenting the material and instrumental levels of the politics of history around the Soviet–Afghan War, based on archival research and the study of contemporary press coverage, the article traces the development of the official treatment of the war in Afghanistan from the end of the war through to the present, and subsequently compares the state's interpretations of the history of that war with those of the veterans' associations. In so doing, it will show how both the state and the veterans' organizations manipulated the history of the war to further their own aims. Thus, the article makes it possible to draw some conclusions about the changing relationship between state institutions and veterans' associations within different settings in Russia. In addition, I also analyze the relationship between the veterans' organizations and the veterans themselves. My analysis of this relationship is based on in-depth oral history interviews with two Soviet veterans, conducted in 2013 and 2015.[11] By comparing their wartime recollections against official statements issued by veterans' organizations, I will explore how the distortion of the political framework has formed the individuals' memories and, in this context, to what extent the veterans participate in the common feelings and perceptions of veterans' groups in today's Russia.

Political Distance and Economic Decline—The State's Handling of the War in the 1990s

The end of the Soviet–Afghan War coincided with a time of political turmoil and economic decline throughout the Soviet Union. Both

---

[10]   B. Schwelling, „Krieger in Nachkriegszeiten – Veteranenverbände als geschichtspolitische Akteure der frühen Bundesrepublik", in *Geschichtspolitik: Wer sind ihre Akteure, wer ihre Rezipienten?*, eds. Claudia Fröhlich and Horst-Alfred Heinrich (Stuttgart: Franz Steiner Verlag, 2004), 69–80, 71.

[11]   The analysis of these interviews is based on the analytical distinction between the *experienced* and the *narrated* past by the sociologist Gabriele Rosenthal. In this context, what has to be underlined first is the biographical relevance of the experience of the life, and second, the relevance of the self-presentation of this experience in the present time; Gabriele Rosenthal, *Interpretative Sozialforschung: Eine Einführung* (Weinheim and München: Beltz Juventa, 2014).

these dimensions had a deep impact on the state's handling of the war and its consequences.

In the immediate wake of the war's end, the Soviet political establishment adopted a detached attitude towards the Soviet–Afghan War.[12] The reasons for this were at least in part connected to the critical examination of the Soviet past which began on the material level of the politics of history in the wake of the political upheaval in the late 1980s.[13] It was in this context, on 24 December 1989, that the Second Congress of People's Deputies of the USSR condemned the Politburo's decision to deploy Soviet troops to Afghanistan.[14] In their opinion, the deployment had violated the Constitution of the Soviet Union, since only the Supreme Soviet had the right to decide whether to deploy troops. Therefore, the Congress deemed the Politburo to be responsible for the violation of norms and the international loss of legitimacy and trust in Soviet foreign policy within the world community that occurred due to the intervention in Afghanistan.[15] However, this condemnation of the deployment by the Congress of People's Deputies applied only to the political decision and did not condemn the actions of the soldiers. According to the Congress, the soldiers had fulfilled their military duty because, "they had been convinced to protect the interests of their home country and provide help for a friendly country."[16] In this context, the decision of the Presidium of the Supreme Soviet on 28

---

[12]   Natalija Danilova, „Kontinuität und Wandel. Die Denkmäler des Afghanistankrieges", *Osteuropa* 55, nos 4-6 (2005): 374.

[13]   See Jan Lipinsky, *Das Geheime Zusatzprotokoll zum deutsch-sowjetischen Nichtangriffsvertrag vom 23. August 1939 und seine Entstehungs- und Rezeptionsgeschichte von 1939 bis 1999* (Frankfurt: Peter Lang, 2004). See also the debates on the evaluation of the protocol at the 8th session of the First Congress of People's Deputies on 1 and 2 June 1989; "Stenogramma vos'mogo zasedaniia S"ezda narodnykh deputatov SSSR (avtorskii ekzempliar)", t. 1, Gosudarstvennyi arkhiv Rossiiskoi Federatsii (GARF), f. 9654, op. 1, d. 19; "Stenogramma deviatogo zasedaniia S"ezda narodnykh deputatov SSSR (avtorskii ekzempliar)", t. 2, GARF, f. 9654, op. 1, d. 22.

[14]   "Zakony SSSR, Postanovleniia i drugie akty S"ezda narodnykh deputatov SSSR, priniatye s 12 po 24 dekabria 1989 goda", t. 2, GARF, f. 9654, op. 1, d. 61, l. 266.

[15]   "Materialy k aktam, priniatym vtorym S"ezdom narodnykh deputatov SSSR, razdavaemye narodnym deputatam SSSR", t. 2, GARF, f. 9654, op. 1, d. 97, l. 104.

[16]   Ibid., l. 105.

November 1989 to declare an amnesty for the soldiers who fought in Afghanistan was not countermanded by the Congress.[17]

Nevertheless, in the 1990s there was no political will to deal with the various consequences of the war. On the one hand, this concerned commemoration. The state authorities did not plan to build a central memorial complex for soldiers fallen in the Soviet–Afghan War immediately after the withdrawal of Soviet troops from Afghanistan. It was only in 1990 that the head of the Chief Directorate for Social Welfare within the Soviet State Committee for Labor recommended in a report to the USSR Council of Ministers and the Ministry of Defense that such a complex be created in the 1991–95 period.[18] However, the financial crisis in Russia prevented the state from building the memorial.[19] In addition, the July 1990 proposal by the Committee for Internationalist Soldiers[20] to introduce a special Memorial Day devoted to this war was never realized.[21] Furthermore, attendance at veterans' commemorations was usually limited to local politicians. High-ranking officials and members of the government only took part in major commemorative days. On the fifth anniversary of the withdrawal from Afghanistan, 15 February 1994, the Minister of Defense participated in related ceremonies.[22] In general, however, most political representatives seem to have avoided being associated with the Soviet Union's last war.

In turn, this lack of willingness to deal with the war significantly affected the care which veterans received. Most politicians seemingly did not feel any responsibility for taking up this issue. This is exemplified by the drawn-out history of the veterans' law

---

[17]   "Postanovleniia Verkhovnogo Soveta SSSR 'Ob amnistii sovershivshikh prestupleniia byvshikh voennosluzhashchikh kontingenta sovetskikh voisk v Afganistane' i materialy, svyazannye s yego razrabotkoi", GARF, f. 9654, op. 10, d. 160, l. 14.

[18]   "Dokumenty o deiatel'nosti Komiteta po delam voinov-internatsionalistov", GARF, f. 9654, op. 7, d. 1314, l. 29.

[19]   See Danilova, „Kontinuität und Wandel", 374.

[20]   The Committee of Internationalist Soldiers was founded by the Supreme Soviet in April 1990 in order to protect the interests not only of the Afghanistan veterans but also of the deployments in, for example, Vietnam, Egypt, and Ethiopia; see Galeotti, *Afghanistan*, 122–25.

[21]   "Dokumenty o deiatel'nosti Komiteta po delam voinov-internatsionalistov", l. 50.

[22]   See "Pomnim, tovarishch, my Afganistan", *Krasnaia zvezda*, 17 February 1994.

which was eventually enacted in the Russian Federation in 1995. This law was meant to clarify the benefits, pensions, and legal status of veterans in general and the Soviet Afghan veterans in particular. However, unlike in Belarus, where such a law was passed as early as in 1992, the Russian law became the object of ongoing political controversy. In addition to the fact that the state could not afford the law, executive-legislature disputes about competences and responsibilities further delayed the progress of the legislation.[23] In this context, Aleksandr Belashov, the chairperson of the Committee for Veterans and Invalids and thus involved in drafting the law, attested that some politicians were obstructing the law's passage. In a Committee session concerning the law on 1 March 1993, Belashov stated: "Those who are against the Supreme Soviet adopting the law will say: 'Who sent them [the soldiers] there? The state did not. They were sent there by some kind of party leadership'."[24] In general, the political handling of the war in Afghanistan during this period can be described as remote and detached, and characterized by a lack of will to deal with the war's consequences.

In addition to the prevalent critical attitude towards the war and its consequences, the Soviet government was also experiencing severe problems maintaining public welfare by the end of the 1980s.[25] Starting in the 1960s and lasting until the beginning of the Soviet–Afghan War, Soviet veterans' policy had been mainly focused on the needs of the veterans of the Great Patriotic War.[26] This exclusive veterans' policy gradually changed with the return of the *afgantsy* into society. In contrast to the handling of Great Patriotic War veterans during the first post-war decade when, for example,

23   Andrea Chandler, *Shocking Mother Russia: Democratization, Social Rights, and Pension Reform in Russia, 1990-2001* (Toronto: University of Toronto Press, 2004), 120.
24   "Protokoly zasedanii Komiteta. Stenogramma zasedaniia Komiteta ot 1 marta 1993 g. po obsuzhdeniiu proekta Zakona RF 'O veteranakh'", GARF, f. 10026, op. 4, d. 2174, l. 43.
25   See Manfred Sapper, *Die Auswirkungen des Afghanistan-Krieges auf die Sowjetgesellschaft: Eine Studie zum Legitimitätsverlust des Militärischen in der Perestrojka* (Münster and Hamburg: LIT, 1994), 150–56.
26   See Natalia Danilova, "The Development of an Exclusive Veterans' Policy: The Case of Russia", *Armed Forces & Society* 20, no. 10 (2009): 13–14.

the reintegration of the war invalids into working life had been seen as the main instrument of social reintegration of veterans,[27] the *afgantsy* were now granted special benefits for serving in Afghanistan as early as three years after the outbreak of the war. Based on the decision made by the Central Committee of the Communist Party of the Soviet Union (CPSU) and the USSR Council of Ministers on 17 January 1983, the relatives of soldiers fallen in Afghanistan were granted the right to compensation payments, and the returning soldiers received preferential claims to housing and access to various educational and training programs.[28] In this way the Soviet leadership sought not only to recognize the achievements of the soldiers in Afghanistan but also to facilitate their transition (back) into civilian life. However, due to the onset of the economic crisis and the growing number of returning soldiers, many of these measures came to nothing.[29] In response, the USSR Council of Ministers attempted countermeasures and adopted a resolution on 9 August 1988 aimed at improving the living conditions of the veterans.[30] As a result, further privileges such as pensions and housing for invalids were granted. Nevertheless, by this stage the state was unable to ensure their sufficient supply. This is shown by a report by the Committee for People's Control to the President of the USSR, Mikhail Gorbachev, in June 1990. According to this report, Soviet veterans were suffering from inadequate provision of housing, health care, and

---

[27] See B. Fieseler, "Soviet-style Welfare: the Disabled Soldiers of the 'Great Patriotic War'", in *Disability in Eastern Europe and the Former Soviet Union. History, Policy and Everyday Life,* eds. Michael Rasell and Elena Iarskaia-Smirnova (New York and London: Routledge, 2014), 18–41; Beate Fieseler, "The Soviet Union's 'Great Patriotic War' Invalids: The Poverty of a New Status Group", *Comparativ. Zeitschrift für Globalgeschichte und vergleichende Gesellschaftsforschung* 5, no. 20 (2010): 34–59.

[28] "Postanovlenie TsK KPSS, Sovmina SSSR ot 17.01.1983 N 59-27", *Best Pravo,* 17 January 1983, http://www.bestpravo.ru/sssr/gn-akty/i2g.htm.

[29] See "Spravki o rezul'tatakh proverok prokuratur Voronezhskoi i Donetskoi oblastei o rabote po osushchestvleniiu nadzora za ispolneniem zakonodatel'stva o l'gotakh dlia voennosluzhashchikh, vypolniavshikh svoi internatsional'nyi dolg v Respublike Afganistan", GARF, f. 8131, op. 28, d. 6309.

[30] "Postanovleniia Soveta Ministerstva SSSR ot 9.08.88 goda № 989 'O dopolnitel'nykh merakh po uluchsheniiu material'no-bytovykh uslovii lits, vypolniavshikh internatsional'nyi dolg v Respublike Afganistan, i ikh semei'", *Libussr,* 9 August 1988, http://www.libussr.ru/doc_ussr/usr_14958.htm.

food.[31] In addition, the resolutions on veterans' welfare adopted by the Central Committee and the Council of Ministers in the 1980s did not define clear administrative or financial responsibilities for the provision of welfare services to veterans. Thus, the process for claiming benefits from the Soviet administrative authorities was lengthy and often fruitless.[32]

Despite the fact that these problems continued throughout the 1990s,[33] many veterans had no choice but to rely on state support. Frequently they were not able to take care of themselves. A total of 10,751 soldiers returned from Afghanistan as invalids.[34] Many suffered from the consequences of traumatic war experiences.[35] Not only the disabled but also the physically unscathed veterans were often in desperate need of state support. During the economic decline, many of them were unable to find employment following their return from Afghanistan. At the end of 1992, more than 30,000 former Soviet–Afghan War soldiers in the Russian Federation were officially registered as unemployed because they lacked sufficient qualifications or work experience.[36]

Due to the political chaos and the state's inability to maintain their support, the veterans were largely on their own. For this rea-

---

[31]   "Materialy proverki 'O ser'eznykh nedostatkakh v vypolnenii postanovleniia S"ezda narodnykh deputatov SSSR v chasti usileniia vnimaniia k veteranam voiny i voinam-internatsionalistam, pervoocherednogo resheniia ikh nasushchnykh problem'", GARF, f. 9527, op. 1, d. 9957, ll. 161–64.

[32]   Danilova, "Development of Exclusive Veterans' Policy", 16.

[33]   See "Porucheniia Predsedatelia VS RF postoiannym komissiiam palat, komitetam VS RF, Ministerstvu oborony RF o rassmotrenii pisem organizatsii veteranov voiny, voinov-'afgantsev', voennosluzhashchikh, Soiuza kazakov po voprosam bezopasnosti RF, sotsial'noi zashchity voennosluzhashchikh, veteranov voin; dokumenty o vypolnenii poruchenii; perepiska s MO RF", t. 4, GARF, f. 10026, op. 5, d. 144, l. 35.

[34]   Grigorii Krivosheev, *Rossiia i SSSR v voinakh XX veka: Poteri vooruzhennykh sil. Istorio-statisticheskoe issledovanie* (Podol'sk: GUP MO, 2005), 617.

[35]   See L.I. Yugova, "Problemy lecheniia i medio-sotsal'noi reabilitatsii byvshich voinov-internatsionalistov", in *Rossiia i Sovetskii Soiuz v lokal'nykh konfliktakh XX stoletiia,* ed. Vladimir Lobovikov (Ekaterinburg: IGU, 2002), 266–72.

[36]   "Perepiska s ministerstvami, vedomstvami, veteranskimi organizatsiiami voinov-internatsionalistov, voinami-uchastnikami voiny v Afganistane", t. 2, GARF, f. 10026, op. 4, d. 2255, l. 5.

son, numerous veterans became involved in criminal activity following their return.[37] In this context, the veterans' suffering did not differ from the suffering endured by the majority of the population of the former Soviet Union during this period. In fact, the *afgantsy* were effectively competing during this period with other, relatively privileged groups such as the veterans of the Great Patriotic War. As a newly appeared group, the *afgantsy* found themselves at the back of the line when it came to state welfare.[38] In 1989 one Afghanistan veteran in Perm', for example, was ranked no. 53 on the waiting list for the allocation of an apartment, and the 52 persons ahead of him on the said list were all veterans of the Great Patriotic War.[39] These economic, political, and social constellations had a deep impact on the Afghan veterans' movement, shaping in particular the veterans' attitudes towards one another as well as towards state institutions.

Veterans in the 1990s: A Shared Sense of State Neglect and Military Fraternity

The lack of interest shown by most politicians and the above-outlined problems surrounding the veterans' welfare fostered unification of the veterans' movement as early as at the beginning of the 1990s. In the 1980s, however, the *afgantsy* did not embody a coherent force. From the middle of the 1980s onwards, many local veterans' groups were established. Nevertheless, due in part to the different positions held during the war, the Afghan War soldiers were far from having a homogeneous "Afghan mentality" or a monolithic vision of the war. Rather, the *afgantsy* movement represented a wide range of opinions and aspirations.[40] This lack of homogeneity also applies to the level of participation in the local veterans' groups. Not every former soldier took part. In the Vershchaginskii region, west of Perm', for example, 52 veterans out of the 83 registered *afgantsy*

---

37   Galeotti, *Afghanistan*, 106.
38   Danilova, "Development of Exclusive Veterans' Policy", 17.
39   "Pis'ma grazhdan sotsial'no-bytovogo kharaktera Redaktsiia gazeta 'Molodaia gvardia'", Permskii gosudarstvennyi arkhiv noveishei istorii (PermGARNI), f. 7677, op. 15, d. 51, l. 28.
40   Galeotti, *Afghanistan*, 103.

were members of the local veterans' organization.[41] It is worth pointing out that this heterogeneity is no peculiarity limited to the *afgantsy*, however; similar patterns (or lack thereof) can also be observed amongst former combatants in the aftermath of all kinds of
armed conflicts.[42]

In his study of the veterans of the Great Patriotic War, the
historian Mark Edele pointed out that they shared less a self-con-
ception as former soldiers than common psychological traits such as
a strong sense of entitlement.[43] Similar traits are also present among
the *afgantsy*. Consequently, the Afghan veterans lobbied politicians
in an effort to foster greater concern for their struggles.[44] First, this
concerned the provision of state support. In this regard, the Committee for Internationalist Soldiers received more than 3,000 requests and complaints from veterans and their family members in
the early 1990s.[45] Second, the veterans demanded recognition for
their military service in Afghanistan in the form of official war commemorations. Thus, for example, in December 1989 twenty-four former Afghanistan fighters, along with members of the Second Congress of People's Deputies, demanded commemoration of their service in Afghanistan in the form of the introduction of a Memorial
Day.[46] Claims of this kind make it possible to conceptualize the *afgantsy* as an "entitlement group" like the Soviet veterans of the Great
Patriotic War.[47]

The feeling of entitlement among the Afghan veterans was
based on the argument that since the state had sent them to Afghan-

---

[41]   "Dokumenty obshchestvennogo ob"edineniia vereshchaginskikh veteranov Afganistana", PermGARNI, f. 1424, op. 1, d. 112, l. 18.

[42]   For a comparative perspective on this topic see Neil J. Diamant, *Embattled
Glory: Veterans, Military Families, and the Politics of Patriotism in China, 1949-
2007* (Lanham: Rowman & Littlefield Publishers, 2010).

[43]   Edele, "Soviet Veterans," 132.

[44]   Aleksandr Liakhovski, *Plamia Afgana* (Moskva: Vagrius, 2009), 560.

[45]   "Dokumenty o deiatel'nosti Komiteta po delam voinov-internatsionalistov", ll.
12–13.

[46]   "Materialy, razdavaemye narodnym deputatam SSSR na vtorom S"ezde
narodnykh deputatov SSSR", GARF, f. 9654, op. 1, d. 98, l. 99.

[47]   See Edele, "Soviet Veterans".

istan, the state therefore also had a responsibility to care for its soldiers after their return.[48] One former soldier reflected these perspectives in letters to a Supreme Soviet deputy and fellow Afghan veteran
at the beginning of the 1990s. In one of these letters he wrote that
he saw the *afgantsy* as having fallen "into the hands of the Soviet
Mafia of bureaucracy, who blame me for having fulfilled my duty to
the country honorably. They've spat on my past, in which people
just like them sent us off to our deaths."[49] The soldier complained
that instead of receiving simple and non-bureaucratic support in
recognition of his service, he now had to struggle with the state institutions in order to obtain the care due to him. His words seem to
convey a certain sense of powerlessness and disappointment with
public officials. However, this feeling of disappointment was evoked
not only by insufficient welfare provision, but also by the official assessment of the war. In his above-quoted 1990 report the head of the
Chief Directorate for Social Welfare also pointed out that the official
condemnation and generally critical media reports on the war had
led to incomprehension and misunderstanding amongst veterans.
Many of the soldiers could not understand why the aims and values
for which they had supposedly fought were no longer valid. They
saw their war and their sacrifices as futile.[50]

To compensate the lack in recognition, many veterans fell
back on well-known values such as military fraternity (*bratstvo*).

---

[48] The historian Karen Petrone argues that the "Afghan veterans expectations' were
raised by the example of benefits and honor accorded to the World War II generation before them"; Karen Petrone, "Coming Home Soviet Style: The Reintegration of Afghan Veterans into Soviet Everyday Life", in *Everyday Life in Russia
Past and Present*, eds. Choi Chatterjee, David L. Ransel, Mary Cavender, and
Karen Petrone (Bloomington: Indiana University Press, 2015), 352.

[49] "Perepiska s ministerstvami", t. 1, GARF, f. 10026, op. 4, d. 2254, l. 61. In his letters to the deputy the veteran commented on the situation in the country and
on his private situation, as well as asking for favors. He asked the deputy, for
example, to find him the address of one of his comrades-in-arms. The cause of
this is that the veteran was writing the letters while serving a prison term. After
returning from Afghanistan in 1987 he had founded a veterans' club in Shatsk.
In connection with his work in the club disputes arose between the local administration and the club members. The veteran did not specify the nature of
this conflict. As a result of the dispute he was sentenced to ten years in prison.

[50] "Dokumenty o deiatel'nosti Komiteta po delam voinov-internatsionalistov", l. 20.

This bond with their fellow soldiers was one of the few reliable constants in their lives. As the above-quoted soldier put it in one of his letters: "In my heart I still believe in the value of brotherhood. Who else would I be able to turn to in difficult times if not my brothers, who I went through hell with?"[51] For many soldiers, this sense of brotherhood and the cohesion of the group was the only thing offering support and assistance to solve their problems; to quote our soldier again, "only the courage and assertiveness of the 'afgantsy' could break through the wall of the bureaucrats' indifference."[52] Thus, the starting point of the unifying process can be seen in the increasing feeling of neglect by the state, which arose within the veterans' movement regarding the lack of provision of welfare and moral support.[53] Here again, there are similarities to the earlier Great Patriotic War veterans' movement.[54]

However, whereas their predecessors, in contrast, only finally acquired their own organizations more than ten years after the war was over, in 1956,[55] the *afgantsy* were able to establish an organized veterans' movement immediately after the war. Against the background of an increasing political self-determination at the end of the 1980s, the veterans seized the opportunity to found veterans' organizations in which the local groups came together. The larger associations enabled the veterans both better organization through self-sufficiency and also greater opportunities for the representation of their interests against the state.[56] Therefore, the founding of the veterans' organizations can be seen as a reaction not only to the veterans' medical, psychological and social problems, but also to the prevailing critical political and social attitude towards the war.[57]

---

[51]   "Perepiska s ministerstvami", t. 1, l. 61.
[52]   Ibid.
[53]   See also Sapper, *Die Auswirkungen des Afghanistan-Krieges*, 183.
[54]   See Mark Edele, *Soviet Veterans of the Second World War: A Popular Movement in an Authoritarian Society, 1941-1991* (Oxford: Oxford University Press, 2009).
[55]   Edele, "Soviet Veterans", 121.
[56]   Galeotti, *Afghanistan*, 108.
[57]   "Perepiska s ministerstvami", t. 1, l. 40.

The case of the Russian Alliance of Veterans of Afghanistan (RSVA) as "sister organization" of the Alliance of Veterans of Afghanistan (SVA) illustrates this point.[58] Veterans founded the RSVA on 20 November 1990. One of its main purposes was to provide legal, political, and economic protection to the veterans.[59] To ensure this, the organization assumed most of the welfare functions usually fulfilled by the state. These included, for example, a range of issues related to ensuring decent living conditions. The association built houses, provided household-related services, and established a special food-trading system for veterans.[60] The support provided by the RSVA also included health care. The RSVA maintained health facilities for veterans and cooperated with universities in providing medical care.[61] Furthermore, the organization raised funds for financing social programs for veterans. These included, for example, projects aimed at the "patriotic education of youth" and the organization of sporting events, such as football tournaments.[62] Thus, veterans' associations of this kind served to provide an institutional framework for veteran self-help. In addition to working to improve the living conditions of the *afgantsy*, the veterans' organizations also tried to exert influence on political decisions. The RSVA, for example, was involved in the drafting of laws, such as the 1995 Veterans Act.[63] In order to gain ground in the political field, the organization also founded the "National-Patriotic Party" (NPP) in spring 1992. As a political party, the NPP acted as the political arm of the RSVA. The founder and first chair of the party was Aleksandr Kotenev.[64]

---

[58] The "Alliance of Veterans of Afghanistan" (SVA) was founded in March 1989 as a union-wide organization. However, the RSVA developed into the main pillar of the SVA and replaced it after the collapse of the USSR. See Aleksandr Kotenev, *Neokonchennaia voina* (Moscow: SVA, 1994).

[59] "1. Obshchie polozheniia", *Ustav RSVA*, 20 November 1990, "Perepiska s ministerstvami", t. 1, l. 31.

[60] "2. Zadachi, funktsii i printsipy deiatel'nosti, 2.1.17", *Ustav RSVA*, ibid., l. 32.

[61] "2.1.8 and "2.1.10", *Ustav RSVA*, ibid.

[62] Concerning military-patriotic education see further Galeotti, *Afghanistan*, 104–5.

[63] "Protokoly zasedanii Komiteta", ll. 2–4.

[64] See Sapper: *Die Auswirkungen des Afghanistan-Krieges*, 190. Aleksander Kotenev went to Afghanistan in 1980 and was injured when his car hit a mine. Back in the USSR he started a scholarly career at the Ministry of Defense's Institute of Military History. In his publications, he shows a critical attitude towards the

The new organizations clearly had the power to attract the veterans. At the end of 1991 the SVA had approximately 300,000 members, for example.[65] The appeal of the associations can be explained at least in part by their ability to secure material benefits for the veterans.[66] This support was focused solely on the *afgantsy* and did not include other social groups. Membership in the SVA/RSVA, for example, was restricted to those who had served in Afghanistan or other "hot spots".[67]

The growing coherence of the *afgantsy* as a group was also reflected in the commemoration of the war during this period. The associations now started to build memorials and monuments. They raised money and requested financial support from state authorities. To date, the RSVA has helped erect about 310 Afghan war monuments in Russia.[68] A main theme of these monuments is the memory of the dead soldiers, expressed in forms that place an emphasis on mourning and fraternity. The aim of these commemorations is to bond the living with the dead. Thus, it is important to note that death is perceived as a constant element of the soldiers' community. This is represented by figures of soldiers carrying their fallen comrade—a common motif of Afghan War monuments. In order to further emphasize this community, the organizations pointedly avoided using state symbols in the monuments. In this context, the sociologist Natalia Danilova has called this form of commemoration a "self-related" veterans' memory.[69]

Soviet military strategy in Afghanistan. At the end of the 1980s he took an increasing interest in the development of concepts for a new social organization, which could solve the problems of social adaptation for the *afgantsy*. In this context Kotenev was one of the founding fathers of the SVA and its Chairperson from 1989 until 1992. In addition, in the 1991–95 period he was also the leader of the RSVA; see "Kotenev, A. A. Neokonchennaia voina", *RSVA* official website, http://www.rsva.ru/content/kotenev-neokonchennaya-voina.

65   Galeotti, *Afghanistan*, 115.
66   Ibid., 104.
67   "6. Chleny Soiuza, ikh prava i obiazannosti, 6.1", *Ustav RSVA*, l. 39.
68   "Istoricheskaia spravka", *RSVA* official website, http://www.rsva.ru/union.
69   Danilova, „Kontinuität und Wandel", 375–50.

The State and Veterans' Organizations in the 1990s:
A Precarious Relationship

Veterans' commemorations reflect not only the process of building coherence amongst veterans as a group but also the problematic relationship between the veterans' associations and the state in the 1990s. At the beginning of this period, the state institutions primarily used the veterans' organizations for political purposes. For their part, the veterans' organizations' role was three-fold: to act as an instrument to secure material supply; to help reintegrate the veterans; and to gain political support for their cause.

Since the work of the veterans' organizations meant that fewer state resources were necessary to provide state welfare, the government promoted the founding of veterans' organizations during the 1990s with the intention of passing this task along to those associations.[70] Hence, both the Council of Ministers and the Presidium of the Supreme Soviet of the Russian Soviet Federative Socialist Republic (RSFSR) advocated the establishment of the RSVA in November 1990 so that the alliance could take over the charitable mission of caring for the veterans and improving their living conditions.[71] For this purpose, the veterans' organizations were granted certain material and fiscal privileges. For example, they are entitled to receive land, buildings, and equipment needed to provide the veterans with material-technical assistance. Additionally, as social organizations they gained permission to pursue commercial activities, and they were allowed to charge the market price for their products and services. Furthermore, veterans' unions were permitted to cooperate with foreign organizations and companies in the form of international trade. These associations were exempt from fees on their foreign exchange earnings.[72]

The founders of these organizations also intended to facilitate the veterans' social reintegration and their linkage to the political system through the organizations themselves. The years of mistreatment had eroded the soldiers' confidence in political institutions,

---

[70]   Danilova, "Development of Exclusive Veterans' Policy", 18.
[71]   "Perepiska s ministerstvami", t. 1, ll. 42–45.
[72]   "Perepiska s ministerstvami", t. 1, ll. 42–45.

and as a result, they often felt resigned to their fate, leading to apathy and a lack of participation in the political and social process.[73] Thus, the above-quoted veteran wrote in his letter to the veteran Supreme Soviet deputy that he wanted to go "to the Red Square and throw his military medals in front of the Kremlin."[74] These sentiments are a clear indication of the veteran's disappointment. He does not want to identify with a country that would send him to war and then refuse to take care of him after his return.

In order to allow the veterans' social reintegration, the organizations also handled the task of "youth military-patriotic education", especially during the Soviet era.[75] Activities of this kind gave the veterans an opportunity to cooperate with the political system and its institutions.[76] Such activities also offered the veterans a meaning for their combat mission, the experience they gained in Afghanistan, and their military knowledge in the aftermath of the war.

In addition, state politicians tried to reintegrate the veterans not only by giving them the task of patriotic education but also by aiming to increase their acceptance within the society. The Soviet–Afghan War catalyzed a decline in acceptance of the legitimacy of Soviet rule and of the Soviet military on the part of the Soviet population.[77] In the course of the war and the public critical discussions from the middle of the 1980s, not only the meaning and purpose of the combat mission, but also the prestige of the soldiers were challenged. Later, in the 1990s, in an effort to counteract these processes and to enhance the social recognition of the *afgantsy*, state officials showed their support for the veterans in a series of public appearances. On these occasions, politicians tended to reiterate the Congress of People's Deputies' condemnation of the war. Crucially, however, they accompanied this with an emphasis on the heroism of the soldiers in fulfilling their duty. Thus, for example, in his speech at the commemoration ceremony marking the fifth anniversary of the withdrawal from Afghanistan, the Russian Minister of Defense,

---

73   "Dokumenty o deiatel'nosti Komiteta po delam voinov-internatsionalistov", l. 20.
74   "Perepiska s ministerstvami", t. 1, l. 61.
75   "1. Obshchie polozheniia, 1.2.7", *Ustav RSVA*, l. 31.
76   Galeotti, *Afghanistan*, 105.
77   Sapper, *Die Auswirkungen des Afghanistan-Krieges*, 230–41.

Army General Pavel Grachev depicted the Afghan veterans as heroes:

> "For us as soldiers it is clear: In this undeclared war the *afgantsy* overwhelmingly showed courage, heroism, and loyalty to the military oath and the homeland. And it is not our fault that the army had to pay with blood for the mistakes of the political leaders; and they paid an immense price for them."[78]

The usage of the personal pronoun "us" indicates that Grachev was speaking to the veterans primarily as a fellow soldier rather than an official representative. However, the official viewpoints of 1989 are also reflected in his comments: Political mistakes had been made, yet the soldiers had heroically fulfilled their military oaths.

Government officials continued using this same set of narratives in the following years. For example, in 1999 President Boris Yeltsin showed his endorsement of the tenth anniversary commemorations by sending a personal greeting to the veterans. In this, he emphasized not only the veterans' bravery and heroism, but also their faithfulness to the military oath, which was why, he said, "we pay a tribute of deep respect to all internationalist warriors."[79] In his address to the ceremony, Prime Minister Yevgenii Primakov also made a point of condemning the war: "The politicians were not up to the mark. This can be said directly... Afghanistan should never have happened."[80] These narratives built on the notions of the "military oath" and "duty" enabled the government officials to underscore the heroism of the soldiers and to justify their actions in Afghanistan. Simultaneously, they also made it possible for the officials to maintain their condemnation of the war without portraying the veterans themselves as in any way implicated by this. Therefore, these narratives served the cause of rehabilitating the Afghan veterans, supporting their social reintegration and lending them new prestige.

By granting privileges and publicly recognizing the soldiers as heroes, state officials were also, of course, trying to strengthen political ties with the veterans and to win their political support. In the

---

[78]   "Dolgoe ekho afganskoi voiny", *Krasnaia zvezda*, 16 February 1994.
[79]   Ibid.
[80]   "Proshchaite, gory, vam vidnei", *Krasnaia zvezda*, 17 February 1999.

wake of the political conflicts of the early 1990s in particular, government officials hoped that the veterans' unions might act as political supporters in the future. Thus, for example, the government supported the establishment of the NPP in 1992. The Vice President and close confidant of Boris Yeltsin, Gennadii Burbulis, acted as chairperson of the party.[81]

In the early 1990s, the state and the veterans' associations had a close relationship. The associations sought to link themselves to government institutions in order to gain more governmental welfare. In addition to veterans' privileges, the associations needed financial support directly from the state to support their work aimed at improving the living conditions of the veterans.[82] Carried by the hope of retaining financial aid, the associations supported the president's political agenda during his conflict with parliament. Thus, the NPP encouraged the "irreversibility of the reforms" and buttressed Yeltsin during the Constitutional crisis in September/October 1993, and the *afgantsy* participated in the storming of the White House in Moscow in early October.[83]

However, this alliance went into decline in the wake of the economic crisis and the deterioration of living conditions. In this context, one issue was the fact that not all veterans' associations had been granted the same rights and benefits by the state. As a result, rivalry arose between the organizations, ultimately leading to confrontation not only with one another but also with state institutions. Beside the SVA and the RSVA, there existed more than twenty other organizations of Afghanistan veterans, all striving and competing for influence and resources in the 1990s.[84] The other associations had grown resentful of the special status enjoyed by the SVA and RSVA. Since its inception, the SVA had been linked closely to the political sphere. Its chairperson, Aleksandr Kotenev, for example, worked as an advisor to the government on veterans' affairs.[85]

---

[81]   Anatolii Gil' Lider, "Narodno-patrioticheskaia partiia", *Panorama*, 1999, http://www.panorama.ru/works/vybory/party/afgan.html.
[82]   "Perepiska s ministerstvami", t. 1, l. 59.
[83]   Lider, "Narodno-patrioticheskaia partiia".
[84]   "Perepiska s ministerstvami", t. 2, l. 47.
[85]   Ibid., t. 1, ll. 165–67.

Through its political contacts, the SVA/RSVA managed to gain a prominent role as the leading veterans' organization. The RSVA, for example, obtained state privileges in 1990 and again in 1992, while the other associations only received these at a later date and never automatically.[86] The other veterans' organizations criticized this special cooperation between the SVA/RSVA and the state authorities, one which they claimed led to unfair preferential treatment for both of these organizations.[87] In this context, the other organizations accused the SVA/RSVA of cheating them out of state benefits and of abusing their status as veterans in order to secure financial benefits for their party. Thus, the organizations pleaded for the same rights which the SVA and the RSVA held. They argued that since they had taken care of the soldiers and their bereaved in the war's aftermath just as the SVA and RSVA had done, they also deserved the same privileges.[88]

However, the competition over influence and privileges did not stop at the level of verbal criticism. At a time when the state was in disarray and lacking assets, the organizations were often either connected to criminal subjects or engaged in criminal activities themselves.[89] The transfer of responsibility for housing and the allocation of flats from the state to the veterans' groups often promoted corruption. In some cases veterans could improve their positions in the queue for an apartment by paying an additional fee to

---

[86]   See "Porucheniia Predsedatelia VS RF postoiannym komissiiam palat, komitetam VS RF, Ministerstvu oborony RF o rassmotrenii pisem organizatsii veteranov voiny, voinov-'afgantsev', voennosluzhashchikh, Soiuza kazakov po voprosam bezopasnosti RF, sotsial'noi zashchity voennosluzhashchikh, veteranov voin; dokumenty o vypolnenii poruchenii; perepiska s MO RF", t. 2, GARF, f. 10026, op. 5, d. 137, ll. 42–43. See also Natalia Danilova, "The Veterans' Policy in Russia: a Puzzle of Creation", *The Journal of Power Institutions in Post-Soviet Societies*, nos 6/7 (2007), http://www.pipss.org/document873.html.

[87]   "Perepiska s ministerstvami", t. 1, ll. 165–67.

[88]   See "Dokumenty o sostoianii i problemakh sem'i, materinstva i detstva, molodezhi, veteranov i invalidov, voinov-internatsionalistov v RSFSR (porucheniia Predsedatelia Verkhovnogo Soveta RSFSR, pis'ma, obrashcheniia, zapiski, perepiska i dr.)", t. 1, GARF, f. 10026, op. 1, d. 2432, l. 250.

[89]   Serguei Alex. Oushakine, *The Patriotism of Despair. Nation, War, and Loss in Russia* (Ithaca: Cornell University Press, 2009), 167.

their veterans' organization. Furthermore, the veterans' organizations reportedly spent only between 9 percent and 24 percent of their financial receipts on the improvement of living conditions for the veterans.[90] The rest evaporated in murky channels. Many veterans' unions used the opportunity to create joint ventures with foreign companies in order to smuggle drugs and alcohol into Russia.[91] In this environment, the rivalry escalated and the organizations used violence in their struggle against one another. On 10 November 1994, the leader of the Union of Invalids of the Afghan war, Mikhail Lokhodei, was killed in a professional bombing. Two years later, at the cemetery during a service commemorating his death, another bomb explosion injured and killed several persons, including his widow and his son.[92]

These attacks can be regarded as a turning point in the relationship between the state and the organizations. Due to the escalating violence, state institutions reduced cooperation with a number of veterans' associations. The attacks were seen as representing a direct challenge to the state, not least because the Lokhodei assassination had been carried out on the professional holiday of the Soviet and later Russian militia forces,[93] and was thus considered a direct attack on the security forces and their reputation.[94]

Even before the attack, the state authorities had been working to try to contain the criminal activities of veterans' groups. The police had raided many of the veterans' organizations. In 1992, for example, the offices of the Sverdlovsk RSVA were searched on suspicion of breach of trust, and tax evasion.[95] As a consequence of the

---

[90] N. Nikulina, "Pokushenie na blagotvoritelnost'", *Vek*, 30 May 1997; Ye. Nedomerova, "Kuda tekut 'afganskie' milliardy?", *Segodnia*, 4 May 1995. See also Oushakine, *Patriotism of Despair*, 166.

[91] Vadim Volkov, *Violent Entrepreneurs: The Use of Force in the Making of Russian Capitalism* (Ithaca, NY: Cornell University Press, 2002), 13.

[92] Oushakine, *Patriotism of Despair*, 168.

[93] "10 noiabria – Den' sotrudnika organov vnutrennikh del Rossiiskoi Federatsii", *Azzeros*, 2014, http://azerros.ru/events-and-comments/20797-10-noyabrya-den-sotrudnika-organov-vnutrennih-del-rossiyskoy-federacii.html.

[94] Oushakine, *Patriotism of Despair*, 167.

[95] "Porucheniia Predsedatelia VS RF postoiannym komissiiam palat, komitetam VS RF, Ministerstvu oborony RF o rassmotrenii pisem organizatsii veteranov voiny, voinov-'afgantsev', voennosluzhashchikh, Soiuza kazakov po voprosam

1994 attack the state reduced and later cancelled the tax benefits and privileges enjoyed by veterans' groups.[96] By doing this, the police were trying to reduce criminal activity. Yet we can also read these developments as marking a new realization on the part of state officials that the veterans' unions had now lost their important role in state welfare. Effectively the state was attempting here to regain its authority in the sphere of social welfare. At the same time, this development can also be seen as indicating the definitive breakdown of the Soviet system of civil-military relations that had previously provided soldiers and veterans with a privileged status in an attempt to guarantee their loyalty to the state.[97]

This breakdown was likewise paralleled in the sphere of "youth military-patriotic education". During Yeltsin's presidency, patriotic education did not play as important a role in the school system as it had during the Soviet era.[98] Therefore, there was less incentive in this regard for the state to support the activities of the veterans' associations. As a result, the organizations now faced new difficulties realizing another of their goals—the veterans' social reintegration.

The deteriorating relationship between the state and the organizations prompted changes in the shape of the veterans' movement. With the elimination of the state privileges, the organizations began to consolidate. Beside their membership dues and government benefits, they had no financial means. Therefore, they were dependent on grants and redistributions which were not always forthcoming. Consequently, many of the associations were dissolved and/or had little choice but to merge with the RSVA.[99] The RSVA "survived" this period because it succeeded in maintaining its contacts on the political level, enabling access to additional resources.[100]

---

bezopasnosti RF, sotsial'noi zashchity voennosluzhashchikh, veteranov voin; dokumenty o vypolnenii poruchenii; perepiska s MO RF", t. 5, GARF, f. 10026, op. 5, d. 140, l. 207.

[96]   Oushakine, *Patriotism of Despair*, 168.
[97]   See Danilova, "Development of Exclusive Veterans' Policy", 18–19.
[98]   Galeotti, *Afghanistan*, 104–5.
[99]   See "Dokumenty obshchestvennogo ob"edineniia komitetov veteranov voiny v Afganistane 'Iskra' zavoda Mashinostroitel'", PermGARNI, f. 1924, op. 1, d. 31, l. 17.
[100]   Galeotti, *Afghanistan*, 117.

However, the intensity and nature of these contacts was no longer comparable to those of previous years. In fact, the veterans' organizations were now moving in the opposite political direction. This can be shown by examining the candidates for the December 1995 parliamentary elections. Having previously supported the president's camp, the NPP now launched the patriotic voting bloc "For the Motherland!" in a coalition with other patriotic organizations in the lead-up to the election. "For the Motherland!" was distinguished by its critical attitude towards the government.[101]

The growing gap between the veterans' organizations and the state during this period can also be demonstrated on the instrumental level of the politics of history. The organizations did not share the state's perspective on the Soviet–Afghan War. Like the state officials, the associations used the notion of "fulfillment of duty" as the cornerstone of their general narrative of the war in the 1990s.[102] However, this notion of duty was divided among the veterans into an internal and an external perspective. Within the group, the veterans adhered to a heroic view on the mission, similar to the state perspective. Thus, for example, in 1993 the RSVA chairperson Kotenev emphasized in a letter to the group's members his sense of honor at having served in Afghanistan.[103] However, in the public sphere, references to duty were combined less with an emphasis on heroism and more with critical reflection on the military operation itself. In this context, the grief, suffering, and sacrifice of the soldiers were invoked and the objectives of the intervention were questioned. Examples illustrating this tendency can be found in numerous statements made by representatives of the veterans' associations in interviews and speeches at anniversaries. In an official statement

---

[101]   Vasilii Timoshenko and Sergei Zaslavskii, *Rossiiskie partii, dvizheniia i bloki na vyborakh v Gosudarstvennuiu Dumu 17 dekabria 1995 goda: Opyt, problemy, perspektivy* (Moscow: Znanie Rossii, 1996), 48.

[102]   "Bolit v dushe Afganistan", *Krasnaia zvezda*, 16 February 1995.

[103]   "Porucheniia Predsedatelia VS RF postoiannym komissiiam palat, komitetam VS RF, Ministerstvu oborony RF o rassmotrenii pisem organizatsii veteranov voiny, voinov-'afgantsev', voennosluzhashchikh, Soiuza kazakov po voprosam bezopasnosti RF, sotsial'noi zashchity voennosluzhashchikh, veteranov voin; dokumenty o vypolnenii poruchenii; perepiska s MO RF", t. 1, GARF, f. 10026, op. 5, d. 141, l. 154.

issued by the Russian Fund for Invalids of the War in Afghanistan (RFIVA) in 1998, for example, the notion of the fulfillment of military duty was linked not to the honor of the soldiers, but to the casualties of the war. Similarly, the RFIVA broached the issue of the pain and grief of the families of the fallen, especially their mothers.[104]

One can see a further example of this critical stance toward the war in a statement by Boris Gromov, the chairperson of the veterans' organization "Battle Fraternity" and also the last commander of the 40th Army.[105] In a 1999 interview, Gromov questioned the meaning of the operation: "Over nine years and two months of bloodshed the soldiers' commitment did not achieve the higher internationalist goals."[106] As a former commander-in-chief Gromov did not have the military aspect of the operation in mind here. Rather, he was concerned with the general political objective behind the intervention: "We achieved no results at the level of previous political interests. Afghanistan was—and is—of great importance for our government according to geopolitical interests. But after we left, we surrendered the country to the tyranny of fate."[107] He criticized the fact that there was neither a clear strategy nor clear guidelines for the Soviet operation in Afghanistan. This, therefore, can be seen as an indictment regarding what the soldiers actually fought for.

The differences in the narratives on the war employed by the state and the veterans' organizations exemplify the growing rift in the relationship between these two sets of actors. Instead of adopting the state narratives of military heroism and working together with the state towards greater social recognition, the associations took a different stance, apparently based primarily on their priority

---

[104] "Nasha Spravka", *Krasnaia zvezda*, 13 February 1998.
[105] After his service in Afghanistan Gromov started a political career. For example, he was a Member of the Congress of People's Deputies in 1989, Deputy Defense Minister between 1992 and 1995, Deputy in the State Duma in the 1996-99 period, and Governor of the Moscow region from 2000 to 2012.
[106] "Nashe boevoe bratstvo bez granits", *Rossiiskaia gazeta*, 13 February 1999.
[107] Ibid.

of gaining material and financial support from the state. In this connection, an emphasis was placed on the victimhood rather than the
heroism of the veterans. The associations denied the state-sponsored heroic perspective in public and instead portrayed themselves
as victims of the war. By doing so, the associations attempted to convince state politicians to take moral responsibility for the veterans
and their welfare. At the same time, by presenting themselves as victims, the associations were also trying to show society that they were
not responsible for what a significant part of the population considered to be a "bad war".[108]

The *Afgantsy* as a Mainstay of National Identity from the 2000s

The remote relations between state institutions and the veterans'
associations changed during the first term of Vladimir Putin's presidency. In the course of the formation of the societal and cultural
militarization that has been increasingly evident as a pillar of Putin's
political system from this period onwards,[109] state actors have taken
more interest in the remembrance of the Soviet–Afghan War.
Putin's actions in this regard have included initiatives in the material field of history politics. For example, in 2001 Putin ordered the
creation of a monument to the internationalist fighters.[110] The monument was unveiled at the memorial complex of the Great Patriotic
War in Moscow on 27 December 2004. In addition, at the end of 2010
the date of the withdrawal from Afghanistan—15 February—was
added to the official commemorative calendar as a "day of remembrance for the Russian countries that did their duty outside of the
home country."[111]

---

108   Galeotti, *Afghanistan*, 150–52.
109   See Lev Gudkov, „Die Fesseln des Sieges. Rußlands Identität aus der Erinnerung
        an den Krieg", *Osteuropa* 55, nos 4-6 (2005): 56–73; Stephen Webber and Jennifer Mathers, *Military and Society in Post-Soviet Russia* (Manchester: Manchester
        University Press, 2006).
110   The RSVA had been lobbying the government for such a monument since 1999;
        see "O Soiuze", RSVA official website, http://www.rsva.ru/union.
111   "Federal'nyi zakon Rossiiskoi Federatsii ot 29 noiabria 2010 g. N 320-FZ", *Rossiiskaia gazeta*, 3 December 2010, http://www.rg.ru/2010/12/03/den-dok.html.

An increased engagement with the Soviet–Afghan War was also initiated on the instrumental level of history politics. Presidents Vladimir Putin and Dmitrii Medvedev participated more frequently in veterans' commemorative events, or at least conveyed greetings. In their content, the presidential statements made on these occasions differ from the historical and political handling of the mission in Afghanistan under President Yeltsin. As in the 1990s, Putin and Medvedev continuously emphasized the heroism and bravery of the soldiers.[112] However, in their statements they also pointed out the relevance of the *afgantsy* for society today. On the fifteenth anniversary of the withdrawal from Afghanistan, for example, Putin noted in connection with his praise for the *afgantsy* that: "Today, Russia needs people who know how to overcome difficulties and solve complex tasks."[113] According to Putin, the experiences and skills that they had acquired in Afghanistan made the veterans particularly useful for the nation. They were especially suitable for carrying out tasks in the field of the "military-patriotic education of youth" and the state security sector.[114]

In addition, the 21th-century presidents gave new meaning to the Soviet–Afghan War itself, linking the notion of internationalist duty to the defense of the homeland. In his 2004 commemorative address on the anniversary of the Soviet withdrawal from Afghanistan, Putin described the protection of "our southern borders" as a primary objective of the operation.[115] Constituting the war as a "Just

---

[112] See "Uchastnikam torzhestvennogo meropriiatiia, posviashchennogo 21-oi godovshchine vyvoda Ogranichennogo kontingenta sovetskikh voisk iz Respubliki Afganistan", *Prezident Rossii* official website, 15 February 2010, http://www.kremlin.ru/events/president/letters/6869.

[113] "Vystuplenie na sobranii, posviashchennom Dni pamiati voinov-internatsionalistov", *Prezident Rossii* official website, 15 February 2004, http://archive.kremlin.ru/appears/2004/02/15/1615_type63374type63376type122346_159652.shtml.

[114] "Uchastnikam torzhestvennogo vechera, posviashchennogo podvigu voinov-internatsionalistov", *Prezident Rossii* official website, 15 February 2008, http://archive.kremlin.ru/text/greets/2008/02/160261.shtml. See also "Pozdravlenie veteranam afganskoi voiny s 20-i godovshchinoi vyvoda Ogranichennogo kontingenta sovetskikh voisk iz Respubliki Afganistan", *Prezident Rossii* official website, 15 Febraury 2009, http://www.kremlin.ru/news/3192.

[115] "Vystuplenie na sobranii".

War",[116] Putin thus rendered the Soviet–Afghan War meaningful not only for the soldiers, but also for the wider Russian population.

Another novelty of the Putin-era discourse in contrast to the 1990s is its acknowledgment of the veterans' suffering during and after the military mission,[117] but now combined with an absence of the critical perspective on the war that was characteristic of the 1990s. Condemnation of the war is no longer a feature of official discourse. Putin qualified the political failure of the invasion in his speech in 2004 by drawing a parallel to the US war in Vietnam, which, as he put it, was similarly driven by the ideological conflicts of the Cold War. In this way, Putin downplayed the Soviet responsibility for the invasion. Moreover, he has reinterpreted the suffering and misery of the veterans as a positive experience. The veterans had mastered their problems because of their fraternity and mutual support. The soldiers had learned these skills during their time in the military, and they transferred them to their civilian lives. In this way, Putin glorified the Soviet–Afghan War as a "school of life" and the *afgantsy* as role models for society. The emphasis on military values and soldierly virtues seemed to play a more important role than debating strategic issues or the suffering and violent experiences of the soldiers. This provides evidence that nowadays history politics is an essential pillar for the government in implementing societal and cultural militarization, and, in this context, an important tool for strengthening the political system in today's Russia.[118]

The commemoration of the Soviet–Afghan War is now being used for the purposes of nation building.[119] In contrast to the state handling of the war in the 1990s, since the 2000s this war has been

---

[116]   For a comprehensive overview of contemporary extensions and alternatives to the just war tradition see Nicholas G. Evans and Adam Henschke (eds), *Routledge Handbook of Ethics and War: Just War Theory in the 21st Century* (New York and London: Routledge, 2013).

[117]   "Vystuplenie na sobranii".

[118]   Wilfried von Bredow has defined militarism as the "dominance of the military as a form of organization of the state and the society and the prevalence of military and warlike categories of thought in the state, society and politics"; Wilfried von Bredow, *Militär und Demokratie in Deutschland. Eine Einführung* (Wiesbaden: VS Verlag für Sozialwissenschaften, 2007), 66.

[119]   Danilova, „Kontinuität und Wandel", 383.

held up as marking an important point of identification for the population. Therefore, the national pertinence of the war and the selfless devotion of the soldiers to their duty and their homeland are highlighted. At the same time, the interests of veterans are also taken into account by the state authorities. Formed in the 1990s, these interests include the demand for recognition and respect for their problems and for attention to be paid to the question of the war's meaning. Thus, the *afgantsy* have now been offered not only a rationale for their combat mission, but also a new level of social re-integration as national heroes and important members of society.

Nevertheless, despite the revised approach towards the Soviet–Afghan War and its consequences, the state commemoration program remains primarily focused on remembrance of the Great Patriotic War, and it is the latter that continues to serve as the main instrument for building social coherence.[120] This same hierarchy of wars can also be seen in the 1995 veterans' law. This law fixes the status of the *afgantsy* as "veterans of combat operations". This provides them with a different set of rights and privileges than the Great Patriotic War veterans, who are designated as "veterans of war".[121]

The 2000s: The Start of a New Cooperation between Veterans' Organizations and the State

One of the consequences of the intensified discussion of the Soviet–Afghan War in the twenty-first century has been a fusion of veterans' organizations with official institutions. This fusion can be discerned in the organizations' shifting interpretations of the war during this period. The narratives employed by the veterans' unions now reflect the official memory politics on the war. The unions' representatives now stress the sacrifice and the importance of the war for the country at commemorative events. Thus, for example, the

---

[120] See also Ludmilla Lutz-Auras, „Auf Stalin, Sieg und Vaterland": Politisierung der kollektiven Erinnerung an den Zweiten Weltkrieg in Russland (Wiesbaden: Springer, 2013).

[121] "Federal'nyi zakon N 5-F3 'O veteranach' ot 12 yanvaria 1995", Rossiiskaia gazeta, 15 January 1995, http://www.rg.ru/1995/01/25/zakon-dok.html. See Danilova, Development of an Exclusive Veterans' Policy, 21.

chairperson of the RSVA, Frants Klintsevich,[122] said in an address to
the State Duma in 2009: "The resulting irreparable damage and casualties in this war were not in vain. Thanks to the ten-year presence
of the Limited Contingent of Soviet Forces the fire of a new world
war was prevented at the borders of our state."[123] Besides the RSVA,
the veterans' association "Battle Fraternity" has also increasingly
used such narratives regarding the war. For its leader, Boris Gromov,
the war was necessary to protect the country against international
terrorism and to prevent drug trafficking: "The Soviet soldier stood
in the land of mountains and desert to fight against the forces of
international terrorism and drug trafficking on the borders of his
country, and that is his great merit."[124] As we saw above, a decade
earlier, in an interview marking the tenth anniversary of the Soviet
withdrawal, he had questioned the meaning of the military operation, but now, on its twentieth anniversary, he expressed a position
identical to the current official perspective on the war. Overall, in
contrast to the 1990s, the organizations have transformed their self-
image as victims of state abuse into one based on the notion of the
heroic and self-sacrificing defense of the country.

The harmonized narrative shared by the veterans' organizations and the state since the 2000s depicts a common view on the
history of the Soviet-Afghan War. This joint picture of the war suggests an increased cooperation between veterans' associations and
the state during Putin's presidency. This has also been reflected in
the RVSA's stance in support of government policy. After the unsuccessful attempts to establish itself as an independent political force

---

[122] Since September 2015 Frants Klintsevich is also a member of the Russian Federation Council and the Deputy Chairperson of the Council's Commitee for Defense and Security. Prior to his current position, he was a "United Russia" deputy in the State Duma, where he served from 1999, including as Deputy Chairperson of the parliamentary group "United Russia" (from 2003), and Deputy
Chairperson of the State Duma Committee for Defense (2011–September 2015).
[123] "Utrennee plenarnoe zasedanie Gosdumy 25 dekabria 2009", *Gosudarstvennaia
duma* official website, 25 December 2009, http://www.duma.gov.ru/news/273/
59025/?sphrase_id=369282.
[124] "Pomnit' vse. Ispolniaetsia 20 let so dnia vyvoda sovetskikh voisk iz Afganistana", *Rossiiskaia gazeta*, 13 February 2009, http://www.rg.ru/2009/02/13/gro
mov.html.

in the parliamentary elections in 1995,[125] the RSVA Party NPP entered Putin's electoral bloc "Unity/Bear" before the elections in 1999. In 2001 the bloc was transformed into the ruling party "United Russia", into which the NPP was duly incorporated. The RSVA also supported "United Russia" in the run-up to the recent parliamentary elections. Before the elections in 2011 the RSVA joined the "All-Russia People's Front",[126] which Putin had founded in May of the same year in order to gain political support.[127] In addition, the RSVA sent its members in particular to the electoral lists of "United Russia".[128] However, the RSVA supported not only the domestic, but also the foreign policy goals of the Russian government. The organization's actions during the current Ukraine crisis since 2014 confirm this thesis. In April 2014 Putin admitted during his annual "Direct Line" conversation with the population that Russian soldiers had received official orders to support, disguised as informal "green men", the separatist movement in Crimea in order to ensure a referendum on independence on 16 March of the same year.[129] However, not only the "green men" but also the veterans' organizations assisted the Crimean separatists. According to the Russian newspaper *Novaia gazeta*, some veterans' organizations travelled to the Crimea in February 2014 in order to observe the Ukrainian military activity at the

---

[125] The bloc "For the Motherland!" did not succeed in winning any seats in the State Duma. See "Rezul'taty vyborov v Dumu II sozyva", *Politika*, 17 December 1995, http://www.politika.su/fs/gd2rezv.html.

[126] "Otdeleniia Soiuza veteranov Afganistana Komi reshili podderzhat' kurs Putina", *Afghanistan.Ru*, 28 November 2007, http://www.afghanistan.ru/doc/10605.html; "OOO KRO RSVA v podderzhku Obshcherossiiskogo narodnogo fronta", *RSVA* official website, 25 May 2011, http://www.rsva.ru/NEWS/50010023/270000729.

[127] J. Hans, „Allrussische Volksfront: Putin gründet eigenen Wahlverein", *Süddeutsche Zeitung Online*, 13 June 2013, http://www.sueddeutsche.de/politik/neue-partei-in-russland-putin-gruendet-seinen-eigenen-wahlverein-1.1695387-2.

[128] About 500 Members of the RSVA were involved with the state authorities of the Russian Federation at different levels and in different positions between 2006 and 2011; "Otchet Predsedatelia CP RSVA A.N. Razumova o rabote Pravleniia Obshcherossiiskoi obshchstvennoi organizatsii Rossiiskii Soiuz veteranov Afganistana za period s fevralia 2006 g. po aprel' 2011 gg", *RSVA* official website, 20 May 2011, http://afgans.rsva.ru/NEWS/50010023/270000708.

[129] "Priamaia linia s Vladimirom Putinom", *Prezident Rossii* official website, 17 April 2014, http://www.kremlin.ru/events/president/news/20796.

Ukrainian–Crimea border and give instructions in propaganda tech-
niques to the local politicians.[130]

The RSVA's support for contemporary Russian domestic and
foreign policy suggests that the organization unlike in the 1990s,
nowadays sees better ways to implement its current objectives. On
the one hand, this applies to financial guarantees for the veterans'
welfare. In the course of the economic recovery since 1999, Putin has
been providing financial support for the veterans' associations.[131] On
the other hand, a further current objective of the organizations comprises the social recognition of veterans.[132] According to the current
charter of the RSVA, one of the organization's core aims is to
strengthen society's moral sense of responsibility towards the veterans to ensure their humane living conditions and consideration of
their interests.[133] In this connection, the new governmental perspective on the war has redounded to the RSVA's advantage. The reconstituted official heroic canon offers the association a useful framework for their self-image. Furthermore, it is now possible for the associations to align themselves with the government's history politics, and simultaneously to harmonize their internal and external
perspectives on the war. Similarly, the newly advocated conserva-
tism and the militarization of society that has characterized Putin's
presidency offer the RSVA a framework toward achieving their goal
of reintegrating the veterans.[134] As the 2012 RSVA charter proclaims,
this reintegration will primarily be accomplished through the use of
the experience and the capacity of the veterans to promote national
spiritual and cultural prosperity in Russia.[135] Currently, as in the
1980s, this is conducted mainly via "youth military-patriotic education". Thus, the organizations can be considered stakeholders of

---

[130]   "Spetsturisty", *Novaia gazeta*, 1 July 2014, http://www.novayagazeta.ru/in-
        quests/64242.html.
[131]   "Putin predlagaet sozdat' pri pravitel'stve sovet po delam veteranov", *RIA
        Novosti*, 19 January 2011, http://ria.ru/society/20110119/323597827.html.
[132]   Author's interview with the RSVA press officer, Moscow, 8 November 2011.
[133]   "2. Missiia Soiuza, 2.3", *Ustav RSVA*, 15–16 December 2012, *RSVA* official website,
        http://www.rsva.ru/content/ustav-rsva.
[134]   See also Achim Spanger, „Unheilige Allianz. Putin und die Werte", *Osteuropa*
        64, no. 1 (2014).
[135]   "2. Missiia Soiuza, 2.5", *Ustav RSVA*.

militarized and national-patriotic values, who try to publicly promote these ideas.

In this context, the main veterans' associations have evolved from genuine veterans' interest groups into an important social pillar for the implementation of state policy since the 2000s. Membership in the RSVA is no longer linked to the status of veteran. Nowadays any adult Russian can join the group.[136] In this context, the membership of the RSVA has swelled to 500,000.[137] Furthermore, counterintuitive as it may seem, on occasion the organizations also support political decisions against the veterans. In 2006, the RSVA deputies in the Duma voted for the *reduction* of state benefits for veterans.[138] Yet at the same time, the alliance should not be considered a mere handmaiden of the state. In fact, an ongoing process of negotiation characterizes the relationship between the state and the organizations. In return for political support, the associations have sought to gain access to financial resources and receive governmental recognition for their service in Afghanistan. In this regard, the objectives of the associations have changed over time. In the 1990s, veterans' welfare was their main concern. In the context of a more favorable economic climate, the RSVA, for example, now considers it more important to call for a political reassessment of the war and specifically, a rethinking of the 1989 Congress of People's Deputies' resolution condemning the war. In 2014 Klintsevich expressed his view that it was wrong to condemn the intervention on political and moral grounds since the war had been about the defense of the Soviet borders.[139] One can also see such attitudes regarding the war on an individual level on the part of the members of the veterans' associations, to which we now turn.

---

[136]   "5. Chleny Soiuza, ikh prava i obiazannosti, 5.1-5.3", ibid.

[137]   "O Soiuze".

[138]   "Spetsturisty".

[139]   "Frants Klintsevich predlagaet Gosdume peresmotret' ofitsial'nuiu negativnuiu otsenku Afganskoi voiny 24 dekabria 1989 goda S"ezd narodnykh deputatov SSSR v svoem postanovl", *RSVA* official website, http://rsva.ru/content/frants-klintsevich-predlagaet-gosdume-peresmotret-ofitsialnuyu-negativnuyu-otsen ku-afganskoi.

Wartime Recollections on the Individual Level in the 2010s

The comparison of two oral history interviews with former officers of the 40th Army gives insights into the shift in the self-perception from victims of state abuse to defenders of the fatherland amongst members of the veterans' organizations. The interviews also shed light on the current basis of social cohesion within the veterans' movement which consists especially of militaristic values.

The interviews with "Igor'" and "Andrei" were conducted in St. Petersburg and Moscow in 2013 and 2015.[140] The interviewees' curricula vitae share structural similarities, both reflecting the form of a typical officer career during this period. Igor' was born in 1951. After finishing school at the age of 17 he decided to follow the family tradition and enrolled in the military academy in 1968. During his military service he was stationed in Central Asia before serving as a commander of an artillery battalion in Afghanistan from 1984 until 1986. Afterwards he was sent to the GDR, inter alia. In 2003, his service came to an end when he reached retirement age. Andrei was born in 1960 and also began his military career at the age of 17, likewise following his family tradition. From 1981 until 1986 he was stationed in the GDR. Subsequently, he commanded a motorized infantry unit in Afghanistan from 1986 until 1988. After several deployments at different locations within the USSR he was retired in 2012. Finally, another parallel in their military career is that during their time in Afghanistan, both officers participated in armed combat against the Mujahidin.

These structural similarities notwithstanding, their lives differ in one pivotal point concerning this analysis. After his retirement, Igor' studied marketing. At the time of the interview, he was working for a telecommunications company. In contrast, Andrei went on to join a small veterans' union in Moscow and is now working in a leading position within this organization.

Neither of the interviewees spoke about the physical and psychological intensity of their combat missions as the veterans did in

---

140   Both names have been changed for data protection reasons.

the late 1980s.[141] Instead, they stressed the sense they had of having fulfilled their duty. However, they differed significantly in the connotations with which they combine this emphasis on the importance of performing one's duty. In this context, there is a striking similarity between the narratives employed by Andrei and those used by representatives of the state and the veterans' associations more broadly.

Why We Were Sent to Afghanistan

The apparent influence of the state and veterans' associations' narratives can be demonstrated through an examination of Andrei's views on the reasons why the USSR sent troops to Afghanistan. In this connection, Andrei pointed out:

> It was right that we were in Afghanistan. However, it was wrong that we left. When we finished the war in Afghanistan, there were only three factories for the production of [illegal] drugs [there]. Furthermore, they were supervised. Now, there are approximately 1,500 officially known factories to be found again. These drugs are crossing our southern borders, coming to Russia through Tajikistan, Uzbekistan and Turkmenistan. In Russia, nowadays, more than 40,000 young Russians die [each year] from drug abuse. Essentially this is a weapon. And this is war against Russia, a war with different instruments.

Andrei describes the mission in Afghanistan as a necessary one, in order to prevent drug trafficking. To endow his service with meaning, Andrei uses similar narrative patterns as the representatives of the state and veterans' associations, based on the notion of protecting the country against external threats.[142] In this way, Andrei transforms the extra-territorial *internationalist duty* into a national issue. He outlines a national threat scenario, which existed not only in the past but also in the present, and which Russia must

---

[141]   See Jan C. Behrends, "'Some Call Us Heroes, Others Call Us Killers.' Experiencing a Sphere of Violence: Soviet Soldiers in the Afghan War (1979-1989)", *Nationalities Papers* 43, no. 4 (2015): 719–34.

[142]   See Margarete Klein, "Russia's New Military Doctrine. NATO, the United States and the 'Colour Revolutions'", *SWP Comments* 9 (February 2015), http://www.swp-berlin.org/fileadmin/contents/products/comments/2015C09_kle.pdf.

withstand by any means necessary. Thus, Andrei links the meaning of the intervention with patriotic and militaristic patterns of thought.

Igor's statements contrast sharply on this point. He describes the mission not as a safeguard mission, but as an "adventure" into which the government had cynically and foolishly sent the soldiers:

> Things started to get interesting when the government realized that Afghanistan was a boiling cauldron. Therefore, the Soviet government sent secret agents there. [...] The Secret Service is a separate caste. It can make correct and false estimations. This depends on the person receiving the data. This person was Leonid I. Brezhnev. He was old, well, certainly there was something wrong with his brain. Who knows, it's hard to say, I'm not a specialist, not a doctor. I just know that it was possible to draw Brezhnev into this adventure. The last straw that broke the camel's back was the murder of Taraki... Taraki was friends with Brezhnev.

This statement reflects the governmental perspectives from the 1990s in the form of political condemnation on the one hand and an emphasis on the fulfillment of the soldiers' duties on the other. According to this narrative, the war against the Mujahidin was based on misconceptions on the part of the political class. The Soviet leadership could have known that an intervention in Afghanistan would be pointless. For Igor', the war was not the soldiers' fault, since they only fulfilled their military duty in this "political adventure". Thus, Igor' does not connect the mission with military necessity. His remarks rather contain critical viewpoints on the decision to send troops into Afghanistan.

The comparison of these narratives suggests that not all veterans have accepted the attribution of meaning handed down by the representatives of the state and the veterans' associations. Andrei, as a leading member of a veterans' association, has turned more towards these narrative patterns than Igor', who is not part of the veterans' movement. Thus, Andrei participates in the newer communicative constructions of the past, and, by doing this, contributes to their consolidation within the group. This indicates that within the veterans' movement it is the heroic perspective rather than the victim's perspective on the war that shapes the self-image of the organized veterans nowadays. Thus, the glorification of the military can be seen as a constitutive element of the veterans' groups' solidarity.

Militarism as Instrument of In- and Exclusion

The different remarks of the two former officers concerning the meaning of the Soviet–Afghan War also support the assumption that militarized patterns of thought constitute the social cohesion of the veterans' groups. Thus, for example, Andrei identified "fraternity" as an empirical value linked to Afghanistan. To him, this implies the cohesion and mutual support which have influenced his path in life. It was due to these factors that he joined one of the veterans' organizations after his time in the army:

> First, we were interested in communicating with each other, to meet and remember. Second, yeah, maybe the organization could assist their comrades to solve problems. In addition, the organization is always linked to the state structure. The organization can represent interests better than one or two single persons. The Union can develop a solution or a proposal or talk to the authorities and they are obliged to respond to it.

It was in order to sustain this sense of fraternity that Andrei joined the veterans' organization. For him, the associations represent mutual appreciation and support in an institutionalized form. Indications of the process of unification of the veterans' movement from the late 1990s can be observed in this context. Consider, for example, Andrei's comment that:

> [w]e also know that there were veterans of the Afghan War who were in Afghanistan but who spent their entire service at the headquarters in Kabul. They never even fired a single shot, but they did fly in planes, they could have been shot down (planes were sometimes shot down)... That is to say, they were under pressure, too, like the other veterans. But nobody draws a distinction between the different categories of veterans. Sometimes it even works in the opposite direction—the closer they were to headquarters, to the leadership, the more medals they got, more than the soldiers who were sitting in the trenches. But every soldier ought to have been decorated.

In his remarks, Andrei downplays the importance of rank and the differing experiences of veterans, which were previously obstacles to the unification of the veterans' movement, especially in the 1980s. In his opinion, the veterans are all brothers in arms and deserve the same recognition. The different types of veterans are not rivals competing for benefits and state support. For him, the *afgantsy* are a self-contained group within which everybody should be treated the same way. This indicates that militaristic patterns of thought currently play an important role amongst the veterans' movement in terms of providing a basis for social cohesion within the movement.

In this context, the associations' claim for recognition by the state plays an important role also on the individual level. As Andrei put it,

> There are different benefits for the veterans of the Great Patriotic War and the participants of military actions in other hot spots. I.e. there is a category "combat veterans" and "veterans of World War II". Nonetheless, we also have been under fire. Maybe Afghanistan was not such a serious war with such a mass of people, nevertheless for a single person—what's the difference? ... There were other roles in the [Red] Army—[people were classified as] participants of the war, but they never even once picked up a weapon and never fired a single shot, throughout the entire period of World War II. And they're considered participants of the war. And we're considered participants of combat actions. It isn't right.

Due to his self-perception as a defender of the homeland, Andrei felt unfairly treated by the state. In his opinion, his accomplishments were comparable to those of the veterans of the Great Patriotic War, and therefore he wanted the same rights, privileges, and recognition by the state. In this context, his argument resembles that of Klintsevich in the latter's push for ending the condemnation of the war. Despite the fact that the state and the veterans' associations collaborate closely in many social and political fields, both of these statements expose what continues to be a large distance between the veterans and the state regarding the claim for recognition.

This attitude can also be found beyond the veterans' movement. Igor's statements concerning the welfare illustrate this:

Society treats the veterans according to their level of social and economic development. Today, the state pays me 1,000 roubles per month for having fought in Afghanistan. What's 1,000 roubles? Converted into euros it's [...] 25?![143] Super! What a great donation! [laughs]

Concerning state welfare, Igor' also reveals a critical attitude:

The state does not remember the war. It doesn't even need the war. [...]. The question is different. Does the next generation need a patriotic education? [...]. If the state has such experience in the form of veterans, it will use them [the veterans] for educational programs.

Igor' is clearly not satisfied, then, with the state's engagement with the history and memory of the war and its veterans. State officials could not ensure adequate welfare, and nor were they interested in remembrance, he claims. In Igor's opinion, the veterans should have been shown more respect and appreciation. For him, then, the state only deals with the war in order to implement its own interests in the form of military-patriotic education. Instead of viewing this as an offer for recognition and social integration, Igor' regards this program as a violation on behalf of the state. On this point, he opposes the associations. His attitude towards military-patriotic education indicates that he is less open to militarized patterns of thought. This can also be deduced from the fact that he did not join a veterans' organization after ending his military career. Unlike Andrei he does not rely on the group. First, Igor' does not agree with either the approach or the perspective of the veterans' associations on the war; in fact, he goes so far as to say that: "The website of the RSVA is one of these sites which does not tell the truth about the war." Second, in his opinion, the associations were not capable of helping to solve the existing problems: "Tasks and problems can be solved more easily if there is a small collective. A large veterans' organization doesn't solve anything." It was more important for Igor' to stand on his own feet and take care of himself, which is why he decided to study after his retirement.

These examples suggest that the prevailing militaristic patterns of thought can be regarded not only as a mechanism of social

---

143   Based on the exchange rate prevailing at the beginning of 2013.

coherence and inclusion within the veterans' movement, but also as a barrier against joining these organizations. Thus, the organized veterans nowadays consider the organizations primarily as a community of common memories and experience,[144] and not only a partnership aimed at achieving practical ends linked to the receipt of sustenance, as was the case in the past, particularly in the 1990s.

Conclusion

The history of the relationship between the state institutions and the veterans' organizations can be seen as an example of how a social group furthered its interests, and subsequently acted as an "entitlement group" cooperating with state institutions in order to reach its goals after the collapse of the Soviet Union. In this context, the *afgantsy* had a great deal in common with the participants of the Great Patriotic War. Like their predecessors, the *afgantsy* demanded recognition of their efforts in the form of improved welfare, and felt neglected by the state due to lack of official support. However, the two "entitlement groups" differ in that the Afghan veterans additionally had to deal with a critical governmental (and social) attitude towards the war in the 1990s.[145] This attitude catalyzed the unification of the different local veterans' groups into larger nationwide associations at the end of the 1980s. In this connection, the different political opportunities for founding wider organizations at the end of the war can be seen as a further difference between the *afgantsy* and the veterans of the Great Patriotic War. Thus, as institutionalized groups they each developed different strategies vis-à-vis the state policy in order to improve the living conditions of the veterans and to foster and shape remembrance of the war.

In the 1990s the veterans' unions acted mostly in opposition to state institutions. This can be exemplified by the memory narratives shared and promoted by the group during this period. The or-

---

[144] See Birgit Schwelling, *Heimkehr – Erinnerung – Integration. Der Verband der Heimkehrer, die ehemaligen Kriegsgefangenen und die westdeutsche Nachkriegsgesellschaft* (Paderborn: Schöningh, 2010).
[145] See Petrone, "Coming Home Soviet Style", 353.

ganizations rejected the government's public attribution of the veterans as heroes and instead presented themselves as victims of state abuse, who had been sent to war and later forsaken. In order to achieve improved welfare, the associations tried to remind the politicians that the latter had a moral responsibility for the veterans. However, since the 2000s a convergence between the state institutions and the veterans' associations can be observed. Within the framework of the cultural and social militarization during Putin's presidency, the Soviet–Afghan War increasingly became a focus of government-sponsored memories, and the soldiers' heroism and national defense became the main objects of remembrance. In this way, the state took the organizations' demand for recognition of their services in Afghanistan into account. On this basis, the associations and governmental actors have been forming an alliance. First, the veterans' organizations support the foreign and domestic policy goals of the state. In this they are surely motivated at least in part by the desire to receive financial support from the state as a reward for their loyalty. Second, they share the same narratives regarding the war. In this way, the organizations seek to generate social recognition. The primary objective in the 1990s was to improve living conditions; this has now given way to the aim of achieving enhanced social prestige. Therefore, the veterans no longer depict themselves as victims; instead, they draw a heroic and militarized picture of themselves and the war. Through a combination of a new politics of history around the Soviet–Afghan War and improved levels of veterans' welfare, political actors managed to swing the veterans' organizations from political opposition over to the government camp.

In addition, over the course of the transformation of the veterans' self-image from victims of state abuse to defenders of the homeland, we can observe not only a closer political cooperation with governmental institutions but also a stronger social coherence within the veterans' groups themselves. The organizations have developed from a genuine community of entitlement into a community of values, based on militarized patterns of thought. This is indicated in the analysis of the oral interviews with the two former officers. The officer who is a member of a veterans' association is much more open-minded to the heroic interpretation offered by the state and the associations than the other. This indicates that the members of the associations are more open to the current official political stance, and, in this way, support the change towards a much closer relationship between state power and their organizations. Furthermore, the other veteran largely denies military values like camaraderie and fraternity. For him personally, it was more important to take care of himself. In addition, he rejects the heroic perspective on the war. Thus, the veterans' organizations nowadays can be seen as both a medium for and a pillar of the militaristic and patriotic political ideology and tendencies in Russia.

Furthermore, in recent times, militaristic and patriotic political ideology has led to cooperation between the veterans' organizations and patriotic social groups such as the abovementioned "Night Wolves". The latter participated, for example, in the veterans' commemorations of the withdrawal from Afghanistan on 15 February 2015 and laid flowers at the Afghanistan Monument at Poklonnaia gora in Moscow[146]—a development which may mark the beginning of a new convergence of these patriotic groups beyond the "Anti-Maidan" movement.

---

[146]   "V Moskve otmetili Den' voina-internatsionalista", *RSVA* official website, February 2015, http://www.rsva.ru/content/v-moskve-otmetili-den-voina-internatsionalista.

Veterans of the Soviet–Afghan War and the Ukrainian Nation-Building Project: from Perestroika to the Maidan and the War in the Donbas[1]

Iryna Sklokina

Abstract: The aim of this article is to consider the process of transformation of the organized Afghan veterans' movement in independent Ukraine and the emergence of its new national historical narrative, with special focus on the Maidan (or "Eurorevolution") of 2013–
2014 and the subsequent war in the Donbas. The case of the Ukrainian
veterans of the Soviet–Afghan War is an interesting example of how a
group with a common experience of Soviet army service and a specific
memorial culture rooted in ideas of "military brotherhood" and "masculine values of courage and dignity", as well as in Soviet nostalgia
and paternalism, can be transformed into an actor of civil society. In
independent Ukraine, the Afghanistan veterans presented their experiences in both national and post-Soviet nostalgic discourses. The
Maidan and war in Donbas seem to have put an end to the supra-na-
tional community of the Afghanistan veterans in post-Soviet space as
the veterans in Russia and Ukraine have joined opposite sides of the
conflict. In the current situation of war, Ukrainian veterans' organizations and public opinion are working together for the creation of a
narrative of a continuous, centuries-long national struggle for freedom and independence. Afghan veterans have occupied the position
of the descendants of the "Great Patriotic War" victors, and of the "fathers" of the new veterans of the ATO in the Donbas—not only

---

[1]   This article is a result of participation in the project "Region, Nation, and Beyond: An Interdisciplinary and Transcultural Reconceptualization of Ukraine"
coordinated by the University of St. Gallen (Switzerland), and the seminar
"Back from Afghanistan", 12–13 February 2015, Center for German Studies, European Humanities University, Vilnius.

through their promotion of this sort of discourse in the media, but also because of their active participation in the current war. The future development of the afhantsi *community and identity and of the newly emerging group of veterans will be an important case for studying many aspects of contemporary developments, such as the transformation of civil society, the social welfare system, public discourses on history and memory, and generational changes.*

Introduction

Nearly 150,000 people from Soviet Ukraine took part in the Soviet military operation in Afghanistan in 1979–89, and 3,360 of them died or were taken into captivity. In 2004 there were 135,648 former participants in the Afghan war in Ukraine.[2] The first registered veterans' organizations emerged during perestroika in 1986–87; in 1990 there were 1,003 Afghanistan veterans' councils in Ukraine, and there are currently more than 1,500.[3] The emergence of the *afhantsi* (as the Afghan war veterans came to be known) as a specific social group and symbolic community, with the largest and most established Ukrainian Union of the Veterans of Afghanistan (the UUVA, founded in June 1990) has been acknowledged by the Ukrainian state—on the symbolic level, by the participation of officials in the memorialization of the war, and on the social level—by establishing social benefits and the use of the judicial category of "veterans–participants of military conflicts on the territory of other states". In spite of the predominantly negative attitude to the Soviet intervention in Afghanistan in Ukrainian society after 1991, in the course of the past twenty-four years, the organized movement of *afhantsi*, with all its dynamism and regional diversity, has succeeded in adapt-

---

2   "Ukrainska spilka veteraniv Afganistanu (voiniv-internatsionalistiv)", *UUVA* website,   http://www.usva.org.ua/mambo3/index.php?option=com_content&task=blogcategory&id=14&Itemid=62. All websites cited in this article were last accessed on 17 July 2015.
3   Serhii Chervonopys'kyi, *Organizovanyi "afhanskyi ruh" v Ukraini: stanovlennia ta rozvytok: zbirnyk statei* (Kyiv: Medinform, 2007), 8.

ing to the new situation, creating a new positive image for the Afghan war veterans, and making significant strides in achieving their social reintegration.

The aim of this article is to consider the process of transformation of the organized Afghan veterans' movement in independent Ukraine and the emergence of its new national historical narrative, with special focus on the Maidan (or "Eurorevolution") of 2013–2014 and the subsequent war in the Donbas. I will try to embrace both the discursive and non-discursive dimensions of this transformation. The discursive dimension here includes public discussion of the Soviet–Afghan War and its ramifications for the newly independent Ukrainian state, for the image and self-image of Afghanistan veterans, and for the changing vision of their place in both the national Ukrainian community and the transnational community of veterans; the non-discursive dimension to be examined here concerns the position of the veterans in political and social life. My analysis draws on a range of sources including the relevant legislation; memoirs and historical literature, especially that produced by the communities of veterans in different regions; press materials; and interviews with activist veterans. I will start by describing the process whereby the Soviet–Afghan War experience has been incorporated into the newly emergent narrative of national (and still post-Soviet) history in Ukraine. Next, I present the position of the veterans vis-à-vis other groups, in Ukrainian society and beyond, as a base for their activity in the third sector; this is followed by an account of the veterans' participation in the Maidan and the war in the Donbas. In my concluding remarks I reflect on the changes that the veterans' movement has undergone, especially during the Euromaidan in 2013–2014 and the subsequent war in the Donbas.

"My left boot is an occupier, and my right one—a liberator": Ambiguous Reflections on the Afghan War Experience in Ukrainian Society

The definitive breakdown of the dominant ideology of "friendship of the nations" and "Soviet internationalist help to fraternal socialist countries" in 1991 made the meaning and relevance of the Soviet mission in Afghanistan extremely vague and doubtful. Almost every popular history book or collection of memoirs published on this topic since then starts by raising problematic questions: "What did we fight for?"; "What was the Motherland we fought for?"; "Why do we need the Afghanistan remembrance now, when we live under a new peaceful state?"[4] Incorporating and assimilating this experience into coherent life histories was especially difficult for the veterans given that the state that had conducted the war and justified it as "fraternal help" and "internationalist duty," the Soviet Union, had ceased to exist.

In the period of perestroika and the early 1990s the dominant opinion on the recent war was strongly negative, and it was broadly condemned as one of the crimes of the Soviet regime. In spite of the fact that the USSR adopted laws that were quite beneficial for the veterans, benefits that were largely later taken over officially by the Ukrainian government in 1994,[5] public opinion took a rather dubious view on the status of "participant of combat actions on the territory of other states", as *afhantsi* were officially designated. In many cases, Afghan war veterans could be and were called "occupants", "aggressors", and even "killers" in polemical texts published on this issue in the 1990s.[6]

---

4   See, for example: Aleksandr Skorobagatyi and Valeriy Kuz'menko, *Afganskii sindrom 20 let spustia* (Dnepropetrovsk: IMA-Press, 2009), 7; Viktor Zaika, *Voina bez pobedy: Kniga o voinakh-internatsionalistakh Donetskoi oblasti, prinimavshykh uchastie v boevykh deistviiakh v Afganistane* (Donetsk: Multipress, 1998), 4; Viktor Bereka, *Povernys' zhyvym dodomu, synu. Naukovo-populiarne vydannia* (Kamianets-Podilsky: PP Moshak M.I., 2006).
5   See Ukraine's veteran laws, available at the website of the Ukrainian Union of the Veterans of Afghanistan (UUVA, in Ukr. УСВА): http://usva.org.ua/.
6   This was in fact mostly characteristic of the perestroika period, but *afhantsi* remember this well, and often mentioned these offensive terms in works published years later: see for example, R. Skrypal and G. Rytchenko, "Kontingent",

The problematic nature of the image of the Afghan veterans and their historical mission was captured well by one of the editors of a collection of memoirs about Afghanistan:

> "My left boot is an occupier, and my right one—a liberator." I wanted to use this phrase for the title of the book, but the afhantsi got obstinate about this. They don't want to hear the word "occupier", because they still consider themselves to be at least heroic internationalist soldiers, if not the real liberators of a brotherly people. Their intention in that country was not enslavement but providing help, and that deserves respect.[7]

This phrase is a reflection of the problematic attitude towards the Soviet heritage in independent Ukraine—on the one hand, there is a rejection of its imperialist and militarist aspects, but on the other, there is a wish to preserve the version of the Soviet–Afghan War as a heroic war.

Some veterans have held onto the traditional Soviet account of the Soviet–Afghan War, where the Soviet soldiers are presented as heroes and defenders.[8] Almost all the memorial books and collections of memoirs argue that the Soviet soldiers in Afghanistan were only fulfilling their duty to defend their country's southern borders, and that they discharged this duty honorably.[9] Many authors refer

---

Internatsionalist (Kharkiv), 2 (2005): 20; N. Razhik, "My shli na voinu yunymi, ne znaiushchimi zhizni...", in *Territoriia chesti*, ed. Svetlana Zadvornaia (Kyiv: Azimut-Ukraina, 2009), 143–47; Ivan Kushnirenko and Volodymyr Zhylinskyi, *Huliaipiltsi—voiny-internatsionalisty* (Zaporizhzhia: Dniprovskyi metalurg, 2014): 109; *Kolybel Chirchikskogo spetsnaza: istoriia i boevoi put' 15-i otdel'noi brigady spetsial'nogo naznacheniia GRU* (Dnepropetrovsk: IMA Press, 2007), 13. One author wrote bitterly, "We are errors and victims"; Anatolii Shamov, *Pritsel sud'by. Poeziia* (Cherkasy: Orfei, 2004), 29.

7   Serhii Bortnikov, preface to: Serhii Bortnikov and Hryhorii Pavlovych (eds), *Afhanistan: Volyns'kyi rakhunok* (Lutsk: Tverdynia, 2008), 7. All translations are mine.

8   For some typical examples, see: *Oni s chest'iu vypolnili prikaz Rodiny. Voinam-internatsyonalistam Stanichno-Luganskogo raiona posviashchaetsia. Ocherki, stat''i, rasskazy* (Lugansk: Press-Ekspress, 2014); Yurii Onipko and Oleh Krivolapov (eds), *Opalennoe nebo Afganistana* (Dnepropetrovsk: IMA Press, 2009).

9   See esp. Volodymyr Lohvynenko, Anatolii Blyzniuk, preface to: Anatolii Kostyria (ed.), *"Afgantsy" Donetchiny. Istoriko-memorial'noe izdanie* (Donetsk: Promin, 2009), 10; Boris Tkach, "Neznamenitaia voina", in ibid. 19-20; Skorobagatyi and Kuz'menko, *Afganskii sindrom, 17*; Kushnirenko and Zhylinskyi, *Huli-*

to the "Afghanistan generation"—the last generation socialized before the advent of capitalism with its anti-human values. This generation is presented as comprising "pure souls", sincere and genuine,
patriots willing to sacrifice their lives for others, the heirs of their
grandfathers who had fought and defeated Nazism.[10] An important
part of this quasi-Soviet discourse is an Orientalist vision of the population of Afghanistan that serves to strengthen a "Soviet identity"
shared by the soldiers (as the ethnic, cultural, and religious differences between them pale in comparison with the "Asian world": "the
non-Russian world, incomprehensible for the logic of Slavs".[11] "No
one could help them except us"—this is another popular justification for the USSR's intervention into the neighboring country. Very
often, the books published by the veterans' unions highlight the
constructive labor performed by the Soviet military contingent,
while tending to depict the local population as primitive, militant,
and unable to solve their economic and social problems. In addition,
this discourse blames the USA for its support of the Afghan guerrilla
opposition and inability to stop international terrorism and drug
business in the world. As the author of one such book put it, "We
were the first to stand in the way of the emerging international terrorism, Islamic extremism, and narcotic terrorism".[12] The difference
between the Soviet soldiers who died in the name of the state and
the recent international forces in Afghanistan made up of mercenaries is important here as well.[13]

  This kind of discourse continues to work as a unifying factor
for the supra-community of veterans from across post-Soviet space.

---

aipiltsi, 3–4; Oleg Krivolapov, "Dush zolotye rossypi," in Opalennoe nebo Afganistana, eds. Onipko and Krivolapov, 13–36; Boris Gromov, preface to: Ivan
Shkvarko (ed.), Bil pamiati. Knyha pamiati pro voiniv Kharkivshchyny, zahyblykh v Afganisrani (Kharkiv: Oryhinal, 1995), 3–4; Sergei Ursov, Vremia vybralo
nas. Liudi, sobytiia, podvigi (Kiev: Varta, 2005).

10   Onipko and Krivolapov, Opalennoe nebo, 6–12; Zaika, Voina bez pobedy, 6.
11   Vladimir Maimeskul, untitled, in Kostyria (ed.), "Afgantsy" Donetchiny, 198. For
     the positive evaluation of the Soviet policy in Afghanistan ("the great mission")
     see esp. in: Velikaia missiia: fakty, dokazatel'stva, svidetel'stva (Nakolaev:
     Shamrai P.N., 2011).
12   Ibid., 10.
13   Yevgenii Podsolenov, "Posle utverzhdeniia—nachali rabotat'...", in: Zadvornaia
     (ed.), Territoriia chesti, 84.

One of the instruments of maintaining the ties between *afhantsi* in different countries is the Committee for Internationalist Soldiers, which is an organ of the Council of the Heads of the Governments of the Member States of the CIS.[14] This organ has worked as an additional tool for lobbying for social benefits for veterans in different countries and has also organized various international programs.[15] Every year delegations made up of the representatives of this Committee along with other veterans and the members of their families hold rallies where the "friendship" and solidarity between the organizations in different countries is symbolically manifested.[16]

The nostalgic quasi-Soviet discourse works in support of "passing on the baton of heroism and patriotism from one generation to another".[17] Many *afhantsi* in Ukraine were and still are involved in the activities of military and patriotic clubs and paratroopers' circles (administered by the former officers of the famous

---

[14]   The Commonwealth of Independent States (CIS) was founded in 1991 as an organization of former Soviet republics. It was then declared that the independent states' policy in various spheres was to be coordinated, and the Council for Internationalist Soldiers subsequently emerged with the Hero of the Soviet Union Ruslan Aushev as its head.

[15]   The Committee has organized international cooperation in social and medical support of the veterans, sanatorium therapy, searching for missing POWs, and organizing conferences on related issues. Another important part of the Committee's activity is connected to commemoration and symbolic recognition of the veterans. It is worth noting that Ukraine participates in the Committee's initiatives but has given it no financial support.

[16]   See "Protokol pro utvorennia komitetu...", *Supreme Council of Ukraine* official web-portal, 13 March 1992, http://zakon4.rada.gov.ua/laws/show/997_644. Interestingly, after the Orange Revolution of 2004–2005, while the Russian official state propaganda, as well as the rhetoric of the Party of Regions, made more extensive use of the myths about the domination of "nationalism" and "banderovshchina" in Western Ukraine, the Ukrainian *afhantsi* tried to preserve friendly relations with their colleagues from other post-Soviet states and to contest these myths. In May 2013, when a meeting of the Coordinating Council was organized by the UUVA, they decided to invite their colleagues to no other city than Lviv—the main city of Halychyna and the self-defined capital of Ukrainian nationalism—in order to shatter the propaganda myths. See the news report on this event: "Ruslan Aushev, Iosif Kobzon ta voiny-internatsionalisty u Lvovi", *Viiskovi novyny Zakhidnoi Ukrainy* channel, 23 May 2013, https://www.youtu be.com/watch?v=LSzB6JXniUc.

[17]   Volodymyr Lohvynenko, Anatolii Blyzniuk, preface to: Kostyria (ed.), *"Afgantsy" Donetchiny*, 10.

"VDV"[18]), which have very close relations with similar organizations across the whole post-Soviet space. In some cases these organizations have produced cadres for radical rightist pro-Russian organizations.[19]

In general, the comparison with the situation in neighboring Russia seems to be a source of frustration for the Ukrainian veterans. Many of them visit Russia on anniversary occasions and maintain personal contacts with other *afhantsi* there. The more solid social support enjoyed by veterans under the Russian state, the much higher pensions for army retirees, and especially the extensive use of patriotic and military rhetoric in public rituals and speeches by officials, together with the stronger ties existing between secondary schools and veterans in Russia—all these things impress the Ukrainian guests greatly. Some veteran activists have even argued that in Ukraine the veterans' movement has fallen into decay, while in Russia "the Afghanistan organization stands firm, and in general patriotism is very popular".[20] In addition, Ukrainian veterans' campaigns

---

[18]   VDV stands for *vozdushno-desantnye voiska*—paratroopers units—the most prestigious and heavily glorified part of the Soviet army. The VDV veterans have perhaps the strongest collective identity of all the different groups of army returnees.

[19]   For example, in Kharkiv the members of the paratrooper club *"margelovtsy"* under the leadership of former *afhantsi* take part in quasi-Soviet rituals at the Memorial to Internationalist Soldiers, where new members swear an oath of fealty to the "brotherly peoples of Ukraine, Russia, and Belarus", and pledge to uphold the glorious traditions of the Soviet army. In this case, we can see the obvious transformation of Soviet ideology into the ideology of the "Russian world" (*russkii mir*) that excludes the "non-Slavic" peoples of the former USSR. The participation of a priest of the Orthodox Church of the Moscow Patriarchate is typical for these rituals. See: Sergei Moiseev, "Delo dlia nastoiashchih muzhchin", *Russkaia Narodnaia Liniia*, 3 March 2011, http://ruskline.ru/analitika/2011/03/04/delo_dlya_nastoyawih_muzhchin/; Kirill Frolov, "Margelovtsy i drozdovtsy ne pustiat v Khar'kov banderovtsev", *Votserkovlenie politiki. Zhurnal Kirilla Frolova. LiveJournal*, 7 May 2011, http://kirillfrolov.livejournal.com/1286875.html. Such clubs of *margelovtsy* exist throughout post-Soviet space but can have ideological differences. Vasilii Margelov (1909–90) was a Soviet army general, commander of the paratroopers, and Hero of the Soviet Union. His grandson Mikhail Margelov is a famous political figure and oligarch in the Russian Federation and is currently the deputy head of the Russian Council for International Affairs.

[20]   Sergei Ivanov, untitled, in: Zadvornaia (ed.), *Territoriia chesti*, 176.

claiming additional social benefits (for example, pensions for parents of fallen soldiers and exemption from paying for utilities) are rooted in such a comparison with Russia and Belarus.[21]

At the same time, the veterans of Afghanistan try to express their experience in national, Ukrainian frameworks as well. This is expressed in the emphasis placed on the suffering of the soldiers, the senselessness of the imperialist campaign in a foreign country, and the differentiation of the Ukrainian group of soldiers from the others. In some cases the explanatory narrative explicitly reveals the reason for the deaths and suffering of the soldiers in Afghanistan, namely: the absence of an independent Ukrainian state and the imperialist policy of the USSR.[22] Memoirs of this kind include references to the importance of meeting fellow-countrymen while in the army, and sometimes the religious and language differences among the soldiers are also highlighted.[23] The Soviet justifications for the intervention are sarcastically rejected, and many aspects of the campaign are criticized, among them the disdainful attitude to the local population, profiteering in the army economic structures, the technical backwardness of the Soviet army, alcohol abuse, black-marketeering, the moral degradation of the command, and violence against younger conscripts (*didovshchyna*).[24]

---

[21] Galina Kazakova, "Moi syn sluzhyl v Gazni...", in Ibid., 160. Many of the benefits were cancelled in Belarus in 2008, and in some parts of Russia some types of benefits were canceled in the 2000s, but in general the financing of the veterans' social support is better in Russia than in Ukraine. See "Belorusskie afgantsy trebuiut vernut' l'goty", *Khartyia 97*, 9 September 2009, http://charter97.org/ru/news/2013/9/9/75375/; "Vernite l'goty afgantsam", *Listok*, 19 March 2014, http://www.listock.ru/35355.

[22] As the inscription on the monument in Dubno (Volyn region) states metaphorically: "If only you [Motherland] had freedom, you would give us a better lot" ("Iakby ty mala voliu, dala b nam krashchu doliu").

[23] Nykyfor Lysytsia, *Nad khrebtamy Hindukusha* (Vinnytsia: Knyga-Vega, 2004); Roman Kindratyshyn, *Karpaty – Hindukush. Shchodennyk, povist', opovidannia, novely, poeziia, narysy, spohady, esei, foto* (Lviv: Kameniar, 2009).

[24] Anatolii Honchar (ed.), *Aviatory. Knyha pam'iati pro zahyblykh v Afganistani viiskovykh aviatoriv* (Vinnytsia: Knyha-Vega, 2004); Kindratyshyn, *Karpaty – Hindukush*. The critique of these aspects is present in the non-national narratives as well: Leonid Moskalenko and Viktor Kucher, *Chest' imeiu* (Lugansk: Luganskaia oblastnaia tipografiia, 2007); Zaika, *Voina bez pobedy*.

However, this nationalizing framework for remembering the Soviet–Afghan War is not aimed at the radical rejection of the Soviet military experience as such. Some authors note that the military skills and the ability to survive in extreme circumstances, developed by Ukrainians in Afghanistan, became important for the participation of the independent Ukrainian state in peacemaking missions for the UN, OSCE and other international forces, as well for the development of the independent state's armed forces.[25] The life histories of many *afhantsi* are traced through the period of independence, thus demonstrating the importance of the Afghanistan experience for future careers, and highlighting their choice in favor of the army of independent Ukraine (many officers and military experts had the option of choosing to continue their service in Russia or other countries after 1991). The very notion of "internationalist duty" is criticized, but not rejected completely. In some memoirs and works of non-fiction the war in Afghanistan, and especially the courage, heroism, and self-sacrifice of the "rank-and-file" soldiers is inserted into a broader narrative about the heroic military efforts of the Ukrainian people, alongside the Kyiv Rus' period, the Cossack wars, the Second World War, and international missions in the 1990s–2000s.[26] In many narratives, the peaceful Ukrainian village (as the "cradle of the nation") is contrasted with the imperialist mission in the foreign and exotic country, but its rank-and-file participants are presented as real heroes and worthy sons of the nation.[27]

One of the characteristic narrative passages in the discourse of the *afhantsi* is contraposition of the higher state leaders and generals, on the one hand, and rank-and-file soldiers, on the other.[28] As the inscription on one monument in the city of Khmel'nyts'kyi reads, "The rulers make mistakes, and it is the people who suffer". In some cases, the discussion of the problem includes blaming the

25   Lysytsia, *Nad khrebtamy Hindukusha*, 3.
26   See, for example: Honchar, *Aviatory*.
27   See, for example: O. Harkusha *et al* (eds), *Afgan, propysanyi u sertsi* (Mykolaiv: Mykolaivska oblasna drukarnia, 2004); Bereka, *Povernys' zhyvym dodomu*; Kindratyshyn, *Karpaty – Hindukush*.
28   Skorobagatyi and Kuz'menko, *Afganskii sindrom*, 7; Ivan Bezena and Petro Koretskyi, *Afganistan zvuchyt v moii dushi: knyha spohadiv i materialiv* (Kryvyi Rih: Sofiivka, 2008), 3; Boris Gromov, preface to: Shkvarko (ed.), *Bil' pam"iati*, 3–4.

Soviet *nomenklatura,* since their children were able to avoid mobilization to the army through personal connections (*blat*) and bribes; by contrast, those who served in the army are portrayed as "ordinary guys", "simple and naive" (an obvious reference to the myth of democratic military comradeship so typical for wars in the modern epoch[29]). This strategy leads to the vindication of the mission of the Soviet soldiers in Afghanistan—the vindication not of its political meaning, but of the personal meaning which it holds for its participants. The positive myth of the veteran is related to the notions of "courage", "dignity", "real masculine merits", and especially—"frontline camaraderie". These concepts made possible the active presence of the veterans of this "shameful war" in the public sphere, as well as their ongoing close relations with other veterans' groups in Ukraine and beyond.

Position in the Public Sphere: "Frontline Camaraderie" Then and Now

The notion of "frontline camaraderie" and the image of the veterans as truth-seekers, as people with a higher sensitivity to social injustice, are set against the "dishonesty" of politicians in the discursive strategies employed in the *afhantsi*'s memoirs.[30] The political sphere is often denigrated as a place of "disgrace" and squabbles over selfish interests. This is why *afhantsi* are supposed to be rather apolitical people: "They [politicians] are trying to divide us into different political camps, that's why it is difficult for us to be united, though *afhantsi* are mostly apolitical people. The majority dislikes politics;

---

[29]   The classic work about this is: George Mosse, *Fallen Soldiers: Reshaping the Memory of the World Wars* (New York, Oxford: Oxford University Press, 1990).

[30]   Characteristic formulas are: "Those who sent the soldiers to the war are perpetrators <...> Officers and soldiers educated in the best traditions of the Russian army, loving the Motherland, generous, believing in the bright future, fulfiled the order with dignity" (Zaika, *Voina bez pobedy*, 6); "The Afghanistan war is a terrible military and political error on the part of the former Kremlin bosses. But nothing can diminish the heroism of our soldiers there" (Ivan Nitochko, *Afhanistan. Chornobyl. Vyprobuvannia trahedieiu. Berezivs'kyi raion* (Odesa: Astroprynt, 2009), 7).

tell them [whom] to vote [for], and they'll vote."[31] It is partly this specific attitude that explains the failure of the successive attempts to establish a political party of *afhantsi*.[32] In fact, the camaraderie myth not only serves to help make personal sense of the war, but creates a specific construct for action in the public sphere (especially for participation in protesting the neo-liberal state policy) and a base for solidarity with other veterans' groups.

The sacred character of the "Great Patriotic War" in Soviet society gave the biggest social capital to the veterans of this war, and other groups usually tend to try to cooperate with them where possible. The official Soviet valorization of the Afghanistan soldier in the late perestroika era was also modeled on the base of the established World War II rituals. The celebrations of Victory Day were usually the occasion of choice for propagating the heroic image of veterans of Afghanistan—"the successors of the traditions of military glory".[33]

In independent Ukraine, the participation of *afhantsi* in World War II commemorations is widespread. For example, they take part in visiting World War II military cemeteries and memorials, in ceremonies marking the unveiling of memorial plaques, and in the work of joint veterans' commissions dealing with the issues of "patriotic education" at schools. In legal terms, in Ukraine there are three categories of war veterans, each entitled to different social benefits: warfare participants, war invalids, and war participants

---

[31]   N. Razhik, "My shli na voinu iunymi, ne znaiushchimi zhizni...", in Zadvornaia (ed.), *Territoriia chesti*, 147.

[32]   In 1992 the Ukrainian Party of Justice was established with the support of the UUVA, but it failed in its successive attempts to be elected to parliament. In 2001 the joint party "Ukrainian Party of Justice - Union of Veterans, Disabled Persons, Chornobyl Disaster Liquidators, and *afhantsi*" (UPS-SVIChA, headed by Chervonopys'kyi) was established, but was likewise unsuccessful. In 2005 this party merged with the Socialist Party of Ukraine. In general, the ideological preferences of *afhantsi* are considered to be closer to leftist parties because of their wish to preserve social benefits and to resist liberal reforms. Soviet nostalgia on the part of the movement plays a certain role here as well.

[33]   See, for example, the case of Kharkiv, where the celebrations for Victory Day (9 May) included the ritual presentation of medals to *afhantsi* as well as send-offs for the new conscripts leaving for Afghanistan: N. Sotnyk, "Zhadaimo vsikh poimenno", *Vechirnii Kharkiv*, 5 May 1988.

(this last category includes people who were born before 1932 and worked on the homefront).[34] This is why the veterans of different wars are often members of the same veterans' councils, and the younger among them can act as representatives for the whole veteran community. The participants of the frontline warfare in World War II are already quite few, and very often they are too old to take part in the public events. This is why schools, clubs, concert halls, and other institutions regularly invite labor veterans, veterans of the war in Afghanistan, or "liquidators of the Chornobyl' catastrophe" to take part in the Victory Day (9 May) festivities. In this way, a sense of continuity between different heroic efforts is built. By contrast, the commemorations of 15 February—the Day of the Withdrawal of the Soviet Army from Afghanistan—are not always attended by the World War II veterans (although the representatives of the local administration and children from nearby schools almost always take part in these ceremonies). This testifies to the different symbolic status of these veterans' groups in Ukrainian society, as well as their wish to cooperate in the struggle for social benefits.

However, in their everyday activities, *afhantsi* cooperate more with the Chornobyl' liquidators and with participants of the UN peacekeeping operations in the 1990s–2000s, as they are much closer to each other in terms of age. Very often the veterans of so-called "local wars" waged by the USSR, such as in Libya, Somali, Angola, and of the Soviet army interventions in Hungary and Czechoslovakia, are the members of a single organization (representing the so-called "internationalist soldiers").[35]

---

[34]   "Zakon Ukrainy pro status veteraniv viiny, harantii iikh sotsialnoho zahystu", *Verkhovna Rada* official website, http://zakon4.rada.gov.ua/laws/show/3551-12.

[35]   In this sense the case of Ukrainian *afhantsi* is different from the Altai case of the Chechen war veterans described by Sergei Oushakine in his *Patriotism of Despair*. Oushakine states that the veterans in Russia do not make use of their experience either for rethinking their relations with the state and calling for its social responsibility or for creating some positive base for self-identification. For Oushakine, the myth of camaraderie serves only for escaping the questions of wider significance of the war and privatization of loss and trauma. See Sergei Oushakine, *The Patriotism of Despair: Nation, War, and Loss in Russia* (Ithaca and London: Cornell University Press, 2009). As I show here, the development of the veterans' movement in Ukraine, in spite of some paternalist illusions, is

In spite of the fact that former Afghanistan soldiers are represented at all levels of the Ukrainian state administration[36] and thus
have the ability to influence the budget process, the legislature's
nominal declarations on social benefits tend to differ greatly from
reality. The draft budget approved at the end of every year usually
makes provisions for reductions or even cancellation of some social
benefits, which results in active public protests by the veterans. The
funding for veterans' organizations comes mostly from local budgets
and private donors, and consequently in some cases their loyalty to
the local administration and regional business bosses is stronger
than to the central government. This factor seems important for explaining their frequent lack of success at the national level as well.

Because political struggle is a constant in independent
Ukraine, which lacks a unified stable "party of power" and a single
state ideology, the *afhantsi* movement is not very strongly connected to the state. The narrative of the Ukrainian military experience in Afghanistan has for the most part not been appropriated by
the state; thus, for example, this experience is underrepresented in
school textbooks, where it is mostly described in the context of
world history rather than national history.[37] In terms of social pro-

---

more related to values of solidarity and serves to oppose the neo-liberal state
policy.

[36] According to the UUVA's official data, in 2005 a large number of veterans were
elected to the local administrative organs: 27 became deputies of oblast councils, 81—city councils, and 222—district councils. See "Ukrainska spilka veteraniv   Afganistanu   (voiniv-internatsionalistiv)",   *UUVA*   website,
http://www.usva.org.ua/mambo3/index.php?option=com_content&task=blog-
category&id=14&Itemid=62.

[37] I. Shynkarenko, "Ob ob"ektivnosti nekotorykh urokov istorii", in Kostyria (ed.),
"Afgantsy" Donetchiny, 130–46. At the same time, the Soviet–Afghan War is one
of the topics featured in school patriotic education programs, and children have
to participate in commemorative actions on 15 February (the date of the withdrawal from Afghanistan), laying flowers at the military cemeteries or monuments, attending concerts at which Afghan war songs are performed, and putting on dramatized shows with poetry. For examples of scenarios for these commemorative events, see: T. Kusa, "Iak dovho tsia viina tryvala", *Shkilnyi svit*, no.
2 (2004): 19–22; T. Serheeva, "Ty vichnyi bil', Afganistan... Vechir-rekviem",
Shkilnyi svit, no. 4 (2007): 7–9; V. Filenko, "Poety ne hynut': Urok pam'iati pro
viinu v Afganistani", *Shkilnyi svit*, no. 4 (2009): 5–7. These commemorative

tection for the veterans, different political ruling groups have combined populist rhetoric with actual underfunding of social programs.

Notwithstanding the fact that the unchallenged leader of the
Ukrainian Union of the Veterans of Afghanistan Serhii Chervonopys'kyi (from 1991)[38] makes a point of highlighting the veterans'
loyalty to the ruling elites and political parties, Ukrainian *afhantsi*
do actively organize street protest actions, and sometimes these are
quite radical. "We have considerable military experience and we are
ready to make use of it"[39]—this formula is an effective argument
used by the veterans in their struggle against the liberalization of
social policy. In 2005 President Viktor Yushchenko liquidated the
Ukrainian State Committee of Veterans' Affairs for financial reasons,
but the ensuing pressure from veterans forced him to restore it in
2007. Nearly 10,000 activists took part in the protests against the
cancellation of veterans' benefits in Kyiv in May 2005.[40] Especially
strong protests were also waged in reaction to the social policy of
President Viktor Yanukovych, who paradoxically represented the
pro-Russian and Soviet-style nostalgic ideological trend, but also
tried to cancel social benefits to veterans and other groups. Along
with the countrywide "language maidan", "taxes maidan",[41] and students' and teachers' protests against reforms in education,[42] the
street protests of the veterans of Afghanistan and Chornobyl' were
quite impressive. In September 2011 *afhantsi*, Chornobyl' veterans,

---

forms are similar to those related to World War II memory, but the events are
not so widespread as the 9 (or 8) May celebrations.

[38]   In December 2013, however, several well-known leaders of the UUVA (including
Serhii Kunitsyn) were excluded from the organization because of a personal
conflict with Chervonopys'kyi. On 8 February 2014 Serhii Kunitsyn and his followers proclaimed the foundation of a new, alternative organization of veterans
(the All-Ukrainian Association of the Veterans of Afghanistan), but at the moment it is unclear how successful it will be. This act does not seem to be related
to the Maidan events.

[39]   *Internatsionalist* (Kharkiv), no. 4 (2005): 5.

[40]   Serhii Chervonopys'kyi, *Politychni ta sotsial'ni naslidky dlia Ukrainy spetsoperatsiii v Afhanistani 1979-1989 rr. i rol' USVA v iih podolanni: monohrafia* (Kyiv:
Medinform, 2008); *Internatsionalist* (Kharkiv), no. 4 (2005): 5.

[41]   Mass protests provoked by the adoption of new tax code and language law (November–December 2010 and July–August 2012, respectively).

[42]   Students protested in October 2010 and schoolteachers in March 2011.

"children of war"[43] and other groups entitled to benefits protested against the governmental attempt to cancel their social benefits and even organized an assault on the Supreme Council of Ukraine; the building was close to being seized, but the leaders stopped the action at the last minute so as to avoid a deeper confrontation. The result was the temporary cancellation of the pension cuts, but in the end the following year's budget, adopted in November, reinstated the original measures.[44] In response there were new protests and several violent attempts to seize the parliament building, leaving one person dead and several wounded.

Characteristically, the temporary acquiescence of the state in retaining the social benefits was related only to those groups who took active part in the protests. Other groups' problems went unnoticed, and *afhantsi* readily stopped protesting upon receiving assurances that the rights of their own group would be respected. Some observers consequently became extremely critical of the protests, noting their orientation towards the rights of narrow groups, and their lack of national solidarity and of real revolutionary potential. "The problems of *afhantsi* and *chornobyl'tsi* are equally important for the civil society activists as the problems of Saturn's satellites. And the activists of popular revolt [*afhantsi* and *chornobyl'tsi*] are absolutely indifferent towards democracy, freedom of speech, European integration, Yulia Tymoshenko and Lina Kostenko", one political commentator noted in late 2011, alluding to the lack of manifestations of national identity and solidarity (in its political or cultural form) among the protesters. For this commentator, the "real" civil society activists were represented by European-minded intellectuals and students, but not by the "mobs" of "conservatives from the popular masses" whose only wish was to get money from the state, as

---

43 In accordance with Ukrainian legislation, a "child of war" is a person who was less than 18 years old in 1945. The social benefits for this category were introduced by the law "On the Social Protection of the Children of War", 18 November 2004.

44 See the detailed account of the protests under Yanukovych and the analysis of the state's strategies aimed at avoiding social accountability in the Ukrainian case in: Mihai Varga, "State Strategies of Resisting Social Accountability: Post-Soviet Insights", *East European Politics and Societies and Cultures* 27, no. 4 (2013): 727–42.

they used to do in the Soviet period, and whose only grievance was based on a nostalgic desire for a kind of return to the Soviet *zastoi* (stagnation) era, which the Ukrainian state was unable to deliver.[45]

However, all of these criticisms could equally be leveled at the post-Soviet civil society as a whole. Many observers have noted that NGOs in the post-Soviet space tend to defend the interests of their leaders or narrow interest groups, and that the greater part of the population distrust any organizational arrangements, and prefer informal, often corrupted personal relations of friends, family, and clans.[46] According to Victor Stepanenko, poll data before 2006 showed that many people in Ukraine described civil society in terms of "an authoritarian-paternalistic model, in which the state controls the NGO's activity and satisfies the citizens' interests".[47] All of this supports Lucan Way's thesis about the weakness of the post-Soviet civil society and its minor role in the protests, whose nature was more spontaneous than organized.[48]

However, amongst the protesters, it was the *afhantsi* who generally demonstrated the highest level of organization in their activity, because of their "military discipline": the call of their leaders in Kyiv "mobilized" the members of the local veterans' unions who immediately came to Kyiv or organized protest actions in their native cities. In spite of the fact that Afghan veterans struggled for the benefits of their own social group, and that they ultimately made no impact on the social policy of the state in general, their actions provided quite a good example for other groups. Protest actions now became an accepted part of everyday life in Ukraine. On the eve of the revolutionary Maidan of 2013–2014, *afhantsi* were considered to

---

[45]   Mykhailo Dubynianskyi, "Buntuiut' vsi!", *Ukrainska pravda*, 28 December 2011, http://www.pravda.com.ua/articles/2011/12/28/6857849/.

[46]   Sarah Phillips, "Prostranstvo pravozashchitnogo aktivizma invalidov v postsotsi- alisticheskoi Ukraine: NPO i grazhdanskoe obshchestvo mezhdu lokal'nym i global'nym", *Zhurnal issledovanii sotsial'noi politiki*, 1 (2012): 43–60; Victor Ste- panenko, "Civil Society in Post-Soviet Ukraine: Civic Ethos in the Framework of Corrupted Sociality", *East European Politics and Societies* 22, no. 4 (2006): 571–97.

[47]   Ibid.

[48]   Lucan Way, "Civil Society and Democratization", *Journal of Democracy* 25, no. 3 (July 2014): 35–43.

be a very well organized and active part of society, and they were proud of this.[49]

Afhantsi on the Maidan: "Fathers and Sons" or "A Human Shield Between the Two Sides"?

Taking into account the long tradition of struggle for social support from the state, as well as the military experience of the Afghan veterans, it is not surprising that they took an active part in the revolutionary events of 2013–2014. Initially, President Yanukovych's rejection of the signing of the European Union Association Agreement on 26 November 2013 provoked no special reaction on the part of the veterans. The liberal reforms, usually associated with pro-European policy, would most probably have all but abolished the *afhantsi* social benefits, which are remnants from the Soviet past. The idea of "European Ukraine" does not seem to have been very attractive, especially for those *afhantsi* holding nostalgic quasi-Soviet views. However, the unnecessarily rigid line taken by the government provoked more and more resistance, coming to involve groups who would otherwise have remained to one side.

During the first period, the protests were rather few and limited to the participation of intellectuals and students opposing the government's decision to suspend preparations for signing the EU Association Agreement. The unexpectedly cruel crackdown by militia on the peaceful student demonstration on 30 November 2013 provoked an outburst of anger all over the country. *Afhantsi* came to the Maidan right after the beating of the student demonstrators. Their motivation was far from being politically loaded: they positioned themselves as "the defenders of our children", as courageous and strong "fathers", real fighters for justice and dignity (in accordance with their own self-image so vividly portrayed in their memoirs

---

49   See, for example, the comment of one *afhanets*: "The Ukrainian government never gave anything to us—neither Tymoshenko, nor Yushchenko, Azarov, or Yanukovych. We struggled for everything. That's how it is!"; Larysa Artemenko, "Kremenchuts'ki afhantsi na Maidani: Za shcho stoiat?", *Telegraf*, 15 February 2014, http://www.telegraf.in.ua/topnews/2014/02/15/kremenchuck-afganc-na-maydan-za-scho-stoyat_10034992.html.

and other writings), whose duty was to protect the weak and vulnerable. As Timothy Snyder put it, "they [*afhantsi*] didn't mean their own sons and daughters: they meant the best of the youth, the pride and future of the country".[50] The same motif is widespread in the personal accounts of veterans who took part in Maidan.[51] Nonetheless, the participation of *afhantsi* in the Maidan did not necessarily equate to enthusiastic support for these young people's ideals. It just meant that the protest needed some sort of self-defense and people with relevant experience.

The metaphor of "fathers and children" reappeared once again in the relations between the *afhantsi* and Right Sector—an organization bringing together the more militant and radical participants of the Maidan with rightist political views. In fact, the *afhantsi*, who now are in their 40s and 50s, could well have been the fathers of the young activists. This metaphor refers to the transmission of the military experience and values of solidarity, mutual help, and comradeship, but in no sense does it indicate the sharing of common political views with the nationalist radicals. This was a specific trait of the Maidan, where traditional ideologies and political doctrines, as well as party leaders, were perceived with bitter skepticism, but the idea of solidarity transcending political and social divisions was welcomed. Paradoxically, Right Sector, that was associated with political radicalism and extremist, violent methods of struggle, became the closest partner for the *afhantsi*. The two groups united primarily because both were trying to physically defend the space of protest from the government forces. On the other hand, the *afhantsi* presented themselves as experienced men able to influence the young

---

[50]   Timothy Snyder, "Fascism, Russia, and Ukraine", *The New York Review of Books*, 20 March 2014, http://www.nybooks.com/articles/archives/2014/mar/20/fascism-russia-and-ukraine/.

[51]   This rhetoric of "fathers" and "children" is present in the personal narratives of *afhantsi* and Officer Corps members who were active on the Maidan. See: Interview with male respondent from Zhytomyr region, 22 December 2013 and interview with male respondent, 6 December 2013, both from "Voices of Resistance and Hope" project, Center for Urban History of East Central Europe Archives; interview with Valeriy Fisun, 31 July 2014 and interview with Valeriy Kubytskyi, 11 March 2014, both from "Maidan: Oral History collection", Ukrainian Institute of National Remembrance Archives.

radicals to become more mild and tolerant, and to teach them how to protest "in a civilized way".[52]

At the same time, the *afhantsi* expressed the same fatherly feelings to militiamen from the internal security troops (standing in front of the protesters) who were largely very young and mercilessly exploited by the Yanukovych regime.[53] In this case, the long tradition of loyalty to the state and ruling party (of whatever orientation) influenced the veterans' position as well. The veterans even compared their own mission in Afghanistan ("we were just sent there to carry out an order, though it was unjust or just fallacious") with the position of the militia and "Berkut" special forces who, they said, were only fulfilling their duty just as the *afhantsi* had done in Afghanistan.[54] However, the growing violence on the Maidan and the use of firearms by the government forces eventually provoked greater engagement of *afhantsi* in the protests.

Oleh Mikhniuk, the vice-chairman of the Ukrainian Union of Afghanistan Veterans, became the commander of the *afhantsi* who physically joined the Maidan, lived at the tent camp, and took part in seizing buildings. In fact, this means that participation in the protest was sanctioned at the highest level of the veterans' organization, though the chairman of the organization, Chervonopys'kyi, presented himself publicly as a neutral actor. Some veterans came out to the Maidan in response to the call of Serhii Kunitsyn—the veteran and deputy of the Supreme Council of Ukraine, member of the "UDAR" party.[55] The 8th *sotnia* (unit),[56] or "*Afhans'ka sotnia*", was formed on the base of the non-governmental organization "*Ofit-*

---

[52]   "Interview with S. Chervonopys'kyi: My proty ekstremizmu", *Hromadske telebachennia*, 4 February 2014, https://www.youtube.com/watch?v=R6K6HD0Q0-A.

[53]   "Afhantsi: my nastavnyky Pravoho Sectoru", *Espreso TV*, 5 February 2014, https://www.youtube.com/watch?v=gi6nAUb7GTY.

[54]   This understanding and empathy towards the policemen who were forced to follow immoral orders is expressed in some personal narratives of *afhantsi*: see interview with Valeriy Fisun (born 1957), 31 July 2014, Ukrainian Institute of National Remembrance Archives, Maidan collection.

[55]   "Vitalii Klychko's UDAR (Ukrainian Democratic Alliance for Reforms)" emerged in 2010 as a personal project of famous boxer Vitalii Klychko.

[56]   The term *sotnia* is borrowed from the Cossack term designating a military unit, later borrowed by the Ukrainian Insurgent Army (UPA) as well.

sers'kyi korpus" ("Officer Corps"). Some other people with no experience of participation in warfare joined the "*Afhans'ka sotnia*" as
well. Their tasks on the Kyiv Maidan were those of policing: pattrol-
ing the perimeter of the square and especially the barricade at
Hrushevs'koho street, monitoring and enforcing the adherence to
armistice agreements, and unveiling provocateurs and pickpockets.
Interestingly, at the same time the *afhantsi* declared themselves to
be neither Maidan nor government supporters. They chose the position of "conciliators", a "living shield" against the radicals from
both sides. This distinctive position can possibly be attributed to the
habitual veterans' strategy of seeking the state's support through
demonstrative loyalty and patriotic rhetoric, and at the same time
lobbying for their interests by means of public protests and the use
of threat of force in the event of the state's undermining of their
social benefits. The official declaration of the UUVA on their website
proclaimed that *afhantsi* did not support any political force or
party.[57] In many public speeches *afhantsi* highlighted the fact that
they were people of different political and religious beliefs and of
different regional backgrounds, but that they were all united by a
wish for deep transformations in Ukrainian politics and society.
When the *afhantsi* and Right Sector initiated a separate dialogue
with the government aimed at achieving the release of hostages,
there were even some fears that the *afhantsi* might try to play their
own game and that this might possibly result in a split in the ranks
of the protesters. The veterans rejected these accusations by under-
lining the difference between the civil and military mentality: "They
simply don't know what it is to rescue your own men [*svoikh*]", they

---

[57]   The same "neutrality" was always highlighted by the leader of the organization
Serhii Chervonopys'kyi, while the rank-and-file members were more frank in
expressing their anti-government positions: "Afhantsi na Maidani—ne za
opozytsiiu i ne proty vlady", *Telekanal Tvi*, 5 February 2014, https://www.you
tube.com/watch?v=6pIqnGMneGs. For Chervonopys'kyi's views, see: S.V. Chervonopys'kyi, *Organizovanyi "afhans'kyi ruh" v Ukraini: stanovlennia ta rozvytok:
zbirnyk statei* (Kyiv: Medinform, 2007); S.V. Chervonopys'kyi, *Politychni ta sotsial'ni naslidky dlia Ukrainy spetsoperatsiii v Afhanistani 1979-1989 rr. i rol' USVA
v iih podolanni: monohrafiia* (Kyiv: Medinform, 2008).

said, alluding to their experience of the sacrificial rescuing of com-rades in the war.[58]

The veterans' key positions are encapsulated by two state-ments that were typical for them not only on the Maidan but also during the whole period of Ukraine's independence: "We don't trust any political force" and "We defend the people". As the leader of the UUVA Serhii Chervonopys'kyi put it at the beginning of February 2014:

> We are standing up to protect the people. We are neither for any political force nor for the power [regime]. Yes, we cooperate with the regime, and we will cooperate with the regime. There used to be an Orange regime—we col-laborated with the Orange [regime], now we have the current regime—we will [cooperate] with this one. Next: at any given time people need help for the families of the fallen, for the disabled, orphans, et cetera, people need help, so our aim is to help people in cooperation with the regime.[59]

The logic of the revolutionary events in Kyiv constantly chal-lenged this position of declared "neutrality," however, and many vet-erans became the backbone of the self-defense units who fought against the governmental attempts to disperse the protesters and to crush the barricades and tents. Their military experience was ex-tremely useful there, particularly for the regular paramilitary train-ing. In February 2014 the number of veterans reached over one thou-sand people constantly present on the Maidan and constantly ro-tated.[60] Serhii Kunitsyn declared that on the Maidan there were over three thousand participants of the Soviet–Afghan War and UN peacekeeping missions, paratroopers, and special units' veterans al-together.[61]

On 15 February 2014 on the 25th anniversary of the troop pull-out from Afghanistan, several columns of *afhantsi* from the Maidan marched to the monument near Kyiv-Pechersk Lavra to pay their

---

58   Artemenko, "Kremenchuts'ki afhantsi."

59   Interview with Chervonopys'kyi, "My proty ekstremizmu."

60   Artemenko, "Kremenchuts'ki afhantsi".

61   Sergei Kunitsyn, "Evromaidan uzhe prinial bolee trekh tysiach veteranov", *Per-sonal web-site of Sergei Kunitsyn*, 14 December 2013, http://kunitcyn.com/in-dex.php?option=com_content&view=article&id=666:evromajdan-uzhe-prinyal-bolee-trekh-tysyach-veteranov-afganistana&catid=9&Itemid=123.

respects to their fallen comrades. The representatives of the Mai-dan-supporting *afhantsi* once again expressed their readiness to be-come observers in the process of negotiations between the protest-ers and the government, as well as to defend the Maidan protesters. "We are here not only to change the regime, but to change the sys-tem", argued one *afhanets*. They also asked for more support from other Afghanistan veterans and urged them to join the street pro-tests physically.[62] At this later stage of the struggle, one can see a change in moods, when the leadership of the veterans still used con-ciliatory rhetoric, while rank-and-file participants were ready to fight to the end, not only to defend the people, but also to dismantle the regime that was so deeply bogged down in corruption, klep-tocracy, and human rights violations.

Some veterans have even claimed that not a single Afghan vet-eran supported the Yanukovych regime,[63] but this was rather wish-ful thinking. Belonging to the same veterans' organization did not preclude different political choices. The common identity nurtured by the activists of the *afhantsi* movement in Ukraine was too fragile and problematic to sustain stronger symbolic ties between its mem-bers. The political differences were of a regional nature as well. In Donets'k, for example, some *afhantsi* played the role of *titushki*—thugs paid by government or local administration to carry out ag-gressive acts against Euromaidan protesters; they attacked Maidan

---

[62]   "Afgantsy prizyvali svoikh sobrat'iev vykhodit' na ulitsy", *Censor.net*, 15 Febru-ary 2014, http://censor.net.ua/video_news/270866/afgantsy_prizyvali_svoih _sobratev_vyhodit_na_ulitsy_i_podderjat_mayidan_my_vyshli_protiv_sistemy _video; see also "Afhantsi rozpovily, sho ne pidut z Maidanu do peremohy", *Dyvys.info*, 15 February 2014, https://www.youtube.com/watch?v=Y2vID4INC GI.

[63]   "Khochu uvidet' afgantsa...", *Espreso.tv*, 14 February 2014, http://espreso.tv/ne w/2014/02/14/veteran_afhanistanu_ya_khochu_pobachyty_zhyvoho_afhancya _yakyy_skazhe_scho_maydan___ce_pohano. At the beginning of February 2014 Chervonopys'kyi highlighted in an interview that there were different groups of *afhantsi*; some supported the Maidan, while others condemned it: Chervo-nopys'kyi, "My proty ekstremizmu..."

gatherings in Donets'k along with Party of Regions followers, *ka-zaki*,[64] and landing forces ("VDV") veterans.[65] In Luhans'k in January 2014 nearly 30 people came to the local Euromaidan and introduced themselves as *afhantsi* and strugglers against "Euro-sodom".[66] Other local veterans' organizations were initially neutral during the Maidan, but finally made important decisions in March and April—the period of revolutionary change amidst the drastic loss of legitimacy of the central power. *Afhantsi* in Kharkiv (in the eastern part of Ukraine) helped to provide security for the Maidan activists attacked by the pro-Russian gathering on 1 March, and in April the local *afhantsi* council denounced the violent seizure of the local administrative building by pro-Putin activists and expressed support for the unity of Ukraine.[67] A similar declaration was issued by the Dnipropetrovs'k organization, as well as by some others in the eastern and southern parts of the country, in this critical period of power vacuum.

After the ousting of Yanukovych in late February 2014, in the situation of uncertainty and demoralization of the army and police, the position of non-governmental organizations was quite important and authoritative for part of the population. In early March when the Russian troops appeared in Crimea, Ukrainian *afhantsi* started to take part in the formation of new army units, loyal to the new government in Kyiv. Many of them joined the special units of self-defense to protect strategic objects in Kyiv and other big cities.

---

64   *Kazaki* are members of the pro-Russian paramilitary organizations who claim to be the descendants of the Don and Kuban Cossacks.

65   "Vlasti Donets'ka priamo predupredili", *Zerkalo Nedeli* news portal, 24 January 2014, http://zn.ua/UKRAINE/vlasti-donecka-pryamo-predupredili-chto-mest nyy-evromaydan-razgonyat-titushki-137376_.html; "Ne obnaruzhyv aktivistov Evromaidana, donetskie titushki pobili svoikh", *Telegraf*, 26 January 2014, http://telegraf.dn.ua/news/ne-obnaruzhiv-aktivistov-evromajdana-donetskie-titushki-pobili-svoih/.

66   Andrei Zhygailo, "Na Evromaidan prishli Afgantsy", *Po-ukrains'ky* newspaper, 11 January 2014, http://gazeta.ua/ru/articles/regions/_na-evromajdan-v-lu-ganske-prishli-afgancy-borotsya-s-evrosodomom/535764.

67   "Khar'kovskie afgantsy obratilis' s zaiavleniem", *Media group "Obiektiv" news*, 10 April 2014, http://www.objectiv.tv/100414/95781.html; "'Afgantsy' pomogali militsii vyvodit' liudei iz KhOGA", *Khar'kov: Kommentarii*, 1 March 2014, http://kharkov.comments.ua/news/2014/03/01/203348.html.

Interestingly, once again the leader of the organization, Serhii Chervonopys'kyi, used the rhetoric of "peacemaking mission" and "standing between", proclaiming that "We stood as a living shield between Berkut and the protesters... we are ready to stand between the Russian troops and our boys [soldiers] who are much less numerous [than the Russian army], and to support dialogue, not to let the situation develop to the shedding of Slavic blood".[68] On 4 March 2014, the UUVA held a conference in Kyiv where its leaders were informed that Ukrainian *afhantsi* in Crimea should act as a "human shield" between Putin's "little green men" and Ukrainian army units, between Crimean Tatars and Russian *kazaki* detachments, in this way disclaiming the thesis about the pro-Russian position of *afhantsi* on the peninsula.[69] Chervonopys'kyi highlighted the veterans' support for the unity and independence of Ukraine, and their readiness to join the army ranks.

Back in the Army Ranks Again: the Participation of *Afhantsi* in the War in the Donbas

However, the neutrality and the idea of being "in-between" became highly problematic once the real warfare began. The war in the Donbas (officially called the "Anti-Terrorist Operation" or ATO) that started in April 2014 led to the crushing of illusions about the possibility of preserving the ambiguous identity of "Slavic unity" or the "Russian world", as well as the effectiveness of appealing to "comradeship" with the Russian veterans of Afghanistan. When the seizure of Crimea started, many activists of the Maidan, especially those with military training, came to military enlistment offices as volunteers. The *afhantsi* were the first to do this and their public call

---

68   "Afgantsy formiruiut podrazdeleniia dlia zashchity tselostnosti Ukrainy", *Ukrinform*, 4 March 2014, http://www.ukrinform.ua/rus/news/afgantsi _formiruyut_podrazdeleniya_dlya_zashchiti_tselostnosti_ukraini_1609690.
69   "Pres-konferentsiia: 'Veterany-afhantsi—za zberezhennia iednosti Ukrainskoi derzhavy'", *Ukrinform*, 4 March 2014, http://www.ukrinform.ua/ukr/ news/pres_konferentsiya_1914541.

to arms evoked reactions from their comrades in Russia who sometimes expressed solidarity with the Ukrainian side.[70] The Ukrainian
veterans became more and more unambiguously involved in the
Ukrainian army: as rank-and-file combatants, officers, instructors,
specialists in logistics, civil volunteers who helped to provide the
army with necessary equipment and consumer goods, organizers of
charitable funds, and so on.[71] Many Afghanistan veterans joined volunteer battalions, and some also joined the army ranks. The 8th
Afhans'ka sotnia from Maidan joined the 24th Battalion of the territorial defense "Aidar" in May 2014. The veterans' combat experience
now became crucial for training the new army cadres, especially in
the context of the low professional skills of the Ukrainian army and
the collapse of its technical base. Serhii Kunitsyn reported in November 2014 that one thousand Ukrainian *afhantsi* were at the front,
and that 74 of them had perished in the ATO in the Donbas to date.
Among the dead was Oleh Mikhniuk—the leader of the 8th *sotnia*
and the deputy head of the UUVA.[72]

The war in the Donbas caused an extremely deep split between the Russian and Ukrainian organizations of Afghanistan veterans. In spite of the fact that the Ukrainian UVA asked its Russian
colleagues not to intervene in the conflict, Russian veterans of many
local wars now became the most active volunteers, hirelings, and
organizers for the flow of soldiers joining the anti-Ukrainian troops
in the Donbas.[73] The Russian veterans mostly followed the official

---

[70] "Veterany-afgantsy gotoviatsia k mobilizatsii", 5 *kanal*, 3 March 2014,
https://www.youtube.com/watch?v=cuV-nkMsY8c.
[71] "V zoni provedennia antyterorystychnoi operatsii zahynuly 74 'afhantsi'", 5
kanal, 18 November 2014, http://www.5.ua/ato-na-shodi/pid-chas-ato-
zahynuly-74-afhantsi-62937.html. Among other things, the UUVA appealed to
President Poroshenko with the suggestion that *afhantsi* be included in commissions dealing with captives: "Chy potribnyi dosvid afhantsiv?", *UUVA* web-site,
http://usva.com.ua/news/732-chi-potrbniy-dosvd-afgancv.html.
[72] "V zoni provedennia antyterorystychnoi operatsii".
[73] The presence of the Russian veterans of Afghanistan and Chechnya—volunteers
as well as professional military men—in the conflict in the Donbas is narrated
by these seasoned fighters themselves: James Rupert, "Direct Translation: A Retired Russian Army Officer Sends Paid 'Volunteers' to Fight in Ukraine", *Atlan-
tic Council*, 27 December 2014, http://www.atlanticcouncil.org/blogs/new-at-
lanticist/direct-translation-how-a-retired-russian-army-officer-sends-volun-

position of the Kremlin with its use of the rhetoric of patriotism, anti-fascism, and military glory. For many of them this was just another in a series of military conflicts that had broken out in the Russian Federation after 1989.[74]

In contrast to their counterparts in Ukraine, who live under a state with more unpredictable social guarantees and no official unified ideology, the Afghan veterans in Russia, though demonstrating the huge potential of an independent civil movement during perestroika, are currently more inclined to express their loyalty to the regime.[75] Deep feelings of belonging to the Russian national imperial project, and an understanding of the personal Afghanistan experience as a part of the greatness of Russia, have led the veterans of the local wars in this country to lean more toward the official state vision of the situation in Ukraine. The specific Afghanistan experience provided the Russian participants of the war in the Donbas with an additional narrative strategy—the idea of an "internationalist duty" to defend "brotherly peoples". Significantly, in the media discourse the Russian intervention in Ukraine is spontaneously compared with the Soviet intervention in Afghanistan—the latter has become a metaphor for any colonial war involving such factors as the covering up of losses, collaboration on the part of the population, the existence of global aims behind the local conflict, and possible negative outcomes for the aggressor.[76]

---

teers-to-fight-in-ukraine; "Veterany chechenskikh voin priekhali voevat' v Donbass", *Nastoiashchee vremia* channel, 10 December 2014, https://www.you tube.com/watch?v=76W-BqyF-sk; "Chechens Now Fighting on Both Sides in Ukraine", *Radio Free Europe*, 1 August 2014, http://www.rferl.org/content/caucasus-report-chechens-fighting-for-ukraine/26558104.html.

[74] See the research on the Chechen war veterans in Russia in: Anne Le Huérou, Elisabeth Sieca-Kozlowski, "A 'Chechen Syndrome'? Russian Veterans of the Chechen War and the Transposition of War Violence to Society", in *War Veterans in Postwar Situations. Chechnya, Serbia, Turkey, Peru, and Côte d'Ivoire*, ed. N. Duclos (New York: Palgrave Macmillan, 2012), 25–51.

[75] Nataliia Danilova, "Geroi v bor'be za svoi prava: dvizhenie invalidov voin v Sovetskom Soiuze i v Rossii", in *Obshchestvennye dvizheniia v Rossii: tochki rosta, kamni pretknoveniia*, eds. P.V. Romanov and E. R. Yarskaia-Smirnova (Moscow: Variant; TsSPG, 2009), 59–72.

[76] "Eks-'aidarivets' Dykyi: Ukraina dlia Rosii—iak Afganistan dlia SRSR", *BBC Ukraine*, 20 February 2015, http://www.bbc.com/ukrainian/politics/2015/02/ 150204_dykiy_aidar_interview_vs; Andrei Skliarov, "Vran'e v nasledstvo. K 26-i

Of course, there are veterans who refused to fight the "brotherly Ukrainian people". For example, in March 2014 groups of veterans from the Russian Federation and Ukraine (Belarusians were invited but did not come) met in a border village in Chernihiv region
near the Soviet "Friendship" monument, thus using the Soviet tradition of the ritualistic "building of peace and friendship between
brotherly peoples". They discussed the situation and declared their
refusal to participate in the possible military conflict between Russia
and Ukraine and their support for the overthrow of the dictator
Yanukovych. They also criticized the propagandistic myths about
the cruel "benderovtsy" who had allegedly seized power in Kyiv, and
finally hailed the semi-humorous slogan "Peace! Friendship! Lard!
[Salo!]".[77] It should be noted that this was, however, the private initiative of just one part of the veterans' communities.

The same wish to prevent the war with the use of "public diplomacy" was present on the Ukrainian side. At a special session of
the Zhytomyr regional council local leaders of *afhantsi* made a public appeal to their comrades in Russia:

> We are on the eve of a fratricidal war between our nations. We must prevent
> this. The military intervention of Russian military forces in Crimea is open
> military aggression and an intrusion into the internal affairs of Ukraine. We
> ask all of you, our warfare comrades, veterans of Afghanistan and all the
> brotherly nations of Russia, to influence your government and to prevent
> war between our countries. We have no reason to fight and there is no rea-
> son to wage war.[78]

In the course of the war, these hopes for mutual understanding vanished.

On the other hand, it is also worth noting that some of the
Ukrainian *afhantsi* joined the ranks of the separatist Donets'k and
Luhans'k "people's republics". Thus, in December 2014 (quite late,

---

godovshchine vyvoda voisk iz Afganistana", *Rufabula* website, 15 February 2015,
http://rufabula.com/author/sklyarov/347.

77 "Ukrainski i rosiiski afhantsi vidmovliaiutsia voiuvaty mizh soboiu", *Televiziina
sluzhba novyn*, 6 March 2014, https://www.youtube.com/watch?v=VtM6FJ7
113g.

78 "Afhantsi zvernulys' do vlady ta boiovykh pobratymiv u Rosii," *Zhytomyr.Info*
channel, 4 March 2014, https://www.youtube.com/watch?v=dqXRJ_2IS7U.

let us note, as by this point Donets'k had already been in the hands of the "people's republic" for several months), the Union of the Veterans of Afghanistan of the Donets'k People's Republic was created.[79] The Veterans' Organization of the "Luhans'k People's Republic" appeared even later, in January 2015.[80] Basically, the same feelings of solidarity and the wish to use the veterans' combat experience to help the young conscripts (along with the fear of "west Ukrainians") were presented as motivation for participation in the war on the side of the so-called Donets'k and Luhans'k People's Republics.[81]

Afhantsi and ATO Veterans: Symbolic Continuity and the Question of Benefits

Since the ATO began in the Donbas in mid-April 2014, the *afhantsi* became preoccupied with helping its participants—not only at the front, but on the home front as well. Moreover, *afhantsi* have been trying to unite all the veterans with different experiences in one category and to lobby their rights together. When the new attempt to cancel the benefits was made in the budget for 2015, *afhantsi* protested against this once again. In this context, Serhii Kunitsyn argued that there should be no difference in the state policy towards the veterans of World War II, the Soviet–Afghan War, and participants of the ATO in the Donbas.[82] Actually, at the government level, in 2014 the State Committee for Veterans' Affairs took on responsibility for the participants of the ATO. The legal category "participant in warfare" and respective benefits have also been applied to this

---

[79]   "DNR, vozlozhenie tsvetov k pamiatniku voinam-afgantsam", *News Front*, 27 December 2014, https://www.youtube.com/watch?v=XS-Vao_7SdU.

[80]   "O respublikanskoi obshchestvennoi organizatsii 'Veterany Luganskoi Narodnoi Respubliki'", *Veterany LNR* website, 15 January 2015, http://www.veterani.club/.

[81]   "Moi afganskie tovarishchi s Zapadnoi Ukrainy voiuiut protiv menia", *Goriachie novosti channel*, 19 April 2015, https://www.youtube.com/watch?v=fMtopb9tNt4.

[82]   "Dlia afgantsev, boitsov ATO i veteranov VOV dolzhen byt' odin zakon,—Kunitsyn", *112 Ukraine channel*, 24 November 2014, http://112.ua/politika/dlya-afgancev-boycov-ato-i-veteranov-vov-dolzhen-byt-odin-zakon-kunicyn-150591.html.

new group of veterans. Still, the lack of resources and bureaucratic obstacles are reducing the level of social support actually delivered, and gaining access to these benefits is still a struggle—consequently, the help of more experienced veteran community members is crucial.

In February 2015 the Chernivtsi Afghan veterans publicly appealed to the local administration with a request that ATO veterans be granted the free use of public transport, land plots for housing, and other benefits, with a view to breaking with the usual state practice of neglecting veterans' problems in Ukraine.[83] In this way, the *afhantsi* expressed their solidarity with the new groups of veterans, but at the same time, they were also giving voice to a feeling of uncertainty about their own future in a state where there is an excess of candidate welfare recipients. "We understand that this is a generational change. We know what kind of attitude towards us existed when we returned from the war in Afghanistan", *afhantsi* from Uzhhorod commented in their appeal to the local administration. In so doing, they revealed both a sense of solidarity with the ATO veterans and acceptance of the fact that there was now another generation of soldiers, traumatized and in need of care and understanding—probably more so, in fact, than the *afhantsi* themselves today.[84]

At the symbolic level, the unity of different veterans' generations is manifested in traditions linked to shared commemorations. In Novoarkhangel'sk (Kirovohrad region) a new memorial called "Heroes Don't Die" (in fact, one of the slogans of the Maidan) was created in honor of soldiers fallen both in Afghanistan and in the ATO in the Donbas. This initiative was supported by donations from the residents of this predominantly rural region, including veterans, businesspersons, and farmers. The slogan on the memorial reads, "We remember the fallen, we care about the living". The memorial plaque depicts two Soviet soldiers, one of whom is assisting in plant-

---

83   "Afhantsi prosiat' vladu stavytysia do voiniv ATO krashche, nizh do nykh", *Telekompaniia TVA*, https://www.youtube.com/watch?v=jlO3x3LnfQk.
84   "Zvernennia voiniv-afhantsiv do vlady m. Uzhhorod", 12 June 2015, https://www.youtube.com/watch?v=oYYUOUMikUo.

ing a tree, and two Afghans: a soldier and a child. Two other memorial plaques are located on the sides of the monument, one with a star (the Soviet military symbol) and the names of the fallen in Afghanistan, the other with the Trident (the symbol of the Ukrainian independent state), and the names of the fallen in the Donbas. In this way both missions, in Afghanistan and in the Donbas, are presented, first and foremost, as a fight against terrorism and for the liberation of the local population. At the ceremonial unveiling of the memorial, the veterans of World War II, the Soviet–Afghan War, and the ATO came together, and the reportage on one of the national channels was titled "A Shared Memory".[85]

There are many other examples of memorials to ATO soldiers that have been erected near the existing World War II memorials, and of shared commemorative events held on Victory Day. In June 2015, President Petro Poroshenko proclaimed that "it would be fair to create a memorial to the Unknown Soldier of *our* Great Patriotic War in Glory Park, near the Unknown Soldier of World War II".[86] The largest museum of the Great Patriotic War, in Kyiv, ran an exhibition called "Family Memory of War. Preserved", with concluding parts titled "Victory Day" and "Cyborgs".[87] These parts included stories of *afhantsi* taking part in the war in the Donbas. In another example, in Kirovohrad, memorial plaques commemorating the fallen in the ATO were installed at a memorial marking a burial site for soldiers fallen in World War II and the Soviet–Afghan War.[88]

In other words, it would appear that a new mythological construct is emerging, in which the veterans of different wars, led by

---

[85]   "Na Kirovogradshchyni vidkryly spilnyi memorial zahyblym pid chas ATO ta afhanskoi viiny", *TSN channel*, 15 May, 2015, https://www.youtube.com/watch?v=oh2hO2iwooM.

[86]   "U Kyevi z'iavyt'sia memorial na chest' zahyblykh v ATO", *Hromadske.tv*, 5 June 2015, http://www.hromadske.tv/society/u-kiyevi-z---yavitsya-memorial-na-chest-zagiblikh-/.

[87]   "Cyborgs" became the nickname for the Ukrainian servicemen fighting for Donetsk airport, and in this case the term is used even more broadly to refer to all the Ukrainian servicemen in the Donbas; Iryna Kotsab'iuk, "Kiborhy-afhantsi", *UUVA* web-site, http://www.usva.org.ua/mambo3/index.php?option=com_content&task=view&id=5810&Itemid=1.

[88]   "U Kirovohradi vidkryly memorial pam'iati zahyblym voinam ATO", *Hromadske.tv*, 8 May 2015, https://www.youtube.com/watch?v=AhzcLeBEiVw.

different states and with different aims, are placed together into a single scheme where the worthy sons of Ukraine fight for independence and freedom against terrorists and foreign aggressors. The Afghan link is not always present in this scheme, but the link between the "Great Patriotic War" and the ATO in the Donbas is omnipresent in mass media. Particularly important here was the case of the World War II veteran Ivan Zaluzhnyi from Zaporizhzhia who lost his grandson in the ATO in August 2014. Zaluzhnyi publicly blamed Putin for his grandson's death and appealed to his comrades in Russia ("with whom we shared a piece of bread back then") with a call to force Putin to end the aggression.[89] The case of Zaluzhnyi was widely publicized, and the Ukrainian Institute of National Remembrance made Zaluzhnyi's story part of a collection of materials it created with the deliberate aim of forming a new tradition of nationwide Victory Day commemoration "in the European spirit of memory and reconciliation".[90] For the 2015 Victory Day commemorations (8 and 9 May), the Information Resistance group[91] created a video in which a soldier fighting in the ATO telephones his grandfather, a veteran of World War II, to congratulate him on Victory Day. They also produced another, similar video clip featuring a granddaughter and grandmother.[92] These videos made a linkage between World War II and the ATO in the Donbas through the stories of ordinary people, their human emotions, and family ties as contrasted to the Soviet traditions of the leadership cult. The family metaphor here symbolizes the nation, while the Russian language

---

[89]   "Vichna slava heroiam! Veteran Ivan Zaluzhnyi vtratyv vnuka u viini na skhodi Ukrainy," *Ukrainian Institute of National Remembrance* channel, 30 April 2015, https://www.youtube.com/watch?v=kRcsPW4lpxo.

[90]   "8-9 travnia. Materialy dlia zavantazhennia", *Ukrainian Institute of National Remembrance* website, http://www.memory.gov.ua/page/8-9-travnya-materiali-dlya-zavantazhennya.

[91]   Information Resistance was launched in March 2014 as a project of the NGO "Center for Military and Political Studies" and is aimed at supporting the national security of Ukraine in the informational space. The project (http://sprotyv.info/en) produces analytics, news reports, and investigations.

[92]   "Ukraina. Den' Pobedy. Babushka", *IS* channel, 27 April 2015, https://www.youtube.com/watch?v=c3EgHMTDtng; "Ukraina. Den' Pobedy. Ded", *IS* channel, 27 April 2015, https://www.youtube.com/watch?v=eQk6Uup EJuA.

used by the characters in the clips alludes to the civic (and multi-ethnic) concept of this nation.

Conclusion

The organized movement of Afghan veterans in independent Ukraine is an interesting example of how a group with a common experience of Soviet army service and a specific memorial culture rooted in ideas of "military brotherhood" and "masculine values of courage and dignity", as well as in Soviet nostalgia and paternalism, can be transformed into actors in civil society. The Eurorevolution of 2013–2014 proved the veterans' potential for emancipation and showed that the veterans' organizations had the capacity to become a real civil society structure, independent from the state and exerting pressure on the state not only with a view to getting social benefits for the group, but also in order to change the whole political sphere and social care in Ukraine. How this potential will develop in the future, however, is still an open question in the current situation of war and deep economic crisis. One can predict that there will also likely be interesting developments on this front in terms of the interaction between the different groups of veterans, old and new. For the moment, it would appear that the Afghan veterans are trying to identify themselves both with the veterans of World War II, as the latter still have very high symbolic capital, and with the new group of veterans from the war in the Donbas. It also remains an open question whether the veterans' activities will ultimately contribute to the creation of a new quality for civil society, which in the Ukrainian case is still very much built upon informal interpersonal relations and spontaneous self-organization, and not on the base of institutions and impersonal trust.

In many cases, the veterans are trying to make themselves useful for the state with their contribution to "patriotic education", but in Ukraine there is no single state ideology, and it is impossible to arrive at a Soviet-style "big deal" whereby the activists work for the benefit of the state in exchange for considerable social benefits. The contiguous tradition of the Ukrainian state to avoid its social responsibility clearly survived the revolution, as the attempts in the fall of 2014 to cut back the veterans' social benefits showed. The new group of veterans of the Donbas war is only starting its struggle with state bureaucracy for the recognition of every participant and consistent fulfillment of the laws on social support. The rhetoric of the state legislation alludes to socialist standards of comprehensive social support, but the practice is rather neo-liberal.

The Maidan and the war in the Donbas in 2014–2015 challenged the very existence of the transnational identity of the "former Soviet–Afghan War veteran", as the majority of veterans in the Russian Federation and Ukraine took opposite sides in this conflict. An important part of this process has been numerous splits in personal relations between not only veterans' groups, but also relatives and friends. The rhetoric of "internationalist duty" has thus been discredited by the mercenaries from Russia who joined the conflict on the side of separatists. The two sides in the conflict use two different myths of the Afghan veteran—the Ukrainian patriot and civil society activist, on one side, and the defender of imperial ideas of a quasi-Soviet polity with Russian statist rhetoric and paternalism, on the other. It is becoming more and more difficult to avoid declaring allegiance to one of these two sides. What we are witnessing in contemporary Ukraine may perhaps be the end of post-Soviet ambivalence and borderland vagueness. This process of delineating new mental borders is a painful one, especially now that some of the Ukrainian *afhantsi* have joined a different project: the self-proclaimed Donets'k and Luhans'k People's Republics.

In the current situation of war, the veterans' organizations and public opinion are working together for the creation of a coherent (though in many respects problematic) narrative of a continuous Ukrainian national struggle for freedom and independence. Afghan veterans have occupied the position of the descendants of the "Great Patriotic War" victors, and of the "fathers", or senior comrades, of the new veterans of the ATO in the Donbas—not only through their promotion of this sort of discourse in *afhantsi* memoir literature and in public commemorations, but also through their active participation in civil disobedience, including the Maidan in 2013–2014, and in the current war. It is still unclear to what extent this new discourse will resemble the Russian official discourse with its broad inclusion of imperial, "national", and Soviet aspects of "military glory" into one teleological narrative construction, especially taking into account the fact that Ukrainian propaganda is tending to cope with the problems posed by its Russian counterpart in a reactive, rather than a proactive, way.

Another significant aspect is that the commemoration of the Soviet–Afghan War has not been discussed in relation to the "Decommunization laws" adopted in April 2015 and aimed at excluding the Soviet (actually, not communist) aspects of memory and identity from the public sphere (the only exception is made for the memorials, monuments, and plaques commemorating World War II—no other wars are mentioned either in the laws themselves or in the related debates). This stands in contrast to the situation in, for instance, Lithuania, where the Soviet–Afghan War was uncompromisingly condemned, and where the veterans were neglected during the post-Soviet period and only recently attained the status of victims of Soviet repression.[93] In independent Ukraine, the Afghan veterans are much more numerous, and their impact and recognition much more visible, both because of the partial inclusion of the Soviet experience into the new national canon and because of the activity of *afhantsi* in the third sector. However, the future development of the *afhantsi* community and identity and of the newly emerging group of ATO veterans, in a Ukrainian state that is simultaneously nationalizing, striving towards "western" values, and fighting a war, will be an important case for studying many aspects, such as the transformation of civil society, the social welfare system, public discourses on history and memory, and generational changes.

---

[93] Vėjūnė Domanskaitė-Gota, Danutė Gailienė and Jurate Girdziušaitė, "The Trauma of War: Research on Lithuanian Veterans of the Afghanistan War after Seventeen Years", *Afganistano karo veteranai*, http://www.afganai.lt/Leidy ba/The_Trauma.pdf.

Post-Soviet Legacies of Afghanistan:
A Comparative Perspective[1]

Jan C. Behrends

Anybody who lived in Russia during the 1990s was familiar with the plight of veterans of the Soviet–Afghan War, the so-called *afgantsy*. Although controversies about the war had begun to disappear from the Russian media and—with a few prominent exceptions—many veterans kept a low profile, they remained highly visible in cities like Moscow and St. Petersburg. Crippled vets—often wearing the beret and the trademark *maika*-shirt—begging in metro stations or in public squares became an iconic image of the transition. Their mutilated bodies were not merely reminders of the vicious fighting on the Hindu Kush. They also symbolized the inability of the post-Soviet welfare state to address the needs of disabled soldiers who had served the USSR in its last war. In a way, the veterans' misery represented at once the legacy of late socialism and the hardship of the post-Soviet transformation. Their fate reminded the public of the cruelty with which the Soviet regime treated its own people. They were mainly seen as victims of a bygone empire, of the draft, the failed medical system and, more generally, of the lost cause of "internationalism." Yet, other perspectives on the veteran's experience have faded away or were never seriously discussed. The Soviet soldier as perpetrator of war crimes was hardly mentioned in the post-Soviet public sphere. The expertise of the *afgantsy* in using military force was often used after 1991 but hardly problematized. Until the state-sponsored rebirth of nationalism and hero culture under Vladimir Putin, the narrative regarding the Soviet–Afghan War was one

[1]   Research for this paper was partially funded by the Leibniz-Gemeinschaft, SAP grant "Physical Violence and State Legitimacy in Late Socialism" and by the Centre for Contemporary History (ZZF) in Potsdam, Germany. I would like to acknowledge the help of Philip Decker, New York, in the editing of this text.

of victimhood. This narrative often blocked any contemplation of the ambivalences and the actual consequences of the war in Afghanistan—consequences for the veterans but also for the societies of the post-Soviet space more broadly.

Returning veterans are a problem for any society. While the question of reward and recognition for military service goes back to ancient times, it gained particular significance in the age of mass-mobilization. After the First World War, failure to re-integrate millions of men returning from the battlefield caused turmoil and is widely seen as a cause of political radicalism and instability throughout Europe.[2] Those who did not find their way back to civilian life used their military skills in the political struggles that marred the continent after the war. After the Second World War, the United States and Great Britain, not wishing to repeat the mistakes that had contributed to war, went to great lengths to ensure a successful re-integration of veterans. They were given privileged access to college education ("GI Bill") and, especially in Britain, to the workplace.[3] West Germany tried to integrate veterans of the Wehrmacht through a generous welfare system in order to appease them politically and win them over to the new republic.[4] By contrast, Stalin's Soviet Union lacked both the resources and the will to establish sim-

---

[2]   See e.g. Hagen Schulze, *Freikorps und Republik 1918–1920* (Boppard: Boldt, 1969); Mimmo Franzinelli, *Squadristi. Protagonisti e tecniche della violenza fascista, 1919–1922* (Rome: Oscar Mandadori, 2004); Antoine Prost, *Les anciens combattants, 1918–1940* (Paris: Gallimard, 2014).

[3]   Michael D. Gambone, *The Greatest Generation Comes Home: The Veteran in American Society* (College Station, TX: A&M Press, 2005); Suzanne Mettler, *Soldiers to Citizens: The G.I. Bill and the Making of the Greatest Generation* (Oxford: Oxford University Press, 2005); Kathleen Frydl, *The GI Bill* (Cambridge, UK: Cambridge University Press, 2009); Alan Allport, *Demobbed: Coming Home after the Second World War* (New Haven, Conn.: Yale University Press, 2009).

[4]   James M. Diehl, *The Thanks of the Fatherland: German Veterans after the Second World War* (Chapel Hill, NC: University of North Carolina Press, 1993); Jay Lockenour, *Soldiers as Citizens: Former Wehrmacht Officers in the Federal Republic of Germany* (Lincoln, NE: University of Nebraska Press, 2001); Svenja Goltermann, *Die Gesellschaft der Überlebenden: deutsche Kriegsgefangene und ihre Gewalterfahrungen im Zweiten Weltkrieg* (Munich: Deutsche Verlags Anstalt, 2009; Jörg Echternkamp, *Soldaten im Nachkrieg. Historische Deutungskonflikte und westdeutsche Demokratisierung* (Berlin: DeGruyter, 2014).

ilar programs. After the "Great Patriotic War" the victorious veterans were disappointed by their state. Stalin's priority was to make his new empire fit for the Cold War. That meant veterans—even disabled ones—had to fully rejoin the labor force.[5] There were few special benefits or entitlements for invalids—not to mention other veterans.[6] Only after decades of struggle would Soviet veterans achieve recognition and some social benefits under the more benevolent rule of Leonid Brezhnev—himself a fellow veteran of the war.[7] Late in their lives they acquired prestige and status as a result of the Soviet cult of the "Great Fatherland War." In any event, the problem of properly "bringing the boys back home" was not limited to the USSR. The USA famously struggled to find a place for the veterans of the Vietnam War after having lost the battle for Indochina in 1973.[8]

How the Specifics of Afghanistan Shaped the Legacy of the Last Soviet War

In order to understand the fate of Soviet veterans of the Afghan War we need to understand the character of that conflict.[9] To begin with, the Soviet leadership only reluctantly came to the rescue of the Afghan regime in the fateful winter of 1979. The USSR was never as committed to this war as the United States had been in Vietnam. In the beginning, Moscow's propaganda pretended there was no war—

---

5   Beate Fieseler, *Arme Sieger. Die Invaliden des „Großen Vaterländischen Krieges" der Sowjetunion* (Cologne: Böhlau, 2013).

6   Mark Edele, "Soviet Veterans as an Entitlement Group, 1945-1955", *Slavic Review* 65, no. 1 (2006): 18–33.

7   Mark Edele, *Soviet Veterans of the Second World War: A Popular Movement in an Authoritarian Society* (Oxford: Oxford University Press, 2008).

8   Wilbur J. Scott, *Vietnam Veterans since the War: The Politics of PTSD, Agent Orange and National Memory* (Norman: University of Oklahoma Press, 2004); Mark Bolton, *Failing our Veterans: The GI Bill and the Vietnam Generation* (New York: NYU Press, 2014).

9   See e.g. Mark Galeotti, *Afghanistan: The Soviet Union's Last War* (London: Frank Cass, 2001); Rodric Braithwaite, *Afgantsy: The Russians in Afghanistan, 1979–1989* (Oxford: Oxford University Press, 2011); Artemy M. Kalinovsky, *A Long Goodbye: The Soviet Withdrawal from Afghanistan* (Cambridge, Mass.: Harvard University Press, 2011).

just an "internationalist mission"—and hid the fighting and the casualties from the Soviet public.[10] For the first couple of years, the myth of "internationalism" could not be questioned. Even when Moscow came around to acknowledge the conflict the lack of legitimacy remained. This lack of legitimacy has characterized the perception of the war ever since. Its strategic and military necessity was not accepted by Soviet society. Therefore it has a different status from other wars of Russian history—especially when compared with the "Great Patriotic War".[11] The Russian veterans of Afghanistan would not be celebrated as defenders of the homeland.

But there were several other reasons for the negative perception of the Soviet–Afghan War. First and foremost, of course, was military stalemate. Since 1945, Soviet society had celebrated a victorious Army it had thought to be invincible.[12] This myth of the Soviet forces was shattered in the mountains of Afghanistan. Another source of disapproval was that this war was fought during the relatively peaceful years of late socialism. The army and society did not necessarily share the same ideals anymore. While public life under Stalin was deeply militarized—especially, of course, in wartime— Soviet society under Brezhnev had different values and ideas. Times were more civil, but much of the military still lived by the outdated rules of Stalin and his henchmen.[13] The times of mobilization and struggle were over and the population was either busy enjoying the

---

[10]   On the Soviet involvement in Afghanistan and the losses, see Grigorii F. Krivosheev, *Grif sekretnosti sniat. Poteri Vooruzhennykh Sil SSSR v voinakh, boevykh deistviiakh i voennykh konfliktakh. Statisticheskoe issledovanie* (Moscow: Voenizdat, 1993).

[11]   On the Cult of the Second World War, see e.g. Nina Tumarkin, *The Living and the Dead: The Rise and Fall of the Cult of World War II in the Soviet Union* (New York: Basic Books, 1994); Jutta Scherrer, „Siegesmythos versus Vergangenheitsaufarbeitung", in *Mythen der Nationen – 1945: Arena der Erinnerungen*, ed. Monika Flacke (Mainz: von Zabern, 2004), 619–57.

[12]   On the Soviet Army's decline in late socialism see William E. Odom, *The Collapse of the Soviet Military* (New Haven, Conn.: Yale University Press, 1998).

[13]   Jan C. Behrends, "War, Violence and the Military during Late Socialism and Transition. Five Case Studies on the USSR, Russia, and Yugoslavia", *Nationalities Papers* 43 (2015): 667–81.

benefits of socialism or, in the case of the younger generation, aspiring toward the sort of consumerism available in the West.[14] Both war and military culture had become alien to much of everyday life in the USSR. The war in Afghanistan brought them back into everyday life.

Furthermore, the war in Afghanistan was quite different from World War Two or, rather, from the way the "Great Fatherland War" was officially remembered. It was fought not on the wide open plains of Eastern Europe but in the mountains of Central Asia. From the very beginning in December 1979, the war in Afghanistan was an extremely violent affair.[15] It was a partisan war fought with little restraint from either side. The logic of violence was more similar to that of civil wars.[16] There were few safe places outside Kabul, but there was no clear front line. Instead of "heroic" tank battles, the war took the form of local scrimmages and raids. The laws of war were hardly ever observed; prisoners were seldom taken and civilians were rarely spared. Millions of Afghans became refugees. Most of the country was turned into a *Gewaltraum*, a space where violence was the dominant resource.[17] Survival within the violent spaces of Afghanistan depended on the adaptation of the combatants to the rules of survival.

During their duty in the Hindu Kush regular Soviet youths were transformed by the wild war they were ordered to fight. They learned to survive, to fight, and to kill. Some of them started to enjoy being violent. For months and years they lived in a space where the weak enjoyed no protection and where the stability (later labeled

---

[14] See e.g. Donald J. Raleigh, *Soviet Baby Boomers: An Oral History of Russia's Cold War Generation* (Oxford: Oxford University Press, 2012).

[15] See Jan C. Behrends, "'Some Call Us Heroes, Others Call Us Killers.' Experiencing a Sphere of Violence: Soviet Soldiers in the Afghan War (1979–1989)", *Nationalities Papers* 43 (2015) (in press); idem, „Afghanistan als Gewaltraum. Sowjetische Soldaten erzählen vom Partisanenkrieg", in *SovietNam. Die UdSSR in Afghanistan*, ed. Tanja Penter and Esther Maier (Paderborn: Schöningh, in press).

[16] Stathis N. Kalyvas, *The Logic of Violence in Civil War* (Cambridge, UK: Cambridge University Press, 2006).

[17] See Jörg Baberowski, „Einleitung. Ermöglichungsräume exzessiver Gewalt", in *Gewalträume. Soziale Ordnungen im Ausnahmezustand*, ed. idem and Gabriele Metzler (Frankfurt am Main: Campus, 2012), 7–27.

"stagnation") of the late socialist USSR seemed far away. Those who survived and returned home brought their experiences as well as their new skill with weaponry with them. For many, we now know, it was only their first encounter with violence. Yet it would haunt them for the rest of their lives. But Afghanistan was also a late socialist experience for those who served there. All the ills of the Brezhnev era could also be found in the Hindu Kush: *Afgantsy* experienced ethnic tension, corruption, drug abuse and irresponsibility of officers while serving in the Army.

Finally, the Soviet–Afghan War may be understood by thinking about the way it coincided with the fall of the Soviet Union. The USSR's defeat on the battlefield was quickly followed by its dissolution. When Mikhail Gorbachev assumed power in 1985, he understood that the war in Afghanistan was a lost cause and ordered that the Soviet Army should retreat as quickly as possible. His decision reflected the problems on the ground in Afghanistan. But it also corresponded to his reform ideas. The ongoing war contradicted the new *gensek's* policies: both Gorbachev's return to détente with the West as well as his attempt to further civilize Soviet politics and society were undermined by the Army's occupation abroad.[18] Still, it took the Soviet leadership four years to finally terminate their engagement in Kabul.[19] When the last Soviet servicemen crossed the Amu Darya River in 1989, Gorbachev's perestroika itself was already in crisis. Roughly three years later, the USSR would disintegrate. At the same time, the war had deeply tarnished the image of the Soviet Army.[20] As such, the veterans of a lost war became veterans of a lost empire. They had to integrate into the post-Soviet reality of 15 sovereign states that would develop along different trajectories.

---

[18]   See Jan C. Behrends, „Oktroyierte Zivilisierung. Genese und Grenzen des sowjetischen Gewaltverzichts 1989", in *1989 und die Rolle der Gewalt*, ed. Martin Sabrow (Göttingen: Wallstein, 2012), 401–23.

[19]   Kalinovsky, *Long Goodbye*.

[20]   Manfred Sapper, *Die Auswirkungen des Afghanistankrieges auf die Sowjetgesellschaft. Eine Studie zum Legitimitätsverlust des Militärischen in der Sowjetunion* (Münster: LIT, 1994).

Yet this is not the only paradox that can be observed when studying Afghanistan veterans. It is worth noting how much the development of civil society under Mikhail Gorbachev was tied to the violent experiences of the Soviet era. *Memorial's* raison d'être was to enlighten the public about the Stalinist terror, the "soldiers' mothers" fought for those victimized by hazing in the Armed Forces, and the *afgantsy*, who had their own violent experiences, fought for the recognition of their status as veterans. Thus, some of the most vibrant and influential civil society initiatives of the late Soviet period were tied to the mass-violence that had characterized Soviet rule from Stalin to Brezhnev. In the last years of the USSR the development of civil society and the legacy of violence were closely connected.

The Meaning of the Soviet–Afghan War for Post-Soviet Space

The associations founded by Afghanistan veterans and their impact on late and post-Soviet society have been studied since the 1990s.[21] It has also been noted that many Soviet officers that served in Afghanistan went on to prominent careers in the Armed Forces or in politics. Still, the impact of the Afghan experience was much broader than these official organizations and prominent figures would suggest. It includes a new culture of war in so-called "goriachie tochki" ("hot spots") as well as specific ways of memorializing these wars that differed from World War Two.[22] The war in Afghanistan also triggered a (pop-)cultural phenomenon, beginning in the 1980s and continuing ever since: songs, poems, music, and movies about the war have profoundly influenced the post-Soviet world. Certain images—like the helicopter gunships ("Mil Mi-24") or soldiers in mountainous terrain are closely associated with this war.

---

[21]   See e.g. Sapper, *Die Auswirkungen des Afghanistankrieges*; Galeotti, *Afghanistan*.

[22]   Serguei A. Oushakine, *The Patriotism of Despair: Nation, War, and Loss in Russia* (Ithaca, NY: Cornell University Press, 2009).

Expressions like "gruz 200" and zinc coffins haunt public memory in Russia and throughout the former USSR.[23]

Looking back from the present, the proficiency of *afgantsy* in the use of military force, their combat experience, and their willingness to use their skills may be seen as more important than the veterans' associations or the impact on pop-culture. The Soviet–Afghan War and the subsequent history of (civil) wars in the (post-)Soviet space—Karabakh, Chechnya, Transnistria, Georgia, and most recently the Maidan and Donbas, to name just the larger conflicts—manifest the significance of violence for the post-Soviet transition. This ongoing succession of wars even suggests a different periodization of late socialist and post-Soviet history. For a long time the rise of Mikhail Gorbachev in 1985 and the resulting liberalization of Soviet politics and society was interpreted as the most important caesura of the last decades of the USSR. Perestroika was seen as a cause for the dissolution of the single-party-state and the Soviet empire, as well as the starting point for a wider democratization of public life, first in the USSR and then in its successor states. The more or less peaceful end of the Soviet Union ("Armageddon Averted") was hailed as yet another example of peaceful change.[24] Many historians argued that 1991 followed in the footsteps of 1989. The history of war and violence in the post-Soviet space, however, points to different causalities. Looking back at the string of armed conflicts, we may consider 1979—the Soviet invasion of Afghanistan—a turning point in Soviet and Russian history. The long peace that had begun in 1945

---

23 "Gruz 200" is the Soviet military code for fallen soldiers that are shipped home. It was first introduced during the Soviet–Afghan War. Cf. the widely read interviews with Afghan veterans by Svetlana Alexievich, *Zinky Boys: Soviet Voices from the Afghan War* (New York: W.W. Norton, 1992). In 2007 a movie called *Gruz 200* directed by Aleksei Balabanov was released in Russia.

24 Cf. Stephen Kotkin, *Armageddon Averted: The Soviet Collapse, 1970–2000* (Oxford: Oxford University Press, 2001). See also Leon Aron, *Roads to the Temple: Truth, Memory, Ideas, and Ideals in the Making of the Russian Revolution, 1987–1991* (New Haven, Conn.: Yale University Press, 2012); Serhii Plokhy, *The Last Empire: The Final Days of the Soviet Union* (New York: Basic Books, 2014).

now ended abruptly and a new age of wild wars erupted.[25] This age of wild wars in the post-Soviet space still continues.

Two arguments support this argument for 1979 as a caesura: first, the forms of conflict after Afghanistan remained similar. Undeclared wars that did not follow international conventions, often characterized by unrestrained violence, became common in the post-Soviet space. Many of the practices first used on the Afghan battlefield—the shooting and torture of prisoners, the raids against towns and villages ("razzia"), the crimes against civilians, the looting—could also be found in post-Soviet conflicts. The formal structures of the Soviet Army disintegrated—a process that started in Afghanistan. A new caste of warriors ("kontraktniki") emerged. Military structures were often gradually replaced by local strongmen and warlords that now not only dominate in the theater of war but also govern vast areas. Chechnya's Ramzan Kadyrov is just the most prominent example.[26] Secondly, the actors have remained the same, i.e. *afgantsy* have been present at many hot spots. This is, of course, not to say that the majority of the *afgantsy* fought in the wars of the 1990s. But a significant number of them did. From the massacre in Tbilisi in April 1989, to the storming of the White House in October 1993, to the two campaigns in Chechnya, the Maidan in Kiev, and the war in Donbas, veterans of the Afghan War have been involved. In fact, *afgantsy* can often be found on both sides of a conflict; they do not necessarily share political goals. Rather, they seem to be bonded by the experience of violence and by their willingness to use it to achieve their goals. Mark Galeotti, who wrote in 1995 that the invasion did not result in the Sovietization of Afghanistan but in the Afghanization of the USSR, certainly was prophetic.[27]

---

[25] Jan C. Behrends, „Ein Jahr der Gewalt. Russlands Staatskrise und der Krieg gegen die Ukraine", *Osteuropa* 65, no. 3 (2015): 47–66. For an overview see Matthew Sussex (ed.), *Conflict in the former USSR* (Cambridge: Cambridge University Press, 2012).

[26] Kimberly Marten, *Warlords: Strong-arm Brokers in Weak States* (Ithaca, NY: Cornell University Press, 2012), 102–38.

[27] Galeotti, *Afghanistan*, 1.

In particular, the Maidan revolution and the subsequent Russian invasion of the Donbas underscore this perspective.[28] War, military action, and violence are seen by all parties as a legitimate resource in political struggle and geopolitical conflict. Both Kiev and Moscow sent "their" *afgantsy* to the front lines and, in some cases, the *afgantsy* themselves volunteered to serve. While protest movements—like in Russia in 2011/12—tend to start peacefully, they can easily be radicalized by police violence.[29] This is not to say that political violence is inevitable. On the contrary: it can usually be traced to specific decisions, personalities, or institutions. Generally, violent conflicts do not randomly break out.[30] They are usually not triggered by differences of language, culture, or memory. Rather, they are started deliberately by those who want to use violent means to achieve political ends. This was clearly the case both on the Maidan and in the Donbas. Those instructed, motivated, and rewarded by Russia waited for orders to destroy Ukrainian statehood and end civil life. They took administrative centers and police stations in targeted areas.[31] The "separatists" used their weapons to establish authority. These armed men had brought their military expertise to these peaceful areas and managed to turn them into a *Gewaltraum* within a matter of days. Many of them had seen the same thing happen before in other post-Soviet conflicts. They knew what they were doing. Expertise in the use of political violence is by no means rare in the post-Soviet realm. And crucially, as I have pointed out, this is

---

[28]   Andrew Wilson, *Ukraine Crisis: What it Means for the West* (New Haven, Conn: Yale University Press, 2014).

[29]   On the Russian protest movement, see Mischa Gabowitsch, *Putin Kaputt?! Russlands neue Protestkultur* (Berlin: Suhrkamp, 2013); Ben Judah, *Fragile Empire: How Russia Fell in and out of Love with Vladimir Putin* (New Haven, Conn.: Yale University Press, 2013), 169–274.

[30]   On understanding violence see e.g. Heinrich Popitz, *Phänomene der Macht* (Tübingen: Mohr Siebeck, 1992); Wolfgang Sofsky, *Traktat über die Gewalt* (Frankfurt am Main: Fischer, 1996); Randall Collins, *Violence: A Micro-Sociological Theory* (Princeton, NJ: Princeton University Press, 2007); Jan Phillip Reemtsma, *Trust and Violence: An Essay on a Modern Relationship* (Princeton, NJ: Princeton University Press, 2012).

[31]   Nikolay Mitrokhin, „Infiltration, Instruktion, Invasion. Russlands Krieg in der Ukraine," *Osteuropa*, 55, no. 8 (2014): 3–16; English version: "Infiltration, Instruction, Invasion: Russia's War in the Donbass", *Journal of Soviet and Post-Soviet Politics and Society* 1, no. 1 (2015): 219–49.

a development that may also be traced back to the war in Afghanistan.

The Afghanistan Veterans: Who Are They?

Academic discourse on this issue tends to focus on the *afgantsy* as actors and as a pressure group in different post-Soviet states. The work presented here shows the consequences of the fall of the Soviet Union for veterans in Russia, Ukraine, and Tajikistan and underscores the differences between these experiences. More broadly, however, the essay by Yaacov Ro'i as well as the following case studies raise the question of whether it makes sense to view Afghanistan veterans as a distinct social group. In many ways, there seems to be more disconnect than cohesion. Networks between veterans are loosely knit and a quarter century after the war narratives differ from country to country. The *afgantsy*, like other former Soviet citizens, were forced to cope with different post-communist settings. While the shared experience of the war continues to matter, the realities of post-Soviet nation building are dividing veterans. Those once bonded by war find themselves in new societies and potentially in new conflicts.

Still, the Afghanistan War remains part of the Soviet legacy. Yaacov Ro'i demonstrates how discourse about the war and veterans originated in the late Soviet era. He points to the fact that the image of the war and of the soldiers who fought in it was contested from the beginning. He also points to the problem of re-integration into civilian life and stresses the social and psychological ordeal veterans faced. It is paramount to remember that we learn more about those who fail to integrate than about former servicemen who lead a normal life or even benefitted from the war experience. Many *afgantsy* became visible because they organized themselves. Upon their return veterans attempted to organize into local and national associations. This movement was initially quite successful. To what extent veterans of the "Great Patriotic War" served as an example to the *afgantsy,* is unclear. Clearly, they struggled for entitlements as well as recognition—a struggle that continues to this day. An interesting question remains the relationship of these organized veterans to the state. While many took a critical stance and were clearly formed out of disappointment, their leaders still professed loyalty to the USSR and its successor states and tried to allocate government resources toward their organizations. Overall, the history of the veterans' associations points to the relative weakness of post-Soviet civil society vis-à-vis the state. They were often reduced to being petitioners. The (post-)Soviet leviathan—although it either could or would not provide adequately —remained the main force in public life. It controlled access to the mass media and to the sparse public resources.

The Russian experience is certainly central to understanding the post-Soviet fate of Afghanistan veterans. Russia was not merely the largest successor of the USSR; it was also the only state that embraced the legacy of the USSR. The Russian Federation viewed itself as the direct heir to the Soviet Union—and to its wars. Michael Galbas explains how the troubled times of the 1990s affected the Afghan veterans' self-perception and social status. In the early years of Yeltsin's presidency there was no functioning welfare system. The collapse of the Soviet identity—which had given meaning to the Afghanistan War with such notions as "internationalism"—left a void. What remained were the official associations as well as the sense of comradeship instilled by the war. Many of the Russian veterans acted like quintessential Soviet citizens: they expected a strong state to care for them. Alas, such a state was not to be found in the 1990s. Still, some of the standard narratives about the war were shaped in these years: the soldiers as those betrayed by incompetent politicians, a sense of duty during a meaningless war, the idea of comradeship in hard times, and a nihilistic heroism.

At any rate, the Chechen Wars confirmed the central role of the military for the Russian state.[32] While the Armed Forces shrank, neither Gorbachev nor Yeltsin reformed them in any meaningful way. The *ésprit de corps* of the Soviet Army—imperial and deeply suspicious of the West—firmly remained in place. While Yeltsin had

---

[32]   On Chechnya, see Valery Tishkov, *Chechnya: Life in a War-Torn Society* (Berkeley, Cal.: University of California Press, 2004); Emma Gilligan, *Terror in Chechnya: Russia and the Tragedy of Civilians in War* (Princeton, NJ: Princeton University Press, 2010); Mark Galeotti, *Russia's Wars in Chechnya 1994–2009* (Oxford: Osprey, 2014).

relied on the army to sustain his power—in 1993 and then 1994/95 against the Chechens—it was Vladimir Putin's all-out revival of militarism that changed the situation for the *afgantsy*. The autocratic president attempted to put a positive spin on the Soviet–Afghan War. He revived the militaristic "patriotic education" for children that had been a trademark of Soviet power. Afghanistan veterans were assigned their place in his resurrected pantheon of Russian heroes. In many ways they now occupy the positions once held by the veterans of the Second World War. Under Putin, the associations of Afghanistan veterans came under strict tutelage of the power vertical. Galbas rightly points to the fact that militarism—as in the USSR— once again serves as a means of in- and exclusion. During the radicalization of the regime in reaction to the conflict with the West and in anticipation of "color revolution," the Kremlin tried to mobilize these veterans as defenders of the existing order. *Afgantsy* were supposed to lead the violent mob of the "anti-Maidan."

The comparison between the Russian case and that of Ukraine is especially instructive. As recent events have shown, Ukrainian society developed quite differently from Russia's after 1991. It never embraced the cult of a strong state and leader in the way many Russians continue to. To a certain degree the Ukrainian elite accepted competitive politics; officials could be voted out of office. The Ukrainian view of the Soviet past is also more ambivalent and contested in Ukraine. Iryna Sklokina discusses the role of Afghanistan veterans during this period of Ukrainian nation-building, i.e. from the 1990s onwards. Many officers with experience in Afghanistan opted to serve in the Ukrainian Army after 1991. Thus, they chose to remain in the cosmos of the (post)Soviet military. Others—like their Russian comrades—tried to struggle for social entitlements. Apart from these welfare issues, Ukrainian *afgantsy* have successfully styled themselves as being apolitical or above the dirty business of post-Soviet power struggles. They have tried to build a moral ground for themselves. Sklokina demonstrates that this "above the fray" attitude does not mean that they shrank from the private sphere or business. On the contrary: Afghanistan veterans have been decisively involved in the turbulent events of the last two years. As members of the "last Soviet generation," they were drawn to the Maidan to protect "their children" from the brutality of Victor Yanukovych's forces. Their attitude may be summed up by the statement "we defend the people." Some *afgantsy* also played a role in the establishment of volunteer battalions to defend Ukraine against the covert Russian invasion in the spring of 2014. Again, their proficiency in fighting wild wars distinguished them. Thus, the anti-politics of Ukrainian *afgantsy* turned out to be quite political. They played and continue to play a role in the ongoing process of Ukrainian nation-building and in the defense of the Eastern border against Russia. Tragically, this role has severed their ties to Russian veterans who found themselves on the other side of the conflict. Former comrades became enemies in this violent post-Soviet theater.

The Tajik case presented by Markus Göransson confirms some of the assumptions about *afgantsy* outlined above. Again it is impossible to identify the local Afghanistan veterans with a particular political position. During the transition and the civil war in Tajikistan the veterans acted in the political arena, but it proved hard for them to rally around a common cause. In a war fought by irregular troops their expertise was, again, valuable and the state tried to enlist them to its side. During the war, however, they split up along the same fault lines as the general population. What really set them apart was their experience of war and their willingness to use force. During the breakdown of order in the early 1990s—which must have reminded the veterans of the situation they had faced across the Amu Darya in neighboring Afghanistan during the 1980s —they tried to style themselves as a force of order and protector of the populace. In general, the cases of Tajik *afgantsy* in the early 1990s, the Armenian veterans that fought in Nagorno-Karabakh, or the Ukrainian veterans in 2014 do not seem to be very different. When called upon, some of the *afgantsy* were willing to use the skills acquired long ago for other regimes and causes. The similarities between the Tajik case and the ongoing war in Ukraine point to the long-term effects of the war in Afghanistan. Afghanistan veterans could be used as a resource for local elites, but they could also defend their own agency.

Some Conclusions

The processes and experiences that began with the Politburo's decision to invade in late 1979 still impact political culture in the post-Soviet sphere. A new type of war was fought at the Hindu Kush, and it resulted in a large number of veterans who had learned to fight such a war. These *afgantsy* returned to the USSR at a time when the single-party-state was collapsing. More than others, they were qualified to engage in the violent struggles that began to shape the post-Soviet sphere. They were the "violent few" of the last Soviet generation.

The war in Afghanistan was shaped by the problems of late socialism. The dysfunctional army, the lack of legitimacy of party rule, the empty concept of "internationalism" as well as the fragmentation of troops along social and ethnic lines were all characteristic of the last Soviet decade. None of these things disappeared after 1991, but problems evolved along with society. The fate of the *afgantsy* and their associations was determined by the post-Soviet situation. Veterans in the Baltic Republics found themselves at home in states that vastly differed from those in Central Asia or even in Russia or Ukraine. The differences between Russia and the other post-Soviet states are instructive. While Ukraine made attempts at nation-building, Russia—already under Yeltsin, then even more radically under Putin—adopted a post-imperial identity. The Russian Federation also embraced the use of military violence in political conflict—in contrast to Ukraine, which remained peaceful until the escalation of the Maidan in the winter of 2013/14 and the subsequent Russian invasion of the Donbas. Different degrees of violence resulted in different opportunities for Afghanistan veterans. Therefore, Russia, Central Asia, and the Caucasus were areas where they were active as warriors. In other states they were active in the civil arena.

In all parts of the former USSR the *afgantsy* struggled for public recognition. On these issues local context was also paramount. While in the Baltic States Afghanistan veterans have presented themselves as victims of communism, Russia has aggressively tried to normalize the Afghan experience by ascribing a new sort of nihilistic heroism to the war. This is expressed in local monuments but also in mass media. In all post-Soviet countries the initial phase of scandalization of the war ended quickly. With different emphasis, Afghanistan veterans are now presented as victims and heroes. The extreme violence in the war, the war crimes and atrocities are hardly remembered anywhere. The memory culture emphasizes the suffering of the Soviet conscripts and soldiers—while the Afghans are mostly out of the picture. Their loss—in numbers far greater—hardly plays a role. Afghanistan has been reduced to being the scenic place where the drama played out—the mountains, gorges, valleys. But the Afghan people do not play a significant role in post-Soviet memory. They are the forgotten people in this conflict.

As discussed above, another issue that united veterans was the fight for social entitlements. This was especially difficult in the 1990s, when the Soviet welfare system collapsed. In the beginning, the *afgantsy* sought international aid—they even turned to Vietnam veterans in the US for support. Over time this struggle was nationalized because welfare was run by the new nation-states. While the struggle for social recognition seems to have been more successful, the fight for concrete entitlements continues. One may argue that Afghan veterans have had experiences with their respective states that are similar to those of veterans of the "Great Patriotic War." Recognition in the form of medals was easier to achieve than material benefits. Overall, post-Soviet states never made it a priority to care for the veterans of this Soviet war. We see a history of neglect throughout the entire post-Soviet sphere.

What is the significance of the Soviet–Afghan War today? As I outlined above, it may be read as the starting point for a history of violent struggle that has shaped the (post-)Soviet experience. The *afgantsy* were often found in the middle of these conflicts. Some of their most prominent names will be remembered in textbooks: Dudaev, Rutskoi, or Grachev. Most, however, will remain as anonymous as the handicapped that begged for bread and money in the Moscow metro during the 1990s. The difference between the *afganets* as a military officer, politician, activist, or beggar reminds us of the complex legacies of the war in Afghanistan. In any case, the war's human cost was high and its consequences long outlived those old men who ordered the last Soviet generation to respond to the call from Kabul for "internationalist help." In the post-Soviet development, the experience of Afghanistan tipped the balance between violence and civility. Thus, a war that was fought far away from most Soviet citizens in the 1980s brought consequences that affected many of them from the 1990s onwards—both veterans and civilians alike.

Faces of the Lithuanian *Afganai*

Anna Reich

Zigmas Stankus, of Miražas Klaipėda
(previous page) Jonas Vaitkūnas in his bedroom
Vilnius, Lithuania

I began working with the Lithuanian Association of Afghan War Veterans in early 2014 with the purpose of creating a photo book portraying the lives of veterans from the Soviet–Afghan War. In addition to the photographic component of this project, I conducted interviews with many veterans, discussing the realities of Post-Traumatic Stress Disorder and the conditions of their lives today. "The first year back was the most difficult, my wife could not relate to me," said Zigmas Stankus, "I drank for one year. Then I changed, I began to adapt to society." Other veterans are unanimous in sharing Stankus' sentiment—the first few years after the war were the greatest challenge. Vytas Lukšys, who was selected by local scouts to fight during the early years of the war, explained that initially no one would dare to bring up any psychological trauma to avoid being stigmatized. "There was no such thing as Post-Traumatic Stress Disorder. The psychological effects of war were not acknowledged," Lukšys described. It is easy to see how the veterans came to be referred to as "invisible people".

Although they wished to assimilate into society, the consensus among the veterans with whom I worked is that the lack of social programs and assistance and the unpopularity of their cause greatly hindered their reintegration into the public. Not only did they want social guarantees and to maintain veteran status after the dissolution of the Soviet Union, but they desired the camaraderie from the past and an understanding that they felt they only received from other veterans. Sergei Ivanov recalls how the veterans' organization grew from this void. "The idea for the club was to talk through trauma. There was no psychological assistance in place for us so we helped each other." Each veteran has a unique set of experiences and perspective from his time in the army, but most imparted some note of positivity as they spoke about the past. "I am not sorry it happened because I saw life," Algimantas Baranauskas, now a customs officer, said, "you can't run away from your fate, but it is good when it ends well."

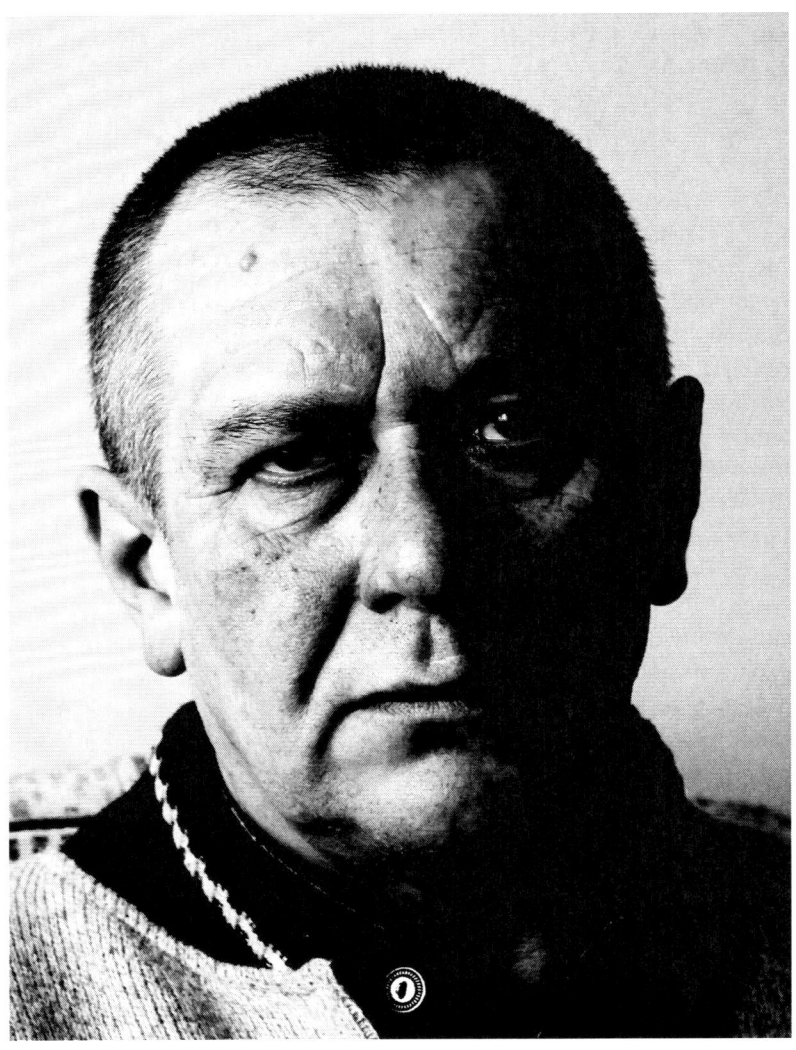

Algimantas Baranauskas in his home
Naujoji Vilnia, Lithuania

Dmitrij Michailov at the Vilnius Afganai Headquarters
Vilnius, Lithuania

Because of his time in Afghanistan, Dmitrij Michailov believes he looks at life differently. "Seeing death makes you appreciate and value life more." Michailov not only received support from other veterans of the Soviet–Afghan War, but also from his mother—a Soviet Army veteran from World War II. They were able to relate their experiences and reach an unlikely understanding that Michailov credits with facilitating a far smoother transition into civilian life.

Jonas Vaitkūnas was selected to be a scout and establish a path from the Soviet Union into Afghanistan before the war officially began. He then returned to Vilnius where he chose soldiers to lead into Afghanistan during the first months of the war in 1980—one of these soldiers was Vytas Lukšys. Vaitkūnas tries never to think of the war. "It is better not to remember," he said, "it is easier to live." All veterans interviewed for this project maintained a consistent assessment of the war. "It was a pointless war," Vaitkūnas echoed what many also stated, "this war lost many lives, many people were injured, and all of that was meaningless and unnecessary. It was a big mistake for Russia. No one asked us if we wanted to go [to Afghanistan]. If we refused to fight we could have been killed because of the rules of the army." Many veterans' views on the past are unified, but a full spectrum of attitudes and positions are represented when discussing politics and Russian relations, especially the situation in Ukraine.

Lithuanian veterans of the Soviet–Afghan War were granted the status of victims of totalitarian rule by the Lithuanian Seimas in December 2014. They hope this leads to further social and institutional acknowledgment.

This project was made possible by the Robert Rauschenberg Foundation's Artist as Activist Program.

More information on the Vilnius Association of Soviet Afghan War Veterans: www.afganai.lt.

Sergei Ivanov, retired Lieutenant of the Soviet Army,
in his living room, Vilnius, Lithuania

Vytas Lukšys, Former President of the Lithuanian Association of Afghan War Veterans

Martyrdom and Memory in Eastern Europe

GUEST EDITED BY

UILLEAM BLACKER AND JULIE FEDOR

-- JSPPS 1:2 (2015) --

Soviet and Post-Soviet Varieties of Martyrdom and Memory[1]

Uilleam Blacker and Julie Fedor

In this special issue, we explore the narratives of martyrdom connected to the history and memory of twentieth-century violence in Eastern Europe. The archetypal figure of the martyr offers a powerful vehicle for remembering the dead, and a potent tool for making and remaking identity, and especially for cultivating national myths. The language and imagery of martyrdom has long been a central part of the memory cultures of Eastern Europe, but in recent decades in particular it has undergone a striking revival. Religiously inflected narratives of the past involving claims to martyrdom have become increasingly prominent throughout the region, from the Russian Orthodox Church's "new martyrdom" discourse on the Soviet persecution of religion to the stories of national sacrifice presented at museums such as the Lonts'kyi Prison museum in Ukraine or the Museum of the Warsaw Uprising in Poland, through to the recent mass canonization of Armenian genocide victims. Images of martyrdom have proliferated especially since the beginning of the war in Ukraine, where they are being used to underpin territorial

---

[1] We gratefully acknowledge support provided by the CEELBAS Research Networks Scheme; the Humanities in the European Research Area Joint Research Programme; Darwin College, Cambridge; and the Australian Research Council's Discovery Early Career Research Awards (DECRA) funding scheme (project DE150100838). The views expressed herein are those of the authors and are not necessarily those of the abovelisted bodies.

claims,[2] calls for retribution,[3] and new national myths.[4] The contributors to this special issue examine a range of manifestations of this mode of remembering in Soviet and post-Soviet space. Our focus is on the distinctive forms which these martyrdom narratives take, and the ways in which these in turn are used to frame and shape identities.

Martyrdom is a key node within a cluster of semantically rich and interlinked concepts—victimhood, sacrifice, persecution—all of which can be used to mount compelling claims to legitimacy and authority, especially in the absence of alternative channels for political expression. To identify a martyr is to enable sacralization. As Katerina Clark has written, "Martyrdom has always been a primary mode of vindication".[5] The figure of the martyr—as a single individual, embodying and personifying a cause or a collective—can exert a strong hold over imaginations and emotions. Stories of martyrdom can offer consolation in the face of untimely death and catastrophe; vindication, entitlement, and a sense of righteousness; and they also have unique mobilizing force. The notion of martyrdom can activate complexes of intense emotions linked to the notion of persecution, and here in particular this discourse can create fertile soil for radical othering and dehumanization.

---

2   The back cover of one recent Russian history of Crimea, for example, proclaims that "The blood of our soldiers, fallen during the Russo-Turkish, Crimean, Civil and Great Patriotic Wars, has been shed on every meter of Crimean soil"; *Istoriia Kryma* (Moscow: OLMA Media Grupp and Rossiiskoe voenno-istoricheskoe obshchestvo, 2015).

3   See for example this text on Novorossiia: "Amidst the roaring of mortars, the burning cities, to the screams of the Odessan martyrs, to the moans of the wounded in Mariupol' and Slaviansk, the young state of Novorossiia is being born"; "Chtoby ni ot kogo ne zaviset'", *Veteran*, no. 19, 20 May 2014.

4   See the *Terra Dignitas* initiative to memorialize the victims of the February 2014 Maidan shootings, known as the "Heavenly Hundred"; Alya Shandra, "Kyiv City Council Launches Open Online Vote for Projects Commemorating Heaven's Hundred", *Euromaidan Press*, 6 April 2015; and "Podcast: Catherine Wanner, War, Grief and Rage: Popular Commemorations of the Maidan", 6 April 2015, http://www.reesblog.pitt.edu/podcast-catherine-wanner-war-grief-and-rage-popular-commemorations-of-the-maidan/ (accessed 30 November 2015).

5   Katerina Clark, *The Soviet Novel: History as Ritual* (Bloomington, IN: Indiana University Press, 2000), 179.

The tendency to cast the dead as martyrs is not, of course, an exclusively "East European" phenomenon. The martyrdom paradigm offers one of the most pervasive and enduring of the narratives that humans have created to make sense of life and death. The Christian tradition is unimaginable without it, and as Joyce E. Salisbury has argued, many present-day beliefs and "indeed simple habits of mind" can be traced to the formative influence of the stories and imagery drawn from accounts of violence against the early Christian martyrs.[6] Salisbury writes that "the influence of the accounts of this ancient violence extended far beyond the creation of new converts... this torture and persecution caused people to see the world as a struggle of good against evil that continues to haunt our cultural memories".[7] The categories and archetypes associated with martyrdom are among the central building blocks of the symbolic and moral universe shared in common across the Western world.

Yet while martyrdom as a discursive formation continues to exert a pervasive influence on Western cultures, the forms which it takes have largely been reconstituted, secularized, and sanitized. We can make out clear traces of the traditions of martyrdom in the modern languages of humanitarianism and human rights,[8] and of nationalism, with its claims to the right to call upon soldiers to sacrifice their lives in the name of the nation.[9] Yet these are for the most part no longer couched in the idiom of martyrdom,[10] which now has an archaic ring to it in English.

---

[6]   Joyce E. Salisbury, *Blood of Martyrs: The Impact and Memory of Ancient Violence* (London: Routledge, 2004), vi.

[7]   Ibid., 1.

[8]   See Stephen Hopgood, *The Endtimes of Human Rights*, where he argues that "At the heart of this [modern humanitarian activism] was the suffering innocent, a secular version of Christ". On the 17th-century shift in Protestant polemic from "martyrology to humanitarianism" see D. J. B. Trim, "Interventions in Early Modern Europe", in *Humanitarian Intervention: A History*, ed. Brendan Simms and D. J. B. Trim (Cambridge: Cambridge University Press, 2011), 38–39.

[9]   See for example Carolyn Marvin and David W. Ingle, *Blood Sacrifice and the Nation: Totem Rituals and the American Flag* (Cambridge: Cambridge University Press, 1999).

[10]   The canonization of the Martyrs of the Spanish Civil War is one notable recent exception.

By contrast, in socialist and post-socialist space we find that martyrdom often takes a number of quite distinctive forms, comprising different mixes of religious and secular language, often mobilizing different sets of emotions, and serving a range of different political and ideological ends. These varieties of martyrdom are in part the products of long-standing cultural traditions in which suffering is not only romanticized and sacralized as a crucible of national identity, but often also valorized as something of inherent value in its own right. The Soviet cult of revolutionary martyrdom with its pantheon of secular saints,[11] and the heroic histories of anti-Soviet dissent, are also strands of these traditions. But perhaps most importantly, the specific forms which the martyrdom paradigm takes in this region have to do with the protracted and tortuous process of remembering and mourning the unacknowledged victims of successive waves of violence experienced in this part of the world in the twentieth century. The decades-long attempted suppression and repression of these memories on the part of socialist regimes in the region have meant that, as Uilleam Blacker and Alexander Etkind put it, "Uncounted or misrepresented, the dead do not lie in peace... Mourning for these dead is often difficult, complex, and incomplete."[12]

The resulting crisis of mourning and remembrance faced by the post-socialist world is comparable in some respects to the watershed experience of the Great War in Western Europe. Seminal histories of memory and mourning such as Jay Winter's *Sites of Memory, Sites of Mourning* (1998), Paul Fussell's *The Great War and Modern Memory* (1975), and George L. Mosse's *Fallen Soldiers: Reshaping the Memory of the World Wars* (1990), focused on British,

---

[11]   On which see Elena Gapova, "Stradanie i poisk smysla: 'moral'nye revoliutsii' Svetlany Aleksievich", *Neprikosnovennyi zapas* 99, 1 (2015), www.nlo-books.ru/node/5953 (accessed 9 June 2015); and Adrienne M. Harris, "Memorializations of a Martyr and her Mutilated Bodies: Public Monuments to Soviet War Hero Zoya Kosmodemyanskaya, 1942 to the Present", *Journal of War & Culture Studies* 5, no. 1 (2012): 73-90.

[12]   Uilleam Blacker and Alexander Etkind, "Introduction", in *Memory and Theory in Eastern Europe*, ed. Uilleam Blacker, Alexander Etkind, and Julie Fedor (New York: Palgrave Macmillan, 2013), 14.

French, and German cultural responses to the unprecedented "encounter with mass death" during the Great War.[13] The scale and nature of the human loss, including enormous numbers of missing people and graves, placed a heavy burden on the old rituals and other practices surrounding mourning, which were no longer adequate to the task of making sense of these deaths.[14] The new rituals and practices that emerged in the aftermath of this encounter with mass-scale mechanized and anonymized killing included the tomb of the Unknown Soldier— sites which offered a surrogate grave, and consolation, and simultaneously becoming sites where, in Mosse's phrase, the nation came to "worship itself".[15]

While they have received less attention to date, the magnitude and nature of the violent deaths experienced in Eastern Europe in the twentieth century present challenges of comparable significance, novelty, and complexity. Indeed the difficulties here are arguably greater. Soldiers killed in the trenches on the Great War's Western Front may have died in new and horrifying ways but there were established military traditions for commemorating and mourning deaths in combat which could be employed here. No such conventions exist when it comes to deaths occurring in the course of such complex situations as genocide, state-run terror campaigns, inter-ethnic violence, state-contrived famine or massacres of prisoners-of-war. As Alexander Etkind puts it in relation to one specific

---

[13]   See in particular "Introduction: A Different Kind of War" in George L. Mosse, *Fallen Soldiers*: Reshaping the Memory of the World Wars (New York and Oxford: Oxford University Press, 1990).

[14]   On which see *ANZAC Remembered*: *Selected Writings by K. S. Inglis* (Melbourne: University of Melbourne, Department of History, 1998).

[15]   Mosse, *Fallen Soldiers*, 35 and passim. Benedict Anderson has famously argued that "No more arresting emblems of the modern culture of nationalism exist than cenotaphs and tombs of Unknown Soldiers. The public ceremonial reverence accorded these monuments precisely *because* they are either deliberately empty of no one knows who lies inside them, has no true precedents in earlier times"; Benedict Anderson, *Imagined Communities: Reflections on the Origin and Spread of Nationalism*, revised ed. (London and New York: Verso, 2006), 9. Significantly, as Kenneth Inglis has pointed out, "in neither of the two nations with the most men to mourn, Russia and Germany, was the tomb of an unknown soldier created"; K S. Inglis, "Entombing Unknown Soldiers: From London and Paris to Baghdad", *History and Memory*, 5, no. 2 (Fall/Winter 1993): 8.

case, "the very nature of the Soviet terror makes it difficult to comprehend, remember, and memorialize".[16] These words also have a
wider resonance for various mnemonic discourses across the region.
Particularly notable in this regard is the status of the Holocaust. In
Western Europe and North America, Holocaust memory is perhaps
the most pervasive and well-developed paradigm of memory of any
event of the 20th century, and is considered, though it displays significant internal variation, a model of coming to terms with a difficult past. The meaning of the millions of deaths that occurred during the Holocaust is, however, far less stable in Eastern European
societies where the paradigm comes into contact with complex in-
terfering factors, such as competing victimhoods, complexes of guilt
over Nazi collaboration, co-participation in atrocities, or the trauma
of the witness.[17]

The situation with regard to remembering and interpreting
the deaths of victims of Soviet terror or the Holocaust is further
complicated by the long period of several intervening decades of
suspended and repressed mourning, by long-standing taboos, and
by ongoing bitter conflicts over the basic facts of the historical record, together with the need to craft national histories for the region's
newly independent states. It is not surprising, then, that we should
find a tendency to fall back on the paradigm of martyrdom which
offers a familiar, reassuring, and often politically convenient way of
representing and making sense of violent death.[18] Yet at the same
time, there are important ways in which the martyrdom paradigm is
inadequate or ill-suited to this task.

---

[16]   Alexander Etkind, *Warped Mourning: Stories of the Undead in the Land of the
Unburied* (Stanford, CA: Stanford University Press, 2013), 11.
[17]   A survey of Holocaust memory in Eastern Europe can be found in the volume
*Bringing the Dark Past to Light: The Reception of the Holocaust in Postcom-
munist Europe*, ed. John-Paul Himka, Joanna Beata Michlic (Lincoln and London: University of Nebraska Press, 2013).
[18]   We see these representations as linked to mourning, following Philippe Ariès
who has described the ways in which the mourning ritual serves to "contain"
the loss of death and to do so by "re-presenting" the death; Ariès cited in Peter
Homans, "Introduction", in *Symbolic Loss: The Ambiguity of Mourning and
Memory at Century's End*, ed. Peter Homans (Charlottesville and London: University Press of Virginia, 2000), 4.

In this introductory essay, we sketch out several distinctive features of the varieties of martyrdom and memory in Soviet and post-Soviet space. First, we note the fact that quite often the term martyrdom is used in unexpected ways here to refer to deaths that would not qualify as martyrdom under the standard definitions. It is conventionally the case that for a death to be characterized as martyrdom, it should involve the individual in question making the choice to die.[19] Under this criterion, the vast majority of deaths as a result of state campaigns of terror and mass killing would of course be disqualified, and yet in many cases this has not prevented the widespread claiming of these victims as martyrs.

Can martyrdom be involuntary? As Jay Winter discusses in his essay in this issue, this is a question that has previously been debated at length by Jewish thinkers in connection to the Holocaust. Some of the current debates on Soviet state terror revisit the same set of issues and in some cases reach similar solutions. Like Shimon Huberband, the Polish rabbi, historian, and writer who, as Jay Winter's essay explains, argued for an inclusive definition of Jewish martyrdom at the hands of the Nazis involving a shift of focus away from how a victim died to how he or she lived, so too, for example, the Russian historian Aleksei Beglov has suggested that our understanding of the "new martyrs", that is, the clergy and laity of the Russian Orthodox Church who suffered as a result of Soviet state repressions, should be based on attention to the victims' everyday lives rather than to the circumstances of their execution and death. Beglov points out that unlike traditional martyrs, the "new martyrs" were "not witnesses, but victims", given that "[i]n the overwhelming majority of cases nobody offered them the chance to preserve their life at the cost of renouncing their faith."[20]

One powerful and original voice in the discussion over "new martyrdom" in Russia is the theologian and cultural theorist Anna Shmaina-Velikanova, who has called for a radical expansion of the

---

[19]   See further Margaret Cormack, "Introduction", in *Sacrificing the Self: Perspectives in Martyrdom and Religion*, ed. Margaret Cormack (Oxford: Oxford University Press, 2002), xii.

[20]   Aleksi Beglov, "Zhizn' vo Khriste", *www.bogoslov.ru*, 23 November 2010, www.bogoslov.ru/text/1249558.html (accessed 3 November 2015).

category so as to include non-believers and all gulag victims who died "for no reason" (*prosto tak*).[21] In this way Shmaina-Velikanova refashions the martyrdom paradigm in an attempt to resist the temptation to seek easy answers to the questions posed by past catastrophes.[22] But more often, in contemporary East European martyrdom narratives, the involuntary nature of the deaths is elided, or rejected. When it comes to the case of ethnically targeted terror campaigns, identifying as a member of a particular national group is recast as an act of volition. The historian Andrzej Nowak, for example, in his defense of the Polish martyrological paradigm and its application to NKVD terror campaigns against Poles, has asserted that:

> [T]hey died... because they were Poles... For Poland, Polishness, was obstructing the realization of the two mighty great powers' plans for imperial expansion... And either we remember that role as an obstacle to two of the most criminal systems in 20th-century history, or we agree with the thesis that there is no role here, there is only the absurdity of the crime and the victim. The Poles who died en masse at the hands of the NKVD did not interpret their Polishness as absurd. They were attached to it, *they chose it voluntarily*. If we don't interpret our Polishness as absurd, as a hump that can already be sawn off, then we ought not to forget those 150 thousand victims [emphasis added – UB & JF].[23]

The vigorous debates that have taken place in Poland over the validity of the national martyrdom paradigm contrast quite sharply with the general tendency across the region. More often, the status

---

[21]   See further A. I. Shmaina-Velikanova, "Neischislimyi sonm muchenikov", undated, available at: http://www.damian.ru/Actualn_tema/shmaina/Shmaina Velik_ru.html and Yu. Balakshina, "Voiti v nasledie tekh, kto otdal zhizn' za Khrista", 4 February 2012, *Preobrazhenskoe sodruzhestvo malykh pravoslavnykh bratstv*, http://www.psmb.ru/aktualnye-temy/usvoen-li-cerkovju-ves-opyt-no-vomuchenikov/statja/voiti-v-nasledie-tekh-kto-otdal-zhizn-za-khrista/   (both accessed 3 November 2015).

[22]   She notes: "We like looking at icons—there we see the martyr not in blood, not in filth, but in Glory. We also like looking at monuments of great scholars and poets killed for resistance, because in this way we build prophets' tombs... But we don't look at ... the ones who died for no reason"; Shmaina-Velikanova, "Neischislimyi sonm muchenikov".

[23]   Andrzej Nowak, *Strachy i lachy. Przemiany polskiej pamięci 1982-2012* (Kraków: Biały Kruk, 2012), 273.

of a particular group of victims of terror as martyrs is simply asserted, even when, or perhaps especially when, as Uilleam Blacker discusses in his contribution, this means avoiding the complexities and ambiguities of the events in question.

Other distinctive aspects complicating the remembrance of 20th-century deaths by violence in Eastern Europe as martyrdom have to do with the factors of anonymity and scale. Conventionally the martyrdom paradigm derives its power from the drama of the individual fate, around which stories can be woven, and imaginations and emotions engaged and mobilized. Yet in this case we are dealing most often with the phenomenon of anonymous mass death, where victims are counted in the millions, as Aleksandr Cherkasov from the "Memorial" Society puts it, "[b]y numbers of zeroes, not as individuals".[24] This has bearing on how the martyrdom framework is applied and adapted, especially when it comes to the case of state terror campaigns, where anonymization of the victims was not incidental but integral to the atrocities in question. It was the result of systematic and deliberate measures that were taken with the express purpose of ensuring that, as Irina Flige puts it, the memory of these events and their victims would be "objectless" or "non-material" (*bespredmetna*). Flige writes that,

> The arrests and executions of '37 were accompanied by a mute anonymity [*glukhaia neizvestnost'*]. Cars without number plates. A muteness of buildings—no signs, no addresses. An absence of written testimonies on the fate of the arrested. Arrest as disappearance, as death; but an unknown death, without a date, without a place, without a body, without a funeral, without a grave.[25]

Indeed, the secrecy surrounding the execution and burial sites was taken to such lengths that even the chekists guarding the Butovo mass grave site on the outskirts of Moscow, for example, for decades

---

24   "Reabilitatsiia repressirovannykh ili reabilitatsiia repressii—chto vybiraiut rossiiane?", *Kul'turnyi shok*, 1 November 2014, http://echo.msk.ru/programs/kulshok/1427774-echo/ (accessed 3 November 2015).
25   Irina Flige, "Sovremennoe istoricheskoe znanie o Bol'shom terrore I publichnaia pamiat' o nem zametno razoshlis'", in *Gorbachevskie chteniia. Grazhdanskoe obshchestvo: nastoiashchee i budushchee. 1937-2007: pamiat' i otvetstvennost'*, ed. O. M. Zdravomyslova (Moscow: Gorbachev-Fond, 2007), 132.

after the killings had no clear idea what they were guarding or why.[26] Some contemporary Russian memory projects place at their center precisely this anonymity and non-materiality, borrowing from the Great War cenotaph model and making reference to "the unknown martyr", representing the most abject, anonymous masses of victims of the gulag,[27] or "the unknown *zek*".[28]

The corrupting effects of the unspoken compact between state and society under late socialism to keep silent about this history and never to mention the names of the victims were for some commentators such as poet and philosopher Ol'ga Sedakova among the most destructive consequences of these events.[29] Key civic memory initiatives in Russia today such as the annual Return of the Names event[30] and the Final Address project[31] are aimed at restoring the individual names of the victims as a crucial step in building a new civil society. But significantly, a strong resistance to concretizing and individualizing the victims of Soviet terror remains a characteristic feature of the Russian state's handling of this memory.[32]

---

[26]   L. A. Golovkova *et al* (eds), *Butovskii poligon. 1937-1938 gg. Kniga Pamiati zhertv politicheskikh repressii. Vypusk 8.* (Moscow: Izd. "Al'zo", 2004), 157.

[27]   Shmaina-Velikanova, "Neischislimyi sonm muchenikov".

[28]   Grigorii Pomerants, "Mogila neizvestnogo zeka", in Zdravomyslova (ed.), *Gorbachevskie chteniia*, 229.

[29]   See her comments on this subject in "Zachem pominat' usopshikh?", *Radio Svoboda*, 6 December 2013, www.svoboda.org/media/video/25182088.html.

[30]   http://www.october29.ru/ (accessed 3 November 2015).

[31]   The Final Address is a civil society project launched in December 2013 and aimed at erecting small memorial plaques to individual victims on residential buildings in Russian cities; see Anna Narinskaia and Grigorii Revzin, 'Proekt "Poslednii adres": nuzhno li otdeliat' zhertv gosudarstvennogo terrora ot palachei i udastsia li dogovorit'sia s vlastiami', *Dozhd'*, 18 December 2013, http://tvrain.ru/teleshow/narinskaja_i_revzin/narinskaja_i_revzin_proekt_poslednij_adres_nuzhno_li_otdeljat_zhertv_gosudarstvennogo_terrora_ot_palachej_i_udastsja_li_dogovoritsja_s_vlastjami-359102/?video (accessed 15 October 2015). According to Arsenii Roginskii, the Final Address plaques represent the first time that the concrete words "was shot" have been used in a memorial of this kind in Russia, as opposed to phrases like "innocently perished" which leave the precise circumstances unspecified; cited in Kirill Mikhailov, "Tochka nevozvrata", *Novoe vremia*, no. 42, 15 December 2014, www.newtimes.ru/articles/detail/91561/ (accessed 3 November 2015).

[32]   This applies even more so to the memory of the perpetrators; on this issue see "Aleksandr Daniel': Peizazh pamiati o sovetskom gosudarstvennom terrore", *Portal Prava Cheloveka v Rossii*, 22 June 2015; Konstantin Eggert, "Pamiatnik

Thus, astoundingly, even though successive Russian presidents have recognized Soviet responsibility for the Katyn massacres, today the Russian judicial system continues to refuse to rehabilitate the victims of the Katyn massacre on the grounds that there is no firm proof that the individuals in question were sentenced and executed. For "Memorial" historian Aleksandr Gur'ianov, this can be read as reflecting a fundamental unwillingness on the part of the current state to move this history out of the realm of anonymity.[33]

The reluctance on the part of the Soviet state and some of its successors to remember individual victims in the context of unimaginably vast waves of mass killing (or their indeed aggressive determination to forget these events) has been the focus of the efforts of numerous civil society and cultural actors both in Russia and in other post-Soviet states. Indeed, outside Russia, as is the case in Ukraine or the Baltic states, for example, the victims of Soviet state terror are often remembered and mourned in a nationalized idiom of martyrdom at the hands of foreign occupiers: the Lithuanian Mausoleum of Anti-Soviet Partisans and Victims of Stalinism, which employs various symbols of martyrdom including a metallic stylized crown of thorns, or the Lonts'kyi Prison Museum in L'viv, which relies on similar imagery and rhetoric, are two prominent examples of this.[34] This kind of externalization is obviously much harder to justify in the Russian case. Nevertheless, attempts are being made in Russia, too, to nationalize victims through the discourse of martyrdom. As Kathy Rousselet has shown, the new martyrdom discourse draws connections between martyrs killed in wars and martyrs killed during the Great Terror, describing both as part of the same

---

zhertvam politicheskikh repressii: dilemma Vladimira Putina", *Deutsche Welle*, Russian translation at inosmi.ru, 16 January 2015, http://inosmi.ru/russia/20150116/225591193.html (accessed 3 November 2015).

33   Aleksandr Gur'ianov, "Katyn'. Problema sostavleniia knig pamiati i reabilitatsiia zhertv", "Memorial" seminar, Moscow, 15 May 2015, available at https://www.youtube.com/watch?v=bIgWbnQSKoQ (accessed 3 November 2015).

34   See Yekaterina Makhotina, "Vil'nius. Mesta pamiati yevropeiskoi istorii", *Neprikosnovennyi zapas* 4(90) (2013), http://magazines.russ.ru/nz/2013/4/19m-pr.html (accessed 22 November 2015). On the Lonts'kyi museum see Uilleam Blacker's article in this issue.

spiritual struggle in the service of a Russia in the state of combat.[35] Thus, during a recent visit to Noril'sk, Patriarch Kirill proclaimed the church's new martyrs of the twentieth century to be "our national heroes".[36]

Another distinctive feature of martyrdom discourses in Russia in particular concerns the sometimes paradoxical ways in which they can be turned to the advantage of the state. This variety of martyrdom entails reversing the positions of victim and perpetrator, and is aimed at legitimizing the state's use of violence against its citizens by casting the agents of the authoritarian state itself as martyrs, persecuted and unjustly maligned. Thus in the Soviet official narrative the chekist was a kind of inverted martyr, whose sacrifice consisted precisely of taking on the terrible but necessary role of executioner in the name of defending the revolution. In the post-Soviet period, martyrdom narratives have also been woven around the fate of the KGB as the doomed but courageous last defenders of the state in the lead-up to the Soviet collapse.[37]

Most recently, we can see examples of this authoritarian martyrdom discourse in the so-called "Anti-Maidan" narratives of the revolution and war in Ukraine. Like all revolutions and like all wars, the events in Ukraine have been accompanied by the emergence of competing cults of martyrdom around the dead. Remembrance of the "Heavenly Hundred", the victims of the February 2014 massacre on the Maidan, has formed the powerful centerpiece of a new version of Ukrainian national identity linked to the narration of these events as a Revolution of Dignity. This is reflected in the constant

---

[35]   Kathy Rousselet, "The Church in the Service of the Fatherland", *Europe-Asia Studies*, 67, no. 1 (January 2015): 52-53. For an overview of positions within the Church on the issue of the Soviet past, see Zh. V. Kormina and S. A. Shtyrkov, "Pravoslavnye versii sovetskogo proshlogo: politika pamiati v ritualakh kommemoratsii", in *Antropologiia sotsial'nykh peremen*, ed. E. M. Guchinova and G. A. Komarova (Moscow: Rossiiskaia politicheskaia entsiklopediia, 2011), 389–413.

[36]   Cited in "Patriarkh pochtil pamiat' muchenikov 'Noril'skoi Golgofy'", *News.ru*, 17 September 2015, http://www.newsru.com/religy/17sep2015/patriarch_norilsk.html (accessed 1 November 2015).

[37]   On chekist claims to martyrdom, see Julie Fedor, *Russia and the Cult of State Security: The Chekist Tradition, from Lenin to Putin* (London and New York: Routledge, 2011).

presence of the Heavenly Hundred as a rhetorical figure in Ukrainian public and political debates, but also in a major project for renovating the public space of central Kyiv, discussed in Uilleam Blacker's chapter, which will permanently and prominently incorporate memory of the victims of the Maidan shootings at the very symbolic heart of the country. In turn, the Russian state and the Anti-Maidan movement has put forward its own narrative of the conflict. This narrative also centers on claims to martyrdom, but on the part of the Berkut riot police, the Odessan victims of 2 May, and the Russian diaspora in Ukraine and elsewhere in post-Soviet space. For the Anti-Maidan, the *berkutovets* was the heroic and unjustly slandered defender of the lawful order against the forces of US-sponsored revolutionary chaos and mayhem. The *berkutovtsy* who were killed on the Maidan have been claimed as "holy sufferers" who sacrificed their lives in order to enable Crimea's reunification with Russia.[38] Here then we are dealing with a martyrdom story which serves to disguise and legitimize armed aggression.

In Ukraine, the war has led to a rise in militaristic rhetoric in public discourse, and this is often linked to historical instances of national martyrdom. Ukraine's Institute of National Memory, which has been revitalized and given new leadership since the Maidan, was instrumental in instituting a new national holiday, the Day of the Defender of Ukraine, on 14 October, which replaces the Day of the Defender of the Fatherland (23 February), which was a essentially continuation of Soviet Army and Navy Day. The new holiday was chosen in response to Russian military aggression, and in a deliberate attempt to distance Ukrainian memory discourse from Soviet practice: 14 October is the Feast of the Veil of Our Lady, which was

---

[38]   See for example, N. Andrievskaia, "Krym-2015: My vse 'Berkut'!", *My vse—"Berkut"* website, 18 February 2015, http://myvse-berkut.su/archives/484 #more-484Viktor Zeiskii, "Rekviem po Berkutu—avtor naiden!", *Proza.ru*, 2014, http://www.proza.ru/2014/02/27/1889;   "Boitsy Berkuta, postradavshie v Kieve, poluchat ot Rossii material'nuiu pomoshch'", *Korrespondent.net*, 16 April 2014,   http://korrespondent.net/ukraine/politics/3350476-boitsy-berkuta-pos tradavshye-v-kyeve-poluchat-ot-rossyy-materyalnuui-pomosch;   "V   chest' ukrainskogo 'Berkuta' predlozhili nazvat' ulitsu v Moskve", *lenta.ru*, 17 December 2013, http://lenta.ru/news/2013/12/17/berkut/ (all accessed 3 November 2015).

a traditional Cossack holiday and is still the official Day of Ukrainian Cossackdom. The date also happens to have been used, partly because of its pre-existing significance, to mark the symbolic founding of the Ukrainian Insurgent Army (UPA) in 1942, and this association features prominently in the Institute's argumentation for the establishment of the new tradition.[39] In the context of the new holiday, the Institute has also recently begun to promote the idea of Ukraine as an "army-nation" (*narod-viis'ko*) that has constantly been engaged in a fight for survival "from the Cossack era to the ATO" (i.e. the "anti-terrorist operation" against separatists and Russian forces in the Donbas).[40] The Institute explicitly draws parallels between past struggles and the present in its activitites, combining energetic initiatives to rehabilitate Ukraine's nationalist martyrs of the Second World War with oral history projects on the current war.[41]

The resurgence in the focus on struggle and sacrifice for the nation in Ukraine has potential implications for wider political relations in Eastern Europe, however. With the victory of the Law and Justice party in the 2015 parliamentary elections in Poland, the patriotic memory politics for which this party is well known is likely to experience a resurgence at state level in Poland, and clashes over the revitalized celebration of Ukrainian nationalist heroes from the Second World War are likely. The wartime activities of the OUN (Organization of Ukrainian Nationalists) and UPA included a campaign of ethnic cleansing and mass murder of Polish civilians in the regions Volhynia and Galicia in 1943, which led in turn to smaller scale but still significant retaliatory violence on the part of Polish forces

[39]   "Metodychni materialy ukrains'koho instytutu natsional'noi pam'iati shchodo vidznachennia 14 zhovtnia", *Ukrains'kyi Instytut Natsional'noi Pamiati*, 2015, http://www.memory.gov.ua/news/metodichni-materiali-ukrainskogo-institutu-natsionalnoi-pam-yati-shchodo-vidznachennya-14-zhovt (accessed 24 November 2015).

[40]   Volodymyr Viatrovych, "Ukraintsi—narod-viis'ko: zakhody 12-14.10 do Dnia zak hyznyka Ukrainy", *Ukrains'ka pravda*, 11 October 2015, http://blogs.prav da.com.ua/authors/viatrovych/561a6adcac233/ (accessed 24 November 2015).

[41]   For the rationale behind the new holiday see the Institute of National Memory website: http://www.memory.gov.ua/news/metodichni-materiali-ukrainskogo-institutu-natsionalnoi-pam-yati-shchodo-vidznachennya-14-zhovt (accessed 24 November 2015).

against Ukrainian civilians. The recognition of the victims of this violence, or lack thereof, continues to be a bone of contention between the two countries, and forceful statements from the new Polish president, Andrzej Duda, and other prominent politicians on the topic, combined with the dominant historical politics in Ukraine at the moment, point to the likelihood that this contentiousness may well continue to escalate.[42] This is only one element of a potential return to national martyrology in Poland, and the most significant instance of this kind of thinking may come as a result of the appointment in November 2015 of Antoni Macierewicz as Polish Defense Minister: since 2010, Macierewicz has been head of a parliamentary investigation into the 2010 Smolensk air crash that killed Polish President Lech Kaczyński and his entourage while on their way to commemorate the Katyn massacres. Macierewicz's commission has consistently worked towards the theory that the catastrophe was caused deliberately, which has helped fuel popular theories in Poland over the involvement of the Russian state. The appointment of Macierewicz at a time of heightened tension over Russia's military aggression in Eastern Europe could, then, see martyrological thinking play a crucial role in the course of relations between Poland and Russia in the near future.

Another, perhaps less predictable consequence of current events for the development of martyrology in the region relates to recent Russian casualties: on the one hand, the Russian troops killed in this conflict go unrecognized, buried quietly and forgotten; on the other, the state seems to be cultivating the image of a different kind of martyr—the special operations soldier killed in the course of covert operations, and a figure who has been at the fore of Russia's recent actions abroad. Over the past year there have been some tentative attempts to grope towards a new symbolic language for commemorating these semi-secret deaths in Russia. There are two new additions to the official Russian calendar which are significant in

---

[42]   Tadeusz Isakowicz-Zaleski, "Andrzej Duda krytykuje gloryfikacji UPA na Ukrainie", *Onet wiadomości*, 17 May 2015, http://wiadomosci.onet.pl/kraj/andrzej-duda-krytykuje-gloryfikacje-upa-na-ukrainie/2hg37k (accessed 24 November 2015).

this context. In February 2015 Putin proclaimed a new annual "Special Operations Day", to be marked on the anniversary of the Crimean operation (earlier, in September 2014, one Duma deputy had proposed instituting a new "Polite People Day", to be celebrated on Putin's birthday).[43] Also, in 2014, the Day of the Unknown Soldier (3 December) was inaugurated in Russia with the aim of, to quote the Defense Ministry, "paying the tribute of memory once more to all those who perished on fronts and whose names have never been successfully established".[44] In another example, a new memorial is currently being planned for the prominent Poklonnaia gora memorial complex in Moscow in honor of soldiers fallen in "local conflicts" and Cold War proxy wars.[45] We might read these new developments as attempts to handle the new reality of undeclared hybrid war and the particular demands that it makes of soldiers and their families. These state initiatives seem tentatively to be aimed at fostering the emergence of a new kind of martyr, whose martyrdom lies precisely in renouncing his right to a name and to an individual grave.

As we hope to have shown in this brief introduction to the topic and its historical and contemporary resonances, the concepts of martyrdom and cultural memory in Eastern Europe have long been interlinked in complex, often convoluted ways, and continue to play an important role in the fast-moving social, cultural and political processes at work in the region today. The papers presented in this special issue aim to unpick some of these complexities in more detail in relation to Russia, Ukraine, Belarus, and the Baltic states.

***

---

[43] "Putin Establishes New 'Polite People' Day in Russia", *Moscow Times*, 27 February 2015.

[44] "V Rossii vpervye otmetiat Den' Neizvestnogo soldata", *Polit.ru*, 3 December 2014, http://polit.ru/news/2014/12/03/unknown/ (accessed 24 November 2015).

[45] Igor' Plugatarev, "Pamiati ne vernuvshikhsia s kholodnoi voiny", *Nezavisimoe voennoe obozrenie*, supplement to *Nezavisimaia gazeta*, 25 April 2014, http://nvo.ng.ru/nvo/2014-04-25/14_monuments.html?id_user=Y (accessed 24 November 2015).

This special issue arose out of a workshop held in Cambridge in December 2013, and opens with the keynote address delivered to that workshop by one of the world's leading thinkers on remembrance and mourning, Jay Winter. In this introductory essay, Jay Winter provides a global survey of cultures of martyrdom. Focusing on attitudes to the Holocaust in Western Europe, Eastern Europe, and among Jews more widely, Winter makes the compelling and perhaps provocative case for recognizing an ever-increasing divergence between Eastern and Western memory cultures, in which attitudes towards martyrdom are a central defining feature. Jay Winter's contribution also emphasizes the destructive effects of the martyrdom paradigm and the ways in which it precludes reconciliation, reminding us that

> when martyrdom enters the equation, there is not enough symbolic space for both communities of victims to enter into national narratives of loss. The language of martyrdom apparently creates a zero sum game: only one set of martyrs can be commemorated at a time.

As Jay Winter puts it in his essay, "languages of martyrdom frame memory and history in very different ways". The remaining articles in the special issue explore different examples of these languages of martyrdom in Ukraine (Uilleam Blacker and Iryna Starovoyt), Russia (Sander Brouwer and Maria Mälksoo), and Belarus (Simon Lewis).

Uilleam Blacker's article traces change and continuity in Ukrainian martyrological traditions, paying particular attention to how martyrdom is inscribed in public space. Blacker argues that these traditions have their roots in the literary paradigm of national martyrdom developed by Ukrainian Romantic nationalist writers in the mid 19th century, and that they continue to hold sway in contemporary Ukraine, in the context of the lives lost during the Maidan protests and the war in the Donbas. Blacker also identifies the different, sometimes conflicting ways in which the martyrological tradition has been manifest in Ukraine and explores the potential for martyrological memory paradigms to exclude important elements of the past from public commemoration.

Sander Brouwer also examines deeply ingrained martyrological ideas, this time in relation to Russia, in his analysis of Karen Shakhnazarov's 2012 film *White Tiger*, explored here as a reflection on Russian narratives of martyrdom aimed at endowing Russian history with transcendent meaning, partly as an antidote to the problems of the present and as a means of sublimating trauma and loss. Brouwer shows how one prevalent narrative of Russian martyrdom takes a distinctive cyclical form, based on the notion of a mystical and eternally recurring struggle between the Russian Empire and its foes, a struggle which periodically demands martyrs in the cause of restoring the Empire. Esoteric as it is, this is a narrative that should be taken seriously; it resonates in particular with the broader popular narrative of Russian martyrdom in the liberation of Eastern Europe from fascism, a discourse that frequently blends into neo-imperialist rhetoric.[46]

While Blacker and Brouwer focus on culture as the locus of martyrology, in the next article in the issue Maria Mälksoo takes the discussion of discourses of martyrdom onto the plane of International Relations, examining how these inflected Russia's relations with its neighbors, particularly the Baltic states, during the Medvedev presidency. Mälksoo explores the official emphasis on Russian victimhood as an example of mimesis, arguing that this emphasis, which is aimed at "normalizing" the country as an actor in international politics, is also resistant to and subversive of the hegemonic European discourse that it imitates, since this mimesis has for the most part comprised symbolic actions emptied of any substance. In the Russian case, the shift towards a "modern" memory politics focused on the victims of Soviet terror has not gone along with any real commitment to protecting individual human rights or pursuing transitional justice.

In the last two papers in the issue, Iryna Starovoyt and Simon Lewis both grapple with issues surrounding the remembrance of anonymous mass martyrdom. Starovoyt examines the ways in which the Holodomor, the artificial famine of 1932-33 that killed millions

---

[46]   See for example Aleksandr Prokhanov's declaration that Ukraine and Poland owe their existence as nations to this act of martyrdom; Aleksandr Prokhanov, "Zabyli o Pobede?", *Argumenty i fakty* (Moscow), no. 1, 21 January 2015.

in Soviet Ukraine, is remembered in post-war Ukrainian literature and cinema. Her panoramic tour of Ukrainian culture of this period convincingly demonstrates the extent to which that culture is soaked in ideas and images of martyrdom in relation to the Holodomor, but also provides an acute analysis of the difficulties of representing and commemorating mass death and exploring its meanings in conditions of political oppression and censorship. Simon Lewis traces the notion of collective mass martyrdom back to the late Soviet period in his study of Belarusian literature and memorials. Focusing in particular on commemoration of the destruction of the village of Khatyn by the Nazis in 1943, Lewis provides an in-depth study of the various ways in which the tragedy has been invoked in Belarusian culture both pre- and post-1991, examining the complex dynamics through which cultural representations negotiate official commemorative discourses.

The papers in this special issue cover mnemonic phenomena as diverse as poetry and political decrees, and span half a dozen countries. We have also included a series of essays on the historiography and memory of one of the region's most famous martyr figures, Stepan Bandera; reviews of several new publications in East European memory studies; and a report on a conference on "The Political Cult of the Dead in Ukraine" that recently took place in Munich. All of these testify to the high level of interest in contemporary martyrological memory practice and discourse in the region. We hope that this special issue will provoke further research on this important topic in memory studies, both within our focus region and beyond it.

War and Martyrdom in the Twentieth Century and After

Jay Winter

Abstract: This article examines the claim that there is a striking con-trast between memory regimes in operation today in different parts of the world. They are differentiated by their approach to martyrdom. The presence of the terms "martyr" and "martyrdom" and their corre-lates varies over time and space, increasing in frequency and signifi-cance the further east you go. In Western Europe, the term martyr faded from use rapidly and irreversibly in the twentieth century; in Eastern Europe, it is still alive and well, informing a host of national and religious movements; and in the Middle East and beyond, the term is not only present but at times radioactive. Islamic radicalism is in-comprehensible without it, and so are other political movements in middle Asia and the Far East. This paper explores the way the lan-guage of martyrdom frames memory and history in different places and in very different ways in the early twenty-first century.

As a prelude to the essays which follow, I want to examine the claim that there is a tripartite set of memory regimes in operation in dif-ferent parts of the world today. They are differentiated by their ap-proach to martyrdom. The presence of the terms "martyr" and "mar-tyrdom" and their correlates varies over time and space, increasing in frequency and significance the further east you go. In Western Europe, the term martyr has faded from use rapidly and irreversibly in the twentieth century; in Eastern Europe, it is still alive and well, informing a host of national and religious movements; and in the Middle East and beyond, the term is not only present but at times radioactive. Islamic radicalism is incomprehensible without it, and so are other political movements in middle Asia and the Far East. This spatial model of sacred and secular forms of remembrance is intended to serve heuristic purposes, and like all useful models, it needs nuance and clarification when applied to individual national or regional cases.

My central premise is that languages of martyrdom frame memory and history in very different ways. In this context, we can see how the varying experience of the two world wars is a critical factor in accounting for these contrasting patterns of the sacralization of remembrance practices. In conclusion I want to suggest that in this distinction lies some of the reasons why there has not been a European commemoration of the Great War, let alone a global commemoration of the outbreak of the 1914–18 conflict one hundred years on. Different languages of sacrifice and martyrdom, referring in different ways to both the First and the Second World Wars, and to the Holocaust within the Second World War, as well as to the crimes of Stalinism in the Soviet Union and its satellite states, have created divergent commemorative paths and very different notions of the role of sacred language in the way we understand the disasters of the twentieth century.

Memory Regimes East and West

Martyrdom is both a trope and a practice framed by religious traditions and revolutionary movements. It is part of a grammar of sacrifice tending to elevate to the sacred level the act of dying for the state or for the church or for the two combined.

This grammar of sacrifice is not universal. It has a history, which differs according to national traditions and the shadow of national disasters. In Britain, without a continuous revolutionary tradition, with a painful but palpable distance from Roman Catholicism, and without an ongoing tradition of conscription for military service, the grammar of sacrifice as "glory" and its attendant words and images constitute a lexicon which faded from the mid-nineteenth century to the present. The language of "glory" was on the wane when Elgar, at the suggestion of Edward VII, tried to raise it up again in "Land of Hope and Glory", and it was simply too shallow a vessel to carry the weight of suffering and loss of life in the Great

War. Thus, the cultural space for the war poets was created long before the Battle of the Somme, in contrast to Ireland and to other countries in both Western and Eastern Europe for whom glory was still a robust, though frequently trivialized, signifier.[1]

After the Great War, the glory brigades dwindled further in much of Western Europe, though it took the fascist temptation and its destruction in 1945 to empty their ranks. A flourish of glorious martyrs to the Resistance took their place for a time (and sometimes even justifiably so), but only for a time, yielding a memory regime in Western Europe which treated war not as an adventure but as an abomination. Since language frames memory, these significant linguistic shifts are part of the de-legitimation of war and of military heroism in Western Europe over the last century. The European project is incomprehensible without this cultural trajectory away from war.

This cluster of developments has had powerful effects on what I term the Western European memory regime. The separation of death in war in Western European cultural and political life from metaphors of martyrdom, glory, transcendence, beatification, canonization, sanctification, and so on, marks it off from Eastern European memory practices, and even more so, from Middle Eastern cultures and from East Asian memory practices too. There is a host of evidence that in Eastern Europe, the Middle East, and in East Asia martyrology is an essential part of the narrative of loss of life in wartime. No longer is this the case in Western Europe. The key divide is the Second World War and the Holocaust. From then on, the Western European memory regime rested on a secularized story of suffering and death in wartime. It took time, but from the 1970s, the story of the murder of European Jewry entered centrally into the history of the Second World War and into the story of the construction of the European Union as a radical departure from war and from martyrdom in war.

---

[1]   Jay Winter, "Beyond Glory: First World War Poetry and Cultural Memory", in Santanu Das (ed.), *The Cambridge Companion to the Poetry of the First World War* (Cambridge: Cambridge University Press, 2013), 242–56.

One complicating factor in the history of the European memory regime was the entry into the European Union of most of the former Warsaw Pact nations. They retained martyrdom as an essential feature of their memory regimes, producing an east-west split which precludes the emergence of any common approach to the history of the Second World War, and to the Holocaust within it. Thus Europe's political union rests on a fundamental cultural divide.

Europe Divided

One way to understand the significance of this split is to borrow from demographic history. In the late 1940s the British demographer John Hajnal published a set of seminal papers on what he termed the European marriage pattern, from the Reformation to the then present. To the west of a line roughly linking Trieste and Danzig, celibacy was a social choice for women. The available statistics indicate that roughly one in five women never married, and that that practice was an enduring one. To the east of that line, celibacy was not a social choice for women; perhaps 3 percent of all women never married, in the sense of remaining single in her childbearing years. And when we move further east again, into Asia west and east, the percentage of women at age 49 who never married is infinitesimal. Thus Hajnal offered us a tripartite interpretation of a European marriage pattern (which is really a Western European pattern, separate from a second Eastern European marriage pattern, and a third non-European marriage pattern.[2]

Borrowing the structure though not the content of Hajnal's still authoritative work, I would like to suggest that there is a parallel tripartite set of memory regimes of a similar kind, and that the presence of the terms "martyr" and "martyrdom" and their correlates varies in each of them, increasing in frequency and significance the further east you go. In Western Europe, the term martyr has faded from use rapidly and irreversibly in the twentieth century; in Eastern

---

[2]   John Hajnal, "European Marriage Patterns in Perspective", in *Population in History: Essays in Historical Demography*, eds. David Glass and D.E.C. Eversley (London: Edward Arnold, 1965), 101–43.

Europe, it is still alive and well, informing a host of national and religious movements; and in the Middle East and beyond, the term is not only present but at times radioactive. Islamic radicalism is incomprehensible without it, and so are other political movements in middle Asia and the Far East.

Memory Regimes

Memory regimes are ways groups of people frame their understanding of the past. These regimes are closely related to what Jan and Aleida Assmann term "cultural memory", in that they go beyond direct experience to privilege the symbolic representations of events whose origins lay outside the reach of contemporaries.[3] These ways of putting the past into the present do not only rely on the voices of those who were there. Instead they extend beyond the generations who sit around the dinner table, and who tell stories about how "I remember when". Even after they pass away, later generations share narratives about what happened in the increasingly distant past. This move is, in Jan and Aleida Assmann's terms, a shift from communicative memory, that of lived experience, to cultural memory, that of imagined experience.

In some cases, these narratives disclose a sacred presence in history. These narratives operate in what I term the sacred memory regime; in others, the story of the past highlights salient groups— Jews, freemasons, gypsies, kulaks, and so on; these are targeted as intrinsically and powerfully evil, and responsible for the suffering of the ancestors of those telling the story. I term this the demonic memory regime. In effect, these two operate together in a world where the presence of God is immanent. In other instances, there is no central agent operating in history: neither the benevolent hand of God nor the malevolent hand of a social or ethnic group is blamed

---

3   On the Assmanns' approach to communicative and collective memory, see Jan Assmann, "Collective Memory and Cultural Identity", trans. by John Czaplicka, *New German Critique*, no. 65, Cultural History/Cultural Studies (Spring–Summer 1995): 125–33, and Aleida Assmann, *Cultural Memory and Western Civilization: Functions, Memory, Archives*, trans. Aleida Assmann and David Henry Wilson (New York: Cambridge University Press, 2011).

for initiating the course of events, chaos, or catastrophe being retold today. I term this set of beliefs the secular memory regime.[4]

These distinctions are highly schematized. In all societies, there are alloys of all three regimes, and occasions when one absorbs elements of the others. And yet, preserving such distinctions helps us see some important divergences in the ways different populations understand their collective past, and act in the present to recall it and even occasionally to go beyond it. At times what James V. Wertsch terms "memory templates" incorporate sacred images and lexicons; at other times, these schematic stories are secular in character, and at still other times, there is a mix of the two.[5] Understanding these cultural practices as dynamic may help us see how war and martyrdom have been configured differently in different parts of Europe and beyond.

Moving in Opposite Directions

What has been at the heart of divergent pathways of remembrance in Europe in recent decades is the question as to how to commemorate the victims of the Second World War, and in particular, how to commemorate Jewish victims of the Nazis alongside other victims. In a nutshell, when martyrdom enters the equation, there is not enough symbolic space for both communities of victims to enter into national narratives of loss. The language of martyrdom apparently creates a zero sum game: only one set of martyrs can be commemorated at a time. To remember both is certainly not logically

---

4   The terms sacred, demonic, and secular are mine. On memory regimes more generally, see: Samuel Moyn, "Two Regimes of Memory", *American Historical Review*, ciii, 4 (October 1998): 1182–6; Eric Langenbacher, "Twenty-first Century Memory Regimes in Germany and Poland: An Analysis of Elite Discourses and Public Opinion", *German Politics and Society,* issue 89, vol. 26, no. 4 (Winter 2008): 50–81; Astrid Erll, "Locating Family in Cultural Memory Studies", *Journal of Comparative Family Studies*, xlii, no. 3 (May–June 2011): 303–18; and Richard Ned Lebow, "The Future of Memory", *Annals of the American Academy of Political and Social Science*, vol. 617, The Politics of History in Comparative Perspective (May 2008): 25–41.
5   James V. Wertsch, "Collective Memory and Narrative Templates", *Social Research*, 75, no. 1 (Spring 2008): 133–56.

impossible; it just is so in reality. On the head of the proverbial pin, there is room, apparently, for only one martyr at a time.

Consider this sculpture in the Dresden City Cemetery, near a series of memorial sites focusing on the Fire Bombing of the city in February 1945 (Fig. 1). It is of a young girl whose arms signal completely opposite directions. At any single site, remembrance of war can move in many directions, but its center of gravity, its core, is grief, mourning, and bereavement.

Figure 1. Sculpture in Dresden City Cemetery. Photo by Jay Winter, 14 February 2012.

The Dresden sculpture follows a long aesthetic tradition separating the language of hope from the language of grief. Consider these three images as iconic representations of horizontality as the language of grief, not that of triumph or glory. The first is Mantegna's "Dead Christ" of 1480; the second is Hans Holbein's "Christ in the Tomb" of 1524, and the third is Kathë Kollwitz's "Widow" of 1920.

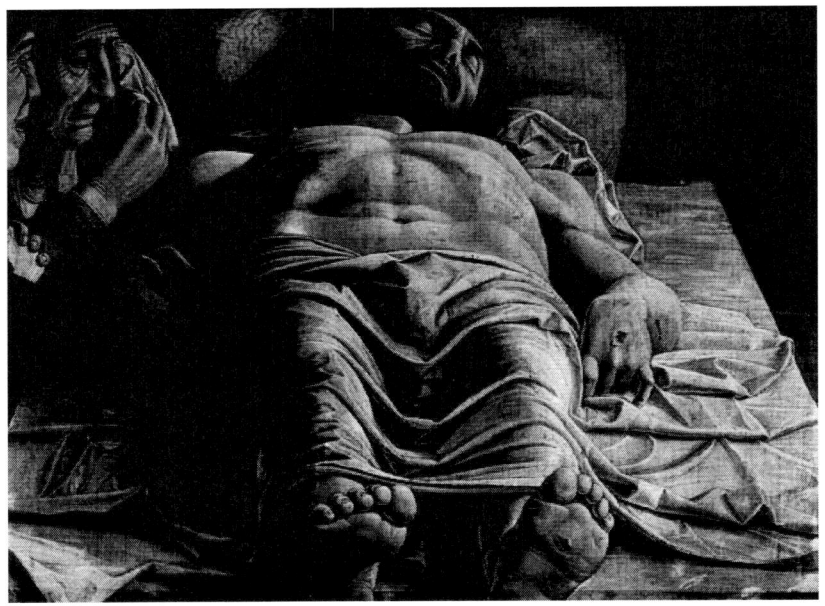

Figure 2. Andrea Mantegna, "The Dead Christ" (1480).

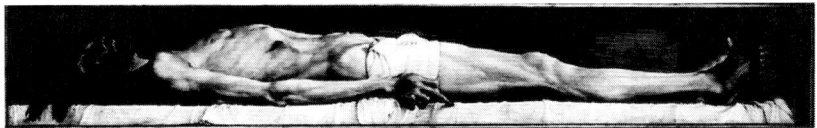

Figure 3. Holbein, "Christ in the Tomb" (1524).

Figure 4. Kathë Kollwitz, "The Widow" (1922).

Each conveys the concreteness of mortality, its denial of divinity or of any uplift at all. The second painting, that of Holbein, is even more barren than Mantegna's painting, in that Holbein strips the scene of any observers. The Marys are not there; no apostle is in mourning. This is a dead body, and in perhaps the greatest visual expression of the Reformation, Holbein tells us visually, that Christ is really dead, with a realistically dislocated finger on his crucified hand. To believe in the Resurrection, the artist tells us, you need faith and faith alone. Kathë Kollwitz, the granddaughter of a Protestant pastor, presents grief in the same weighty horizontality, with the widow's body literally brought down to earth together with her child (Figs. 2-4). No verticality here; like Mantegna and Holbein, the harsh materiality and irreversibility of death grounds our imagination, and prevents us from lifting off into vertical flights of hope or redemption.

These are exceptional works of art, departing from a vertical tradition of celebrating the martyrdom of those faithful even unto death. Starting with the crucifixion itself, and the Assumption of the Virgin Mary, configurations of sainthood have been relentlessly vertical in both the Roman Catholic or Eastern Orthodox traditions; examples are too numerous to catalogue. The reason is evident: martyrs and martyrdom redeem suffering and death.

The staggering death tolls of the First World War precipitated a resurgence of the language of martyrdom in many countries in both Western and Eastern Europe. But the configuration of the carnage of the Second World War was complicated by two parallel developments. The first was the suppression of the murder of Eastern European Jewry within Communist narratives of victimhood; the second was the underground survival of the Roman Catholic and Orthodox narratives of victimhood, both of wartime violence and of the post-war repression of religious life after 1945. These narratives only partially overlapped with more general memories of Soviet communist crimes not only against those identified by their religious practices, but against the entire Soviet population. These narratives of both Nazi and Communist crimes never merged. Indeed, they became more and more distant, as Jewish narratives of victimhood lost the aura of martyrdom both among Jews and in an increasingly secularized post-war world. More on that below.

The key point is that when narratives of martyrdom fade away, narratives of war lose their sacred aura and their potentially redemptive force. This is the key to the post-redemptive character of Western European memory regimes. Martyrs redeem; dispense with martyrs and redemption ceases to be a narrative framework for war and the victims of war and political repression.

However varied are different Eastern European historical memories, they all were marked indelibly by the twin phenomena of Soviet rule and Nazi occupation. Hitler's genocidal project was different from that of Stalin's crimes, though had Hitler completed his mission to destroy every single Jew in Europe, he could have used Auschwitz and other camps to destroy the Polish people as well.

Another way of putting the point is this. The crimes of Stalin were ecumenical; he killed groups and individuals, believers and unbelievers alike, for myriad "reasons"; the murder of the Jewish people stood apart as a project which cannot be reduced to just another chamber of horrors in the history of totalitarianism. The Shoah stands apart, and so do monuments to its victims. They cannot be absorbed into the national narratives of victimhood to both Nazi and communist crimes.

The Polish Case

In the Polish case, the language of martyrdom is still alive and well, but it collides with an entirely separate narrative, that of the Holocaust. The two cannot be braided together precisely because of the religious notation of Polish national suffering, and the difficulty (to say the least) of using Christology to represent the Holocaust. It is for this reason that we select Poland as a site of contestation between sacred and secular memory regimes. What has happened there is not the same as what has happened elsewhere in Eastern Europe, but provides insights into the development of varying languages of commemoration elsewhere.

To illustrate this point, let us return for a moment to the Dresden sculpture pointing in opposite directions.

Figure 5. Warsaw street sign: divergent sites of memory. Photo by Jay Winter, 24 October 2013.

Here (Fig. 5) is a street sign in Warsaw, which I photographed in in October 2013, the second from the top right-hand arrow of

which indicates that the monument to the heroes of the Jewish Warsaw ghetto uprising of 1943 is 350 meters to the north, that to the
heroes of the Polish rising of 1944 is in the opposite direction, 550
meters to the south, and the monument to the murdered and fallen
in the East, that is those victims of Soviet crimes, is 450 meters to
the east. This sign invites us to move in different directions to commemorate different narratives, still framed in heroic language. Over
time those narratives have diverged radically, to the point that they
are incompatible today.

At the center of the Jewish commemorative landscape is the
Umschlagplatz, or the point from which Jews living in the Warsaw
Ghetto were deported to be murdered in Treblinka, 60 kilometers
away. The Umschlagplatz memorial is understated and marked by a
presentation of the first names of those people who went from that
point to their deaths (Figs 6 and 7).

*Figure 6. Umschlagplatz memorial, Warsaw. Photo by Jay Winter,
24 October 2013.*

Figure 7. Names at the Umschlagplatz, Warsaw. Photo by Adrian
Grycuk (Own work), via Wikimedia Commons.

Here is a map indicating the location of the monument in relation to the rest of the Ghetto (Fig. 8).

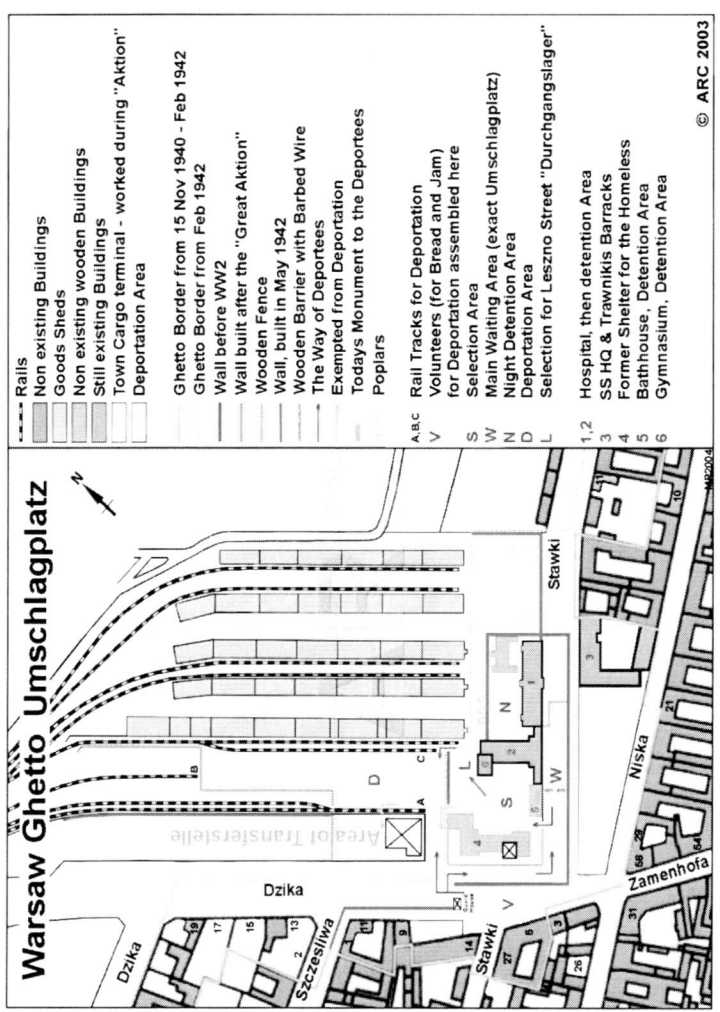

Figure 8. Map taken from www.deathcamps.org/occupation/umschlagplatz.html. Reproduced with kind permission. © by Michael Peters, Germany. www.deathcamps.org.

This monument is at the point of the deportation zone; other parts of the ghetto are difficult to mark precisely, since when Warsaw was rebuilt after the war, the streets of the Muranow district which housed the Ghetto were set out differently than they had been before the war.

The Monument to the Murdered and Fallen in the East, is very different indeed (Figs 9–12).

Figure 9. Railway ties, Monument to the Murdered and Fallen in the East, Warsaw. Photo by Jay Winter, 24 October 2013.

Figure 10. Katyn railway tie, Monument to the Murdered and Fallen in the East, Warsaw. Photo by Jay Winter, 24 October 2013.

Figure 11. Carriage of crosses, Monument to the Murdered and Fallen in the East, Warsaw. Photo by Jay Winter, 24 October 2013.

The way of the Cross is manifest in a railway via Dolorosa, indicating sites of Polish martyrdom on railway ties, leading to a Golgotha of dozens of crosses, pointing east accusingly to Russia. It is an impressive monument. The name of Katyn is clearly visible on one of the railway ties in the monument. The monument is located near the northern boundary of the ghetto. This monument to the Murdered and Fallen in the East is unmistakably an appropriated site, one turning a part of the ghetto, near its north-eastern limits, a place of Jewish suffering, into a site of Christian martyrdom.

Figure 12. Monument to the Fallen and Murdered in the East, War-saw. Photo by Jay Winter, 24 October 2013.

This monument was designed by Maksymilian Biskupski, and inaugurated in 1995, on the 56th anniversary of the Soviet invasion of Poland on 17 September 1939. The monument commemorates not that date or event, but primarily the martyrdom of Poles following that invasion. The railway tracks bear the names of the places that mark the deportation or execution of Poles, including Katyn.

Consider for a moment the juxtaposition of these two memorials. In this contrast, we see symbolic representations of the way Jewish and Polish memory regimes move in opposite directions. The horizontality of Jewish names is entirely distinct from the verticality of the cross. The language of martyrdom makes it inevitable that the two remain distant, incompatible, indeed at odds with each other.

This distinction stands despite the fact that there is a small Jewish element in the ensemble of crosses in the railway wagon Biskupski placed at the end of the Monument to the Murdered and Fallen in the East. The presence of a Jewish star on a tombstone amongst a sea of crosses appears as a footnote, a minor addition, to an overwhelmingly Roman Catholic site of memory.[6]

The same point was made by Reinhard Koselleck in the *Frankfurt Allegemeine Zeitung* in 1993, when Helmut Kohl decided to inaugurate a monument in the Neue Wache in Berlin by using a ballooned version of a Käthe Kollwitz Pietà to symbolize the victims of war and dictatorship.[7] Using the crucifixion as the symbolic language of commemoration, either through the myriad crosses in Warsaw or the Virgin and dead Christ in Berlin, leaves no room for Jewish memory or Jewish commemorative practices. It fractures the painful past and negates any idea of bringing together the two narratives of loss (Fig. 13).

Figure 13. Kathë Kollwitz, Pietà, in Neue Wache, Berlin. Attribution:
By Drrcs15 (Own work), via Wikimedia Commons.
Source: *https://upload.wikimedia.org/wikipedia/com-*
mons/8/8e/Statue_in_the_Neue_Wache.JPG. Image licensed under CC BY-SA-4.0
(http://creativecommons.org/licenses/by-sa/4.0/legalcode).

---

6   There are also a Muslim symbol and several Orthodox crosses.
7   Reinhart Koselleck, "Bilderverbot. Welches Totengedanken?", *Frankfurter Allgemeine Zeitung*, 8 April 1993.

Memory Bridges

One possible metaphor for a way out of this division between memory regimes is to imagine bridges between the two. Here again, Warsaw hosts an imaginative monument to this precise point. There is a nearly invisible replication of the wooden bridge linking the two parts of the ghetto at Chłodna Street. It points to a vanished crossing point, and to our replication of the safety and perhaps the indifference of all of us who pass under it (Figs 14 and 15).

Figure 14. Memorial Bridge between two parts of the Warsaw ghetto. Photo by Jay Winter, 24 October 2013.

*Figure 15. Bridge between southern and northern parts of the War-
saw ghetto, June 1942. Attribution: Bundesarchiv, Bild 101I-270-0298-
14 / Amthor / CC-BY-SA 3.0.*

Source: https://commons.wikimedia.org/wiki/File:Bundesarchiv
_Bild_101I-270-0298-14,_Polen,_Ghetto_Warschau,_Br%C3%BCcke.jpg. Image licensed under CC BY-SA 3.0 DE (https://creativecommons.org/licenses/by/3.0/de/le-
galcode; in English: https://creativecommons.org/licenses/by-sa/3.0/legalcode).

But such a bridge simply joins two parts of the ghetto, and not
the narrative of Polish loss to that of Jewish loss. Images of martyrdom to represent the Second World War and the Holocaust within
it inevitably lead to cultural collisions and divergences as between
different memory regimes. The more Christological iconography is
used to characterize or symbolize Polish, or Russian, or Belarusian
or Ukrainian suffering in the war, the harder it is to integrate the
Jewish catastrophe in the general catastrophe of the Second World
War. To be sure, this iconographic divide is not universally respected. Marc Chagall shocked his Jewish contemporaries by representing the Holocaust by portraying Christ as a Jew on the Cross,

dressed only in a prayer shawl.[8] Suffice it to say that here the exception proves the rule.

And the rule is that the more the Holocaust has come into
moral prominence, the less sacralized the Western European
memory regime has become. Martyrdom is an Eastern European
trope in part because it comes out of a living faith, one with little if
any room in it for the story of the Holocaust.

It is this particularly Christological iconography which makes
a major difference not only between commemorating Jewish suffering and Christian suffering, but in the configuration of monuments
in secularized Western Europe as opposed to less secularized Eastern Europe, where the Church played a central role in standing
against the Soviet empire. In sum, memory regimes with martyrdom
at their core in Eastern Europe are radically different from memory
regimes in Western Europe, and are likely to become even more radically different as time goes on.

This general interpretation still requires qualification when
applied to different national cases. I have used Polish examples, and
recognize that commemorative motifs and practices vary in important ways in all the other countries of the former Soviet bloc.[9]
Not only is it an error to take "Eastern Europe" as a single entity,
either under communism or after its downfall,[10] but the recent history of religious life in Poland is no sure guide to what is going on
elsewhere. The memory wars that have emerged in the Baltic states
cannot be taken as guides to what has happened in the Balkans, and
the Russian case cannot be treated as a guide to what is happening

---

8   See Marc Chagall's "White Crucifixion" (1938), available at the Art Institute of
      Chicago website, http://www.artic.edu/aic/collections/artwork/59426.
9   Stefan Troebst und Johanna Wolf (eds), *Erinnern an den Zweiten Weltkrieg:
      Mahnmale und Museen in Mittel- und Osteuropa* (Leipzig: Leipziger Univer-
      sitätsverlag, 2011).
10   Larry Wolff, *Inventing Eastern Europe: The Map of Civilization and the Mind of
      the Enlightenment* (Stanford: Stanford University Press, 1994); Maria Todorova
      (ed.), *Remembering Communism: Genres of Representation* (New York: Social
      Science Research Council, 2010); and Claus Leggewie, "A Tour of the Battle-
      ground: The Seven Circles of Pan-European Memory", *Social Research*, lxxv, no.
      1, Collective Memory and Collective Identity (Spring 2008): 217–34.

in countries which have entered the European Union. But while recognizing national and regional or sub-national specificities, we must not lose sight of the gap which separates Jewish and non-Jewish commemorative forms not only in Poland but also elsewhere in Eastern Europe, however that region is defined.

More specifically military monuments present fewer problems, but here again, what links a certain kind of heroic visual language, Jewish and Christian alike in Poland, separates that kind of representation in the East (or in Israel or China) from Western European sculpture, installations, and other forms of visual art. There is a clear overlap between the presentation of the martyrdom of those with the strength to rise in revolt in Warsaw, Jews in 1943, and non-Jewish Poles in 1944. The imagery of the monument to the 1944 uprising in Krasiński Square, designed by sculptor Wincenty Kućma and architect Jacek Budyń near the Supreme Court is scarcely distinguishable from Nathan Rapaport's socialist realist sculpture of 1948, the last site of the Jewish committee leading the uprising now in front of the new Museum of the History of Polish Jews (Figs 16–17). Notice the verticality of the larger-than-life Jewish hero, drawn from a shared romantic tradition.

Figure 16. Wincenty Kućma and Jacek Budyń, Monument to the 1944 Uprising. Photo by Jay Winter, 24 October 2013.

*Figure 17. Natan Rapoport, Monument to the Heroes of the Warsaw
Ghetto Uprising, with Mordechai Anielewicz at center right (1948).
Photo by Jay Winter, 24 October 2013.*

Jewish Memory Regimes

This tradition is shared only to a point, however, with new emphases
emerging during the Holocaust itself. It is important to note the extent to which martyrology has faded as a central element in Jewish
memory regimes since the Holocaust. In the past, the notion, eluci-
dated classically by Yosef Chaim Yerushalmi, that Jews have memory
but not history, depended on a belief that time was circular, that the
mythical recurred year in and year out, and that, for instance, when
the Jewish people celebrate Passover, they really do leave Egypt on
the very evening they celebrate. In a more somber register, each Jewish catastrophe registers and echoes the destruction of the two Tem-
ples, marked by Tisha B'av, a fast day in the summer.[11]

---

[11]   Yosef Chaim Yerushalmi, *Zachor. Jewish History and Jewish Memory* (Seattle,
WA: University of Washington Press, 1982).

First, the massacres of the Great War and then the Holocaust changed both the premise and the practice of Jewish memory. Historical time drove a wedge into the circularity of mythical time; there would be no celebration of Passover, no Exodus, no miracle in the spaces of Eastern Europe where Jewish life had been destroyed. In addition, the creation of the State of Israel was another historical rupture making it difficult, though not impossible, for Jews to continue to think that every year is like every other year, and every enemy of the Jewish people resembles Haman from the Book of Esther.[12]

Such changes were evident during the war itself. Even during the years of destruction 1939–45, Orthodox Jews began to take a broader view of what martyrdom meant. Some even went so far as to redefine it entirely, not as dying in sanctification of the name, *bekiddush hashem*, but living as sanctification of God, *al kiddush Ha'Hayyim*. Others were not so open-minded, and saw the Holocaust as yet another instance of the eternal return of the sufferings God metes out, for reasons only He knows, to the chosen people. Perhaps the best way to present the development of ideas about Jewish martyrdom is to say that for many, though not for all, the Holocaust complicated the discussion in radical ways.

The key issue, indeed the central problem was the significance of intention or choice in the fate of those facing death as Jews in the Holocaust. This matter was discussed by rabbis in Warsaw and elsewhere while the Holocaust was under way. One of the most remarkable texts on this question was written by a Polish rabbi and polymath, Shimon Huberband. He was born in 1909 into a rabbinic family and took his Smicha, or ordination, with his grandfather. He was not only a rabbi but an historian, a writer, and a poet. He published widely on Talmudic and secular topics. He was even the author of a book on Jewish physicians in his hometown of Piotrków in the Łódź district in the seventeenth century.

At the outbreak of the war, he and his family fled their home, but his wife and child were killed in bombing in the nearby town of

---

12   Jay Winter, "The Great War and Jewish Memory", *Yearbook of the Simon Dubnow Institute*, xix (2014), 1–23.

Sulejów. Thereafter in shock, Huberband travelled north to Warsaw, and began a new life working for the Jewish Social Self-Help Organization. He was director of the organization's religious section. Despite contracting typhus, he worked alongside Emanuel Ringelblum to document Jewish life in the Warsaw ghetto by placing these documents in milk cans buried for posterity. The project is now known as the Oneg Shabbat archive (Fig. 18). The term in Hebrew means the joys of the Sabbath, a name showing the stark affirmation of Jewish belief in extremis.[13]

---

[13]   Samuel Kassow, *Who will Write our History: Emanuel Ringelblum and the Oyneg Shabes Archive* (Bloomington, Ind.: Indiana University Press, 2007).

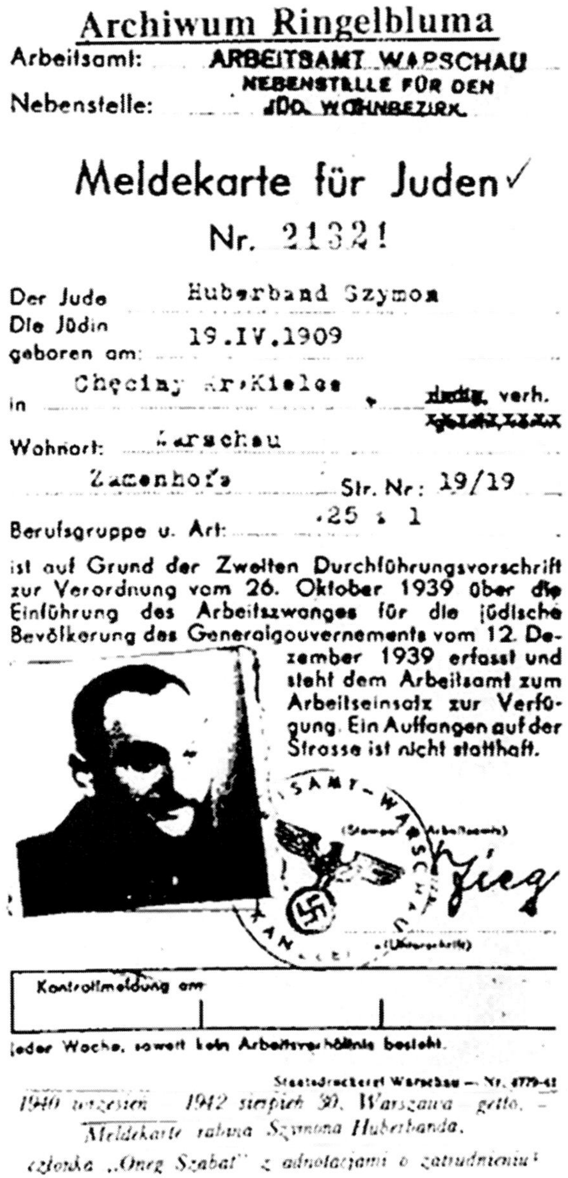

Archiwum Ringelbluma

Arbeitsamt: ARBEITSAMT WARSCHAU

Nebenstelle: NEBENSTELLE FÜR DEN JÜD. WOHNBEZIRK.

Meldekarte für Juden ✓

Nr. 21321

Der Jude / Die Jüdin: Huberband Szymon

geboren am: 19.IV.1909

in: Chęciny Kr. Kielce, ledig. verh. geschieden

Wohnort: Warschau

Zamenhofs Str. Nr.: 19/19

Berufsgruppe u. Art: 25 : 1

ist auf Grund der Zweiten Durchführungsvorschrift zur Verordnung vom 26. Oktober 1939 über die Einführung des Arbeitszwanges für die jüdische Bevölkerung des Generalgouvernements vom 12. Dezember 1939 erfasst und steht dem Arbeitsamt zum Arbeitseinsatz zur Verfügung. Ein Auffangen auf der Strasse ist nicht statthaft.

(Stempel d. Arbeitsamts)

(Unterschrift)

Kontrollmeldung am

jeder Woche, soweit kein Arbeitsverhältnis besteht.

Staatsdruckerei Warschau — Nr. 4779-41

1940 wrzesień – 1942 sierpień 30, Warszawa getto. – Meldekarte rabina Szymona Huberbanda, członka „Oneg Szabat" z adnotacjami o zatrudnieniu

Figure 18. Identity card of Shimon Huberband.

Huberband's astonishing work in Yiddish, later published in Hebrew and English under the title *Kiddush Hashem*, is a wide-ranging study not only of how Jews died, but of how Jews lived. He documents the daily rhythms of Polish Jewry, especially in Warsaw, in the midst of the Holocaust. On 18 August 1942, Huberband and his second wife were deported from the Umschlagplatz in Warsaw to Treblinka where they were murdered.

The fragments Huberband collected showed many different forms of the stubborn refusal of Jews to give up even the traces of their collective life. Teaching Hebrew went on, among different Jewish groups in the ghetto, Zionists and anti-Zionists alike. The non-observant shared other forms of defiance, rescuing Torah scrolls and sacred books, symbols of their collective life which meant more to them at the end of their lives than they had before.

The topic of martyrdom was central to Huberband's work, and yet, not despite, but perhaps because, of the catastrophe he saw in front of his eyes, he took a very liberal and open-minded view of the subject of *Kiddush Hashem*. Huberband departed from the way martyrdom was understood in traditional Jewish scholarship in 1942, by opening the door to active *Kiddush Hashem*. Yes, Jews were killed without having done a thing. That was passive martyrdom. In contrast active sanctification of the Lord existed by living a Jewish life and not only by dying.[14] The Ethics of the Fathers captured the dilemma: when there are no human beings around, be one.

There is a spectrum of possibilities in Huberband's discussion of martyrdom. The door was open to admit virtually any Jew who died in the war to the ranks of the martyrs. And yet there was considerable discussion about the significance of a willed act, of volition, rather than simply being Jewish and in the wrong place at the wrong time.

After the Holocaust, the argument within Jewish thought on who was a martyr continued. The broad consensus of rabbinic thinking was that *Kiddush Hashem* requires a decision to give up one's life rather than commit idolatry or murder or incest. Since the

---

[14]   Shimon Huberband, *Kiddush Hashem: Jewish Religious and Cultural Life in Poland During the Holocaust* (New York: Yeshiva University Press, 1987), 247.

victims of the Nazis, in the overwhelming majority of cases, had no choice that would save their lives, and since many of them had no interest even in preserving a Jewish identity, the concept of martyr-dom in its older forms was in need of review, and even of revision.

We have seen that Huberband was open to the possibility that all victims were martyrs. He parted company therefore from earlier (and later) chroniclers who emphasized conscious choice. Perhaps one way to put Huberband's position is that Jews as Jews were forced to make not a religious but an existential choice—to go on living, whether or not they practiced Jewish law. The Nazis took that choice away from them, and rendered them martyrs despite themselves, as it were. What Huberband did was to make living as a Jew and not dying as a Jew the focus of his affirmation of faith.

Those holding different opinions still were stuck on the no-tion of affirmation, of choice. Those who wrote of the First Crusade's Rhineland killings note that in most cases Jews were indeed given a choice to preserve their lives by accepting baptism, and many in-deed did take this option. The language of martyrdom is very strong in these chronicles—as in the rabbinic texts about the Jewish victims of Roman persecution. Evidently, the Holocaust was sufficiently shocking to enable even the most strictly Orthodox to see that their secular, unbelieving Jewish brothers and sisters, with whom they had only one thing in common, shared their fate. That common des-tiny accounts for the distinction Huberband made between active *Kiddush Hashem*—evidently present in his case and the case of those who created the Oneg Shabbat archives—and passive *Kiddush Ha-shem*, which was one way to describe the fate of those swept away in the Holocaust who made no such choice. How else can one de-scribe the predicament of more than one million children murdered by the Nazis?

The French novelist André Schwarzbart, traversed the same difficult field in his novel *The Last of the Just* (1959), confronting the myth of the Lamed Vav, the thirty-six just men on whom the fate of the world resides. The last of the just is perhaps the last of the mar-tyrs, who like the director of the Warsaw orphanage, Janusz Kor-czak, accompanied his children to the end, speaking to them of leg-ends of redemption (Fig. 19).

Figure 19. Janusz Korczak, leading his children to the Umschlag-
platz, Warsaw Jewish cemetery. Author: Jolanta Dyr.
Source: https://commons.wikimedia.org/wiki/File:251012_Janusz_Korczak_monu-
ment_at_Jewish_Cemetery_in_Warsaw_-_03.jpg. Licensed under the Creative Com-
mons Attribution-Share Alike 3.0 Unported license (https://creativecommons.org/li-
censes/by-sa/3.0/deed.en).

But Schwarzbart ends his book by interpolating the names of the death camps between every single word of the mourner's prayer, the Kaddish. The holy prayer for the dead is splintered by the Shoah, and so, the author suggests, is any idea of claiming that one million Jewish children murdered in the Shoah were martyrs. The language of martyrdom is too frail to bear that weight. The consequences of this change were significant within what may be termed the post-Holocaust Jewish memory regime.

Others configured the problem of choice in different ways. Zionists in Israel had pointed out to the Jewish population of Poland and elsewhere the danger of remaining in Europe in no uncertain terms, and yet the mass of Jews there had not listened. Furthermore, and this mattered in the militant society of the Yishuv or Jewish set-tlement of Palestine and after 1948, of Israel, the acts of resistance in Warsaw and elsewhere, of which Huberband's work was a salient instance, were isolated and unrepresentative of what some Zionists (and sometime Zionists like Hannah Arendt) took to be the over-whelmingly passive response of Jews to their fate. When in 1953, a day was chosen to mark the Holocaust in the Israeli calendar, it was given the name of Yom Hashoah v'ha G'vurah, the day of Catastro-phe and Heroism. To remember the murders alone gave too much place to passivity; to braid together victimhood and heroism brought the active element documented by Ringelblum and Huber-band and many others into the heart of the story. It was a tale com-patible with a Zionist view of history. Hence in the State of Israel, martyrdom was the right word for those who rose in revolt; perhaps their heroism enabled those who did not revolt to enter the martyrs' pantheon, holding on to their coattails, as it were. And perhaps not. Most importantly, the Israeli day of remembrance was not the tra-ditional fast day of lamentations, Tisha B'av. The Shoah was not part of the circular calendar of Jewish martyrdom. It was part of the lin-ear calendar of history, leading to the establishment of the State of Israel.

This binary position on suffering and heroism presents insta-bilities in Jewish narratives of the Holocaust. The notion of armed resistance as heroic is clearly present in the Rapoport memorial which presents both a plaque of abjection, "The Last March" on one side of the monument, and another plaque of muscular resistance fighters, symbolizing the Warsaw Ghetto uprising, suitable for the Arc de Triomphe, on the other. Both are there, and yet the relation-ship between the two is left to the imagination.

There is a contemporary political dimension to this problem too. Many object to the appropriation of the Shoah by the Israeli state to justify whatever policies it adopts in the ongoing conflict with Palestinians. Many others object to the use of religious imagery of any kind to describe the Shoah. The very word is an attempt to bypass the sacred origins of the term "Holocaust", signifying a burnt offering entirely consumed by fire. There was nothing sacred about the slaughter of six million Jews; for such commentators, the religious language of martyrdom is anathema.

The same is true for artists like Anselm Kiefer, who uses images drawn from Jewish mysticism, but braids them together with entirely different elements of broken glass and metal, to configure catastrophe in ways utterly remote from martyrdom. Here are two instances of his post-martyrological art (Figs 20–21).

Figure 20. Anselm Kiefer, "Breaking of the Vessels" (1990). Lead, iron, glass, copper wire, charcoal, and Aquatec. Installed: 12 ft. 5 in. x 27 ft. 5 1/2 in. x 17 ft. (378.5 x 836.9 x 518.2 cm). © Anselm Kiefer.

Figure 21. Paul Klee, "The Angel of History" (1919) and Anselm Kiefer, "Bird-song" (Sprache der Vögel) (1989). Lead, steel, wood, oil, plaster, resin and acrylic. 114 3/16 x 194 1/8 x 66 15/16 in. (290 x 493 x 170 cm). © Anselm Kiefer. Photo © White Cube (Ben Westoby).

The first refers directly to the Kristallnacht, with the broken glass and burnt books. But it is located in a kabbalistic legend about theodicy. How did evil get into the world? The kabbala tells us that when God wanted to create the Universe, he withdrew and created space for it, and then put the creative material for all forms of life in sacred vessels. But the big bang, the act of creation, was so powerful, that these vessels smashed, and jagged pieces of them fell into the world. Thus evil came out of infinite good. Here we see pathos, not myth; irony, not the affirmation of the faithful. Mystical, not martyrological, poetry.

Kiefer is not Jewish, but has understood the Jewish predicament about martyrdom in profound and important ways. The second of his installations, "Birdsong" or "Die Sprache der Vögel" makes the same point. It was first designed in 1989, and it has been part of his repertoire ever since. It tells the story of rabbi Chanina ben Teradion, wrapped in the Torah and burned at the stake by the Romans for teaching the Torah in public. When asked by his students what he saw in his last moments, the rabbi answered, "I see the parchment is burning but the letters are taking wing".

Burning parchment is one of Kiefer's *idées fixes*; but here he references not only rabbinic legends, but also another vision of catastrophe beyond martyrdom. I refer to Paul Klee's Angel of History, which Klee painted seventy years before Kiefer, and on which he irresistibly comments. The commentary extends to Walter Benjamin's reading of the painting, which Klee gave to him, as a vision of the catastrophe in which he lived. Klee's angel stands before this catastrophe and cannot even close his wings around him. He cannot save us. He can only witness. Kiefer's installation "Birdsong" is Klee's angel without a face, a post-humanist and post-Holocaust meditation on the end of the language of martyrdom and the sacred world in which it flourished.

Conclusion

My conclusion is a mixed one. The language and imagery of Christian spirituality and sacrifice, still present in commemorative forms throughout Eastern Europe, has slowly vanished from Western European commemorative practices and art. The conceptual gap between East and West is deep and likely to deepen further. This collision was unavoidable, and has grown in significance and intensity over time, as the Holocaust entered centrally into Western narratives of the Second World War.

In Russia itself, the language of martyrdom has grown for other reasons. The Vatican takes considerable time before it beatifies and canonized its saints. Not so the Russian Orthodox Church, as Polish sociologist Zuzanna Bogumił has shown.[15] It has canonized nearly two thousand martyrs over the past couple of decades.

The mugshots taken by the NKVD followed the arrest of millions of Soviet citizens. Among them were priests, nuns, and devout men and women who died for their faith. The Russian church was able to take these photographs and put gold foil around them, producing instant iconography out of the very records of the killers.[16]

---

[15]   I am grateful to Dr Bogumił for discussions on this subject in Cambridge and Warsaw.

[16]   Zuzanna Bogumił, "Do *Milieux de mémoire* Still Exist in Eastern Europe?", Cambridge conference on Martyrdom and Memory, 13 May 2013.

Perhaps here the foundational distinction Pierre Nora made in the 1980s about the memory boom matters here. Without agents of memory living in broad communities of remembrance, Jewish commemorative practices are bound to focus on what he termed *lieux de mémoire,* traces of a vanished past, in Poland, Russia, Belarus, and Ukraine. Christian notation there is imbedded in *milieux de mémoire,* animated by present-day practices and recent family memories. Perhaps that leaves us with only one choice: to proliferate monuments like the building opposite the Yiddish theater in Warsaw on which between 2008 and 2014 Jewish faces were displayed. The name of the project was "I Can Still See Their Faces".[17]

The building itself is empty, as much a *lieu de mémoire* in Nora's sense of an empty relic, as one could imagine. So much of Jewish Warsaw, like Jewish Saloniki and Jewish Czernowitz, has completely vanished, with virtually no trace left on the streets where Jewish life flourished. Secular commemoration of the staggering losses of the Second World War is the only way to build bridges from an intolerable past to the very different world we inhabit today.

I have claimed that there are three overlapping but distinctive memory regimes in operation in different parts of the world today. They are differentiated by their approach to war and martyrdom. The presence of the terms "martyr" and "martyrdom" and their correlates varies over time and space, increasing in frequency and significance the further east you go. In the first of the three, the Western European memory regime, the term "martyr" largely has faded from use; its decline has been rapid and irreversible in the twentieth century, and especially after the Holocaust; in Eastern Europe, where a different memory regime operates, the notion of "martyrdom" is still alive and well, informing a host of national and religious monuments, most of which refer not to the 1914–18 war but to the Second World War and the Soviet period; and in the Middle East and beyond, there is a third memory regime in which the braiding

---

[17]   "I ciągle widzę ich twarze", located at ul. Próżna (B-3), in Warsaw. The project was part of a wider initiative under the same name organized by the Szalom Foundation and its head Gołda Tencer. Images can be found here: https://commons.wikimedia.org/wiki/File:PL_Warszawa,_judaica,_ul_Prozna,_I_ciagle_widze_ich_twarze_(1).jpg.

together of war and martyrdom is not only palpable, but at times programmatic. Anti-colonial struggles adopted this framework, and more recently, Islamic radicals have done so, creating commemorative practices in parts of Asia and the Far East quite different from those in Europe.

Consider just one instance. In central Tokyo, the Yasukuni monument is a sacred site of martyrdom. All those who died for the Emperor are worshipped here. By giving their lives for the Emperor, they become gods. At the side of the monument, there is a museum in honor of the kamikaze pilots who committed suicide in ramming their planes into Allied ships, much like Al Qaida "martyrs" did to the Twin Towers in New York. The political fallout is considerable whenever a Japanese prime minister visits the shrine, and yet they still do. The sacred nature of martyrdom is alive and well in contemporary Japan. And though they might contest it, Communist Chinese images of the martyrs of the Long March and the Revolution are not significantly different. All inhabit a sacred space in which lives lost in war are touched with something divine. This is what separates Western European commemorative practices from those in Eastern Europe and in Asia.

It is the fading away of the lexicon of martyrdom in the Western European memory regime that distinguishes the commemoration of 1914–18 there from commemoration of the Second World War, in which the subject of the Holocaust has become more and more important over time. The theme of martyrdom is still present in Holocaust commemoration, but not in stable ways. During the war itself, indeed in the heart of the Warsaw ghetto, there was a shift in Jewish thought on the Holocaust which distinguishes between dying *al Kiddush Hashem*, to sanctify the name of the Lord, and living as sanctifying the Lord, *be Kiddush HaChaim*.

Still, some groups use the language of martyrdom to describe the Holocaust, but most do not. Primo Levi abjured the notion of martyrdom, which preserves a sacred framework in which to place the Holocaust. For him, there was a simple choice. Either Auschwitz existed, or God exists. Most people follow his lead in making commemoration of the Holocaust a non-religious act.

The screen memory of the Second World War has had major effects on how we remember the First. In Western Europe, commemorating both world wars has moved out of the register of martyrdom into the register of pacifism. In doing so, it has enhanced its popular appeal, especially to men and women in secularized societies. That is what will draw tens of thousands to pilgrimages and other commemorative gestures in the coming years.

There is a second case which seems to me to be exceptional. It is the case of Gallipoli. Turkey, together with Australia and New Zealand, has created a variant on the theme of martyrdom which appeals to religious and secular alike. Theirs is the story of the birth of their nations, and their emergence as separate entities from the two empires they served in the Great War. In Turkey, this story has both a Kemalist form, with its secular nationalism uninflected by Islam, alongside an Islamic form, in which the Ottoman fallen are martyrs whose blood made the emergence of modern Turkey possible. This is part of the reason why admitting the Armenian genocide is so difficult. It compromises the story of martyrdom at Gallipoli by shifting the focus to other martyrs—Armenian martyrs—massacred or left to die of thirst in Anatolia and the Syrian desert. Conflicting stories of martyrdom compromise the story of the birth of the Turkish nation. It is only by seeing both Turkish soldiers and Armenian civilians as victims not martyrs that that gap can be bridged. Don't hold your breath: the force of the martyrs' tale is still surprisingly strong.

In 2014, the centenary of the outbreak of the First World War, we can see palpable evidence of the existence of divergent memory in Western and in Eastern Europe. First, in no sense was there a European (let alone a global) commemoration of the global war of 1914–18. In Russia and Poland, 1914 is not a date in the calendar; in contrast, 1917 and 1918 are years of "liberation" for the two countries, the first from the war and Tsardom, the second from domination by Poland's imperial neighbors. Consequently, commemoration of the centenary of the war's outbreak there is largely a non-event in Poland, Russia, Belarus, and Ukraine, where so much of the war on the Eastern front was fought.

-- JSPPS 1:2 (2015) --

Further east in Asia, silence will greet the centenary, save for the voices of family members visiting the thousands of Commonwealth War Graves Commission cemeteries scatted across the globe. This contrast should not cause much surprise. Commemoration happens when groups of people agree on a specific meaning or moral value in a past event or events. With respect to the Great War, millions of men and women now give the Great War a pacifist meaning, one in which the family history of war is the family history of a lost generation of ten million men.

In Western Europe, our secularized commemorative language now has little room left in it for images of martyrdom. A turn away from war is a turn away from the glory of war and its association with both martyrdom and sacrifice. The two are not the same, though the sacralization of sacrifice is the essence of martyrdom. When the suffering on active military service and the loss of millions of lives in the Great War are no longer framed as matters of martyrdom and glory, but as matters of regret, then the nature and meaning of commemoration is bound to change as well.

It may take longer for there to be changes in the language used to commemorate those who died in the Second World War. The period since the end of Soviet rule in Eastern Europe is still very brief; perhaps by 2045, the centenary of victory over Nazism will be commemorated in similar ways in Eastern and Western Europe. This is by no means sure, but if it occurs, it will mark a coming together of memory regimes which have tended to separate European commemorative practices in the recent past.

Martyrdom, Spectacle, and Public Space: Ukraine's National Martyrology from Shevchenko to the Maidan

Uilleam Blacker

Abstract: The article traces the concept of martyrdom through Ukrainian cultural history from the 19th century to the present. It identifies a tradition of martyrological thinking in Ukrainian culture and commemorative practices, arguing that this paradigm begins and is manifested prominently in literature, before spreading much more widely in Ukrainian culture in the twentieth century. The article argues that religiously inflected Romantic nationalist ideas, language and imagery have dominated since the formulation of the concept of Ukrainian national martyrdom in the 19th century, and that these have been evident in various ways in official and unofficial uses of public space, from the creation of Taras Shevchenko's grave as a site of national memory in the late 19th century down to commemoration of the victims of the Maidan shootings in 2014. Finally, the paper identifies potential problems with the paradigm of martyrology in terms of what it includes into and excludes from Ukrainian memory culture.

The image of the martyr can be found at the beginnings of the modern Ukrainian national project, in the writings of the Romantic writers and activists of the mid-19th century as they cast their memories, and those of their readers, back to the Cossacks who laid down their lives in battle against enemies bent on subjugating Ukraine. The Cossack period was a golden age of liberation in the eyes of Taras Shevchenko and others, and was ended by the brutal strength of the Tsarist Empire, whose leaders "crucified" Ukraine.[1] The image can

---

[1]   Images of crucifixion recur in Shevchenko's work. One of the most famous instances is his poem "Son" (The Dream, 1844), in which he refers to Peter I and

also be found in the present, in the discourse of memory and commemoration that surrounds the most recent deaths in the cause of
Ukrainian national self-determination during the Maidan protest of
2014 and the subsequent war in eastern Ukraine. This article will
trace martyrological thinking through Ukraine's cultural history, focusing on cultural representations and public commemorative practice, and argue that this Romantically-inflected paradigm has been
at the heart of Ukrainian cultural identity since the 19th century in a
consistent, though shifting way.

Martyrdom, Meaning, and Public Space

In all of the catastrophes that have beset Ukraine in the twentieth
century, Ukrainians have died, sometimes in their millions; each of
these catastrophes also brought setbacks for the Ukrainian national
project. While many Ukrainians willingly gave up their lives for the
national cause, and many others died involuntarily for their dedication to that cause, the deaths among Ukrainians in the 20th century
were, of course, mainly not in the service of Ukraine. In the case of
the many Ukrainians who died fighting in the Red Army, they could
be said to have done so fighting against the Ukrainian national
cause. Those who did suffer and die consciously for Ukraine may
also present their own complications: they themselves may have
been perpetrators of violence, as well as victims, a fact that can compromise their status as hero and martyr. At the same time, while
many Ukrainians have become victims of repression and violence
because of their nationality, many of the catastrophes that affected
Ukrainians also affected others: the Nazi occupation of World War
II took a proportionally heavier toll on the Jewish population of the
territory of today's Ukraine than on Ukrainians, while Poles in the
(now) western Ukrainian territories also suffered heavily from the
Soviet invasions; likewise, the famines that affected east and central
Ukraine in the early 1930s affected other ethnicities in the region,
and also occurred in southern Russia and Kazakhstan.

Catherine II as "That *first* that crucified/Our Ukraine/And the Second who finished off/The widow-orphan"; Taras Shevchenko, "Son", *Kobzar* (Kyiv: Radians'ka shkola, 1986), 197.

As a paradigm of memory, however, martyrology avoids the kind of complexity outlined here, ignoring diversity among groups, the paradoxes of individual fates and motivations, or the moral ambiguity of those it wishes to canonize; it also tends to ignore the degree of willingness on the part of the martyr, appropriating those who might be more accurately described as involuntary victims of violent death.[2] Martyrology is interested in unambiguous, spectacular impact. For these reasons, martyrdom has generally, since the concept entered into Christian thought and practice at least, been a public event designed to have powerful propagandistic impact. Early Christian acts of martyrdom were what George Bowersock has described as "a conspicuously urban affair": Roman punishment of Christians took place in public spaces, often as part of entertainments in the amphitheaters, or at the agora, the temple, or in public spaces beside city prisons.[3] Roman spectacles, according to Bowersock, performed propagandistic functions, reinforcing imperial, social, political, religious, and gender hierarchies, and the execution of Christians was often an integral part of this show.[4] The spectacular public executions of Christians also, however, served a propaganda purpose for those Christians, providing them with a stage on which to demonstrate their faith. Christian martyrs of the early church actively sought out public platforms for their self-sacrifice, often traveling to cities in order to solicit martyrdom. They appropriated and subverted the Roman spectacle in order to be able to

---

[2]   There are, of course, many different types of death that may be interpreted as martyrdom. In some cases, death may be deliberately sought, while in others it may be recognized by an actor as a likely, if undesirable, result of their actions; others may die for a cause having underestimated the likelihood of their death; at the opposite end of the spectrum, people may die in the context of political violence entirely unwillingly, even ignorant of the reasons for their death, but still be framed in later commemoration as martyrs. The question of voluntary martyrdom is one of the thorniest in religious scholarship on the topic: in Catholic religious thinking, for example, those who display an over-eagerness to sacrifice themselves as martyrs may be frowned upon. See Candida Moss, "The Discourse of Voluntary Martyrdom: Ancient and Modern", *Church History* 81, no. 3 (2012): 531–51.

[3]   George Bowersock, *Martyrdom and Rome* (Cambridge: Cambridge University Press, 1995), 41. See also Elizabeth Castelli, *Martyrdom and Memory* (New York: Columbia University Press, 2004), 6–7.

[4]   Bowersock, *Martyrdom and Rome*, 54.

speak to and impress the assembled crowds.[5] The use of public space and spectacle by both authorities and martyrs was thus a battle over the minds of the city's inhabitants between the exercise of power on the one hand, and self-sacrifice on the other. This was a battle in which both sides sought to make maximal impact, with a maximally unambiguous message.

Martyrdom, Elizabeth Castelli argues, must have meaning, and it must have an audience that will absorb that meaning.[6] Public spaces provided the platform on which early Christian martyrs could create and convey that meaning through spectacle. Yet while the initial performance was important, the meaning of martyrs' deaths was formulated to a great degree after the event, through the memory work of martyrology. Accounts of witnesses, the preserved writings of martyrs themselves, as well as official documentation of the deaths, all constituted the culture of martyrology. The spectacular nature of the martyrs' deaths was retained in the accounts: the vivid, gruesome stories of public execution were central to the effectiveness of the myth, which presented the martyrs as heroes who could eclipse the idolatrous spectacles of the Empire.[7] While the initial acts were of course crucial, it was really in martyrology that the meanings that were attached to the deaths were formulated and spread.

Romanticism and Spectacle

It was precisely the combination of the spectacular nature of martyrdom and its potential for aesthetic and narrative elaboration that was appealing to Romantic nationalist writers like Shevchenko. According to the scholars of Polish Romanticism Maria Janion and Maria Żmigrodzka, the fondness for the language of martyrdom among poets like Adam Mickiewicz was linked to the belief in the blending of literature with reality, word with deed, via which the Romantics and their co-conspirators believed they could recover control over the unpredictable and hostile forces of history that had cast Poland

---

5   Ibid., 42.
6   Castelli, *Martyrdom and Memory*, 34.
7   Ibid., 105–26.

into statelessness and partition.[8] This blurring of the boundaries between literary and intellectual endeavor and the "theatricalization" of acts of defiance and resistance resonates strongly in the works and ideas of Mickiewicz's contemporaries in Ukraine, with whom the Polish poet and many of his contemporaries had personal contacts, and on whom they exerted a significant influence.[9]

An important example of the influence of Mickiewicz on the Ukrainian Romantic movement is the writer and historian Mykola Kostomarov's *Knyhy buttia ukrains'koho narodu* (Books of Genesis of the Ukrainian People, 1846), the programmatic statement of the Brotherhood of Cyril and Methodius, a group of Ukrainian intellectuals that included Taras Shevchenko. Kostomarov at once modeled the text on Mickiewicz's poetic-political pamphlet *Księgi narodu polskiego i pielgrzymstwa polskiego* (Books of the Polish People and of the Polish Pilgrimage, 1832), which was written in Paris in the wake of the failed uprising against the Russian Empire of 1831, and yet also subverted it, placing the ordinary Cossacks in the messianic/martyrological role in place of Mickiewicz's Polish nobles, who had, for Kostomarov, themselves contributed to the victimization of Ukraine. Both texts ground the national culture in strident religious language and imagery, framing the national projects in sacred terms, and in each case, the nation emerges as suffering great tortures, collectively and via individual martyrs, in a sense also death, in order to rise again. In each case the national project is intertwined with religion, in the Polish case with Catholicism, in the Ukrainian case with Orthodoxy. Kostomarov's text threads its narrative from the creation through Christ and the early Christian church down to the period in which it was written, establishing a continuity between early Christian martyrs and their suffering at the hands of the Roman empire and the "torment" of the Ukrainian Cossacks, "an equal

---

8   Maria Janion and Maria Żmigrodzka, *Romantyzm a historia* (Warsaw: PIW, 1978), 7.

9   See George Grabowicz, "Pol's'ko-ukrans'ki literaturni vzaemyny: pytannia kul'turnoi perspektyvy", *Do istorii ukrains'koi literatury: doslidzhennia, ese, polemika* (Kyiv: Osnovy, 1991), 138–69. Unless otherwise indicated, all websites cited in this article were accessible on 17 August 2015.

Christian brotherhood", at the hands of the Polish "Pany" (or land-owners) and then the subsequent "idol and tormentor" of Ukraine, the Tsar.[10]

As was the case with the Polish Romantics, the oppression of the Ukrainian Romantic poets for their beliefs and writings, most notably Shevchenko, turned the writers themselves into martyr-metonyms for the wider Russian imperial oppression of Ukrainian language and culture that characterized the second half of the 19th century: not only were Ukraine and its writers and intellectuals vic-timized by the Tsar, but the language and culture themselves be-came martyred. In an article written in 1917, the critic Serhii Ye-fremov (who would himself join the ranks of Ukraine's intellectual martyrs with his death in the Gulag in 1939) described the "long chain" of oppressive measures taken against Ukrainian language, lit-erature, press, and publishing in the Russian Empire as the "martyr-ology of the Ukrainian word", referring to the contemporary state of affairs as a "temporary death" for that word.[11]

Shevchenko was arrested in 1847 and tried along with other members of the Brotherhood of Cyril and Methodius in what Ye-fremov called "the first death blow" for Ukrainian literature.[12] Shevchenko received the harshest sentence of all those on trial: he was sent into military exile, and banned from writing and painting for a decade. The poet dreamed of returning to Ukraine, but after his exile he was only able to make one short trip back, during which he was again arrested and forced to return to Russia, where he re-mained under police surveillance until his death in 1861. He did, however, return to Ukraine after his death: almost three months af-ter his burial in St Petersburg, the repatriation of his remains to Ukraine was organized by a group of his followers in order to fulfill the desire expressed both privately and in his famous poem "Zapo-

---

[10]   Mykola Kostomarov, *Knyhy bytiia ukrains'koho narodu* (Paris: Franko-ukrains'ke vydavnytstvo, 1947). The words used in relation to the torment of Cossacks and the Tsar as "tormentor"—"muchyt'" and "muchytel'"—are pho-netically related to the Ukrainian word for martyr, "muchenyk".
[11]   Serhii Yefremov, "Martyroloh ukrains'koho slova", *Kyiv* 5 (1991): 121–27 (121/127).
[12]   Ibid., 123.

vit" (Testament, 1845) to be buried in the Ukrainian steppe over-looking the Dnipro river. After visiting a number of towns in Russia and Ukraine, his remains were brought to Kyiv, where, despite offi-cial injunction, they were carried through the city by hundreds of people then taken by boat down the Dnipro to the town of Kaniv and buried at Chernecha Hora, a hill overlooking the river. At a fu-neral service held at the Cathedral of the Assumption in Kaniv, the priest announced that "here, on one of the highest hills of the Dnipro, as on the mountain Golgotha, like Our Lord's Cross, a cross will be raised that will be seen on this and on the other side of the Dnipro".[13]

The reburial of Shevchenko, the creator and then embodi-ment of the national martyrdom myth, also coincided with the abo-lition of serfdom in the Russian Empire, and the timing and nature of the event, according to the dissident Yevhen Sverstiuk, took on an almost mythological or religious significance that would be im-portant for later generations:

> And this miracle happened in 1861, during the celebrations for the abolition of serfdom, when the spirit of freedom was awakened in the people and Shevchenko's words rang like a psalm. Ukraine needed its prophet, its mar-tyr for truth and its herald of God's truth. And he was recognized as such during the second funeral service, in May 1961 [sic – 1861].[14]

As promised at his funeral service, a wooden cross was indeed erected after the burial, on top of a mound built by locals and friends of Shevchenko. The cross was later replaced by a cast iron one in the early 1880s, during general renovations of the site funded by public donations; at the same time the first, modest Shevchenko museum was opened at the site.[15]

The so-called Tarasova Hora (Taras's Hill) became a site of pilgrimage for nationally conscious Ukrainians soon after the burial.

---

[13] V. M. Mel'nychenko, "Shevchenka shanuie ioho Bat'kivshchyna", in *Ukraina Tarasa Shevchenka: istorychni kraeznavchi narysy*, eds. R. V. Man'kovs'ka and V. M. Mel'nychenko (Kharkiv: Folio, 2014), 59.
[14] Yevhen Sverstiuk, "Shevchenko ponad chasom. Data 22 travnia", *Prosvita Pol-tava*, 22 May 2012, http://www.prosvita.poltava.ua/?p=1610.
[15] Mel'nychenko, "Shevchenka shanuie ioho Bat'kivshchyna", 60.

Its associations with the new national "prophet", as well as its evocative resemblance of the Cossack burial mounds that feature prominently in Ukrainian folklore and in Shevchenko's own poetry, turned it into what Serhy Yekelchyk calls "a sacred place" and "one of the central symbols in the semiotic network of the modern Ukrainian national identity".[16] The grave and its resident quickly became the focus of "myth creation and symbolic thinking", with large numbers of pilgrims, including intellectuals, clergy, and peasants, treating the site as though it contained the remains of a saint, even prostrating themselves in front of it. The site was consequently seen as a potential flashpoint for Ukrainian nationalist mobilization: Tsarist authorities consistently denied requests for a monument to be built, while local Polish landlords asked for the removal of the grave, fearing it might incite the kind of uprisings against them that Shevchenko had described in his work.[17] In 1911 and 1914, on the fiftieth anniversary of Shevchenko's death and one hundredth anniversary of his birth, the authorities circulated instructions across Ukraine to prevent commemoration, and dispatched police units to prevent demonstrations at the grave.[18] The authorities' fears had some foundation: in 1891, for example, the first Ukrainian organization in the Russian Empire to openly campaign for Ukrainian independence, the Brotherhood of Taras, was founded at the site by a group of students.[19]

During Soviet times, the figure of Shevchenko was appropriated by the authorities, and his writings used selectively for their anti-Tsarist, egalitarian message. Commemoration was permitted, though carefully controlled. Throughout the 1920s and 1930s the site at Kaniv was gradually expanded with new memorials and museums, with a temporary monument erected in 1923, and a major sculpture finally installed in 1939, at the same time as another major

---

[16] Serhy Yekelchyk, "Creating a Sacred Place: the Ukrainophiles and Shevchenko's Tomb in Kaniv (1861-ca. 1900)", *Journal of Ukrainian Studies* 20, nos 1–2 (1995): 15–33 (20).

[17] Ibid., 22–25.

[18] Mel'nychenko, "Shevchenka shanuie ioho Bat'kivshchyna", 16.

[19] Yekelchyk, "Creating a Sacred Place", 31.

monument was also erected in Kyiv. Major, officially sanctioned anniversaries in Kaniv, such as those in 1961 and 1964, attracted tens of
thousands of visitors. According to Yevhen Sverstiuk, however, the
monuments, particularly the Kyiv one, and the date of the 1861 reburial (22 May) became important for unofficial celebrations of
Ukrainianness from the 1960s onwards, and were strictly policed by
the Soviet authorities, who would arrest students and activists who
came to lay flowers, recite poetry, and sing at the monuments.[20]

Martyrdom as Cultural Paradigm

Under the powerful shadow of Shevchenko's transition from subject
to object of martyrology, Ukraine's great literary figures have tradi-
tionally been perceived through the lens of suffering and self-sacrifice for their culture. This is manifested most powerfully in relation
to the remarkably vibrant generation of writers who emerged in the
1920s in Soviet Ukraine and were murdered by the regime in the
1930s. Even against the background of the horrors of the Stalinist
terror across the Soviet Union, the fate of Soviet Ukrainian professional writers in the 1930s—about 80 percent of whom were murdered—stands out as particularly brutal.[21] Until the Thaw period,
the memory of this decimated generation was prohibited, and even
then could only be partially discussed; it was actively promoted by
Ukrainian intellectuals in emigration, however, notably by the
writer Viktor Petrov (who wrote under the pseudonym Domon-
tovych), in whose war-time writing documenting the fate of these
writers "the first coherent thesis of martyrology was formulated",[22]
but perhaps most famously with the landmark publication of the
anthology under the title *Rozstriliane vidrodzhennia*—or "executed

---

[20]   Sverstiuk, "Shevchenko ponad chasom", and Yekelchyk, "Creating a Sacred
        Place", 31. According to Yekelchyk, the site at Kaniv lost its popularity with its
        appropriation by the authorities in the later Sovet period.
[21]   Yurii Lavrinenko, "Literatura vitaizmu, 1917–1933", in *Rozstriliane vidrodzhen-
        nia: antalohiia 1917-1933*, ed. Yurii Lavrinenko (Kyiv: Smoloskyp, 2008), 929–56
        (955).
[22]   Halyna Hryn, "The Executed Renaissance Paradigm Revisited", *Harvard Ukrain-
        ian Studies* 27, nos 1-4 (2004–2005): 67–96 (68).

renaissance"—in 1959, by the Polish émigré journal *Kultura* and under the editorship of the critic Yurii Lavrinenko. The term "executed renaissance", which had been suggested to Lavrinenko by the editor of *Kultura* Jerzy Giedroyc, proved to be an apposite one, encapsulating not only the martyrdom of those responsible for the 1920s cultural rebirth in Ukraine, but also, for Lavrinenko, pointing towards the potential power of the legacy of these writers for the resurrection of Ukrainian culture: as Lavrinenko puts it, citing a poem by Shevchenko, "in the 'Great Dungeon' [to which the Soviets had consigned Ukrainian culture] after twenty five years lie not relics, but the living, young, powerful, and vitalistic spirit of rebirth".[23]

The sophisticated analytical essay by Lavrinenko in the anthology, which is cited above, represents more than just a martyrological text, and his anthology was a major achievement in bringing the work of these writers to light. The formulation "executed renaissance" (in many ways, of course, simply descriptive of these writers' fate) also helped to shape the image of this literary generation as martyrs to the Soviet system, and in doing so elided the artistic and political complexity of the group it described.[24] The term, to cite Yevhen Sverstiuk's essay in a later edition of the anthology, has "gone into history and has defined the fate of Ukrainian culture after the revolution and the lost war. And at the same time, this metaphor embraces the dead and the living [a reference to Shevchenko's poem "My Friendly Epistle..."—UB], who have not been executed, but have been deprived of the freedom to create".[25]

The "executed renaissance" thus appears as a further link in the "chain" of violence that Yefremov identifies, and the image of these writers that circulates in Ukraine today is dominated by their martyrdom. In the post-1991 period, when open publication of these writers' work and discussion of their fate became possible, this image was magnified and widely disseminated in projects such as the initiative "Martyroloh Ukrainy" (Martyrology of Ukraine), led by the writer Oleksa Musienko, who in 1991, as the first of a number of

23   Lavrinenko, "Literatura vitaizmu", 956.
24   Hryn, "Executed Renaissance", 68–69.
25   Yevhen Sverstiuk, "Pro Rozstrilane vidrodzhennia (suchasni refleksii)", in *Rozstriliane vidrodzhennia*, 957–62 (957).

"martyrological" initiatives, published the book *Z poroha smerti: pysmennyky Ukrainy – zhertvy stalins'kykh represii* (From the threshold of death: Ukrainian writers, victims of Stalinist repressions). The book represents a partial list of the writers who fell victim to the "Stalinist Golgotha", and frames them as part of a wider Moscow-based persecution of "Ukrainian literary culture" and "Ukrainianness" that extends from the victimization of individual writers to the larger tragedy of the Holodomor and far beyond:

> [...] for several centuries already Ukrainian literature, like no other literature in the world, has been drowning in its own blood. For apart from the Stalinist terror, it has been ruined and bled dry by Tsarist terror, and, in the lifetime of a single generation, it was set upon by the White, Red, Polish-Noble, German-Fascist, and Brezhnev terrors. It remains for us to wonder how this nation survived at all, and did not lose the gift of the artistic Word.[26]

Musienko's project is a perfect example of Marko Pavlyshyn's influential idea, that the Ukrainian cultural canon has been and still is constructed not as a mere genealogy of writers, but as an "iconostasis" of saints and martyrs, from Shevchenko in the 19th century down to Vasyl Stus, the dissident poet who died in the Gulag in 1985, and whose complex, philosophically rich verse is eclipsed by his image as a rugged, undefeated national martyr.[27] Stus, who Pavlyshyn singles out as having suffered particularly from his work being seen through this particular prism, was key to the continuation of the writer-martyr myth in Ukraine, and his posthumous commemoration echoed that of Shevchenko: Stus's remains (alongside those of fellow dissidents Iurii Lytvyn and Oleksa Tykhyi) were transferred to Kyiv and reburied in a ceremony attended by 30,000 people in 1989.[28] As was the case with Shevchenko and his "Testament", with

---

[26]   Oleksa Musienko and Valerii Huzhva, *Z poroha smerti: pysmenyky Ukrainy – zhertvy stalins'kykh represii* (Kyiv: Radians'kyi pysmennyk, 1991); an online version can be found at *Ukrains'ke zhyttia v Sevastopoli*: http://ukrlife.org/main/ev shan/martyrolog.htm.

[27]   Marko Pavlyshyn, *Kanon ta ikonostas* (Kyiv: Chas, 1997); on Stus, see Marko Pavlyshyn, "Martyrology and Literary Scholarship: the Case of Vasyl' Stus", *The Slavic and East European Journal* 54, no. 4 (2010): 585–606.

[28]   Tom Rowley, "Documentary Film and Dissident Reburial in the Soviet Union 1989-91", paper given at the conference Martyrdom and Memory Wars, held at the University of Cambridge, 13 May 2013; Natalia Shostak, "To Whom Does a

Stus's reburial his famous line "My people, I will return to you/and in death will return to life", with its Christian echoes, was seen to have been fulfilled, much like a biblical prophecy.[29]

While Shevchenko's reburial provided a model of martyrological practice that could function with cultural figures like Stus, the site of his grave at Kaniv would also prove an inspiring location not only for nationally conscious Ukrainians who gathered there on the anniversaries of the reburial, but also for those seeking to spectacularly perpetuate the martyr tradition. In 1978, for example a Ukrainian nationalist activist, Oleksa Hirnyk, dramatically underlined the connection between late Soviet opposition and Romantic nationalist valorization of the spectacular deed when he burned himself alive on Shevchenko's grave, protesting against the Russification and colonization of Ukraine. Hirnyk was not the first to take such drastic action: in 1968, Vasyl Makukh, a former soldier of the anti-Soviet wartime resistance movement, the UPA (Ukrainian Insurgent Army), burned himself alive on Kyiv's main street, Khreshchatyk, on the day of the celebration of the October Revolution, in protest against the Warsaw Pact invasion of Czechoslovakia, and also against the Russification of Ukraine under Soviet rule.[30]

It is worth remembering that a key slogan used in protest against the Warsaw Pact invasion was "For our freedom and for yours", which has its roots in the Polish Romantic uprisings of the 19th century against Tsarist rule and attempts to persuade Russians to sympathize with the Polish cause.[31] The slogan was used by Soviet dissidents during their famous protest on Red Square in August 1968 in opposition to the invasion of Czechoslovakia, and also by Ryszard

---

Poet Belong: The Reburial of Vasyl' Stus as a Ritual of Cultural Appropriation", *Spaces of Identity* 2.3, no. 4 (2002), http://www.yorku.ca/soi/_Vol_2_3/PDF/Shostak.pdf.

[29]   Vasyl' Stus, "Yak dobre te, shcho smerti ne boius' ya", *Vybrani tvory* (Donets'k: Bao, 2011), 96.

[30]   V. Ovsienko, "Makukh, Vasyl' Omelianovych", *Dysydents'kyi rukh Ukrainy: virtual'nyi muzei*, 14 July 2007, http://archive.khpg.org/index.php?id=1184404827; B. Krasavtsev, "Vasyl' Makukh – liudyna yaka zhorila za Ukrainu", *Radio Svoboda*, 14 November 2011, http://www.radiosvoboda.org/content/article/24770217.html.

[31]   Norman Davies, *God's Playground: a History of Poland. Volume II: 1795 to the Present* (Oxford and New York: Oxford University Press, 2005), 50.

Siwiec, a former member of Poland's wartime resistance movement, the Home Army, when he burned himself alive in Warsaw's Centennial Stadium during a harvest festival in the same year. While neither Makukh nor Hirnyk are known to have used the slogan, their actions fit very much into this paradigm of neo-Romantic national opposition, which reached its zenith in the 1960s and 1970s with a wave of similar self-immolations across the Soviet Union and Eastern Bloc. It is notable that the national movements in all countries in which such instances occurred—Ukraine, Poland, Czechoslovakia, and Lithuania—developed in the mid- to late 19th century under the influence of Romantic intellectual/literary national liberation movements with their emphasis on "theatricalization" and the blending of word and deed. What these gestures also show, however, is that during the twentieth century, Ukrainian martyrology had shifted away from its literary-intellectual roots in the 19th century and from the involuntary martyrdom of figures like Shevchenko towards a more radical, voluntary, and violent paradigm.

Twentieth-Century Martyrology: Kruty and Stalinist Terror

The reason for the escalation and radicalization of Ukrainian martyrdom and martyrology lay in Ukraine's 20th-century history, which repeatedly created the conditions for the appearance of new national martyrs. One of the first examples of this came in 1918, during the conflicts that followed the end of the First World War and which provided space for the establishment of the short-lived Ukrainian People's Republic, when a group of several hundred Ukrainian soldiers, some of them students, fought the battle of Kruty in 1918 against superior Bolshevik forces, suffering heavy losses.[32] The self-sacrificial fight at Kruty, which is intimately connected to Ukraine's failed but symbolically important attempt to establish statehood at the time, entered deep into Ukrainian martyrological thinking. There were immediate commemorations under the short-lived Ukrainian People's Republic (UNR), and the poet Pavlo Tychyna

---

[32]   Orest Subtelny, *Ukraine: A History of Ukraine* (Toronto: University of Toronto Press, 1988), 352.

hailed the young men who died, in a poem laced with biblical references, as "martyr-Ukrainians".[33] While the "heroes of Kruty" were
erased from the official Soviet discourse that soon took over in most
of Ukraine, their memory survived in the Ukrainian diaspora and in
western Ukraine, in interwar Poland, where the events were an in-
spiration for, among others, the radical Organization of Ukrainian
Nationalists (OUN) and later for the OUN's military wing, the
Ukrainian Insurgent Army (UPA). Official commemorative activity
recommenced immediately after the collapse of the USSR, culminating in the inauguration of a major memorial at the site of the battle
in 2006, opened by Viktor Yushchenko, which incorporated a chapel
and a large cross-shaped pool. Another, smaller memorial marks the
burial place of some of the fallen in Kyiv—the site of the original
UNR memorial—with the words from John 15:13 "Greater love hath
no man than this, that a man lay down his life for his friends". Yushchenko's presidency also saw the renaming of a number of streets
after the "heroes of Kruty". More recently, Kruty was referenced in a
much-photographed piece of graffiti on the Maidan, just near the
end of Instytuts'ka Street, where many young men died fighting government forces: "Nashi Kruty tut"—Our Kruty is Here.

    After the establishment of Bolshevik power in Ukraine, a dif-
ferent mythology was dominant—that of the martyrs of the Civil
War and Revolution.[34] Yet while this new martyrology was developing, the early 1930s saw the Soviet state inflict perhaps the greatest
tragedy in Ukraine's modern history: the Holodomor, or artificial
famine, of 1932–33, which killed several million Ukrainians (though
it also affected other parts of the USSR). While memory of this tragedy was strictly suppressed in the Soviet Union, and the deaths had
little to do with voluntary political martyrdom, the victims would
later, especially in emigration, then in Ukraine after 1991, particularly during the presidency of Viktor Yushchenko, come to serve as

---

33   Pavlo Tychyna, "Pam'iati trydtsiaty" [1918], *Zibrannia tvoriv u dvanadtsiaty tomakh*, vol. 12 (2) (Kviv: Naukova dumka, 1990), 110.
34   On the wider Bolshevik martyrdom culture, see Catherine Merridale, *Night of Stone: Death and Memory in Russia* (London: Granta Books, 2000), 118–23.

metonyms for the broader martyrdom of the Ukrainian nation.[35] Yushchenko's push, both at home and abroad, to have the famine recognized as an act of genocide perpetrated against Ukraine as a nation was precisely an attempt to cement Shevchenko's image of a crucified nation in national and international law.[36] Yushchenko's policy also included the construction of a memorial and museum in central Kyiv, opened in 2008 for the 75th anniversary of the famines, which is now the focal point for yearly commemorations, and is on the standard itinerary for visiting heads of state. Part of the museum's exhibition is a copy of the *National Book of Memory of the Victims of the Holodomor of 1932-33 in Ukraine*, published in 2008 by the Institute for National Remembrance, which contains a "martyrology"—the names of the known victims of the famines—for each region of Ukraine.[37]

Ukraine's Churches and the National Martyrdom Discourse

Another key element of Ukraine's modern martyrology has been, of course, religion. Christian imagery was prominent in the works of the Ukrainian Romantic writers, and sites and practices of national martyrdom of the late 19th century, most notably Shevchenko's grave and the commemorative events that took place there, were religious in character and involved the participation of clergy. While this element was absent from Soviet martyrdom narratives for obvious reasons, post-independence martyrology in Ukraine widely incorporates Christian aesthetics and language. Ukraine's various churches

---

[35] On Holodomor commemoration see David R. Marples, *Heroes and Villains: Creating National History in Contemporary Ukraine* (Budapest and New York: Central European University Press, 2007), 35–77.

[36] On the problem of the Holodomor as genocide see ibid.; Hiroaki Kuromiya, "The Soviet Famine of 1932–1933 Reconsidered", *Europe-Asia Studies* 60, no. 4 (2008): 663–75; George G. Grabowicz, "The Holodomor and Memory", in *Hunger by Design. The Great Ukrainian Famine and Its Soviet Context*, ed. Halyna Hryn (Cambridge, MA: Harvard University Press, 2008); and Georgiy Kasianov, "Ukraine: *Holodomor* and Nation Building", *Pro et contra* 13, nos 3–4 (May–September 2009).

[37] *Natsional'na knyha pam'iati zhertv Holodomoru 1932-33 rokiv v Ukraini* (Kyiv: Vydavnytstvo Oleny Telihy, 2008). Online version available here: https://archive.is/20121222074350/www.memory.gov.ua/ua/publication/content/1522.htm.

play a key role in the development of the discourse of national martyrdom through participation in state-sponsored commemoration
and through the promotion of their own modern martyrs.

Since the 1980s, there have been numerous publications that
aim to recover the memory of the martyrs of Ukraine's churches,
notable among them being two volumes entitled *Martyroloh
ukrains'kykh tserkov* (martyrology of the Ukrainian churches) published in 1987 under the editorship of the human rights activist,
scholar and writer Osyp Zinkevych, the first dealing with Orthodox
martyrs, and the second with Catholic ones.[38] All of Ukraine's
churches have celebrated their respective "new martyrs" of the communist period, often inscribing these into a wider narrative of national suffering. In 2011, the Ukrainian Orthodox Church of the Kyiv
Patriarchate—the most influential church in Ukraine today—declared the second Sunday after Pentecost to be the Day of the All-
Church Commemoration of the New Martyrs and Confessors in
Ukraine and in Other Lands in the 20th Century who Suffered for
Christ and the Orthodox Faith, referring in official statements to the
"warlike and godless" powers of the 20th century who, like the "ancient Roman pagans" had persecuted the Ukrainian church.[39] The
minority Ukrainian Autocephalous church, meanwhile, commemorates a Memorial Day of the Holy Ukrainian New Martyrs on 27 November, the date on which the church's first Metropolitan, Vasyl
Lypkivs'kyi, was executed by the NKVD in 1937. The Autocephalous
church considers Lypkivs'kyi a saint, and he is the subject of a memorial in Ternopil and several commemorative plaques and icons.
A street was named after him in Kyiv in 2007, while in 2014, shortly
after the Maidan protests, the town of Lypets' in the Vynnytsia region renamed part of its Lenin Street after him, with the other part

[38] *Martyroloh ukrains'kykh tserkov v chotyr'okh tomakh: dokumenty, materiialy,
khrystyians'kyi samvydav Ukrainy*, eds. Osyp Zinkevych, Taras Lonchyna (Toronto: Smoloskyp, 1987).
[39] "Zhurnal No. 22: Zasidannia sviashchennoho synodu ukrains'koi pravoslavnoi
tserkvy Kyivs'koho patriarkhatu", *Ukrains'ka Pravoslavna Tserkva Kyivs'koho
Patriarkhatu*, 27 August 2011, http://www.cerkva.info/uk/synod/1766-synod-27-
08-11.html.

being named for the Heroes of the Maidan.[40] Finally, in relation to the Orthodox churches, it is important to acknowledge the influence in Ukraine of the Ukrainian Orthodox Church of the Moscow Patriarchate, which effectively promotes the memory of its own New Martyrs in Ukraine, serving thus as a pro-Russian counterbalance to the nationally-oriented martyrdom myths of the other churches.[41]

The Ukrainian Greek Catholic Church (UGCC) is the most influential church in the western part of Ukraine, but also "sees itself as the church best qualified, or indeed the only one qualified, to be called a Ukrainian National Church", even though its members represent only around 11 percent of the Ukrainian population.[42] In late and post-Soviet Ukraine, the UGCC's martyrs have been a key part of the Church's attempts to assert itself both in terms of the wider Christian and Catholic context, but also as the Ukrainian national church. In 1981, the church published a special issue of one of its journals entitled *Church of Martyrs*, with an essay by Patriarch Iosif Slipyi, who himself spent eighteen years in Soviet prisons before being expelled from the Soviet Union, dedicated to its clergy that had fallen victim to the NKVD.[43] Twenty years later, in 2001, twenty-eight "new martyrs", UGCC victims of Soviet repression, were beatified on the request of the UGCC by Pope John Paul II.

A key part of the discourse legitimizing these new martyrs has been the brutal ways in which they were killed. While the fate of these individuals was genuinely horrific, stories surrounding them also reached beyond established facts into the realm of myth, incorporating details of suffering and death that were borrowed from Christian martyrdom mythology, thus deliberately inscribing the

---

[40]   "Vulytsiu Lenina pereimenovano", *Nash Lypovets'*, 22 July 2014, http://lipovets.co m.ua/index.php/ainmenu-29/14-/350-vulytsiu-lenina-pereimenovano.html.

[41]   On the New Martyrs in Russia, see Julie Fedor, "Setting the Soviet Past in Stone: The Iconography of the New Martyrs of the Russian Orthodox Church", *Australian Slavonic and East European Studies* 28, nos 1-2 (2014): 124–53.

[42]   Sophia Senyk, "The Ukrainian Greek Catholic Church Today: Universal Values versus Nationalist Doctrines", *Religion, State and Society* 30, no. 4 (2002): 317–32 (319). See also "Bil'shist' naselennia Ukrainy vidnosyt' sebe do Pravoslavnoi tserkvy Kyivs'koho patriarkhatu", *Fond Demokratychni Initsiatyvy im. Il'ka Kucheriva* [no date; based on statistical information gathered in December 2014]; http://dif.org.ua/ua/publications/press-relizy/bilshist-naselgo-patriarhatu.htm.

[43]   *Tserkva muchenykiv*, special issue of *Vidhomin' liubovi*, 2 March 1981.

new martyrs into an old tradition.[44] As Castelli notes, it was precisely the brutal nature of the deaths of the Christian martyrs that made martyrology so effective, providing evocative narrative material and powerful images of a spectacular profession of faith that was sure to leave an impression on its audience, and the same dynamic seems to apply in this case.[45]

World War II

Without doubt, the greatest focus for martyrology in contemporary Ukraine is World War II. In this regard, two main narratives of heroic martyrology dominate: that of the Red Army and Soviet partisans on the one hand, and that of the anti-Soviet nationalist resistance movement, the UPA, on the other. As Nina Tumarkin and others have discussed, the USSR's massive losses in the war were instrumentalized by the authorities to sacralize the victory over Nazism and legitimize the post-war geopolitical order, bringing "new myths of martyrs and saints" that were dramatically and ubiquitously imposed on public spaces across the Soviet Union.[46] This was a martyrdom myth that was imposed from above, but also shared from below by those whose relatives had died in the service of the Red Army or among the partisans. The Ukrainian Insurgent Army, on the other hand, formed the focus for narratives of national martyrdom among many anti-Soviet Ukrainians, particularly in the west of the country.

The UPA, OUN, and their martyrs, such as the prominent OUN leader Stepan Bandera (who was assassinated by the KGB in 1959) or the commander of the UPA Roman Shukhevych (who killed himself to avoid being captured by Soviet security services in 1950), represent a controversial part of Ukrainian martyrology, given the crimes that members of these organizations committed against

---

44   Kateryna Budz, "Martyrdom as a Response to Violence", unpublished paper presented at the workshop "Violence and its Aftermath in Soviet and Post-Soviet Contexts", Zhytomyr, 2011.

45   Castelli, *Martyrdom and Memory*, 6–7, 34, 39.

46   Nina Tumarkin, *The Living and the Dead: the Rise and Fall of the Cult of World War II in Russia* (New York: Basic Books, 1994), 76.

Polish, Jewish, and Ukrainian civilians during the war. The interwar and wartime national movement in western Ukraine became increasingly different from what it had been under the UNR, and previously among the Romantic nationalist intellectuals of the 19th century, and certainly contrasted with the left-wing strands of Ukrainian nationalism that existed in Soviet Ukraine between the wars: as in much of Europe, in the 1930s, Ukrainian nationalist politics became increasingly dominated by the radical right. The nationalism of the OUN focused far more on ideas of race and ethnicity, and pursued its goals through an increasingly violent philosophy, which culminated in brutal acts of ethnic cleansing during World War II.[47] Commemoration of the OUN and UPA tends to ignore these less palatable aspects of their history and focus on their fight against Soviet subjugation, and on the brutal repressions suffered by their members at the hands of the Soviets: those who were not executed during or after the war often spent years or decades in Soviet prisons, often undergoing horrific tortures. As Yuliya Yurchuk points out, in contemporary discourse on the OUN and UPA "the fight for independence turns the UPA soldiers into martyrs, or even almost into saints, and the duty of remembering is constructed as a moral duty of each Christian".[48] Their memory is channeled through the same historical myths favored by the Romantics—through Cossackdom, with many motifs of the discourse seemingly borrowed from Romantic literature: Yurchuk points out the use, for example, of the motif of the "insurgents' graves" in commemorative discourse, which echoes the emphasis placed by Shevchenko on the graves of the Cossacks in his work. The discourse is also couched in powerful religious rhetoric, which has at times been supported by Ukraine's churches.[49] The intense Christianization of the memory, as Yurchuk

[47] Oleksandr Zaitsev, "Ukrainian Integral Nationalism in Quest of a 'Special Path' (1920s–1930s)", *Russian Politics and Law*, 51, no. 5 (September–October 2013): 11–32.
[48] Yuliya Yurchuk, *Reordering of Meaningful Words: Memory of the Organization of Ukrainian Nationalists and the Ukrainian Insurgent Army in Post-Soviet Ukraine* (Stockholm: Stockholm Studies in History, 2015), 184.
[49] Ibid., 90, 126, 164.

notes, lends the martyrology weight and makes it harder to challenge.[50]

Commemoration of these organizations causes friction within Ukraine, as many, particularly in the south and east of the country, subscribe more to the Red Army Victory myth, and either view the nationalists as German collaborators or are indifferent to them.[51] While local memory practice in western Ukraine has celebrated the OUN and UPA, national governments have treated these organizations with some distance, and it was only at the end of Viktor Yushchenko's rule, when his popularity was already all but gone, that a major commemorative gesture was made at state level, with the awarding of the title of Hero of Ukraine to Bandera in 2010 (a decision that was annulled under Yanukovych). A further development came in 2015, however, when the Ukrainian parliament approved a package of so-called "decommunization" laws, which were co-authored by the historian and head of the Ukrainian Institute of National Remembrance Volodymyr Viatrovych. The laws have provoked controversy by their insistence on state recognition of those who fought for Ukraine's independence in the anti-Soviet nationalist resistance alongside the existing recognition of the sacrifices made by those who fought in the Red Army and with the partisans, even potentially introducing legal consequences for questioning the heroism of nationalist fighters.

The "decommunization" laws, in theory, entail the exhaustive removal of Soviet symbols and monuments from public space across Ukraine, lending official legislative backing to the kind of practice already seen in the wave of destruction of Soviet monuments that took place following the Maidan protests. However, the laws also specifically recognize the sacrifice of those who fought in the Soviet armed forces in order to defeat Nazism, and specifically guarantee respect for memorials, cemeteries, and monuments that commemorate that victory. This aspect of the laws also plugs into pre-existing

---

50   Ibid., 184.
51   See Viktoria Sereda, "Regional Historical Identities and Memory", *Ukraïna Moderna* 12, no. 2 (2007): http://uamoderna.com/images/archiv/12_2/4_UM_12_2 _Statti_Hrytsak.pdf.

practice in Ukraine, since Red Army graves and memorials are generally respected throughout the entire territory of Ukraine. There is, however, potential for conflict and contradiction within the laws in their dual aims to eliminate Soviet symbols and monuments from public space, when monuments to the victory over fascism were such a central part of the Soviet public commemorative landscape: while the law on "the condemnation of the Communist and National Socialist (Nazi) regimes, and the prohibition of propaganda of their symbols" provides an exception for "memorial structures located within burial sites, honorable burial sites", it is unclear what happens to Red Army memorials that are not attached to places of burial.[52]

The complexity and ambiguity in contemporary Ukraine's attitude to the Soviet Great Patriotic War martyrdom myth could be seen in the events that marked the anniversary of the end of the war in 2015: instead of holding only the traditional 9 May Victory parade—a Soviet practice that has persisted in independent Ukraine—the government announced, as part of the same wave of legislation that produced the "decommunization laws", that an additional "Memorial and Reconciliation day" on 8 May would be added, introducing a more European-style somberness to the celebration in contrast to the bombast of Soviet celebrations that still characterizes Russian Victory Day parades. To this end the Institute for National Remembrance also introduced a new symbol for the commemorations already in 2014: the black and red poppy, which appears in both Ukrainian folk culture but also, notably, in British and Commonwealth Remembrance Day commemorations, and which, according to the Institute's director Volodymyr Viatrovych, is "a traditional Ukrainian symbol, which appears in Cossack *dumy* as a symbol of spilled Cossack blood. On the other hand, the red poppy is a European symbol of the victims of the First and Second World Wars."[53] The red and black colors also happen to be associated with the OUN

---

[52]   *Ukrainian Institute of National Remembrance*, 9 April 2015: http://www.memo ry.gov.ua/laws/law-ukraine-condemnation-communist-and-national-socialist-n azi-regimes-and-prohibition-propagan.

[53]   Volodymyr Viatrovych, "Maky pam'iati", *Ukrains'ka Pravda*, 8 April 2015: http://blogs.pravda.com.ua/authors/viatrovych/5524cbea80744/.

and UPA, though this was not officially cited as a reason for choosing them. Kyiv's most visible Soviet monument, the Motherland statue that stands above the city's World War II museum, was decorated with a giant wreath of poppies.

The hybrid nature of the two-day commemorations of the war in 2015, retaining elements of Soviet, Ukrainian, and European practices, is fairly typical of Ukraine's martyrologies, and of its memory culture more widely.[54] In this sense, the country's most prominent site of World War II commemoration, the Museum of the History of Ukraine in World War II, at the base of Kyiv's Motherland monument, is also telling. The museum was opened in 1981, and is surrounded by an extensive memorial complex featuring typical Soviet relief sculptures displaying the heroic struggle, death, and suffering of Soviet soldiers, partisans, and civilians, as well as an alley of Soviet Hero Cities. The museum has been redesigned and its narrative reframed to an extent since Ukrainian independence, and the recent moves towards decommunization prompted an official name change from the previous Museum of the Great Patriotic War; but the predominance of Soviet aesthetics and symbolism persists. Visitors are greeted by a monumental bronze Soviet soldier standing over a smashed fascist eagle and swastika: only today the soldier is draped in a Ukrainian flag. The museum also overwhelmingly focuses on the Red Army and partisans, with only one small additional window about the UPA, and no attempt made to explain the relationship between these organizations. The two sets of heroes and martyrs, the Soviet and the nationalist, sit alongside one another, but are not brought into any kind of dialogue, and the problem of the incompatibility of competing martyrdoms is simply left unresolved. Notably, other potential narratives of heroism and suffering, most obviously that of the suffering of Jews in the Holocaust, are almost entirely absent from the museum, which still uses the Soviet term "peaceful Soviet citizens" (in parts of the display that clearly date from the original museum) to refer to the Nazis' victims, even

---

54   On Ukraine's pluralist memory culture see Andriy Portnov, "Memory Wars in Post-Soviet Ukraine (1991–2010)", in *Memory and Theory in Eastern Europe*, ed. Uilleam Blacker, Alexander Etkind and Julie Fedor (New York and Basingstoke: Palgrave Macmillan, 2013), 233–54.

when these were overwhelmingly Jews: again, potential muddying of the waters of the narrative(s) of heroic martyrdom is avoided.[55]

While the museum in Kyiv retains much of the cult of the Soviet war martyrdom, only cautiously introducing the nationalist narrative, other sites take a different approach. One such site is the Prison on Lonts'kyi Street museum in L'viv, in the development of which Volodymyr Viatrovych (then head of the Center for the Study of the Liberation Movement that was based in the museum) played a key role. The museum was opened in 2009, in a former jail that was the site of the torture and murder of many Ukrainians, including nationalist activists, by the NKVD during World War II, though it was also used by the Nazis, and had functioned as a prison under the interwar Polish and pre-World War I Austrian authorities, when it had also held Ukrainian nationalist activists. During World War II, the site became a focal point for the L'viv pogrom of 1941, in which members of the nationalist underground participated, and which was sparked in part by the Nazis' opening up of the NKVD prison to reveal the mutilated bodies of the victims of Soviet atrocities; blame for these crimes was projected onto the city's Jewish population.[56] While the prison in reality was the site of the suffering and death of people of various nationalities, some, but certainly not all, for their political beliefs, the present museum frames it overwhelmingly as a site of national—and nationalist—martyrdom. Its exhibit focuses predominantly on Soviet crimes against Ukrainians, giving prominence to OUN activists, and culminates in a visit to the courtyard,

---

[55] I discuss the relationship of Holocaust commemoration to Ukrainian national narratives in more depth—including in relation to the World War II museum in Kyiv—in my forthcoming monograph *Memory, Forgetting and the Legacy of Post-1945 Displacement in Eastern Europe* (Routledge, forthcoming 2016).

[56] On memory of the L'viv pogrom see John Paul Himka, *Ukrainians, Jews, and the Holocaust: Divergent Memories* (Saskatoon: Heritage Press, 2009). On Ukrainian memory of the Holocaust see: John-Paul Himka, "The Reception of the Holocaust in Postcommunist Ukraine", in *Bringing the Dark Past to Light*, eds. John-Paul Himka and Joanna Beata Michlic (Lincoln, NE: Nebraska University Press, 2013), 626–62. I discuss the museum and its context in more detail here: Uilleam Blacker, "Urban Commemoration and Literature in post-Soviet L'viv: a Comparative Analysis with the Polish Experience", *Nationalities Papers* 42, no. 4 (2014): 637–54.

once an execution site, which is dominated by a large cross surrounded by gruesome pictures of the corpses of torture victims.

The museum's online mission statement identifies its four "main ideas":

> The triumph of good (sacrifice/victims [*zhertv*] in the name of independence and freedom) over evil (torture, occupation, death, enslavement)
>
> The greatness of the struggle and sacrifice for the independence of Ukraine.
>
> Other than Ukrainians, other nations also suffered, and Ukrainians fought for independence both for themselves and for all.
>
> It is impossible to kill the thirst for freedom, and thus freedom itself, via physical destruction.[57]

The martyrological approach is clear from the language used here, while the problem of the darker side of some of the organizations celebrated in the museum is elided by casting "other nations" as beneficiaries of the Ukrainian national struggle, not victims of it. This framing hides the fact that, while some of those who appear in the museum (such as some 1960s dissidents) certainly supported the rights of other nations on Ukrainian territory, the prominently-celebrated OUN is in fact well known for its desire to forcibly remove non-Ukrainians from what it considered ethnically Ukrainian lands.[58]

The Lonts'kyi museum's discursive tactic of homogenizing those who suffered on its territory in terms of ethnicity and political ideals is part of a wider attempt to inscribe a coherent narrative of national heroism and martyrdom onto the mnemonic map of L'viv. Situated not far from the museum is a controversial monument to Stepan Bandera, which was erected in 2007. This district of L'viv also

---

[57]   *Tiurma na Lonts'koho: Natsional'nyi muzei-memorial zhertv okupatsiinykh rezhymiv: Misiia*: http://www.lonckoho.lviv.ua/muzej/misiya.

[58]   Karel C. Berkhoff and Marco Carynnyk, "The Organization of Ukrainian Nationalists and Its Attitude toward Germans and Jews: Iaroslav Stets'ko's 1941 Zhyttiepys", *Harvard Ukrainian Studies* 23, nos 3/4 (1999): 149–84; and Gabriel N. Finder and Alexander V. Prusin, "Collaboration in Eastern Galicia: The Ukrainian Police and the Holocaust", *East European Jewish Affairs* 34, no. 2 (2004): 95–118 (96).

experienced a significant wave of street renaming in honor of nationalist wartime heroes after 1991: the museum, for example, is on Stepan Bandera Street, which between 1944 and 1961 was named after Stalin, and from 1961–91 bore the typical Soviet name of Peace Street. In 1997, a dramatic monument to the victims of political oppression was unveiled opposite the site of the prison on the initiative of former political prisoners. The combination of the museum and the two monuments along the same street creates what Tarik Cyril Amar has called an "axis of national suffering and nationalist triumph".[59]

The "axis" is not confined to this one area of L'viv, however. Another monument, installed in 1999 near the site of another former Soviet prison, at Zamarstyniv, designates the site the "Ukrainian Golgotha". Not far from the Zamarstyniv memorial, a new project for the city called "Territory of Terror", construction of which began in late 2014, looks set to expand on the national narrative of Ukrainian suffering as laid out at Lonts'kyi. The project is being sponsored by and run under the aegis of the L'viv City Council, a member of which, Taras Choliy, who is also a producer of historical films about western Ukraine and a civic activist, is its director. The new complex will be constructed on the site of the wartime L'viv ghetto and also the location of a former Soviet transit prison, which was set up in 1944, and from which the Soviet authorities sent local prisoners on to the Gulag. The plans do incorporate the story of the Jewish experience of the ghetto, but the project's website gives greater prominence to the Ukrainian narrative of suffering at the hands of two totalitarian regimes (an approach recognizable from analogous sites in the Baltic states or Hungary, such as the Museum of Occupation in Riga or the House of Terror in Budapest).[60] Though at the time of writing it is too early to say, it seems possible from the plans detailed on the website that the new museum may represent one of Ukraine's

---

[59] Tarik Cyril Amar, "Different but the Same, or the Same but Different? Public Memory of the Second World War in Post-Soviet L'viv", *Journal of Modern European History* 9, no. 3 (2011): 373–94.

[60] For further information see the project website, *Terytoria teroru*: http://territoryterror.org.ua/uk/.

most spectacular sites for the commemoration of national martyr-dom, while trying to balance this with respectable nods to the experiences of other groups whose fates are linked to its location.

Post-Soviet Martyrdom and Martyrology: from Gongadze to Nihoyan

While the end of Soviet rule opened the way for public commemoration of earlier national martyrdom in Ukraine, it did not mean that the country stopped producing martyrs. Despite the fact that independent Ukraine has been a much freer place than Soviet Ukraine, there remains a widespread perception that insidious remnants of the Soviet system have never quite been cast off: indeed, much of the discourse around the "decommunization laws" has been about finally achieving the sharp break with the past that was not achieved in 1991. The cause of ridding post-Soviet Ukraine of the lingering legacy of corruption and violence found its own martyr, in 2001, when the journalist Georgy Gongadze was murdered after his investigations into high-level corruption in the Ukrainian government. Many believe that members of the political elites, including President Leonid Kuchma, may have been involved in the killing.[61] Though he was far from a deliberate martyr for the national cause, Gongadze was nevertheless inscribed into the pantheon of national martyrs: in 2005, President Yushchenko, post-Soviet Ukraine's greatest adherent to the Romantic national tradition, awarded Gongadze the title of Hero of Ukraine (an honor he also bestowed upon Stepan Bandera five years later), and in 2008 a dramatic memorial to Gongadze and other murdered journalists was opened in central Kyiv.

The most significant re-emergence of martyrdom discourse in post-Soviet Ukraine came in February 2014, however, when more than 100 protesters were killed by security forces during the Maidan protests against the corrupt and abusive regime of President Viktor Yanukovych. The murdered protesters quickly became known as the

---

[61]   "Ukraine's ex-President: Catching Kuchma", *The Economist*, 31 March 2011, http://www.economist.com/node/18488564.

Nebesna sotnia (usually translated as Heavenly Hundred): the name *sotnia*—literally, a military unit of one hundred fighters—was used widely on the Maidan for the units of the Maidan Self-Defense, and has its roots among the Zaporizhian Cossacks of whom the Ukrainian Romantics were so fond (though it was also used by the UPA, for the same reason). The Heavenly Hundred quickly became the focus for spontaneous and then later official commemoration practices, during which references to Romantic literature were plentiful: while Shevchenko's image was omnipresent around the Maidan protests, the famous line from his poem "The Caucasus", "Boritesia—poborete!", or "Fight and you will overcome!", became a symbol of the protesters more widely, and of the Heavenly Hundred in particular. Improvised memorials and shrines transformed central Kyiv in the weeks and months following the protests, creating a powerful topographical martyrology around the locations of the deaths. Shortly after the change of regime, a series of large crosses were installed at the murder sites, which were linked into an improvised *khresna doroha*, or stations of the cross, that followed the route of the deaths from the bottom of Hrushevs'kyi Street, where it intersects with Khreshchatyk, to a small, wooden chapel on top of the hill on Instytuts'ka Street, overlooking the Maidan. A plaque on the chapel wall describes it as "The Chapel of the Pure Heart of Our Lady and the New Martyrs of the Ukrainian People (The Heavenly Hundred)" (Kaplytsia Neporochnoho Sertsia Materi Bozhoi i Novomuchenykiv Ukrains'koho narodu [Nebesna sotnia]). The above-mentioned graffiti inscription referring to the martyrdom of the Kyiv students in 1919—"Our Kruty is Here"—is only meters away from the crosses.[62] The events also sparked a wave of street renaming in honor of the Heavenly Hundred: in Kyiv's case, this was a bottom-up phenomenon, when a section of Instytuts'ka began to be called after the Heavenly Hundred, with improvised street signs installed by protesters, but later it became official. Perhaps the most overt use of Christian

---

[62] Catherine Wanner discussed the sacralization of space via commemoration of the dead of the Heavenly Hundred at a lecture at the University of Pittsburgh in April 2015 entitled "War, Grief and Popular Commemoration of the Maidan", http://www.reesblog.pitt.edu/podcast-catherine-wanner-war-grief-and-rage-popular-commemorations-of-the-maidan/.

martyrdom symbolism among the early Maidan commemorations was an "Alley of the Heavenly Hundred", created inside Ukraine's parliament in April 2014, which featured rows of photographs of the killed protesters, each one ringed by a crown of thorns.

The largely spontaneous initiatives outlined above powerfully inscribed the spectacle of the Maidan martyrology into Kyiv's urban space, and the authorities acted quickly to facilitate and capitalize on this phenomenon. On 2 February 2015, the Ukrainian government adopted a resolution on its "sacred duty" to "commemorate the sacrifices suffered by the Ukrainian people in defending their freedom and democracy", which will include a wave of public commemorative events, memorials, and museums.[63] The Ministry of Culture, Kyiv City Administration, and the Kyiv Department of Urban Planning and Architecture announced a major competition for plans to redevelop central Kyiv, entitled "Territory of Dignity" after the popular name for the protests, the "Revolution of Dignity", to reflect on and commemorate the Maidan.[64] The competition, for which James Young, the well-known scholar of Holocaust memorials and jury member for the 9/11 memorial in New York, acted as consultant, included four elements: a memorial to the Heavenly Hundred, a Museum of the Maidan, a revamped public space around the Maidan, and the renovation of the Ukrainian House, the building off the Maidan which served as one of the centers for the protest activities.

Immediately after the announcement, sketches began to appear on social media, mostly featuring the "Heavenly Hundred" as angels being taken to heaven. Interestingly, however, the organizers of the competition made clear stipulations that while they wanted to maintain respectful and emotionally powerful commemoration of the Heavenly Hundred as a key element of the project, they also

---

[63]   Law of Ukraine: "Pro uvichnennia pam'iati pro Revoliutsiu hidnosti 2013-2014 rokiv", 06 February 2015, http://w1.c1.rada.gov.ua/pls/zweb2/webproc4_1?pf3511 =53918 (accessed 31 March 2015).

[64]   On the plans for redevelopment see Anna Ustenko, "Bol'shie plany: kakim budet obnovlennyi tsentr Kieva" (interview with Anna Bondar, coordinator of the architectural competition), *Dream Kyiv*, no date, http://dreamkyiv.com/majdan/ (accessed 31 March 2015).

wanted the emphasis to be on creating a pedestrian-friendly, usable space, "without creating memorials of death in the shape of wreaths and crosses" and avoiding "naturalism, nationalist kitsch [*sha-rovarshchyna*], and Soviet symbols".[65] These guidelines show a clear awareness among the project organizers of the pitfalls of overbearing, kitsch nationalistic urban martyrology, which so often also falls back on the clichés of Soviet monumentalism.

After competition entries were received, a period of public consultation was launched, which included numerous public meetings, an open-air display on the Maidan, and a website that allowed internet users to vote for projects that they liked, though the final decision was made by a competition jury which included architects, historians, writers, artists, and museum professionals from Ukraine and abroad.[66] Many of the dozens of proposed projects incorporated precisely the kind of martyrological aesthetics that were discouraged in the guidelines, including crosses, chapels, a domed church devoted to the "Great Martyrs of the Maidan", pietas, Virgin Mary statues, references to sainthood, halos, and angels. There were numerous uses of traditional national symbols, such as the *kalyna* (viburnum), and several projects that used nationalist symbols and slogans. Muscular, socialist realist aesthetics were also present. A significant number included citations from Shevchenko, some the famous line from "The Caucasus" mentioned above. In the short texts accompanying the projects, the words martyr and martyrdom are mentioned repeatedly, and there are references to the "Ukrainian Golgotha".

The competition organizers and jury stayed true to the original stipulations, however, and announced in June 2015 winning projects that avoided overtly martyrological imagery and text. The project for redesigning the Maidan came from a company from Taiwan, and focused on producing a green public space with provision for public events and public art, while the winning project for the Ukrainian House was by a team of Ukrainian designers and artists

---

[65]   The word *sharovarshchyna* comes from *sharovary*—traditional Cossack trousers often worn by folk dancers in kitsch displays of national dance and music.

[66]   For a full list of jury members see the Kyiv local authority website *Terytoria hidnosty/Terra Dignitas*: http://terradignitas.kga.gov.ua/pro-konkurs/zhuri.

who proposed turning the building into a multipurpose arts and cultural center with an outdoor cinema. The winning designs for most important element of the project for this discussion—the memorials to the Heavenly Hundred—came from an Italian team, although a Ukrainian design that proposed creating a "constellation of martyrs" on Instytuts'ka Street came second. The Italian project envisages a "path of memory" on Instytuts'ka made up of maple trees representing the dead protesters, each one growing out of a "wound"—a rectangular opening in the paved path. While the references to wounds and the use of trees as symbolizing "rebirth" bear some relation to Christian martyrological language and imagery, the connection is oblique and subtle. No award was made for the final part of the project, the Museum of the Maidan, as none of the proposed projects were deemed appropriate.

Post-Maidan, not Post-Martyrology

In the context of the planned redevelopment of the Maidan, it is interesting to speculate on how Kyiv's Maidan commemoration, and Ukraine's culture of martyrology, will develop in future. The eventual shape of the Kyiv projects and the way in which martyrdom is framed in them will undoubtedly send a strong signal as to the place of martyrological thinking in contemporary Ukrainian culture, and whether the commemoration of the "Revolution of Dignity" represents a continuation of previous traditions, or a break from or modification of them. Just as Shevchenko's burial site served as a martyrological locus for the concentration of national feeling in the late 19th century, at a time of considerable growth and evolution in the Ukrainian national project, so the Maidan martyrs' memorials will serve as crucial node in "the semiotic network of the modern Ukrainian national identity" in the context of the present upheavals.

Commemoration has, of course, been predominantly Christian and nationally Ukrainian in its symbolism. Religious symbols and the state symbols of Ukraine are omnipresent, as are references to Ukrainian culture, such as folk motifs, citations from Shevchenko or images of him, or images of Cossacks. The highly emotive funeral service for the victims that was held on the Maidan on 21 February

2014 demonstrates the influence of national(ist) martyrological motifs: as the coffins were carried through the crowd, the folk song "Plyve kacha po Tysyni" (A Duck Swims on the Tysyna) was played and the crowd chanted "Glory to the Heroes". Both the song and the slogan have associations with the UPA, though in neither case is this association exclusive, and it is debatable to what extent those in the crowd would have been aware of the links.[67]

Yet while most of those killed on the Maidan were ethnic Ukrainians, there were also people of Jewish, Armenian, Belarusian, and Russian origin among them, and there are signs that the Maidan martyrology recognizes this, and has moved towards a more civic, rather than ethnic, conception of national identification. Indeed, it is telling that the organizers of the project for renewing central Kyiv have chosen to try to avoid nation-centric, religiously-inflected martyrological clichés and focus rather on usable civic spaces: this reflects precisely the more progressive, pro-European, liberal side of the protests, which were, after all, made up to a large degree of Kyiv's generally pro-European middle classes, among whom the level of civic—rather than ethnic nationalist—engagement is generally high.[68] In this sense the choice of the project title, "Territory of Dignity", rather than anything with nationalist connotations, is telling. The commemorative activity has been generally multi-ethnic and multi-faith: religious leaders other than Christian have been present at ceremonies and prayers, and Jewish and Muslim organizations have broadly supported the Maidan and the commemoration of those who were killed. The chapel to the "Heavenly Hundred" at Instytuts'ka is ecumenical, though under the care of the Greek Catholic church. The fact that the Maidan's first victims included people of non-Ukrainian ethnic origin has not been covered up or down-

---

[67]   See Olesya Khromeychuk, "Gender and Nationalism on the Maidan", in *Ukraine's Euromaidan. Analyses of a Civil Revolution*, ed. David R. Marples and Frederick V. Mills (Stuttgart: Ibidem/Columbia University Press, 2015), 123–46 (126).

[68]   Olga Onuch, "Maidans Past and Present: Comparing the Orange Revolution and the Euromaidan", in *Ukraine's Euromaidan*, ed. Marples and Mills, 27–56 (46–48).

played, but rather emphasized as part of a discourse that has generally tried to stress Ukraine's unity in diversity against a common threat.

It is telling in this regard that one of the faces of the Heavenly Hundred, and the first protester shot dead by the government snipers, was Serhii Nihoyan, a Russophone student of Armenian origin from Dnipropetrovsk. One of the first and largest street shrines established after the shootings was dedicated to Nihoyan, while photographs of the rugged, bearded protester, with a passing resemblance to Che Guevara or even Christ, became some of the most reproduced images of the Maidan. His likeness spread widely on the Internet and through posters and graffiti stencils around Kyiv. A memorial to him was built in his home village, Bereznuvativka near Dnipropetrovsk, and a street was also named after him, as was a major street in Dnipropetrovsk (previously Kalinin Prospect—a telling choice for renaming, given its associations with the Soviet leader). A similar suggestion has been made for the square by the Dynamo stadium in central Kyiv, where Nihoyan was killed. The protester has also been made a Hero of Ukraine.

Another factor that lent particular poignancy to the figure of Nihoyan was his appearance in the video project "Nash Shevchenko" (Our Shevchenko), initiated by the theater director Serhiy Proskurnia in 2013 for the 200th anniversary of the poet's birth, which featured films of people across Ukraine reciting lines of Shevchenko's poetry, and happened to coincide with the protests. In one of the most viewed clips of the project, Nihoyan stands on the Maidan barricades and reads part of Shevchenko's "The Caucasus", including the line "Boritesia—poborete!"[69] In the spirit of the slogan "For our freedom and for yours", Shevchenko wrote the poem in 1845 about the struggles of the peoples of the Caucasus against Russian imperial aggression. He imagines the mountain peoples as Prometheus, chained to a rock and tortured by the Russian imperial eagle—an image that resonates with his image of a crucified Ukraine; yet he also laments the needless death in the service of the empire of a

---

[69]   The project videos are available on YouTube. For Nihoyan's clip see *76 – Serhii Nihoyan. Nash Shevchenko*, 22 December 2013: https://www.youtube.com/watch?v=CyFqqstK7eo.

friend, Yakiv de Balmen, to whom the poem is dedicated, and who died serving in the Russian Imperial army in the Caucasus. "The Caucasus" is thus in part a reflection on martyrdom, on the meaningfulness or otherwise of death, suffering, and struggle: the Caucasian peoples' struggle is ennobled as one in the service of freedom; De Balmen's death is tragically devoid of meaning. There are clear resonances with events in Kyiv in February 2014, with the war in eastern Ukraine, and in particular with Nihoyan's death: much in the spirit of Shevchenko's poem, Nihoyan was part of a fight for human dignity that transcended national boundaries. This latter point is key in this most recent development of Ukrainian national martyrology, and speaks to a return to Shevchenko's open, solidarity-based model of national identification.

It is not yet clear, however, what direction the Maidan martyrology will take. While the paradigm is still firmly in place, there does appear to be a willingness to try to modify or soften the language of martyrology, and the initial tendencies in Kyiv introduce a civic, rather than ethnic-national understanding of self-sacrifice. This does not challenge martyrology, but rather fills it with a different content. The question as to whether martyrdom itself is a desirable or productive paradigm of memory is not being asked, and with the horrific escalation of the war in the east, it becomes harder and harder to question self-sacrifice in the service of the nation. Indeed, the valorization of such sacrifice is now being actively promoted by some Ukrainian official bodies, such as the Institute of National Memory, whose head Volodymyr Viatrovych has made public statements about Ukrainians as being historically a "nation–army" (*narod-viis'ko*), and which makes clear links in its activities between the heroism and sacrifice of contemporary soldiers and those of soldiers from the past, especially the UPA.[70] It is notable also that in November 2015 two prominent Ukrainian journalists started a petition to have a monument to Vasyl' Makukh, the UPA veteran who burned himself alive in central Kyiv against rule from Moscow,

---

[70] Volodymyr Viatrovych, "Ukraintsi – narod-viis'ko: zakhody 12-14.10 do Dnia zakhyznyka Ukrainy", *Ukrains'ka pravda*, 11 October 2015, http://blogs.prav da.com.ua/authors/viatrovych/561a6adcac233/ (accessed 24 November 2015).

erected on Khreshchatyk. It is clear that this kind of gesture is find-ing a renewed resonance in today's Ukraine.[71]

Yet there are questions related to the nature of martyrological thinking that could be discussed in relation to both the victims of the Maidan violence and the war in eastern Ukraine. It is worth con-sidering, for example, not only what kind of martyrdom is being nar-rated, and what is being excluded from that narrative, but also whether the very mode of narration of martyrology excludes certain aspects of memory. Here it is worth recalling the function that mar-tyrdom and martyrology fulfill in terms of articulating and reinforc-ing the meanings and hierarchies that were outlined at the begin-ning of this paper. Only one of the 106 people included in the Heav-enly Hundred narrative, for example, was a woman. This reflects the fact that women's roles in the "revolution" were different: while some women did rise to prominence in the protests and the subse-quent conflict, their roles were in the main behind the scenes, in less visible and glorified positions.[72] While a number of women were at the frontlines of the street fighting, most were not, and often those who wished to be there were physically excluded by male counter-parts. If the paradigm of martyrology, which remembers those who fought and died, is dominant, then "the other half of the Maidan", which was marginalized from the epicenter of violence, is excluded from memory. This problem persists in even more alarming fashion in the context of the war in eastern Ukraine, where female volun-teers are present on the frontlines without official recognition as a result of the inbuilt sexism of Ukrainian military structures, which

---

[71] 'Kyiany zbyraiut' pidpisy na monument chlenu UPA, scho pidpalyv sebe na Khreshchatyku', *Hromads'ke radio*, 24 November 2015: http://hromadskera-dio.org/2015/11/24/kyyany-zbyrayut-pidpysy-na-monument-chlenu-upa-shcho-pidpalyv-sebe-na-hreshchatyku (accessed 24 November 2015).

[72] Khromeychuk, "Gender and Nationalism". Women's roles in protest in Ukraine and beyond are the focus of a forthcoming special issue, "Gender, Nationalism and Citizenship in Anti-Authoritarian Protests in Belarus, Russia and Ukraine", *Journal of Soviet and Post-Soviet Politics and Society* 2, no. 1 (forthcoming 2016), ed. Olesya Khromeychuk.

refuse to recognize women as equal participants in violent combat.[73] At the same time, the violence, often sexual, suffered by civilian women in the conflict areas is still poorly recognized.[74] The problem of lack of visibility of women lies at the heart of martyrological thinking more generally, as Castelli has pointed out: female martyrs in the early Christian church were often imagined to have somehow become masculine through their courageous self-sacrifice. Since martyrdom involves male attributes and privileges like courage, participation in violence, authority, and the right to act and speak, then women cannot participate as women, in Castelli's words, "the 'feminine' is present [...] only as a shame-steeped other—the embodiment of a failure of masculine nerve".[75]

It may be that the discourse of martyrology will shift to become more inclusive in relation to gender, as it seems to have done in relation to ethnicity. The figure of Nadia Savchenko, the pilot who was captured in 2014 by the pro-Russian rebels in eastern Ukraine and placed on trial in Russia for the murder of two journalists, and who has repeatedly gone on hunger strike protesting her innocence and the violation of her rights, may, tragically, facilitate such a shift: the at times "masculinized" portrayal of Savchenko in the media also lends plausibility to Castelli's thesis. Martyrology in Ukraine clearly is capable of shifting and re-aligning its content, moving away from traditional nationalism towards civic patriotism, from bombastic pathos to more subtle, civic public displays; it could also shift its focus away from spectacular masculine heroism, though this remains to be seen. One thing is certain, however: as long as violent conflict and death remain facts of everyday life in Ukraine, and the country remains locked in a grim struggle for its survival, it is unlikely that martyrology itself will fade from prominence in public

---

[73] "Maria Berlins'ka: daite zhinkam mozhlyvist' lehal'no zakhyshchaty Batkivshchynu", *Hromads'ke* Radio, 4 July 2015, http://hromadskeradio.org/gromadska-hvylya/mariya-berlinska-dayte-zhinkam-mozhlyvist-legalno-zahyshchaty-batkivshchynu.

[74] Antonina Vikhrest, "All-enveloping Silence Persists around Rape in Ukraine conflict", *Women Under Siege Project*, 15 January 2015, http://www.womenundersiegeproject.org/blog/entry/all-enveloping-silence-persists-around-rape-in-ukraine-conflict.

[75] Castelli, *Martyrdom and Memory*, 60.

space, in commemorative practices, and as a wider paradigm of national memory.

The Eternal Martyr:
Karen Shakhnazarov's *White Tiger* as a Cinematic Reflection on Russian Martyrdom

Sander Brouwer

Abstract: *The contemporary official attempts to reconstitute a national self-image through a reinterpretation of Russia's history show strong elements of self-heroization as well as self-victimization. This renewed orientation towards the past focuses in particular on the victory of the Stalinist regime in World War II: heroism and victimhood are intertwined here in a very complex way. The new master narrative allows for an interpretation of Russia's 20th-century history in which the millions of Russian victims of the Soviet regime are recast as martyrs who died for the cause of defending or rebuilding the transhistorical Russian Empire. This paper analyzes Karen Shakhnazarov's film* White Tiger *(2012) as an artistic reflection on, or perhaps criticism of, such attempts to construct a transhistorical if not justification, then at least meaning, behind Russian history. Shakhnazarov thus takes issue with recent popular Russian films like* We are from the Future *I and II (2008 and 2010) or* Fog *I and II (2010 and 2012), films that, contrary to* White Tiger, *clearly sustain the idea that in a most literal way direct lessons for the present can be learned from the—unequivocally readable—past.*

There are in my view two main reasons why the theme of martyrdom is very relevant for contemporary Russian culture. The first is that it fits very well with official attempts to reconstitute a national self-image through a reinterpretation of Russia's history, especially, but not exclusively, that of the 20th century. These attempts may be observed starting around 2005 (cf. Koposov 2011) but are very obvious since Vladimir Putin's re-election as president in 2012.[1] The second is that this self-image contains strong elements of self-heroization as well as self-victimization; as such it has become one of the main mechanisms for lifting Russia's acute problems out of the sphere of the everyday (Max Weber's *das Alltägliche*) and into the lofty sphere of transcendent meaning and destiny.

Karen Shakhnazarov's film *White Tiger* (2012) may be seen as an artistic reflection on, or perhaps criticism of, such attempts to construct a transhistorical if not justification, then at least meaning, behind Russian history. As is well known, this renewed orientation towards the past focuses in particular on the victory in World War II (cf. Lutz-Auras 2012). A particularly touchy subject here is, of course, the positive evaluation of the figure of Stalin that has been apparent for some time already in Russia, and which seems to be becoming stronger (cf. Walker 2008; Levada-Center 2012, 2013). Heroism and victimhood are intertwined in a very complex way here: the role Stalin is alleged to have played in the Great Patriotic War is presented as a kind of excuse for the Gulag. Thus, for instance, in the notorious school history textbook by A. Filippov, which was endorsed by the government in 2007, it is stated that the Stalinist terror was "the price of the great achievements of the Soviet Union" (Filippov 2007: 90). As Alexander Etkind observes: "Filippov's textbook does not deny the mass violence of Stalin's era but entertains the radical transformation of its meaning" (Etkind 2009: 633); it puts forward the idea that "the mass violence of the early Soviet era helped to shape the New Soviet Man, the tortured Bolshevik version of the Übermensch" (ibid.: 634).

This renewed cult of the Victory, for which Stalin gets the main credit, coincides with or forms part of a new master narrative that has become very clear since the beginning of Putin's second term in 2004. This is a narrative of an essentially unchanging and thus transhistorical Russian Empire which is at times threatened with so-called "systemic crises" designated as Times of Troubles

---

[1]   The literature on this phenomenon is vast and expanding quickly. For an analysis of its reverberations in Russian society see *Radio Free Europe/Radio Liberty*'s interview with Kirill Kobrin and Andreas Umland (Whitmore: 2015).

("Smuty"; see Brouwer, in press), in which internal enemies collab-orate with external foes to undo the Empire, but after which order is restored by the next strong leader; this is a narrative in which his-torical periods are connected not syntagmatically, in a series of causes and effects, but paradigmatically, as a chain of equivalent pe-riods. Such a narrative allows for an interpretation of Russia's 20th-century history in which the millions of Russian victims of the Soviet regime are recast as martyrs who died for the cause of defending or rebuilding the transhistorical Russian Empire.

To ascribe the introduction of such a conception to Kremlin spin doctors manipulating the public for national or international political reasons is perhaps too one-sided—although such factors undoubtedly play their role. Serguei Oushakine in his *Patriotism of Despair* (2009) has described how in the 1990s new forms of social bonds were constructed far beneath the level of the government and the state, from which large societal groups felt totally estranged (teachers, academics, neo-communists, veterans of the wars in Af-ghanistan and in Chechnya, veterans' mothers, patriots). These bonds can summarily be described as based on the principle of mar-tyrdom: the common Russian man in the late 1980s and '90s was perceived by these groups as perishing in a cyclically repetitive Rus-sian Tragedy. This tragic death, as Giesen (2004; see below) shows, guarantees the lofty nature of the cause for which the martyr dies, which is above life and death—the cause of the Russian people. It may well be that the Putin spin doctors instinctively and/or con-sciously pick up this mood, this model, and try to re-inscribe the state in it, strongly accentuating the identity of the Russian people, the Russian state, and the Russian Empire.

Before taking a closer look at Shakhnazarov's cinematic re-flections on this Russian self-image of martyrdom based on a cycli-cal historical model, let us reflect some more on these concepts. The construction of martyrdom is a cultural mechanism aimed at some-how coping with the violent loss of human life, an event that cannot be integrated in life as it is normally experienced. To construct the one who has lost his life as a martyr means to assert that he has lost that life not for nothing, but that his death contributes to establish-ing or perpetuating some supra-individual, even transcendent

cause. In contrast to the victim, who dies *passively* and unexpectedly, as a result of the aggression of others, the death of the martyr
is an *act* of self-sacrifice. It is seen as a gift of one's own life, a contribution to a cause that is higher than human, mundane, profane
life. Indeed, it could be said with Bernhard Giesen that "cultures of
martyrdom center on this ultimate sovereignty of the voluntary
death: let reality perish, but never give up the sacred cause" (Giesen
2004: 76). Although martyrdom is originally a religious concept—
the martyr dies for his belief—modern martyrs may die for secular
notions such as the nation, the party, humanity at large, a way of
life, freedom, *Lebensraum*. Martyrdom belongs to the realm of the
political myth discussed by Girardet (1986), who sees the construction of such myths as resulting from a feeling that reality falls short
of explaining the total picture of life. Reality can only fully be
grasped, as far as myth is concerned, by taking recourse to the realm
of the unseen. Heroes and martyrs by their existence establish such
a realm and confirm it.

Nevertheless, we should not forget that the construction of
martyrdom is also a *traumatic* mechanism. Giesen's holding on to
the "sacred cause" and its concomitant denial of reality is a reaction
to shocking events that are seen as part of a reality that is doomed,
fundamentally flawed, lacking "ultimate transcendent foundations",
in Dominick LaCapra's words (2001: 46). LaCapra offers a most in-
sightful approach to these kinds of traumatic mechanisms. Let me
briefly remind the reader of the distinction LaCapra makes between
"structural" and "historical" trauma, although such a condensation
must by necessity relentlessly reduce the elegance and subtlety of
LaCapra's argument, especially his avoidance of binary schematiz-
ing.

According to LaCapra, one radical pole in the spectrum of
possible reactions to the traumatic loss of one's security/integ-
rity/sense of belonging is to take the attitude that there never really
has been such a security and such belonging: they had in fact always
been illusory and in reality absent. In psychological terms one might
call this a defense mechanism: it was *not* the traumatic event that
shattered something, its impact has *not* been that essential. Not that
such a defense mechanism is of any use—the impact becomes no

less radical as a result. This type of reaction is mostly associated with Freud's melancholia: it leads to a state of perpetual reliving, acting out, of the horror—there seems to be no possibility to relegate it to some point in the past, to see it as a past experience—the trauma is "structural", not "historical". LaCapra points to the fact that by stressing the "absence" of pre-trauma integrity, one easily loses the sense of the real crime, fails to recognize the real perpetrator—the evil is interpreted in terms of a kind of primordial sin, a perpetual state of fall from grace (one thus misses the opportunity, in the first place to punish the perpetrators, but in the long run also to learn lessons for the future, perhaps to prevent others from becoming the same sort of perpetrator; in other words: viewing one's "loss" as "absence" may easily lead to passivity and resignation).

The other radical pole of reaction to a traumatic event is to neglect the possibility of "absence" and focus exclusively on "loss": radically fixing the event in a historical moment, a "before" and "after", absolutizing and idealizing the security and the sense of belonging before the event; ascribing the aggression of the traumatic event to a totally alien force, which acts for incomprehensible, unpredictable reasons and is solely responsible for the violence (while the victim is totally innocent); and especially, striving to retrospectively wipe out the event and fully restore the happy state imagined to have existed before it: punish the enemy, or forever remove him, and thus perhaps even gain from the event by making sure that there can never be another possibility for the traumatic event to repeat itself. Thus, while structural trauma, according to LaCapra, is "related to (and even correlated with) transhistorical absence (absence of/at the origin)" (77), seeing the traumatic event as "historical" and "specific" (78) enables the victim to restrict it to a certain historical time span, and to distinguish more clearly between victims, perpetrators, and bystanders.

LaCapra furthermore describes the peculiar but often observed mechanism of *conflation* of loss and absence, of historical and structural trauma. The conversion of "historical" loss, of the lives of concrete people, under specific historical circumstances, by specifically motivated perpetrators, into absence, "bears striking witness to the impact of trauma and the post-traumatic" that may "induce a gripping response whose power and force of attraction can be compelling" (46).

To my view, the creation of martyrdom is just such a response, but under a different sign: it translates the loss not into absence, but into "presence". The martyr has through his sacrifice become part of "ultimate transcendent foundations" that justify the suffering, transforming it into something transhistorically charismatic, into heroism, thereby denying the merely historical, the everyday, *das Alltägliche* (Max Weber's term as applied in Giesen [2004: 76]), as something of secondary importance. Constructing the victim as a martyr constructs the nature of the conflict in which he suffered as essentially transcending the reality in which the harmful events took place, transcending history. It is the translation of historical loss— not into metaphysical *absence*, but into metaphysical *presence*, which thus turns out to be a kind of positively charged variant of "melancholia": LaCapra is right in maintaining that structural trauma "is often figured as deeply ambivalent, as both shattering or painful and the occasion for *jouissance*, ecstatic elation, or the sublime" (80).

***

Before discussing Shakhnazarov's *White Tiger*, let us take a brief look at a work of literature in which an artistic reflection on the historical model we have just described is presented, and in which the theme of return from a martyr's death is introduced: Dmitri Bykov's novel *Justification* (*Оправдание*, 2005). The book is concerned with the problem of Empire and its continuity over time, and shows a great awareness of the "traumatic" mechanisms that are involved in the way these themes function in contemporary Russian society. Characteristically, it uses the theme of a return from the dead for its main characters. As I had occasion earlier to write on this type of literary text:

> the deep confusion over the continuity of time (the way the present is connected with the past), in these texts, shows that they are concerned, in a direct or indirect way, with a traumatic displacement. They are trying to reflect on the loss of certain fixed ways of living after 1991, plus the renewed confrontation in the wake of it with the undigested Soviet past, and the impossibility of

defining one's own position towards it, recognizing it as *one's own* past (Brouwer 2010a).

In *Justification*, we follow a Moscow historian, Slava Rogov, in his investigation, in the 1990s, of the fate of a number of Gulag victims. Rogov believes that he is able to uncover the reason why a small number of these Gulag victims returned home some time after the war. These returns are described in eerie detail in the book as Rogov reconstructs them. He becomes convinced that the real reason behind Stalin's purges in the 1930s was that they were meant to "filter" the whole population (indeed, the plans were to send *everyone* to the camps) in order to select the very few who would not break under torture, and would refuse to sign any confession or to denounce anyone. These few would then be isolated and trained to lead the country, and form the nucleus and elite of its shock troops in the catastrophic war that had already been foreseen—but also in the ensuing battle for world dominance. After the war, when they had done their jobs, they were set free and returned home—unsuccessfully in all cases, since they had now become totally alienated from any normal life. Rogov then sets out to find a village that is rumored to have housed many of these elite members before they were sent on their mission. He finds it, or at least he thinks so, but it appears to be populated by members of a weird sect in which sadomasochistic replayings of public torture take place. Initially, Rogov has a hard job trying to find out what exactly the rules of conduct are in this place: everybody is constantly sentenced for all kinds of violations of unstated laws, but never is there an explanation of what rule exactly has been violated and how. Eventually, he discovers that there are no rules at all, and that it all boils down to gaining the upper hand in each separate situation by convincing your opponent that you know a rule or law that he has violated. Finally Rogov escapes, but drowns himself in a Siberian marsh. The narration then ends with explaining the events that Rogov took for the return of the Gulag elite never took place, all died in the camps, Rogov must have merely imagined things.

Boris Noordenbos writes of this theme of victims of the Stalin regime seeming to reappear from death, literally becoming "revenants":

> What is at stake is an undecidedness between two seemingly incompatible attitudes towards Russia's twentieth-century history and identity: the returnees, being the conceptual pivot of the story, function as the spectral revenants from a violent past and as the corporal embodiments of recovered losses; as spectres they stand for the unmourned collective traumas of Soviet terror, while as flesh-and-blood people they represent the hope that the empire that inflicted these traumas might (and should) be restored (Noordenbos 2013: 174).

Rogov's suicide in the end certainly serves as a symbol of the failure of this obsessive search to heal the rupture of time and turn the victims into martyrs. The strangely magical structure of space in the novel, in which Rogov constantly gets lost and only then reaches his goal when he is lost—only to be once more deceived—creates an acute sense that a reconstruction of the Stalinist Empire with its conscious goals and firm coordinates is doomed, as well as any attempt to place oneself in the history of that Empire and find some connection with it.

I would suggest that this chronotopical confusion in the literary or artistic search for the Imperial Sublime, for an image of the Soviet empire as the high point in the development of Russia as an Empire, the exultation of that Empire and the striving for its restoration in the future, is Bykov's comment on the way historical traumas are figured as structural ones in contemporary Russia. The loss of lives is seen as necessary for the preservation of a higher goal, a goal that will always demand sacrifices, martyrs.

***

Karen Shakhnazarov's *White Tiger* is the latest of the film-maker's series of investigations into Russian historical traumas over the recent and not so recent past. In the early 1990s, in films like *City Zero* (1990) and *Dreams* (1993), he reflected on the confusion in the heads of ordinary people after the Soviet worldview to which they had been accustomed was totally discredited. In *Vanished Empire* (2008), the theme of historical discontinuity returned in a much more general historiosophical frame: the fall of the Soviet empire is placed in a wide historical perspective through a series of allusions to early Persian empires; while at the same time, through painstakingly accurate visual and auditory detailing, the vanished everyday life of the Soviet 1970s is made intensely present for the viewer.

In 1998, Shakhnazarov became the head of Mosfilm studios, and since then he has developed into one of the leading figures in Russian cultural life. As such, he has not always been able to remain neutral in the political field—in April 2014 he signed an open letter in support of President Putin's moves to seize the Crimea and Russia's hostile politics towards Ukraine. As a film director, however, his position has arguably been much more aloof and reflective. In this article, I am interested in that second hypostasis of Shakhnazarov, the "implied" or "abstract" author[2] of *White Tiger*.

The main character of that film, the tank driver Ivan Naidenov is seriously wounded in battle and given up on by the doctors, but miraculously rises from certain death to become an avenger devoted, in an Ahab-like manner, to destroying a mythical Nazi tank. He never really does so and eventually disappears in his chase, like a mythical eternal hunter. The tank also disappears, and seems to transform into a symbol for Nazism itself, which hides but is not completely destroyed, and, as a small scene at the very end of the film suggests, is waiting to be resurrected at any moment. The film thus positions itself right in the middle of the contemporary renewed Russian discourse about a perceived "eternal" Western Russophobia that is allegedly reappearing today. This discourse is played out, as can be observed on an everyday basis, not only in Russian mass media (TV, the blogosphere), but very prominently also in the cinema (cf. Norris 2012a: 117–28).

In the 1990s, while there was no lack of films about recent and contemporary armed conflicts, like the Afghan and Chechen wars,

---

[2]   For a definition of these terms (obviously a variant of Wayne Booth's "implied author" (see Booth [1961]), based on an extensive discussion of the concept in critical literature, see Schmid (2013).

the theme of World War II seemed rapidly to disappear from Russian literature as well as from cinema: "virtually no films about World War II appeared for almost a decade after the Soviet Union disintegrated" (Smorodinskaya 2010: 89). In the Putin era, however, we witness "a deluge" of films on World War II, as well as many television series, almost all of them "action and adventure films" (ibid.: 90). Literature started to catch up with this tendency somewhat later. Mikhail Kononov's *The Naked Pioneer Girl* (2005) seems to have been the first novel of the 2000s to use the war theme, and then in 2007 there appeared *Sleep and Believe: A Blockade Novel* (Спать и верить. Блокадный роман) by Andrei Turgenev (Viacheslav Kuritsyn), and in 2008 Il'ia Boiashov's *Tank Man, Or the White Tiger*, which became the basis for Shakhnazarov's film.

I focus on Karen Shakhnazarov's screen version of Boiashov's story, because this film reflects in an interesting way on the rather crude ways in which the bulk of contemporary Russian war films present the war experience as having a clear and unequivocal meaning and a direct and non-negotiable relevance for our times. As extreme reference points for such an approach I would mention the two hugely popular *We are from the Future* films, the first one from 2008 (director Andrei Maliukov), and the second from 2010 (directed by Aleksandr Samokhvalov and Boris Rostov). The first film, which was not only a box office success but was shown as a four-part miniseries on the state-owned RTR (Rossiia) TV channel on 9 May (Victory Day) 2008, is about a group of egoistic youngsters living the good life in St. Petersburg. At the beginning of the film they are representative of contemporary atomized society, focusing merely on personal success and hedonism, and make easy money by selling war medals that they dig up themselves on the battlegrounds around St. Petersburg/Leningrad. They love to immerse themselves in the fiction of first person World War II shooters—while knowing little about the real Great Patriotic War. One critic calls them "'smart-arse' gravediggers, historical cynics, disrespectful exploiters of the past" (Dolgopolov 2008).

Through some kind of time warp they are transported to 1944, where they are taken for real Soviet soldiers and are forced to fight in a real battle. Thus they learn the meaning of real courage, real sacrifice and real love—above all, real love for the Fatherland. They acquire "an appreciation of the toughness of the ancestors and how the symbols of yesteryear are relevant today (...). This movie makes the War appear as something fresh and relevant" (ibid.). It seems to be a matter not so much of "we are from the future" as "the past is in our present" and guides us there.

In the sequel to this film, two members of the previous group travel to Ukraine to participate in a reenactment of a battle between the Nazis and Ukrainian UPA separatists, on the one hand, and So- viet forces on their way to liberate the Motherland, on the other. When the two arrive in the reenactment camp, they are confronted by a group of jingoist Ukrainian nationalists who behave in a very hostile manner toward the modern "moskali". One of the Ukrainian organizers even announces over a megaphone that "here in 1944, our fathers and grandfathers laid down their heads for the freedom of [our] native Ukraine." And so the battle to be reenacted is a copy of the one in the present, the Ukrainian youngsters indeed donning Nazi helmets while drinking beer and listening to Western hard rock sung in Ukrainian.

Later, however, the two Russians and two of the Ukrainians are transported to 1944 and, as one might expect, the plot "rips the Ukrainians away from their iniquitous idolatry of the UPA and con- verts them almost instantly to the Red Army's true gospel of anti- fascism" (McVey 2010). Russians and Ukrainians are reunited: "we can have our conflicts in the twenty-first century, but to return there, we will have to stick together", as one of them says. And in the end Russians and Ukrainians indeed unite in defending the So- viet Fatherland, in the spirit of, as McVey notes, "the recent state- ment in *Izvestiia v Ukraine* by the Russian ambassador to Ukraine, Mikhail Zubarov: 'I am convinced that we are not only fraternal na- tions—we are a single nation'" (ibid.).

Both of the *We are from the Future* films are based on the idea that in a most literal way direct lessons for the present can be learned from the—unequivocally readable—past. They implicitly connect both periods with a time-transcendent, "eternal" truth that hangs over all of Russia's history and that, if perhaps temporarily forgotten, should and can be brought back in memory.

The literary prototype for *White Tiger*, Boiashov's *Tank Man*, largely seems to fit in with such a description—at least the story seems designed to draw the reader into co-experiencing the past, the spirit of battle in all its madness and debilitating aggression. It is a World War II variant of the Moby Dick story, the Tank Man chasing the White Tiger like Ahab chasing the White Whale, in an endless and ever more senseless self-chosen mission that becomes its own *raison d'être*. After the tank battle near Prokhorovka in 1943, a tank driver is found with a 90 percent burned body in a destroyed tank. He miraculously recovers, but cannot remember his name or any part of his past. No one can explain the recovery: in the film (not in the book) the doctors refer to his condition as "a rare case of retrograde amnesia." The tank driver is renamed Ivan Ivanovich Naidenov (formed from *naidenysh*—foundling) and sent back to the front. As his superiors note, "warriors do not need a memory"; Naidenov himself concurs: "I remember that I am a Russian tank driver, what else do I need to know?" His only drive in his new life is to destroy the German tank that had by some miracle not succeeded in killing him, and which keeps destroying one Soviet tank after another: a mysterious invulnerable German tank dubbed the "White Tiger", that materializes out of nowhere, does its devastating work, and seems to vanish into thin air. At the same time, Naidenov himself is shown to have acquired supernatural powers: he can hear tanks speak and uses this information to determine what is happening in battle. By the end, the war is won, but Naidenov insists that the White Tiger has not been defeated, sets out to hunt it down, and in the last sentence is probably shot down by a combined Soviet and American tank unit.

Some internet reviewers regard the story as a new kind of (historical/superhero) fantasy, meant to keep the memory of World War II alive for the contemporary Russian younger generations by making the horrors through which tank crews lived more accessible. Shakhnazarov's film, however, adds two key scenes to the Boiashov plot that radically alter the focus of the material from that of the novel. A large part of the film, following the book, shows Naidenov's crew tracking the mysterious tank and engaging it on a couple of occasions, as the Red Army advances into Europe. But by adding, after that series of events, further scenes (the penultimate and last ones of the film), Shakhnazarov fundamentally shifts the focus of his film away from the war plot itself, and transforms it instead into a reflection upon the status of memory in contemporary Russia, and memory of the war in particular. In the first added scene, after some street impressions showing the end of the war and the convoying of German POWs in Berlin, we see German generals, led by Field Marshal Wilhelm Keitel, surrender to Zhukov and other Soviet generals in a meticulous reconstruction of the original scene on 8/9 May in Berlin-Karlshorst—the hall, the position of every participant, the words spoken, the glances exchanged, even the sash on Keitel's marshal's staff. Everything is filmed in painstaking detail, as if the viewer were present at the real thing. Afterwards the German generals eat a meal that features frozen strawberries with cream, commenting that it is the first time they have had this treat (the scene, as Shakhnazarov noted in an interview, came from Keitel's memoirs, written in his Nuremberg cell).

There then follows a baffling second and final scene, where an aged Hitler is talking to someone sitting in a chair listening attentively, in a lavishly decorated hall. Several commentators call this silent listener a newspaper correspondent (Norris 2012b, Plakhov 2012), but one can only conclude that a dead Hitler (the monologue is apparently spoken long after Germany's defeat) can find himself only in Hell and his companion therefore can only be Satan himself. Indeed, Shakhnazarov himself hinted at the figure being the Prince of Darkness (Dodolev 2012b).

Hitler opens his monologue by saying: "We have known each other too long and too well. Too much connects us for me to hide my thoughts from you".[3] Let me quote at some length what he then says:

---

3   The translations here and below are my own—SB.

The war has been lost. (...) Europe has been destroyed.

Poor Germany. (...) The German people will be the scapegoat for everything. (...) And we, I and Germany, we will stand before the world as the idiosyncratic outcast of humankind, as the progeny of Hell.

But we simply found the courage to make real what all Europe was dreaming about.

We said, "If you are thinking about it, let us finally do it." (...)

Have we not realized the secret dreams of every European inhabitant? (...)

They always disliked the Jews. They always feared Russia, that dark and gloomy country in the east. That centaur, savage and foreign to Europe.

I said, "Let us simply solve these two problems." Solve them once and for all.

Did we invent something new? No. We simply brought clarity to all those matters for which Europe wanted clarity, and that is all.

As long as the Earth orbits around the sun... As long as heat and cold exist, storms and sunlight... so long struggle will exist, including struggle between peoples and nations. (...) War is a natural, normal thing. War is going on always and everywhere. It has no beginning and no end. War is life itself. War is the original condition.

We will return to what is said here in a moment. Striking in itself is the decisive way that this "Epilogue in Hell" changes the way we perceive the events depicted in the film. Andrei Plakhov writes that "the sharp genre and stylistic turns rather interfere with appreciating the film as a coherent whole, they break the rhythm and the suspense. But (...) precisely these turns give us greater [aesthetic] pleasure, adding an intriguing unpredictability" (Plakhov 2012). The director himself declared that this mix of documentary realism and mystical fantasy was deliberate (Dodolev 2012a), though it remains for the viewers to interpret what exactly that purpose may have been.

This last scene introduces an impossible chronological perspective in a film that had hitherto, in the narrative of the Tank Man Naidenov, offered the traditional cinematic illusion of making the viewer feel present in the historical past, and had followed the approach to history as a reiterative process—precisely as expressed in films like *We are from the Future*. That perspective is enhanced in the Keitel scenes, where the viewer becomes a direct witness of history. But now suddenly we are outside of space and time, and it becomes clear that Hitler and the Tank Man think in the same way: the opposition between Russia and the West is for both an eternal one. In some crucial periods it will take the form of a fierce struggle, of war (which is when the German Spirit—or the Spirit of the West, for that matter—will materialize in the form of the White Tiger), while in other periods the antagonism may soften or become blurred. This striking equivalence between Hitler and the Tank Man alone already shows that we should be careful in taking the idea about the eternal enmity between Russia and the West as the director's view. Shakhnazarov is not merely adapting Boiashov's story for the screen; the added scenes place the story of the Tank Man in a wholly different light.

The obvious mystical character of the final scene contrasts heavily with the preceding episode with Keitel, which is done in the extreme, meticulous, documentary style known from many Soviet war films. In *White Tiger*, the viewer is even further drawn into the illusion that he is present in the past when, after the public treaty-signing session, he is taken into the generals' private backroom where he is witness to their trivial quotidian chat about frozen strawberries with cream.[4] But the Hitler scene destroys that illusion *within* the film, "bares the device", as the Formalists would say. Both scenes taken together lift the film from a story about something in the past to a reflection on how to represent that past in the present, how to remember the past. As a result, the Soviet experience of World War II is drawn into the field of reflection. The film questions

---

[4]   Another subtle way of drawing the viewer into co-experiencing the traumatic historical present is the naturalistic attention to visual and auditory detail in the preceding parts. Much as the historical details in *Vanished Empire* contributed to the feeling of being carried back into the 1970s (for many Russian viewers, the time of their youth), the realistic and somewhat, it seems, over-amplified clanking of the old Soviet tanks in *White Tiger* suggests "being there" together with Naidenov, who seems mysteriously able to "understand" the tank sounds.

the contemporary semi-official axiom that World War II is an experience that is directly available, in a non-mediated way, to the present generation to guide its behavior.

As I have said, the war films of the Putin area revive not only
the war theme itself; they also, in their extreme form, strive to blur
the distinction between that past and the present—as is clearly evident in the two *We are from the Future*. In doing so they also return
to a central late Soviet ethical and historical-ideological axiom. Indeed, the "war trope" has rightfully been called "an indispensable
part of [Soviet cinema's] symbolic structure" (Prokhorova 2010: 51),
shaping the way generations were thought to relate to each other.[5]
What is important to keep in mind here is that the literal "making-
present" of these films reflects an all-pervasive ethical rhetoric of
temporal presence in the Soviet ideology. As Shpagin writes:

> The myth of the Great Patriotic War was very effective. For instance, in the
> film from the fifties *The Case of the Gaudy Gang* [Дело «пестрых»], a pros-
> ecutor tries hard to get a confession out of a criminal, who, however, doesn't
> give in, until finally the main card is played: "Do you know who your father
> was?" The criminal doesn't know, he was raised in an orphanage. Then the
> father is revealed to have been a war hero, "he died for you, and you obstruct
> us in building communism!" The criminal breaks down immediately and re-
> pents. In the kolkhoz comedy of the '60s, *The Apple of Discord* [Яблоко
> раздора], the chairman visits a small time speculator and makes her feel
> ashamed, saying: "You, Petrovna, were side by side with us in the war, you
> helped the partisans, and now look at how you behave!" She blushes with
> shame and gives up her black trade forever. What happens in this and other
> cases is a conversion to the Soviet faith, a partaking in the Eucharist, and the
> reward is a spiritual cleansing (Shpagin 2005).

The Putin-era films (and this is something that can be observed not
only in films on World War II) recycle not only the Soviet discourse
on the war, but also the cyclical or "presentist" model of history that
is so characteristic of the era's worldview.[6] This presentist model is

---

5   "The relationship between fathers and sons was at the heart of Soviet utopian
     imagination, asserting historical and ideological continuity between genera-
     tions, while also marking moments of traumatic rupture and transition"
     (Prokhorova 2010: 51).
6   We may also remember that the first film of the Putin era "World War II film
     deluge", Nikolai Lebedev's *Zvezda* of 2002, was itself a remake of Aleksandr

at the moment part and parcel of the Russian government's discourse, with its talk of the "Kiev fascist junta" as though the Nazi ideology of the 1930s and '40s had suddenly become alive again; and it can be witnessed in every individual or group rhetoric that somehow follows or is connected with this discourse.[7]

The film *White Tiger* consciously posits its story in this worldview. It was a stroke of genius that Shakhnazarov chose Boiashov's story about a man without a memory, without a past, and without parents, as the protagonist for his artistic reflection. Only when there is no real *memory* of the past can there be such a literal obsessive *repetition* of that past in the present. And in that sense Naidenov's behavior can be read as traumatic—and Shakhnazarov's film as a film on historical trauma.

In Boiashov's text, the motif of Ivan's resurrection from the dead is there to help develop the supernatural level of the battle with the mythical monster (Ivan is called a living corpse, the doctors call him "Tanatos", he is "as it were from the other world"). He is also called "Akakii Akakievich" a few times (Gogol's "little man" from *The Overcoat* who also avenges himself after death), which may be connected with still more interesting literary allusions, but these subtleties in the end serve merely to put his battle in a certain wider context. In the film, however, the motif of life after death connects Ivan with Hitler, and this puts his *revenant*-features in the context of a past that hauntingly keeps returning in the present. Naidenov is un-dead, or rather, he has died as a martyr and returns as the Eternal Martyr.

Ivanov's *Zvezda* of 1949. Indeed, the time warp device from *We are from the Future* itself recycles a device from two Soviet films: the Russian/Estonian *Small Requiem for a Harmonica (Маленький реквием для губной гармошки/Väike reekviem suupillile*, Veljo Käsper, 1972) and *If This Happens to You (Если это случится с тобой*, Igor' Nikolaev, 1973).

7   Witness, for instance, the march of Ukrainian government-loyal POWs on the streets of Donetsk by Eastern Ukrainian rebel soldiers on 17 June 2014, at which, behind the column, street cleaning machines watered the roads exactly like those on the streets of Moscow during the German POW march on 17 June 1944. See *Ukraine: Donetsk Parades POWs* (about 00.00.20 - 00.00.25) and *March of German Prisoners* (about 00.00.50-00.00.55).

Naidenov is also a man without a childhood.[8] It is no coinci-
dence that for his pseudo-documentary episode Shakhnazarov
chose Wilhelm Keitel signing the German surrender: this is an obvious quote from Tarkovsky's first feature film *Ivan's Childhood* (1962),
in which actual historical footage of the scene is shown (true, for
only ten seconds or so). Ivan Ivanovich Naidenov resembles Tarkovsky's Ivan, of course, in his stubborn determination to fight the enemy to the end, but even more importantly in the absence of a past,
of a childhood, symbolized in Tarkovsky by the absence of a father;
indeed, as Helena Goscilo aptly writes, in Tarkovsky's film even all
the attempts of the respective surrogate fathers are rejected by Ivan
(Ivan's mother, on the other hand, is very present in his dreams;
however, only in the form of the obsessive reliving of the moment
of her death). Furthermore, there may be an echo in *White Tiger*,
especially in the words spoken by Hitler on the ongoing war, of the
famous quote from the end of *Ivan's Childhood*, "can it really be that
this is not the last war on earth?" ("неужели это не самая
последняя война на земле").

Ivan's Childhood was the first important film to break with the
Soviet axiom that World War II was something to be remembered
as a heroic model for the present, an indubitable moral, political,
and national anchor that gives direction to history, and teaches how
to live in the present and the future. The function of this quote in
White Tiger seems obvious: there cannot be a direct line from the
past to the present, no equation of the two, nothing can be taken
from the past to the present in an un-mediated way. The Keitel episode seems to do just that, but the illusion is broken by the mystical
scene with Hitler in hell. Interestingly, during the Keitel scene a re-
porter trips over something and falls, for a moment drawing every-

---

8   Of course, this places the film in a tradition of symbolizing epochal historical
ruptures through generational ones. Alexander Mitscherlich's "generation without fathers" (*Auf dem Weg zur vaterlosen Gesellschaft*, 1963) was the first study
to call attention to this psycho-cultural topic. Its prominent presence in the
symbolic structure of many modern Russian films is analyzed in Goscilo and
Hashimova (2010). The topic has a much longer prehistory in Russian culture,
though; see Brouwer 2010b, passim.

body's attention. I have not been able to find this detail in any description of the real historic event, so I presume that Shakhnazarov added it, and I read it as a symbolic failure of the witness illusion.

Thus, *White Tiger* positions itself in a debate, or perhaps rather a missing debate, about the way the 20th century should be remembered in Russia, aiming right into the middle of its vortex, World War II, as the pivotal episode of the Soviet historical discourse. It is not easy to establish the background for the return of the obsession with World War II and, moreover, the positive evaluation of it, in contemporary Russian culture, which, as outlined above, is connected with a re-evaluation of the figure of Joseph Stalin. In very broad terms, I think it would be correct to search for an answer along the lines drawn by Paul Gilroy in his *Postcolonial Melancholia* (2004), in which he analyzes Britain's "continued citation of the anti-Nazi war" and interprets it as a reaction of a trauma, still not overcome, over the loss of imperial greatness.[9] I am not sure whether I agree with Gilroy in his analysis of British contemporary society, but it seems correct to me to extrapolate it to the post-Soviet-imperial cultural trauma that became so apparent especially after the humiliating experience of the 1990s, when economic and social troubles aggravated the negative mood.

***

To conclude: Shakhnazarov's film takes issue with a construction of the traumatic past as part of a cyclical tragedy in which the Russian people plays the role of the martyr. I would suggest that this type of "active suffering" can and should be differentiated from other types of historical suffering constructed in post-1991 Eastern Europe.

---

9   "Th[e] memory of the country at war against foes who are simply, tidily, and uncomplicatedly evil has recently acquired the status of an ethnic myth" (Gilroy 2004: 89). Of course, the comparison between the ex-Soviet and the ex-Imperial British situation is very problematic. The point, however, is not to compare two political constellations, but the mechanism of projecting feelings connected with the traumatic experience of one series of events onto a wholly different set of events.

In the case, for instance, of Poland, from the point of view of position-taking towards Russia the situation is quite clear: the Poles are victims, and the historical events can be "worked through" as loss. And although the sky has not cleared in many respects, it is possible to observe the beginning of such a working through: monuments are being erected, there is a debate on who suffered, who inflicted the pain, and who were bystanders. I am not suggesting that all is well: eruptions of renewed acting out of suffering may occur, as with the Smolensk plane crash of 2010 in Poland;[10] perhaps the discussion about who was guilty and who innocent could be more open, as the Jedwabne case clearly shows.[11] And although certainly the self-images of Poles show some traits of martyrdom, in the sense that their victims died for others—metonymically for Poland, or perhaps for the right Catholic faith, or perhaps even to save the world[12]— still there is a process of discussion about events, while the events themselves are ever more clearly relegated to the past. I would see films like Wajda's *Katyń* (2007) or Smarzowski's *Róża* (2011) in this light, at least as a tendency, at least at the moment. The mere existence of exhibitions and museums in Poland that follow this pattern would suggest so. By contrast, in the Russian case one finds more traces of the confusion/conflation of loss with absence— or presence in this case, but these are, as I have argued, from the point of view of trauma studies, two sides of the same coin.

REFERENCES

Boiashov, Il'ia (2008) *Tankist, ili "Belyi tigr"*. St Petersburg: Limbus-Press.
Booth, Wayne (1961) *The Rhetoric of Fiction*. Chicago, IL: University of Chicago Press.

---

[10]   Cf. Przylipiak (in press). For a detailed discussion of the background see Etkind *et al* (2012).
[11]   See Gross (2001); Polonsky and Michlic (2004).
[12]   See Jerzy Hoffman's film *Battle of Warsaw 1920* of 2011, in which the traditional myth of Poland as "antemurale christianitatis" is translated into a myth of Poland as the world's defender against Bolshevism.

Brouwer, Sander (2010a) "Agency and Memory in Polish, Russian and Ukrainian Films and Novels". Paper at the Memory at War Inaugural Workshop, Cambridge (June 2010). http://www.memoryatwar.org/publications-list/Brouwer Agency and Memory Paper June 2010.pdf (accessed 28 February 2014).

--- (2010b) "First Love, but not First Lover: Turgenev's Poetics of Unoriginality", in R. Reid and J. Andrew (eds) *Turgenev: Art, Ideology and Legacy*. Studies in Slavic Literature and Poetics; Vol. 56. Amsterdam: Rodopi, 87–106.

--- (in press) "From Empire to Smuta and Back. The Mythopoetics of Cyclical History in Russian Film and TV-Documentaries", in S. Brouwer (ed.), *Contested Interpretations of the Past in Polish, Russian, and Ukrainian Film. Screen as Battlefield*. Leiden: Brill, 2016.

Bykov, Dmitrii (2005) *Opravdanie*. Moscow: Vagrius.

Dodolev, Yevgenii (2012a) "Interv'iu: Karen Shakhnazarov o svoei rabote—lente 'Belyi tigr'", *Moscow 24*, 28 September. http://www.m24.ru/videos/3265 (accessed 28 February 2013).

--- (2012b) "'Belyi tigr' Shakhnazarova", Blog Yevgeniia Dodoleva, 28 September. http://www.mk.ru/blog/posts/1634-belyiy-tigr-shahnazarova.html (accessed 28 February 2013).

Dolgopolov, Greg (2008) "Adventure Tourism to 1942 as a Rite of Passage", review of *We are from the Future* (*My iz budushchego*, 2008), *KinoKultura* no. 22. http://www.kinokultura.com/2008/22r-future.shtml (accessed 28 February 2014).

Etkind, Alexander (2009) "Stories of the Undead in the Land of the Unburied: Magical Historicism in Contemporary Russian Fiction", *Slavic Review*, 68(3): 631–58.

Etkind, Alexander, Rory Finnin, Uilleam Blacker *et al* (2012) *Remembering Katyn*. Cambridge, Oxford, Boston, MA: Polity.

Filippov, Aleksandr (2007) *Noveishaia istoriia Rossii, 1945–2006 gg. Kniga dlia uchitelia*. Moscow: Prosveshchenie.

Giesen, Bernhard (2004) *Triumph and Trauma*. Boulder, CO: Paradigm Publishers (Yale Cultural Sociology Series).

Gilroy, Paul (2004) *Postcolonial Melancholia*. New York, NY: Columbia University Press.

Girardet, Raoul (1986) *Mythes et mythologies politiques*. Paris: Éditions du Seuil.

Goscilo, Helena and Hashamova, Yana (eds) (2010) *Cinepaternity: Fathers and Sons in Soviet and Post-Soviet Film*. Bloomington, IN: Indiana University Press.

Goscilo, Helena (2010) "Fraught Filiation: Andrei Tarkovsky's Transformations of Personal Trauma", in H. Goscilo and Y. Hashamova (eds) *Cinepaternity: Fathers and Sons in Soviet and Post-Soviet Film*. Bloomington, IN: Indiana University Press, 247–81.

Gross, Jan Tomasz (2001) *Neighbors*. Princeton, NJ: Princeton University Press.

Koposov, Nikolay (2011) "'The Armored Train of Memory': The Politics of History in Post-Soviet Russia", *Perspectives on History*, January.

https://www.historians.org/publications-and-directories/perspectives-on-history/january-2011/the-armored-train-of-memory-the-politics-of-history-in-post-soviet-russia\ (accessed 28 February 2014).

LaCapra, Dominick (2001) *Writing History, Writing Trauma*. Baltimore, MD: The Johns Hopkins University Press.

Levada-Center (2012) "Kolichestvo negativnykh otsenok lichnosti Stalina sredi rossiian za 15 let sokratilos' pochti v tri raza", 18 October. http://www.levada.ru/18-10-2012/kolichestvo-negativnykh-otsenok-lichnosti-stalina-sredi-rossiyan-za-15-let-sokratilos-poc (accessed 28 February 2014).

--- (2013) "Rossiiane o roli Stalina v istorii: initsiave vozvrashcheniia Volgogradu nazvaniia Stalingrad", 4 March. http://www.levada.ru/04-03-2013/rossiyane-o-roli-stalina-v-istorii-initsiative-vozvrashcheniya-volgogradu-nazvaniya-stali (accessed 28 February 2015).

Lutz-Auras, L. (2012) *"Auf Stalin, Sieg und Vaterland!" Politisierung der kollektiven Erinnerung an den Zweiten Weltkrieg in Russland*. Wiesbaden: Springer.

March of German prisoners in Moscow 1944. https://www.youtube.com/watch?v=vr1mVoaYUYLU (accessed 28 February 2015).

McVey, David (2010) "Review of *We Are from the Future 2* (*My iz budushchego 2*, 2010)," *KinoKultura*, no. 30. http://www.kinokultura.com/2010/30r-future2.shtml (accessed 28 February 2015).

Noordenbos, Boris (2013) *Messages from the Black Hole: Post-Soviet Literature in Search of a Russian Identity*. S.l.: s.n. Proefschrift Rijksuniversiteit Groningen.

Norris, Stephen M. (2012a) *Blockbuster History in the New Russia: Movies, Memory, and Patriotism*. Bloomington, IN: Indiana University Press.

--- (2012b) "Review of Karen Shakhnazarov: *White Tiger* (*Belyi tigr*, 2012)", *KinoKultura*, no. 38, http://www.kinokultura.com/2012/38r-belytigr.shtml (accessed 28 February 2015).

Oushakine, Serguei (2009) *The Patriotism of Despair: Nation, War and Loss in Russia*. Ithaca, NY: Cornell University Press.

Plakhov, Andrei (2012) "Potustoronnie boevye deistviia. 'Belyi tigr' Karena Shakhnazarova", *Kommersant" S-Peterburg*, no. 82 (4867), 10 May. http://www.kommersant.ru/doc/1930592 (accessed 28 February 2013).

Polonsky, Antony, and Michlic, Joanna (eds) (2004) *The Neighbors Respond: The Controversy over the Jedwabne Massacre in Poland*. Princeton, NJ: Princeton University Press.

Prokhorova, Elena (2010) "Mending the Rupture: The War Trope and the Return of the Imperial Father in 1970s Cinema", in H. Goscilo and Y. Hashamova (eds) *Cinepaternity: Fathers and Sons in Soviet and Post-Soviet Film*. Bloomington, IN: Indiana University Press, 51–69.

Przylipiak, Mirosław (in press) "'I Am Afraid of this Land'. The Representation of Russia in Polish Documentaries about the Smolensk Plane Crash", in S.

Brouwer (ed.), *Contested Interpretations of the Past in Polish, Russian, and Ukrainian Film. Screen as Battlefield*. Leiden: Brill, 2016.

Schmid, Wolf (2013) "Implied Author", *The Living Handbook of Narratology*. http://www.lhn.uni-hamburg.de/article/implied-author-revised-version-uploaded-26-january-2013 (accessed 2 July 2015).

Shpagin, Aleksandr (2005) "Religiia voiny. Sub"ektivnye zametki o bogo-iskatel'stve v voennom kinematografe", *Iskusstvo kino*, no. 5, May. http://kinoart.ru/archive/2005/05/n5-article10 (accessed 28 February 2013).

Smorodinskaya, Tatiana (2010) "The Fathers' War through the Sons' Lens", in H. Goscilo and Y. Hashamova (eds) *Cinepaternity: Fathers and Sons in Soviet and Post-Soviet Film*. Bloomington, IN: Indiana University Press, 89–113.

Ukraine: Donetsk Parades POWs mirroring 1944 Moscow Nazi POW parade. https://www.youtube.com/watch?v=0cz7A2bxU4Y (accessed 28 February 2015).

Walker, S. (2008) "The Big Question: Why is Stalin Still Popular in Russia, despite the Brutality of his Regime?", *The Independent*, 14 May. http://www.independent.co.uk/news/world/europe/the-big-question-why-is-stalin-still-popular-in-russia-despite-the-brutality-of-his-regime-827654.html (accessed 28 February 2015).

Whitmore, B. (2015) "Podcast: Putin's History Channel". *Radio Free Europe/Radio Liberty*, 19 June. http://www.rferl.org/content/podcast-putins-history-channel/27081590.html (accessed 28 February 2015).

In Search of a Modern Mnemonic Narrative of Communism: Russia's Mnemopolitical Mimesis during the Medvedev Presidency

Maria Mälksoo[*]

Abstract: *This article examines the politics of memory in Russia during the Medvedev presidency (2008–12). It suggests an understanding of the proposals for a "new historical doctrine" in Russia during this period through the lens of mimesis. Russia's search for a "modern" mnemonic narrative of communism could be interpreted as an attempt to "normalize" the country as an actor in international politics. The paper engages critically the question of whether the calls for mnemonical modernization subscribe to, or rather challenge, the Western power to define the normative meaning of what constitutes the proper way of coming to terms with the violent past. It problematizes the link between "mnemonical modernization" and international "normality" in contemporary Russian politics. The article argues that the emphasis on the volume of national suffering and martyrdom has not been matched with the discussion of the issues of responsibility in the calls to establish a "new historical doctrine" about communism in contemporary Russia.*

"We Need a Modern Narrative"

Russia's eclectic reckoning with its communist past and its glaring eschewal of transitional justice has received a fair share of criticism

---

[*] I acknowledge the financial support of the European Union via the European Social Fund's Mobilitas post-doctoral programme (grant no. GSHRG060MJ), HERA Memory at War project (grant no. MSHRG10039) and the Estonian Research Council (grant no. ETF8295). I am grateful to Prof. Viatcheslav Morozov for encouragement and engagement with an earlier draft of this paper.

across the disciplinary boundaries of political science, law, and contemporary history (e.g., Adler 2012a, b; Andrieu 2011; Nuzov 2014; Satter 2012; Schlögel 2013; Stan 2009). The controversial politics of memory[1] during the Putin era, in particular, has been denounced as aimed at constructing a new national mythology of the positive legacies of the communist period in Russian history, rather than accounting for the crimes of the antecedent regime. While human rights organizations, such as the "Memorial" Society, have dug into the social memory of communism in earnest ever since the gradual collapse of the Soviet system, the political elites have generally avoided contemplating issues of responsibility and guilt in the context of the Second World War, the Soviet suppression of Russia's neighboring nations and states, and mass repressions inflicted on the Russian nation itself. The preferred frame of public remembrance regarding the violent legacy of communism has been the victimhood if not outright martyrdom of the Russian people. The tendency to evade questions of accountability by foregrounding the immensity of the Russians' own suffering under the Soviet regime is hardly surprising against the backdrop of a significant degree of continuity between the Soviet and post-Soviet elites in contemporary Russia (Gill 2013; Sakwa 2011).

Yet, during Dmitry Medvedev's presidency (2008–12), the need for a new mnemonic narrative of communism that would be more suitable for Russia's international image and desired symbolic status in international society, was acknowledged in the official circles of the country. In June 2010, Konstantin Kosachev, Chair of the State Duma Committee for International Affairs, published an article wherein he argued that the damage to Russia's reputation was beginning to outweigh the advantages brought by defending the Soviet past on the international arena (Kosachev 2010). Accordingly, he called for devising a "set of principles, a 'historical doctrine' of

---

[1]   The notions "mnemopolitics" and "politics of memory" are used interchangeably here, referring to the political coordination and sanctioning of particular narratives of the past, generally manufactured, although hardly ever entirely controlled, by elites. Likewise, "mnemonic" is used as shorthand for "memory-related" in the text. For a "Historically Realist" take on the politics of memory, see Berger (2012).

sorts", in order to clarify Russia's position with regard to the Soviet past in terms that would be easily comprehensible to its foreign partners. According to Kosachev, such a strategic move would enable a sharp distinction to be drawn between historical evaluations of Soviet actions at the domestic and international levels. Emphasizing that while Russia fulfilled all the international obligations of the USSR as its successor state, it could not be held morally or legally responsible for the actions and crimes committed by the Soviet authorities, Kosachev sought to protect Russia against possible future demands for compensation for the victims of Soviet crimes as well as to deflect East European attempts at provoking Russia into aggressive responses on the historical memory front (Fedor 2010; Torbakov 2011).

The eminent Russian foreign political heavy-weight Sergei Karaganov, head of the Russian Council on Foreign and Defense Policy and the chairman of the Standing Committee on Historical Memory[2] under the Presidential Council for the Development of Civil Society and Human Rights delivered, in his turn, a quite remarkable programmatic speech on the issue of policy on the Soviet past at a meeting with President Medvedev in Yekaterinburg on 1 February 2011. This meeting was organized by the Presidential Council for the Development of Civil Society and Human Rights, a consultative body established for assisting, informing, and advising the president in the exercise of his constitutional responsibilities vis-à-vis human rights, freedoms, and civil society institutions.[3] It brought together historians and representatives of social organizations, the "Memorial" Society among them. Setting out his vision for reconstituting the Russian identity through a re-evaluation of the Soviet past, Karaganov claimed that Russian society could not regain its self-respect until it faced up to the "terrible sin" that was the revolution and the subsequent decades of totalitarian rule (Karaganov

---

[2]   Established in 2011, see further at: http://president-sovet.ru/about/commissions/permanent/read/5/ (accessed 11 June 2015).

[3]   See http://en.kremlin.ru/structure/councils#institution-18 (accessed 10 June 2015). For a discussion, see Owen (2012).

2011a). Invoking the notion of *samogenotsid* (or self-genocide)[4] to describe the Civil War and the Stalinist terror, Karaganov's Yekaterinburg speech built upon some of the points he had previously made in another programmatic piece, evocatively titled "The Russian Katyn" (Karaganov 2010). In his Yekaterinburg speech, Karaganov defined the victims of Soviet terror as "the best" of society, and called upon contemporary Russian society to identify with these victims, instead of the perpetrators (Karaganov 2011a).[5] He made the case for launching a state-run mass movement aimed at memorializing and honoring the victims of political repressions during the Soviet period. Arguably, the benefits would include the creation of a new patriotic elite with a real sense of responsibility for the country; and the earning of respect and good will internationally.[6]

Accordingly, the Committee on Historical Memory proposed a list of measures in 2011 aimed at adjusting the Russian collective remembrance of the Soviet experience in the interests of Medvedev's modernization strategy. The cornerstone of these draft proposals was the idea that Russia should aim to take a leading role in the struggle against totalitarian legacies in post-Soviet and post-communist space, as the country which had suffered most of all. Russia should accordingly spearhead a large-scale memorialization

---

[4] The focus on Stalin's USSR´s responsibility for domestic genocide evades, however, the discussion of its international genocidal activity in the Second World War (see further Shaw 2013: 78; Naimark 2010; Werth 2008).

[5] Quite symptomatically, his speech nonetheless displayed the blurring and thus fundamental relativization of the categories of victims and perpetrators: "We all should bow low to the millions of victims. After all, the butchers were victims, too." Later on in the speech, he argued that: "all countries of the former Soviet Union ... were among the victims—and among the executioners, too" (Karaganov 2011a).

[6] "Some fear that recognizing in full the horrors of the Gulag and declassifying all the archives would damage the prestige of the country. They will not. Perpetuation of the memory of the victims of the totalitarian regime can only evoke respect. /--/... Russia is one large Katyn, with the thousands of graves of millions of the best citizens of the USSR. By paying respects to their memory in all the villages and cities, from where they were sent to labor camps or for death, to their mostly nameless graves, we shall regain not only self-esteem, but also the respect of all normal people in the world. After all, we shall do so ourselves, without coercion or pressure from outside, not by compulsion, as losers, but voluntarily" (Karaganov 2011a).

campaign throughout the former Soviet space, with the possibility of eventually expanding this to the broader European level, since allegedly "all Europe was a victim, all Europe was guilty of the tragedies of the twentieth century—of the two world wars, of the two totalitarianisms, of the most severe schism, which has yet to be overcome completely" (Karaganov 2011c). The proposals included renaming the Day of Popular Unity (4 November) as the Day of Remembrance of the Victims of the Civil War and National Reconciliation, reflecting the view that the totalitarian regime had waged war against the people of Russia from 1917 to 1991, and raising the status of 30 October, the Day of Remembrance of the Victims of Political Repression in the Russian calendar of political remembrance. In addition, the development of a state-supported public campaign for the mass construction of monuments to victims of the totalitarian regime, and the opening up of the archives was called for. These steps were devised to prepare the ground for the political and legal assessment of the crimes of the communist regime in order to "de-totalitarianize" Russian public consciousness. As Karaganov maintained in his Yekaterinburg speech, the aim of the project on the "Perpetuation of the Memory of the Victims of the Totalitarian Regime and National Reconciliation" was "de-Stalinization and de-Communization of the Russian public mind and our country in general".[7] Its main goal was to "ensure transformation of the consciousness of both Russian society and the Russian elite", for:

> modernization of the country will be impossible either at the technical or on the political level without changing the consciousness of society, without nurturing the people's sense of responsibility for themselves and for the country, the feeling of pride in it, albeit bitter at times (Karaganov 2011a).

What should we make of these mnemopolitical moves? Did these calls for mnemonical modernization subscribe to, or rather challenge, the Western power to define the normative meaning of what constitutes the proper way of coming to terms with a violent past? This process is generally understood as engaging transitional justice, that according to a 2004 report by the UN Secretary General,

---

[7] For the full transcript of the event, see "Stenograficheskii otchet" (2011).

comprises "the full range of processes and mechanisms associated with a society's attempts to come to terms with a legacy of large-scale past abuses, in order to ensure accountability, serve justice and achieve reconciliation" (UN SecGen 2004: 3). Yet, while Medvedev lent his support to some of the good intentions behind the project on the "Perpetuation of the Memory of the Victims of the Totalitarian Regime and National Reconciliation", his backing of the "Memorial" Society-driven request for a political-legal judgment of the crimes of the communist regime was not forthcoming (see "Stenograficheskii otchet" 2011). To date, Russia's official record in the legal, political, administrative and symbolic dimensions of addressing the legacy of the Soviet regime has remained at best half-hearted, if not outright revisionist during the consolidation of the current illiberal government. The harassment of "Perm-36" and the consequent "self-liquidation" of the NGO managing the country's most important museum of Gulag,[8] along with the increasing political pressure on civil society organizations, including the "Memorial" Society which was originally involved in the drafting of proposals for the perpetuation of the memory of the victims of political repressions, and the Sakharov Center, are particularly evocative reminders of Russia's mnemopolitical reversal during president Putin's third term in the office. The Russian case has accordingly been described as a good counterexample of transitional justice for its "faux" or pseudo-transitional justice interventions that have been aimed not at democratization and the protection of victims' rights so much as at legitimizing the new political elite (Andrieu 2011).

This article suggests an understanding of the calls for a "new historical doctrine", as aired from the country's official quarters during the Medvedev presidency, through the lens of mimesis. I subsequently conceptualize the Medvedev-era "de-Communization" campaign as an attempt to sustain the "legitimate exceptionalism" of Russia's way of dealing with the Soviet past while seeking to do away with being cast as a failure of post-communist transitional justice, or, in a sense, an "abnormal" state (cf. Hagström 2015; Lawson and

---

8   See further http://www.perm36.ru/ru/novosti/novosti/724-ano-zakryvaetsya-rabota-prodolzhaetsya.html (accessed 11 June 2015).

Tannaka 2011). Below I outline the argument for understanding Russia's quest for a "modern" mnemonic narrative as an attempt to "normalize" the country internationally. Taking a cue from Ayşe Zarakol's (2014: 313) suggestion that historical stigmatization of non-Western states, inter alia Russia, contributes both to their compliance with and rejection of particular international norms, I understand the most recent state-supported "de-Stalinization" campaign as an example of mimesis, rather than a wholehearted attempt at compliance with the (Western) norm of transitional justice. The search for an internationally passable mnemonic narrative about Russia's relationship towards the Soviet past as put forth during the Medvedev presidency closely reflects Russia's ongoing quest for a specific status in international society. As Zarakol (2014: 313) observes, "emulation and non-compliance are at times the two sides of the same coin". Instead of providing a safe route to "international normalcy" then, mimesis ultimately threatens the order as defined by the "normal" (Ibid.: 316).

My main claim is that the emphasis on the volume of national suffering and self-victimization discourse in the Medvedev-era calls to establish a "new historical doctrine" about the communist period was not matched by engagement with the issues of responsibility and accountability. Depicting Russians as the people who suffered most in the Soviet period not only helped to circumvent the international implications of the violence perpetrated by the communist regime, but also implied a sense of vindication through the emphasis on Russia's self-sacrifice, as though Russians suffered and died also for others in the community of nations of the former USSR, thus obfuscating the allocation of clear responsibility. While Russians were invited to identify with the persecuted, the persecutors remained an unidentified tragic force. The allusions of overwhelming Russian martyrdom under the Soviet regime hence enabled the continuing instrumentalization of a selective remembrance of the Soviet experiment for contemporary political benefit.

"Why Be Happy When You Could Be Normal?" (cf. Winterson 2011)

Symbolically, the calls for renewed de-Communization of Russia under Medvedev appeared to be quite a radical rupture compared to Vladimir Putin's previous terms in the office of the president of the Russian Federation which were characterized by the explicit distancing of the country from bearing any historical responsibility for the crimes of the Soviet regime. Putin's second term in office (2004–2008), in particular, was marked by various attempts to reconnect with the proud moments of Russia's communist past, leading to the securitization and sacralization of the victory of the Great Patriotic War, along with the state-orchestrated pompous public remembrance of this event.

The apparent mnemopolitical shift during Medvedev's presidency has been regarded as an obvious ploy aimed at bringing Russia's mnemopolitical arsenal in line with Medvedev's modernization strategy in order to win more "hearts and minds" in Europe, and generally improve relations with the West (Sherlock 2011). The acknowledged need for a modern mnemonic narrative of communism tallied with a broader strategic objective to improve and project Russia's "soft power" more efficiently abroad.[9] Just as Lavrentii Beria, the Minister of Internal Affairs and the first de-Stalinizer, as unlikely as this might seem, recognized that de-Stalinization was "a strong weapon in the struggle for power" (Khlevniuk, cited in Adler 2002: 77), a similar logic was discernible in Karaganov's contemporary invocation of the term. Since at least the Khrushchev era, de-Stalinization has been a way of breaking with the immediate

---

9   As bluntly exemplified by Karaganov, yet again, in the following excerpt: "Russia should fight for positions on the market of ideas and images, since they are playing a much greater role today than ever in the past. The alternative is an inevitable loss in international competition. This fighting requires up-to-date propaganda tools, but not only them. One must understand what brands, images and ideas can be sold. And it is even more important to ensure that Russian intellectuals, who are the main producers of ideas and images for the country and for the whole world, begin to side with their homeland and—at least partially—with the government. But this is again a problem of our inner organization, which we will have to restructure anyway. If we do not, the result will be a flop in international competition" (Karaganov 2012).

past, distancing oneself from the ideology and/or actions of one's predecessors *inter alia* with the aim of "bending with the political winds" (Ibid.: 77–78).

I would like to offer an alternative, or rather complementary, reading of Russia's mnemonical reputation management here, utilizing insights from post-colonial theory. Taking my cue from Bhabha (1994) in particular, Russia's search for a "modern" mnemonic narrative could be interpreted as a hybrid attempt to "normalize" the country as an actor in international politics. I depart from the premise that Russia's search for a modern mnemonic narrative is a response to the hegemonic construction of East European memory of the twentieth century as different from an implicit or explicit European "standard account". The Russian quest for mnemonical modernization thus emerges as part of its quest for international "normality", with "modernity" in mnemopolitics functioning as the equivalent of such normality.

Yet, in order to account more substantively for the Medvedev-era "de-Stalinization"[10] campaign, as it was curiously dubbed, I suggest that it might be better understood as a form of resisting the hegemonic European discourse about what constitutes a "normal relationship" vis-à-vis one's violent past. This strategy of resistance entails seemingly playing along with the terms of the dominant discourse, yet ultimately only mimicking, rather than filling out the discourse with real actions aimed at "coming to terms" with one's past in earnest. If we view these mnemopolitical moves in Russia towards "modernizing" its collective assessment of the communist experiment as merely a strategic case of paying lip-service to the European expectations about how one should handle the criminal legacy of the totalitarian period, then we miss the power of the mimetic to potentially redefine the mimicked subject (that is, the European

---

[10]   The concept of de-Stalinization goes way back to the mid-twentieth century. According to Adler (2002: 239), "[a]fter the death of Stalin, state policy traversed the spectrum from de-Stalinization to re-Stalinization to de-Stalinization to de-Sovietization". It is perhaps only symptomatic that the most recent calls for de-Sovietization have been dubbed as "de-Stalinization" in popular media yet again. On the intricacies of previous rounds in the long process of Russian de-Stalinization, see also van Goudoever (1986).

conception of a link between democratization and the society's ability and will to deal with a violent past). Besides the concern for symbolic power, there are vital issues of respect, recognition, and ontological security (or the security of a state's self-defined identity) (cf. Mitzen 2006; Steele 2008) involved in the quest for "mnemonical modernization". As Karaganov put it:

> In reality, its [the project's] main aim is to modernize the consciousness of the Russian people, as well as that of all the peoples of the USSR, who were left badly wounded by seventy years of the Communist, totalitarian regime. One of the main ways of dealing with this trauma is through showing respect to the millions who perished in Communist times: by building monuments for them and tending their graves. In cultivating this sense of respect for them people will learn to respect themselves, and each other. It is about giving people back that sense of self-respect. This was not developed as an anti-Stalin initiative. De-Stalinization happened in the sixties and later. As I see it, this program deals at the fundamental level with restoring people's faith in themselves (Karaganov 2011b).

Russia's post-Soviet mnemopolitical hurdles have indeed been exacerbated by the lack of a clearly distinguishable "self" to which Russia could have returned after the collapse of the Soviet Union in order to sustain the consistency of its collective "selfhood". It is hardly surprising, against that backdrop, that contemporary Russia's state-sanctioned memory politics regarding its relationship to the Soviet past might be described as ambivalent, to say the least. Victory in the "Great Patriotic War" and the mass crimes of the very regime that governed and led the country through that war sit uneasily together in the modern Russian mnemonical template, marking the poles of ontological security and insecurity, respectively. Russia's difficulties in reckoning with the communist past have been magnified by the complicated demands of facing the "other in oneself".

During his first two terms in the office of the president, Vladimir Putin generally distanced Russia from any historical responsibility for the crimes of the Soviet regime.[11] Gradually, the attempts

---

[11]   This sentiment has been generally shared societally as well, as arguably the vast majority of Russians refuse to admit any collective responsibility for the Soviet regime. Partly, this is due to the fact that there has hardly been another case

to selectively pick and choose which bits and pieces of the Soviet past to cherish and which to forget became more varied with cautious recognition also of the darker chapters of the Soviet legacy, as exemplified by Putin's symbolic visit to a key site of the Stalinist Great Terror, the Butovo killing field on 30 October 2007, and his remarks at the commemoration ceremony of the victims of Katyn on 7 April 2010 (see Mälksoo 2012, for further discussion). Medvedev, in his turn, forcefully declared his conviction that the "memory of national tragedies is as sacred as the memory of victories" (Medvedev 2009). As a rule, Russia's post-Soviet mnemopolitical dynamics has nonetheless been replete with status-conscious trajectories of an ongoing quest for ontological security as a state in international society. Societally, furthermore, Russian people have equally sought to retain a basic ontological consistency throughout the tumultuous post-Soviet decades—in spite of the fundamental difficulties they have faced in integrating the Soviet experience into a coherent and positive national "self". If anything, it was the decade of the 1990s which invited "almost universal condemnation" in Russia (Prozorov 2008: 208). The immediate post-Cold War "memory thaw" proved to be ultimately indecisive, and was followed by attempts to re-connect with aspects of the previous socio-political predicament in order to find some stability after the sudden rupture in the ontological sense of the "Russian self" as a result of the collapse of the Soviet Union, further intensified by the chaotic onslaught of brutal capitalism of the early 1990s. Against that backdrop, it is perhaps not so striking that sociological polls have persistently quoted significant percentages of the Russian population as regarding Stalin as someone who "did more good than bad for the country" (Garagozov 2008: 20), and have indicated a general lack of a sense of any responsibility for the crimes committed under the Soviet regime (Adler 2005; Khapaeva 2009). In the past two years, Stalin's popularity among Russians has soared even further (Monaghan and Gladkova 2015). The issue here might be not so much ignorance as indifference, or "an intentional desire to ignore the dark sides of

---

but the Soviet Russia where the boundaries between perpetrators, accomplices and victims have been so blurred (Viola 2013; Khazanov 2008: 300–1).

the Soviet past" (Khazanov 2008: 294). Consequently, attitudes towards the Soviet past are conceived as "a matter of values much more than of knowledge" (ibid.; cf. Forest *et al* 2004: 374). When the overarching value is the security of the self, the aspects endangering that security tend to get glossed over or rejected entirely.

All the more dangerous for Russia's successful post-communist healing, argue those analysts who have noticed the tendency towards shunting the tragic legacy of the Soviet period into the sphere of personal remembrance and embracing only the heroic in the public commemoration practices in contemporary Russia (e.g., Garagozov 2008: 27; Khazanov 2008: 295; cf. Tumarkin 1994; Merridale 2000). Some are fiercely critical: according to Khapaeva's diagnosis, for instance, Russian society is "seriously ill" with a "partial amnesia that makes its historical memory strangely selective". Not only are there "no political debates or hot intellectual discussions on how the Soviet crimes influenced and continue to influence contemporary Russian society", but there is also "no intellectual or political force that would make post-Soviet society face the issue of historical responsibility" (Khapaeva 2009: 359). Not surprisingly against that backdrop, there has been no lustration in post-Soviet Russia, no criminal prosecution of perpetrators of crimes in connection with the administration of the Soviet justice, thus leaving "the evil ... insufficiently personified" (Khazanov 2008: 298). The overall Russian memory of Stalinist repressions has been characterized as victim-based, not perpetrator-centric (see further Roginski 2008). Nonetheless, the prospect of building an official central monument to the victims of political repressions in Russia has become realistic only recently.[12]

It is pertinent to inquire here, whether Russia's long-time difficulties related to acknowledging the criminal legacy of its predecessor, the USSR, have been determined by the internally generated obstacles to self-reflection, or have been rather externally generated as a result of Russia's insecurity in its relationships with Europe/the West. As Zarakol (2010: 4) has suggested in the context of Japan and Turkey, intersubjective pressures to handle one's past in a particular

---

[12]   See further http://konkurs.gmig.ru/ (accessed 11 June 2015).

way matter more at times when traditional self-routines are broken—and are more likely to create ontological insecurity outside the West. Indeed, it might be reasonable to claim that Russia's difficulties in fully reckoning with its forebear's legacy are related to the complicated demands of ontological security due to the still continuing openness of its international belonging (cf. Zarakol 2010: 6). Russia's general non-compliance with the Western norm of transitional justice reflects its sensitivity towards the particular origin of that norm (cf. ibid.: 313). Yet, its occasional emulation of the transitional justice discourse reveals an equal obsession with its perceived position in the socially stratified international society of established and still liminal members.

Mnemopolitics as Mimesis

Departing from the Lacanian point that the making of the self is a narrative act (Epstein 2011), I suggest that the Medvedev-era calls for a "new historical doctrine" in Russia be understood through the lens of mimesis. Following the tripartite distinction of a Canadian psychologist and cognitive neuroscientist Merlin W. Donald, mimicry, imitation, and mimesis refer to different degrees of intensity of the action of (appeared) replication and resemblance. While *mimicry* refers to "the deliberate reduplication in action of a perceived event without careful attention to, or knowledge of, its purpose", and *imitation* pays closer attention to the purpose of reduplication, *mimesis* purposefully reduplicates an event for communicative purposes, taking into account the audience (Donald 2005: 286). It should be noted, though, that mimesis remains "an umbrella term that includes imitation and mimicry", for the levels of mimetic action are not distinguished by any discrete boundaries. Rather, Donald argues, the three levels form "a scale of successively more abstract or 'intelligent' versions of reduplicative action". Mimesis is the most complex of the three, as it requires the understanding of not only the purpose of the action, but its various social ramifications and interpretations in context as well (Ibid.: 286–87).

Similarly to President Medvedev's modernization strategy in general, the quest for a new historical doctrine of communism utilized terms explicitly borrowed from the Western liberal democratic discourse while not subjecting the country to the actual demands of that discourse, attempting to sustain a specifically "Russian way" of handling the communist past instead. Likewise, it is important to remember that the Soviet modernizing project remained "vitally attached" to the Western modernizing project in the first place (Buck-Morss 2002: 68). The presentation of the Russian "alternative" is therefore hardly an alternative: by following the rules of dominating discourses on dealing with the totalitarian legacy, Russia produces the effect of ambivalence—as it has done often on previous occasions in history (Morozov and Rumelili 2012), thus reproducing its subject position of liminality. We are witnessing an instance of subtle resistance here: what substantively speaking constitutes a challenge to the master discourse of democratic reckoning with the totalitarian legacy is legitimized in Russia by presenting hybrid demands within the rules of recognition of the dominating discourse so that Russia's difficult past might be handled on its own terms. A subtle, hybrid resistance of this kind is allegedly more empowering than outright opposition or exclusion (Bhabha 1994: 110; for further discussion, see Polat 2011: 1259–60 and 1268). Through mimicry and semblance of the "master discourse", yet without following up on the demands of that discourse with actual policies of transitional justice not just in symbolic, but also legal-political terms, Russian mnemopolitical "modernization" effectively constitutes an act of subversion of the said discourse. Such mimicry enables the subjugated to reverse its subjugation to the hegemonic discourse (see ibid.: 1268). More generally, the search for a "modern mnemonic narrative" of communism is an offspring of Russia's mimetic politics—its mimicking of the forms and language of the Western discourse of *Vergangenheitsbewältigung*[13] without substance, or symbolic *activity* without real *action* (cf. Känd 2013).

---

[13]   The German term for the process of coming to terms with the totalitarian past has become a universal shorthand for a general phenomenon in post-war Euro-

In that sense, the mimetic move in Russia's official mnemo-political line during the Medvedev presidency sought to particularize the universalist discourse on "modern" social memory management. The result is the subversion of "democratic memory work" as a fixed, universal referent (cf. Polat 2011: 1260). The above-quoted statements by Karaganov and other members of the Russian political elite thus underscore the irrelevance of pondering whether and how Russia can *modernize* in the sphere of its dealing with its communist legacy. Instead, they highlight how Russia reproduces, reconfigures, and subverts the Western discourses of democratic *Vergangenheitsbewältigung* through its own representational practices (cf. Rumelili 2012: 497). Russia's particularism is hardly constitutive of a non-hegemonic or "democratized" understanding of what constitutes proper "memory work" in International Relations (IR), however. As Rosa Vasilaki rightly points out, particularism in the form of regional IR schools is often merely "the mirror-image of the logic underpinning Western dominance: based on the idea of uniqueness of a 'special' civilization, culture or nation, its 'special' place in the world and its 'special' mission, they often produce their own versions of hegemony and imperialism" (Vasilaki 2012: 7; cf. Makarychev and Morozov 2013). Russian representatives' calls for a new historical doctrine that would be more suitable to the country's foreign political interests seek to, on the one hand, reposition Russia as part of the West/Europe, essentially reproducing the terms of the Western discourse on "good memory work". On the other hand, the limited, and as such, subversive, way Russia substantiates its turn towards condemning the violent legacy of communism only reproduces its own ambiguity vis-à-vis "Western standards", as well as ultimately sustaining its liminal position in European (identity) politics (Rumelili 2012: 498). As Morozov and Rumelili have aptly pointed out:

> Russia's role as a Europe-maker is presently determined by the fact that it is unhappy about its exclusion from the European political space, [and] tries to

---

pean mnemopolitics, betraying thus the particularist origins of the contemporary Western "rule of thumb" in dealing with the legacies of totalitarian rule according to a set of normative expectations and standards.

challenge this exclusion, but this challenge is certainly very far from being a radical one. Instead of confronting western/EU hegemony, Russia, in Gramscian terms, prefers to wage a war of position whose main parameters are defined by the hegemonic force. This inevitably leads to a situation where hegemony is being reproduced and even, precisely due to this challenge, tends to consolidate (Morozov and Rumelili 2012: 42).

Russia's mimesis of de-Communization under Medvedev thus ultimately emerges as a productive hegemonic, rather than explicitly counter-hegemonic strategy, for it has arranged discursive elements of the dominant discourse so as to "promote the goal, the aims and the objective of a hegemony" (Herschinger 2012: 76). Whether or not it really will follow the suggested course of condemning the crimes of the communist regime in the form of real actions in this direction remains to be seen. While retrospective justice can involve either perpetrators, victims or both, it defeats the purpose of its main goal (that is, justice) if any distinction between the two categories is eschewed by collapsing everyone, victims and perpetrators alike, into the category of "victims" of a greater tragic force.[14] The Russian state has generally encouraged regarding the Stalin-era crimes as "tragedies" and has conceived of the Russian people as first and foremost victims. Selective demonization of the supreme leader and his henchmen has allowed the Russian people to be absolved of all responsibility and to avoid grappling with the difficult questions of complicity, intentional and unintentional, making it essentially seem as if the Soviet regime existed without the Soviet people (Ferretti 2003: 55, 58). The result, as Maria Ferretti claims, is that the Russian people suffer from a "memory disorder"—since the mourning for the victims of the Soviet regime has not been completed, a sense of (unhealthy) melancholia has ensued which

---

[14]   Cf. Karaganov and Fedotov (2011): "One cannot demand that victims assume responsibility for the barbarities committed against them! At the same time, we must explicitly condemn the heinous crimes of the totalitarian regime and declare that we do not have (and do not want to have) anything in common with them. Not the slightest shade of blame must rest on those Soviet people who had to live in those difficult years, who grew grain, built houses, hunted down thieves, served in the army, and composed symphonies. They lived the only possible kind of life in those inhuman times. But we must renounce the crimes of that regime."

continues to hinder the construction of a new democratic identity for Russia (cf. Etkind 2013).

Hence, there has been a general inclination to handle the repressive Soviet legacy, both societally and by the current regime in Russia, as a series of essentially nameless, and thus also agentless tragedies (Etkind 2009; Khazanov 2008). It is difficult to admit the criminal legacy of the predecessor state if one is simultaneously attempting to inherit the "good legacy". Such mnemonical cherry-picking is hardly consistent. Yet, admitting self-critically to a certain agency inherited from the Soviet Union would inevitably require Russia to reconsider its sense of self, to revise its current major identity-narrative. The temptation to emphasize the "good" legacy at the expense of disregarding the "bad" is naturally human—and thus always present. Russia's long-time reluctance to reckon with the criminal legacy of communism should not be particularly puzzling against that backdrop, but rather consistent with its attempts to maintain the basic consistency of a positive sense of its social "self".

Conclusion

The question of to what extent the current Russian regime can adapt to the de-legitimization of the Soviet regime without destabilizing itself to the core, remains a valid one. Without acknowledging and denouncing the role of state security structures in the criminal legacy of the communist experiment, the coming to terms with the Soviet past in Russia would hardly meet the bulk of implicit and explicit Western criteria of full-scale *Vergangenheitsbewältigung*. Transitional justice was originally conceived as "handmaiden to liberal political transitions" (Sharp 2015), or a core component of modernization based on the Western democratic model. Russia's *osobyi put'* of coming to terms with its communist past points towards a diversion from this model. As regards lustration, and assessment of the role of the security structures in the previous regime's criminal legacy, this sort of "coming to terms with the past" is unlikely to happen in a Russia governed by a former KGB-operative, actively setting the standards of the "new normal" in Russia's post-Soviet neighborhood via its political and military engagement in the

Ukrainian crisis. The initiatives of the Standing Committee on Historical Memory under the Presidential Council for the Development of Civil Society and Human Rights aimed at acknowledgement of the mass crimes of the communist regime still remain to be matched by atonement for these crimes, and the recognition of the full human worth of their victims. Except for the rehabilitation of the victims of the communist political repressions, a clear structural, political, and symbolic break with the past is yet to happen in contemporary Russia. Without facing the entire moral and political implications of the communist experience, Russia's "breaking with its communist past" remains incomplete (Satter 2012: 300–305). The 2014 "memory law" targeting the "dissemination of intentionally false information about the activities of the Soviet Union during the Second World War" and the "rehabilitation of Nazism" (for discussion, see Koposov 2014; Kurilla 2014; Mälksoo 2015) is a painful reminder of the fact that the trend towards "mnemonical modernization" has apparently gone into full reversal after Putin's return to the presidency in 2012.

What, then, does the Medvedev-era search for a modern mnemonic narrative tell us about Russia's readiness to revise its central narrative of a national "self"? Medvedev's administration apparently understood the positive political effects of softening the hardline stance on boasting the achievements of the Stalin era at the price of belittling the crimes of his regime. It was gradually dawning upon the political elite that the absence of denials and selective glorification of the communist past would likely facilitate Russia's rapprochement with the states formerly in its sphere of influence, as well as create a benevolent atmosphere for the EU-Russia partnership for modernization.

However, the suggested path of victim-centric remembrance of the darker chapters of the Soviet period does not firmly indicate a willingness for self-critical memory work that would also consider the issues of agency, responsibility, and regret along with depicting oneself as the greatest victim, or greatest martyr of all. While moral masochism and a cult of suffering are allegedly symptomatic for the Russian psyche and its cultural tradition (Rancour-Laferriere 1995), relating to the Soviet past primarily through a sense of martyrdom can hardly be considered a constructive way of engaging with and learning from the past (cf. Etkind 2013). Common catchphrases about overcoming the negative heritage of the past amount to no more than hollow parroting here. Instead, one can only agree with Denis Sekirinsky (2011), the academic secretary of the National Committee of Russian Historians, that what is needed in order to overcome the negative heritage of Russia's communist past is the emancipation of people, first and foremost, by "turning them into personalities and citizens able to think independently, make their own decisions and be responsible for their behavior."

References

Adler, N. (2002) *Beyond the Soviet System: The Gulag Survivor*. New Brunswick and London: Transaction Publishers.

_____ (2005) "The Future of the Soviet Past Remains Unpredictable: The Resurrection of Stalinist Symbols amidst the Resurrection of Mass Graves", *Europe-Asia Studies* 57(8): 1093–119.

_____ (2012a) "Reconciliation with—or Rehabilitation of—the Soviet Past?", *Memory Studies* 5(3): 327–38.

_____ (2012b) "'The Bright Past', or Whose (Hi)story? Challenges in Russia and Serbia Today", *Filozofija i društvo* XXIII(4): 119–38.

Andrieu, K. (2011) "An Unfinished Business: Transitional Justice and Democratization in Post-Soviet Russia", *The International Journal of Transitional Justice* 5(2): 198–220.

Berger, T. U. (2012) *War, Guilt, and World Politics after World War II*. Cambridge: Cambridge University Press.

Bhabha, H.K. (1994) *The Location of Culture*. London: Routledge.

Buck-Morss, S. (2002) *Dreamworld and Catastrophe: The Passing of Mass Utopia in East and West*. Cambridge, Mass.: MIT Press.

Donald, M. W. (2005) "Imitation and Mimesis", in N. Chater and S. Hurley (eds), *Perspectives on Imitation: From Neuroscience to Social Science: Imitation, Human Development and Culture*. Cambridge, Mass.: MIT Press, 283–300.

Epstein, C. (2011) "Who Speaks? Discourse, the Subject and the Study of Identity in International Politics", *European Journal of International Relations* 17(2): 327–50.

Etkind, A. (2009) "Post-Soviet Hauntology: Cultural Memory of the Soviet Terror", *Constellations. An International Journal of Critical and Democratic Theory* 16(1): 182–200.

_____. (2013) *Warped Mourning: Stories of the Undead in the Land of the Unburied*. Stanford, CA: Stanford University Press.

Fedor, J. (2010) "Kosachev Offers Another Sign of Shift in Official Russian Position on the Soviet Past", *Memory at War: Blog*, 29 July. http://cam-
bridgeculturalmemory.blogspot.com/2010/07/kosachev-offers-another-
sign-of-shift.html (accessed 28 May 2015).

Ferretti, M. (2003) "Memory Disorder: Russia and Stalinism", *Russian Politics
and Law* 41(6): 38–82.

Forest, B., J. Johnson and K. Till (2004) "Post-Totalitarian National Identity:
Public Memory in Germany and Russia", *Social and Cultural Geography* 5(3):
357–80.

Garagozov, R. (2008) "Historical Choice and the Characteristics of Collective
Experience", *Journal of Russian and East European Psychology* 46(1): 19–51.

Gill, G. (2013) *Symbolism and Regime Change in Russia*. Cambridge: Cambridge
University Press.

van Goudoever, A.P. (1986) *The Limits of Destalinization in the Soviet Union:
Political Rehabilitations in the Soviet Union since Stalin*. New York: St.
Martin's Press.

Hagström, L. (2015) "The 'Abnormal' State: Identity, Norm/Exception and Japan",
European Journal of International Relations 21(1): 122–45.

Herschinger, E. (2012) "'Hell Is the Other': Conceptualizing Hegemony and
Identity through Discourse Theory", *Millennium: Journal of International
Studies* 41(1): 65–90.

Känd, K. (2013) "Euraasia Liit—unelm, vimm või tegelikkus?", *Diplomaatia* 116.

Karaganov, S. (2010) "Russian Katyn", *Rossiiskaia gazeta*, 22 July.

_____. (2011a) Speech at a meeting of the Council on Civil Society and Hu-
man Rights. Yekaterinburg, 1 February. http://karaganov.ru/en/news/230
(accessed 28 May 2014).

_____. (2011b) "When Will Russia be Free from Totalitarian Mentality?", Val-
dai Discussion Club, 20 July. http://valdaiclub.com/history/28660.html
(accessed 28 May 2014).

_____. (2011c) "Roman s tiranom bez kontsa?", *Rossiiskaia gazeta*, 8 April.
http://www.rg.ru/2011/04/08/repress.html (accessed 11 June 2015).

_____. (2012) "Russia in the World of Ideas and Images", *Russia in Global
Affairs*, 21 October. http://eng.globalaffairs.ru/pubcol/Russia-in-the-
World-of-Ideas-and-Images-15709 (accessed 28 May 2015).

Karaganov, S. and M. Fedotov (2011) "The Judgment Century", *Rossiiskaia
gazeta*, 27 July.

Khapaeva, D. (2009) "Historical Memory in Post-Soviet Gothic Society", *Social
Research* 76(1): 359–94.

Khazanov, A. (2008) "Whom to Mourn and Whom to Forget? (Re)constructing
Collective Memory in Contemporary Russia", *Totalitarian Movements and
Political Religions* 9(2-3): 293–310.

Koposov, N. (2014) "Pamiat' v zakone: Pro istoriiu", *Russkii zhurnal*, 8 April.
http://www.russ.ru/Mirovaya-povestka/Pamyat-v-zakone (accessed 28 May
2015).

Kosachev, K. (2010) "Sovetskaia li Rossiia?", *Ekho Moskvy*, 29 June.

Kurilla, I. (2014) "The Implications of Russia's Law against the 'Rehabilitation of Nazism'". *PONARS Eurasia Policy Memo* 331 (August). http://www.ponarseurasia.org/sites/default/files/policy-memos-pdf/Pepm331_Kurilla_August2014_0.pdf (accessed 28 May 2015).

Lawson, S. and S. Tannaka (2011) "War Memories and Japan's 'Normalization' as an International Actor: A Critical Analysis", *European Journal of International Relations* 17(3): 405–28.

Mälksoo, M. (2012) "Nesting Orientalisms at War: World War II and the 'Memory War' in Eastern Europe", in T. Barkawi and K. Stanski (eds.), *Orientalism and War*. New York: Columbia University Press, 177–195.

————— (2015) "'Memory Must Be Defended': Beyond the Politics of Mnemonical Security", *Security Dialogue*: 1-17, DOI: 10.1177/0967010614552549 (ahead of print article).

Makarychev, A. and V. Morozov (2013) "Is 'Non-Western Theory' Possible? The Idea of Multipolarity and the Trap of Epistemological Relativism in Russian IR", *International Studies Review* 15(3): 328–50.

Medvedev, D. (2009) "Pamiat' o natsional'nykh tragediiakh tak zhe sviashchenna, kak pamiat' o pobedakh", *Address on the Day of Remembrance of the Victims of Political Repression*, 30 October. http://kremlin.ru/events/president/news/5862 (accessed 28 May 2015).

Merridale, C. (2000) *Night of Stone: Death and Memory in Twentieth Century Russia*. New York: Penguin.

Mitzen, J. (2006) "Ontological Security in World Politics: State Identity and the Security Dilemma", *European Journal of International Relations* 12(3): 341–70.

Monaghan, J., Gladkova, Y. (2015) "Was Stalin's Terror Justified? Poll Shows More Russians Think It Was", *The Moscow Times*, 31 March. http://www.themoscowtimes.com/news/article/was-stalins-terror-justified-poll-shows-more-russians-think-it-was/518298.html (accessed 28 May 2015).

Morozov, V. and B. Rumelili (2012) "The External Constitution of European Identity: Russia and Turkey as Europe-makers", *Cooperation and Conflict* 47(1): 28-48.

Naimark, N. (2010) *Stalin's Genocides*. Princeton: Princeton University Press.

Nuzov, I. (2014) "The Role of Political Elite in Transitional Justice in Russia: From False 'Nurembergs' to Failed Desovietization", *U.C. Davis Journal of International Law and Policy* 20(2): 273–321.

Owen, Catherine (2012) "Is the Presidential Council for Civil Society and Human Rights 'Democratic'? Implications for Russian Governance, *Foreign Policy Centre*, 5 December. http://fpc.org.uk/articles/573 (accessed 11 June 2015).

Polat, N. (2011) "European Integration as Colonial Discourse", *Review of International Studies* 37(3): 1255–72.

Prozorov, S. (2008) "Russian Post-Communism and the End of History", *Studies in East European Thought* 60: 207–30.

Rancour-Laferriere, D. (1995) *The Slave Soul of Russia: Moral Masochism and a Cult of Suffering*. New York and London: New York University Press.

Roginski, A. (2008) "Fragmented Memory: Stalin and Stalinism in Present-day Russia", *Eurozine*, 5 December. http://www.eurozine.com/articles/article_2009-03-02-roginski-en.html (accessed 28 May 2015).

Rumelili, B. (2012) "Liminal Identities and Processes of Domestication and Subversion in International Relations", *Review of International Studies* 38(2): 495–508.

Sakwa, R. (2011) *The Crisis of Russian Democracy: The Dual State, Factionalism and the Medvedev Succession*. Cambridge: Cambridge University Press.

Satter, D. (2012) *It Was a Long Time Ago, and It Never Happened Anyway: Russia and the Communist Past*. New Haven and London: Yale University Press.

Schlögel, K. (2013) "The Cube on Red Square: A Memorial for the Victims of Twentieth-century Russia", in M. Silberman and F. Vatan (eds), *Memory and Postwar Memorials: Confronting the Violence of the Past*. London and New York: Palgrave Macmillan, 31–50.

Sekirinskiy, D. (2011) "Why We Still Cross Swords on Stalin?", Valdai discussion club, 11 May. http://valdaiclub.com/history/24900.html (accessed 28 May 2015).

Sharp, D. N. (2015) "Emancipating Transitional Justice from the Bonds of Paradigmatic Transition", *International Journal of Transitional Justice* 9, no. 1: 150–169.

Shaw, M. (2013) *Genocide and International Relations: Changing Patterns in the Transitions of the Late Modern World*. Cambridge: Cambridge University Press.

Sherlock, T. (2011) "Confronting the Stalinist Past: The Politics of Memory in Russia", *The Washington Quarterly* 34(2): 93–109.

Stan, L. (2009) "Former Soviet Union", in L. Stan (ed.) *Transitional Justice in Eastern Europe and the Former Soviet Union: Reckoning with the Communist Past*. London and New York: Routledge, 222–46.

Steele, B. J. (2008) *Ontological Security in International Relations: Self-Identity and the IR State*. New York: Routledge.

"Stenograficheskii otchet" (2011) *Stenograficheskii otchet o zasedanii Soveta po razvitiiu obshchestva i pravam cheloveka*, Yekaterinburg, 1 February. http://kremlin.ru/events/president/transcripts/10194 (accessed 28 May 2015).

Torbakov, I. (2011) "History, Memory and National Identity: Understanding the Politics of History and Memory Wars in Post-Soviet Lands", *Demokratizatsiya* 19(3): 209–32.

Tumarkin, N. (1994) *The Living and the Dead: The Rise and Fall of the Cult of World War II in Russia*. New York: Basic Books.

UN Secretary General (2004) *The Rule of Law and Transitional Justice in Conflict and Post-Conflict Societies* 8 U.N. Doc.S/2004/616, 23 August.

Vasilaki, R. (2012) "Provincialising IR? Deadlocks and Prospects in Post-Western IR Theory", *Millennium: Journal of International Studies* 41(1): 3–22.

Viola, L. (2013) "The Question of the Perpetrator in Soviet History", *Slavic Review* 72(1): 1–23.

Werth, N. (2008) "Crimes of the Stalin Regime: Outline for an Inventory and Classification", in D. Stone (ed.), *The Historiography of Genocide*. Basingstoke: Palgrave Macmillan, 400–19.

Winterson, J. (2011) *Why Be Happy When You Could Be Normal*. Alfred A. Knopf Canada.

Zarakol, A. (2010) "Ontological (In)Security and State Denial of Historical Crimes: Turkey and Japan", *International Relations* 24(1): 3–23.

_____. (2014) "What Made the Modern World Hang Together—Socialisation or Stigmatisation?", *International Theory* 6(2): 311–32.

Holodomor, Amnesia, and Memory-(Re)Making in Post-War Ukrainian Literature and Film

Iryna Starovoyt

Abstract: *This article examines Ukrainian works of literature and film that sought to preserve the memory of the Holodomor (the Ukrainian Great Famine of 1932–33) during the period when the Holodomor was still unmentionable in the Soviet press and largely unknown or forgotten elsewhere in the world, from the mid-1930s to mid–1980s. While this half-century was generally characterized by the cultural and social forgetting of the Holodomor, there were writers and film-makers who attempted to preserve its memory in their works. The article approaches the memory work performed in these texts as a response to the phenomenon of mass martyrdom and the collectivization of suffering that was invented by the twentieth-century totalitarian regimes. The point of contact between totalitarian martyrdom and memory may be read out of the ancient Greek literal meaning of the term "martyr"—a witness. In this ancient tradition, however, the martyr dies for a cause. In contrast, totalitarianism created the phenomenon of mass martyrdom, characterized by a drive precisely to suppress the memory of the witness, to prevent the act of witnessing. Ukrainian writers who addressed the Holodomor both in the USSR and in emigration set out to resist this by rescuing this memory and encoding it in culture through the articulation of a mnemonic anti-narrative.*

The Holodomor (the Great Famine of 1932–33) was a non-story for more than fifty years. However, during these years it remained a nexus of trauma and conspiracy. The suffering of the famine victims was to some degree masked by the prevailing focus on the atrocities of the Holocaust, the Second World War, partisan warfare, and the post-war Soviet/anti-Soviet reign of terror. Party activists—bystanders and enablers, and those somewhere in between, many thousands of Ukrainians among them—became accustomed to a form of doublethink about their own involvement in the famine, in part because, in order to deflect criticism of the regime, Stalin had circulated among top Party officials a contrary explanation for what was happening: that the responsibility for the famine lay with enemy sabotage, opposition, and the peasants themselves (Graziosi, 2015: 246–247). The public space for a discussion was missing until the era of *glasnost'*, a period that was dominated by a focus on retrospective news, as one after another, historical revelations captured the public's attention. This article takes as its subject the period when the Holodomor was not mentioned in the Soviet press, when it was not known by this name, when it was impossible to imagine an official commemoration of the event in Ukraine. The half-century from the mid–1930s to the mid–1980s represented, instead, a type of cultural and social forgetting. My focus is on Ukrainian works of literature and film that preserved the memory of the famine trauma and tried to find ways to voice that trauma. On the one hand, their authors were confronting censorship and denial (in the attempts to remember the famine in the Soviet Union); meanwhile, others were struggling with the stigma of the famine survivor who was later exposed to the Second World War's ravages (in the attempts to mourn at distance, in emigration). I will attempt to reconstruct how this transfer of knowledge happened and how the mnemonic anti-narrative was gradually articulated, saved from incineration, and encoded in culture.

Over the past three decades the memory and history of the Holodomor has been uncovered, becoming a symbol of the senseless suffering and deaths of millions of civilians in a time of peace with the ensuing prohibition on mourning or remembering them. It has also become, for many Ukrainians, an introduction to the dark age of totalitarian atrocities and a centerpiece of a new national identity based on victimhood.

The Holodomor forces one to consider the issue of mass martyrdom and collectivization of suffering that was invented by the twentieth-century totalitarian regimes. The point of contact between totalitarian martyrdom and memory may be read out of the ancient Greek literal meaning of the term "martyr": μάρτυς, mártys—a witness. In this ancient tradition, however, the martyr dies for a cause. His or her suffering, refusal and death are a test, a trial. In contrast, totalitarianism created the phenomenon of mass martyrdom, characterized by a drive precisely to suppress the memory of the witness, to prevent the act of witnessing.

The Holodomor throws these issues into sharp relief. The martyrs killed by the famine could not recant and be saved. The result of a devastating experiment in biopolitics, the famine allowed the Soviet government to eliminate those it considered undesirable and hostile to its rule,[1] the kind of "other" that Giorgio Agamben has called "not only political adversaries but an entire category of citizens who for some reason cannot be integrated into the political system" (Agamben, 2010: 2). Survivors and their heirs sensed that what has come to be known as the Holodomor represented an act of politically motivated mass killing, and in this sense their martyrdom took an unusual form. They became dangerous witnesses, but not to any divine deeds or miracles; rather, they were victim witnesses, dangerous because they were able to testify to the death and destruction wrought in the name of Bolshevik modernization. As the bare fact of the Famine was insistently denied and suppressed by the Soviet regime, the inhuman suffering of the Holodomor victims was transformed into pseudo-suffering. We now know that a major ef-

---

[1]   On the Holodomor, see Conquest (1986); see also the findings of the US Commission on the Ukrainian Famine in Mace (1988), and of the International Commission of Inquiry into the 1932–33 Famine in Ukraine, in Luciuk and Hrekul (2008: 245–351). Among published memoirs see: Kravchenko (1946); Pidhainy (1955); Dolot (1985). Diplomatic reports of the event have been disclosed and published since the 1980s in many European languages. There are also historians, including V. Danilov, R. W. Davies, S. G. Wheatcroft, and V. Kondrashin, who maintain that the famine was an unplanned result of Stalin's anti-peasant campaign in Soviet Ukraine. Davies and Wheatcroft describe this as "a famine crisis which had been caused partly by [the Soviet leadership's] wrongheaded policies, but was unexpected and undesirable" (2004: 441). They list a number of contributing factors, but their primary emphasis is on the famine as a consequence of rapid industrialization.

fort was made to block the martyr narratives arising out of the famine, indeed to erase all traces of their existence. The state leadership denied that there had been a famine and continued to destroy the evidence. It was claimed that any talk of famine was part of an international conspiracy by the "imperialist West" to besmirch the Soviet Union. Any revelations about it were classified as attacks on the Fatherland (Graziosi, 1996: 46-70). Thus, the victims of the famine not only lost their lives, but lost all dignity in death, as any trace of their personal existence was obliterated. Their descendants were forbidden to mourn them. Survivors were ashamed or incapable of mentioning the victims, even in a whisper.

How, then, if at all, were these catastrophic events remembered and reflected in Ukrainian literature? By the time of the famine, several Ukrainian writers had already presented literary challenges to Soviet state violence. In the early Soviet period, perpetrators who reduced people to objects and free thinking to a set of clichés had been portrayed in Mykola Khvyl'ovyi's story *Ia (Romantyka)* (I [A Romance]) in 1923. Khvyl'ovyi (real name Mykola Fitiliov) was a Ukrainian proletarian writer who, after a peripatetic upbringing, courted many risks as a war veteran, artist, and polemicist, became a leader of the new Ukrainian literature in Soviet Kharkiv, and dared to oppose Joseph Stalin and his ideology. Yevhen Pluzhnyk, one of the finest poets of this generation, who has been compared to Rainer Maria Rilke, and also a novelist based in Kyiv, was similarly vocal about revolutionary atrocities and the victimizing impersonal force of Soviet power. His poem *Galilei* (Galileo, 1926) and novel *Neduha* (Illness, 1928), which gave him notoriety in the eyes of the Kremlin, were both banned from circulation shortly after publication. The first writer to address the subject of the famine was Mykola Kulish, the most famous Ukrainian playwright of the twentieth century. Kulish wrote two plays—his first *97* (1924) and his final play, *Proshchai, selo* (Farewell, Village, 1933)—reflecting on the post-revolutionary struggle, humiliation, and then destruction of the traditional Ukrainian village through collectivization and famine. The Soviet censors forced him to revise *97* and to rewrite and rename *Proshchai, selo*. All of these authors were subsequently persecuted:

Khvyl'ovyi committed political suicide in 1933, Pluzhnyk died of tuberculosis in the Solovetskii camp in 1936, and Kulish was labeled a "counterrevolutionary", expelled from the Communist party, sentenced to an isolation cell and murdered during the mass executions of political prisoners marking the twentieth anniversary of the October Revolution.[2] After the purges of the 1930s no Soviet writer attempted to address the themes of famine, repression, and resistance openly until after Stalin's death, while the theme was ignored by Western writers.

There were, however, some writers who did begin to approach the topic in the late 1930s. One such writer was Yuri Klen, a Ukrainian writer who, because of his German origins (his real name was Oswald Burghardt) escaped the repressions in Kyiv and Kharkiv by re-emigration to Germany in the early thirties. Being outside and relatively safe, Klen expressed the intuition that unless the atrocity was attested, the memory of the traumatic events could be aborted and life would go on as if *nothing* had happened. His poem *Prokliati roky* (The Accursed Years, 1937) was written at the peak of the Soviet purges; it is saturated with the idea of witnessing, and uses an epigraph from Pushkin's *Boris Godunov*:

It's not in vain that the Lord

Made me the witness of so many years.[3]

Недаром многих лет

Свидетелем Господь меня поставил.

---

2   More information on these writers' lives and works in the context of their generation can be found in Khvyl'ovyi, 1986; Hryn, 2004–2005; Kratochvil, 1999; Stech, 2002; Shapoval, 2009; Shkandrij, 1992.
3   All translations are mine unless otherwise indicated—IS.

The writing here came out of deathly silence:

Who knew that, who was keeping track of the deaths and executions?

Where is the movie to show you the famine

of that accursed 33rd year?

Хто знав, хто вів смертям і стратам лік?

Де фільм, який вам показав би голод

Отой проклятий 33-й рік? (Klen 1937)

Klen favors *enargeia*—the visual over the verbal, memory-image over memory-narrative[4]—although he knew well that visual documentation of the famine of 1932–33 was forbidden and that any occasional surviving pictures were later destroyed. Writing a poem supplied a substitute for writing a testimony—literature in history's stead, literature for the sake of future inquiry. The poet seems to be turning around the desecrated memory, struggling for some penetrating image and not attaining it. In an effort to achieve some perspective on this contemporary martyrdom, *The Accursed Years* alludes to ancient texts like the Old Testament or episodes in classic Roman history and medieval martyrologies. One stanza imitates the diction of a chronicle from the time of Kyivan Rus':

In days of yore, as the Chronicle would say, there being plague *[mor]* and famine *[glad]*.

Во врем'я оно – Літопис би сказав, – бисть *мор* і *глад* (Klen 1937)

This line came closest to the term later adopted by Ukrainians for the famine: the Holodomor.

---

4   *Enargeia*—the fact before the eyes, vividness, actualization. In ancient historiography and rhetoric it described an effort to make the reader a spectator. "If *enargeia* was the purpose of the *ekphrasis* [the description of a work of art], truth was the result of *enargeia*. We can imagine the sequence of this type: historical narration—description—vividness—truth" (Ginzburg, 2012: 12).

In *The Accursed Years*, Klen attacked his former Kyivan friend and fellow neo-classicist Maksym Ryl's'kyi, who figures in the work as *poeta Maximus*, now a timid proletarian poet and anthem-writer, servile to Stalin. (Curiously, the poet who glorifies the rotten leadership of pigs and writes the anthem for *Animal Farm* is called Minimus in Orwell's story).[5] Klen reminded Ryl's'kyi of who he had once been and how he had changed after imprisonment.[6]

Ryl's'kyi responded to the blow in a roundabout way, five years later, from evacuation in Ufa, with an important poem called *Zhaha* (Thirst, 1942), in which he also ventured to address the Great Famine, and in which he may have attempted to redeem himself in the face of Klen's charge. He did this by portraying specters ("silhouettes") marked by the Holodomor, without, however, breaking the code of silence surrounding this subject, blurring his subject to avoid omnipresent censorship by using a stream-of-consciousness technique. His poem emphasizes the unimaginable mass scale of the events and the nature of the victims' suffering. His protagonist is also tormented by a torrent of shocking semi-memories, the rendering of which serves not so much to remember but rather to anonymize the martyrs again:

---

[5] George Orwell was the first Western writer to make the case against collectivization and its consequences in his anti-Stalinist *Animal Farm: A Fairy Story* (1945). He opposed the British diplomatic whitewashing of Soviet orthodoxy and its crimes. Orwell had his own encounter with Stalinism and the Soviet secret police (NKVD) in the 1930s in Spain, which he described in *Homage to Catalonia* (1938). Orwell's *Animal Farm* was translated into Ukrainian by a young historian, Ihor Ševčenko, and published in 1947 in the Displaced Persons camps in post-war Europe, where a quarter of a million refugees from Soviet Ukraine found themselves.

[6] Ryl's'kyi was an established poet, translator and full member of the Academy of Sciences of the Soviet Union. He debuted in 1910 and reached acclaim in the 1920s as one of the Ukrainian Neoclassicists. His poetry provoked fierce attacks during Stalin's purges. He was arrested for five months in 1931, and then declared himself reformed and went on to publish the conformist collection *Znak tereziv* (The Sign of Libra, 1932). He was one of the few Ukrainian writers who managed to live through the Stalinist terror and become one of the main poets in the ranks of the official Soviet versifiers. On the story of his imprisonment, see Ilienko (1994).

There are many, many, many of them.

Dark lines on skeletal faces.

Some were disfigured, others only scratched.

Many were killed and all were tortured.

Їх багато, багато, багато.

Темні зморшки на лицях худих.

Тих скалічено, тих лиш підтято.

Тих убито, а мучено – всіх. (Ryl's'kyi 1983: 42–43)

The ubiquitous *Thirst* was perhaps exactly the image that Yuri Klen had tried and failed to create some years before: a (carefully crafted) euphemism for the Great Famine. This writing could be framed as a phobic regime of remembrance: the author is speaking about total evil and still feels a direct and immediate threat, almost a decade after the events took place.

Amongst the prolific writings of the Ukrainian diaspora, the texts on the famine were seen as important but, perhaps surprisingly, far from central in the shared Ukrainian twentieth-century memory. In these texts, the image of a collective victim dominated, and the formula chosen was to present every human fate as a piece in a vast mosaic of pain. It is worth mentioning that unlike most Eastern Ukrainians displaced from their home villages and rural towns, none of the major émigré writers who tried to bear witness to the suffering of Holodomor victims was a survivor himself, and only Todos Osmachka, another World War I veteran, an expressionist writer and educator, who had spent the early 1930s in the Kuban, then a largely Ukrainian region, had witnessed some part of it, before being taken to a mental institution. But all these writers had lost relatives and friends to the terror-famine. They saw their duty as secondary witnesses in helping to give voice to primary ones and in making the unspeakable more available for contemplation and mourning. By the end of World War II, before the Iron Curtain was put in place, a vast wave of political emigration brought to the West about 400,000 expatriates from Ukraine, a few thousand Holodomor survivors and, as we know now,[7] some perpetrators among them. For most of them, "all that they knew about the famine was that it once happened. And that Stalin provoked it" (Kryvenko 1993).

In the post-World War II Displaced Person camps memories were shared and several stories finished and published in subsequent years—most notably Osmachka's *Plan do dvoru* (Plan to the Courtyard, 1951) and Vasyl Barka's *Zhovtyi kniaz'* (The Yellow Prince, 1963). All these titles had no prospect of being made available to Soviet readers, and thus the authors could be more outspoken, as there was no longer a question of censorship for them. Barka confessed in private that he felt bereft of the resources of speech. His novel is written in a modern realistic manner, and he warned that his stories were capable only of speaking on *behalf* of victims, of repeating, rather than testifying. In the early 1960s one might attribute this to the lack of direct experience; a similar feeling persisted, however, into the 1990s, and would appear to be linked to a more profound crisis of witnessing that surfaced around this time (Felman and Laub 1992: 81-84).

The Tormented Body of Memory: Kostets'kyi and Grossman

Who is a survivor? How can somebody, if he or she is a writer, break through the survivors' muteness and give expression to the horror of survival, to something one can hardly bear to contemplate? Ihor Kostets'kyi (Eaghor G. Kostetzky)—one of the few Ukrainian writers in the diaspora to take the wounds of Soviet collective memory to their sadomasochistic limits—describes the following:

> They take a piece of a soaked white bread. When the soaked bread is kneaded in such a way that you get a four-cornered lump, then beat it

---

7   One example of such a late admission is the posthumously published memoir of a Holodomor perpetrator, Dmitrii Goychenko (1903–93), who made his way into emigration after World War II; see Goichenko (2010).

against the stone floor. Almost no-one will think to knead it that well. Maybe it's a fortunate thing that one will knead and then leave it, and then another will take over. And then they put the little lump into a jacket and ironed pants, attach a tie and roughly rub his brain with books from all four sides. An old-world mother rests on a small bench, groans now and again, and then asks them at night: "Are you happy, my children?" And the son answers her: "How, mum, can a Slavic person be happy?" He says this once, twice. And then forgets it.

Беруть кавалок намоченого пшеничного хліба. Коли намочений хліб вим'яти так, щоб вийшла з нього чотирирога штучка, то бий нею хоч об кам'яну долівку. Та рідко хто здогадається так вим'яти. Може в тому й щастя, що один вимне та й покине, а тоді другий. А тоді вже вбирають кавалок у піджак і в прасовані штани, ще й краватку чіпляють, і грубо-грубо з чотирьох вітрів книгами їй мозок натирають. Лежить старосвітська матінка боком на короткій лаві, лежить і крекче зрідка, а тоді вночі та й питається: чи щасливі ж ви, діточки. А син і одвічає: - як же може, матусю, слов'янська людина та щасливою бути. Так скаже враз і вдруге. А тоді забуде. (Kostets'kyi 2005: 39).

The split personality, the Gogolian double, and the loss of one's identity were recurring images in Kostets'kyi's reflective prose. The above, rather mysterious, quote about a man, kneaded as a lump of dough, comes from a short story *Tsina liudskoi nazvy* (The Price of a Human Name, 1945) in which Kostets'kyi's protagonist Pavlo Palii, a well-established Ukrainian painter and a refugee of World War II, while in a fever, has a nightmare which meanders over the loss of his name and identity: a younger fellow with the same name, also a painter, but with an entirely different style, joins the small community of displaced (Soviet) Ukrainians in a post-war German town. Palii is irritated by this mismatch, which threatens to ruin his artistic reputation. He then approaches the younger Palii and tries to persuade and bribe him into taking on a pseudonym. The younger man refuses to abandon what is in fact his real name, and also realises that for the old Palii the name they share is a pseudonym, and that the older man now fears that the two may be mistaken for one another, which could damage the reputation he has built up over twenty years. One loss redirects the protagonist's memory to another loss that is related to the psychosomatic trauma of famine; as he speaks of himself:

A man without a name is a man that eats grass. Whether he survives or not.

Людина без імені це людина, що їсти траву. Виживе чи не виживе. (Kostets'kyi 2005: 41).

Pavlo Palii is stricken by anxiety and recurrent attacks of panic. His syntax is broken, deliberately hard to understand, as he ponders over the topic of hatred of and revenge on the inhuman system, telling himself that the force of the revenge will destroy the avengers. And then he encounters the haunting image of a man who walks through the war with a sack of potatoes. Ironically, the potato-bearer's small strategy is far more effective than many others, and his method of survival is shown to be a mark of genius:

He harnessed his oxen and took off from Poltava to Cologne and then to Buenos Aires, his woman at the back of the farm cart. Who are you? A guy with no name. What are you carrying? A bit of wit and my inhuman ingenuity and my inhuman humanity.

Запріг воли, і від Полтави до Кельну і до Буенос-Айресу, і баба позаду на возі. Хто такий. Чолов'яга без імені. Що везеш. Шматок дотепу і нелюдську свою винахідливість і ще нелюдську свою людяність. (Kostets'kyi 2005: 42).

The survivor is a human living through the inhuman and bearing that stigma, the wound inflicted on his "own being capable of everything" (Agamben 2002: 77).

The nature of memorial space on the Soviet side of the Iron Curtain resembled a self-erasing palimpsest, offering itself ever anew as a semi-blank sheet. The future-oriented Soviet state was reluctant to allow any retrospective rituals of mourning except the yearly commemoration of official and unknown victims of the Revolution and Great Patriotic War. Against the backdrop of millions of invisible martyrs with no graves it developed a detailed topography of memorials called "graves of the unknown soldier"[8] (again, "a person with no name"), often featuring an empty tomb. In the Soviet

---

[8]   War graves of the Unknown Soldier have also existed in many other countries since World War I. In the Soviet case, this practice was established much later, from the late 1960s. In Soviet towns and villages these graves developed a new

Union both the Holodomor and the Holocaust remained unspoken in the post-war "coalition of silence" (Giesen, 2004: 120), which functioned as an imperative to forget. This practice was known in ancient times as *damnatio memoriae* whereby memory was destroyed and dishonored in the spirit of blaming the victim. Celebratory remembrance rituals of the Soviet "Great" Victory in the "Great Patriotic War"—an archetypal restoration of justice—were employed to deny or screen the horrors of the interwar and wartime periods.

A shared memory requires communication. It is best secured within communities of memory (Margalit 2002: part 2). When repression and censorship were reversed after Stalin's death and millions of political prisoners were released due to the policies of de-Stalinization, the memory of the 1932–33 famine was nevertheless still not articulable in public. There was, however, an attempt made by a few of the Soviet writers and film-makers related to Ukraine to point to it in some extra-communicative way, through the interstices of a "double inscription" (Bhabha 1994: 108). Inspired by Bakhtin, Homi Bhabha contemplates the historical surmounting of the "ghostly" or the "double" in cultural texts but also associates this figure with the uncanny process of the warping of identity, of, as Bhabha puts it, citing Freud, "the doubling, dividing and interchanging of the self" under the systemic pressure, say, of ideological censorship. The Holodomor was underrepresented, true, but the link to its memory was very real and for the generation of survivors and perpetrators, even the smallest hint was enough to evoke it.

One of the most important attempts to address this theme was made by Vasily Grossman, known for his early depictions, both fictional and non-fictional, of Stalinist and Nazi atrocities. He was correspondent for the Soviet army's newspaper during World War II and famous for his courage on dangerous front-line missions. After the war, three decades before Gorbachev's *glasnost'*, he finished his second novel *Zhizn' i sud'ba* (Life and Fate, 1959) set against the

---

function as they not only marked a place of (safe) mourning, but also redirected collective memory away from the images of the horrific events which took place here both during the war and in peacetime, and away from the (mass) unmarked graves of the victims of famine and terror, whose memory was obliterated in public commemoration.

backdrop of the Battle of Stalingrad. In the novel, Grossman indicted the abhorrent conditions of Stalinism, which the war and its human cost only enlarged. The KGB censors seized the manuscript and the typewriter used to write it. Grossman was not daunted by this, and started his last novella, *Vse techet* (Everything Flows, 1963), an even more bitter assault on Stalin and Stalinism, which in his view had turned the whole country into one big labor camp. Both novels stand for the kind of double inscription that Bhabha describes, which in this case we might call *Soviet anti-Soviet* literature, and both comment on a society in which open discussion of the past is lacking, though remembrance of that past is not. The relationship in *Everything Flows* between Ivan, the Gulag returnee, and Anna, the former grain-requisitions activist, leads to her ambiguous testimony of the famine: the testimony of a victim among other victims and of a perpetrator among other perpetrators. Here, Grossman tackled the moral consequences and echoes of terror, proclaiming that there were "No innocents among the living" ("Нету среди живых невиновных") (Grossman 1989: part 4).

Grossman did, however, feel that some change in the memorial space had taken place due to the fact that under Khrushchev the state had admitted its guilt, at least in part. He included in his novel a sequence of confessions of Stalinist horrors (with no easy attribution of blame). One of these was a first-person account by a Holodomor collaborator named Anna, now in her forties and dying of cancer. In the face of her imminent death she is haunted by the question of non-memory and non-repentance:

And there is nothing left. And where is that life, where is that horrible suffering? Is there really nothing left? Is it possible that no one will answer for all that? And that it will all be forgotten without a trace?

И ничего не осталось. А где же эта жизнь, где страшная мука? Неужели ничего не осталось? Неужели никто не ответит за это все? Вот так и забудется без следа? (Grossman 1989: part 11).

Everything Flows was translated into English as *Forever Flowing*, and published in the US in 1972. It was published in its original form in the Soviet Union in 1989, twenty-five years after the author's death (though not two hundred years later, as Khrushchev's ideologist Suslov had foretold). In his opus magnum *Life and Fate*, along with the unfinished *Everything Flows,* night whispers of mourning-memory during the Khrushchev Thaw were accompanied by a warning that, as the generation of survivors was now dying out, testimony was in danger of being lost forever.

When We See the Pain of Others: Illienko and Tiutiunnyk

From despair comes an understanding that if any mediation of the aftermath is to remain it will remain in culture, through the transmission of narratives and images, no matter how warped or fragmented. Even during the Khrushchev Thaw, the public non-memory of terror functioned as a dominating practice. The "state of emergency" shielded off access to non-official recollections that might influence feelings and bring about some dissident bonds of mnemonic solidarity. For sure, there were grassroots attempts to outwit this top-down expurgation. But Yuri Illienko's film *Krynytsia dlia sprahlykh* (A Well for the Thirsty, 1965), based on Ivan Drach's screenplay, was more than just that. While his generation was generally focused on the theme of the war and victory, Illienko was concerned with the victory over forgetting. Except for one or two episodes, his film contained nothing for Soviet censors to cut—not only because he was hiding from censorship, but because he had consciously set out to make a film that would be universal in its appeal. The whole piece triggered a memory of collective suffering that had long been blocked. *A Well for the Thirsty* was produced by and for the "1.5 generation"—the generation of child victims and survivors. In the film's titles its genre is defined as "film-parable".

The parable is centered on an old man living in seclusion and on his fixation on some sensual, bodily recall. The man is chased by his painful memories and is dissociated from real time. He is still taking care of his well, which is now rarely used. In the opening scene he comes back to an empty home, sits at the bench, and struggles to cope with the auditory hallucinations of funeral weeping and lamenting mixed with the giggles and screams of a child, drifting in from the past. His nerves betray him and he turns all his photos to face the wall, then doing the same with a mirror. But the giggling goes on. Then we see him laying alive in the coffin which he has hewed for himself, and we watch his children arriving late for his (faked) funeral, at a complete loss, not even able to spot his fresh grave, never mind mourn for him. Viewers of the film would have been all too aware that there was only one major tragedy in this village—as in the many other neighboring villages—and the unflinching trauma in the film hovers on the border of the taboo against recalling that during the famine it was not possible to comfort the dying, to bury the dead, and to mourn them as humans do.

None of the film critics in the Soviet Ukraine dared to point to Holodomor memory. But many of them, I believe, knew fairly well what the film-makers knew: to point to this memory was to ascribe an origin to the protagonist's numbness. Through the lens of the screenwriter and film director, *A Well for the Thirsty* conveyed the omnipresence of an extreme suffering at every moment. Stark black-and-white and half-silent, the film was addressed to those who witnessed, struggled through, and still remembered the famine, escaping recollection in fear and silence. The silence is active here, recalling Elaine Scarry's observation that:

> To witness the moment when pain causes a reversion to the pre-language of cries and groans is to witness the destruction of language; but conversely, to be present when a person moves up out of that pre-language and project the facts of sentience into speech is almost to have been permitted to be present at the birth of language itself (Scarry, 1985: 6).

The film's central metaphor—the well and those dying of thirst—makes a direct link to Ryl's'kyi's earlier poem *Zhaha* (Thirst) and takes his trope to a place of dangerous significance in the eyes of the censors. The metonymic likeness drawn here is between bread for the hungry and sweet water for the thirsty.

A Well for the Thirsty engaged in an uneasy dialogue with Dovzhenko's high-profile film *Zemlia* (Earth, 1930) and its promotion of collectivization. In *A Well for the Thirsty* the after-effects of collectivization are presented as a violent and traumatogenic change. What Dovzhenko was promoting through his film and what actually took place never overlapped. For those in the know, casting

Dmytro Miliutenko as a protagonist for *A Well* was a happy choice. An outstanding actor and one of the few survivors of the legendary Les Kurbas theater company,[9] in the film he was able to pass along the long-lasting effects of the catastrophe without words and with minimal gestures, reduced to his basest self.

In *A Well for the Thirsty,* the Ukrainian village is depicted as a ghostly wasteland. It comes into view almost empty, with long streets of abandoned farmhouses and bricked-up windows. Its silence is heavy and resounding. The film shows the way that famine and the destruction of traditional family-based farming entered the collective unconscious, making people emotionally deprived and uprooted, and affecting their attitudes and relationships. The village community is gone. There is hardly any normal life to which people could now return. The imperative to survive has dominated the values of care. In this moral vacuum elderly people are unable to speak while younger ones are equally unable to listen to them. Re-examined by official censorship, *A Well for the Thirsty* was removed from screens shortly after the premiere, and remained banned until 1987 (Hoseiko, 2005: 191).

Hryhir Tiutiunnyk, another Holodomor survivor who débuted as a writer in the 1960s, was mesmerized by *A Well for the Thirsty,* by its combination of softness and brutal honesty and by its high resolution depiction of human suffering. The film led him to begin to wonder whether Holodomor amnesia perhaps mirrored something in today's reality. After the film's premiere screening at Dovzhenko Film Studio, "the breakthrough-spring", as he called the experience of watching the film, he wrote his *Autobiography*—never published in his lifetime—leaving a direct testimony:

---

[9]   Les Kurbas, a philosophy student at the University of Vienna before World War I, later moved back to Ukraine where he organized and directed the avant-garde *Berezil* theater. At its height Kurbas' theater employed nearly four hundred actors and staff members and ran six actors' studios, a directors' lab, a design studio, a theater museum, and ten specialized committees. He trained an entire generation of Ukrainian actors and directors. He was dismissed from his position and sent to the Solovetskii camp, where he managed to create a prison theater; he was executed in 1937. See further Makaryk (2004).

In 1933 our family became swollen with hunger and my grandfather, the father of my father, Vasyl Feodulovych Tiutiunnyk, died—he was still not gray
and all his teeth were strong (and I still don't know where his grave is), and
I at this time—when I was one and a half—stopped walking (though I already knew how to)—stopped laughing and talking.

У тридцять третьому році сімейство наше опухло з голоду, а дід, батько
мого батька, Василь Феодулович Тютюнник, помер—ще й не сивий був
і зуби мав до одного міцні (я й досі не знаю, де його могила), а я в цей
час—тоді мені було півтора року—перестав ходити (вже вміючи це ро-
бить), сміяться і балакать перестав. (Tiutiunnyk, 1984, 1: 20)

In the late 1960s and early 1970s, Tiutiunnyk gradually developed into a Soviet writer of anti-Soviet memory retrieval. Against
the backdrop of Brezhnev-era censorship, which strove to control
the scope of public discourse, he was telling his stories in a world
where history could never be neutral. He aimed to find a niche
where story-telling on anxiety-provoking topics still had some
chance of coming out in print. That slot opened in Soviet teenage
literature, which proved also to be a genre peculiarly well-suited to
his task, as we shall see below.

In 1972 Tiutiunnyk wrote in his diary: "I can write only with
memories". Linking together a narrative from what is essentially
anti-narrative, Tiutiunnyk came up with the idea of generational autobiography: "No, it was not my own childhood anguish, not my
hunger, and not my own father—guilty with no guilt—that I wanted
to recall, but the grief of my entire generation and of many wrongly
accused fathers" ("Ні, не свої жалі дитинства, не свій голод, не
свого без вини винного батька хотів я згадати, а жалі всього
мого покоління і багатьох без вини винуватих батьків") (Tiutiunnyk, 1984, 1: 116).

Writing is inadequate but necessary, in Tiutiunnyk's view. According to Susan Sontag, essentially, "no 'we' should be taken for
granted when the subject is looking at other people's pain" (Sontag
2003: 7). For Tiutiunnyk's protagonists, the subject experiencing
pain is always "I", but is not, at the same time, confined to the ego-
tism of suffering; instead, this pain makes him/her sensitive to other
people's sorrow. Tiutiunnyk finds some advantages in writing under
censorship since it makes him more acute and inventive in his craft

of the double inscription (Shevchenko 1998: 66). Most often he tries to look into a situation when adolescence first confronts the family memory taboo. A teenager becomes an interrogative witness far too young to comprehend the story but nonetheless a perfect listener, embodying one's "hope of being heard" and recognized (Felman and Laub 1992: 82). His short stories evolved around a generational shock-memory which, in Avishai Margalit's terms, might have been *common* but which in the given time and space was "by no means a *shared* one" (Margalit 2002: 51).

Tiutiunnyk's prose was first tagged as "war prose" but it soon became less and less compatible with the dominant Soviet historical narrative on the Great Patriotic War. At the same time, it clearly resonated with readers. Top Soviet critics singled out his cathartic stories for praise. His new books came out in print runs of 250,000 copies and were bestsellers. By the mid-1970s his works were translated for the first time both inside and outside of the Soviet Union, in twenty different languages; significantly, however, in what we might read as a marker of the power of his prose, subversive of the Soviet master narrative, he was prevented from publishing in Ukrainian.[10]

Tiutiunnyk was frustrated by his image as a writer for teenagers. His major concern is in fact what Kostets'kyi called "inhuman humanity". As his protagonist is often a twelve-year-old boy, the stories are seen through the eyes of a child but, if read thoroughly, they are far too much even for adults to bear. The boys' understanding is often bound up with compassion and self-imposed guilt. To survive into adulthood they go through situations where nobody is innocent and even those who seem to be right are right in the wrong way.

Tiutiunnyk writes for those for whom terrible events happened one after another, or for those who experienced one and the same terror three times over—we are reminded that the local population of the places depicted in his stories endured three wars (World War I, the Civil War of 1919–21, and World War II) and three grain procurements followed by famines (under War Communism in 1921–22, under Stalin in 1932–33, and in the year following the

---

[10]   For more details see Starovoyt (2015).

"Great Victory" over Nazi Germany, 1946), thus emptying the slogans on the impending happy future of "meaning and credibility" (Sontag 2003: 12). "'Well, how could you compare!'", cries out the protagonist of *Dyvak* (The Oddball, 1963):

> Symin is as healthy as a church bell, and young. And soon I'll be lying under the earth with the chickens scratching the dirt over me. 'Cause you tell me, what health can I have when I've been through three hungers and three wars in one life! And now divide it up for yourself: every ten years either one or the other.

> "Прирівняв! – Симін здоровий, як бедзвін, і молодий. А мене вже скоро й курка лапою загребе. Бо де ж те здоров'я візьметься, скажіть, коли на мій вік три голодовки випало і три війни! От і поділіть: на кожні десять років або те, або те" (Tiutiunnyk 1984, 1:50).

Tiutiunnyk's hidden work of mourning developed a new quality that allowed for the (re)direction of the readers' attention. In his stories, peripheral moments float to the center. Some part of a hard conversation remains unspoken. As an author he often operates through what is known in experimental psychology as the Stroop effect—the interference caused by conflicting word stimuli (Stroop 1935). The propaganda setting (from formal agenda-setting guidelines through to informal codes of silence) challenges one's selective attention. Readers have to train their ability to choose and to focus on the things that propaganda half-truth might prefer them to ignore. In the condition which Tiutiunnyk calls in his diaries "castrated truth" the brain and emotions of the reader adopt marginal focalizers rather than central ones. So the author writing under censorship finds his readers (also reading under censorship) less prone to errors in decoding his message and breaking through traumatic silence.

Conclusion

In this article I have told the story of Holodomor memory prior to any official Holodomor iconography. This memory was troubled in two aspects: by paralysis when approaching the theme and by resistance to the demand to forget it. The notion of *martyrdom* when

applied to those who perished and to those who survived has in recent decades tended to be viewed through the filter of the genocides
of the twentieth century. From an increasing distance, in this particular configuration of ideologically motivated and unrestrained
torture and mass killing, there will surely be attempts to determine
whether these people can be said to have been martyred, even
though their suffering was involuntary and did not produce spiritual
heroes. As the history of martyrdom entered the twentieth century,
it grew in scale and mixed with the story of totalitarian fanatics. The
rhetorical tropes later elaborated around "Stalin's martyrs" arose out
of the compulsion to draw a connection between the mistreated innocence and passivity of victims and the extreme cruelty inflicted
on them on behalf of the state. Stalinism produced not so much people who were eager to give their lives for their political faith, as people who were prepared to sacrifice others' lives. It perpetrated society's habituation to horror and the erasure of the memory of guilt-
less victims, who must be executed and then forgotten. The recognition of that past was seen as a major threat to the regime and many
efforts were invested to make sure that the victim would never turn
into μάρτυς, the witness.

The unmasking of the profound historical deceit about the
Holodomor in the late 1980s in Soviet Ukraine seemed to generate a
sort of delayed (vicarious) shock. Though the dramatic comeback of
Holodomor memory did become possible, as in Oles Yanchuk's film
Famine-33 (1991)—aired first on the state TV channel the night before Ukrainians voted to leave the Soviet Union—it was partially blocked and addressed rather in a pattern of deterritorializa-
tion of collective (or, rather, collected) memories: since the 1930s,
the public sphere as agora had ceased to exist for Soviet citizens living under a regime that ensured the complete absence of open discussion. The Chornobyl 4th reactor's sarcophagus and its 30 kilome-
ter exclusion zone came to stand as a stark symbol of the Soviet
state's violence, secrecy, and criminal neglect; now it was joined by
the Holodomor, a kind of black hole in the recent past—a frighten-
ing socioscape of man's inhumanity, a place of pandemonium and
convulsion.

It is worth considering further why recognition of the Holod-omor should have been so troubling to Soviet and now to post-So-viet Russian identity, and why none of the other revelations about Soviet mass martyrdom had such a great potential to debunk the Soviet ideology and its moral vacuum. Holodomor stories slowly found their way to Soviet Ukrainians (both Russian- and Ukrainian-speaking), reconnected with family histories, and were transformed into post-Soviet, and then anti-Soviet memories.[11] Meanwhile, in So-viet and post-Soviet Russia, the troubling memory layers that lay be-yond the visible surface of the triumphant narrative of Communism were mostly ignored or just avoided. As Aleida Assmann writes, "The memory of Stalin's terror has had a contested and fragmented his-tory, fuelling the national narratives of victimhood of some post-So-viet states on the one hand and disappearing from Russian political memory almost entirely on the other" (Assmann 2013: 27). Those who ignored it preferred instead to follow the pattern of denial dur-ing *glasnost'* and the Soviet Union's dissolution, gradually retreating into rehabilitation of Stalin and Stalinism in the context of a wider neo-Soviet trend.[12]

Moving from the West to the East of Europe one stumbles upon strategies of forgetting which undo the life of signs and change the scene of mediation to the point when more memorials would not help. Alienation and the displacement of terror-loaded memory has now been transmitted across three generations. For almost fifty

---

[11]   A national survey carried out in fall 2010 (seventy-seven years after the events and twenty-five years since Gorbachev's *glasnost'*) revealed a divide in Ukraine between a community of memory and a non-communal community of oblivion. While the first group was openly negotiating the social and cultural catastro-phes of the Holodomor years and was biased on whether it was (61 percent) or was not (25 percent) genocidal in nature, the second group followed the tradi-tional Soviet view that there was no major famine, or thought that it was the result of natural calamities or knew nothing about the famine (10 percent), or declined to give their opinion (14 percent). By the year 2014, the community of memory had expanded to 72 percent and dominated opinion all over Ukraine, including in the Donetsk region. See: Sotsiolohichna hrupa *Rating*, "Dynamika stavlennia do Holodomoru: lystopad 2014", 17 November 2014, http://www.rat-inggroup.com.ua/products/politic/data/entry/14115/ (accessed 17 January 2015).
[12]   "Opros: bol'she 50% rossiian podderzhivaet Stalina", *BBC Russkaia sluzhba,* 20 January 2015, http://www.bbc.co.uk/russian/russia/2015/01/150120_russia_sta-lin_poll (accessed 20 January 2015).

years, official commemoration was dissonant and hostile to idioms of living memory and tried to eradicate the crossing point between the official and the private. The short-lived period of de-Staliniza-tion brought pioneering attempts to visualize the Holodomor's af-ter-effects (like Illienko's *A Well for the Thirsty* [1965]) and to trans-form them into literary narratives (like Hryhir Tiutiunnyk's and Va-sily Grossman's autobiographical writings). Single attempts to voice lacunas in traumatized remembrance, to somehow reconnect with the shocking collective past, were soon banned by the censors. By 1989, the existing handful of isolated communities of memory had been lost and much of the pandemonic testimony was actually re-imported from the diaspora. What followed was an attempt to pro-mote the Holodomor memory as a national one. The top-down ap-proach peaked with Yushchenko's presidential adaptation and neg-ative sacralization of the Holodomor memory in 2005–2009. His at-titude of state-supported appropriation was a reversal of the decades of silencing: to make the Holodomor victims' memory public and obligatory along with the Holocaust, to enact it as an official remem-bering, as a *lieu de mémoire*, and to reinstall it as anticolonial and all-Ukrainian, uniting a nation in commemoration. This brought a new wave of cultural production along with heated discussions about inheritance of guilt. The Holodomor memory's rapid promo-tion then had a polarizing effect on Ukrainian-Russian political re-lations and mental borders, making it clear that Russian society had missed its opportunity to free the repressed past as it ignored ques-tions of guilt and responsibility. The NKVD and KGB archives were never fully opened to researchers. Unmourned victims, unpunished culprits, and the toxic "plume of atrocities" (Bykov 2015) engulf a major swath of the post-Soviet Russian-speaking space. Hiding from such a heritage slows its post-Soviet transition down to the mini-mum and ultimately, pulls it back into a colonial frame.

REFERENCES

Agamben, G. (2010) *State of Exception.* Transl. Kevin Attell. Chicago: University of Chicago Press.

Agamben, G. (2002) *Remnants of Auschwitz: The Witness and the Archive.* New York: Zone Books.

Assmann, A. (2013) "Europe's Divided Memory", in U. Blacker, A. Etkind, J. and Fedor (eds) *Memory and Theory in Eastern Europe.* New York: Palgrave Macmillan, 25–42.

Bhabha, H. K. (1994) *The Location of Culture.* London and New York: Routledge.

Bykov, D. (2015) Interview on *Osoboe mnenie,* 28 January, http://echo.msk.ru/programs/personalno/1481074-echo/ (accessed 28 January 2015).

Conquest, R. (1986) *The Harvest of Sorrow: Soviet Collectivization and the Terror-Famine.* Oxford: Oxford University Press.

Davies, R. W. and Wheatcroft, S. G. (2004) *The Industrialisation of Soviet Russia 5: The Years of Hunger: Soviet Agriculture, 1931-1933.* Hampshire and New York: Palgrave Macmillan.

Dolot, M. (1985) *Execution by Hunger: The Hidden Holocaust.* New York: W.W. Norton.

Felman, S. and Laub, D. (1992) *Testimony: Crises of Witnessing in Literature, Psychoanalysis, and History.* New York: Routledge.

Giesen, B. (2004) *Triumph and Trauma.* London: Paradigm.

Ginzburg, C. (2012) *Threads and Traces: True, False, Fictive.* Berkeley, CA: University of California Press.

Goichenko, D. (2010) *Krasnyi apokalipsis: skvoz' raskulachivanie i holodomor.* Kyiv: A-ba-ba-ha-la-ma-ha.

Graziosi, A. (1996) *The Great Soviet War: Bolsheviks and Peasants, 1917–1933.* Cambridge, Massachusetts: Harvard University Press–HURI.

Graziosi, A. (2015) "Stalin's Solution: Soviet Ukraine, 1932/1933", in D. Curran, L. Luciuk, and A. G. Newby (eds), *Famines in European Economic History: The Last Great European Famines Reconsidered.* Oxford and New York: Routledge, 227–56.

Grossman, V. (1989) *Vse techet, Oktiabr'* 6. Available at: http://lib.ru/PROZA/GROSSMAN/techet.txt.

Hoseiko [Hosejko], L. (2005) *Istoriia ukrains'koho kinematohrafa. 1896–1995.* Kyiv: Kino-Kolo.

Hryn, H. (2004–2005) "The Executed Renaissance Paradigm Revisited", *Harvard Ukrainian Studies* 27(1–4): 67–96.

Ilienko, I. (1994) "Lashtuiuchys v dalekyi shliakh. Maksym Ryl's'kyi u slidchykh spravakh DPU-NKVS", in *U zhornakh represii.* Kyiv: Veselka, 60–121.

Illienko, Y. (1965) *Krynytsia dlia sprahlykh* (film, Dovzhenko Film Studio, Kyiv, Ukrainian SSR, 73 min).

Khvylovy [Khvyl'ovyi], M. (1986) *The Cultural Renaissance in Ukraine: Polemical Pamphlets, 1925–1926*, trans. with an introduction by Myroslav Shkandrij. Edmonton: CIUS Press.

Klen, Y. (1937) *Prokliati roky.* Available at: http://www.ukrcenter.com/ Література/Юрій-Клен/23991-1/Прокляті-роки-повністю (accessed 30 June 2015).

Kostets'kyi, Ihor (2005) "Tsina liuds'koi nazvy", in *Tobi nalezhyt' tsilyi svit.* Kyiv: Krytyka, 36–45.

Kratochvil, A. (1999) *Mykola Chvyl'ovyj—eine Studie zu Leben und Werk.* Munich: O. Sagner.

Kravchenko, V. (1946) *I Chose Freedom: the Personal and Political Life of a Soviet Official.* New York: Scribner's.

Kryvenko, O. (1993) "Marhinal'na moia Ukraina". Republished in *Istorychna Pravda*, 13 May 2013. http://www.istpravda.com.ua/columns/2011/04/9/350 61/ (accessed 13 May 2015).

Luciuk, L. Y. and Hrekul, L. (eds) (2008) *Holodomor: Reflections on the Great Famine of 1932-1933 in Soviet Ukraine.* Kingston: Kashtan Press.

Mace, J. A. (ed.) (1988) *Investigation of the Ukrainian Famine 1932–1933: Report to Congress.* Washington DC: Government Printing Office.

Makaryk, I. R. (2004) *Shakespeare in the Undiscovered Bourn: Les Kurbas, Ukrainian Modernism, and Early Soviet Cultural Politics.* Toronto: University of Toronto Press.

Margalit, A. (2002) *The Ethics of Memory.* Cambridge, MA and London: Harvard University Press.

Orwell, G. [1945] (1987) *Animal Farm: A Fairy Story*, in *The Complete Works of George Orwell.* Vol. 8. London: Secker and Warburg.

Orwell, G. (1947) *Kolhosp tvaryn: kazka.* Trans. Ivan Cherniatyns'kyi (Ihor Shevchenko). [Munich]: Prometei.

Pidhainy, S. O. (ed.) (1955) *The Black Deeds of the Kremlin: A White Book, vol. 2. The Great Famine in Ukraine in 1932-1933.* Detroit, MI: Globe Press.

Ryl's'kyi, M. (1983) *Zibrannia tvoriv u dvadtsiaty tomakh.* Tom tretii. Poezii 1941–1950. Kyiv: Naukova dumka.

Scarry, E. (1985) *The Body in Pain: The Making and Unmaking of the World.* New York and Oxford: Oxford University Press.

Shapoval, Y. (2009) *Poliuvannia na "Val'dshnepa." Rozsekrechenyi Mykola Khvyliovyi.* Kyiv: Tempora.

Shevchenko, A. (1998) *Vichna zahadka liubovi: Literaturna spadshchyna Hryhora Tiutiunnyka, spohady pro pys'mennyka.* Kyiv: Radians'kyi Pys'mennyk.

Shkandrij, M. (1992) *Modernists, Marxists, and the Nation: The Ukrainian Literary Discussion of the 1920s.* Edmonton: CIUS Press.

Sontag, S. (2003) *Regarding the Pain of Others.* New York: Picador.

Starovoyt, I. (2005) "Kotyhoroshky: dity vijny u prozi Hryhora Tiutiunnyka", *Ukraïna Moderna*, 6 June. http://uamoderna.com/md/starovoyt-tutunnyk (accessed 30 June 2015).

Stech, M. R. (2002) "The Concept of Personal Revolution in Mykola Kulish's Early Plays," *Journal of Ukrainian Studies* 27(1–2): 107–24.

Stroop, J. R. (1935) "Studies in Interference in Serial Verbal Reactions", *Journal of Experimental Psychology* 18: 643-62. Available at http://psychclassics.yorku.ca/Stroop/ (accessed 11 August 2015).

Tiutiunnyk, H. (1984) *Tvory. Knyha 1: Opovidannia, Knyha 2: Povisti.* Kyiv: Molod'.

Overcoming Hegemonic Martyrdom:
The Afterlife of Khatyn in Belarusian Memory

Simon Lewis

Abstract: *This article examines the contested memory of civilian victims of the Second World War in Belarus, from the late Soviet period to the present day, focusing on the site of Khatyn, a Belarusian village whose residents were burned to death in March 1943. In the official Soviet interpretation, victimhood had redemptive meaning attached to it: according to the state, those murdered at Khatyn and other burned villages died for the freedom of the USSR. Literature, however, contested the state's monolithic memorialization. Works by authors such as Ales' Adamovich foregrounded meaningless suffering and traumatized memory, and thereby gave voice to individual experiences that were at odds with the state's triumphalism. The discursive conflict between different narratives within Soviet Belarusian society laid the foundations for further contestation after the dissolution of the Soviet Union. Since 1991, Khatyn has been reevaluated and subjected to further criticism, whilst it has also been a major legitimizing instrument for the authoritarian regime of Aliaksandr Lukashenka. The article ends with an analysis of a recent Czech novella, Jáchym Topol's* Chladnou zemí, *which shows how Khatyn can be remembered without being restricted to the realm of the nation. It is argued that Topol's transnational treatment of wartime victimhood may contain a key to Belarus overcoming the lingering legacy of Soviet-era martyrdom.*

Recent years have seen the rise to prominence of the politics of victimhood in Eastern Europe. Burning issues that were suppressed under communism, such as the Polish-Ukrainian conflict of 1943–44 in Volhynia, anti-Semitic pogroms in Jedwabne (1941) and Kielce

(1946), and the Katyn massacre (1940), have inspired strings of re-criminations that have affected both inter-state relations and do-mestic politics and culture. The importance of victimhood as a cat-egory in memory discourse is reflected in the development of a scholarly literature that analyzes its application.[1] In most accounts, however, the "culturally celebrated status of victimhood"[2] tends to be understood as a narrative of historical injury that is developed through open public debate within a stable political system. By con-trast, the ways in which the major political and economic transfor-mations of 1989 and 1991 in Central and Eastern Europe have corre-sponded to changes in memories of victimhood are yet to be sub-jected to thorough examination. This article seeks to address this gap by analyzing the obfuscation of suffering by official memory in Soviet Belarus and the manner in which literature in the late-Soviet period and cultural developments in the post-Soviet era have rede-fined the terms of public debate. Focusing in particular on the case of Khatyn, a major Soviet-era memorial to the civilian victims of Nazi terror, it argues that the construction of a memory of victim-hood is an important strategy in the narration of collective identity. In Belarus, competing memories of violence have sought to gain dominance in order to define the nation, and opposition to the So-viet myth of national martyrdom has been an important feature of this contested discourse.

---

[1]   Whilst the literature on victimhood is vast, I am particularly indebted to the following contributions: Daniel Levy and Natan Sznaider, "Memories of Univer-sal Victimhood: The Case of Ethnic German Expellees", *German Politics & Soci-ety*, 23, no. 2 (2005): 1–27; Jeffrey K. Olick, *The Politics of Regret: On Collective Memory and Historical Responsibility* (New York: Routledge, 2007); Jie-Hyun Lim, "Victimhood Nationalism in Contested Memories: National Mourning and Global Accountability", in *Memory in a Global Age: Discourses, Practices and Trajectories*, eds. Aleida Assmann and Sebastian Conrad (Basingstoke: Palgrave Macmillan, 2010), 138–62; Andrzej Nowak, "Murder in the Cemetery: Memorial Clashes over the Victims of the Soviet-Polish Wars", in *Memory and Theory in Eastern Europe*, eds. Uilleam Blacker, Alexander Etkind and Julie Fedor (New York: Palgrave Macmillan, 2013), 149–71.

[2]   Daniel Levy and Natan Sznaider, "The Politics of Commemoration: The Holo-caust, Memory and Trauma", in *Handbook of Contemporary European Social Theory*, ed. Gerard Delanty (London–New York: Routledge, 2006), 289–97 (289).

In many languages of Central and Eastern Europe, there is a semantic slippage between the concepts of "sacrifice" and "victim-hood", i.e. between the meaningful death of a subject whose demise (whether or not willing) is intended as a symbolic transaction that will bring future dividends, and the passive death that brings nothing but loss. In languages including German (*Opfer*), Polish (*ofiara*) and Russian (*zhertva*), the same word connotes both ideas, potentially giving rise to situations of confusion or conflation. Yet as Aleida Assmann points out, there is also a fundamental contrast in memory discourse between what she calls "heroic memory of victimhood" (*heroisches Opfergedächtnis*) and "traumatic memory of victimhood" (*traumatisches Opfergedächtnis*). Remembering violence and loss in terms of the former is "easy" and involves rendering the victim as a martyr: death is attributed a symbolic teleology within a religious or national master narrative. Traumatic memory, on the other hand, may take "decades or even centuries" to develop at the level of the collective, and its lack of articulation may lead to the "psychic wounds of trauma being passed on to subsequent generations".[3] Thus, the heroic and traumatic modes of remembering are opposed to each other heuristically: the creation of martyr myths can only defer the necessary memory work of coming to terms with loss.

In the Soviet Union, heroic memory was not merely an "easy" default option, but a key component of hegemonic official ideology: the cult of victory in the Great Patriotic War. The civilian victims of the war were turned into martyrs who died for the glory of the Soviet Union. However, in the countries on the western periphery of the former Soviet Union including Belarus, two waves of mass violence coincided in space and time: atrocities were carried out by both the Stalinist authorities and the Nazi occupation forces. Yet in memory, there existed an imbalance, whereby official Soviet discourse precluded discussion of the former and loudly proclaimed the evil of the latter. In asserting collective victimhood whilst denying its role as a perpetrator, the Soviet state effectively repressed two distinct

---

3   Aleida Assmann, *Der lange Schatten der Vergangenheit. Erinnerungskultur und Geschichtspolitik* (München: C.H. Beck, 2006), 74–76. All translations are my own, unless otherwise indicated.

traumatic memories: the martyr myth deferred the possibility of reckoning with both the Nazi and the Stalinist crimes.

Nonetheless, a traumatic concept of wartime victimhood was articulated in Belarus, chiefly in imaginative literature of the Thaw era. This literature was politically subversive and an important component of mnemonic dissidence; by giving voice to individual hardship, it effectively ensured the survival of an alternative war memory. In the aftermath of the collapse of the Soviet Union, the martyr myth was further discredited, and brought into competition with the resurfaced memory of Stalinist atrocities. I argue that in the post-Soviet era, however, the memory of victimhood in Belarus has become polarized between two dominant discourses that both create unitary myths. Caught in the midst of a zero-sum game that instrumentalizes their memory, the victims themselves are under threat of being paradoxically forgotten. A possible antidote to this forgetting is discovered in a novella by Czech writer Jáchym Topol (*Chladnou zemí*, 2009, translated as *The Devil's Workshop*, 2013), whose delicate treatment of the memory of East European violence, including at the Belarusian site of Khatyn, may contain a key to Belarusian memory releasing itself from the lingering hold of Soviet-style martyrdom.

The Sacrificial Victim

Whilst the cult of victory in the Great Patriotic War was central to claims of Soviet legitimacy throughout the Union,[4] in the BSSR it was presented as the *raison d'être* of the republic. Just as the very notion of the Great Patriotic War—"a specifically Soviet war virtually removed from the rest of humanity's experience of that conflict

---

4   Nina Tumarkin, *The Living and the Dead: The Rise and Fall of the Cult of World War II in Russia* (New York: Basic Books, 1994); Amir Weiner, *Making Sense of War: The Second World War and the Fate of the Bolshevik Revolution* (Princeton: Princeton University Press, 2001); Nina Tumarkin, "The Great Patriotic War as Myth and Memory", *European Review*, 11 (2003): 595–611; Vladislav Grinevich, "Raskolotaia pamiat': Vtoraia mirovaia voina v istoricheskom soznanii ukrainskogo obshchestva", *Neprikosnovennyi zapas* 2–3 (2005), http://magazines.russ.ru/nz/2005/2/gri24.html (accessed 15 June 2014).

and elevated to mythical status"[5]—served to present the Second World War as a bilateral conflict between the Soviet Union and Nazi Germany, so the narration of a Belarusian "all-national partisan struggle [*vsenarodnaia partizanskaia bor'ba*]" endowed war memory with a sense of specificity that was conducive to the making of a national myth. Within this framework, accounts of the mass murder of civilians were embellished with formulaic demonization of both the Germans and their supposed ideological heirs in the western world, which contrasted both implicitly and explicitly with the moral and historical rectitude of the Soviet Union.

The semantics of "genocide" played an important role in the official narrative of collective victimhood and transcendental glory. The memory of Nazi crimes was inscribed into a narrative of mass terror aimed specifically at the Soviet Union: for example, an account by one of the most prominent and productive official historians in Belarus claimed that "the German-fascist invaders set themselves the aims of destroying the socialist state, seizing and utilizing for their own interests its huge material resources, annihilating millions of Soviet people, and turning an exactly calculated number of remaining people into slaves."[6] Whilst actively promoting the term "genocide",[7] this accenting of generalized "Soviet" victimhood masked the fact that the Germans had singled out Jews for total extermination.[8] The presentation of the Soviet state itself as the victim

---

[5]   Mark von Hagen, "From 'Great Fatherland War' to the Second World War", in *Stalinism and Nazism: Dictatorships in Comparison*, ed. Ian Kershaw and Moshe Lewin (Cambridge: Cambridge University Press, 1997), 237–50 (238).

[6]   V.F. Romanovskii, *Zabveniiu ne podlezhit* (Minsk: Belarus', 1985), 5.

[7]   E.g.: "Terror, mass murder of Soviet people, a policy of genocide were the basis of [the occupying] regime"; *Natsistskaia politika genotsida i "vyzhzhennoi zemli" v Belorussii, 1941-1944*, ed. V.E. Lobanok, I.F. Klimov, V.F. Romanovskii, A.A. Filimonov (Minsk: Belarus', 1984), 21.

[8]   Zvi Gitelman, "Politics and the Historiography of the Holocaust in the Soviet Union", in *Bitter Legacy. Confronting the Holocaust in the USSR*, ed. Zvi Gitelman (Bloomington and Indianapolis: Indiana University Press, 1997), 14–42; Shalom Cholawski, "The Holocaust and Armed Struggle in Belorussia as Reflected in Soviet Literature and Works by Emigres in the West", in *Bitter Legacy*, 214–29 (esp. 214–17); Il'ia Al'tman, "Memorializatsiia kholokosta v Rossii: istoriia, sovremennost', perspektivy", *Neprikosnovennyi zapas* 40–41 (2005), http://magazines.russ.ru/nz/2005/2/alt28.html (accessed 15 June 2014).

---

therefore entailed the erasure of the historical fact of the planned destruction of the Jews, but it also contributed to the politicization of all deaths of the occupation period.

Remembrance of the dead was subordinated to the dominant myth of the "heroism" of the Soviet partisans. Thus, for example, the introduction to a 1965 compilation of archival documents concerning Nazi atrocities in Belarus forges a link between Nazi crimes and the glory of the Soviet Union:

> The Hitlerite hangmen subjected the Belarusian people to torture and suffering hitherto unseen in history. [...] Over the course of the occupation in the territory of Belarus, over 2.2 million Soviet citizens were exterminated by the Hitlerites [...]. The terror and violence of the Hitlerite invaders did not break the will of the Belarusian people, which from the first days of the Patriotic War raised itself to a sacred war against the Fascist enslavers—they [the Nazi measures] only strengthened the people's resistance. Love of the Soviet Fatherland and hatred of the enemy, the striving to defend their freedom, independence, [and] the socialist state lifted the popular masses up against the German fascists and their "new order". [...] This was a genuinely all-national war behind enemy lines.[9]

Here, the generalized description of civilian suffering is followed by a statistic, after which the Nazi atrocities are explicitly named as a cause of partisan heroism. This logic effectively constitutes a step-by-step elision of individual suffering and loss: first, Nazi crimes are described in terms of their perpetrators, i.e. blackening the enemy is the principal motive, although personal suffering is implied and mentioned; second, the victims are brought together under a single number, and thereby deprived of ethnic, gender or geographic difference—they are stripped of their individuality; third, the dead and wounded are left behind altogether as the focus is shifted to the partisan heroes. Death fades out of the picture, and is replaced by the triumph of the Soviet state.

---

[9]   *Prestupleniia nemetsko-fashistskikh okkupantov v Belorussii v 1941-1944 gg. Dokumenty i materialy*, ed. Z.I. Beluga, N.I. Kaminskii, A.L. Manaenkov, A.V. Semenova, A.A. Faktorovich, I.P. Khovratovich, G.N. Shevela (Minsk: Belarus, 1965), 8.

Combatant deaths were treated in a similar fashion to the nameless thousands of murdered civilians: their deaths were rendered as sacrifices. For instance, one history quotes the newspaper *Pravda*, saying that "When the fearless defenders of the Soviet Union's borders ran out of ammunition, they blew themselves up with grenades".[10] A memoir by Pavel Proniagin, the former head of the partisan movement in Brest region, describes the deaths of comrades-in-arms solely in terms of the bonding effect those deaths had on the living: "[t]he names of extolled partisan commanders, like military emblems, called upon and inspired the people's avengers to glorious military deeds in the struggle against the hated enemy."[11] Similarly, the war memoir of Piotr Kalinin, former chief of staff of the Belarusian partisan movement, ends with images of the celebration of victory, including a comment that "[t]he memory of fallen patriots lives in the hearts of Belarusians and all of the nations of the great Soviet Union. The losses did not break the fortitude of the partisans."[12] Official censorship did not allow for the description of pain, hardship or fear in these heavily depersonalized narratives;[13] similarly, there was no place for death, unless framed as a "loss" (*utrata* or *poteria*), i.e. a form of collateral damage suffered by the collective in pursuit of the great cause.

The process of appropriating victimhood for state ideology is essentially similar to what Elaine Scarry calls the "disowning" of injury. For Scarry, "the main purpose and outcome of war is injuring", yet the very structure of warfare necessitates an abstraction of memory away from the individual body:

---

[10]   *Pravda*, 25 June 1965, cited in V.F. Romanovskii, *Protiv falsifikatsii istorii Belorussii perioda Velikoi Otechestvennoi voiny* (Minsk: Nauka i tekhnika, 1975), 15.

[11]   P.V. Proniagin, *U samoi granitsy* (Minsk: Belarus', 1979), 111.

[12]   P.Z. Kalinin, *Partizanskaia respublika* (Moskva: Voennoe izdatel'stvo ministerstva oborony SSSR, 1964), 334.

[13]   Kenneth Slepyan, *Stalin's Guerrillas: Soviet Partisans in World War II* (Lawrence: University Press of Kansas, 2006), 60–103.

[war] requires both the reciprocal infliction of massive injury and the eventual disowning of the injury so that its attributes can be transferred elsewhere, as they cannot if they are permitted to cling to the original site of the wound, the human body.[14]

This act of disowning can be achieved in a number of ways, the main categories of which are "omission" of historical facts and "redescription" of events.[15] The official Soviet narrative of civilian martyrdom employed both mechanisms to transfer the site of agency to the collective. Emplotting the losses of war within the triumphant victory narrative, it omitted individual accounts of the experience of suffering, replacing them with statistics and politically charged images of enemy brutality; at the same time, these generalized (redescribed) depictions of injury were further removed from the original act of violence by being inscribed into the myth of partisan glory. However, if disowning injury is a structural necessity for the waging of war for Scarry, the Soviet discourse of victimhood fulfilled a clear political function: it ensured the hegemony of Soviet memory models and thus the Soviet identity of the Belarusian people. The rhetorical fusion of martyrdom and victory resulted in a discourse of sacrificial redemption. This commemorative economy placed minimal value on the loss of individual life, subsuming personal suffering into a narrative of collective triumph. It was the political body that both suffered and retaliated, and finally claimed victory.

Martyrdom and Glory

The most important Soviet-era symbol of Belarusian martyrdom (and arguably, of Soviet martyrdom more broadly) is the Khatyn Memorial Complex, an open-air museum built on the site of the village of Khatyn',[16] 60 kilometers north-east of Minsk. Here, 149 residents, including seventy-five children, were forced into a barn and

---

<p>14   Elaine Scarry, <em>The Body in Pain. The Making and Unmaking of the World</em> (New York–Oxford: Oxford University Press, 1985), 63–64.</p>

<p>15   Ibid., 80.</p>

<p>16   To differentiate between the village eviscerated in 1943 and the memorial complex which now stands in its place, the form Khatyn', with an apostrophe to</p>

burned alive on 22 March 1943. The memorial complex, which was opened in 1969, commemorates the civilian victims of the Nazi occupation, including 628 villages which were destroyed, like Khatyn', together with their residents.

The history of memorialization at Khatyn shows the site's trajectory from a symbol of local mourning to a shrine of national martyrdom. Until the middle of the 1960s, a series of minor memorials marked the mass grave of the villagers: the three unmarked crosses that initially commemorated the tragedy were soon replaced by an obelisk crowned by a red star; i.e. the monument was secularized. Then, a plaster sculpture entitled "The Grieving Mother" was added in 1964, effectively restoring Christian symbolism, official atheism notwithstanding.[17] Inconspicuously fulfilling a symbolic need for a local audience, the early memorials at Khatyn were no different to many others dotted around the country. Little is known of their histories, and they have now been overshadowed by the monumental memorial complex that has replaced them. In 1965, the decision was taken in the highest Party echelons to build a larger memorial. Piotr Masherau, the head of the republic (1965–80), took a personal interest in the Khatyn project from the very outset. He is said to have specifically commissioned a memorial which would "convey through the tragedy of the village of Khatyn' the tragedy of the entire Belarusian nation".[18]

The Khatyn memorial was intended from its inception as part of the nationwide commemorative landscape that emphasized Soviet triumph. In one of the first pieces of correspondence on the matter, a note from the BSSR Minister of Culture Mikhail Minkovich to Masherau, the planned Khatyn museum is included in a list of measures aimed at:

---

mark the soft sign, will be used for the former, and Khatyn, bearing no apostrophe, will be used for the latter.

[17]   V.I. Adamushko, I.A. Valakhanovich, N.E. Kalesnik, N.V. Kirillova, V.D. Selemenev, V.V. Skalaban (eds), *Khatyn'. Tragediia i pamiat'. Dokumenty i materialy* (Minsk: NARB, 2009), 4.

[18]   L.M. Levin, *Khatyn': avtobiograficheskaia povest'* (Minsk: Asobny Dakh, 2005), 92.

commemorating the victims of fascism and the incinerated villages, the warriors and partisans who fell in the struggle for freedom and the independence of our Country, the active work of the underground fighters, the places
where partisan brigades and units were stationed, the sites where partisans
and warriors of the Red Army battled against the German-fascist invaders...[19]

Explicitly a memorial to the victorious partisan war, the
Khatyn project was planned and legislated for in conjunction with
the Mound of Glory, a giant obelisk on the outskirts of Minsk. Both
monuments were designated to be unveiled in time for the 25th anniversary celebrations of the "liberation" of Belarus by the Red Army,
in 1969.[20] Of these two principal monuments in the Minsk region,
however, it was Khatyn which had its grand opening linked to the
calendar anniversary of the liberation: 3 July. The ceremony began
at Victory Square in the center of Minsk, followed by a military pro-
cession to the new memorial. The two sites were symbolically linked
by a transfer of fire: a torch was lit from the eternal flame at the
Victory Monument and carried over to Khatyn, where a new eternal
flame was ignited. Tellingly, the day's events were described using
the hyphenated adjective *torzhestvenno-traurnyi* ("triumphant-
mournful'"), further reinforcing the inseparability of glorification
and grief.[21] The official speeches delivered at Khatyn were filled with
images of heroism, martyrdom, and redemption. Deputy Prime
Minister Vladimir Lobanok set the tone when he spoke of the imperative of commemoration: "The wounds of the war are healed. But
we cannot and will never heal our spiritual wounds. In the people's
memory, those *who paid for our freedom with their lives* will always
be alive".[22] Transforming the victims of atrocity into a sacrifice made
for the sake of salvation, Lobanok attributed to the villagers of
Khatyn' an agency they never had, in effect implying that they gave
up their lives willingly in exchange for the defeat of the Germans
and the return of Soviet power. The victims are similarly instrumentalized by a large inscription prominently displayed at the memorial
site. On a large concrete structure which represents the barn in

---

[19]   Adamushko *et al*, *Khatyn'*, 133.
[20]   Ibid., 151.
[21]   Ibid., 171–72.
[22]   Ibid., 173, emphasis added.

which the people were killed, the deceased villagers are made to speak to the living, using the words:

> Good people, remember. We loved life and our Motherland, and we loved you, our dear ones. We were burned alive by fire. Our request to all of you: may your grief and sorrow turn into courage and strength, so that you can secure eternal peace and rest on the Earth, in order that from today onwards, people should never die anywhere in the vortex of fires!

Turning the villagers of Khatyn' into loyal Soviet citizens who "loved their Motherland", the authorities spoke on their behalf, and by extension, for all of the victims of the occupation. The dead villagers became puppets of memory.

A number of written narratives published from the late 1960s onwards served to further establish the connection between Khatyn and the myth of Belarusian devotion to Soviet rule.[23] For example, a "documentary short story" by Mikalai Andrushchanka, published in parallel in both Belarusian and Russian and bearing the title of *Khatyn'*,[24] tells the pre-war history of the villagers of Khatyn' in rosy shades of patriotism, heroism and idyllic harmony which resulted from the spread of the October Revolution to Belarus:

> The villagers were proud of their fellow inhabitants Uladzimir Iaskevich and Vasil Karaban. The former fought against the whites in the civil war and earned a medal. The latter died a hero's death on the Karelian Isthmus in 1940. Stsiapan Fedarovich, Hauryla Rudak and Mikola Zhalabkovich likewise never returned, giving their lives for the Motherland... [...] They loved this place, although they had lived less comfortably before the revolution. [...] The population of Khatyn' started to rise only under Soviet rule. [...] Together, as a collective [in the "Red Star" collective farm, established in 1930], the people of Khatyn' earned their happiness, and the happiness of their children. (8-11)

The story indexes pre-war revolutionary martyrdom as a virtuous act ("a hero's death", "giving their lives"), and sets the stage

---

[23]   In addition to the two prose works analyzed below, see the poetry collection: Ales' Bachyla (ed.), *Slukhaitse—Khatyn'!* (Minsk: Mastatskaia litaratura, 1975).

[24]   M. Andrushchanka, *Khatyn'* (Minsk: Belarus', 1969); N. Andriushchenko, *Khatyn'* (Minsk: Belarus', 1969); hereafter, the Belarusian version will be cited. Further references to this text are given after quotations in the text, parenthetically.

for further service and sacrifice. Just as Soviet rule delivers happiness and fulfillment, the onset of war and occupation brings out the very best in Soviet dedication from the villagers: "[t]here is nothing more to it: the partisans enjoyed the full support of the population. The residents of Khatyn' shared with the partisans everything they owned" (17). Moreover, a former partisan commander named I.D. Rakhman'ko is quoted as saying:

> The residents of Khatyn' inspired us, the partisans, by their unbreakable devotion to Soviet power. [...] The people of Khatyn' believed in the Soviet regime, they believed that in the end, the Red Army would win. Even in the most difficult days of the occupation, they celebrated revolutionary holidays. (18)

The genre of this account as a "documentary short story" allows each of these statements to go unattributed. Outwardly fictional, yet purporting to convey historical facts, the narrative offers no actual documentary evidence to support its arguments, and whilst the figure of "I.D. Rakhman'ko" need not be fictional, there is no contextualization of where, when or why he said the above—his statement merely provides a façade of corroboration.

Andrushchanka continues by describing the Khatyn' massacre itself, showing in no uncertain terms that it was motivated by a "barbaric" German hatred of the Soviet way of life:

> Everyone knew that the punishers swarm in suddenly, they hang, they shoot, not discerning whether their victim is an old man or a child. The barbarians destroyed people along with their homes. Such a fate was met by Khatyn' and its people. (20)

However, at no point in this narrative is it pointed out that indirectly, the massacre was caused by partisans: the Khatyn' raid was triggered by a partisan raid on a German division, and the occupation forces burned down the village in an angry act of retribution. Therefore, partisans were not the perpetrators of the crime, but their actions were certainly an important link in the chain of events leading up to it. As Timothy Snyder explains:

Since partisans hide among civilians, they bring down, and often intend to bring down, the occupier's retaliation against the local population. Reprisals then serve as recruitment propaganda for the partisans, or leave individual survivors with nowhere to go but the forest.[25]

It follows that the moral ambiguity of the partisans' motivations actually made their heroization somewhat incompatible with the Khatyn narrative. Andrushchanka avoids this pitfall by ignoring the provocatory role of the partisans altogether.

Another Khatyn text, Anton Bialevich' *Khatyn': Bol' i gnev* ("Khatyn': Pain and Fury") (1975),[26] is similar to that of Andrushchanka,[27] but does differ in that it offers some treatment of the lead-up to the crime. Here, the partisans' actions are interpreted as eminently justifiable:

> The occupiers were very afraid of the partisans. And for good reason: they were under attack from them through day and night. The soldiers of the forest sabotaged the enemy's cars, tanks and motorcycles on the Lahoisk-Pleshchanitsy road. [...] The people's avengers ambushed the fascists and gave them no room for comfort. Every bush, every tree would shoot at them. (22)

In this highly partial version of events, the partisans are cast as popular defenders and their military actions as inherently good, such that any consequences are rendered beyond judgment. Therefore, the possibility that there is any causal relation between their skirmishes and the reprisal actions is overlooked. Furthermore, Bialevich's account attaches an innate positive value to the growth of the partisan movement, a value which atones for the deaths at Khatyn':

> People sighed: "Oh, disaster, disaster, Khatyn' has burned down, its people have burned, every last person has burned." The people, clenching their fists

---

[25]   Timothy Snyder, *Bloodlands: Europe Between Hitler and Stalin* (London: Bodley Head, 2010), 234.

[26]   A.P. Belevich, *Khatyn'. Bol' i gnev* (Moskva: Politizdat, 1975). Further references to this text are given after quotations in the text, parenthetically.

[27]   Bialevich, better known as a poet, writes in a more verbose style than Andrushchanka, featuring more grandiosely poetic language and verses from his own and others' poetry. His text's overall narrative structure and representation of the past, however, are essentially the same as those of Andrushchanka's book.

in anger, said: "we need to join the partisans. We can't sit around at home, that would be sinful. We need to go to the partisan forests, and beat the savage enemy. To drive out the invaders from our native land." And people from nearby settlements and villages joined the partisans. The all-national force grew, gained strength, and became even more fearsome. (29)

Thus, the teleological thrust of this narrative foregrounds the glory of the partisan resistance, with the victims of Khatyn' gently pushed into the shadows as they are made into martyrs.

Both Andrushchanka and Bialevich conclude their narratives with descriptions of the efforts undertaken to commemorate the victims, presenting the Khatyn memorial as a "tribute from the descendants to those who didn't submit to the enemy, who weren't brought to their knees"[28] and a symbol of "stern national memory [*surovaia narodnaia pamiat*]".[29] Thus, they posit Khatyn as a site of *collective* remembrance, impelling citizens to align their individual knowledge of the past with the master narrative of sacrifice and triumph. The final line of Andrushchanka's text is in the imperative mood: "People, do you hear the ashes of the people of Khatyn' knocking on your hearts? So be vigilant!" (46) The command of vigilance impels readers to subscribe to the official narrative of martyrdom.

---

[28]   Andrushchanka, *Khatyn'*, 43.
[29]   Belevich, *Khatyn'*, 54.

Figure 1. Khatyn Memorial, Belarus, 14 May 2008.
Author: John Oldale.
Source: https://commons.wikimedia.org/wiki/File:Khatyn_Memorial,_Be
larus.jpg. Image licensed under Creative Commons Attribution-Share Alike 3.0 Unported license (https://creativecommons.org/licenses/by-sa/3.0/legalcode).

    The one adult survivor of Khatyn', whose voice as a witness to
the massacre remains on record, reveals the discrepancy between
the official narrative of collective sacrifice and the historical experience of trauma—despite the authorities' efforts to incorporate his
story into their own interpretation of events. Iosif Kaminski inspired
the signature piece of the memorial complex, a six-meter tall sculpture which depicts a man carrying his charred, dead son (see Figure
1). Entitled the "Unconquered Human" (Belarusian: *Niaskorany cha-
lavek*, Russian: *Nepokorennyi chelovek*), it monumentalizes defiance, as manifested in its gigantic proportions and rigidly upright
posture. Meanwhile, the distorted facial features and the son's limp
corpse symbolize mourning. Thus, the overall effect is, again, both
triumphant and mournful: *torzhestvenno-traurnyi*. According to the
protocol of a witness statement taken in 1961, however, Kaminski's
experience was very different from that suggested by the sculpture.
His testimony states that, rather than stoically emerging from the

burning barn bearing his son's body, he had been shot and was lying, injured and burned, on the snow-covered ground near the barn when the perpetrators left the scene. His son called to him for help. According to Kaminski's statement: "I crawled over, lifted him slightly, but saw that bullets had ripped him in half. My son Adam managed to ask 'is Mummy still alive?', and then he died on the spot." Unable to move, Kaminski was later found by a relative from a nearby village and carried away.[30] Even when read through the cold and dispassionate transcription of a KGB officer, Kaminski's account screams out in humiliation and pain, not spirited invincibility. At the opening ceremony of the Memorial Complex in 1969, Kaminski broke down in tears as he gave his speech, which markedly differed in tone from the measured pathos of the party officials: "Every time I think of Khatyn', my heart spills over in blood. [...] All that was left of the village was chimneys and ash".[31]

Kaminski's sincere, tortured expression of suffering reflected the wartime experiences of countless thousands of Belarusian civilians (including those of Jewish ethnicity), who endured excruciating bodily pain and irredeemable loss. Film footage of the memorial complex's opening ceremony shows long lines of ordinary citizens attending to express their mourning; their intentions, surely, did not resonate uniformly with the unvarying monotone of redemptive memory which officialdom assigned to the day's events and to the museum itself.[32] The lived experiences of these individuals were largely absent from public discourse of the war: such memories deviated from the official myth of all-national heroism. These voices of suffering were not, however, stifled in their entirety. The fragile testimonies of shattered selves were preserved, in particular, by imaginative literature.

---

[30]   Adamushko *et al, Khatyn'*, 31.
[31]   A video recording of the speech is available on the official website of the Khatyn Memorial Complex: http://khatyn.by/photo/clip3.avi (accessed 15 June 2014); see also Adamushko *et al, Khatyn'*, 176.
[32]   From the official website of the Khatyn Memorial Complex: http://khatyn.by/photo/clip4.avi and http://khatyn.by/photo/clip2.avi (accessed 15 June 2014).

Trauma and Disorientation

In the Soviet Union, especially after the onset of the Thaw, literature had a liminal role between officialdom and dissent. Whilst authors belonged to centrally-funded unions and published in state-owned journals, the work they produced could often test the boundaries of ideological acceptability and enter into conflict with state-produced myths. As Il'ya Kukulin argues:

> Paradoxically, in the USSR, censored literature was the basis not only of official, but also of unofficial memory. Since officially unsanctioned sources of information about the past were prohibited, literature—as personal expression—inevitably became an indirect means of legitimating private biographical memory. What was required was not an Aesopian language but a system of preterition, which, by endowing fictional characters with certain traits, and arranging semantic accents in a certain way, allowed the reader to finish the thought. Even works about the war that were published (including those that became part of the official Soviet canon), in many ways either referred directly to or alluded to many readers' private experience. Readers would extract from those texts things never mentioned in the papers or on the radio.[33]

In Belarus in the late-Soviet period, the Second World War was as central to literature as it was to official ideology, and the central tenets of official war memory were subtly but overtly challenged by Belarusian writers. Moreover, in line with Kukulin's insight, it was private experience that was foregrounded in order to provide an alternative memory of the war.

The author who most prominently subverted the cult of martyrdom in Belarus was Ales' Adamovich (1927–94), a noted prose writer, essayist and literary critic whose major fictional works all focused on the theme of the Second World War. His *Khatynskaia povest'* ('A Khatyn Story'), a novella published in both Russian (1972)

---

[33] Il'ya Kukulin, "The Regulation of Pain. The Great Patriotic War in Russian Literature from the 1940s to the 1970s", trans. Mischa Gabowitsch, *Eurozine*, 6 May 2005, http://www.eurozine.com/articles/2005-05-06-kukulin-en.html (accessed 20 February 2015).

and Belarusian (as *Khatynskaia apovests'*, 1976),[34] is the most strident example of a literary critique of ideological martyrdom. It was
conceived in 1965 and written largely between 1968 and 1971; i.e. the
book's composition was roughly concurrent with the state's project
to build and triumphantly unveil a memorial shrine at the former
site of Khatyn'. The story begins and ends with a group of former
partisans travelling to the recently opened memorial complex, and
unfolds as an alternating dual narrative: the first-person narrator describes his impressions as he journeys to Khatyn with his former
comrades-in-arms, but also digresses frequently to recount his wartime experiences as a teenage fighter. At the core of his wartime past
are two episodes in which he encounters the kind of Nazi brutalities
commemorated at Khatyn: firstly, he returns to his native village in
the midst of hostilities to find it deserted, and after a delay discovers
that his entire family has been burned to death in a barn; secondly,
he directly experiences a similar atrocity in a neighboring village,
being forced into a barn for mass incineration before the perpetrators inexplicably release their victims once the fire has been lit.
Thus, in telling his wartime past, the narrator-protagonist attempts
to come to terms with his suffering. Narration emerges as a per-
formative act, whereby the text itself bears the burden of potentially
enacting some form of healing. In stressing personal injury rather
than collective victory, Adamovich's novella presents a story that re-
pudiates the central tenets of the official narrative of the Great Patriotic War.

It is at the physical level that Florian, the narrator-protagonist, is most prominently scarred by the war. The first line of the
story reveals that its protagonist is a "person in dark glasses, with a
white metallic stick in his hand" (5), and Florian's blindness is a recurring motif through which the novella emphasizes the lasting impact of wounds. Importantly, it is never revealed how exactly this
impairment is acquired: there are vague references to a "white flash"
(73) that shocks Florian as he looks on at a scorched and dying man,

---

[34]   The Russian-language text from the author's Soviet-era *Collected Works* will be
cited here: Ales' Adamovich, *Sobranie sochinenii v chetyrekh tomakh*, 4 vols
(1981–84), III (1982), 5–198. Further references to this text are given after quotations in the text, parenthetically.

as well as a suggestion that "a physical injury" (*fizicheskaia travma*) (implicitly, the experience of nearly being burned to death) (73) played a role. Florian's unattributed injury thus resonates with Cathy Caruth's notion of trauma as an unknowable and haunting residue: "trauma is not seen in the simple violent or original event in an individual's past, but rather in the way that its very unassimilated nature—the way it was precisely *not known* in the first instance—returns to haunt the survivor later on."[35] Also in line with Caruth's concept, a number of narratorial digressions reveal that blindness is a physical state that ceaselessly "haunts" Florian, for example:

> When a person loses his sight, the first horror is that you cannot open your eyes, you keep trying to, but you can't do it. This condition repeats itself endlessly in your dreams. And at the same time, you suffer a different torment: you can't close them either. Your eyes are always open, you are alone with the world. And with yourself, with your memory... (32)

The emphasis on memory as lonesome, troubling, and painful reinforces the notion that the wartime past is not triumphant; instead, it is a source of deep-lying trauma.

In addition to physical injury, a disjuncture between memory and identity is a major theme of *Khatynskaia povest'*: the stream-of-consciousness narration presents an individual who is psychologically scarred and whose post-war identity is fragmented and uncertain. In stark contrast to the self-assured military heroes of official narratives, Florian admits to an ontological distance between his post-war and wartime selves. Addressing himself, he muses:

> But you, Florian Petrovich, owe the partisan Fliora[36] a great deal [...], for the fact that you made it here [*vyshel siuda*]... Sometimes I see that Fliora—my eighteen-year-old self—completely from without. He is certainly not inside me, he remained there (44–45).

By ascribing a distinct identity to himself as a teenager through the differentiation of names and the use of the third person pronoun,

---

[35]   Cathy Caruth, *Unclaimed Experience: Trauma, Narrative and History* (Baltimore, London: Johns Hopkins University Press, 1996), 4; original emphasis.
[36]   Fliora is a diminutive version of the name Florian.

the narrator suggests that the rupture with the past is unbridgeable; yet it is this precisely this rupture that defines him. Paradoxically, the life of Florian Petrovich has been both determined by the war—he "made it here", i.e. the origin from which he "exited" (*vyshel*) in order to arrive "here" is a constitutive but unnameable part of his biography—but he is also separated from his childhood experiences. In other words, he has created a psychological screen between the past and the present, and has kept himself in denial since the end of the war. Indeed, the trip to the Khatyn memorial is conceived as a form of reckoning with repressed memories, a "meeting with our own selves" (44). The central question *Khatynskaia povest'* poses is whether any sense can be made of suffering, and it answers firmly in the negative. Inscribing no redemptive value to wartime hardship, the novella meditates upon the fracturing of individual subjectivity for decades after the event.

The loss of psychological equilibrium is inscribed into the very fabric of the novella: the narration wavers between the present and past tenses, creating an effect of disorientation. For example, as the veterans come together in the post-war part of the story, the narrator-protagonist identifies his former comrades by their voices and reflects on individual characters:

> Kostia the Chief-of-Staff, with him an open field seems crowded: he nudges everyone, gives you a hug and makes you laugh. [...] Twenty-two or twenty-three years old... He was. But he is (was) loved: he knew what he was doing, he was a good fighter. (8)

Florian's chaotic mixing of the past and present tenses is a symptom of his trauma: unable to process the passage of time, he effectively relives the war as he contemplates it. He admits that "I perceive these people in the bus [to Khatyn] as mediators [*posredniki*] through whom I communicate, *as if with living people*, with the Kostia, Zuenok and Vedmed that I knew and saw many years ago" (43; original emphasis). In other words, to adapt a Freudian distinction, Florian does not *remember*, but mentally *repeats* conversations with his wartime comrades.[37] This conflation of temporal perspectives is further emphasized in the recollection of Florian's wartime memories: there is an uneasy alternation between past- and present-tense narration (for example, in adjacent scenes, "the Germans, who had been lying on their machine guns, prepared themselves, and a row of executioners [*karateli*] stepped away from the walls of the barn" vs. "they push us, press against us from somewhere beyond the well, next to the barn, machine guns rattle noisily, but even they do not drown out the human screams"; 127, 136). In such cases, the use of the present tense to describe past occurrences does not merely heighten the drama and tension; rather, the narrator's temporal slippage is a device that betrays the extent to which he is psychologically fixated on his terrible experiences.

In addition to presenting a traumatized narrator whose persona implicitly disputes the commemorative triumphalism of the Soviet state, *Khatynskaia povest'* also engages with official mythology through a mixing of genres. Adamovich's novella is an example of documentary prose,[38] superficially similar to the Khatyn texts by Andrushchanka and Bialevich. It opens with three epigraphs that contextualize the story as based on historical fact, including a set of documentary statistics on the number of villages burned in the BSSR during the war.[39] In addition, at the crucial moment in which Florian is about to be burned with a group of villagers, the story's narration shifts from the first-person account of its protagonist to direct quotation of historical testimonies: by Iosif Kaminski (see above) and other survivors of Nazi atrocities against civilians in Belarus, as

---

[37] Sigmund Freud, "Remembering, Repeating and Working-Through (Further Recommendations on the Technique of Psycho-Analysis II)", in *The Standard Edition of the Complete Psychological Works of Sigmund Freud*, ed. by James Strachey and Anna Freud, 24 vols (London: Hogarth Press and the Institute of Psychoanalysis, 1953–1974), XII, *Case history of Schreber, Papers on Technique and Other Works* (1958), 146–56.

[38] Adamovich published a number of works that hybridized prose fiction and documentary history, including his novels *Karateli, ili zhizneopisanie giperboreev* ("The Chasteners, or a Biography of the Hyperboreals", 1980) and *Blokadnaia kniga* ("The Book of the Blockade", co-written with Daniil Granin, 1977–81).

[39] Similar statistics were cited at the beginning of several works of official history, e.g. Lobanok *et al*, *Natsistskaia politika*.

well as written reports left by German soldiers. The effect is a dramatic morphing of realms, from fiction to recent history: Florian's suffering is told by people whose full names and places of residence are given. Their statements are full of despair and anguish, of the kind that was absent from official accounts. Thus, whereas in Andrushchanka and Bialevich, fact is fictionalized to corroborate official myth (and features no actual documentation despite claiming to be "documentary"), in Adamovich, an outwardly fictional novella is fused with fact to give voice to those whose experiences were obfuscated by the state. *Khatynskaia povest'* bears witness not to the Belarusian victims' Soviet patriotism, but to what its narrator calls the "terrible loneliness of death" (181).

The story finishes with a faint suggestion that remembering does bring some kind of healing. The end of Florian's narrative coincides with the characters completing an official tour of the Khatyn memorial: in this way, two parallel acts of memory are simultaneously brought to a close. Florian and his companions begin to leave, and "the sound behind us [of bells sounding regularly at the museum] becomes weaker, my stick, our steps, the voices of the walking group become louder and more usual [*gromche, pryvychnee*]" (198). Thus, the final outcome is the beginning of a process of normalization, which comes when the individual (Florian) has both faced up to his own torments (through the detailed and honest recollection of his wartime past) and mourned the loss of others (through ritual commemoration at a site of loss). The centrality of narrative to this process of atonement is instructive: the novella advances its own text as a necessary condition of its final positive outcome. In other words, *Khatynskaia povest'* can be read as a broader metaphor for the requirement that literature engage in the work of mourning in order for society to come to terms with the losses of the war. In Soviet Belarus, such mourning was necessarily subversive because of the state's reliance on a myth of triumph that precluded the development of a discourse of loss.

Khatynskaia povest' was one of a series of literary works that created a trend of "counter-memories", in the Foucauldian sense of a subjugated discourse that goes against the grain of hegemonic official history.[40] For instance, Adamovich also co-authored the book *Ia z vohnennai vioski* ("I Came from a Village Ablaze", with Ianka Bryl' and Uladzimir Kalesnik, 1975),[41] a non-fictional compilation of oral testimonies by survivors of incinerated villages. The book's emphasis on "raw", individual, oral testimony pre-empts Holocaust scholar Lawrence Langer's argument that redemptive narratives which attach meaning to suffering are unsustainable if spoken testimonies are taken into account.[42] Langer prioritizes oral testimony over the inevitable artificiality of written memoirs: the latter, through the array of literary devices used, strive to narrow "the abyss separating words from the events they seek to animate".[43] Arguably, the fragmented first-person narration of *Khatynskaia povest'* also strives to replicate the effect of a non-literary account; in *Ia z vohnennai vioski*, however, the unmediated pain of individual suffering is conveyed directly in hundreds of relived personal experiences. Five of these accounts are also presented in an audio recording that accompanies the book, allowing readers to perceive the tremor in survivors' voices.[44] There is also a clear hint that these testimonies have been manifestly ignored by the state's commemoration of the war. Adamovich, Bryl' and Kalesnik leave the last words of their preface to one of their survivors, who says: "And no-one knows that we had a disaster just like the one at Khatyn'. It's a good thing you came, for I'm alone... You see, I can't even tell you—I'm

---

[40] Michel Foucault, *"Society Must Be Defended": Lectures at the Collège de France, 1975-1976*, trans. David Macey (New York: Picador, 2003). For a concise analysis of Foucault's ideas see: José Medina, "Toward a Foucaultian Epistemology of Resistance: Counter-Memory, Epistemic Friction, and Guerrilla Pluralism", *Foucault Studies*, 12 (October 2011), 9-35.

[41] Ales' Adamovich, Ianka Bryl', Uladzimir Kalesnik, *Ia z vohnennai vioski* (Minsk: Mastatskaia litaratura, 1975). This book has been translated into several languages, including English—as *Out of the Fire* (Moscow: Progress Publishers, 1980).

[42] Lawrence Langer, *Holocaust Testimonies. The Ruins of Memory* (New Haven and London: Yale University Press, 1991).

[43] Ibid., 42.

[44] This took the form of a vinyl record in a sleeve attached to the book's cover.

crying...".[45] The people's ignorance and the witness's loneliness combine with the unspeakable trauma of wartime experience, and the breaking of silence emerges as a political act.[46]

Post-Soviet Polarization

In the aftermath of the collapse of the USSR, the state-sanctioned restrictions on discourse were lifted. As the horizons of permissible expression broadened, so the reconstitution of a de-Sovietized subjectivity within new political borders became a narrative imperative. In Belarus, the fact that heroic and traumatic discourses of memory had co-existed in the Soviet period was conducive to a proliferation of competing narratives about Khatyn after 1991. These fall into two broad categories, along political lines: state-sanctioned discourse continues to emphasize military triumph whilst also nationalizing the memory of the war,[47] and opposition accounts dispute both the veracity and the significance of the Khatyn myth. Whilst these renewed arguments about wartime atrocities typically claim to present historical *truth*, they are often equally concerned with *identity*: the re-appropriation or purported demystification of Khatyn is strategically linked to the narration of a post-Soviet Belarusian nationhood.

---

45   Adamovich *et al*, *Ia z vohnennai vioski*, 5.
46   Another example of Adamovich's struggle against official war memory is a documentary film for which he co-authored the script: *Khatyn', 5km* (dir. by I. Kolovskii, Belarusfilm, 1968) was never publicly screened in the USSR because its treatment of the Khatyn theme was considered too negative by state censorship. Other examples of Belarusian literary works that challenged the official narrative of civilian suffering during the war include Viktar Kaz'ko's novella *Sud u slabadze* ("A Village Trial", 1978) and Barys Sachanka's short stories *Daroha u Khatyn'* ("The Road to Khatyn'", 1983) and *Zabytyia selishchy* ("Forgotten Settlements", 1984).
47   The role of Second World War memory in contemporary Belarusian state discourse has been analyzed by several scholars, e.g.: Per Anders Rudling, "'For a Heroic Belarus!': The Great Patriotic War as Identity Marker in the Lukashenka and Soviet Belarusian Discourses", *Sprawy Narodowościowe* 32 (2008): 43–62; David R. Marples, *"Our Glorious Past": Lukashenka's Belarus and the Great Patriotic War* (Stuttgart: ibidem-Verlag, 2014).

Several scholars have argued that Belarus is unique among post-Soviet states in that a neo-Soviet narrative of nationhood remains a potent political force, alongside a revisionist Belarusian nationalism: according to this view, therefore, Belarusian nationhood is split between eastward- and westward-facing, or Eurasian and European, discourses.[48] The Russocentric narrative propounded by the Lukashenka regime holds that Belarusians were oppressed by the Poles and Lithuanians (conceived in ethnolinguistic terms) throughout pre-modern history, until the Russian Empire intervened at the end of the eighteenth century. In this account, the process of Belarusian self-realization began in harmonious union with Russia, and truly flourished in the Soviet period in which Belarus developed its own political and cultural institutions.[49] Meanwhile, a broad swathe of opposition activists and figures of culture conceive of Belarus as part of "pan-European" civilization: they insist on a civilizational border that separates Belarus from Russia and contrast the times of Tsarist and Soviet domination with an unambiguously positive era of national freedom that preceded them.[50] Whilst these dominant forms of Belarusian nationhood offer cardinally different views of identity, they are also similar in that a mythical notion of the past predominates in each. Belarusian identity is essentialized, historicized and totalized: it is condensed into a set of knowable and definable traits, treated as a historical constant with a linear past, and rendered an absolute category that tolerates no overlap with

---

[48]   David R. Marples, *Belarus: A Denationalized Nation* (London and New York: Routledge, 1999); Natalia Leshchenko, "A Fine Instrument: Two Nation-building Strategies in Post-Soviet Belarus", *Nations and Nationalism*, 10 (2004): 333–52; Nelly Bekus, *Struggle Over Identity: The Official and the Alternative "Belarusianness"* (Budapest, New York: Central European University, 2010); Alexandra Goujon, "Memorial Narratives of WWII Partisans and Genocide in Belarus", *East European Politics & Societies*, 24 (2010): 6–25.

[49]   See e.g. V.A. Mel'nik, *Osnovy ideologii belorusskogo gosudarstva* (Minsk: Vysheishaia shkola, 2009).

[50]   Perhaps the best textual example of this version of Belarusian nationhood is the book: Aleh Dziarnovich (ed.), *Naiias'neishaia Rech Paspalitaia. Tsyvilizatsyia—Kul'tura—Relihiia—Palityka—Avantura—Heroika—Uspamin* (Mensk: Lohvinau, 2007). A number of popular illustrated histories have also appeared that idealize the pre-Soviet past, e.g.: Uladzimir Arlou and Z'mitser Herasimovich, *Kraina Belarus'* (N.p: n.p., 2003).

other national identities.[51] Since the collapse of the Soviet Union, this polarizing politics of memory has engulfed Khatyn, generating competing interpretations of wartime victimhood.

The first steps towards the re-evaluation of Khatyn were made, in fact, during Perestroika: whereas the civilian massacres commemorated at Khatyn had previously been touted vaguely as "fascist" crimes, the identities of individual perpetrators were made public in a series of revelatory newspaper articles in late 1990.[52] It turned out that the individuals responsible included local collaborators, many of them Ukrainian national activists before and during the war.[53] Closed trials had been conducted for several individuals in 1973-75 and 1986, ending in death sentences, but collaboration was a taboo subject for official memory and knowledge on the subject was suppressed. The notion that the Soviet state had hidden the truth gained traction in revisionist accounts that proliferated after 1991. For example, a book entitled *Raspiataia Khatyn'* ("Khatyn Crucified", 2005) claims: "All these years they have been trying to convince us that Khatyn' died exclusively at the hands of the Nazis. Is it not time to tell the truth?"[54] A documentary film aired in 2008 makes a similar claim. Bearing the title *Prauda o Khatyni* ("The Truth about Khatyn'"), it advances four central arguments, each of which retrospectively debunks a major pillar of Soviet war-related mythology. The film tries to demonstrate that Khatyn' was destroyed by local collaborators; that those collaborators were former soldiers of the Red Army; that the partisans were culpable because they provoked the Nazis and their auxiliaries; and that the Khatyn memorial was planned in Moscow to cover up the truth about the Katyn massacre—the murder of 22,000 Polish military officers in

---

51   Graham Smith, Vivien Law, Andrew Wilson, Annette Bohr, Edward Allworth, *Nation-building in the Post-Soviet Borderlands. The Politics of National Identities* (Cambridge: Cambridge University Press, 1998), 15–16.

52   V. Roshchin, "Neizvestnaia Khatyn'", *Rabochaia tribuna*, 10 November 1990, 1, 3; V. Zdaniuk, "Khatyn' sozhgli politsai", *Vo slavu rodiny*, 20 November 1990, 3.

53   For detailed historical analysis see: Per Anders Rudling, "The Khatyn' Massacre: A Historical Controversy Revisited", *Holocaust and Genocide Studies*, 26 (2012): 29–58.

54   Elena Kobets-Filimonova, *Raspiataia Khatyn'* (Minsk: Bellitfond, 2005), 5.

1940 by the NKVD—by virtue of the two names' phonetic similarity.[55] In this reappraisal, Khatyn's importance to Belarusian memory is not disputed; rather, it is argued that as a symbol of grief, Khatyn has been distorted by Soviet ideology. As a *Dictionary of [Belarusian] Freedom* puts it, "during Perestroika Khatyn gradually took its place among the new symbols of the Belarusian tragedy."[56]

This re-examination of Khatyn is part of a commemorative economy in which other sites of memory—in particular, places where memory of Stalinist atrocities is enshrined—gain symbolic significance. The most prominent "rival" site is the Kurapaty forest on the outskirts of Minsk, a mass burial ground of victims of the NKVD which has been a major rallying point for political opposition groups since its discovery in 1988; the fact that the post-Soviet Belarusian authorities have refused to elevate it to the status of a major state memorial has been an issue of heavy contention.[57] A direct comparison between Khatyn and Kurapaty is made, for example, by publicist Sergei Vaganov, who in 2008 accused the state-owned media of shying away from "recognizing, at last, the tragic equality of Khatyn and Katyn,[58] of Khatyn and Kurapaty".[59] The application of

---

[55] *Prauda o Khatyni* (Belsat, 2008). The Katyn claim has been made by several historians, including Norman Davies in his *Europe: A History* (Oxford: Oxford University Press, 1996), 1005.

[56] "Slounik svabody", *ARCHE*, July 2000, http://arche.bymedia.net/7-2000/ch700.html (accessed 12 March 2015).

[57] In 1988, two Belarusian archaeologists caused a nationwide stir when they published a newspaper article announcing the discovery of mass graves at Kurapaty that contained the remains of victims of political murder carried out by the NKVD during the Stalinist Terror. See David R. Marples, "Kurapaty: The Investigation of a Stalinist Historical Controversy", *Slavic Review*, 53 (1994): 513–23; Alexandra Goujon, "Kurapaty (1937–1941): NKVD Mass Killings in Soviet Belarus", in *The Online Encyclopedia of Mass Violence*, 27 March 2008, http://www.massviolence.org/Article?id_article=182 (accessed 25 July 2014); Alexander Etkind, Rory Finnin, Uilleam Blacker, Julie Fedor, Simon Lewis, Maria Mälksoo, Matilda Mroz, *Remembering Katyn* (Cambridge: Polity, 2012), 81–86.

[58] In recent years, Katyn has become an increasingly important symbol of Belarusian memory, due in part to the fact that several thousand (as yet unidentified) victims of the Katyn massacre were killed in Belarus, and many victims are believed to have been natives of Belarus. See ibid., 84–86; Simon Lewis, "Vozmozhna li belorusskaia pamiat' o Katyni?", *Novaia Europa*, 24 April 2013, http://n-europe.eu/article/2013/04/24/vozmozhna_li_belarusskaya_pamyat_o_katyni (accessed 20 April 2015).

[59] Sergei Vaganov, "Po kom molchit kolokol", *Narodnaia volia*, 28 March 2008, 1.

a mnemonic arithmetic that generates "equality" between sites of Nazi and Stalinist terror is part of an anti-regime discourse that seeks to disinherit the Soviet legacy.

The Belarusian state authorities, on the other hand, have retained Soviet-style tropes of martyrdom and incorporated Khatyn into official memory as a symbol of national loss. The memorial complex underwent an expensive renovation in 2004, and is regularly commemorated in official speeches and publications. For example, in a speech delivered at the reopening of the memorial in July 2004, president Aliaksandr Lukashenka directly challenged the revisionist reappraisals of Khatyn: "Terrible were the corrosion and lies of nationalism, which devoured the memory of the glory and sacrifices of our people. But the Belarusian people has had its say, and its word is unshakable: the memory of our glory and sacrifices is untouchable!"[60] Lukashenka's characteristically contradictory rhetoric simultaneously demonizes "nationalism", associated with political opposition, and appeals to Belarusian national patriotism. In its insistence on both "glory" and "sacrifice", it draws closely on the Soviet hybridization of triumph and loss, whilst obscuring the actual history of the war by forging a neat identity divide between perpetrators and victims: "fascists bestially murdered peaceful citizens".[61] Moreover, the state attaches redemptive meaning to the suffering of the victims: "the martyrs of Khatyn' died thinking of our lives, of the immortality of our peoples!"[62] This neo-Soviet nationalization of civilian death is an important legitimizing instrument in the identity politics of the present day: it is designed to foster loyalty both to the regime and to the national narrative it propounds.

The current official Khatyn discourse is supported by a body of literature, for instance a book of oral testimony: *Nashchadki vohnennykh viosak* ("Descendants of the Burned Villages", 2009). Although it explicitly refers to its literary predecessor compiled by

---

60   "Vystuplenie Prezidenta Respubliki Belarus' A.G. Lukashenko pri poseshchenii Gosudarstvennogo memorial'nogo kompleksa 'Khatyn'" prezidentami Belarusi, Rossii i Ukrainy", *newsby.com*, 1 July 2004, http://www.newsby.org/news/2004/07/01/text11417.htm, accessed 20 March 2015.

61   Ibid.

62   Ibid.

Adamovich, Bryl' and Kalesnik, this collection differs greatly in that it has a clear propagandistic message: it is the fruit of a "patriotic initiative" designed to counter the "re-writing of the history of the Great Patriotic War—the history of national tragedy, national struggle and national Victory".[63] Its pages of personal histories of suffering at the hands of the "fascists" are overtly rendered as weapons in a memory war: they serve a dogmatic "truth of the war, to which there is no alternative nor can there be".[64] The truth in question is the "feat of the [Belarusian] people, who did not surrender, who rescued the country, Europe and the world from fascist occupation".[65] The author therefore takes heroic memory of victimhood to unprecedented heights, claiming messiah status for Belarus.

The polarization of Khatyn memory in the post-Soviet era is therefore a contestation of historical "truth" that aims to set the terms for defining the Belarusian nation. Yet a striking feature of this split is that neither major narrative aims to grapple with the complexities and contradictions of the wartime past. There is a meaningful difference between the Soviet-era mnemonic resistance of authors like Ales' Adamovich and the anti-state discourse after 1991: whereas the former exposed the glaring omissions of official mythmaking by indirectly appealing to personal experiences of suffering, the latter operates on the same terms as the state's glorification by producing competing unitary "truths". What is largely missing from the contemporary Belarusian discourse of wartime victimhood is, in the words of Holocaust scholar Dominick LaCapra: "judgment that is not apodictic or ad hominem but argumentative, self-questioning, and related in mediated ways to action"; such a mode of retrospection should be based on "distinctions that are not purely binary oppositions but marked by varying and contestable degrees of strength or weakness."[66] Amidst the black-or-white treatments

---

[63]   Tatstsiana Padaliak, *Nashchadki vohnennykh viosak* (Minsk: Litaratura i masta-tsva, 2009), 5.

[64]   Ibid., 144.

[65]   Ibid.

[66]   Dominick LaCapra, *Representing the Holocaust: History, Theory, Trauma*, (Ith-aca, NY and London: Cornell University Press, 1996), 210.

that instrumentalize Khatyn as a tool for the promotion or vilifica-
tion of Soviet-style identity models, the victims of war are under
threat of being consigned to oblivion.

Khatyn Transnationalized

Whereas Khatyn has become caught in a zero-sum game within Belarusian memory politics, it has recently received a more nuanced
treatment outside the country: a novella by Czech author Jáchym
Topol adds a comparative and transnational dimension to the
memory of wartime loss. *Chladnou zemí* ("Through a Cold Land",
2009; translated into English as *The Devil's Workshop*, 2013)[67] is
composed of two halves: the first part is set in the former Nazi concentration camp of Terezín (Theresienstadt) in the Czech Republic,
and the second in Belarus, in Minsk and Khatyn. Although it refers
to real historical events and places, the novella is a grotesque fantasy
and an allegory of memory. The structure and framing of the novella
imply a necessary link between the horrors of the twentieth century
in different European countries, in particular the Holocaust, Nazi
atrocities on the Eastern front and the Stalinist Terror; yet at the
same time, the story's content problematizes the preservation of
memory. The novella creates a tension between competitive and
cosmopolitan memory, warning against the vested interests and
narrow horizons that can compromise transnational efforts to come
to terms with pan-European disaster. Topol's commentary on
Khatyn can be interpreted in terms of Michael Rothberg's proposal
that "we consider memory as *multidirectional*: as subject to ongoing
negotiation, cross-referencing, and borrowing; as productive and
not privative."[68] Khatyn emerges from *Chladnou zemí* as a potentially vital node of an expansive memory dialogue that may help Europe to achieve reckoning with its violent past.

---

[67]   Here, the English translation is cited: Jáchym Topol, *The Devil's Workshop*,
trans. by Alex Zucker (London: Portobello Books, 2013); further references to
this novel are given after quotations in the text, parenthetically.

[68]   Michael Rothberg, *Multidirectional Memory: Remembering the Holocaust in the
Age of Decolonization* (Stanford: Stanford University Press, 2009), 3; original
emphasis.

The story's first-person narrator, a young man whose name is never revealed, grows up in present-day Terezín. Inspired by "Uncle" Lebo, a camp survivor who takes it upon himself to preserve the material remains of the town's terrible past, the protagonist becomes an expert in memorialization: the two of them, with a gradually expanding circle of supporters, transform the deserted town into a vast monument to the war dead that attracts thousands of tourists and global media attention. The Czech state authorities see the new memorial as a threat, and destroy it by force, using bulldozers. At this climactic moment, the narrator-protagonist is recruited by a pair of Belarusians, who plan to use his expertise and contacts to create a similar museum in Belarus. They lure him to Minsk, from where he will help to promote a new memorial at Khatyn.

In Belarus, however, it is not the state, but the advocates of commemoration who pose a threat to memory. According to the Belarusian memory activists, their new Khatyn should be a global symbol for Belarusian national martyrdom, a martyrdom that encompasses murders by the Stalinist NKVD, the Holocaust, and wartime Nazi atrocities against Belarusian civilians. They are resentful and uncompromising, and they conceive their narrowly nationalistic project in purely competitive terms: "They say all the death camps were in Poland. That's bullshit! All the tour operators only go to Auschwitz! But that's going to change" (96); "the Katyn massacre was a walk in the park compared to this [mass executions of Belarusians by the NKVD]" (98). Moreover, as is gradually revealed to the protagonist's horror, his hosts will go to brutal and extraordinary lengths to achieve their aims: the "museum" they have started to create employs mechanized and mummified corpses of individuals who experienced wartime atrocities. These macabre puppets of memory bear witness to the events they have "survived" by reproducing their oral testimony in their original human voice. The biggest cause of alarm for the protagonist is the discovery that the Belarusians have murdered his friend Lebo and turned him into such a mechanized doll: this revelation acts as the trigger that convinces the narrator-protagonist of the need to flee. The story ends with him in hiding, in peril but nonetheless full of hope. The final sentences read as follows: "We'll make it somewhere. Save ourselves. Yeah, it might work out" (159).

The novella's open and optimistic ending appears to intimate the possibility of healthier, more open-ended memory models prevailing, despite the brutal horrors of the Belarusians' attempts at memorialization. In the closing pages, the narrator-protagonist encounters a German woman named Ula, who is researching the wartime history of the region and whose efforts are aimed at achieving both historical understanding and penitent mourning. Ula's father had been responsible for the wartime massacre of an entire Soviet village (i.e. an equivalent of Khatyn'). He committed suicide after the war, and Ula was left with the burden of coming to terms with his crimes: "There's no way to understand the cruelty. Our minds aren't equipped for it. But it dawned on me that I had to balance out the horror myself. [...] I became a researcher. And it helped me" (156). Significantly, Ula studies not German crimes against Soviet civilians (i.e. the atrocities of her father's generation), but the Stalinist murders in the 1930s and early 1940s at NKVD killing fields in Belarus, which have been hushed up by the government. Ula's memory work, in other words, seeks to mollify her own trans-generational perpetrator guilt by bridging the different mid-twentieth-century traumas that affected Eastern Europe. Unlike the Belarusian museum creators, who see Khatyn solely in terms of "our" losses, Ula understands the historical complexities of the fact that the victims of both Stalinism and Nazism were of various nationalities:

> Was it Soviets killing Soviets, or Germans murdering Soviets and Jews, or Germans and Soviets killing other Soviets? Then on top of that, consider that here they were divided into Belarusians and Russians and Ukrainians and Ruthenians, and of course there were also Poles and Balts [...]. (154)

Thus, the introduction of Ula at the story's end counterbalances the preceding episodes in which Belarusian memory activists strive to indiscriminately appropriate all of the different victims under the unified sign of Belarusianness. Ula advances an imperative to conceptualize both history and identity in all their contradictoriness, an imperative also accepted by the narrator-protagonist. The "we" of the novella's closing sentences, cited above, refers to an emerging partnership and understanding between the two characters, which can also be understood as a bonding of memories: their nascent friendship symbolizes an intertwining of the memories of the Holocaust (Terezín), Nazi atrocities against non-Jewish civilians (Khatyn and other sites in Belarus, including the massacre committed by Ula's father), and the crimes of the Stalinist NKVD.

Topol's novella has not been translated into Belarusian or Russian,[69] and it is perhaps not surprising that the author himself has expressed an apprehension about the potential reception: Topol has admitted he is "afraid" of the reaction a translation will receive, as he fears he may "insult the Belarusian reader".[70] Yet despite the unfavorable portrayal of the principal Belarusian characters, the central idea of Belarus as a vital depository of memory about the recent past, memory that must be released from the clutches of politicized forgetting and commemorative manipulation, reveals a profound concern with the legacy of the war and totalitarianism in Belarus. By structurally linking Belarusian memory to the site of Terezín through a Czech youth and his German companion, *Chladnou zemí* invites readers to engage in a transnational dialogue about the meaning of the terrible past; meanwhile, through its satirical grotesquerie, it indicates the dangers of declining to participate in such dialogue. Topol's novella can therefore be read as an antidote to the polarization and instrumentalization of Khatyn memory in today's Belarus. Mikhail Bakhtin wrote that:

> The resistance of a unitary, canonic language, of a national myth bolstered by a yet-unshaken unity, is still too strong for heteroglossia to relativize and decenter literary and language consciousness. This verbal-ideological decentering will only occur when a national culture loses its sealed-off and self-

---

69 Anon., "'Belaruski' raman chekha Iakhima Topala pakul' ne zatsikaviu vydautsou u Belarusi", *Radyio Svaboda*, 27 September 2010, http://www.svaboda.org/content/article/2169019.html (accessed 25 July 2014).

70 Cited in Anon., "Chekhi pishuts' pra Belarus'", *news.21.by*, 29 July 2010, http://news.21.by/culture/2010/07/29/118009.html (accessed 25 July 2014).

sufficient character, when it becomes conscious of itself as only one among *other* cultures and languages.[71]

The "unitary canonic language" of the Soviet martyrdom myth has maintained a strong grip on contemporary Belarusian memory of the Second World War, shaping the contours of debate on both sides of the political divide. However, Topol's engagement with Khatyn points towards the viability of a pluralistic, "decentered" and open-ended attitude to the past: *Chladnou zemí* suggests that by abandoning competitive martyrdom and recognizing the interrelations and commonalities shared by sites such as Khatyn, Katyn and Kurapaty, Belarus would be better equipped to overcome the joint legacy of Nazi occupation and Soviet domination.

Conclusion

A recent analysis by Serguei Oushakine argues that Khatyn is an example of "postcolonial estrangement" in the post-socialist Belarus, whereby the articulation of a narrative of victimhood is said to demonstrate Belarusian culture's inability to "carv[e] out in colonial history a space untouched by the imperial presence".[72] Oushakine describes the ruptures within Belarusian memory, including the competing versions of Khatyn that have proliferated since Perestroika, and concludes that the common desire to locate Belarusian identity in a space "between Stalin and Hitler" is a symptom of "perpetual alienation between different enemies".[73] This treatment amounts to a normative diagnosis based on historical judgment: it implies that Belarus *should* recognize Stalinist and Nazi atrocities as a constituent part of its national history, rather than external impositions—and suggests that if the country does not do so, it must be

---

[71]   Mikhail Bakhtin, *The Dialogic Imagination: Four Essays*, ed. Michael Holquist, trans. by Caryl Emerson and Michael Holquist (Austin, TX: University of Texas Press, 1981), 370; original emphasis.

[72]   Serguei Alex. Oushakine, "Postcolonial Estrangements: Claiming a Space between Stalin and Hitler", in *Rites of Place*: *Public Commemoration in Russian and Eastern Europe*, ed. Julie Buckler and Emily D. Johnson (Evanston, IL: Northwestern University Press, 2013), 285–314 (308).

[73]   Ibid., 301.

"estranged" from its own past. A major constituent flaw of Oushakine's argument is that it fails to differentiate between political actors: it treats official Soviet mythmaking and literary works by Ales' Adamovich as part of the same monolith, and lumps together statements made by Lukashenka and opposition figures. The result is a methodological fallacy: because this analysis mistakes antagonistic narratives within a diachronically developing socio-political field for a single confused voice, it imagines a jumbled and irrational claim to Belarusian victimhood.

The above examination has shown that any estrangement of memory is not in fact a function of Belarusian self-alienation, but a historically contingent product of the ideological hegemony of the myth of martyrdom. The Soviet authorities in Belarus sought to maintain a symbolic monopoly over war memory in order to construct a narrative of Belarusian loyalty to the Soviet project. This involved the multiplication of tropes of heroic death and devoted sacrifice, which obscured the suffering of thousands of individuals in Belarus. In the late Soviet period, such personal experiences were given voice by works of literature that foregrounded trauma rather than triumph. In the aftermath of the collapse of the USSR, attempts to loosen the hold of Soviet martyrdom were continued, but memory has been polarized between a nationalizing neo-Soviet version of the war and revisionist attempts to de-Sovietize memory. Yet as Jáchym Topol shows, historical victimhood is not neatly sealed within national categories, and memory need not be either. Since a defining quality of Soviet mythmaking was the creation of a closed and totalized truth, the overcoming of martyrdom will involve a process of opening up, both spatially and conceptually.

CONFERENCE REPORT

The Political Cult of the Dead in Ukraine (Munich, 9–11 July 2015)

"The Political Cult of the Dead in Ukraine" was the topic of an international conference held, in cooperation with the University of St. Gallen, at the Ludwig Maximilian University of Munich on 9–11 July 2015. In their welcoming speeches **Guido Hausmann** (Munich) and **Carmen Scheide** (St. Gallen) pointed out not only the topicality of research on the political cult of the dead in Ukraine in relation to the Euromaidan in 2013/14 and the Ukrainian–Russian war in the east of the country. They also stressed the effects these recent events have had on the historical research within Ukraine itself. The purpose of the conference was therefore to enable a deeper understanding of and provide new analytical approaches to Ukrainian traditions of the political cult of the dead in their regional dimensions and to place the human sacrifices and victims of the Euromaidan within a broader historical context.

The first panel on "The Concept and the Formation of the Political Cult of the Dead in the Ukrainian Lands in the First Half of the 20th Century" was opened by **Guido Hausmann**. In his presentation he asked how to apply the concept of the political cult of the dead to the history of Ukraine. He pointed out that Western European concepts used for Eastern Europe and Ukraine in particular might not be able to explain the political cult of the dead in Ukraine. To understand existing distinct Ukrainian traditions in commemoration we have to consider the historical–political traditions, religious differentiation, the strong role of the regions, and the low level of national and cultural integration of and within the country. In addition, we also need to challenge the received idea of a strict civil–military divide in Ukraine.

Christoph Mick (Warwick) showed in his presentation how interwar Poland gave meaning to war and how it alienated the Ukrainian and the Jewish minorities in the process. In Poland, in contrast to Western Europe, the First World War played no role in the official state remembrance. Memory practices focused on the battles the new Polish state fought with neighboring countries over its borders. The 1919 battle for Lviv played an especially big role in the development of a political cult of the dead which focused totally on Polish victims and blended Ukrainian victims out. Therefore Ukrainians were not able to identify with this cult, and this in turn strengthened the idea of an independent Ukrainian state in the region.

The last presentation in this panel was delivered by **Andryj Ljubarec** (Kyiv). Ljubarec questioned the traditional concept of a dualistic vision of modern Ukrainian cultural memory and disclosed the high level of instrumentalization and politicization of the memory of the 1918 Battle of Kruty, fought between Bolshevik and Ukrainian People's Republic forces. The discourse about this battle in Ukrainian society has changed several times. At first, in 1918, the Ukrainian government tried to ease criticism about its responsibility for the death of the fighters by reburying some of them. In the 1930s, nationalists celebrated Kruty as a victory, and they continue to do so today. Under Viktor Yushchenko's presidency the commemoration of the battle was encouraged in the form of "rally-requiems" on several occasions. The speaker used this example to illustrate the changes in commemoration depending on the political context.

The second panel about "The Legacy of World War II in and beyond Ukraine" was opened by **Serhy Yekelchyk** (Victoria), who analyzed the evolving Soviet politics of memory concerning World War II at the Eternal Park of Glory in Kyiv. He showed how, after a short period without centralized memory politics, the commemoration was taken over by the Soviet state under Stalin. The subsequent construction of the first memorial to the Unknown Soldier in 1957 can in turn be seen as a part of Khrushchev's de-Stalinization. The memorial and the surrounding park became the symbolic center of war remembrance in the Ukrainian SSR. Under Brezhnev however, a new memorial park was built and opened in 1981, since the Western concept of the Unknown Soldier and the connected rituals proved incompatible with the celebration of Soviet military power. In independent Ukraine under Viktor Yushchenko the Eternal Park of Glory was redefined as a memorial site by the construction of a monument and a museum to the victims of the Holodomor.

Ekaterina Makhotina (Munich) showed in her presentation how official monuments and memorials to fallen soldiers were used to make (monumental) sense of World War II in the Soviet Union and in post-Soviet Russia. She demonstrated that the process of forming memory by memorials in the Soviet Union was much more eclectic and ambiguous than centralized and state-controlled. In the second part she presented how the materialized memory in post-Soviet Russia (was) changed, through its geopolitical instrumentalization, from the victory of the Soviet people to a victory and triumph of the Russian state.

How independent Ukraine dealt with its communist heritage in material and spiritual forms was the topic of **Oleksandra Gaidai**'s (Kyiv) presentation. Her research focused on the removal of Lenin statues in post-Soviet Ukraine. She delineated how the public opinion towards these statues was conditioned by political circumstances and identified different phases which were mostly not characterized by state policy, but rather depended on local authorities. The "Leninfall/Leninopad" of 2013/14 was, however, directly connected to the Euromaidan and shows how the "forgotten" Lenin statues in the cities were now "rediscovered" as a symbol of Soviet–Russian oppression.

Kateryna Kobchenko (Kyiv) illuminated how female soldiers of the Red Army were celebrated as heroines of World War II and highlighted the transformation of these political cults of the dead in contemporary Ukraine. She identified the function of the war heroines as the symbolic personification of the Motherland and a means to popularize women's participation in the war, which was important, and to demonstrate the new possibilities the Soviet state had opened up for women. The celebration of women as heroes/heroines of war is still visible in independent Ukraine. But with the construction of a modern national war narrative, a "ukrainization" of the heroes and heroines of World War II has occurred, which has also meant the rehabilitation of women who had been stigmatized as enemies by the Soviet state.

The third panel on the Soviet legacy in Ukraine was opened by **Oksana Myshlovska** (Geneva) with a presentation on the Bandera Cult in Western Ukraine from 1991 to 2015. Within the past twenty years the commemoration and monumentalization of Bandera has moved beyond the areas where he lived and which are directly connected to him. He was even promoted to a national hero in 2010 by President Yushchenko. Before the Euromaidan, the popularization of Bandera was influenced by the Svoboda party on various occasions such as marches and rallies. Symbols and slogans of the OUN (Organization of Ukrainian Nationalists) and UPA (Ukrainian Insurgent Army) were used for mobilization during the Euromaidan but reinterpreted and integrated into new rituals, especially with the commemoration of victims of the Euromaidan and the "Anti-Terrorist" Operation in Eastern Ukraine. At the same time there is, due to the heroization, no space for questioning controversial issues at the local level.

Polina Barvinska (Odesa) analyzed the uses of the past via the example of the remembrance of fallen Soviet soldiers and sailors in today's Odesa. The commemoration of the defenders and liberators was always strongly celebrated in the city, especially since Odesa was one of the first four cities to be honored as Hero Cities in the Soviet Union. Since the independence of Ukraine the glorification of the dead soldiers of World War II has undergone a transformation. Next to the state, new actors play a role in this process, and the dedicated memorials in Odesa are used by various groups, often with opposing world-views and values. For example, the nationalization of the commemoration in Odesa led to clashes with pro-Soviet activists. Since 2014 however, it is possible to forecast the de-communization, but, evidently, not the de-heroization of the Soviet soldiery, who defended and liberated Odesa, and this will surely lead to yet another transformation of the city's commemorative landscape and practices.

The regional diversity in the commemoration of the fallen soldiers of the Soviet–Afghan war in Ukraine was the topic of the presentation by **Iryna Sklokina** (Lviv/Kharkiv). Her research focused on the Zhytomyr, Kharkiv, and Donbass regions. She showed how the organized movement of *afhantsi*, despite the negative image of Afghan war in 1991, managed to form a positive commemorative culture around them in the context of a new national historical narrative. Her presentation also highlighted the regional differences

in the commemoration, which was influenced by transborder cooperation with Russian Afghan veterans' societies in the Kharkiv region until the Euromaidan. At the same time there is a common motif in the commemorations in Ukraine. The *afhantsi* are strongly
connected with the veterans of World War II—they are seen as their
descendants, but also as the "fathers" of the new veterans of the Euromaidan and the "Anti-Terrorist Operation" in Eastern Ukraine.

The panel was closed by **Mariana Hausleitner** (Berlin) who
focused on the multicultural commemoration in the city of Cherniv-
tsy since 1993. She analyzed different phases in the history of the
commemoration of the city's past. Before World War II, 40 percent
of the city's population was Jewish. Most of the Jewish population
were killed in the Holocaust, which led to a rise of the Ukrainian
population from 10 to 80 percent, due to the influx of Ukrainians
into the city. Under the Soviet state the multicultural history of the
city was not part of the official state memory. However, the independence of Ukraine has brought about the commemoration not
only of the Jewish past, but also of the German and Romanian history of the city: different memorials to Jewish, German and Romanian authors, funded by foreign donations, were erected after 1991.
At the same time the former fighters of the OUN and UPA, some of
whom collaborated with the Wehrmacht, are celebrated as martyrs
for the country's independence. Consequently, it is hard to predict
which aspects and versions of the regional history will be given pref-
erence in the near future.

The presentation by **Andriy Portnov** (Berlin) on post-Maidan Dnipropetrovsk opened the last panel of the conference, which
focused on "Ukraine in Revolution and War 2013–2015". His research
showed how the city surprisingly became the bastion of civic
Ukrainian nationalism after the annexation of Crimea by the Russian Federation and the outbreak of the war in the neighboring Donbass oblast. He demonstrated how different grass-roots, private and
to some degree also state actors played an important role in the formation of the pro-Ukrainian nationalism which was accompanied
by the removal of some, but not all, Soviet memorials. Sketching out
an agenda for further research, he argued that there was a need for
Ukraine to develop a new analytical language to describe itself and

be described—a language which might acknowledge heterogeneity and contestation as not necessarily a sign of weakness.

Olesya Khromeychuk's (East Anglia) speech focused on the dilemmas of remembering World War II nationalist military organizations in contemporary Ukraine in the case of the Waffen-SS "Galicia" Division. She demonstrated how the division has been included in the mnemonic landscape since 1991 but only as fighters who played a marginal part in the country's independence. She also highlighted how the most recent events such as the laws "On the Legal Status and Honoring the Memory of Fighters for Ukraine's Independence in the Twentieth Century" have reinforced the division's peripheral place since it has been neither openly excluded from nor included in the heroic narrative. Khromeychuk showed how this approach to the memory of Ukrainian collaboration leads to problems in the deeper understanding of the historical events as well as for reconciliation between the different veterans of World War II and their descendants in today's Ukraine.

The thanatological discourse of the Revolution of Dignity in Ukraine was the topic of the last presentation by **Milena Milenina** (Kyiv). Her research analyzed oral tributes commemorating victims of the Euromaidan protests, mostly given during funeral dinners or cemetery visits. These texts bear similarity to folk necrotic texts of the modern city including biographical stories about the deceased. The biographies of the deceased were construed by the interpreters' assessment of the Euromaidan. There was also a recognizable shift in support towards the Euromaidan movement after the events on Instytutska Street, during which several people were killed, which also had an influence on the oral texts. Also a change within in the texts dedicated to the Heavenly Hundred is visible since the Euromaidan was victorious and the new government officially recognized them as heroes. But especially their biographical data united the conflicting approaches to the interpretation of the Euromaidan.

In the final discussion several central aspects emerged. First of all, participants raised the question of whether the civil–military divide, which was obviously important for the historical observation, especially in the case of Soviet commemorations, is still useful for researching contemporary political cults of the dead in Ukraine

and in other countries as well. Another key question was the definition of the political. Is there a strict divide, and does it make sense
to separate political and public cults of the dead, or should the idea
of "hybrid" cults taken in consideration? Also, the term "sacrifice"
should be defined more precisely, since there is a divide between a
personal sacrifice and a person being sacrificed by someone else. Another outcome of the conference was that we can hardly, in the case
of memorials, speak of a distinct Soviet–Ukrainian political cult of
the dead. In addition the lack of research on political cults of the
dead in rural areas was seen by many participants as a problem
which should be tackled in future research. Overall, the conference
provided a good opportunity for an exchange between international
scholars. It also showed that there are many topics concerning the
political cult of the dead in Ukraine still to be researched. A publication containing the respective contributions is to follow.

Michael Störk
Master's student of East European Studies
Ludwig Maximilian University of Munich

De-Mythologizing Bandera:
Towards a Scholarly History of the Ukrainian Nationalist Movement

Stepan Bandera (1909–59), the leader of the radical Ukrainian nationalist movement, is, perhaps, the most controversial figure in the history of Ukraine. One has only to compare the titles of some of his biographies, *Stepan Bandera—Symbol of Revolutionary Determination*, by Petro Mirchuk;[1] *Stepan Bandera—a Life Dedicated to Freedom*, by Mykola Posivnych;[2] and, finally, *Stepan Bandera: The Life and Afterlife of a Ukrainian Nationalist: Fascism, Genocide, and Cult* by Grzegorz Rossoliński-Liebe, published by *ibidem* in 2014.[3] In this collection of review essays, we use Rossoliński-Liebe's recent book as a departure point for a wider discussion on the current state of the historiography on Bandera and on Ukraine's recent past more broadly.

Who was Stepan Bandera: an uncompromising revolutionary, a freedom fighter, or a fascist and an ideologue of "genocidal nationalism"? Not only historians, but also ordinary Ukrainians diverge radically in their answers to this question. As opinion polls demonstrate, of all historical figures about whom respondents are asked, Bandera divides Ukrainians most of all (the figures who most unite Ukrainians in negative attitudes are Vladimir Putin and Joseph Stalin).[4]

The style and the content of the Ukrainian debates on Bandera resemble the Russian polemics of the 1860s about the hero of

---

[1]   Petro Mirchuk, *Stepan Bandera—symvol revoliutsiinoii bezkompromisovosty*, 2nd ed. (New York and Toronto: Orhanizatsiia Oborony Chotyriokh Svobid Ukrainy, 1992).

[2]   Mykola Posivnych, *Stepan Bandera—zhyttia, prysviachene svobodi* (Toronto and L'viv: Litopys UPA, 2008).

[3]   Grzegorz Rossoliński-Liebe, *Stepan Bandera: The Life and Afterlife of a Ukrainian Nationalist: Fascism, Genocide, and Cult* (Stuttgart: ibidem, 2014).

[4]   "Nostalgia for the Soviet Union and the Attitude to Particular Personalities", *Rating Group Ukraine*, 5 May 2014, http://ratinggroup.ua/en/research/ukr aine/nostalgiya_po_sssr_i_otnoshenie_k_otdelnym_lichnostyam.html (accessed 30 November 2015).

Ivan Turgenev's *Fathers and Sons*, the essence of which one critic summaries as follows: "Is Mr Turgenev's Bazarov a caricature that should be ridiculed, or is he an ideal that should be emulated?"[5] In the same way, contemporary debates about Bandera and his associates are mostly confined to the question whether they were fascist criminals who should be branded with shame, or national heroes to whom monuments should be erected and whose example should serve for the education of today's youth.

In other words, a war of two historical myths is being waged (or a war between myth and anti-myth) with the characteristic binary opposition of light and darkness, with no gray in between. In the mythologized historical consciousness, Stepan Bandera, his Organization of Ukrainian Nationalists (OUN) and the Ukrainian Insurgent Army (UPA) are either placed on the totally light or the completely dark side; there is no middle ground.

The book by Rossoliński-Liebe that is the subject of discussion in the current issue takes the debate on Bandera to a new and more academic level. As noted by one of the reviewers, Yuri Radchenko, this book is the first academic biography of Bandera, and that is the greatest achievement of its author. At the same time, it continues and develops the tradition of historiography of the OUN that aims at "exposing" its darker side. Over several hundred pages the author argues that Bandera and his OUN were not actors in the national liberation movement, but rather fascists, racists, and organizers of mass killings of civilians. However, unlike previous journalistic attacks on Bandera, his followers and activities, Rossoliński-Liebe's book has a solid foundation in theory and archival sources, meaning that the apologists of the leader of the OUN will no longer be able to simply dismiss it as a piece of "anti-Ukrainian propaganda".

In this introduction I will not analyze in detail the contents of the book, as this has been done meticulously elsewhere in this issue

---

5   Dmitrii Ivanovich Pisarev, "Posmotrim!" (1865), available at http://az.lib.ru/p/pisarew_d/text_1865_posmotrim.shtml (accessed 30 November 2015).

by André Härtel and Yuri Radchenko. I shall focus on just one fundamental question that forms the main point of my differences with
both the author and the reviewers.

Both Rossoliński-Liebe and the two reviewers agree on the
characterization of the OUN as a fascist movement and, subsequently, of Bandera as a fascist leader. Indeed, in the late 1930s and
early 1940s the OUN had much in common with the fascist movements. Certainly, the concept of "Ukrainian fascism" has a right to
exist as one possible explanatory scheme, since it undoubtedly offers
plausible explanations for certain facts.

A certain methodological reservation must be made here.
When we claim that this or that political movement was fascist, we
do not reveal its "true" nature, but simply use a chosen typological
scheme in order to place the movement under investigation in a
comparative context. Thus, those who consider the OUN to be a fascist organization therefore suggest that a) we will understand the
ideology and practices of the OUN better if we compare it with the
Italian National Fascist Party, the National Socialist German Workers' Party, the Romanian Legion of the Archangel Michael, etc., than
with the political movements of any other type; b) we will understand the phenomenon of fascism better, if, in addition to the above
organizations, we also include in our analysis the OUN.

In my view, both of these assumptions are misleading. The
OUN's ideology and practices do correspond to some interpretations within the framework of the theory of "generic fascism", yet
these are all based on the study of ultra-nationalist movements in
nation-states. Serving as it does to elide the fundamental differences
between the nationalist movements of nations with and without
states, the concept of "Ukrainian fascism" ultimately generates more
theoretical and practical problems than it helps to solve. According
to this logic, using the framework of fascism, one would have to construct a subcategory of "national liberationist fascism", which would
seem to be a contradiction in terms.

Rossoliński-Liebe apparently senses this logical contradiction, as he consistently uses scare quotes for phrases such as "liberation movement" and "liberation struggle" in relation to the OUN
and the Ukrainian Insurgent Army. Thus, for example, he writes that

the "'liberation struggle' or 'liberation war' practiced by the OUN and UPA could not have been liberation because it was not necessary to kill several thousand civilians to liberate Ukraine" (p. 541). Yet in fact there is no reason why atrocities against civilians should necessarily preclude the recognition of the OUN as a national liberation movement. Such practices were more often the rule than the exception in the history of twentieth-century national liberation movements, and in this respect the OUN was fairly typical.

Historian John-Paul Himka's approach is more consistent, as he does not consider the national liberationist nature of the movement to be an obstacle to recognizing it as fascist. He asks a rhetorical question: "Does the fact that OUN was also a national liberation movement make it not fascist? The Ustashe was also a national liberation movement—was it too not fascist? The Viet Cong was a national liberation movement—was it therefore not communist?"[6]

In other words, according to Himka, a national liberation struggle can be combined with any ideology, including fascism. Indeed, certain well-known historical national liberation movements adopted liberal, conservative, socialist, communist, and other doctrines. Does this mean that the national liberation struggle is innately un-ideological? Such a claim would suggest that nationalism is not an ideology. However, nationalism is an ideology, albeit of a kind different to liberalism, communism, and so on. Unlike the latter, nationalism in itself does not contain a vision of the future socioeconomic and political system. It focuses on achieving and maintaining the "autonomy, unity, and identity" of the population that is considered to be a "nation".[7] Therefore, in order to be a fully-fledged ideology, able to mobilize the masses, nationalism must borrow elements from other social and political doctrines. Through this process combinations are formed such as liberal, conservative, or socialist nationalism, national-communism, etc.

---

6   John-Paul Himka, "The Organization of Ukrainian Nationalists and the Ukrainian Insurgent Army: Unwelcome Elements of an Identity Project", *Ab Imperio*, no. 4 (2010): 87.
7   Anthony D. Smith, *Nationalism: Theory, Ideology, History*, 2nd ed. (Cambridge: Polity, 2010), 9.

However, unlike liberalism or communism, *fascism itself is an extreme form of nationalism* (Rossoliński-Liebe partially agrees with this, although his explanation of the relationship between these concepts (pp. 33–34) is not distinguished by clarity or consistency). Therefore, when considering the relationship between fascism and national liberation movements, an internal typology of nationalism should be taken into account, in particular the division of nationalisms into those of stateless nations and nations with a state. The former group considers the national revival as, first of all, the overcoming of oppression, and the creation of one's own state; for the latter group, the national revival means the strengthening of the state, filling it with "real" national content, and sometimes also the cleansing of the national community of "hostile" elements, external expansion, imperialism, and national messianism. Undoubtedly, the first type of nationalism can turn into the second. Yet the abstract and theoretical arguments about what the state will be like acquire practical significance only after the first task of achieving the state has been fulfilled. When we employ the term "fascism" for nationalist movements of nations with and without states, we elide the important differences between them.

Rossoliński-Liebe not only rejects the classification of the Ukrainian nationalist movement as national-liberationist, but also spurns the much more neutral term "integral nationalism", which, starting with John A. Armstrong's 1955 monograph,[8] has been widely adopted in the historiography as a label for the OUN's ideology. Rossoliński-Liebe puts forward two main arguments justifying his position here:

> First, neither did the OUN use the term "integral nationalism," nor did it identify itself with the ideology of integral nationalism. Second, the OUN and its leaders did not claim the "traditional hereditary monarchy" and a

---

[8]   John A. Armstrong, *Ukrainian Nationalism, 1939–1945* (New York: Columbia University Press, 1955); idem, *Ukrainian Nationalism*, 2nd ed. (New York: Columbia University Press 1963; reprint, Littleton, CO: Ukrainian Academic Press, 1980); 3rd. ed. (Englewood, CO: Ukrainian Academic Press, 1990). See also: idem, "Collaborationism in World War II: The Integral Nationalist Variant in Eastern Europe," *Journal of Modern History*, 40, no. 3 (1968): 396–410.

number of other features typical of integral nationalism, as did Maurras, the father of this ideology (p. 25).

Even if the first statement were accurate, it would be difficult to consider it a compelling argument. After all, the fact that members of the OUN did not call themselves fascists and even officially objected to this term does not prevent Rossoliński-Liebe from labeling them as such. In any case, in actual fact the author is mistaken: the OUN activists, albeit infrequently, did use the term "integral nationalism" to define their ideology—Iulian Vassyian did so in 1928,[9] for example, and so did the newspaper *Nash Klych* (Our Call) in 1933.[10] The OUN's detractors from the Ukrainian Catholic camp also used the term (in a negative sense).[11]

Rossoliński-Liebe's second objection is equally unconvincing, since the concept of "integral nationalism", which was introduced into academic usage by Carlton J. H. Hayes,[12] has long ceased to be associated with monarchism in the style of Charles Maurras. Its meaning as used by Hayes and Armstrong is essentially synonymous with the concept of "ultranationalism", which Rossoliński-Liebe, following Roger Griffin and Stanley G. Payne, includes in his list of the criteria for fascism (pp. 29–30, 33).[13]

While I do not reject the concept of "Ukrainian fascism" out of hand, I would argue that this is not the most accurate or useful description for the OUN and Bandera. Instead, I propose that they

---

9   Iu. Vassyian, "Do holovnykh zasad natsionalizmu", *Rozbudova Natsii*, 1 (1928), ch. 2, p. 40; reprinted in Oleh Protsenko, Vasyl' Lisovyi (eds.), *Natsionalizm: Antolohiia* (Kyiv: Smoloskyp, 2000), 206.
10   S. O., "Soiuznyky bol'shevyzmu", *Nash Klych*, 14 May 1933, p. 3. It is possible that the cryptonym "S. O." was used by Bandera's close ally, Yaroslav Stets'ko.
11   "Borot'ba z neistnuiuchymy nebezpekamy", *Meta*, 26 March 1933, p. 1.
12   Carlton J. H. Hayes, *The Historical Evolution of Modern Nationalism*, 3rd ed. (New York: Russell and Russell, 1968), 164–224.
13   See Roger Griffin, "Introduction", in *World Fascism: a Historical Encyclopedia*, vol. 1, eds. Cyprian P. Blamiers with Paul Jackson (Santa Barbara, CA: ABC-CLIO, 2006), p. 2; Andreas Umland, "Zhirinovskii as a Fascist: Palingenetic Ultra-Nationalism and the Emergence of the Liberal-Democratic Party of Russia in 1992–93", *Forum für osteuropäische Ideen- und Zeitgeschichte*, 14, no. 2 (2010): 195.

be viewed as instances of what I call *ustashism*.[14] That is, they should be viewed in the context of the revolutionary ultranationalist (integral-nationalist) movements of stateless nations, such as the Croatian Ustaša (before 1941), the radical wing of Hlinka's Slovak People's Party (before 1939) or the Internal Macedonian Revolutionary Organization. Movements of this type had certain features in common with fascism, but their primary aim was not reorganization of an existing state according to totalitarian principles, but the creation of a new state, using all available means, including terror, to this end. The history of the Ustaše movement shows that if the conditions are "favorable", ustashism can evolve into real fascism. This did not eventuate in the Ukrainian case because the Nazis dispersed Stets'ko's government and imprisoned Bandera and other leaders of the OUN in 1941, thereby preventing a repeat of the Croatian scenario in Ukraine.

It should be emphasized that the radical ethnic nationalism of the OUN, although it differed from fascism, was not more humane or less prone to violence. This is evidenced time and again by Rossoliński-Liebe's findings, which describe in detail the mass violence the OUN and the UPA perpetrated in relation to Poles, Jews and Ukrainians during the war, although this had no direct relation to Bandera, who at this time was imprisoned in a German concentration camp. Therefore, André Härtel is right when he writes below that:

> While ongoing debates about the differences and similarities between Ukrainian radical nationalism and e. g. German National Socialism or other fascist movements might be fruitful for the general conceptual delineation between nationalism, ultranationalism, and fascism, they should not lead to a relativization of the inhumane, xenophobic, and totalitarian character and policies of the OUN/UPA before and during the Second World War.

On the other hand, one cannot reduce the activity of the OUN and UPA *only* to xenophobia and totalitarianism, forgetting about

---

[14]   For further info see Oleksandr Zaitsev, "Fascism or Ustashism? Ukrainian Integral Nationalism in Comparative Perspective, 1920s–1930s", *Communist and Post-Communist Studies*, 48, nos. 2–3 (June–September 2015): 183–193.

their lasting struggle against the even more inhumane and totalitarian Soviet regime, which for most participants was a struggle for freedom.

The main problem with Rossoliński-Liebe's arguments is not the fact that he considers the OUN and Bandera to be fascists—such an explanatory diagram may have a certain heuristic value— but rather that his *a priori* scheme often prevails over his facts. I do not agree with Yuri Radchenko when he criticizes Rossoliński-Liebe below for having failed to use this or that source. In fact, the source base of the book is more than sufficient, and in any case covering all possible sources on such a broad topic is simply impossible. What matters is how the historian uses his sources while selecting and interpreting the facts.

As I have argued elsewhere, a conscientious historian must take into account not only those facts that support his working hypothesis, but also the ones that do not.[15] Unfortunately, Rossoliński-Liebe is not always sufficiently scrupulous in observing this rule. At times the text reads as though he were consciously or unconsciously adjusting the facts to fit into an *a priori* scheme of "fascism", "racism" and "genocidal nationalism". He rightly points to the elements of racism in certain brochures written by OUN members, yet he ignores the criticism of Nazi racism which appears in a number of other texts, in particular, in the official OUN publication, *Rozbudova Natsii*.[16] He sees fascism everywhere, even in the greeting "Glory to Ukraine!", groundlessly attributing its invention to a small and little-known Ukrainian Union of Fascists (pp. 34, 563), when in actual fact it had been widespread back in the time of the Ukrainian Revolution of 1917–20,[17] that is, several years before the formation of the Union

---

15   See further my forthcoming review of Rossoliński-Liebe's book in *European History Quarterly*.

16   Ievhen Onats'kyi, "Ideol'ogichni i taktychni rozkhodzennia mizh fashyzmom i natsional-sotsializmom", *Rozbudova Natsii*, nos 5/6 (1934): 142–149; idem, "Kul't uspikhu", *Rozbudova Natsii*, nos. 7/8 (1934): 162-169. See also V. Obukhovych [Stepan Okhrymovych], "Vid vydavtsiv" [a foreword to the translation of the extracts from Hitler's *Mein Kampf*], *Tsentral'nyi derzhavnyi arkhiv vyshchykh orhaniv vlady ta Upravlinnia Ukrainy*, f. 3833, op. 2, spr. 40, ark. 3.

17   See for example Sviatoslav Shramchenko, "Liniinyi korabel'-drednavt Chornomors'koi Flioty 'Volia': Istorychnyi narys", *Litopys Chervonoi Kalyny*, XI, no. 5

of Ukrainian Fascists. Citing documentary sources, he uses the translation "totalitarian power of the Ukrainian nation" (p. 181), even though the word "totalitarian" is not present in the original, which instead refers to the "sovereign, indivisible, total [*povna*] power of the Ukrainian people".[18] Contradicting his own declaration in the Introduction, where he states that "the study does not suggest that all Ukrainians who were in the OUN or UPA were fascists or radical nationalists" (p. 48), in later chapters the author often depicts the OUN as an ideological monolith, which it was not. Fascism, Nazism, anti-Semitism, totalitarianism, terror had both their supporters and critics in the ranks of the organization, yet the author carefully cites only the supporters.

However, the demand for complete objectivity is a utopian one: it is simply unachievable for a single researcher. As Karl Popper wrote, "science and scientific objectivity do not (and cannot) result from the attempts of an individual scientist to be 'objective', but from the friendly-hostile co-operation of many scientists. Scientific objectivity can be described as the inter-subjectivity of scientific method".[19] This is also a fair statement in relation to history as a "critical human science".[20] That is why the "friendly-hostile" discussion of the different interpretations of the phenomenon of Bandera in an academic environment is necessary if we are to move towards a more accurate account of the history of Ukrainian nationalism.

Yet the Bandera problem also has significance that goes far beyond academic debates. It is important for understanding the current problems and the possible scenarios for the future development of Ukrainian society. Times of revolution and social transformation

---

(1939): 7; Vsevolod Petriv, *Viis'kovo-istorychni pratsi. Spomyny* (Kyiv: Polihraf-knyha, 2002), 556–7, 603; Iurii Horlis-Hors'kyi, *Kholodnyi Iar: Dokumental'nyi roman*, 10th ed. (Kyiv and Drohobych: Vidrodzhennia, 2008), 31.

[18] Orest Dziuban (ed.), *Ukrains'ke derzhavotvorennia: Akt 30 chervnia 1941: Zbirnyk dokumentiv i materialiv* (L'viv and Kyiv: Piramida, 2001), 25.

[19] Karl R. Popper, *Open Society and Its Enemies* (Princeton and Oxford: Princeton University Press, 2013), 424.

[20] Jo Guldi and David Armitage, *The History Manifesto* (Cambridge: Cambridge University Press, 2014).

always produce a process that Hayden White calls "retrospective ancestral constitution".[21] This process consists in society's rejection of the old "ancestry" and choosing of new "ideal ancestors", whose activity they consider a model for the present and for the building of an ideal future. A similar process has been taking place in Ukraine, starting with the time of *perebudova* (*perestroika*) and the collapse of the USSR, and the Euromaidan has given it a new impetus. Ukrainian society is getting rid of the old, Soviet-imperial "ancestry", and establishing (or reviving) an alternative "ancestry". This has been and continues to be associated mainly with the carriers of (real or imagined) democratic traditions: from the Zaporizhzhian Cossacks to the Soviet-era dissidents. However, with the aggravation of the problem of geopolitical and civilizational choice (with Europe or with Russia?), the nationalists and historians associated with them are attempting with ever greater persistence to impose their own list of "ideal ancestors" on Ukrainians, with Bandera, the OUN and UPA most prominent among them. At the same time, they do not understand, or do not wish to understand, that such an "ancestry" severely impedes not only integration into the European Union, but also the consolidation of the Ukrainian nation.

In his exclusive emphasis on the "fascist", "racist" and "genocidal" nature of the Banderite movement, and his complete denial of the presence of liberationist and democratic elements within it, Rossoliński-Liebe goes to the other extreme. Yet he is certainly right to argue that the cult of Bandera, which is currently prevalent in western Ukraine, is an important factor that has prevented Ukrainians from critically reassessing their history. Ukraine needs a radical demythologization and desacralization of its past, and the first academic biography of Stepan Bandera, for all its shortcomings, will surely contribute to this, at least through encouraging broad academic and public discussions of the kind featured here in this journal.

Oleksandr Zaitsev
Ukrainian Catholic University, L'viv

---

[21]   Hayden White, *The Fiction of Narrative: Essays in History, Literature, and Theory, 1957–2007* (Baltimore, MD: Johns Hopkins University Press, 2010), 132–5.

Bandera's Tempting Shadow: The Problematic History of Ukrainian Radical Nationalism in the Wake of the Maidan

Gregorz Rossoliński-Liebe's biography of Stepan Bandera, the leader ("Providnyk") of the "Organization of Ukrainian Nationalists" (OUN/OUN-B) from 1940–59, arrives at a time when debates about Ukrainian nation-building, the legitimate role of the Ukrainian state in writing a "national historical narrative", and finally the appropriate reference points for such a narrative in Ukraine's uneasy history have taken on international significance.[1] Ukraine's current post-revolutionary context and the war against Russian-supported separatism have provoked Ukrainian elites and the general public alike to sharpen the historical image of a "political nation" trying to finally find itself. In such a violent and unstable environment, the temptation to resort to and highlight the more radical phases, actors, and organizations of a nation's history—an understatement in the case of Bandera and the OUN, as Rossoliński-Liebe's study demonstrates—is understandably big. Therefore, any such deep and genuine scholarly contribution to the study of the history of Ukrainian nationalism should be warmly welcomed by Ukrainian and international audiences.

The book is as much a biography of Bandera as it is a history of Ukrainian nationalism and its main institutional proponents in the 1930s and 1940s. It furthermore covers Bandera's "afterlife" beyond his assassination in 1959 and discusses the considerable impact of his "personal cult" on post-Soviet Ukraine's political culture. After introducing Bandera's life prior to his assumption of a leading position in the OUN, the author discusses the role of two crucial trials during the early 1930s, which in many ways became the origin of the

---

[1]   See for example the letter by many renowned international and Ukrainian historians and other scholars asking President Petro Poroshenko not to sign the "De-Communization Laws" of 9 April 2015, and the subsequent scholarly debate at krytyka.com, available at: http://krytyka.com/en/articles/open-letter-scholars-and-experts-ukraine-re-so-called-anti-communist-law.

"Bandera cult". In the second part, Rossoliński-Liebe provides a detailed account of the "Ukrainian National Revolution" initiated by
the OUN simultaneously with the German attack on the Soviet Union in 1941, whose final aim was the creation of a totalitarian and
monoethnic Ukrainian state. The latter part of this chapter and the
chapter following it focus on the systematic extermination of Poles
and Jews in Eastern Galicia and Volhynia during the Second World
War and discuss the pivotal role of both the OUN and UPA in the
organization and legitimization of genocide. This longer section
concludes with a chapter on the brutal war between Ukrainian nationalists and the Soviets after 1944, which resulted in tens of thousands of dead on both sides and around 200 000 deported Ukrainians by the mid-1950s. The third part of the book studies Bandera and
the cult around him from four different perspectives: his personal
life, beliefs, and politics up to his assassination; his role in Soviet
propaganda; the growing "Providnyk"-cult, especially in the diaspora community, after his death; and the impact the OUN leader
and the ideology of his movement have had on post-Soviet Ukraine.

The "Providnyk" and the Individual's Role in History

While it is generally a difficult task to assess an individual's historical contribution, the question of Bandera's agency when it comes to
OUN "homeland" activities in the 1930s and 1940s is especially difficult to answer. Because the "Providnyk" spent almost the entire period under study in prisons, camps, under home arrest abroad, or in
exile, his impact, especially on terrorist activities and ethnic violence, requires extensive explanation and a discussion of what are
often highly subjective sources. Yet Rossoliński-Liebe manages to
demonstrate how Bandera's early fascination for fascism and the
radicalism with which he promoted a racially "pure" Ukrainian state
(from p. 106) led to his justification of mass murder for the sake of
"liberating" the Ukrainian nation at the L'viv trial in 1936 (p. 159),
and to the ultimate call for systematic ethnic violence against "Muscovites, Poles, and Jews" in a crucial 1941 document entitled "The
Struggle and Activities of the OUN in Wartime" (p. 181). Notwithstanding those legal facts, Rossoliński-Liebe rightly argues that the

"moral, ethical and political responsibility" weighs more heavily in Bandera's case, especially considering that he never condemned or even regretted the results of his "Ukrainian National Revolution" (p. 239).

Another crucial factor supporting an interpretation of Bandera as a key historical actor with a strong influence on the OUN movement is the considerable "cult" which apparently elevated the "Providnyk" to the status of an almost superhuman being in the eyes of his followers (p. 98). The cultish adoration of the OUN leader seems to have its roots especially in his charismatic behavior at the Warsaw and L'viv trials and in the narrative of Bandera's "suffering for the national liberation" in prisons abroad (p. 285), an episode which tends to be somewhat exaggerated by his followers. The "cult" but also the special conditions of arrest mostly granted to Bandera during the war provided him with almost unchallenged authority and ample opportunity to continue to exert leadership and to communicate with his subordinates throughout this period. The cult even went so far as to claim that, after the end of the Second World War, the "Providnyk" was still able to use his aura to deceive Western security agencies about his then waning influence and thereby gain their considerable financial and informational support (from p. 330). From 1944 onwards even Soviet propaganda contributed to an equation between Ukrainian nationalism and the "banderovtsy" (p. 405), and thus helped to reinforce the cult.

Cleaning Up All Myths: the OUN's Ideology and Systematic Ethnic Violence

The central contribution of the book is however the deep study, evidence, and coherent interpretation Rossoliński-Liebe provides on the mass atrocities committed by members of the OUN-B, the UPA (Ukrainian Insurgent Army), and other Ukrainian radical nationalist and paramilitary formations during the Second World War. Because OUN and UPA veterans, Bandera himself, and also many Ukrainian and even international historians have managed and manage to the present day to negate the atrocities and portray the actors as morally and politically unassailable "fighters for freedom and liberation" (see

Chapter 10), such an informed clean-up is still deeply necessary and timely. Systematic ethnic violence, especially against Jews and Poles, Rossoliński-Liebe argues, was well prepared ideologically by the OUN/OUN-B. Following its main ideological "spin-doctors", Dmytro Dontsov and Mykola Stsybors'ky, the "OUN actively put the anti-Semitic components of the ideology of Ukrainian nationalism into practice" (p. 81) and programmatically prepared a fascist totalitarian dictatorship with rights granted to "ethnic Ukrainians alone" (p. 83).

In 1941, the OUN, with its "National Ukrainian Revolution", began to implement its program of the ethnic cleansing of Ukrainian territory, supported by factors such as the German attack on the Soviet Union and the Nazis' own genocidal plans, but also the preceding NKVD terror against ethnic Ukrainians. Rossoliński-Liebe convincingly demonstrates how Ukrainian militia, "established and co-ordinated" by the OUN-B (p. 200), and other OUN-dominated formations such as the "Nachtigall batallion" systematically killed Jews in "well-organized" pogroms and mobilized the Ukrainian population to take part (pp. 212-13). Although Rossoliński-Liebe mainly has to rely on hitherto neglected testimonies of Jewish, Polish, and Ukrainian survivors to prove his claims, there are also plenty of official documents demonstrating how Ukrainian radical nationalists wanted to "solve" the "Jewish problem" (p. 218). This also holds true for the deliberate ethnic cleansing of Poles in Eastern Galicia and especially Volhynia from 1943 on, when "(...) the UPA was the army that the OUN-leaders expected to 'cleanse' the Ukrainian race" (p. 268). While it is also acknowledged that Polish formations were engaged in a considerable amount of anti-Ukrainian atrocities at the time, the author convincingly shows how the OUN and UPA had learned from the Germans' genocidal actions how to "annihilate an entire ethnic group in a relatively short time" (p. 260) and used the same practices to systematically kill between 70 000 and 100 000 Poles by 1945 (p. 271). In short, Bandera and his movement longed as much for the implementation of a completely inhumane, totalitarian, and racist order as they did for Ukrainian national liberation.

Ukrainian Radical Nationalism in Comparative Perspective

On that basis, the author also makes considerable efforts to explain the fascination of many Ukrainians with the "Bandera cult" right up to the present day. Especially for the growing but also very diverse Ukrainian diaspora after the war, the "Providnyk" and the memory of the OUN and UPA's fight for "national liberation" seem to have become necessary symbolic and cultish objects for preserving a sense of unity and durability during the Cold War (Rossoliński-Liebe calls them "charismatic communities", p. 416). Yet, the question remains how much of the contemporary defense and even admiration of many ordinary Ukrainians and Ukrainian historians for Bandera and the OUN/UPA is acceptable. An answer to this question can only be found by analyzing Ukrainian radical nationalism in the larger context of other European ultranationalist and fascist movements of the inter-war and war periods and by reflecting on the historical memory of all Ukrainians.

There are indeed some points one should consider before equating Ukrainian radical nationalism too easily with both German National Socialism and Italian Fascism. First, the special ferocity and growing fanaticism of Ukrainian radical nationalism during the inter-war and war periods become more explicable if one considers the specific experiences of Ukrainians during the 1930s: the famine caused by Stalin's collectivization, Polish discrimination, and the NKVD terror and deportations. It is also an established fact that the Western Ukrainian lands had been the heart of what Timothy Snyder famously called the "bloodlands", where reciprocal ethnic cleansing and genocide led to almost entire de-humanization on all sides during the Second World War.[2] Second, while German and Italian fascisms were revolutionary movements aiming at a total reorganization of existing states, Ukrainian radical nationalism was first of all about acquiring statehood—a claim which was moreover violently opposed by Poles, Soviets, and also Germans.[3] Finally,

---

[2]   See Timothy Snyder, *Bloodlands. Europe Between Hitler and Stalin* (New York: Basic Books, 2012).

[3]   Some scholars claim that the lack of a Ukrainian state distinguishes the OUN/UPA from fascism and fascist movements of the inter-war and war period and allows a classification of it as "Ustashism" instead. See Oleksandr Zaitsev,

Ukrainian radical nationalism was, as Rossoliński-Liebe repeatedly points out, a Western Ukrainian phenomenon (pp. 243–44). Ukrainians from Central and Eastern Ukraine, who shared the cruel "camp-like" reality of the "Reichskommissariat Ukraine" during the Second World War,[4] did not sympathize with the OUN and were occasionally even targets of its terror.

Therefore, it seems hardly appropriate to simply equate the OUN, which was and is understood by many Ukrainians first of all as a national liberation movement, with the Nazis. Nor is it appropriate to expect Ukrainians today to apply the same "*Tätervolk*" ("Nation of Perpetrators") attitude to themselves as for example the Germans do. However, it speaks volumes about the treatment of history in present-day Ukraine when even a "liberal group" of contemporary Ukrainian historians tends to "romanticize" OUN-UPA violence and/or sees Bandera and his movement solely in the perspective of the country's ongoing fight for sovereignty (see the discussion from p. 519).[5] The ideological and political similarities of the OUN/UPA to fascist movements of the time are still too obvious to warrant such an interpretation. Notwithstanding the OUN's prior quest for national liberation, neither its most important ideologists nor Bandera himself ever left any doubt that a future Ukrainian state should be a totalitarian dictatorship based on fascist principles.[6] For those aims, ethnic cleansing and genocide were seen as legitimate means by the "Providnyk" and the rest of the OUN/UPA leadership. Consequently, while ongoing debates[7] about the differences and similarities between Ukrainian radical nationalism and e.g. German

---

"Fascism or Ustashism? Ukrainian Integral Nationalism in Comparative Perspective, 1920s–1930s", *Communist and Post-Communist Studies* (2015, in press).

4   See Karel Berkhoff, *Harvest of Despair. Life and Death in Ukraine Under Nazi Rule* (Cambridge, MA: Harvard University Press, 2004).

5   On this contested issue see further Yuri Radchenko's review in this issue.

6   The OUN leadership "democratized" its official program only after it became clear that Germany would lose the war and that the fate of the movement and a future Ukrainian state would depend on the Western allies instead. However, as Rossoliński-Liebe demonstrates, these changes were mostly of a pseudo-nature, while Bandera in particular seems to have never distanced himself from his inter-war and wartime convictions; see pp. 264–65 and 346.

7   See for example Zaitsev, "Fascism or Ustashism", and Alexander J. Motyl, "On Nationalism and Fascism, Part One", *World Affairs Journal*, 10 June 2013, http://world affairsjournal.org/blog/alexander-j-motyl/nationalism-and-fascism-part-1.

National Socialism or other fascist movements might be fruitful for the general conceptual delineation between nationalism, ultranationalism, and fascism, they should not lead to a relativization of the inhumane, xenophobic, and totalitarian character and policies of the OUN/UPA before and during the Second World War.

Bandera, the OUN and Post-Maidan Ukraine

Almost inevitably, Rossoliński-Liebe's book is also a valuable contribution to debates among political scientists interested in post-Maidan Ukraine, in the increasingly heterogeneous development of the post-Soviet space, and in the still highly interconnected politics of memory and identity formation of the region. For example, it raises the question of the degree to which contemporary Ukrainian voters are still attracted by radical right-wing ideologies and parties such as the Svoboda Party,[8] or how Ukrainian nationalist debates were affected by the experience of independence in 1991, by the transformation of the modern Ukrainian state ever since, and finally by the war against Russian-supported separatism since 2014.[9] What value system lies behind the now supposedly more consolidated political nation, and how does it perceive its neighbors? Moreover, it is disturbing to see how much Rossoliński-Liebe's reflections on the significance of propaganda and counter-propaganda in the inter-war and war periods have in common with the propaganda or "media wars" carried out by Russian or pro-Russian and to some degree pro-Ukrainian officials and media-outlets of the present.[10] What are the

---

[8]   Based on survey data, Lena Bustikova for example argues that the pre-2014 support for Svoboda was a result mostly of voters' fears related to the character of the Ukrainian state under the Yanukovych regime and of economic threats, rather than of distinguished ideological positions. See Lena Bustikova, "Voting, Identity and Security Threats in Ukraine: Who supports the Ukrainian 'Svoboda' Party?", *Communist and Post-Communist Studies* (2015, in press).

[9]   Here, Ivan Gomza has lately made a contribution, whose methodology and approach could also be used for an analysis of the Ukrainian nationalist movement after 1991 or the war in the Donbass. See Ivan Gomza, "The Elusive Proteus: A Study in Ideological Morphology of the Organization of Ukrainian Nationalists", *Communist and Post-Communist Studies* (2015, in press).

[10]   See e.g. the related contributions in the first issue of this journal devoted to "The Russian Media and the War in Ukraine".

medium- and long-term political consequences of war propaganda, and how successful are current civil-society-led projects and campaigns to counter propaganda and establish a liberal and ethically committed media space? Finally, what role will the history of Ukrainian nationalism and specifically Bandera and the OUN play in the understandable endeavor of Ukraine's post-Maidan government and society to sharpen the historical image and memory of the nation?

While studies conducted by Rossoliński-Liebe and other scholars have generally called into question the standard Ukrainian image of Bandera and the OUN as "fighters for national liberation", there is another major reason why the "Providnyk" and his movement are not suitable reference points for any national historical narrative: there is still hardly any other topic which is so divisive between Western and Eastern Ukrainians as radical Ukrainian nationalism or Bandera and the OUN.[11] While it is almost unavoidable under current Ukrainian circumstances that history should be excessively used for political purposes, acting politicians should be aware of how much damage playing with the "national card" will do to the apparently newly found national consensus. Although it is true that the Ukrainian political nation seems to extend much further geographically than many observers thought before 2014, this consensus surely does not include a shared interpretation of Ukraine's past. Yet, with his signature under the controversial "De-Communization Laws" of 9 April this year,[12] current President Poroshenko unfortunately missed an opportunity to separate historical debates from contemporary politics and risks making the country's history a divisive issue again.

André Härtel
Friedrich Schiller University of Jena

---

[11]   See e.g. Ivan Katchanovski, "Terrorists or National Heroes? Politics and Perceptions of the OUN and the UPA in Ukraine", *Communist and Post-Communist Studies* (2015, in press).

[12]   Poroshenko signed the "De-Communization Laws" on 15 May 2015, under: http://www.rferl.org/content/ukraine-poroshenko-decommunization-law/27019045.html.

From Staryi Uhryniv to Munich: The First Scholarly Biography of Stepan Bandera[*]

The thought that Ukrainian society is still far from a scholarly discussion on the role of the figure of Stepan Bandera in the history of Ukraine and Eastern Europe struck me yet again during a visit to L'viv in April 2015. During my stay, I made a return visit to the "Prison on Lonts'kyi Street" Museum, with the aim of finding out whether the exposition there had changed at all since my last visit in summer 2010. A quick survey of the museum revealed that little had changed, but I did happen upon an event being held in the same building: the launching of a brochure by Mykola Posivnych devoted to the life of Stepan Bandera.[1] The author's talk ran for roughly an hour and was mostly hagiographical in nature. Posivnych failed even to touch upon the problem of the OUN's participation in crimes against Jews, Poles, and Ukrainians who did not share their views. Moreover, judging by the questions from the floor following the presentation, the audience gathered there fully supported this version of Bandera's biography. In response to my questions about the anti-Semitic component in the OUN's ideology, Posivnych, and several individuals from the audience, cited "arguments" and "sources" that remained on the methodological level of debates from back in 1991.

---

[*] This text is an expanded and revised version of an article originally published on the *Ukraïna Moderna* site under the title "Vid staroho Uhryniva do Miunkhena: istoriia ta spadok. Persha naukova biohrafia Stepana Bandery", 16 May 2015, http://uamoderna.com/md/radchenko-bandera-biography-review. It is based on research enabled by the support of the L. Dennis and Susan R. Shapiro Fellowship (Center for Advanced Holocaust Studies, United States Holocaust Memorial Museum), the European Holocaust Research Infrastructure Fellowship (Zentrum für Holocaust-Studien, Institut für Zeitgeschichte, Munich, Germany), the Petro Jacyk Visiting Fellowship and the Anne Tanenbaum Centre for Jewish Studies (CJS) Visiting Fellowship at University of Toronto, as well as a stipend from the German Historical Institute in Warsaw. I am grateful to Per Anders Rudling, Yaroslav Hrystak, and John-Paul Himka, for valuable advice during the writing of this article.

[1] Prezentatsiia knyhy Mykoly Posivnycha "Stepan Bandera" v "Tiurmi na Lonts'koho", 5 April 2015, http://prostir.museum/ua/event/3075.

Unfortunately, despite all the political, historical, and pseudo-historical discussions over the past quarter of a century following the fall of communism in Ukraine, not a single(!) scholarly biography of Stepan Bandera has ever been written in Ukraine. As the saying goes, nature abhors a vacuum, and so it is foreign scholars who have taken up the study of Bandera's biography. This study by Grzegorz Rossoliński-Liebe, a post-doctoral fellow at the Berlin Free University, published in 2014 in Stuttgart, is a case in point. This book comprises the author's doctoral dissertation. While I have a complicated personal attitude towards the author as a speaker/lecturer,[2] he is to be commended for undertaking the first ever attempt at a scholarly biography of Bandera, as well as an analysis of the historical memory of Bandera in the Ukrainian diaspora and in independent Ukraine. When I received this book by post in January this year, the first thing that struck me was its size. The book is 652 pages long, and 559 of these comprise solid text. Even by German scholarly standards, Rossoliński-Liebe has produced "a weighty tome".

Both a quick glance and a careful reading of the book will confirm that Rossoliński-Liebe has examined a large volume of archival sources, and that he is clearly also very well-versed in the historiography, not only in English, German, and Polish, but also in Ukrainian and Russian. In the course of researching the book, the author worked in German, Polish, Ukrainian, US, Canadian, and British archives. At the same time, there are some important gaps here when it comes to archival research. For example, while Rossoliński-Liebe did conduct archival work in Kiev, he nevertheless did not utilize documents from the OUN Archive, which contains a large number of Melnykite documents, including those devoted to the 1920s-40s. Although the book does contain references to the Provincial Archives of Alberta, Rossoliński-Liebe did not (at least, according to the book's references) work in many of the Canadian archives holding useful information for researchers on this topic. Of course, it would be impossible for one individual to cover all of Canada's archives, especially given that documents connected to the Ukrainian

---

[2]   See further Yuri Radchenko, "Pro ukrains'kyi "radykal'nyi natsionalizm", "fashyzm", "natsional-bil'shovyzm" ta kul'turu dyskusii", *Ukraïna Moderna*, http://uamoderna.com/blogy/yurij-radchenko/liebe-bandera.

diaspora are dispersed widely across the expanses of that huge country and the travel costs that this would entail. This being said, materials in the Peter Potichnyj Collection on Insurgency and Counter-Insurgency in Ukraine, which is held in the Thomas Fisher Rare Books Library (Toronto)[3] or the "Oseredok" Ukrainian Cultural and Educational Center archive (Winnipeg)[4] could have shed additional light on the questions raised by Rossoliński-Liebe in this book.

While Rossoliński-Liebe's book does contain references to "oral history" materials, he has made scant use of this type of sources here. For example, the author ignores almost entirely the Shoah Foundation database and the collection of interviews conducted by Patrick Desbois' team at Yahad-In Unum. The Shoah Foundation database comprises a collection of interviews with Jews who lived through the Holocaust, and also with the Righteous Among the Nations. It was created in the 1990s, but in many respects it is invaluable when it comes to studying the OUN's attitude towards Jews. The Yahad-In Unum collection is made up of interviews with non-Jewish witnesses of the Holocaust. These sources mostly comprise eyewitness accounts recorded in the late 2000s. It is a widely known fact that the majority of "Ukrainian" eyewitness accounts of the events of the summer of 1941 in Galicia and Volhynia deny the occurrence of pogroms or the participation of OUN-created structures in any such actions. Sources from this collection sometimes yield very useful data for researchers. For example, one Melnykite asserted that a pogrom did take place in L'viv in the summer of 1941, but, and this is the interesting part, he attributed its execution not to the "Ukrainian People's Militia" created by the government of Yaroslav Stets'ko, but to the "Nachtigall" battalion which was subordinate to the Abwehr.[5] Rossoliński-Liebe's takes an uncritical approach to some "recollections" cited in the book, such as Yevgenii Nakonechnyi's *Shoa u L'vovi*.[6] The author of this book was ten years old in 1941, and it is very likely that he based these "recollections" on family narratives rather than his own experience and its interpretation.

---

3   http://www.library.utoronto.ca/fisher/collections/findaids/potichnyj.pdf.
4   http://www.ukrainianwinnipeg.ca/oseredok/.
5   United States Holocaust Memorial Museum (USHMM), RG-50.589.0187.01.01.
6   Yevhen Nakonechnyi, *"Shoa" u L'vovi: spogady* (Lviv: Piramida, 2006), 286 pp.

Rossoliński-Liebe's book is divided into ten chapters. The author analyzes the history of the Ukrainian radical right during the interwar period, Bandera's political development, the "Ukrainian national revolution" of 1941, the OUN's crimes during the war, Bandera's post-war activities, and the Bandera cult in the Ukrainian diaspora and in independent Ukraine up until the end of President Viktor Yushchenko's rule. Not all sections of the monograph are equally successful when it comes to originality of research and analysis. The best is the fourth chapter, devoted to the events of the summer of 1941, when the OUN made an attempt at realizing the idea of "Ukrainian national revolution" and, collaborating with the Germans and taking part in pogroms of Jews, tried to create their own state. The least successful is the fifth chapter, in which Rossoliński-Liebe attempts to analyze the events of 1941–43, when Bandera was no longer in Ukraine. Particularly unsuccessful are the parts of the monograph devoted to the crimes perpetrated by OUN military formations against Poles and Jews. In these sections the author mostly cites other scholars and offers no original analysis of the events under discussion.

Characteristic of Rossoliński-Liebe's texts and statements is a disrespectful attitude towards studies of the history of the OUN produced in Ukraine or by Ukrainians. His monograph on Bandera displays similar tendencies. The book includes quite a long introduction setting out the metholodological, conceptual, terminological and theoretical framework. On pages 26–33 Rossoliński-Liebe analyzes the highly politicized issue of the correlation between the OUN's ideology and European fascism. It is telling that here the author cites many scholars of nationalism (including scholars from Eastern Europe), but makes no mention whatsoever, for example, of the discussion between Oleksandr Zaitsev and Taras Kurylo conducted in the liberal L'viv internet publication Zakhid.net.[7] Judging by his bibliography, Rossoliński-Liebe is familiar with Zaitsev's

---

Taras Kurylo, "Shche raz pro OUN ta fashyzm", *Zaxid.net*, 15 March 2012, http://zaxid.net/home/showSingleNews.do?shhe_raz_pro_oun_ta_fashizm&objectId=1250264; Oleksandr Zaitsev, "OUN i fashyzm: sim tez do dyskusii", *Zaxid.net*, 30 March 2012, http://zaxid.net/home/showSingleNews.do?oun_i_fa shizm_sim_tez_do_diskusiyi&objectId=1251429.

monograph on the history of the Ukrainian radical right during the interwar period. In this book, which is based on years of work in a range of archives and libraries, Zaitsev set out his theory that there exists a specific type of integral nationalism, which he calls "Ustash-ism", and which has the capacity to be transformed into "fully-fledged" fascism upon creation of an independent state. This is an original if problematic idea,[8] but what is indicative here is the fact that Rossoliński-Liebe does not engage with this valuable research and the debates taking place in Ukraine.

I have criticized Rossoliński-Liebe elsewhere for a failure to formulate clear definitions when employing terms such as "fascism", "Ukrainian radical nationalism", and "Ukrainian fascism".[9] Here, in writing, the author defines his terms more clearly than he has done during oral presentations of his work. But the monograph does also contain terms that remain undefined. Thus, for example, in the introduction Rossoliński-Liebe writes of the need to distinguish between "conservative or military regimes like Antonescu's, Horthy's or Piłsudski's, and fascist regimes like Mussolini's Italy and Hitler's Germany, and also regimes, which at times were fascist but in the long term combined *national-conservatism* with fascism, like Franco's and Salazar's" (my emphasis—YR) (p. 33). From the text it is unclear what exactly Rossoliński-Liebe means by the term "national-conservatism" or which political parties represented and represent it, in the author's view. What the author means by "Ukrainian genocidal nationalism" (p. 531) is likewise unclear. The author provides no explanation of what is meant by this term. Is he referring to OUN ideology from 1929? Or 1941? Does he mean OUN-B or OUN-B? A similar lack of clarity is associated with his use of the phrase "fanatical and suicidal nationalism" (p. 532).[10]

---

8   For my critique of Zaitsev's theory, see Yurii Radchenko, "Rassuzhdeniia nad knigoi Aleksandra Zaitseva *Ukrainskii integral'nyi natsionalizm* ili Ukrainskie pravye radikaly v kontekste epokhi", *Forum noveishei vostochnoevropeiskoi istorii i kul'tury. Russkoe izdanie*, no. 2 (2014), http://www1.ku-eichstaett.de/ZIMOS/forum/inhaltruss22.html.

9   Radchenko, "Pro ukrains'kyi 'radykal'nyi natsionalizm'".

10   Certain terms are discussed in more detail by the author elsewhere: G. Rossoliński-Liebe, "The Fascist Kernel of Ukrainian Genocidal Nationalism", *The Carl Beck Papers in Russian and Eastern European Studies*, no. 2402 (May 2015).

The greater part of the book is devoted not so much to Bandera's biography as to the history of the OUN-B, its ideology, and its political and military practices. For this reason the book's title is not always a good fit for its content. For example, a large number of pages are devoted to the OUN's ideology and to events in Ukraine in 1941–44, a period when Bandera was imprisoned by the Germans and hence unable to exert any influence on events in Ukraine.

Paradoxically enough, at times Rossoliński-Liebe himself (evidently inadvertently) repeats the postulates and theses of OUN propaganda. It is a well known fact that one of the political and commemorative rituals carried out by Ukrainians in interwar Poland was the digging up of graves or burial mounds of Ukrainian Sich Riflemen. A wide range of political groups participated in such actions, from the OUN to the Communist Party of West Ukraine (the KPZU). Rossoliński-Liebe repeats the postwar version of these events set out by the Banderite "party historian" Petro Mirchuk and writes that it was precisely the OUN leaders who instructed their subordinates to create symbolic burial mounds even at sites where no Ukrainian soldiers were buried (p. 101), not mentioning the participation in such actions of other groups.

It remains an open question how strong the influence of biological racism was on the pre-war OUN ideology. Rossoliński-Liebe asserts that "[i]n Ukrainian nationalism, racism and eugenics appeared in the context of purifying the Ukrainian nation, culture, and language of foreign—in particular, Polish, Russian and Jewish—influences, in order to obtain a pure Ukrainian 'race'" (p. 111). It is not entirely clear whether Rossoliński-Liebe is referring here to the OUN or to a broader context. As I see it, racism penetrated more deeply not the OUN ideology but the world-view ideals of the National Unity Front (FNYe) headed by Dmytro Paliiv. Reichsführer-SS Heinrich Himmler in his speech to German officers of the SS "Galician" division on 1 February 1944 asserted that the FNYe "was very close to national-socialism in its worldview".[11] One of the famous propagandists of racial anti-Semitism on the pages of the FNYe

---

[11]   *Yad Vashem Archives*, M 53. F.N.274 (Central State Archive of the Chief Institutions of Power in Ukraine). P.8.

newspaper *Peremoha* was Rostyslav Yendyk, whose works were even translated into German in the Third Reich.[12] It is interesting to note that after the war Yendyk attempted to defend a post-doctoral work on "The Anthropological Structure of Ukraine with Comments on the Paleo-Anthropology of Eastern Europe" at the Ukrainian Free University in Munich, where representatives of the Melnykite and Banderite OUN were influential. Among the authors of positive appraisals of Yendyk's work was the "leading race researcher" of the now defunct Third Reich, Hans Günther. Some of the reviewers criticized Yendyk's "study" for "the presence of a large number of factual errors", while one reviewer wrote that "the author is a fanatical racist".[13] As a result the work was not successfully defended. What is noteworthy, however, is the fact that it was considered and that one of the Third Reich's chief "race researchers" was brought in as an expert consultant.

Rossoliński-Liebe pays a good deal of attention in the book to the Second Great Congress held in Kraków on 31 March–1 April 1941 (pp. 176–81). This Congress formalized the differentiation of OUN-B as a separate organization and passed a series of resolutions which, in the author's opinion, comprised a decisive step towards fascism on the part of the political group of Stepan Bandera's supporters. The political course adopted by OUN-B in April 1941 was totalitarian, xenophobic (and anti-Semitic) and differed little from fascist programs adopted elsewhere in Eastern Europe at the time. What is interesting is the fact that the Resolution passed by the Great Congress did not include any pro-Hitler slogans. But the situation here is not a straightforward one. In the lead-up to the Great Congress OUN-B created a Political Commission, comprising Stepan Len'kavs'kyi as head, together with members Ivan Mitrynha, Borys Levyts'kyi, Lev Rebet and Vasyl' Ryvak. The Commission, like the OUN-B leadership, included those who were in favor of including in the program a point "on full solidarity with national-socialist Germany" and who tried to make it "identical" with the ideology of the NSDAP. We do not know with certainty who the supporters of this

---

[12]   *Arkhiv Ukrains'koho Vil'noho Universitetu*, Fond Rostyslava Yendyka.
[13]   Ibid.

program were or what Bandera's position was at the time, but according to Levyts'kyi's testimony, Mitrynha and Len'kavs'kyi, known
for their anti-Semitic statements,[14] spoke out against including pro-
Hitler points in the OUN-B program.[15]

Rossoliński-Liebe also analyzes a document entitled "The
Struggle and Activities of the OUN in Wartime", which essentially
became the program of what the organization's leadership called the
"Ukrainian National Revolution". The program was actively put into
practice in the summer of 1941 on the territory of Galicia and
Volhynia and (in part) later also on the territory of Transdnipro
Ukraine. Rossoliński-Liebe, like the majority of historians taking a
critical approach to the OUN's heritage, cites large extracts from this
text, in which Jews are depicted as an "enemy" ethno-religious group
from the point of view of Ukrainians. In addition, the document
states that "ethnic minorities" are divided into "friendly" (representatives of "enslaved peoples") and "hostile" ("Russians, Poles, Jews")
(p. 181). It is telling that OUN-M also produced similar instructions
on creating organs of self-government, police, propaganda, and collaboration with the German army. Although anti-Semitic elements
were characteristic of Melnykite propaganda throughout the entire
war, it is telling that the hierarchy of "hostile" and "friendly" peoples
and the attitude to be held towards them was spelt out more clearly
by the Banderites.[16]

Upon creating the Banderite Ukrainian National Government
(UDP) Yaroslav Stets'ko brought several former members of Ukrain-
ian parties into this government. Thus, former activists of the
Ukrainian National Democratic Alliance (UNDO) Yulian
Pavlykovs'kyi and Oleksandr Maritchak were formally members of
the UDP.[17] Rossoliński-Liebe comments on the inclusion of non-
Banderites into the government as follows: "Such cooperation with

---

14   Radchenko, "Pro ukrains'kyi 'radykal'nyi natsionalizm'".
15   "Natsional'nyi rukh pid chas Druhoi svitovoi viiny: interv'iu z B. Levyts'kym",
      Dialohy, 1979. Chyslo 2. 14.
16   *Arkhiv OUN* (Kyiv), F.1, op.1, spr. 266, ark. 1-4.
17   Yaroslav Stets'ko, *30 chervnia 1941 r. – proholoshennia vidnovlenia derzhavnosti
      Ukrainy* (Toronto, New York, London: Liha vyzvolennia Ukrainy, 1967), 226–27.

other parties or political camps was quite typical of some of the fascist movements, which needed to consolidate their power. The National Socialists, for example, cooperated with other political blocs, mainly with conservatives and national conservatives before they established their regime and eliminated other political parties" (p. 217). This passage shows that Rossoliński-Liebe does not fully understand the situation that had taken shape in Western Ukraine from 1939 to 1941. During the "accelerated" Sovietization underway in Galicia and Volhynia, as elsewhere throughout the territories "newly incorporated" by the USSR in 1939-40, all local political institutions and parties that had been functioning prior to the Bolsheviks' arrivals were now destroyed. Therefore it is incorrect to compare the OUN's actions after 1939 to Hitler and Mussolini's cooperation with conservatives and other radical right-wing groups on the path to establishing dictatorship, because in 1941 the UNDO, for example, no longer existed as a structure. In precisely the same way in 1944 the Banderites included into the Ukrainian Supreme Liberation Council (*Ukrains'ka Holovna Vyzvol'na Rada*, UHVR) on a purely formal basis several politicians who were non-members of the OUN-B.

In his discussion on the "Ukrainian National Revolution" period, Rossoliński-Liebe describes the celebrations held in Stanisławów (now Ivano-Frankivsk) to mark "liberation from the Bolsheviks". Here, Hungarian military servicemen took part in these events together with members of the OUN-B and the local population. The celebrations were accompanied not only by the slogans "Glory to Ukraine!", "Glory to Stepan Bandera!", and "Glory to Adolf Hitler!", but also by slogans such as "Glory to the allied Hungarian army!". Rossoliński-Liebe does not comment at all on the OUN's cooperation with the Hungarian army in the context of the fact that among the slogans put forward by OUN-B in 1941 there were, in addition to anti-Soviet, anti-Semitic, anti-Russian, and anti-Polish slogans, also anti-Hungarian ones. Thus, amongst the proclamations issued by the OUN-B's Homeland Executive [*Kraievyi provid*] on 1 July 1941 was the following exhortation: "People! Know! Your enemies are Moscow, Poland, Magyars, Jews—these are your enemies!

Destroy them!"[18] This is particularly interesting in view of the fact that the Hungarian army had intervened and stopped several pogroms in Western Ukraine (p. 236).

Rossoliński-Liebe locates the "Ukrainian National Revolution" geographically in Galicia and Volhynia, and chronologically in the summer of 1941. Consequently, the OUN's activities in central, eastern and southern Ukraine are left outside the field of his study. Rossoliński-Liebe writes little about the OUN-M's actions in central Ukraine (pp. 242–45) or about the Banderites' service in the ranks of the Ukrainian auxiliary policy (pp. 256–60), and he does not touch at all on the topic of the participation of members of "expedition groups" in the creation of police and self-government organs in east and south Ukraine. In some cities of east Ukraine Banderites were so well entrenched in police and self-government organs that they remained in place there until the end of the German occupation. True, it was necessary for them to conceal their party affiliation (this applies to the Banderites from autumn 1941, and the Melnykites from winter 1941–42).

The UPA's participation in the extermination of the Jews remains one of the most problematic and politicized issues in this history. In his study Rossoliński-Liebe cites a large number of testimonies of Jewish Holocaust survivors, materials from postwar trials, and German documents indicating the participation of armed formations of Banderites in the persecution and murder of Jews in the 1943–44 period (pp. 275–76). There is no doubt that the Banderite UPA took part in such actions, and that in 1944 it killed "its own" Jewish doctors because the Security Service (SB) suspected them of sympathizing with the Soviet regime. It is significant that for the Ukrainian rebels who initiated the struggle against the Germans, Jews remained ideological enemies. In 1943 one cadet from the UPA officers' school noted that Jews should be considered "agents of Moscow imperialism, once tsarist, and now proletarian, but all the same first we must beat the *moskali*, and then any remaining Jews

---

18   *OUN u 1941 rotsi* (Kyiv: Instytut istorii Ukrainy, 2006), 261.

[*nedobytkiv*]".[19] Jews were exterminated in the same way by Polish and sometimes also by Soviet partisans. The problem is that in their testimony, the Jews who survived attacks by Ukrainian partisans differ in how they identify the attackers. Holocaust survivors called the armed attackers "banderivtsy", "bul'bivtsy", or simply "Ukrainians". This is very similar to the way in which, when describing the events of 1941, Jews call the pogromists (including "Ukrainian national militia" personnel) not "ounivtsy" or "banderivtsy", but simply "Ukrainian nationalists", or more often, "Ukrainians". Consequently, for scholars using Jewish recollections, it is difficult to identify any group of perpetrators precisely as Banderites, Melnykites, *bul'bivtsy*, or simply criminal elements.

In his analysis of the mass killings by the UPA of the Poles and Jews who had survived persecution by the Germans and collaborationists in Volhynia in 1943-44, Rossoliński-Liebe offers four factors facilitating this: "first, to the social and political situation of Ukrainians in the interwar period or even before; second, to the military aims and strategies of the UPA; third, the tone that the Nazi occupation and Nazi ideology had set; and fourth, the fact that there was no strong administration in these territories at a time when the front was changing" (pp. 279–80). Of course, all these factors played a role in influencing events. At the same time, however, Rossoliński-Liebe ignores the factor of the accelerated "Sovietization" of Volhynia in the 1939–41 period, when the Bolsheviks brought to the region their methods of rule and of struggle against real and imagined enemies of their regime, important elements of which were repressions, deportations, forced nationalization of property, and the killing of prison inmates during the retreat of the summer of 1941.

Rossoliński-Liebe does mention the Ukrainians who helped Jews and Poles during the period of German occupation. Thus, he writes of the 2,472 Ukrainians awarded the status of Righteous among the Nations by Yad Vashem (p. 280). It is significant that among them was OUN-B activist Fedir Vovk. During the German occupation Vovk saved a Jewish family. We know that several UPA

---

[19]   *Archiwum Akt Nowych*, Archiwum Wiktora Poliszczuka, Sign.153 (Dokumenty dotyczące OUN-UPA z zawodu Centralnego Państwowego Archiwum Wyzszych Organow Wladzy w Kijowe, Kserokopie), 186–87.

detachments hid Jews, who went on to survive the war.[20] The author provides no commentary on this "other" side of events. This issue presents historians with a great many questions. How many members of the OUN and UPA took part not only in exterminating, but also in saving Jews? If there were such cases, then whose initiative was this: that of the individual, or the local leadership? What were the motivations? We know that Wehrmacht soldiers and NSDAP members also saved Jews during the war; Oskar Schindler is the classic example. The lack of research on this topic encourages speculations "from the other side", when OUN supporters use what were essentially isolated and exceptional cases of OUN rescues of Jews in an attempt to deny the anti-Semitic nature of the OUN during the war. This tendency is exemplified by the position of Volodymyr Viatrovych, who takes the case of Fedir Vovk and uses it to try to prove that the views of this one member of the OUN were shared by practically all members of the party.[21] Often even moderate organizations in Ukraine adhere to a similar position on this issue. On one occasion, during my visit to Ukraine in winter 2015, a Ukrainian liberal nationalist organization in Kharkiv invited me to give a lecture on my research. At the time I was writing an article on the biography of a Melnykite who had joined Einsatzgruppe D during the war and took part in the murder of Jews in Ukraine and Russia, as well as in "anti-partisan actions" in Belarus. I drafted an abstract and sent it to the organizers. They in turn informed me that "one must bear in mind" that "this kind of presentation" could be used by pro-Russian activists in Kharkiv, and that one needed to "balance" the theme by including discussion of how OUN members saved Jews. I replied that I had not encountered any such cases in the course of my professional study of the primary sources, and cancelled my lecture.

---

[20]   Yakiv Suslens'ky, *Spravzhni heroi* (Kyiv: Instytut natsional'nykh vidnosyn i politolohii Akademii nauk Ukrainy, 1993), 14–15; *Mandyk Khasman – evrei z UPA (siuzhet TVi za 02.02.2012)*, http://www.youtube.com/watch?v=qKm_aySS8oY.

[21]   Volodymyr Viatrovych, "Istoriia z hryfom 'Sekretno': Fedir Vovk – ukrains'kyi natsionalyst ta pravednyk narodiv", *TSN*, 7 February 2013, http://tsn.ua/analitika/fedir-vovk-ukrayinskiy-nacionalist-ta-pravednyk-narod iv-svitu-281088.html.

Rossoliński-Liebe also discusses the OUN-B program adopted at the Great Congress in August 1943 (pp. 262–65). This program, as is well known, was an attempt for propaganda purposes to depart from fascist ideology and to break free of the ideological quagmire and trap which was dragging all the European radical right down to the bottom of a fraternal grave in the deep swamp together with Hitler and the Third Reich. Rossoliński-Liebe asserts that this renunciation of the "Führerprinzip", national discrimination, anti-Semitism, and left-wing rhetoric in the economic sphere, was an attempt to smooth over relations with Great Britain and the United States (p. 265). It is well known, at the same time, that this "democratization" was merely a propaganda move undertaken against the backdrop of the extermination of the Polish population of Volhynia and of the Jews who had survived the attacks carried out by Nazis and their collaborators. But the difficulties that the OUN members themselves had with this program, especially when it comes to "solving the Jewish question", is shown very well by a secret discussion between Dmytro Dontsov and Iosyp Pozychaniuk that took place in 1944. Dontsov, while he was never an OUN member, had always been an authority for Banderites. This is how Dontsov was described in a 1973 obituary by Volodymyr Makar, a member of the OUN-B and of the UHVR General Secretariat of Foreign Affairs:

[A] great Human Being, who already in his lifetime earned the honorable rank of creator of Ukrainian spirituality, of a new worldview... the creator of revolutionary Ukrainian nationalism.

...[T]his was one of the greatest, epochal figures of the Ukrainian nation, on a par with Taras Shevchenko, Ivan Franko, Lesia Ukrainka, who—like the ancient prophets of old—were seized by a great fanatical faith in the Truth of Ukraine and her inevitable victory.

For sixty years—two complete generations—Dmytro Dontsov formed the spirituality of the Ukrainian people and the Ukrainian nation.[22]

---

[22] *Thomas Fisher Rare Book Library (Toronto, Canada)*, The Peter J. Potichnyj Collection on Insurgency and Counter-Insurgency in Ukraine, Box 66, Folder "Dmytro Dontsov".

Until the end of his life Bandera conducted a correspondence with the author of *Natsionalizm*. Three years before his death he wrote to Dontsov at Easter: "Permit me to send you warm wishes on the holiday of Christ's Resurrection—[to wish you] joyful celebrations and a regathering of strength for continued irreplaceable work in preparing our people for the national Resurrection".[23] Before the war, Dontsov's works, which praised Hitler, Mussolini, Degrelle and Franco, were read enthusiastically by members of the radical right in Western Ukraine. Dontsov adhered to a radical anti-Semitic position. He called the left-wing liberals, his political opponents, "defenders of yid democracy" and "*shabesgoi*".[24] It is significant that Dontsov remained a person who hated Jews and equated them with Bolshevism even after the war. In a letter to a banderite on 22 June 1950 he commented on how in Montreal a Ukrainian football team had played a match against a Jewish team, and criticized OUN-B member Serbin for "calling on young people to play with the Bolshevik-yids". According to Dontsov, "the Ukrainians beat the yids up in that match, but then the yids beat up two Ukrainians, alleged 'Hitlerites'... yid and communist pamphlets were distributed at that match".[25]

Pozychaniuk represented the moderate left wing of the OUN, but his attitude to Jews was also highly problematic. He was thirty years younger than Dontsov and had a completely different life experience. After graduating from Nizhyn Pedagogical Institute Pozychaniuk joined the Komsomol. He lived for a long period in Moscow and Leningrad. In 1940 he was sent to L'viv University, which had already been Ukrainianized by this point. It was at this time that Pozychaniuk underwent some kind of ideological break. He made contact with the OUN underground, and was personally acquainted with Bandera. When the German troops entered L'viv he joined the OUN expedition groups and headed for the East, where he was arrested and sent first to Kraków, and then to Auschwitz together with a group of 140 OUN members. The circumstances of his liberation from Auschwitz are not quite clear. According to one version, "the

---

23   *Libraries and Archives Canada*, MG 31, D 130, Vol 5, S. Bandera.
24   *Biblioteka Narodowa*, Archiwum Dmytra Doncowa (1883–1973), Mf. 80378.
25   *Libraries and Archives Canada*, MG 31, D 130, Vol 3, G. Gabora.

Volhyniaks and Pozychaniuks managed to lie their way out of it in the interrogations and they were released".[26] It is unknown whether Pozychaniuk took part in the pogrom in L'viv in the summer of 1941, but there are testimonies indicating that even during the period when he cooperated with the Bolsheviks he still adhered to anti-Semitic views. As one of his friends put it, "Pozychaniuk, like all members of the Komsomol, had a negative attitude towards the 'older brothers'—the Russians and the Jewish communists. Complaints were made against the Russian and Jewish instructors who were sent from other regions to work with the Ukrainians."[27]

During a discussion in 1944 Dontsov accused the OUN of having passed a new program that resembled the Central Rada's declaration during the 1917 Revolution. As an example, Dontsov read out that the OUN was "in favor of equal rights for yids". He stated: "The program contains not a hint of Ukr[ainian] historical traditions, either social, national, or political, and this is not only the traditions of the Cossacks but also the recent traditions of the rebel movement of 1917–21 with their xenophobia against the interlopers from the north, anti-Semitism, religiosity, and private-property tendencies".[28] Even against the backdrop of the genocide unleashed against the Jews by the Nazis with their allies and collaborators, Dontsov wrote: "The mentality and politics of world Jewry is harmful for the Ukrainian nation and statehood. The struggle against Jewry is in the interests and the tradition of the Ukr[ainian] nation".[29] Pozychaniuk's response to this recognized that "[t]hese 'Comments' were written ... by a person holding authority (indeed, to this day) in Ukrainian circles",[30] and that it was only for this reason that he was

---

[26]   *Thomas Fisher Rare Book Library (Toronto, Canada)*, The Peter J. Potichnyj Collection on Insurgency and Counter-Insurgency in Ukraine, Box 86, Folder "Petro Dushyi", Lyst Petra Baliia do "Litopysu UPA", 5 August 1988.

[27]   *Thomas Fisher Rare Book Library (Toronto, Canada)*, The Peter J. Potichnyj Collection on Insurgency and Counter-Insurgency in Ukraine, Box 96, Folder "Josyp Posichniuk".

[28]   "Materialy do dyskusii nad prohramoiu OUN (poshyrenniu ne pidliahaie)", *Arkhiv Vyzvol'noho Rukhu*, http://avr.org.ua/index.php/viewDoc/10692/.

[29]   Ibid.

[30]   Ibid.

responding. In the response, Pozychaniuk at times completely rejects the notion that there was a place for any discrimination on ethnic or racial grounds in the new OUN program: "For us the enemy must be defined not by race, but by the degree of hostility to our ideas and by activeness of his activities against us". But when it came to the "Jewish question" he had very specific views. He acknowledged that anti-Semitism was a constituent element of the OUN's ideology, but argued that at this stage the anti-Jewish propaganda should be ceased: "despite all our traditions on the Jewish question, we should now depart from anti-Semitism to the maximum possible degree".[31]

It is interesting to note that the Banderites succeeded in definitively "departing" from anti-Semitism in their propaganda only in 1944—at the time when this discussion was being carried out. For example, in 1944 a pamphlet entitled "Who are you dying for, brothers" and signed "Ukrainian rebels" was produced for Ukrainian Red Army soldiers. The pamphlet said, among other things, that Red Army soldiers were dying for "the new big world empire of blood-sucker-tsars, for the new tsardom of cannibal Stalin, for a clique, for the party, for fat-bellied, well-fed yid commissars, for the beloved NKVD, for the Kaganoviches, Molotovs, Litvinovs, Vyshinskys, and thousands of others, who, the expense of the people's blood, of plundered property, cavort at banquets and make plans for building the new world empire". In their personal correspondence the members of OUN-B, even while using leftist rhetoric, continued to exploit the old anti-Semitic stereotypes. Thus, on 6 December 1944, one OUN activist wrote to a friend that the "progressive call of the new human being" came "from the healthy soul of the Ukrainian worker and peasant. *And not from the heads of yids* [my emphasis—YR].[32] Even though Pozychaniuk did condemn the extermination of the Jews, he felt no sympathy for them whatsoever. For him, the ban on anti-Semitism was a kind of tactical move: "This doesn't mean that we're

---

31   *Thomas Fisher Rare Book Library (Toronto, Canada)*. The Peter J. Potichnyj Collection on Insurgency and Counter-Insurgency in Ukraine. Box 76. Folder "Underground Publications OUN (b)".

32   *Thomas Fisher Rare Book Library (Toronto, Canada)*, The Peter J. Potichnyj Collection on Insurgency and Counter-Insurgency in Ukraine, Box 81.

in favor of Jewry... No. We are simply discarding that which cannot be used". He went on to add the cynical phrase: "All the more so since today the Jewish problem no longer exists in Ukraine... After the German practice it's hard (if not stupid) to play that card today".[33]

In his analysis of the image of Bandera and Banderites in Soviet propaganda Rossoliński-Liebe notes that it was precisely in 1947 that a change took place in the terms used by Soviet propagandists to designate members of the OUN-B and Ukrainian rebels. If from 1944 they had been called "Ukrainian-German nationalists", from 1947 they were referred to as "Ukrainian bourgeois nationalists". Precisely at a time when the "Cold War" was gathering pace the Soviets were trying to identify the Ukrainian resistance with the defense of capitalism in the mass imagination. The author notes correctly that it was precisely after this that the Ukrainian underground began to print on a mas scale literature in which the OUN and UPA were shown as democratic (almost left-wing) structures which had nothing in common with collaboration with Nazism or the extermination of different ethnic groups; instead, they were knights who had fought all Ukraine's enemies for her independence. The chief rebel author of such texts was Petro Fedun (Poltava). For Rossoliński-Liebe all these declarations from the Ukrainian underground were mere propaganda with the aim of improving the UPA's image at home and abroad. He does not analyze the contacts between left-wing representatives of the Ukrainian emigration and the left wing of the Ukrainian underground after the Second World War or, for that matter, the left "deviations" in the OUN milieu.[34] These topics have in general received little scholarly attention. The newspaper *Vpered*, the organ of the left wing of the Ukrainian Revolutionary-Democratic Party (URDP) was published in Munich from 1949 through 1959. The newspaper's editors were very negatively disposed towards Bandera; they condemned the terror exercised by his supporters, called for the building of "democratic socialism", and took a negative line on the Soviet socio-economic model. Articles

---

[33] "Materialy do dyskusii".
[34] On Ivan Mitrynha's left-wing group see: Radchenko, "Pro ukrains'kyi 'radykal'nyi natsionalizm'".

appeared in *Vpered* in which authors supported the UPA's struggle against the Bolsheviks, but at the same time, criticized Bandera as a totalitarian leader and a "reactionary". One such publication asserted that:

> Mr Bandera does not see the new truths. At a time when THERE [in Ukraine—YR] UHVR, UPA and SB are becoming independent of any political party, when even the OUN has a different ideological face and the brand "banderivtsy" looks like a historical misunderstanding—at the same time HERE [in West Germany—YR] Mr Bandera dictates from the tribune of the "vozhd'" ideological formulas "obligatory for all", gives orders to commanders of military units, makes decisions on mandates which he has not issued and in the foreign press lowers the UPA to the role of his own personal army.[35]

Publications of UPA leftist propagandists such as Osyp Diakiv-Hornovyi appeared on the pages of *Vpered*.[36] The fourth issue for 1950 is of great interest. The front page carried a message of sympathy from the URDP's Central Committee and the *Vpered* editors in connection on the occasion of the death of UPA commander-in-chief Roman Shukhevych. It is difficult to say whether the left-wing publicists producing such texts had a clear understanding of who Shukhevych was, and whether they would have known for example about his participation in the "anti-partisan" actions in Belarus in 1942. Two long letters were also published in this issue. The first was penned by one of the URDP's founders, who was also leader of its left wing, Ivan Maistrenko, who wrote under the pseudonym "A. Babenko". The author of the second letter was Petro Fedun (Poltava). On behalf of the URDP Central Committee it was reported that "correspondence with the Homeland [*z Kraiem*] is beginning a theoretical discussion, which will have large significance, both for the Homeland and for the emigration".[37] In his letter, Maistrenko praises Poltava and Hornovyi: "The existence of the Ukrainian underground with views outlined in the books by O. Hornovyi and P. Poltava, is of exceptional significance not only from the perspective

---

35   E.B., "Ukrains'ka natsional'na revolutsiia i natsionalistychna reaktsiia", *Vpered*, no. 3 (1950).
36   O. Hornovyi, "Nashe stanovishche do rosiis'koho narodu", ibid.
37   Povidomlennia TsK URDP, *Vpered*, no. 4 (1950).

of the Ukrainian cause, but also on the universal-historical scale".[38] He evaluated very highly the activities being carried out by the nationalists in Ukraine. At the same time, Maistrenko wished to clarify several points. The majority of Ukrainian right-wing radicals who had been oriented towards the fascist regimes of Europe up until the mid-1950s, had now begun to praise the Francoist system of rule in Spain. Therefore Maistrenko was interested in Poltava's attitude towards "reactionary movements and tendencies (Franco, De Gaulle, Dewey, Churchill, etc.)".[39] He was also interested in Fedun's attitude towards private property and the class struggle. But the main issue was what people like Hornovyi and Poltava thought about Bandera and Dontsov's actions in the West. As we know, Bandera and Dontsov had actively criticized the OUN's 1943 program and the publications being produced by Hornovyi and Poltava. According to Maistrenko, Dontsov was continuing "to orient the emigration towards fascist ideas".[40]

Fedun's response was very restrained and diplomatic, and avoided "unpleasant" issues. He did not raise the issue of attitudes towards right-wing postwar dictatorships, and he denied the fact that the OUN in Ukraine was moving across to Marxist positions and supporting class struggle. He said nothing about Dontsov, but did add a restrained aside on the conflict between Bandera and the leading rebels in the Homeland:

> We also believe that certain disagreements which have emerged between the OUN in Ukraine and ZCh OUN [*Zakordonna chastyna* or Foreign Branch of the OUN] are only a temporary phenomenon, caused for the most part by the isolation of both parts of the organization. All these disagreements—all of us in the Lands [*na Zemliakh*, i.e. lands populated by ethnic Ukrainians] believe and are striving towards this, on the foundation of the experience in The Lands, on the foundation of the OUN's success in Ukraine, in the name of creating a Ukrainian nationalist movement as the most progressive and the most healthy, both on Ukrainian soil and on a broader scale.[41]

---

[38] Lyst Babenka, ibid.
[39] Ibid.
[40] Ibid.
[41] Lyst P.M. Poltavy, ibid.

The letter closed with very warm words addressed at the left-ist emigration:

> From the field of the liberation battle in Ukraine I send a revolutionary greet-ing to you and your party! I wish you and all your friends great success in the name of the cause shared by all patriots—liberation of our Ukrainian peo-ple... oppressed for centuries. We would be glad to see members of your party alongside us in the struggle against the Muscovite-Bolshevik occupiers in the Ukrainian Lands.[42]

Maistrenko wrote a commentary on this letter by Fedun. Maistrenko viewed Fedun's similar position with regard to the con-flict between ZCh OUN and the nationalists in Ukraine as a positive tendency. In this publication he compared Bandera to Stalin: "Ban-dera's misfortune lies in the fact that he, like his teacher Stalin, be-lieves more not in an idea, and not in an apparatus, not in ethics, but in tactics and cunning. One can be certain that this will lead Bandera where it led Stalin".[43] Describing Fedun's position, Maistrenko admitted indirectly that the Banderite OUN was a fas-cist organization:

> The new generation of nationalists in Ukraine, raised on the ideas of the Homeland OUN, is moving further and further away from ZCh OUN. The liberation movement will have ever greater chances of success on all the Ukrainian lands together when it distances itself from everything on which the stamp of fascism still remains.[44]

It is difficult to say now exactly how many people among the Ukrainian diaspora shared the views of the *Vpered* editors. Most likely this was a very small group. As we know, the Banderites dom-inated the political field of the postwar Ukrainian camps for dis-placed persons. Nevertheless, it is important to be aware that this position did exist.

Rossoliński-Liebe devotes several pages of his monograph to the biography of the writer and pro-Soviet propagandist Yaroslav

---

[42]   Ibid.
[43]   Ibid.
[44]   Ibid.

Halan (pp. 392–94). For the most part he has not used here new documents which have the capacity to shed new light on the activities of this individual. It is significant that in the course of over twenty years of Ukrainian independence, not a single scholarly biography of this complex figure has been published. While Halan was glorified during the Soviet period, the situation looks highly ambiguous from the perspective of independence. Thus, in Galicia, for example, all plaques and street names bearing his name have been removed, while on the territory of central and eastern Ukraine they remain in place. It will be interesting to observe what happens to them in the context of the current government's "decommunization". Was Halan always a Stalinist? Or was he broken by circumstances? It is especially interesting in this context to note that Halan repeated the Banderite version of the beginning of the conflict between Ukrainians and Poles in Volhynia in 1943. He asserted that the extermination of the Poles in Volhynia was a response to the persecution of Ukrainians in Pidlashshia.

Rossoliński-Liebe also writes about the politicization and popularization of the term "banderivtsy" by Soviet propaganda organs:

> The word "Banderites" was an important component of the Soviet propaganda discourse, at least since 1944. All kinds of people who opposed Soviet policies in some way, or were accused of opposing them, could be classified as Banderites, especially if they had some sympathy for nationalism, or if they or their relatives were in the OUN or the UPA. The word "Banderites" had a very derogatory meaning and basically meant a traitor of the Ukrainian nation, a Nazi collaborator, a fascist, an enemy of the Soviet Union, a murderer with blood on his hands, or a spy for Western intelligence services. The word was frequently used to discredit anti-Soviet dissidents and other political opponents (pp. 402–3).

It is interesting to note that in a different section of the text the author effectively uses the term "banderivtsy" as a synonym for "UPA soldiers", although we know that, for example, the last UPA commander Vasyl' Kuk placed a ban on using the term for soldiers.[45]

---

[45]   Dmytriy Vvedeneev, *Odisseya Vasiliya Kuka*, Xfilespress, http://xfilespress.com/odisseya-vasiliy-kuk.aspx.

It is also significant that in the mass understanding, on the part of both Red Army soldiers and the local population, the Ukrainian nationalist resistance movement was not viewed as synonymous with "banderites" or linked to Bandera in 1944. The discourse did sometimes feature the figure of Taras Borovets' (Bul'ba), who was arrested by the Nazis in autumn 1943 and who had been an inmate of the Sachsenhausen concentration camp together with Bandera. In one UPA report from 1944, a meeting between a Red Army soldier and local peasants is described: "A Red Army soldier comes in and asks a woman: 'Is Bul'ba here?' The woman answers in the affirmative. There, under the bench. The startled Red Army soldier jumped up and a minute later calmed down after he found under the bench not the rebel Bul'ba, but potatoes" (in Ukrainian and Belarusian "bul'ba" means "potato").[46]

Rossoliński-Liebe writes about the Spanish dictator Franco's positive attitude towards Bandera after the war. The Caudillo even invited the Providnyk to visit him in Spain, but Bandera turned down the invitation after deciding to stay in Munich (p. 362). After the war Banderites often enjoyed friendly relations of this kind with radical right-wing and (post)fascist movements. For example, Yaroslav Stets'ko was an acquaintance of the leader of the Romanian fascist and anti-Semitic "Iron Guard" Horia Sima, who lived in Spain after the war,[47] while his wife Slava Stets'ko maintained good relations with the editor-in-chief of the neo-fascist journal *Nation Europa*, former SS-Sturmbannführer Arthur Ehrhardt.[48] Rossoliński-Liebe writes that in December 1959 the pro-Banderite journal *Homin Ukraïny* printed a sorrowful text on the occasion of the death of the Ustaša leader Ante Pavelić, referring to him as a "great patriot" and "fighter for independence" (p. 415). But in parallel to this, when they needed to show the victimized history of the Ukrainian radical right and of Ukrainians in general during World War II, circles close to the OUN-B published materials devoted to the crimes of the Ustaše

---

[46]   *Thomas Fisher Rare Book Library (Toronto, Canada),* The Peter J. Potichnyj Collection on Insurgency and Counter-Insurgency in Ukraine, Box 75, Folder "Ukrainian Insurgency".

[47]   *Libraries and Archives Canada,* MG 31, D 130, Vol. 5, Yaroslav Stetsko.

[48]   *Libraries and Archives Canada,* MG 31, D 130, Vol. 5, Nation Europe.

(including crimes against Ukrainians). Thus for example a collection of reminiscences and articles entitled *In the Struggle for a Ukrainian State*, which recounted the martyrology of OUN-B and OUN-M members during the war, also included a text by a Ukrainian priest from Yugoslavia, Yurii Myz', who wrote of the death of several dozen Ukrainians in the Jasenovac concentration camp in 1944. Myz' asserted that:

> [t]he ideology taken on by the Ustaše was essentially identical to the Hitlerite [ideology]. Once holding power in their hands, the Ustaše began to exterminate Jews, gypsies, and ... Serbs, of whom there was no small number on the territory of the NDH [the Independent State of Croatia established by the Ustaše —YR].[49]

One of the methodological problems associated with Rossoliński-Liebe's work is the fact that he tends to see everything in "black-and-white" terms. For example, he calls the current director of the Ukrainian Institute of National Memory Volodymyr Viatrovych a "radical right historian" (p. 451), effectively placing him in the same category as another Ukrainian public-political figure, the former chief ideologue of the Svoboda Party, now an advisor to the head of the Ukrainian Security Service Yurii Mykhal'chyshyn, to whom part of the book is also devoted. Viatrovych and Mykhal'chyshyn both hold Ukrainian doctoral degrees, in history and political science respectively. On several occasions I have criticized Viatrovych as a propagandist and apologist for the OUN-B, who tries to pass himself off as an academic historian. At one point he even succeeded in receiving a stipend from the Harvard Ukrainian Research Institute, and he later he wrote a book about the 1943 events in Volhynia which has been sharply criticized by various historians.[50] Viatrovych is not considered a serious historian in the

---

[49] Roman Myz', *Ukraintsi gynuly tez v Iugoslavii. Yasenovats, V borot'bi za Ukrains'ku Dershavu. Essei, spogady, svidcheniya, litopysania, dokumenty Drugoi svitovoi viiny* (Winnipeg: Svitova liga ukrains'kikh politychnykh v'iazniv, 1991), 918–19.

[50] Grzegorz Motyka, "Neudachnaia kniga", *Ab Imperio*, 17 June 2012, http://net.ab imperio.net/node/2570.

West, nor has he published his work in peer-reviewed journals. Nevertheless, to label him as "radical right" would be an exaggeration. The same cannot be said of Mykhal'chyshyn, known as an apologist for Joseph Goebbels, Horst Wessel, Léon Degrelle, Primo de Rivera, and other "social-revolutionaries" or "conservative revolutionaries", as he calls them. The speed with which Mykhal'chyshyn, who was the Svoboda Party's chief ideologue, disappeared from the country's public life against the backdrop of the unfolding of the clashes on the Maidan in the winter of 2013–14 and the intensification of the war in the Donbas in 2014 leads one to wonder whether Mykhal'chyshyn may have been nothing more than a provocateur. It is interesting to note in this connection that some of the theses put forward by Viatrovych and Mykhal'chyshyn coincide. For example, like Viatrovych, Mykhal'chyshyn uses the term "Ukrainian-Polish war" as a label for the killings of the Polish population in Volhynia in 1943.[51] He takes pride in these events, calling them a "merciless Ukrainian Reconquista", whose result was "revenge for the defeat of the ZUNR ... an ethnically pure Ukrainian Volhynia".[52]

It is no secret that Holocaust studies are often used by Russian and Polish (mostly from *kresowiacy* circles) nationalists with the aim of attacking Ukrainian statehood.[53] For example, the Party of Regions parliamentary deputy Vadim Kolesnichenko has long been engaged in such activities. His "International Anti-Fascist Front" on at least two occasions illegally published (in awful Russian translation and with highly tendentious introductions) studies by Western scholars on the history of the OUN and UPA, including texts by Rossoliński-Liebe.[54] Rossoliński-Liebe has actively condemned both

---

[51]   Nakhtigal' & Zirka z neba, "Nash Bandera", *Vatra*, http://www.vatra.cc/yev ropa/nash-bandera.html.

[52]   Ibid.

[53]   *Kresowiacy*—the ethnic Polish population and their descendants from the so-called "Eastern Borderlands", formerly part of Poland, and present-day Western Ukraine, Western Belarus, and Lithuania.

[54]   Petro Solod'ko, "Yak Kolesnichenko oskandalivsia pered zakhidnymy istorykamy", *Istorychna Pravda*, 5 June 2012, http://www.istpravda.com.ua/columns/2012/06/5/87087/; "Kolesnichenko potsupyv chuzhu pratsiu", *Istorychna Pravda*, 9 April 2103, http://www.istpravda.com.ua/short/2013/04/9/120043/.

Kolesnichenko's piracy and his instrumentalization of these works, but he makes no mention of this in his monograph. It is also odd that Rossoliński-Liebe fails to make any comment here on the books about the OUN and UPA written by Aleksandr Diukov, director of the Moscow-based "Historical Memory" Foundation. The latter is known for its instrumentalization of the Holocaust and other mass killings from the World War II period with the aim of helping the Kremlin to attack Ukraine and the Baltic states. Of course, one needs to approach Diukov's works with great caution, but at the same time, one also needs to remember that he has been provided with privileged access to documents from the FSB Archive which is currently effectively closed to scholars.

Stylistically, the book leaves something to be desired. Rossoliński-Liebe takes a paragraph to say what could be said in a sentence, and a page to say what could be said in a paragraph, a problem that apparently arises out of an inability to analyze and a tendency to replace analysis with description. Thus, for example, pages 396–98 are devoted to the topic of monuments on the territory of Western Europe that were erected with the aim of commemorating local civilians and *chekist* victims of Ukrainian nationalists. This material is potentially fascinating, but the author merely lists the dates on which the monuments were unveiled and describes their inscriptions. He provides no analysis, and does not investigate, for example, whether the given commemorative form differed from that used in other regions, what role the local party organs played in the erection of these monuments, or what the post-1991 fate of these monuments has been.

Before leaving office in early 2010 the Ukrainian President Viktor Yushchenko awarded Stepan Bandera the rank of Hero of Ukraine. On the one hand, this prompted a host of political speculations; on the other, it provoked an academic debate, in which apologists for Bandera and the OUN also took part. One result of this was the publication of the book *Strasti za Banderoiu*.[55] Rossoliński-Liebe divides the participants of that debate into three groups: 1)

---

[55]   Tarik Cyril Amar, Ihor Balyns'kyi, Yaroslav Hrytsak (eds), *Strasti za Banderoiu* (Kyiv: Grani-T, 2010).

historians with a critical approach to Bandera's legacy (John-Paul Himka, Franziska Bruder, David Marples, Per Anders Rudling, the author himself); 2) "'liberal" and 'progressive' Ukrainian scholars such as Yaroslav Hrytsak, Andrii Portnov, Vasyl' Rasevych, and Mykola Riabchuk"; and 3) defenders of Bandera (Volodymyr Viatrovych, Marco Levytsky, Askold Lozynskyj) (p. 520). In my view the criteria used with regard to the second group identified here are excessively vague and the criticisms made of their work not always valid. Thus Rossoliński-Liebe cites an article by Hrytsak that was published in 1996,[56] without noting that the author, who, incidentally, acknowledges that he is not a specialist on the history of the Holocaust,[57] had changed his position on certain issues in the intervening period.[58] In various articles published over the course of the past decade Hrytsak has recognized that members of the OUN and the UPA took part in the persecution and extermination of the Jewish population.[59] Furthermore, in his role as editor of *Ukraïna Moderna* Hrytsak has often offered Ukrainian and foreign historians the opportunity to publish texts critical of the OUN, UPA and their heritage in the journal and on its website.

Rossoliński-Liebe reproaches Andrii Portnov for using the term "integral nationalism" to describe the OUN's ideology. Rossoliński-Liebe writes that "[f]ollowing [John A.] Armstrong, [Portnov] called the OUN-UPA 'integral nationalists' and suggested that their cult would be a legitimate pursuit" (p. 523). In fact, Armstrong himself used the term in the 1950s so as to avoid creating trouble over the issue of the OUN's legacy at a time when the Cold War was gathering pace and many Ukrainian radical right-wing activists were actively collaborating with Western intelligence services, such that labeling CIA personnel "fascists" at that time could

---

56   Yaroslav Hrytsak, "Ukraintsi v antytvreis'kykh aktsiakh", *I*, 8 (1996), http://www.ji.lviv.ua/n8texts/hrycak.htm.

57   Yaroslav Hrytsak, "Moia vidpodid' Grzegorzu Rossolinski-Liebe", *Ukraïna Moderna*, 30 June 2012, http://www.uamoderna.com/blog/172.

58   Rossoliński-Liebe has also made other unjustified attacks on Hrytsak; see Grzegorz Rossoliński-Liebe, "Świat w mroku and Its Reception in Ukraine", *Ab Imperio*, http://net.abimperio.net/node/2573.

59   See for example Yaroslav Hrytsak, *Strasti za nazionalizmom: stara istoria na noviy lad. Essei* (Kyiv: Krytyka. 2011), 228, 243.

well have cost a scholar his career.[60] Furthermore, the term "integral nationalism" was conceived not by Armstrong but by Carlton Hayes, and was also actively used by, for example, Peter Alter.[61]

It is clear that Rossoliński-Liebe finds all forms of extremism abhorrent. He condemns the attempts at rehabilitating Stalin currently underway both in contemporary Russia and in several regions of Eastern Ukraine (p. 526). He is also critical of Polish right-wing radicalism. He devoted one of the subsections of the book to a comparison of the Bandera cult with other authoritarian and totalitarian leadership cults (pp. 526–29). In his description of the cult surrounding Polish right-wing politician Roman Dmowski, Rossoliński-Liebe asserts that the manner in which Dmowski was commemorated by the Polish diaspora during the Cold War is very similar to the Ukrainian diaspora's veneration of Bandera:

> Like the Bandera worshipers, Dmowski admirers have denied or diminished the anti-Semitic and extremist views expressed by him and the Endecja movement and have prized his patriotism and his devotion to the process of establishing a nation state. They have also propagated distorted nationalist versions of Polish history. They have denied the Polish involvement in the Holocaust and have presented the Poles as tragic but brave heroes and martyrs, and the victims of their neighbors, in particular Germans and Russians (p. 527).

Rossoliński-Liebe compares the Ustaša cult of Ante Pavelić in independent Croatia with the cult of Bandera and the OUN in Ukraine after 1991 (p. 529). It is significant that the Ustaša cult became very popular against the backdrop of the war for independence and the rule of President Franjo Tudjman. At that time, Serbs came to be referred to as "Četnici" and Croatians as "Ustaše" in the propaganda of the warring parties. We are currently witnessing something similar happening in connection to the conflict in the Donbas, where the Ukrainian army and volunteer battalions are often called "banderites". As Croatia moved forward towards integration into the

---

[60]   For Armstrong's discussion of "integral nationalism", see John A. Armstong, *Ukrainian Nationalism*, 2nd ed. (Littleton: Ukrainian Academic Press, 1980), 20-21.
[61]   Unfortunately, Portnov did not specify exactly what he meant by the term "integral nationalism"; see Andrii Portnov, "Kontekstualizatsiia Stepana Bandery", *Strasti za Banderoi* (Kyiv: Grani-T, 2010), 392.

EU and NATO, the Croatian state authorities had to renounce the cult of the Ustaše and their leader. Although this was a very painful process, it brought results. It is no longer possible for any respectable Croatian politician to praise Pavelić or to use the Ustaša greeting "Ready for the Homeland!" ("Za dom spremni!"). It seems to me that the situation regarding the struggle with aggressive nationalism is better in Croatia not only because the Croatian state had a more favorable starting position and more competent politicians but also because the Ustaše received their statehood from Hitler and actively collaborated with the Nazis until the end of the war. By contrast, the members of the OUN, even though the OUN was a variant of East European fascism whose members killed Poles, Jews, and Ukrainians who did not share their views, also in part became victims of the Nazi occupation regime. For this reason it is sometimes very difficult to explain to the layperson that it is possible to be an ideological fascist and simultaneously a victim of the Nazi SD, to spend time in a Gestapo prison or concentration camp and even to die there.

At times Rossoliński-Liebe interprets the OUN and UPA in a very specific way, comparing them with other nationalist movements and partisan armies in Europe. For example, he accuses Polish intellectuals Mieczysław and Ksawery Pruszyński, who compared the relationship between the Ukrainian nationalist movement (including its radical-right segment) and the Polish state with the British-Irish or Spanish-Catalonian analogy, of "romanticizing" the OUN. But why exactly should this qualify as "romanticization"? The IRA, which in many respects can be compared to the Ukrainian Military Organization (UVO), also included activists who initially fought London for independence and later began to sympathize with the ideas of fascism and Benito Mussolini. One such example was Eoin O'Duffy. In 1930 he founded the Army Comrades Association. Members of this society wore blue shirts and, like members of the OUN before 1943, greeted one another with the "Roman salute". O'Duffy's men fought in Spain on Franco's side and attempted to collaborate with the Nazis during World War II.[62]

---

[62]   "From a Free State Hero to a Buffoon in a Blueshirt", *Irish Independent*, 2 December 2006, http://www.independent.ie/opinion/analysis/from-a-free-state-hero-to-a-buffoon-in-a-blueshirt-26349279.html.

Rossoliński-Liebe is inclined to compare the UPA to the "Forest Brothers" in the occupied Baltic states (p. 532). In parallel, he avoids comparing the UPA to the Polish partisans. In Ukraine and amongst the Ukrainian diaspora it is currently very fashionable to compare the UPA with the Polish Home Army (AK). In my view this approach is not quite justified, since the founders of the AK were representatives of the Polish government-in-exile, which was not comprised exclusively of right-wing and radical-right-wing figures. Bandera's UPA on the other hand was founded as a military formation of the OUN-B. Later on its ranks were joined by many people holding different views, including peasants who lacked a clear political or world-view orientation. It would be more accurate to compare the "early UPA" (1943–44) to the Polish National Armed Forces (Narodowe Siły Zbrojne, NSZ). The founders of that partisan movement were on the radical right. The NSZ was notorious for its anti-Semitic slogans and murders of Jews. Like the OUN, the AK and NSZ in the Polish underground tried to keep control over the auxiliary German-organized "blue police".[63] Finally, like the OUN, after the Red Army's victory at Stalingrad the NSZ came to see not Nazi Germany but the USSR as the main enemy.

Rossoliński-Liebe takes a sharply critical approach to the cult of the OUN, UPA, and the SS "Galicia" division in Ukraine and among the Ukrainian diaspora. But what is striking here is that he discusses this subject very much from the perspective of an outsider; nor does he offer Ukrainian society any suggestions for a way out of this trap. As Stirlitz put it in the popular Soviet TV series, "It's always easier to criticize and get angry. Putting forward a reasonable program of action is always harder". By contrast, the Polish historian Tomasz Stryjek offers very interesting advice on how to handle the OUN and UPA heritage and on how it might be combined with, for example, elements of the Soviet past. Stryjek outlines his vision for a new national narrative in which:

> the role of hero, victim, criminal, and witness would be carried out by separate individuals, rather than by nations or organizations as a whole [my empha-

---

[63]   "Policja Granatowa", https://www.youtube.com/watch?v=9bC5cohHjwg.

sis—YR]. The same individuals can be evaluated in different ways in different periods of their biography. There would be obvious criminals—both
those for whom this was the only role they played in their life, and those who
sooner or later themselves became victims. And the heroes [of this narrative]
would be those who saved the lives of other people, irrespective of the group
belonging or the role played by those whom they saved.[64]

This approach would be equally well suited to the Ukrainian case, it
seems to me.

To sum up: this is not an ideal book, but it is to be welcomed
as the first scholarly biography of OUN leader Stepan Bandera. Post-
Soviet Ukrainian scholarship has yet to reach the methodological
level enabling the production of serious scholarly work on this subject. The scholars writing critical histories of the OUN and UPA either live or spend most of their time outside Ukraine. I hope that
this situation will soon change, and that no amount of legislative
acts[65] or threats by radicals[66] will succeed in arresting this process
of change. The historical field in Ukraine frequently suffers from an
inability to separate text from author. In this connection I would
recommend that Rossoliński-Liebe's critics first read his book, so as
to form their own opinion of his work and then, even better, to write
their own book on the subject! It is my hope that the publication of
this book and, perhaps, its future translation into Ukrainian, will
serve not to intensify the old conflict between radicals, which has
already brought bloody consequences in the Donbas, but to stimu-
late scholarly academic discussions—Ukraine's own version of the
Polish debates over the tragedy at Jedwabne.

Yuri Radchenko
Center for Research on Inter-Ethnic Relations
in Eastern Europe, Kharkiv

---

[64]   Tomasz Stryjek, "Fashyzm chy integral'nyi natsionalism? OUN u suchasnykh
publichnykh dyskusiakh i v istoriografichniy ta politologichniy perspektyvi",
Ukraïna Moderna, no. 20 (2014): 147.

[65]   "Komentari istorykiv pro Zakon 'Pro pravovyi status ta vshanuvannia pam'iati
bortsiv za nezaleshnist' Ukrainu u XX stolitti'", *Politychna Krytyka*, 14 April 2015,
http://ukraine.politicalcritique.org/2015/04/aktualni-komentari-zakon-pro-
vshanuvannya-bortsiv-za-nezalezhnist/.

[66]   "Ukrainofobia ne proide!", *Pravyi Sector Info*, available at http://banderivets.o
rg.ua/ukrayinofobiya-ne-projde-zayava.html.

REVIEWS

Nataliya Danilova. *The Politics of War Commemoration in the UK and Russia*. Houndmills, Basingstoke: Palgrave Macmillan Memory Studies, 2015. xv, 280 pp.

In this ambitious comparative work, Nataliya Danilova, Lecturer in the Department of Politics and International Relations at the University of Aberdeen, explores the ways in which war commemorations in the contemporary United Kingdom and Russia "potentially evoke nationalistic sentiments, normalise warfare and militarise societies at the cultural level" (xi). She argues that those who participate in national commemorations for the dead should also take political responsibility for the current conflicts in which the nation's soldiers fight. If commemorations provide comfort for families and support for soldiers alone, they become "depoliticised"—detached from the political conditions that create and sustain war—and also "decontextualised,"—as they omit discussion and debate about the specific military conflicts in which the nation participates. Such commemorations allow a "remembrance without politics" that serves as a "justification of future conflicts" (xi-xii). By showing similarities between war commemorations in Britain, a society with strong democratic traditions, and the authoritarian Soviet Union and increasingly anti-democratic Russia, Danilova provocatively suggests that, despite these ideological differences, "in both countries, the politics of war commemoration is capable of subverting political debate and limiting the scope of public deliberation over modern wars and the role of the national armed forces" (218).

Danilova considers the commemoration of British soldiers in the Falklands War of 1982, the Gulf War of 1990-91, the Iraq War of 2003-2009, and the Afghanistan War of 2001-2014. On the Soviet/Russian side, she explores the remembrance of Russian soldiers in the Soviet Afghan War of 1979-89 and the two Chechen Wars of 1994-96 and 1999-2009. Danilova's book is extremely well researched and her careful analysis is sensitive to the many particularities of both societies. She underlines the strong similarities in the ways commemorations function without minimizing the distinct characteristics of each case.

A great strength of the work is the broad spectrum of commemorations that Danilova explores in both the British and Soviet/Russian cases. She investigates the British media in general, war memorials and the National Memorial Arboretum, internet memorials, and commemorative events on Armistice Day and Remembrance Day. The Russian section contains a parallel analysis of commemoration of the war dead in the Soviet and then Russian media, of war memorials and the Serafimovskoe Cemetery in St. Petersburg (an example of patterns of local commemoration), of internet memorials, and of Victory Day celebrations.

Danilova points out that contemporary British soldiers are "the successors of the 'glorious dead'" (208) of the First World War. While this is certainly the case, it is important to remember that the commemoration of the First World War in Britain is itself contested terrain in which narratives of national honor compete with other persistent narratives about the futility of a war where "lions" (British troops) were led by "donkeys," callous generals who sent tens of thousands to the slaughter needlessly. Danilova's work is at its best when she includes analysis of resistance to the dominant narratives of war commemoration such as the white poppy peace movement in Britain, or when British shoppers completely ignore the two minutes of silence on Armistice Day. While I agree that decontextualized and military-centered support for the soldiers as heroes or venerated victims of war can undercut these oppositional currents, it is important not to flatten the uneven texture of popular responses to commemoration into uniform support for military endeavors.

Recent events in Russia bolster Danilova's arguments about the use of commemoration of the Second World War to mobilize patriotic sentiments in contemporary Russia while skipping over the messy Afghan and Chechen conflicts. Her book went to press before the 9 May 2015, "Immortal Regiment" (*Bessmertnyi Polk*) parades, in which purportedly millions of Russian citizens marched with pictures of their relatives who had served in the Second World War, creating direct personal relationships with the war dead and veterans of the war that ended seventy years ago, instead of with the living veterans of the Afghan and Chechen wars. Danilova also effectively shows the ways in which the private commemorations of the families of Afghan and Chechen war dead simultaneously challenge and support the current government. While on the one hand, the relatives, most notably led by committees of soldiers' mothers, confront the authorities and demand recognition for the sacrifice of their sons, this "patriotism of despair" as Serguei Oushakine calls it, seeks for the lost and unrecognized soldiers to be incorporated into the national narrative, thus upholding the nation. Yet, here too, it is important to underline, perhaps even more than Danilova does, that despite the growing overall ideological consent to the militarization of the Russian nation, if draft dodging and passive resistance to cooperation with the military persist, this consent will not translate into effective military action or state legitimacy.

The Politics of War Commemoration is a timely book that demonstrates the ways in which modern states use the commemoration of the war dead to promote and support messy, ambiguous, and conflict-ridden military campaigns. Yet, as the American example of anti-Vietnam protest and the Soviet example of the collapse of support for the war in Afghanistan in the mid-1980s show, what seems to be a powerful pro-war consensus can sometimes collapse under the weight of new political circumstances and social formations. Danilova's outstanding work allows us to see the building blocks of military ideology at work as they are arranged and rearranged by states and social forces to build (or destroy) consensus.

Karen Petrone
Department of History
University of Kentucky

Rodric Braithwaite, *Afgantsy: The Russians in Afghanistan 1979-89*
Oxford: Oxford University Press, 2013. 417 pp.

"In Afghanistan", recalls Ruslan Aushev, a former Soviet officer in Afghanistan, "we did not have the task, as many say, of defeating

anybody. The main task for us in Afghanistan was to secure. To secure the transport of goods, to protect communications, to help the
Afghan army" (Larina *et al* 2014). Indeed, many studies have tried to
analyze the tasks of the Soviet troops during their ten-year long
presence in Afghanistan, to unravel the military and diplomatic implications of this conflict, which became the major combat mission
of the Soviet forces after World War II. Among these publications
we find the groundbreaking Russian account by Alexander Liakhovskii (1995), as well as the books by Gregory Feifer (2009) and Artemy
Kalinovsky (2011). The causes and the long-term consequences of
the war, however, still remain to be fully disclosed. Rodric
Braithwaite, the former British Ambassador to Moscow between
1988 and 1992, has delivered one of the best English-language accounts of the war. His book, *Afgantsy*, benefits from the author's
acquaintance with Soviet diplomatic circles and stands out because
it is based to a large extent on Russian sources. Among the Russian-
language works he exploits are Liakhovskii's *Tragediia i doblest' Afgana* (1995), Varennikov's *Nepovtorimoe* (2001), and Gai and Snegirev's *Vtorzhenie. Neizvestnye stranitsy neob"iavlennoi voiny* (1990)—
the latter in particular is a key source on which Braithwaite draws
time and again.

   This book is hence of interest for all scholars concerned with
the Soviet war in Afghanistan and for a broader audience interested
in this dramatic chapter of Cold War History. Braithwaite begins the
first section of his book, "The Road to Kabul", with a concise sum-
mary of Afghan history from the 17th century. He pays close attention
to the country's most recent history, following the overthrow of
president Mohammed Daud in 1978. Two things emerge in these
opening chapters: first, there was a long-standing diplomatic and
economic interaction between the USSR and Afghanistan well before the Soviet military machine was set in motion. The intervention
can only be grasped against the backdrop of these intense relations
and of the presence of hundreds of Soviet technical advisers working
in Afghanistan prior to the intervention. Second, the Soviet leadership was extremely reluctant to dispatch troops. However, it is a rather superficial preliminary conclusion to say that the Soviet Union
"slithered towards military intervention because they could not

think of a better alternative" (p. 57), or because they were driven by emotions (p. 74). The first section of the book closes with a highly interesting account of dissenting voices within the USSR. While there were also debates at the Politburo level, it cannot be stressed enough that the Soviet Union, even under Brezhnev, was anything but a unitary, monolithic political entity. There was dissent, there were doubts, and, at least in part, these could also be voiced. The Academy of Sciences, for example, repeatedly raised concerns about sending Soviet soldiers (whom Braithwaite consistently calls "the Russians") to Afghanistan.

The 125-page long central section of the book is devoted to the "Disasters of the War". It gives an account of the conflict from the creation of the 40th Army to its downfall. The 40th army is the true protagonist of this book: Braithwaite skillfully retells the drama of this unit and its individual soldiers, arguing that their fate was sealed from the very beginning. The Soviet troops were neither materially nor psychologically equipped for the war to come. Prepared for a conventional conflict on the battlefields of Europe, the Red Army had to fight a counter-insurgency war. However, either the Soviet troops continued to apply the conventional war framework on Afghanistan, or they adhered to the belief that their task was basically a peaceful one: Braithwaite, echoing Ruslan Aushev, claims that this task was not to occupy the country but "to secure the towns and the road between them" (p. 123) and to protect a socialist revolution from outside interference (p. 126).

The Soviet war in Afghanistan was a counterinsurgency war, "a war without fronts" (p. 230). Thus, the numbers of battles won did not determine the outcome of the war. It was a complex affair of military and political factors, both domestic and international. Braithwaite successfully tackles the former issues and discusses the "four distinct phases" of the war that are "usually" distinguished (p. 139). Braithwaite contradicts Liakhovskii's overall negative picture of the 40th army, underscoring that at least in part it succeed in adapting. However, it would be worthwhile to pursue further research to buttress this claim. Chapter Seven, *The Nation Builder,* is probably one of the most interesting sections of the whole book, because it looks beyond the pure military issues of the war. In many telling anecdotes drawn from Russian literature, Braithwaite presents the role of soldiers, advisers, and women, and discusses their day-to-day routines in the cities and in the countryside. However, the book provides neither a systematic account of the massive financial side of the Soviet nation building effort, a task better fulfilled, for example, by Robinson and Dixon (2013), nor a discussion of the cultural policies pursued by the USSR in Afghanistan. The author also looks at the activities of soldiers beyond the battlefield and off-duty (pp. 188ff) and even to their artistic production. This section confirms that certain claims about the war were Western myths. These include for example the fighting morale of Central Asian soldiers (p. 121), the impact of American Stingers (p. 205), or the Soviet toy-like mines (p. 235).

The final section of the book deals with the retreat of the Soviet troops from Afghanistan. It is in this section that the author assumes a more political point of view (esp. on pp. 272–82), highlighting the political process initiated by Mikhail Gorbachev after he took power. Gorbachev wanted to get out of Afghanistan as quickly as possible. Still, he wanted to do so in an orderly manner, that is, with a regime in place that could hang on with Soviet material assistance but without Soviet troops. Gorbachev and his Foreign Ministry were also concerned about the USSR's reputation in the Third World in the event of an overly sudden Soviet retreat. Mohammed Najibullah was the Kremlin's pick to reach out to all warring parties and initiate a process of reconciliation. The issue of "building socialism", however, became a completely secondary task (p. 273). Braithwaite is at his best when he combines the political history of the decision to retreat taken at the top echelons of the Soviet state (ch. 12) with stories from the ground, showing how soldiers experienced their departure (also ch. 11). Finally, *Afgantsy* takes a look at the period after the Soviet withdrawal, both in Russia and in Afghanistan. To the surprise of many observers, Najibullah's government survived until 1992, when the collapse of the USSR resulted in an end to financial and material supportl. The Kremlin's new ruler, Boris Yeltsin, cut all aid to Afghanistan's central government and started dealing with Ahmad Shah Masud and General Dostum's Northern Alliance. Kabul fell to the Taliban in September 1996. For the veterans of the war, the return home meant a protracted process of adaptation to civilian life in countries traumatized by the collapse of the Soviet empire and with shattered economies. In most former Soviet republics, veterans had to struggle for recognition.

Rodric Braithwaite has produced a highly interesting, accessible and instructive book that is empirically rich and well written. The author discloses an impressive level of detail on a range of aspects of the Soviet war in Afghanistan, from the role of women to soldiers' exact wages. His extensive use of Russian sources is a strong point of the book, but in some respects it also determines the book's weaker sides. It is conducive to Braithwaite's aims because it unravels many particulars of the war previously unknown to the English-language reader. The book's appeal derives first and foremost from the individual stories and dramas it retells, from Colonel Sidorov who sacrificed his life to save that of his comrades in arms (p. 211), or from Nikolai Bystrov, the POW turned Masud's bodyguard (p. 263). However, this approach can be disadvantageous: the story built around these individual experiences is prone to take over the Soviet perspective and to romanticize the soldiers' experiences, losing sight of the big (political) picture. Too often the book indulges in the veterans' memories, retelling the story of the war from the perpetrators' perspective, without questioning their accounts. Is this the lesson *Afgantsy* tries to teach: that there are no perpetrators and no victims in a counterinsurgency war? Braithwaite often abstains both from moral judgments and from political analysis. For example, he delivers little hints as to why the USSR was drawn into the quagmire of this war. Westad (2007), in contrast, has advanced an interesting argument that Third World regimes often successfully managed to push the super-powers into certain policies by threatening to switch sides. Focusing entirely on the Soviet soldiers' perspective as this work does, it also comes as no surprise that the Afghan view on the conflict is completely absent. The Afghans did not matter to the Soviet soldiers—they barely appear in the soldiers' accounts, and hence they evidently matter little to the author of this book, too. Bringing in an Afghan or even a post-colonial perspective is not Braithwaite's aim, just as it has not been the aim of Liakhovskii

(1995) or Feifer (2009): these books retell the Soviet soldiers' experiences, and they do this very well. Accordingly, when the Afghan population is mentioned at all, it appears rather monochromatic. Braithwaite puts much stress on the alleged religiosity of the population (which has become a cliché when discussing Afghanistan) and sees the "religious factor" as cause and determinant for their actions (pp. 48, 122, 123). Braithwaite claims that the population was "not ripe for socialism" (p. 48) or that it had no interest in the fruits of modernity that the USSR allegedly offered the country, that they preferred "their own ways" (p. 123). These statements put undue weight on religion and do not reflect the complexity of Afghan society and of the international context in which they were located. Again, Braithwaite takes over the Soviet view on the war while, and, with a pinch of orientalism, he implies that Afghanistan is stuck in backwardness. Religion certainly was a mobilizing force but it is safe to say that it was not the only factor that drove resistance. Other key reasons for resistance were that the fruit of modernity was poisoned—that it came along with a high degree of structural, epistemic, and bluntly physical violence exercised by the country's "socialist" leadership and by the Soviet occupiers. Afghanistan was a *Gewaltraum*, in which, however, the state, supported by Soviet troops, became a primary source of violence. Finally, Braithwaite, at times, seems to put the violence exercised by the invaders and the resistance on the same level (pp. 123, 232-234), disregarding the fact that, as Frantz Fanon famously argued in *The Wretched of the Earth* (1961), violence might be the only appropriate answer to colonialism. Parallels to the Western war in Afghanistan since 2001 are scarce (pp. 181, 304, 227, 236). There are more comparisons to the British experience (pp. 129-31), however, all these comparisons remain unsystematic. The scholarly value of this book lies first and foremost in having incorporated a wide array of sources, especially, Russian ones. Researchers analyzing events during the Soviet presence in Afghanistan will greatly benefit from the detailed bibliography. However, the book is widely lacking in a hypothesis to be tested, or an argument to be advanced. Indeed, there is no proper "conclusion", but rather an "epilogue" and technical "annexes".

Hence, Braithwaite keeps his promise: he puts the veterans, the *Afgantsy*, and their memories at the center of his work, leaving aside a political and economic analysis of the conflict. The book is an excellent, well-sourced English-language chronicle of the war in Afghanistan and most certainly a highly delectable read. It is an indispensable companion for any future work on the Soviet war in Afghanistan.

Philipp Casula
Department of History
University of Zurich

REFERENCES

Feifer, Gregory (2005) *The Great Gamble: The Soviet War in Afghanistan*. New York: Harper.
Kalinovsky, Artemy (2011) *A Long Goodbye*. Cambridge, MA: Harvard University Press.
Larina, Kseniia, Shargunov, Sergei and Aushev, Ruslan (2014) "Sovetskie voiska v Afganistane: Vzgliad v istoriiu spustia 25 let", *Ekho Moskvy*, 14 February, http://www.echo.msk.ru/programs/year2014/1257300-echo/#element-text
Liakhovskii, Aleksandr (1995) *Tragediia i doblest' Afgana*. Moscow: GPI Iskona.
Robinson, Paul and Dixon, Jay (2013) *Aiding Afghanistan: A History of Soviet Assistance to a Developing Country*. London: Hurst & Co.
Westad, Odd Arne (2007) *The Global Cold War*. Cambridge, MA: Harvard University Press.

E. S. Seniavskaia, *Istoriia voin Rossii XX veka v chelovecheskom izmerenii: problemy voenno-istoricheskoi antropologii i psikhologii. Kurs lektsii*. Moscow: RGGU, 2012. 332 pp.

This work reviewed here is a textbook for tertiary level students, and this genre naturally imposes its own specificities on the presentation of the material. We do not have the right to expect wide discussion or deep immersion in bibliographical sources here; students expect unambiguous definitions and clear disciplinary boundaries. But this book does provide a sound basic introduction to the author's concept of military-historical anthropology.

The author of this book, Elena Seniavskaia, is a renowned Russian historian, professor, and leading researcher at the Institute of Russian History in the Russian Academy of Sciences. Her areas of expertise include 20th-century Russian military history, social history, the history of everyday life, historical psychology, military psychology, and military sociology. She positions herself as the founder and leader of the emerging field of military-historical anthropology and psychology. In addition, she is laureate of the Russian Federation State Prize for Young Scholars, awarded for outstanding achievement in the field of science and technology, and laureate of the Russia-wide media contest "Patriot of Russia 2008". Finally, the author is well known in the Russian academic context for a series of scholarly works and textbooks on various themes, including *1941-45. The Front Generation: An Historical-Psychological Study* (Moscow: IRI, RAN, 1995); *The Human Being at War: Historical-Psychological Essays* (Moscow: IRI RAN, 1997); *The Psychology of War in the 20th Century: The Historical Experience of Russia* (Moscow: ROSSPEN, 1999); *Russia's Adversaries in the Wars of the 20th Century: Evolution of the "Enemy Image" in the Consciousness of Army and Society* (Moscow: ROSSPEN, 2006).

The structure and content of the book is set out in the form of eight lectures. The first chapter is devoted to military-historical anthropology as a new branch of historical inquiry. It covers the description of war as a social historical-psychological phenomenon; the author's concept of military anthropology; and the historiography of military anthropology.

The second lecture examines issues surrounding the use of sources for military anthropology, via the example of the Great Patriotic War. Here the author unpacks the concept of the subjectivity of sources and its main forms; sources of private provenance; oral history materials; poetic folklore song; and also literary fiction and military prose.

The third lecture looks at the human being in the extreme conditions of war, as the key theme addressed by military anthropology. It explores such themes as war as a liminal situation; the heroic "breakthrough" and panic in war; combat psychology and soldiers' fatalism; everyday life at the front; the time and space of war; and the existential experience of frontline soldiers.

The fourth lecture is devoted to "leaving war behind" as a socio-psychological problem for combatants. It covers topics such as post-traumatic stress disorder, the "Afghan syndrome", and the "lost generation" of Afghan war veterans.

The fifth lecture discusses the psychology and ideology of war; the image of war as a phenomenon of social consciousness; the typology of enemy images, and of the symbols and myths of war; religiosity and atheism at war; and soldiers' superstitions.

The sixth lecture describes the Russian army in the wars of the 20th century. It discusses the specificities of the psychology of the rank-and-file soldiers and of commanders; their relations in combat situations; military-professional categories; and the relationships between different branches of the armed forces.

The seventh lecture is devoted to the military anthropological approaches to socio-demographic and gender issues. Topics covered here include the particularities of age-group structure and psychology, and the situation of women in times of war, from the pre-revolutionary setting through the Soviet epoch and the Afghan experience.

The concluding final lecture focuses on the topic of war in historical memory, from the theoretical-methodological aspect to the historical memory of the First and Second World Wars in Russia and in the West. The section ends with a discussion of the actualization of historical memory via jubilee dates.

Thus, in this textbook, which is a continuation of the author's previous academic books, the author sets out a new direction in scholarship, that of military-historical anthropology as a "new interdisciplinary branch of scholarship, integrating the achievements, subject areas and research tools of military psychology, sociology, pedagogy, history, cultural studies, medicine, and other disciplines that study the human being in conditions of military activity" (Seniavskaia 2012: 9). According to the author, the fundamental novelty of this approach lies in its integrated systematic study of the human being in the context of military history (ibid.: 19).

The author's approach is underpinned by three methodological sources: the *Annales* school of history; philosophical hermeneutics and existentialism; and the Russian historiography on military psychology and military history. The existing Western socio-histor-

ical fields of military anthropology, military ethnography, war studies, and so on[1] are not examined by the author beyond citing individual works in order to demonstrate the lack of developed works
on the theme. The main corpus of academic materials referenced
here date to the 1960s-80s, and no 21st-century works on the theme
are cited. In this respect the author's claim to be pioneering a new
discipline is unfounded; in fact, this area of studies has long been
developing successfully in global scholarly space. There are numerous recent works that deal precisely with such themes as the human
dimension of war, the life experience of the soldier or officer im-
mersed both in the events of war and in his everyday experience,
both in informal interaction with his fellow servicemen at the front,
and in correspondence with loved ones at the home front. Contemporary military sociology and history has turned its face to "the little
man" at war and his experiences,[2] and also, in the German context
of the Second World War, to the double role of aggressor and victim.
The classical question of how soldiers succeed in overcoming on an

---

[1]   See for example the following works from the 2000s: Raymond C. Kelly, *Warless
Societies and the Origin of War* (Ann Arbor: University of Michigan Press, 2000);
Keith F. Otterbein, *The Anthropology of War* (Chicago: Waveland Press, 2009);
Mark Rose, *The Archaeology of War: Human Conflict since the Dawn of Civiliza-
tion* (New York: Hatherleigh Press, 2005); Alisse Waterston (ed.), *An Anthro-
pology of War: Views from the Frontline* (New York: Berghahn Books, 2008);
Paul Richards (ed.), *No Peace No War: Anthropology of Contemporary Armed
Conflicts* (Oxford: James Currey, 2005); George R. Lucas Jr., *Anthropologists in
Arms: The Ethics of Military Anthropology* (Lanham, MD: Altamira Press, 2009);
Robert A. Rubinstein and Kerry Fosher (eds), *Practicing Military Anthropology:
Beyond Expectations and Traditional Boundaries* (Bloomfield, CT: 2012); David
H. Price, *Weaponizing Anthropology: Social Science in Service of the Militarized
State* (Petrolia, CA: CounterPunch, 2011).

[2]   See Jason Crouthamel, *An Intimate History of the Front: Masculinity, Sexuality,
and German Soldiers in the First World War* (New York, NY: Palgrave Macmillan, 2014); Sönke Neitzel and Harald Welzer, *Soldaten: Protokolle vom Kämpfen,
Töten und Sterben* (Frankfurt am Main: S. Fischer, 2011); David Funkel, *The Good
Soldiers* (New York, NY: Farrar, Straus and Giroux, 2009); Jennifer Keene, *World
War I: the American Soldier Experience* (Lincoln: University of Nebraska Press,
2011); Nikolaus Buschmann and Horst Carl (eds), *Die Erfahrung des Krieges:
Erfahrungsgeschichtliche Perspektiven von der Französischen Revolution bis
zum zweiten Weltkrieg* (Paderborn: Ferdinand Schöningh Verlag, 2001); and
Christopher R. Browning, *Ordinary Men: Reserve Police Battalion 101 and the Fi-
nal Solution in Poland* (New York, NY: Harper Collins, 1998).

everyday basis the life-threatening situation of war,[3] its risks and uncertainties, finds an answer in the description of the everyday dimension of war. This includes both specific work related to war, and
also leisure activities aimed at taking a break from war. And like all
work, war work has its own ethic. In the case of the war work ethic,
its drive is to motivate, to justify, to reward with meaning. In this
way, the discursive polarization of front and Motherland in a tense
dynamic of convergence-divergence comprises the basic framework
that lends meaning to war labor, that demands its intensity, and that
legitimizes the sacrifices it entails.

The abovementioned hermetic nature of this study in turn has
led here to self-limitation when it comes to the selection of methodological tools. The author's quest for the human dimension of war
leads her to focus on personal documents in the form of letters to
and from the front, so-called "frontline correspondence". A whole
tradition has formed around the analysis of this particular genre of
sources, yet the related literature is rarely cited here and the author
does not take it into account in her analysis.[4] If we turn to another

---

3   Tino Käßner and Antje Käßner, *Wofür wir kämpfen: Wie der Krieg in Afghanistan unser Leben veränderte* (München: Irisana, 2011); Birgit Schneider, *From Soldiers to Citizens: The Civil Reintegration of Demobilized Soldiers of the German
Wehrmacht and the Imperial Japanese Army after Unconditional Surrender in
1945* (Washington: Washington State University, 2010); Tobias Pietz, *Demobilization and Reintegration of Former Soldiers in Post-War Bosnia and Herzego-
vina: An Assessment of External Assistance* (Hamburg: Institut für Friedensfor-
schung und Sicherheitspolitik, 2004); Benjamin Bieber, *Wie Kriege enden: Die
Reintegration von Soldaten in Nachkriegsgesellschaften* (Hamburg: Kovac,
2002).

4   Examples of this literature include: G. I. Zlokazov, "Soldatskie pis'ma s fronta v
kanun Oktiabria", *Svobodnaia mysl'*, no. 10 (1996): 37–46; N. A. Lokteva, "O
chem rasskazyvaiut pis'ma s frontov Pervoi mirovoi (Po dokumantam Gosarkh-
hiva Samarskoi oblasti)", *Ekho vekov*, no. 1 (2005): 31–35; B. I. Zhuchkov and V.
A. Kondrat'ev, "Pis'ma sovetskikh liudei perioda Velikoi Otechestvennoi voiny
kak istoricheskii istochnik", *Istoriia SSSR*, no. 4 (1961): 55–69; V. A. Somov,
"Pis'ma uchastnikov Velikoi Otechestvennoi voiny 1941-1945 gg.", *Voprosy istorii*, no. 8 (2003): 131–35; L. N. Pushkarev, "Chelovek na voine (istochniki po izu-
cheniiu mentaliteta frontovikov v gody Velikoi Otechestvennoi voiny)", *Etno-
graficheskoe obozrenie*, no. 3 (2000): 109–21; T. A. Bulygina, "Pis'ma s fronta kak
istochnik istorii povsednevnosti v gody Velikoi Otechestvennoi voiny", in
*Stavropol'e: Pravda voennykh let. Velikaia Otechestvennaia v dokumentakh i iss-
ledovaniiakh* (Stavropol': 2005), 530–40; A. I. Balandin, "Sbor dokumental'nykh
pamiatnikov Velikoi Otechestvennoi voiny", in *Voprosy sobiraniia, ucheta,*

type of source—narrative interviews—we discover that the author is apparently unfamiliar with contemporary narrative sociology and narratology, even though these are actively used by Russian oral history scholars.[5] Consequently, the author turns to a survey questionnaire drafted by Konstantin Simonov(!), and uses it as the foundation for her own empiricial studies—evidently on the assumption that the nature of war in the perception of its participants is a static phenomenon that changes little over time.

The book's section on historical memory provides yet another example of the consequences of remaining outside the well-trodden paths of global historical-anthropological analysis. Again, the body of literature presented here is peculiarly distorted. Here the author introduces her own set of concepts: documentary memory, interpretive memory, narrative memory, and actualized memory of mass consciousness (Seniavskaia 2012: 252). The author writes as though the famous works by Jan and Aleida Assmann, Maurice Halbwachs, Geoffrey Hartman, Pierre Nora and many others had never been written. As though it were possible to imagine a "narrative memory" outside interpretation, mass consciousness outside internalized ideologemes, or historical perceptions of the past that do not contain already interpreted historical events.

Since the author broadly weaves psychological resources into the direction being developed here, obviously, she ought not to have passed by the studies in memory produced by Markowitsch, Tulving, and others;[6] or the research of Russian scholar V. Nurkova,[7] all of whom have argued on the basis of experimental data that the

---

khraneniia i ispol'zovaniia dokumental'nykh pamiatnikov istorii i kul'tury. Ch. 1 (Moscow: 1982), 126–57; "Frontovye pis'ma uchastnikov Velikoi Otechestvennoi voiny kak istoricheskii istochnik tema dissertatsii i avtoreferata po VAK 07.00.99, kandidat istoricheskikh nauk Ivanov, Anton Yur'evich, Avtoreferat Dissertatsiia Artikul 373048 God: 2009.

5   We shall cite only names here: I. Trotsuk, V. Semenova, Ye. Yarskaia-Smirnova, Ye. Zdravomyslova, A. Temkina, Ye. Trubina, and others.

6   H. J. Markowitsch, "Die Errinerung von Zeitzeugen aus der Sicht der Gedaechtnisforschung", BIOS. Zeitschrift fuer Biographieforschung und Oral History, 1 (2000): 30–50; E. Tulving, "Episodic and Semantic Memory", in Organization of Memory, eds. E. Tulving and W. Donaldson (New York: Academic Press, 1972), 381–402.

7   V. Nurkova, Svershennoe prodolzhaetsia: Psikhologiia avtobiograficheskoi pamiati lichnosti (Moscow: Izd-vo Universiteta RAO, 2000).

existence of non-pre-interpreted historical perceptions, narratives and memories of the past is impossible. Consequently, the understanding of historical memory proposed by the author seems rather disjointed.

Finally, there is one important figure of silence in this work, and it concerns precisely the topic that stands at the center of Seniavskaia's work: the war in the memory of Russians. Why does it remain so important for Russian collective identity? Why is it that state ideology continues to draw upon and renew this resource, despite the fact that veterans, as the social group carrying the experience of World War Two, are now passing away? An answer to this question has in part been given by sociologists. The issue lies in the so-called culture of war and in negative identity. Thus, the famous Russian sociologist, based on the experience of many years (1996-2003) of conducting representative public opinion surveys, Lev Gudkov, director of VTsIOM, concluded that the Great Patriotic War and Victory in that war represented the most important and positive event in contemporary Russian history, a conclusion that led him to propose his thesis on "war as culture".[8] It is precisely the symbol of the war that forms the semantic field on which the major ideological conflicts are played out in contemporary Russia. The hyper-exploitation of the past Victory leads to the constant making-present of the war experience, to the unending search for new methods of commemoration, so as to further extend the life of this event, which remains the most important for Russians. Indeed, there is a sense in which we might read this very textbook, with its drive to lend a human dimension to a heavily institutionalized past event, as an example of precisely this kind of approach to historical time.

Elena Rozhdestvenskaya
The National Research University
Higher School of Economics, Moscow

---

8   L. Gudkov, "'Pamiat'' o voine i massovaia identichnost' rossiian", *Neprikosnovennyi zapas*, nos 2–3 (40–41) (2005), http://magazines.russ.ru/nz/2005/2/gu5.html (accessed 7 July 2015).

Polly Jones, *Myth, Memory, Trauma: Rethinking the Stalinist Past in the Soviet Union, 1953–70*. Yale University Press, 2013. xii, 362 pp.

The surge of books and articles about memory over the past couple of decades has created a new field of Memory Studies at the crossroads of history, literature and cultural studies. The field has not yet elaborated its own distinct comprehensive or specific methodology, and so the new literature is very diverse in its approaches; upon starting to read a book or article one can expect to find the logic of the author unfamiliar. As a historian by training, I always prefer books written with a historian's attention to the primary sources, analyzing details, people's motives, and the institutional logic that created and reformed people's memory at the crucial turning points in their countries' development. Polly Jones' book is exactly this kind of reading. Some might even argue that the absence of quotations from the founding figures of Memory Studies like Maurice Halbwachs should disqualify the book from the field of Memory Studies (despite the use of related key words in the title) making it just another "traditional history", but I would disagree: the problems that the author solves deal with the mechanisms of the social work of memory based on the use of a multitude of primary sources.

　　Polly Jones addresses one of the most important periods in the USSR's development. After Stalin's death the Soviet leaders made a decision to reveal the (partial) truth about the crimes of the regime. Yet at the same time they certainly did not want to lose power or destroy the Communist state; that is why theirs was an extremely difficult task. The author is right when she calls Khrushchev's 1956 Secret Speech denouncing Stalin an "unprecedented intervention in Soviet memory: an attempt to reveal and judge the complex truth about a (indeed, the) leading Bolshevik, without entirely forgetting or demonizing him" (p. 18). The discussions and vacillations about the national traumatic memory resulted in what we now consider a very important period of the nation's history; moreover, it can help us to understand better some of the problems that Russian society is facing now, another half a century later. Indeed, reading Polly Jones' book demonstrates to us that the major divisions in the arguments about Stalin in today's Russia were already present in the discussions of the late 1950s-60s: the combination of terror and victory over Nazi Germany, Stalin's personal traits and immanent features of the Communist regime, successes in science and the destruction of peasant lives were juxtaposed in the debates after the XX Congress of the Communist Party denounced Stalin's "cult of personality". Even the major argument used by neo-Stalinists today had already appeared in that epoch: Stalin's "leadership of the war and the construction of socialism" (p. 45).

One of the best features of the book is the presence of multiple voices of the people reacting to Khrushchev's Secret Speech, the renaming of Stalingrad as Volgograd, or Konstantin Simonov's war novel. There is also some attention paid here to the institutional side of the fight, and thus the Moscow Writers' Union, the journal *Voprosy Istorii* and Moscow State University's Department of Party History are treated as actors in the debates of the late 1950s. In order to obtain all this wealth of primary sources, Polly Jones spent a great deal of time in the Russian archives, including regional ones.

During Stalin's time in the Kremlin he became an embodiment of state power and communist ideas, the author reminds us, and that is why an attack on Stalin was for many witnesses a suicidal attack on the state. The latter was proved, from the Stalinists' point of view, by local unrest in the USSR, the crisis in Poznan, and especially by the Budapest uprising, all happening just months following the Secret Speech. Those events were, in turn, reasons for the issuance of a "closed letter" in late 1956 that effectively decreased the level of criticism toward Stalin set by the Secret Speech. The result was ambivalent. Stalin lost his godlike status but did not make his way into the camp of perpetrators. It was only five years later, at the 22nd Party Congress, that the next step in de-Stalinization was taken; but after Khrushchev's dismissal in 1964 the state froze further discussions. The problems of the traumatic Past were posed during the Khrushchev epoch but the de-Stalinization agenda was not fulfilled. The resulting ambivalence could be seen even in the portrayal of Stalin in the second decade of the third millennium.

Indeed, reading the book in contemporary Russia forces the reader to compare the de-Stalinization and later "normalization" of

Stalin's memory described by Polly Jones to historical politics now-adays. Thus, the popular response to the Secret Speech called, among other things, for some sort of lustration, which never did take place in the USSR or Russia; even now we hear lamentations that it never happened. The 1961 debates over renaming Stalingrad also look unfinished: in the 2010s the Communists still appeal to the city's world fame as Stalingrad just as the Stalinists did 54 years ago (p. 118). Finally, reading the author's formulation of the approach that the Soviet state chose to promote on this issue also reminds us of very recent discussions in post-Soviet Russia: finding a "balance between deconstructing the Stalin cult and reinforcing the Stalin-era usable past" (p. 103; see also p. 243).

There are also important differences between the two epochs: the author analyzes two major fields on which the battle around Stalin's name was unleashed: history and literature. This is definitely different from the current situation, where history plays an enormous role while literature is relatively neglected. The reasons for the importance of literature in the late USSR could be specially addressed.

What is missing from this rich and important book? It seems that the author shies away from formulating the questions to which she helps to find answers here. Why does the memory of Stalin still divide Russian society sixty years after his death? And why is the memory of the war still the glue that most unites Russians as a nation? The book gives us some hints but Polly Jones does not offer responses to these questions. The reasons for the de-Stalinization and the vacillations between vindication and condemnation of Stalin throughout the entire period researched for the book could also be addressed with better focus. The author mentions Khrushchev's struggle for power as one of the reasons behind these developments, but does not elaborate that important hypothesis.

There are also other questions raised by the material that would be worth addressing. What alternatives to de-Stalinization existed at that time? It seems that the author wanted to touch upon this theme when she mentioned the Chinese approach to the memory of Mao (p. 98), or when she compared the Khrushchev epoch to the Gorbachev era (pp. 129–30). It might also be interesting to compare forcible memory change (like the de-Nazification of Germany) to the voluntary decision of the regime itself, as was the case in the Soviet Union.

Overall, this is an important book that provides the reader with a better understanding of the unfinished de-Stalinization of Russia, its successes and natural limits, and gives us a new base for understanding the current turns in Russia's historical politics.

Ivan Kurilla
European University at St. Petersburg

Violeta Davoliūtė, *The Making and Breaking of Soviet Lithuania: Memory and Modernity in the Wake of War*. London and New York: Routledge, 2013. 212 pp.

This book offers a fresh perspective on the Soviet period of Lithuania's history. The historical narrative that Davoliūtė masterfully creates in the book goes beyond the ideas of genocide and oppression of the Lithuanian people and Lithuanian nation during the Soviet period. The book raises the issue of the agency of Lithuanian elites and local leaders of the Communist Party as well as posing the question of their responsibility for what occurred in Lithuania during the Soviet period. Therefore, Davoliūtė's research raises very sensitive issues for Lithuanian nation building.

The structure of the book is determined by the periodization of Lithuanian as well as Soviet history. Eight chapters cover the interwar period when independent Lithuania was established; World War II and its consequences for the changes in the ethnic structure of Vilnius; late Stalinism and Khrushchev's Thaw as the time of the rise of Lithuanian modernity; the Brezhnev era in the late 1960s–1970s, conceptualized as "the rustic turn" in Lithuanian culture; and, finally, the 1980s as the time of *perestroika* and *glasnost'* in Soviet history and of the national and political awakening of the Lithuanian people. Regarding each of these periods, Davoliūtė manages to show the continuity of Lithuanian history. By doing this, she challenges those historians who tend to consider the history of Soviet Lithuania "as an abyss, as an abnormal gap between two periods of normality" (p. 176). In this sense, the book takes an important step towards acknowledging and making sense of the experience of the majority of the Lithuanian people who tried to live their lives under the given political circumstances.

The book is nevertheless dedicated mostly to the experience of the Lithuanian intelligentsia whose representatives became the active part of the national renaissance during late socialism. One of the aims which Davoliūtė successfully achieves in her book is to demonstrate how the *Sąjūdis* movement that has become the symbol of the Lithuanian national revival and resistance was formed within—and not outside of or in opposition to—the Soviet system. As the author's argument goes, the autonomy of the cultural elite after de-Stalinization, as well as overlaps between national and Soviet interests in cultural policy, laid a foundation for the development of the modern national culture during the Soviet period. It was this development, which initially had no clear political mission, that made the Lithuanian national resistance possible during the later periods of Soviet history.

A particularly important discussion in the book is concentrated around the history of Vilnius and Lithuanization of the city after World War II. The book makes it clear how this mostly Polish and Jewish city became the center of the Lithuanian national idea and how "the theme of Vilnius as the ancient cradle of Lithuanian identity was blended seamlessly into the communist narrative of reconstruction and the creation of new identities" (p. 67). Hence the book contributes significantly to the literature on the history of Vilnius and the "Vilnius question" as one of the cornerstones of Lithuanian history.

While this is primarily an historical study, it also has a strong interdisciplinary influence. Davoliūtė uses a number of theories from cultural studies and sociology. Her sociological explanation of the behavior of Lithuanian intellectual elites seems particularly well justified and appealing. As Davoliūtė maintains, the loyalty to the

Soviet regime which the post-war Lithuanian intelligentsia demonstrated was connected to the fact that, for this generation, Soviet
rule was closely associated with urbanization and upward mobility.
Although the negative consequences of rapid urbanization and
modernization that Lithuania experienced are also scrutinized in
the book, the author also claims that the career path taken by the
famous Lithuanian poet Justinas Marcinkevičius and his peers, born
in villages in the 1930s, would have been hardly imaginable had they
come of age during the interwar period or World War II. Again, a
whole complex of factors such as the post-war anti-Soviet insurgency in the rural areas of Lithuania, the loss of Lithuanian, Polish,
and Jewish cultural elites in the course of pre-war deportations, Holocaust and post-war resettlement, and the educational promotion
of the peasantry during late Stalinism created the space for the birth
of a new Lithuania elite with a local (village) background and cosmopolitan aspirations. Having been cut off from the bonds of traditional family and sharing the same experience of "modern loneliness" (p. 85), these people formed a strong sense of a solid community that was participating "in a great historical project" (p. 85) under Soviet supervision.

However, the author also describes the sense of disillusion-
ment in the modernity project that the Lithuanian intelligentsia experienced in the middle 1960s. In Chapter 6, which represents a culminating moment of the book, Davoliūtė makes a strong argument
about the famous visit of Jean-Paul Sartre and Simone de Beauvoir
in 1965 as a turning point for Lithuanian intellectuals whose international ambitions were crushed by Sartre's disinterest in the literature and culture produced in the Lithuanian language. This led to
a significant shift in the development of Lithuanian culture which
from that point "instead of looking forward to the future life in modern city, [...] turned backward, and began a profound reflection on
what was being lost during the transition" (p. 120).

As Davoliūtė argues, the disappointment in modernity was
not a peculiarly Lithuanian phenomenon but was also observed
throughout the USSR in general. Here the author draws parallels between Lithuanian and Russian literature where village prose started
developing approximately in the same period, in the late 1960s. This

is only one example of how the book puts Lithuanian Soviet history in a transnational perspective, comparing Lithuanian developments to those of other Soviet republics and states of the Communist bloc. At this point, however, the author fails to acknowledge some important literature such as, for instance, Alexei Yurchak's famous book *Everything Was Forever, Until It Was No More*. It seems to this reviewer that by employing Yurchak's perspective in the introductory part of the book, Davoliūtė's study could have gained from the more sophisticated discussion about agency/structure as the modes of approaching the Soviet history. This omission, however, does not undermine the high quality of Davoliūtė's book and its significant importance for the understanding of the history of Lithuania (and that of other Soviet republics) during the Soviet period.

Olga Sasunkevich
European Humanities University
Lithuania

Olga Malinova, *Aktual'noe proshloe: Simvolicheskaia politika vlastvuiushchei elity i dilemmy rossiiskoi identichnosti.* Moscow: ROSSPEN, 2015. 207 pp.

Our lives are largely dependent upon what we tend to forget and what we still remember. Images and symbols alluding to different events in the present and past also play significant roles in the social construction of people's identities. This new book by the prominent Russian scholar Olga Malinova deals with how Russia's ruling elites used its national past in the changing ideological contexts from the rule of Boris Yeltsin up to the second presidency of Vladimir Putin (1991–2014). Olga Malinova is currently a chief research fellow of the Institute of Scientific Information for Social Sciences (Russian Academy of Sciences), professor at the Moscow State Institute of International Relations, and professor at the National Research University Higher School of Economics. She is also a former (2008–2010) president of the Russian Political Science Association and a renowned Russian expert in the field of identities, the politics of representation, and political discourse analysis, as well as the editor-in-chief of the journal *Symbolic Politics*. Her previous books include *Russia and "the West" in the Twentieth Century: Transformation of Discourse about Collective Identity* (Moscow: 2009); *Ideas and Symbolic Space of Post-Soviet Russia: Dynamics, Institutional Environment, Actors* (ed. by Olga Malinova, Moscow: 2011); and *The Construction of Meanings: the Study of Symbolic Politics in Modern Russia* (Moscow: 2013).

The title of her new book, *The Actual Past: Symbolic Politics of the Ruling Elite and Dilemmas of Russian Identity*, speaks for itself. The word "actual" (*aktual'noe,* which can mean both "actual" and "current" or "topical") stands here for the highly topical historical narratives currently in use by Russian ruling elites to legitimize their political power. The issues of the past discussed here include the post-Soviet revisions of the historical symbols of "the Great October Revolution" and "the Great Patriotic War" (World War II). Using narrative analysis Olga Malinova deconstructs successive presidents' annual speeches to the Russian parliament from 1994 until 2012 as well as the repertoire of commemorative speeches by presidents Vladimir Putin and Dmitrii Medvedev from 2000 until 2014. Based on the results of her research Olga Malinova divides the post-Soviet symbolic politics of the Russian state into four periods. The first period lasts from the early to mid-1990s (approximately until Yeltsin's re-election as president in 1996). This period largely continued the critical stand on the USSR and its totalitarian regimes that had started during perestroika. In a situation of sharp opposition between Boris Yeltsin and Russian parliament (1993) the Russian president refused to undertake any systematic attempts to create a new "infrastructure of memory". The latter was required to successfully inscribe a new narrative of the post-Soviet transition from communism towards Western ideals of liberal democracy into the collective memory of the Russian nation.

The second period marked by Olga Malinova lasted approximately from 1996 until Putin's rise to power. Instead of a total rejection of the Soviet past Boris Yeltsin turned towards seeking "reconciliation and national accord". This was when the November 7th holiday of the Great Russian Revolution was replaced with the Day of Reconciliation and Accord. In 1998 the remains of the Russian tsarist family (assassinated in 1918) were reburied in St. Petersburg with Yeltsin inviting the descendants of the Romanov family to come and witness Russia's attempted reconciliation with its own past. Soon annual Moscow military parades dedicated to the anniversaries of the "Great Patriotic War" returned to Red Square. However that did not help Yeltsin to resolve the conflict between the present and past inside the country as he struggle to push through "democratic reforms" that were often unpopular with the Russian people (and in particular among nationalistic circles).

Olga Malinova assigns the beginning of the third period of Russian symbolic politics to Vladimir Putin's rise to power in 2000. The emphasis on continuity between the heritage and achievements of the Russian Empire and the USSR enabled the new Russian president to incorporate into the construction of Russian identity new symbols and episodes of collective memory coinciding with the promotion of the idea of Russian identity as based on belonging to a "derzhava" (or "great power"). The Russian word "derzhava" can be interpreted either as a state, an empire, or even a mighty and advanced civilization. In taking this course, the Putin government announced the state as the key institution binding together the Russian macropolitical community. The notion of belonging to a mighty "derzhava" also sought a significant level of civilizational sovereignty which resulted in the concept of Russian "sovereign democracy", particularly popular in 2006-2007. However during Putin's first term and later Medvedev's presidency concepts like sovereign democracy proved too eclectic and therefore had little potential to solidify a Russian sense of national belonging.

According to Malinova the fourth and final period of symbolic politics started around 2011-2012. The December 2011 street protests pushed Russian political elites (particularly in the lead-up to the spring 2012 presidential elections) to construct more consistent narratives on Russian identity. An example is Vladimir Putin's article "Russia: The National Question" published on 23 January 2012 and subtitled "Self-Determination of the Russian People: A Multi-ethnic

Civilization Sealed with a Russian Core". At the same time the promotion of a more uniform version of identity politics coincided with
attempts by ruling elites to control public debates over the past
through quasi-think tanks and by means of memorial acts like the
2014 law on criminal responsibility for public dissemination of false
information on the activities of the Soviet Union in World War II.

Taken as a whole, Olga Malinova's book contains pretty much
everything an inquisitive reader or researcher in Russian area studies would want to know on this subject. The book features a thorough review of literature in the chosen field, an accurate and mind-
ful use of a scientific method, sharp analysis of the practices of political power in contemporary Russia, and elaborate research on the
discursive construction of national identity in Russia's public
sphere. Perhaps one thing is missing—there is no analysis of the
most recent events of 2014 like the Olympic Winter Games in Sochi
and the crisis in Ukraine. Feasibly these are topics for Olga Malinova
to address in her next book.

Sergei Akopov
National Research University "Higher School of Economics"
St. Petersburg (Russia)

FELIX ACKERMANN teaches historical anthropology and applied humanities as a DAAD visiting associate professor at European Humanities University (Vilnius). His recent publications focus on the link between migration, memory, and urban space in the post-Soviet borderlands of Belarus, Lithuania, and Poland, and include: *Palimpsest Grodno. Nationalisierung, Nivellierung und Sowjetisierung einer mitteleuropäischen Stadt (1918–1991)* (Wiesbaden: Harrassowitz, 2010).

JAN C. BEHRENDS, senior research fellow at the Centre for Contemporary History (ZZF) in Potsdam, Germany, teaches East European History at Humboldt Universtität zu Berlin. His relevant publications include: "Moscow's War against Ukraine. Comments from a Historical Perspective", *Cuadernos de Historia contemporánea* 36 (2014); "'Some Call Us Heroes, Others Call Us Killers'. Experiencing Violent Spaces: Soviet Soldiers in the Afghan War", *Nationalities Papers* 43, no. 5 (2015); and "Ein Jahr der Gewalt. Russlands Staatskrise und der Krieg gegen die Ukraine", *Osteuropa* 65, no. 2 (2015). In press: "Afghanistan als Gewaltraum. Sowjetische Soldaten erzählen vom Partisanenkrieg", in: Esther Meier and Tanja Penter (ed.), *SovietNam. Die UdSSR in Afghanistan 1979-1989* (Paderborn: 2015).

UILLEAM BLACKER is Lecturer in Comparative Russian and East European Culture at the School of Slavonic and East European Studies, University College London. He is co-author of *Remembering Katyn* (Polity, 2012) and co-editor of *Memory and Theory in Eastern Europe* (Palgrave-Macmillan, 2013). He is currently working on a monograph on urban space, cultural memory, and the legacy of post-WWII displacement in Poland, Russia, and Ukraine, to be published by Routledge in 2016.

SANDER BROUWER is assistant professor of Russian literature and cultural history at the University of Groningen, the Netherlands. He publishes on Russian literature and culture from the 17th to the 21st centuries (Avvakum, Pushkin, Gogol, Turgenev, Pelevin). He was a member of the HERA-funded international collaborative project *Memory at War: Cultural Dynamics in Russia, Poland, and Ukraine* (2010–2013). He is the editor of *Contested Interpretations of the Past in Polish, Russian, and Ukrainian Film. Screen as Battlefield* (to be published by Brill Publishers in 2016).

JULIE FEDOR is Lecturer in Modern European History and ARC Discovery Early Career Researcher in the University of Melbourne's School of Historical and Philosophical Studies. She is the author of *Russia and the Cult of State Security* (Routledge 2011), co-author of *Remembering Katyn* (Polity 2012), and co-editor of *Memory and Theory in Eastern Europe* (Palgrave-Macmillan 2013) and *Memory, Conflict and New Media* (Routledge 2013). Her current research project examines the politics of memory in contemporary Russia.

MICHAEL GALBAS is a PhD candidate at the Department of History/Eastern European History, University of Konstanz. He holds an MA in Eastern European Studies and a BA in History and Politics from the University of Konstanz. In 2014 and 2015 he completed a research visit in Russia, which was funded by the German Historical Institute Moscow and the German Academic Exchange Service (DAAD). The present article is based on research undertaken for his PhD. In his research he analyzes the memories of the Soviet–Afghan war in today's Russia.

MARKUS GÖRANSSON is a PhD candidate at the Department of International Politics, Aberystwyth University. He holds an MA in Conflict Studies and Human Rights from Utrecht University and a BA (Hons.) in Modern History from the University of Oxford. In 2013 and 2014, he was a Junior Research Fellow at the University of Central Asia (UCA) Dushanbe, generously assisted by Sunatullo Jonboboev, senior research fellow at the UCA, Dilovar Butabekov, head of UCA Khorugh campus and Bohdan Krawchenko, director general of the UCA. In 2013, he was also a visiting researcher at the Academy of Sciences of the Republic of Tajikistan, where he received implausibly helpful support from Sakina Karimova. The present article is based on research undertaken for his PhD.

ANDRÉ HÄRTEL is an Associate Professor and DAAD-Lecturer in German and European Studies at the Kyiv-Mohyla Academy in Kyiv, Ukraine. Prior to this he worked as a Lecturer in International Relations at Friedrich-Schiller-University Jena (Germany) and as a Political Advisor at the Council of Europe in Strasbourg (France). His book and PhD thesis "Westintegration oder Grauzonenszenario? Die EU- und WTO-Politik der Ukraine vor dem Hintergrund der inneren Transformation (1998–2009)" was published by LIT in 2012. He also held a research fellowship at Oxford Brookes University (UK) in 2007/2008 and was the first coordinator of the Master's Program in German and European Studies at the Kyiv-Mohyla Academy in 2006/2007.

SIMON LEWIS completed a PhD in Slavonic Studies at the University of Cambridge in 2014. His dissertation analyzed the interaction of memory narratives in Belarus in Belarusian-, Polish- and Russian-language texts between the nineteenth century and the present day. He is a co-author of the collective monograph *Remembering Katyn* (Polity, 2012) and has published articles on Belarusian literature, cinema, and politics. In 2014–15 he was a Visiting Scholar at the Social Memory Laboratory at the Institute of Sociology, University of Warsaw. From January 2016 he will be a Postdoctoral Research Fellow at the Institute of East European Studies, Freie Universität Berlin.

MARIA MÄLKSOO is Senior Researcher in International Relations at the University of Tartu and currently a Visiting Fellow of the Centre for International Studies at the LSE. She was a member of the HERA-funded international collaborative project *Memory at War: Cultural Dynamics in Russia, Poland, and Ukraine* (2010-2013). She is the author of *The Politics of Becoming European: A Study of Polish and Baltic Post-Cold War Security Imaginaries* (Routledge, 2010) and a co-author of *Remembering Katyn* (Polity, 2012). Her work has appeared in *Security Dialogue, International Political Sociology, Review of International Studies, European Journal of International Relations, Communist and Post-Communist Studies*, and in several edited volumes. Her current research focuses on the international implications of Russia's political handling of its communist past.

YURI RADCHENKO is Director of the Centre for Research on Inter-Ethnic Relations in Eastern Europe (Kharkiv) and Lecturer at the Institute of Oriental Studies and International Relations "Kharkiv Collegium". He received his PhD in History from V. Karazin Kharkiv National University in 2012. He has held research fellowships at Yahad-In Unum in Paris, the German Historical Institute in Warsaw, the Anne Tanenbaum Centre for Jewish Studies at the University of Toronto, the Institut für Zeitgeschichte in Munich, Göttingen University, the Centre for Advanced Holocaust Studies at the US Holocaust Memorial Museum, and elsewhere. He has published numerous works on the history of the Holocaust, Ukrainian-Jewish relations, collaboration in Eastern Europe, and the history of right radical movements in Europe.

ANNA REICH is a visual artist and an assistant professor at Augustana College in Sioux Falls, South Dakota. Her photographic work investigates memory and identity. Reich has exhibitied throughout the US and in Australia, Iceland, Lithuania, and Russia. She has received numerous grants including a travel grant from the Foundation for Contemporary Art (2013), a Fulbright Research Fellowship (2013-14), and an *Artist as Activist* Research Grant from the Robert Rauschenberg Foundation (2015).

YAACOV RO'I is professor of history emeritus at Tel-Aviv University. He has written and edited several books and many articles on Soviet history, including: *Islam in the Soviet Union from World War II to Gorbachev* (Christopher Hurst/Columbia University Press, 2000); *Islam in the CIS: A Threat to Stability?* (Royal Institute of International Affairs/Brookings Institution, 2001); (edited) *Muslim Eurasia: Conflicting Legacies* (Frank Cass, 1995); (edited) *Democracy and Pluralism in Muslim Eurasia* (Frank Cass, 2004); and (edited) *The Jewish Movement in the Soviet Union* (Woodrow Wilson Center and The Johns Hopkins University, 2012).

IRYNA SKLOKINA (PhD 2014) is a historian currently based at the Center for Urban History of the East Central Europe in Lviv, Ukraine. Her PhD dissertation examined the official Soviet policy on the memory of the Nazi occupation of Ukraine using the example of

Kharkiv. She graduated from V. N. Karazin Kharkiv National University with a major in Ukrainian history, and holds a master's degree in History (2008). She has worked at Kharkiv National University and the Kowalsky Eastern Institute of Ukrainian Studies (Kharkiv), and is a member of the Kharkiv Historical and Philological Society, and a participant of several international projects about historical memory and oral history, including "Region, Nation and Beyond: An Interdisciplinary and Transcultural Reconceptualization of Ukraine" (research sub-topic: "The Political Death Cult of Fallen Soldiers in Ukraine in the Past 20 years").

IRYNA STAROVOYT is an Associate Professor in the Theory of Literature and Comparative Studies in the Philology Faculty at Ivan Franko National University of L'viv. She was a visiting lecturer at the College of Eastern European Studies at Przemyśl, and Post-Doctoral Research Associate in the Faculty of Arts at the University of Groningen (2012–13); and a member of the HERA-funded international collaborative project *Memory at War: Cultural Dynamics in Poland, Russia, and Ukraine.* Her current research focuses on the neglected twentieth-century generational memories and the new traumatic context of their re-telling in Eastern Europe. She has published essays on Ukrainian modern literary narratives of becoming and belonging, the ethics and sensitivity of memory, and conflictual mental mapping.

JAY WINTER, Charles J. Stille Professor of History at Yale, is an historian of twentieth-century Europe, focusing in particular on the First World War. He received his PhD and DLitt degrees from the University of Cambridge, where he taught and was a Fellow of Pembroke College from 1979 to 2001. He won an Emmy award as co-producer of the BBC/PBS eight-hour television series "The Great War and the shaping of the twentieth century" (1996). He is the author of *Sites of Memory, Sites of Mourning* (Cambridge University Press, 1995), and editor-in-chief of the three-volume Cambridge history of the First World War, published in French and English in 2014.

OLEKSANDR ZAITSEV is Professor of the Modern History of Ukraine at the Ukrainian Catholic University in Lviv. He is the author of

Ukrainian Integral Nationalism of the 1920s and 1930s: Essays in Intellectual History (Kyiv: Krytyka, 2013); co-author and editor of *Nationalism and Religion: the Greek-Catholic Church and the Ukrainian Nationalist Movement in Galicia, 1920s–30s* (Lviv: Ukrainian Catholic University Press, 2011); and editor of a special issue of the journal *Ukraïna Moderna* (no. 20, 2013), "Fascism and Right Radicalism in the East of Europe" (all publications in Ukrainian). His current research examines ultra-nationalism in the stateless nations of interwar Eastern Europe in comparative perspective.